Worldwide Volunteering
For Young People

This directory complements The Worldwide Volunteering for Young People
search and match database,
widely used in schools, universities and careers offices.
The database is available from
Worldwide Volunteering,
Higher Orchard, Sandford Orcas,
Sherborne, Dorset DT9 4RP
Tel/fax 01963 220036
Email: yfb@worldvol.co.uk
Website: http://www.worldwidevolunteering.org.uk

Worldwide
Volunteering
For Young People

W.W.V○L.

Compiled by Roger Potter

How To Books

Published by How To Books Ltd,
3 Newtec Place, Magdalen Road,
Oxford OX4 1RE. United Kingdom.
Tel: (01865) 793806. Fax: (01865) 248780.

Third edition 2001

British Library Cataloguing in Publication Data
A catalogue record for this book is available from
the British Library

Cover design by Shireen Nathoo Design.
Produced for How To Books by Deer Park Productions
Typeset by PDQ Typesetting, Stoke-on-Trent, Staffs.
Printed and bound by Athenaeum Press, Gateshead, Tyne & Wear.

NOTE: The material contained in this book is set out in good faith
for general guidance and no liability can be accepted for loss or
expense incurred as a result of relying in particular circumstances on
statements made in the book. The laws and regulations are complex
and liable to change, and readers should check the current position
with the relevant authorities before making personal arrangements.

Contents

Contents

Foreword

Young people have enormous talent, enthusiasm and idealism. They have a real contribution to make to society and they want to make their voices heard. Volunteering is a wonderful way for them to show what they are capable of.

Volunteering is a three-way process and benefits everyone. For the individuals, groups or causes that volunteers help the value is evident. Volunteers themselves are often surprised by how much they gain from the experience: horizons are widened, doors opened, new challenges met, fresh friendships made, confidence built. I remember my own experiences with nothing but affection in every respect.

But there is a third aspect of volunteering and that is the way in which all of us gain from the altruism, co-operation and energy that volunteering releases. Society as a whole profits not only from the tangible benefits to the recipients of voluntary effort, but also from the enhanced maturity and experience that those who have volunteered bring to all other aspects of their lives. The more that people volunteer the better becomes the fabric of society. Not only that, it's fun as well – letting your life take a new outlet outside of school, college, university or even as a break from a full-time job.

No one sort of volunteer work is better than another. This new book demonstrates the enormous range of opportunities that exist around the world. There is something for everyone. The important thing is that anyone who wants to volunteer should find an opportunity to match their particular circumstances and aspirations – whether it's a week in the county next door or six months in Kathmandu.

If this guide helps you to find the right volunteering opportunity it will provide an experience you will never forget and one in which there are no losers – only winners. Good luck!

RICHARD BRANSON

Preface

Welcome to the third edition of *Worldwide Volunteering for Young People*, a directory of worldwide volunteering opportunities.

The directory contains a mass of information about some 800 volunteer organizations with over 250,000 annual volunteer opportunities throughout the UK and 214 countries overseas. A unique feature is its focus on volunteering by 16–25 year olds. All the organizations listed have opportunities for this age group, though many also have openings for younger and older volunteers. This wealth of precisely focused information makes *Worldwide Volunteering for Young People* the UK's most comprehensive directory of its kind.

You will be amazed at the enormous variety of opportunities on offer. But before going directly to directory entries you may find it helpful to spend a few moments reading this preface in order to make best use of the vast amount of information available.

Sifting through so many organizations each with its different aims and requirements can be a daunting task, but the aim of the directory is to make this process as easy as possible. First, it is crucial to build up a clear picture of exactly what sort of volunteering you are looking for, and the guide is structured to help with this.

In order to build a profile of your ideal volunteering opportunity you will need to consider a variety of questions. Which cause or group of people would you like to help? Where do you want to volunteer? How long for? Starting when? What skills do you wish to use and how much, if anything, can you afford to contribute to the cost of your project? Your responses to these and other questions will determine which organizations best suit you. The guide will pinpoint them and supply a mass of valuable information about each one.

VOLUNTEERING FOR ALL

There are many reasons why people volunteer. A motive common to all must be idealism – the wish to make a contribution to society, to do something for others or for a worthwhile cause without too much concern for personal reward.

But volunteering is not a one-way process. It is perfectly reasonable for volunteers to recognise that as well as giving, they themselves *gain* from the experience, and many choose to volunteer for precisely this reason.

A well-researched and well-chosen volunteer project, for instance, cannot fail to widen your experience, increase your self-confidence and offer exciting challenges. It is likely to take you to new places where you will meet new people with backgrounds and circumstances that differ widely from your own.

People are often surprised by the range of skills and interests that can be used in volunteering. Whether you are interested in accountancy or zoo-keeping there are opportunities that will allow you to use and develop your particular talents. The starting point for many volunteers is the realization that they have something unique to contribute!

Then there are the longer term rewards of volunteering. Employers and university admissions tutors, amongst others, increasingly value evidence of volunteering when selecting candidates for jobs and university places. They recognize the initiative and determination shown in becoming involved and demonstrating an awareness of others, and the ability to organize yourself and work as part of a team that the experience will demand.

Don't spend too much time worrying about *why* you want to volunteer. Far more important is the fact that you want to get involved. The purpose of this guide is to make it easier for volunteers to translate their initial enthusiasm for volunteering into a worthwhile placement.

SAFETY WARNING!

Please remember that *Worldwide Volunteering for Young People* is a reference book designed to help you to find organizations that will suit your own requirements. Whilst every effort is made to ensure that the information is correct and up to date we cannot accept responsibility for errors or omissions. Volunteers should always check with organizations in whose work they are interested.

Neither How To Books nor Worldwide Volunteering for Young People have any financial or other interest in any organization contained in the directory. Nor does inclusion in either the database or directory guarantee the quality of any specific project, organization or activity.

Neither How To Books nor Worldwide Volunteering for Young People can be held responsible for arrangements that individuals or groups may make with any organization in the directory. Volunteers are strongly advised to satisfy themselves on the management, financial, safety, health and all other aspects of a project before enrolling on it.

WORLDWIDE VOLUNTEERING FOR YOUNG PEOPLE

Worldwide Volunteering for Young People is a registered charity whose aim is to make it easier for young people around the world to identify and take part in appropriate volunteering projects. The publication complements the Worldwide Volunteering for Young People search and match database which is available in many schools, universities, careers centres, volunteer bureaux, libraries and other information sources. The database enables volunteers to make more sophisticated searches of the information and is updated every six months.

Worldwide Volunteering for Young People welcomes feedback from readers, who are invited to send comments and suggestions to Worldwide Volunteering for Young People, Higher Orchard, Sandford Orcas, Sherborne, Dorset DT9 4RP. Telephone and fax: (01963) 220036. Email: yfb@worldvol.co.uk
Website: http://www.worldwidevolunteering.org.uk

Roger Potter
Director
Worldwide Volunteering for Young People

Introduction
Tom Griffiths

Volunteering, whether at home or overseas, has never been a more beneficial activity. It is encouraged by universities and valued by employers. Not only will you learn about who you really are and how you react to others, you will mature and develop a character that you probably never knew existed. It could be the most amazing, exciting and challenging time of your life.

Volunteering, however, should not be taken lightly. 'The Challenge' should be taken up in a responsible manner. No one will congratulate you for taking up a scarce place, only to drop out in a few weeks when you get bored or let others down who have come to rely on you. You should not be embarking on this journey to score 'cool points' with your mates, to impress your parents or because you think that it is deemed to be the right thing to do.

Do it because you want to. Do it because you have something to give and because you are happy to give it. Do it because of the self-satisfaction of making a difference to the lives of others. Placement organizations are not after 'shining knights' out to save the world, but young people with an infectious energy and enthusiasm to pass on to others.

Don't wait until it's too late to find that you have missed out. Where do you dream about visiting? What do you dream about doing? Whatever your answer is . . . that should be your placement. Now, let this book do the rest!

Life. There is no rehearsal.

Good luck.

Tom

Tom Griffiths, previous 'Young Travel Writer of the Year' is author of *The Virgin Student Travellers' Handbook* and founder of the Gap Year Company Ltd, independent web site www.gapyear.com, *The Gap Year* magazine and free e-mail www.fireball.co.uk.

How To Use This Book

ALPHABETICAL LISTINGS

The first section of the guide (pages 1–444) lists the volunteer
organizations alphabetically and gives detailed information about
each one. An explanation of directory entries is given below. If you
already know the name of an organization you can go straight to its
entry for further information.

Alternatively you may want to browse through the alphabetical
section to familiarize yourself with the scope of volunteering on offer
and the sort of information available for each organization.

Another way of using this section is to find more information
about an organization that looks right for you once you have
identified it in the cross-referencing section.

CROSS-REFERENCING

For many volunteers the cross-referencing section of the guide will be
the first port of call. All organizations are listed by the cause or
group of people that they help. There are 23 causes:

Addicts/Ex-addicts
Aids/HIV
Animal welfare
Archaeology
Architecture
Children
Conservation
Disabled (learning
  and physical)
Elderly people
Environmental causes

Health care/medical
Heritage
Holidays for disabled
Human rights
Inner city problems
Offenders/Ex-
  offenders
Poor/homeless
Refugees
Teaching/assisting
  (nursery, primary,

secondary, mature,
English as a
Foreign Language
– EFL)
Unemployed
Wildlife
Work camps
  (seasonal)
Young people

So if you think you'd really like to do something to help the
homeless, turn to that particular cause in the Index by Cause on pp
478–510. Any of the organizations listed there will provide you with
the opportunity to fulfil that ambition.

If you've always wanted to visit Malawi and would like to find an
organization that will take you there, turn to the Index by
Worldwide Placement on pages 445–477. You will, in fact, find 19
organizations listed there that offer placements in Malawi. Now look
them up in the directory section for further information.

INDIVIDUAL ENTRIES

Details about each organization in the alphabetical section give you all the information you need to make contact with that organization and in most cases a very great deal more. Entries depend entirely on information provided by individual organizations. Some are more complete than others. However, the format of each listing is identical and a complete entry will contain information under the following headings and in the following order:

Full address, contact details and name including telephone, fax and e-mail address and web site where available.

A description provided by the organization itself outlining its aims and activities and giving volunteers a feel for the work of the organization.

Number of projects worldwide and in the UK.

Starting months and **time commitment** required, ranging from a minimum of one week to a maximum of a year or more.

Age requirement. If no ages are listed it is safe to assume that the organisation has placements for anyone aged 16–25.

Details of **causes helped.**

Activities in which volunteers may be involved.

Total number of volunteers under the age of 26 placed by the organization in a year.

When to apply. Note that it is always sensible to apply as early as possible. The best projects are very rapidly filled.

Whether volunteers work alone or with others.

Volunteers with disabilities.

Qualifications required if any, e.g. linguistic ability, first aid, academic qualifications etc.

Details of any specific **equipment/clothing** required.

Health requirements.

Costs to volunteers. Note that organizations are asked to state typical costs including travel to and from destinations outside the UK but *not* including travel costs within the UK. Costs are based on figures supplied by organizations in 2000/2001. Always check for up-to-date details.

Benefits to volunteers. Details of accommodation provided, insurance if provided, help with travel expenses, pocket money etc.

Training. Details of what, if any, pre-placement training is given.

Supervision. Whether the volunteer is supervised at the placement.

Nationalities accepted.

Interview and selection details.

Certification. Are volunteers provided with references, certificates of attendance etc?

Charity number if a UK registered charity.

Worldwide placements listed by continent and country.

UK placements listed by county.

Where relevant, information is also given to enable **volunteers with offending backgrounds** to establish whether organizations are able to place them.

Headings are omitted from an organization's listing where the relevant information is not available.

Because this information is presented in a standard format from entry to entry it is possible to refine the cross-referencing facility by eliminating, for example, organizations whose start date or time commitment required do not suit the individual volunteer.

The huge variety of opportunities contained in this directory offers volunteers a really wide choice. Whether you are looking for a six-month placement in a developing country for which you will have to raise a great deal of money, or whether you want a short-term local project where all your expenses and even a pocket money allowance will be paid, there is something here for you. The important thing is to become involved and who knows – it could be the start of a great adventure.

A–Z Directory of
Volunteer Organisations

A

1990 TRUST, THE

South Bank Technopark
90 London Road
London
SE1 6LN UK

Tel: +44 (0) 20 7717 1579
Fax: +44 (0) 20 7717 1585
e-mail: aadams@gn.apc.org
Contact: Mrs Audrey Adams

The 1990 Trust aims to promote good race relations, engage in policy development and articulate the needs of the Black community from a grassroots Black perspective. In so doing we will ensure that the real issues affecting the lives of people of African, Asian and Caribbean descent are addressed. Our ultimate aim is to bring about long-term improvements in people's lives by fighting for the elimination of racism in all its forms. The work of The 1990 Trust is founded on the principle that Black people have an inalienable right to complete freedom, justice and equality. The very nature of our work and the environment in which we operate therefore determines our status as a civil/ human rights organization. In working to achieve our goals, we will: ensure that everything we do is informed by the views and experiences of ordinary Black people in different communities throughout the United Kingdom; embrace totally the principle of networking and aim to do so with as many organizations and individuals as relevant and possible; engage a 'community development' approach to our work of a type which enables Black people in their communities to take part in initiatives which will improve their lives economically, socially and environmentally; uphold the ideal of Asian, African and Caribbean people working together, as we view this as the most effective means of eradicating racism and racial disadvantage in the United Kingdom. Volunteers with an offending background are accepted.

Total projects worldwide: 4
Total UK projects: 4
Starting months: January–December.
Time required: 4–52 weeks.
Age requirement: 16 plus.

Causes: Aids/HIV, children, elderly people, environmental causes, human rights, inner city problems, refugees.
Activities: Accountancy, administration, campaigning, community work, computers, development issues, fundraising, group work, international aid, library/resource centres, marketing/publicity, newsletter/journalism, religion, research, scientific work, social work, translating.
Vols under 26 placed each year: Few of a total of 10.
When to apply: All year.
Work alone/with others: Both.
Volunteers with disabilities: Possible.
Qualifications: Specialist skills welcome e.g. law graduates, interest in immigration/race, women's issues, human rights, IT, sustainable development.
Health requirements: Nil.
Costs: Travel.
Benefits: Standard/normal benefits.
Interview details: Interviews take place at The 1990 Trust offices.
Certification: References provided when applying for paid employment.
Charity number: 1012898
Worldwide placements: *Africa* (Ghana, Nigeria); *Asia* (India); *Central America* (Jamaica).
UK placements: *England* (Leicestershire, London).

ABANTU FOR DEVELOPMENT

1 Winchester House
11 Cranmer Road
London
SW9 6EJ UK

Tel: +44 (0) 20 7820 0066
Fax: +44 (0) 20 7820 0088
e-mail: people@abantu.org
Contact: Programme Manager

Abantu for Development is a non-governmental development organization that was founded in 1991 by African women. 'Abantu' means 'people' in several African languages. The main focus of our work is on providing training, information and advice on identifying resources which ensure long-term survival of organizations, networking and lobbying for a role in policy and decision making for refugee and African women. Our aims are: to increase the participation of Africans, especially women, in the political and economic structures of African countries; to eradicate the cultural, legal and political obstacles for women to attain economic independence and equality before the law; to ensure that the advancement of women's interests benefits the entire community; to promote and nurture public awareness of development issues with a gender perspective, which shows an understanding of women's position in society. We achieve these by: supporting African people to empower themselves through a participatory and people-centred method of training to develop skills in the area of policy analysis, economics, healthcare, the media and the environment; providing both support and networking opportunities for trainers and consultants to create an increased pool of competent Africans. Abantu's programmes fall into four categories: training and capacity building; advocacy, public awareness and networking; research, information and publications; institutional development of Abantu. Volunteers are taken on to support activities and projects within these four programmes usually under the supervision of the various programme officers and the line manager.

Total projects worldwide: Varies.
Total UK projects: Varies.
Starting months: May.
Time required: 4–12 weeks.
Age requirement: 16 plus.
Causes: Aids/HIV, human rights, refugees.
Activities: Administration, computers, development issues, fundraising, marketing/publicity, newsletter/journalism, research.
Vols under 26 placed each year: 3 of a total of 4.
When to apply: March.
Work alone/with others: Both.
Volunteers with disabilities: Possible.
Qualifications: Minimum A-level.
Health requirements: Nil for UK. For Africa innoculations and anti-malarial pills.
Costs: Subsistence for all. Travel if overseas.
Benefits: London travel expenses subsidized.
Training: One week induction course.
Supervision: Line manager and other programme officers.
Interview details: Interviews take place at our offices.
Certification: Written reference.
Worldwide placements: *Africa* (Ghana, Kenya, Nigeria).
UK placements: *England* (London).

ABBOT HALL ART GALLERY AND MUSEUM OF LAKELAND LIFE
Abbot Hall
Kendal
Cumbria
LA9 5AL UK

Tel: +44 (0) 1539 722464
Fax: +44 (0) 1539 722494
e-mail: ct@abbothall.org.uk
Web: www.abbothall.org.uk
Contact: Mrs Cherrie Trelogan

Abbot Hall and the museums we look after – Abbot Hall Art Gallery, Museum of Lakeland Life and Kendal Museum of National History and Archaeology – have a particularly wide range of displays, from fine arts through archaeology and geology to natural history and social history. There is an opportunity for people to gain experience in museum and art gallery careers. We have organized a series of structured sessions which will be delivered twice a week by museum and gallery staff. This will allow students the opportunity to combine practical skills with formal instruction and the opportunity for questions and discussion. Subjects will cover education, finance, collections management, marketing and customer care etc.

Total projects worldwide: 3
Total UK projects: 3
Starting months: January–December.
Time required: 12–52 weeks (plus).
Age requirement: 18 plus.
Causes: Archaeology, children, conservation, elderly people, heritage, teaching/assisting (nursery, primary, secondary), young people.
Activities: Administration, arts/crafts, computers, conservation skills, group work, manual work, marketing/publicity, newsletter/journalism, research, teaching, technical skills.
Vols under 26 placed each year: Many but only 2 at a time.
When to apply: All year – as early as possible.
Work alone/with others: Both.
Volunteers with disabilities: Possible.
Qualifications: English language.
Equipment/clothing: General smart appearance and a set of old clothes for messy work.
Health requirements: General good health.
Costs: Food, electricity and other power,

telephone calls and transport (all within walking distance).
Benefits: Lodging can be provided for two students at a time subject to availability. (No availability for lodging until the end of 2001.) Insurance is covered by the Trust.
Training: A new programme of induction sessions is being started this year. Two hour-long sessions per week will be given by staff ranging from collections management to finance. These are in addition to ongoing training through practical tasks.
Supervision: One member of staff is allocated to supervise.
Interview details: Prospective volunteers are interviewed at Abbot Hall.
Certification: Reference on request.
Charity number: 526980
UK placements: *England* (Cumbria).

ABBOTS LANGLEY SKILLS DEVELOPMENT CENTRE
Jacketts Field
Abbots Langley
Hertfordshire
WD5 0PA UK

Tel: +44 (0) 1923 267011
Contact: Alan Thompson

Abbots Langley SDC is a day care service and part of SCOPE East Region. (SCOPE is an organization for people with cerebral palsy.)

Total projects worldwide: 1
Total UK projects: 1
Starting months: January–December.
Time required: 2–52 weeks (plus).
Age requirement: 21 plus.
Causes: Disabled (learning and physical).
Activities: Arts/crafts, caring (general and day), computers, cooking, counselling, DIY, driving, gardening/horticulture, group work, manual work, teaching.
Vols under 26 placed each year: Varies.
When to apply: All year.
Work alone/with others: With staff and other volunteers.
Volunteers with disabilities: Generally no – but possible for some supervision/training.
Qualifications: Nil but driving licence would be useful.
Equipment/clothing: Sensible, everyday clothes and sturdy shoes.
Health requirements: A certain amount of lifting required so unsuitable for anyone with back problems.

Costs: Travel costs to and from the unit.
Benefits: Free sandwiches.
Interview details: Interviews take place at Abbots Langley SDC.
Certification: Reference on request.
Charity number: 208231
UK placements: *England* (Hertfordshire).

ACET (AIDS Care Education and Training)
PO Box 3693
London
SW15 2TG UK

Tel: +44 (0) 20 8780 0400
Fax: +44 (0) 20 8780 0450
e-mail: acet@acetuk.org
Contact: Operations Director

ACET's aim is to provide unconditional care for people living with Aids/HIV and to reduce the number of new infections through schools' education and practical training.

Total projects worldwide: 15
Total UK projects: 9
Starting months: January–December.
Time required: 1–52 weeks.
Age requirement: 18 plus.
Causes: Aids/HIV, health care/medical, teaching/assisting (secondary).
Activities: Administration, caring (general, day and residential), cooking, driving, gardening/horticulture, group work, religion, teaching, visiting/befriending.
Vols under 26 placed each year: 16 of a total of 80.
When to apply: As soon as possible.
Work alone/with others: Alone.
Volunteers with disabilities: Only if the person can undertake practical household chores.
Qualifications: Nil.
Health requirements: Nil.
Costs: Travel to and from training.
Benefits: Travel and experience of working in the community.
Certification: Certificate or reference on request.
Charity number: 299293
Worldwide placements: *Africa* (Tanzania, Uganda); *Asia* (Thailand); *Australasia* (New Zealand); *Europe* (Czech Republic, Ireland, Slovakia).
UK placements: *England* (Bedfordshire, Buckinghamshire, Essex, Hampshire, Hertfordshire, Kent, London, Northamptonshire, Surrey, E. Sussex,

W. Sussex, Warwickshire, West Midlands);
Scotland (Dundee City, Glasgow City);
Northern Ireland (Belfast City, Derry/
Londonderry); *Wales* (Cardiff, Newport, Vale
of Glamorgan).

ACORN CHILDREN'S HOSPICE
103 Oak Tree Lane
Selly Oak
Birmingham
B29 6HZ UK

Tel: +44 (0) 121 414 1741
Fax: +44 (0) 121 471 2880
Contact: Mrs Vinu Gupta

Acorn Children's Hospice requires volunteers
to work for a few hours a week for a
minimum of a year, to build up a relationship
with a child or children. Thereafter,
volunteers could come for a minimum of a
full week at a time.

Total projects worldwide: 1
Total UK projects: 1
Starting months: January–December.
Time required: 1–52 weeks.
Age requirement: 17 plus.
Causes: Children, disabled (learning and
physical), health care/medical, holidays for
disabled.
Activities: Arts/crafts, catering, cooking,
fundraising, visiting/befriending.
Vols under 26 placed each year:
Approximately 50.
When to apply: All year.
Work alone/with others: Normally in pairs.
Volunteers with disabilities: Possible.
Qualifications: Experience of working with
children, especially with disabilities.
Health requirements: Nil.
Costs: No accommodation provided.
Training: Training is spread over periods of 2
months.
Certification: Reference on request.
UK placements: *England* (West Midlands).

ACROSS TRUST, THE
Bridge House
70–72 Bridge Road
East Molesey
Surrey
KT8 9HF UK

Tel: +44 (0) 20 8783 1355
Fax: +44 (0) 20 8783 1622
e-mail: acrosst@across.org.uk

Web: www.across.org.uk
Contact: The Group Organizers

The Across Trust provides accompanied
holidays and pilgrimages in Europe for
chronically sick and severely disabled persons
of all ages, backgrounds, religion etc. Groups
(normal size 24) travel on board the
jumbulance, a purpose built jumbo-
ambulance, fully equipped for the needs of
the disabled traveller. Individual and group
applications are very welcome. The trust has
provided over 90,000 holiday places since
1973. Volunteers with an offending
background may be accepted once the
sentence is spent.

Total projects worldwide: 115
Total UK projects: 100
Starting months: March–October.
Time required: 1–52 weeks.
Age requirement: 16 plus.
Causes: Aids/HIV, children, disabled
(learning and physical), elderly people, health
care/medical, holidays for disabled, young
people.
Activities: Caring (general and residential),
group work.
Vols under 26 placed each year: 6,000 of a
total of 14,000.
When to apply: March – October.
Work alone/with others: With others.
Volunteers with disabilities: Possible.
Qualifications: Any, including doctors and
nurses.
Equipment/clothing: Leisure clothing.
Health requirements: Good health.
Costs: All expenses.
Benefits: Accommodation at all locations.
Interview details: No interview necessary, but
for first-time volunteers a written reference is
required.
Charity number: 265540
Worldwide placements: *Asia* (Israel); *Europe*
(Austria, Belgium, Denmark, France,
Germany, Ireland, Italy, Poland, Portugal,
Spain, Vatican City).
UK placements: *England* (throughout);
Scotland (throughout); *Northern Ireland*
(throughout); *Wales* (throughout).

ACTION AGAINST HUNGER –
OVERSEAS
1 Catton Street
London
WC1R 4AB UK

Tel: +44 (0) 20 7831 5858
Fax: +44 (0) 20 7831 4259
e-mail: clc@acf.imaginet.fr
Contact: Cathy Lennox-Cook

Action Against Hunger – Overseas intervenes in crisis situations to bring assistance to the victims of war and famine. Our approach to emergency relief is always coupled with the long-term objective of enabling the affected population to regain their self-sufficiency. The first victims of famine are nearly always the same: women, children and minority groups. Action Against Hunger combines experience and expertise to provide appropriate responses, through its four main approaches to the fight against hunger which are complemented by disaster preparedness: nutrition, food security, water, health.

Total projects worldwide: 34
Total UK projects: 0
Starting months: January–December.
Time required: 52 weeks (plus).
Age requirement: 24 plus.
Causes: Health care/medical, poor/homeless, refugees.
Activities: Accountancy, administration, agriculture/farming, building/construction, caring (general), community work, computers, development issues, forestry, international aid, outdoor skills, research, technical skills.
Vols under 26 placed each year: 3 of a total of 30.
When to apply: All year.
Work alone/with others: With others usually.
Volunteers with disabilities: Not possible.
Qualifications: Doctors, nurses, nutritionists, water engineers, agronomists, logisticians, administrators. All volunteers must have had at least one year's previous experience.
Equipment/clothing: Depending on location of post.
Health requirements: Certificate of good health and innoculations where necessary.
Costs: Nil.
Benefits: £500 per month after tax plus travel, board and lodging. We provide medical evacuation, personal accident, personal and public liability, life assurance.
Training: Three 3-week briefings according to technical profile. Security 1/2-day briefing for all.
Supervision: Report to line manager/co-ordinator.

Nationalities accepted: Only EU or USA residents.
Interview details: Prospective volunteers are interviewed in London.
Certification: Referral if necessary. Reference provided.
Charity number: 1047501
Worldwide placements: *Africa* (Angola, Burundi, Cameroon, Chad, Congo Dem. Republic, Congo Republic, Ivory Coast, Ethiopia, Guinea, Liberia, Mali, Mozambique, Niger, Sierra Leone, Somalia, Sudan, Tanzania, Uganda); *Asia* (Afghanistan, Cambodia, Indonesia, Korea (North), Laos, Myanmar (Burma), Sri Lanka, Tajikistan); *Europe* (Bosnia-Herzegovina, Russia, Yugoslavia); *Central America* (Guatemala, Haiti, Honduras, Nicaragua); *South America* (Colombia).

ACTION AGAINST HUNGER – UK
1 Catton Street
London
WC1R 4AB UK

Tel: +44 (0) 20 7831 5858
Fax: +44 (0) 20 7831 4259
Contact: Cathy Lennox-Cook

Action Against Hunger – UK: for more details of the organization, see the entry for Action Against Hunger – Overseas, above. Volunteers are needed in our London offices for general administration, recruitment, IT specialist work, translation, communications and the Disaster Preparedness Unit.

Total projects worldwide: 1
Total UK projects: 1
Starting months: January–December.
Time required: 1–12 weeks.
Age requirement: 18 plus.
Causes: Human rights, poor/homeless, refugees.
Activities: Accountancy, administration, computers, development issues, newsletter/journalism, research, translating.
Vols under 26 placed each year: 15 of a total of 20.
When to apply: Up to 6 weeks in advance.
Work alone/with others: With others in the London office.
Volunteers with disabilities: Possible. Small lift to 4th/5th floor.
Qualifications: Nil.
Health requirements: Nil.
Costs: Nil.

Benefits: Travel paid up to Zone 4.
Supervision: Head of department supervises.
Interview details: Prospective volunteers are interviewed in London.
Certification: Reference on request.
Charity number: 1047501
UK placements: *England* (London).

ACTION AID
Hamlyn House
McDonald Road
Archway
London
N19 5PG UK

Tel: +44 (0) 20 7561 7582
Contact: Katherine Fairley

Action Aid is one of the UK's largest international aid agencies, working directly with over five million of the world's poorest people in 27 countries across Asia, Africa and Latin America. We aim to improve the lives of children, families and whole communities in poorer countries. We support their needs and rights, working with local organizations and community groups so that change is appropriate and long-lasting. We work in emergency situations created by war, drought, floods, famine and the displacement of people. We also work to avert crises, particularly food shortages and famine. We work with governments and organizations to improve the policies and practices that have an impact on people living in poverty. We produce educational material for schools – used in half the schools in the UK – so that young people better understand the lives of people in developing countries. We do not send volunteers to our overseas projects.

Total projects worldwide: 3
Total UK projects: 3
Starting months: January–December.
Time required: 6–52 weeks.
Age requirement: 18 plus.
Causes: Children, human rights, poor/homeless, refugees.
Activities: Accountancy, administration, computers, development issues, fundraising, international aid, library/resource centres, marketing/publicity, research, translating.
Vols under 26 placed each year: 40 of a total of 50.
When to apply: All year.
Work alone/with others: Either.
Volunteers with disabilities: Possible.

Qualifications: Depends on the task.
Health requirements: Nil.
Costs: Nil.
Benefits: Travel expenses reimbursed. For 5 plus hours per day we give £3 towards lunch.
Interview details: Prospective volunteers are interviewed at the office where they will work.
Certification: Written reference.
Charity number: 274467
UK placements: *England* (London, Somerset).

ACTION HEALTH/SKILLSHARE INTERNATIONAL
The Gate House
25 Gwydir Street
Cambridge
CB1 2LG UK

Tel: +44 (0) 1223 460853
Fax: +44 (0) 1223 461787

e-mail: info@skillshare.org
Web: www.skillshare.org
Contact: Skills Development Unit

Alternative address:
176 New Walk
Leicester
LE1 7JA UK
Tel: +44 (0) 116 254 1862
Fax: +44 (0) 116 254 2614

Action Health is an operating programme of Skillshare International. We develop primary healthcare training programmes in partnership with communities in Asia and Africa. We respond to requests for assistance by sending qualified health professionals (trainers) to transfer identified skills in order to meet basic health needs. Action Health and its trainers work with the aim of fostering community education, participation and empowerment. Our goal is to help communities become self-reliant.

Total projects worldwide: 16
Total UK projects: 0
Starting months: January–December.
Time required: 52 weeks (plus).
Age requirement: 22 plus.
Causes: Aids/HIV, disabled (learning), health care/medical.
Activities: Development issues, international aid, training.
Vols under 26 placed each year: 2 of a total of 12.

When to apply: 6–12 months before departure.
Work alone/with others: Varies.
Volunteers with disabilities: Possible.
Qualifications: Fully qualified health professionals with a minimum of 2 years post-qualification experience. Contracts range from 1 to 2 years. Doctors, midwives, health visitors, occupational/physio/speech therapists.
Health requirements: Nil.
Costs: Medical insurance required.
Benefits: Housing, food, insurance, round-trip air fare and visas, monthly allowance, pre-departure orientation, local support, paid leave, pre-departure lump sum and resettlement grant on return, language training as required, National Insurance cover.
Training: Residential pre-departure orientation course.
Supervision: Local programme manager.
Interview details: Selection day in the UK.
Certification: We provide references.
Charity number: 1067006
Worldwide placements: *Africa* (Tanzania, Uganda); *Asia* (India).

ACTION PARTNERS MINISTRIES
Bawtry Hall
Bawtry
Doncaster
S. Yorkshire
DN10 6JH UK

Tel: +44 (0) 1302 710750
Fax: +44 (0) 1302 719399
e-mail: info@actionpartners.org.uk
Contact: David Baker

Action Partners Ministries is a Christian agency facilitating partnerships for cross-cultural missions to Africans worldwide. We are committed to bringing the unreached to salvation in Christ, to discipling and training for Christian service, to meeting people's spiritual, emotional and physical needs and to assisting Africans into worldwide mission. We engage in a variety of projects in partnership with indigenous movements and institutions that cover such areas as medical, rural development, educational and relief work. Volunteers with an offending background may be accepted depending on the circumstances.

Total projects worldwide: 5

Total UK projects: 5
Starting months: January–December.
Time required: 3–52 weeks.
Age requirement: 18 plus.
Causes: Children, elderly people, health care/medical, teaching/assisting (nursery, primary, secondary, mature).
Activities: Administration, agriculture/farming, building/construction, caring (residential), manual work, religion, teaching, technical skills, visiting/befriending.
Vols under 26 placed each year: 27 of a total of 37.
When to apply: End April for summer projects. Otherwise 6 months ahead.
Work alone/with others: Either.
Volunteers with disabilities: Not usually as based in Africa but depends on extent of disability.
Qualifications: Committed Evangelical Christians. Otherwise depends on work to be done.
Equipment/clothing: Suitable for Africa.
Health requirements: Good general health. Volunteers for more than a month have medicals.
Costs: All costs – travel, insurance, board and lodging.
Benefits: Allowances come out of total support costs as raised by volunteer. Residential re-union provided.
Training: Residential orientation course provided.
Supervision: For summer team; a team leader will accompany volunteers. For other placements, local supervision.
Nationalities accepted: This office usually covers volunteers from the UK, Ireland and Holland.
Interview details: Prospective volunteers are interviewed at our office at Bawtry, South Yorkshire.
Certification: References on request for those who have volunteered for over 6 months.
Charity number: 1037154
Worldwide placements: *Africa* (Benin, Cameroon, Chad, Congo Dem. Republic, Congo Republic, Egypt, Ethiopia, Ghana, Nigeria, Sudan).
UK placements: *England* (Leicestershire, London, Merseyside, Nottinghamshire, S. Yorkshire).

ACTIV FOUNDATION – RECREATION DEPARTMENT
134 Dundas Road
Inglewood
Perth
6052 Western Australia

Tel: 00 61 8 9370 5466
Fax: 00 61 8 9272 2922
Contact: Simon James, Volunteer
Co-ordinator (Recreation Department)

ACTIV Foundation is a not-for-profit, non-government organization providing services to people with intellectual disability and their families, in the areas of accommodation, employment, respite and recreation. ACTIV Recreation provides many leisure and holiday options for people with intellectual disability to access community facilities. We are always looking for people to volunteer some time either regularly or on an ad-hoc basis. When you offer your services to ACTIV Recreation, staff will ask what your interests are and what time you have available. These are then matched with the programmes that we conduct. People visiting Perth, Western Australia, are welcome to volunteer with us, on one or more of the programmes. Our mission statement is: 'To enable people with intellectual disability to enjoy their life and use their abilities to reach their potential and gain a greater independence.' Volunteers with an offending background may be acceptable if offences are not applicable to this line of work. International police clearances are required.

Total projects worldwide: 90
Total UK projects: 0
Starting months: January–December.
Time required: 1–6 weeks.
Age requirement: 18 plus.
Causes: Children, disabled (learning), elderly people, holidays for disabled, young people.
Activities: Arts/crafts, caring (general and day), cooking, driving, group work, outdoor skills, sport, summer camps, visiting/befriending.
Vols under 26 placed each year: 400 of a total of 800.
When to apply: As early as possible.
Work alone/with others: With others.
Volunteers with disabilities: We are unable to place people with disabilities as volunteers need to be mobile – wheelchair users unsuitable.

Qualifications: Some driving. Caring attitude plus interest in people with intellectual disability.
Health requirements: Reasonable level of fitness.
Costs: Only personal spending money.
Benefits: All food, transport, accommodation and entry to tourist attractions paid for while on programme.
Interview details: Interviews take place at our recreation centre.
Certification: Reference on request.
Charity number: 19589
Worldwide placements: *Australasia* (Australia).

ADDACTION – COMMUNITY DRUG AND ALCOHOL INITIATIVES
67–69 Cowcross Street
Smithfield
London
EC1M 6BP UK

Tel: + 44 (0) 20 7251 5860
Fax: + 44 (0) 20 7251 5890
e-mail: edwards@addaction.org.uk
Web: www.addaction.org.uk
Contact: Karen Edwards, HR Adviser

Addaction – Community Drug and Alcohol Initiatives would be interested in volunteers for our many London-based (and other) projects, and also possibly fundraising/administration volunteers for our Central Office in London.

Total projects worldwide: 26
Total UK projects: 26
Starting months: January–December.
Time required: 2–10 weeks.
Age requirement: 16 plus.
Causes: Addicts/Ex-addicts, offenders/Ex-offenders.
Activities: Administration, counselling, fundraising, library/resource centres, marketing/publicity, research, social work, training, visiting/befriending.
When to apply: All year.
Work alone/with others: With others.
Volunteers with disabilities: Possible – we are an Equal Opportunities Organization.
Qualifications: Nil.
Health requirements: Nil.
Costs: Nil.
Benefits: Fares, travel and meals – all out-of-pocket expenses. Addaction's insurance covers liability.

Training: 6 months structured volunteering programme.
Supervision: Volunteer co-ordinators supervise.
Certification: Reference provided.
Charity number: 1001957
UK placements: *England* (Derbyshire, Devon, London, Staffordshire, E. Sussex, W. Sussex, West Midlands).

ADEPT IN COVENTRY LIMITED
PO Box 165
Coventry
CV1 1ZU UK

Tel: + 44 (0) 24 7623 0606
Fax: + 44 (0) 24 7623 1706
e-mail: info.adept@pop3.hiway.co.uk
Web: www.adept.org.uk
Contact: Roger Smith

ADEPT is a community development organization, which assists the efforts of people and groups from disadvantaged communities in Coventry and Warwickshire to improve quality of life or equality of opportunity, and/or to regenerate the social and economic fabric of their areas. We also provide consultancy and research services and have a community accountancy service and a training service. We are a company limited by guarantee, a registered charity, and a community development trust. Volunteers with an offending background could be accepted.

Total projects worldwide: 1
Total UK projects: 1
Starting months: January–December.
Time required: 26–52 weeks.
Age requirement: 22 plus.
Causes: Human rights, inner city problems, unemployed.
Activities: Accountancy, administration, campaigning, community work, development issues, fundraising, group work, marketing/publicity, research.
Vols under 26 placed each year: 1 or 2.
When to apply: All year.
Work alone/with others: With staff.
Volunteers with disabilities: Dependent on disability – must be mobile.
Qualifications: Graduates.
Health requirements: Nil.
Costs: Nil.
Benefits: Limited expenses but no wage.
Interview details: Interviews take place in Coventry.
Certification: Certification possible in some circumstances. Reference on request.
Charity number: 1018919
UK placements: *England* (Warwickshire, West Midlands).

ADVENTURE FOUNDATION OF PAKISTAN
Adventure Foundation
Garden Avenue, National Park Area
Islamabad
44000 Pakistan

Tel: 00 92 51 825805
Fax: 00 92 51 272538
e-mail: adventure@pimail.com.pk
Contact: Mr Afdab Rana

Adventure Foundation of Pakistan promotes outdoor activities and 'thrill' sports for youth and other interested individuals in Pakistan. Activities include downhill skiing, rock climbing, hiking, windsurfing, bicycling, canoeing, mountaineering, and hot air ballooning. We strive to develop an 'action-orientated education system' that encourages members to: achieve self-awareness; learn practical skills; appreciate Pakistan's national wilderness; participate with others in community spirit efforts; develop physical fitness. We follow the philosophy and concepts of Outward Bound and conduct training courses at adventure training centres to prepare members for organized outings and offer advice to members who plan private excursions. We provide special training courses for disabled individuals and plan special outings to accommodate their needs. We offer courses in swimming and life saving. We are planning to establish a mountain and wilderness guides training centre. We sponsor international youth exchange programmes with other adventure sports organizations. We offer financial assistance to underprivileged members for all courses and outings.

Total projects worldwide: 1
Total UK projects: 0
Starting months: June.
Time required: 3–4 weeks.
Age requirement: 21–25
Causes: Children, conservation, environmental causes, holidays for disabled, young people.
Activities: Conservation skills, first aid, group

work, outdoor skills, summer camps.
Vols under 26 placed each year: 30.
When to apply: By 15 April.
Work alone/with others: With others.
Volunteers with disabilities: Not possible.
Qualifications: Mountaineering, rock
climbing, camping and river running.
Equipment/clothing: Trekking/mountain
boots, rock climbing shoes, sleeping bags,
mat and pack.
Health requirements: Nil.
Costs: Return air fare to North West Frontier
Province, Pakistan.
Benefits: Board and lodging plus £4 per day
pocket money.
Nationalities accepted: Neither Indian nor
Israeli volunteers are accepted.
Interview details: Applicants from abroad are
interviewed by post.
Certification: Certificate or reference
provided.
Worldwide placements: *Asia* (Pakistan).

ADVENTURE PLUS (A plus)
Hill Grove Farm
Dry Lane
Crawley
Witney
Oxfordshire
OX8 5NA UK

Tel: + 44 (0) 1993 703308
Fax: + 44 (0) 1993 708433
e-mail: enquiries@adventure plus.org.uk
Web: www.adventure plus.org.uk
Contact: Helen North, Administrator

Adventure Plus (A Plus) was started in 1990
and is a registered non-denominational
Christian charity. Our aim is to reach out to
young people through outdoor pursuits and
adventure holidays. These take place mainly
in Oxfordshire but we also run activities in
the Brecon Beacons, Forest of Dean, Wye
Valley, North Wales etc. We currently employ
a small core team of permanent staff and are
supported by around 300 volunteers without
whom we could not operate. We offer
'affordable accessible adventure' to many
children and young people by being a very
low cost organization based within 90
minutes of London, Birmingham, Bristol and
Southampton. In 2000 approximately 2,000
young people came through our programmes
of camps and courses. We encourage campers
to return each year particularly to our open

summer camps held each August. We then
hope they will become leaders at the age of
18. We believe that there is a real need for
stimulating moral and spiritual guidance for
today's young people when only too often we
see the results of juvenile crime, drug and
alcohol abuse. We also try to provide this
guidance in a framework of adventure and
fun. Volunteers with an offending
background may be accepted depending on
the offences.

Total projects worldwide: 40
Total UK projects: 40
Starting months: January–December.
Time required: 1–52 weeks (plus).
Age requirement: 18 plus.
Causes: Children, inner city problems, young
people.
Activities: Administration, arts/crafts,
catering, cooking, first aid, fundraising,
group work, music, outdoor skills, religion,
sport, summer camps, teaching, theatre/
drama, training.
Vols under 26 placed each year: 2 gap year
plus 15 others of a total of 20.
When to apply: All year.
Work alone/with others: With others.
Volunteers with disabilities: Possible.
Archery, arts and crafts, music, drama could
be suitable for disabled volunteers.
Qualifications: Nil but for outdoor pursuits
governing body qualifications needed (BCU/
RYA/MLTB etc.).
Equipment/clothing: Provided by A Plus.
Health requirements: In view of our
programmes we need fairly fit volunteers.
Costs: We ask volunteers to pay the costs of
staying on our camps/courses (£11 per day)
maximum £100 per annum.
Benefits: Training weekends offered where
skills and qualifications are gained.
Volunteers are covered by A Plus employees'
liability insurance cover.
Supervision: Provided by staff.
Interview details: Prospective gap year
volunteers are interviewed. Others are not
interviewed but 2 references are followed up
before a volunteer can start.
Certification: Reference on request.
Charity number: 802659
UK placements: *England* (Berkshire,
Cumbria, Derbyshire, Dorset,
Gloucestershire, Oxfordshire, Shropshire);
Wales (Conwy, Gwynedd, Powys).

ADVENTURE SERVICE CHALLENGE SCHEME
10 Aubreys
Letchworth
Hertfordshire
SG6 3TZ UK

Tel: +44 (0) 1462 676865
Fax: +44 (0) 1462 676865
Contact: Tony Freeman

Adventure Service Challenge Scheme is similar to the Duke of Edinburgh's Award but there is no connection. It is for 8–14 year olds (and beyond for those who for one reason or another are not ready to progress into D of E). Volunteers are needed to get involved either administratively or by taking youngsters on expeditions and training them in the skills laid down by the scheme.

Total projects worldwide: Various.
Total UK projects: Various.
Starting months: January–December.
Time required: 1–52 weeks.
Age requirement: 18 plus.
Causes: Children, disabled (learning and physical), offenders/Ex-offenders, teaching/assisting (primary, secondary), young people.
Activities: Administration, community work, development issues, fundraising, group work, newsletter/journalism, outdoor skills, research, social work, summer camps, teaching, training.
When to apply: All year.
Work alone/with others: Both.
Volunteers with disabilities: Possible.
Qualifications: Driving licence essential.
Health requirements: Nil.
Benefits: Out-of-pocket expenses.
Certification: Certificate or reference on request.
UK placements: *England* (Bedfordshire, Cambridgeshire, Cheshire, Cumbria, Derbyshire, Herefordshire, Lancashire, Leicestershire, London, Manchester, Merseyside, Northamptonshire, Northumberland, Nottinghamshire, Rutland, Shropshire, Staffordshire, Tyne and Wear, Warwickshire, West Midlands, Worcestershire, N. Yorkshire, S. Yorkshire, W. Yorkshire); *Wales* (throughout).

AFASIC – UNLOCKING SPEECH AND LANGUAGE
347 Central Markets
Smithfield
London
EC1A 9NH UK

Tel: +44 (0) 20 7236 3632/6487
Fax: +44 (0) 20 7236 8115
Contact: Norma Corkish, Chief Executive

AFASIC represents children and young people who have difficulty in using speech or language. The disabilities range in severity from an inability to articulate speech to a failure to understand the basic elements of language and will in many cases not be associated with physical or intellectual impairments. Half a million children have difficulties severe enough to hinder their ability to learn without specialist help. AFASIC provides advice, information and support through newsletters three times a year, seminars/workshops for parents and professionals, 50 self-help groups throughout the country, weeks/weekends for children and young people to develop communication skills and self-confidence.

Total projects worldwide: 5
Total UK projects: 5
Starting months: January–December.
Time required: 1–52 weeks.
Age requirement: 18 plus.
Causes: Children, disabled (learning and physical), holidays for disabled, teaching/assisting young people.
Activities: Caring (general), summer camps, teaching.
Vols under 26 placed each year: 30–40
When to apply: 19 January onwards.
Work alone/with others: With others.
Volunteers with disabilities: Not possible.
Qualifications: Essential to speak English.
Equipment/clothing: Suitable clothing for outdoor activities including watersports.
Health requirements: Good health.
Costs: Own travel expenses although volunteers can often share transport.
Interview details: Interviews take place in Birmingham, London or Manchester.
Charity number: 1045617
UK placements: *England* (Cumbria, Derbyshire, Dorset, London); *Wales* (Conwy).

AFPIC – ACTION FOR PEOPLE IN CONFLICT
Silverbirch House
Longworth
Abingdon

Oxfordshire
OX13 5EJ UK

Tel: +44 (0) 1865 821380
Fax: +44 (0) 1865 821384
e-mail: afpicuk@gn.apc.org
Web: www.oneworld.org/afpic/index
Contact: Dee Tyrer

AfPiC's mission is to rebuild the lives of individuals and communities damaged by conflict. This presents four different volunteer opportunities: 1. We are particularly interested in volunteers who would work at our head office in Longworth in marketing and promotions; general office work; volunteer recruitment and placement; events. 2. We have two charity shops but intend to open more and can offer accommodation to one or two volunteers for this type of work. 3. In Southampton we have a project to convert an old inshore minesweeper into a 'pirate radio' station in Ireland. Volunteers to work on the refitting of the ship are very welcome. 4. In Kenya we are helping to run an orphanage for street children in Thika. Volunteers are now wanted there all the year round. During 2001 volunteers may also be needed in Sierra Leone, the Balkans and India. Placement in the Balkans would be via The Balkan Sunflower Project and in India via IndiaCares who are based in Bangalore. We would happily consider volunteers with an offending background.

Total projects worldwide: 5
Total UK projects: 2
Starting months: January–December.
Time required: 2–52 weeks.
Age requirement: 16 plus.
Causes: Children, human rights, refugees, teaching/assisting (EFL), work camps – seasonal, young people.
Activities: Administration, building/construction, campaigning, computers, counselling, development issues, driving, fundraising, group work, international aid, marketing/publicity, newsletter/journalism, research, work camps – seasonal.
Vols under 26 placed each year: 20.
When to apply: All year.
Work alone/with others: With others.
Volunteers with disabilities: Possible.
Qualifications: Driving is an advantage. An interest in the charity's mission is a main requirement.
Health requirements: Nil.

Costs: Approximately £750 covers travel and insurance for Kenya and India.
Benefits: Volunteers working on 6 month work placements in the UK received £200 per month to cover costs. Accommodation is subsidized. We have public liability insurance which covers volunteers and we take out individual insurance for volunteers going overseas.
Training: UK – no training required. Overseas – pre-briefing essential.
Supervision: Office work – Director of Development. Retail work – Retail Co-ordinator. Southampton – Pirates for Peace Project Manager. Kenya – Representative in East Africa (Alice Jukes).
Interview details: Interviews take place either in Longworth or at a mutually convenient location.
Certification: Certificate or reference provided.
Charity number: 1060894
Worldwide placements: *Africa* (Kenya, Sierra Leone); *Europe* (Bosnia-Herzegovina).
UK placements: *England* (Oxfordshire).

AFRICA AND ASIA VENTURE
10 Market Place
Devizes
Wiltshire
SN10 1HT UK

Tel: +44 (0) 1380 729009
Fax: +44 (0) 1380 720060
e-mail: av@aventure.co.uk
Web: www.aventure.co.uk
Contact: The Director

Africa and Asia Venture is for hard-working, adventurous school leavers who wish to spend part of their year out gaining cultural and work experience with youth in Africa, in either Kenya, Zimbabwe, Tanzania, Uganda, Malawi or Botswana; or in India or Nepal and contributing towards its development. We also have some plans available for recently qualified graduates. Volunteers are placed in pairs as assistant teachers in selected schools for one term. Depending on their skills and attributes, and the requirements of the schools, volunteers assist in a variety of subjects ranging from English, science, music and vocational activities to clubs and sports. Schools are chosen with location, work opportunities, accommodation and security in mind, and placements do not deprive local teachers from working. There are also a few opportunities for attachment to community-related and conservation projects. In Kenya these include working in National Parks such as Tsavo. Following the placement, participants have 2–3 weeks for independent travel and the complete programme is rounded off with a group safari to places of interest such as Lake Turkana in Northern Kenya or the Zambezi River in Zimbabwe. In India the group will travel to the splendours of Rhajasthan and in Nepal to game parks or trek in the Himalayas. For details contact our Devizes office.

Total projects worldwide: 80–90
Total UK projects: 0
Starting months: January, February, April, May, August–November.
Time required: 16–20 weeks.
Age requirement: 18–23
Causes: Children, conservation, environmental causes, health care/medical, teaching/assisting (nursery, primary, secondary), wildlife, young people.
Activities: Arts/crafts, building/construction, caring (general), community work, conservation skills, music, sport, teaching, theatre/drama.
Vols under 26 placed each year: 410–430.
When to apply: At least 6 plus months before departure and preferably as early as possible.
Work alone/with others: In pairs.
Volunteers with disabilities: Not possible.
Qualifications: Studied to A-level, thereafter assessment interview.
Health requirements: Volunteers must be in good health.
Costs: £2,290 plus air fare and extra spending money.
Benefits: 4-day orientation course on arrival, food and accommodation as well as final safari, charity contribution, travel and medical insurance.
Training: 4-day orientation course on arrival.
Supervision: Provided by our director or representative.
Nationalities accepted: British passport holders only.
Interview details: Interviews take place in Devizes or in regional area.
Certification: Reference on request.
Worldwide placements: *Africa* (Botswana, Kenya, Malawi, Tanzania, Uganda, Zimbabwe); *Asia* (India, Nepal).

AFRICA CENTRE
38 King Street
Covent Garden
London
WC2E 8JT UK

Tel: +44 (0) 20 7836 1973
Fax: +44 (0) 20 7836 1975
e-mail: africacentre@gn.apc.org
Contact: Dr Adotey Bing

The Africa Centre is a charity established in 1961 to inform and educate the British and European public about Africa. We have over 100,000 visitors per year. We have entertainment: music, food, exhibitions, performances and children's workshops. We give information: databases, resource room, fact sheets, courses, responses to telephone and written enquiries. Advocacy: talks, lectures, conferences, debates, radio, cultural awareness, training. We have something for everyone, especially African community groups, teachers and school children, UK NGOs working in Africa, UK national institutions, large-scale employers, politicians, journalists and the media, UK business people with African connections, academics and students, African NGOs and African entrepreneurs. Volunteers with an offending background may be accepted.

Total projects worldwide: 1
Total UK projects: 1
Starting months: January–December.
Time required: 1–52 weeks (plus).
Age requirement: 18 plus.
Causes: Children, human rights, unemployed, young people.
Activities: Administration, development issues, fundraising, marketing/publicity, newsletter/journalism, research.
Vols under 26 placed each year: 20 of a total of 30.
When to apply: All year.
Work alone/with others: Mixed.
Qualifications: Nil.
Health requirements: Nil.
Benefits: Travel costs in London and lunch provided.
Supervision: Provided by the programme co-ordinator.
Interview details: Interviews are conducted at the Centre.
UK placements: *England* (London).

AFRICA INLAND MISSION
2 Vorley Road
Archway
London
N19 5HE UK

Tel: +44 (0) 20 7281 1184
Fax: +44 (0) 20 7281 4479
e-mail: enquiry@aim-eur.org
Web: www.aim-eur.org
Contact: Angela Godfrey, Associate Personnel
Director

Africa Inland Mission gives an opportunity
for young people to be involved in cross-
cultural communication and to look at the
work of missionaries first hand. Placements
are made in rural schools for 8–12 months.
Teams doing a practical project and church
work go for seven weeks each summer.

Total projects worldwide: 11
Total UK projects: 0
Starting months: January, July, August.
Time required: 7–52 weeks.
Age requirement: 18 plus.
Causes: Teaching/assisting (secondary EFL),
young people.
Activities: Accountancy, administration,
religion, teaching.
Vols under 26 placed each year: 24 of a total
of 30.
When to apply: September – May.
Work alone/with others: Alone, in pairs or
in teams of 6–8 people.
Volunteers with disabilities: Not possible.
Qualifications: Post A-level or graduates,
teachers. Committed Christians.
Health requirements: Must be in good health.
Costs: Approximately £4,000 including
travel, insurance, living and administration
costs. Full health insurance is required and is
part of the 'budget' raised by the volunteer.
Benefits: Housing provided.
Training: 4 days of teacher training and 4
days of orientation.
Supervision: Given at the placement by a
national, head teacher or church leader. Local
missionary co-ordinators in most countries.
Interview details: 2 interviews for 12-month
volunteers.
Worldwide placements: *Africa* (Central
African Republic, Comoros, Kenya, Lesotho,
Madagascar, Mozambique, Namibia,
Seychelles, Sudan, Tanzania, Uganda).

AFRICA TREE CENTRE
PO Box 90
Plessislaer 4500
Natal
South Africa

Contact: Mr R.T. Mazibuko, Founder

Africa Tree Centre's founder, R.T. Mazibuko,
has been one of the foremost proponents of
tree planting and forestry education in South
Africa. Through drought, flood, starvation
and oppression, he continued to plant trees,
and educated and inspired many other
Africans to do the same. They still continue
today and the Africa Tree Centre trains youth
in tree planting and gardening. Volunteers
are often needed for tree planting.

Total projects worldwide: Many.
Total UK projects: 0
Starting months: January–December.
Time required: 1–52 weeks (plus).
Age requirement: 16 plus.
Causes: Conservation, environmental causes.
Activities: Conservation skills, forestry,
gardening/horticulture, manual work,
training.
When to apply: All year.
Work alone/with others: With others.
Volunteers with disabilities: If able to do
manual work, tree planting.
Qualifications: Nil.
Equipment/clothing: Outdoor clothes.
Health requirements: Nil.
Worldwide placements: *Africa* (South Africa).

AFRICAN CONSERVATION EXPERIENCE
PO Box 58
Teignmouth
Devon
TQ14 8XW UK

Tel: +44 (0) 1626 879700
Fax: +44 (0) 1626 879700
e-mail: info@afconservex.com
Web: www.afconservex.com
Contact: Rob Harris

African Conservation Experience aims: to
give young British people the opportunity to
experience conservation in Southern Africa;
to bring foreign income and information
exchange for conservation in Southern Africa.
Volunteers are given the opportunity for
hands-on conservation work which may
include research projects on endangered
species, animal counts, game capture, fire

break burning, soil and water conservation projects, educating local tribal children about conservation, anthropology of bushmen, removal of exotic vegetation, re-establishment of indigenous fauna and flora, watching and recording animal habits and movement, maintenance of game fences and roads, hiking trail construction and many other conservation related activities. It is hoped that a long-term relationship will continue between the reserve and the volunteer on research programmes, etc. in colleges, universities and UK conservation establishments.

Total projects worldwide: 16 plus.
Total UK projects: 0
Starting months: January–December.
Time required: 4–12 weeks.
Age requirement: 18–35
Causes: Animal welfare, archaeology, children, conservation, environmental causes, teaching (primary), wildlife.
Activities: Agriculture/farming, arts/crafts, conservation skills, manual work, outdoor skills, research, scientific work, social work, teaching, technical skills, training.
Vols under 26 placed each year: 100 plus.
When to apply: As early as possible, All year.
Work alone/with others: Mostly in teams of up to six – sometimes alone with supervisor.
Volunteers with disabilities: Not possible.
Qualifications: Driving licence and language ability preferable. Some conservation experience useful. It is essential that volunteers have enthusiasm for conservation.
Equipment/clothing: Sleeping bag, day sack, mosquito net, water bottle, plain coloured clothing, good walking boots, binoculars useful. A full kit list is provided.
Health requirements: Volunteers must be fit and healthy.
Costs: £1,795–3,500 depending on reserve, duration and timing plus pocket money. Insurance compulsory – can be arranged by volunteer or African Conservation Experience.
Benefits: The cost includes all travel, food and accommodation.
Training: At the reserve.
Supervision: Work experience co-ordinator on each reserve.
Nationalities accepted: No restrictions providing visas can be obtained.
Interview details: Introduction weekends for groups of 10 held almost monthly in Devon.

Certification: Reference on request.
Worldwide placements: *Africa* (South Africa, Zimbabwe).

AFRICAN REGIONAL COUNCIL OF THE WORLD

Federation for Mental Health
Anchor House
Cairo Road
PO Box 50209
Lusaka
Zambia

Tel: 00 260 5 223024
Fax: 00 260 5 224585
Contact: Isaac Mwendapole, President

Total projects worldwide: 23
Total UK projects: 0
Starting months: January–December.
Time required: 1–52 weeks (plus).
Age requirement: 25 plus.
Causes: Disabled (learning), health care/medical, human rights, poor/homeless, refugees.
Activities: Community work, counselling, development issues, fundraising, newsletter/journalism, research, social work, training.
When to apply: All year.
Volunteers with disabilities: Possible, except visually or hearing impaired.
Equipment/clothing: Only presentable clothing which must include a tie (m) or below-knees dress (f).
Health requirements: Nil.
Costs: Air travel return to Zambia, membership $50, all subsistence.
Certification: Certificate or reference provided.
Worldwide placements: *Africa* (Burkina Faso, Chad, Mali, Senegal, Zambia).

AFS INTERNATIONAL YOUTH DEVELOPMENT

Leeming House
Vicar Lane
Leeds
W. Yorkshire
LS2 7JF UK

Tel: +44 (0) 113 242 6136
Fax: +44 (0) 113 243 0631
e-mail: gillian.woods@afs.org
Contact: Gill Woods
Web: www.afsuk.org

AFS International Youth Development has

voluntary work opportunities in Latin America and South Africa. More than just travel, you can spend six months in Latin America and South Africa living with a volunteer host family, and working alongside local people on community social projects, dealing with issues such as health, education, the environment, community development and working with underprivileged children and people with disabilities. AFS is an international, voluntary, non-governmental, non-profit organization that provides intercultural learning opportunities to help people develop the knowledge, skills and understanding needed to create a more just and peaceful world. AFS has been running programmes since 1947 and is the only organization of its kind to receive a citation from the UN in recognition of its work for world youth. AFS International Youth Development is the UK partner in the international AFS network of 55 different countries worldwide. Volunteers with an offending background may be accepted, assessed on an individual basis.

Total projects worldwide: 8
Total UK projects: 0
Starting months: January, February, July.
Time required: 20–24 weeks.
Age requirement: 18–29
Causes: Addicts/Ex-addicts, Aids/HIV, children, disabled (learning and physical), elderly people, environmental causes, health care/medical, human rights, inner city problems, poor/homeless, teaching/assisting.
Activities: Caring (general), community work, development issues, group work, outdoor skills, teaching, theatre/drama, training.
Vols under 26 placed each year: 40 of a total of 50.
When to apply: All year but 4 months before departure.
Work alone/with others: With others.
Volunteers with disabilities: Possible – each applicant is assessed.
Qualifications: Nil.
Health requirements: Good health essential.
Costs: £2,950. Comprehensive insurance cover is included in contribution costs.
Training: Selection, language, materials, weekend orientation.
Supervision: Local contact and office support.
Nationalities accepted: No restrictions but participants must be resident in the UK.

Interview details: Prospective volunteers are interviewed in Manchester, Leeds or London.
Certification: Certificate or reference provided.
Worldwide placements: *Africa* (South Africa); *Central America* (Guatemala, Honduras, Panama); *South America* (Bolivia, Brazil, Colombia, Peru).

AGAPE CENTRO ECUMENICO

Segreteria
10060 Prali
Torino
Italy

Tel: 00 390 121 80 75 14
Fax: 00 390 121 80 76 90
Contact: The Secretary

Agape Centro Ecumenico is an international ecumenical community centre in a remote part of the Italian Alps, used for national and international conferences, study camps, courses and other meetings on ecological, peace, Third World, political, cultural, theological and women's issues. An international service group made up of volunteers works alongside the resident community during the summer months. The work is varied and can include kitchen duties, housework, cleaning, working in the coffee bar, laundry, babysitting, maintenance, construction or repair work. There are opportunities for volunteers to take part in the conferences. Applicants should be willing to make a contribution to the collective life of the community, 36 hours, six days per week. Volunteers are sometimes taken on outside the summer period.

Starting months: June, July, August.
Time required: 4–8 weeks.
Age requirement: 18 plus.
Causes: Work camps – seasonal.
Activities: Manual work, religion, work camps – seasonal.
Vols under 26 placed each year: 55.
When to apply: February or sooner.
Work alone/with others: With others.
Qualifications: Basic Italian an advantage.
Health requirements: Anti-tetanus vaccination.
Costs: Travel expenses and pocket money.
Benefits: Board and lodging.
Worldwide placements: *Europe* (Italy).

AGE CONCERN ENGLAND (THE NATIONAL COUNCIL ON AGEING)
Astral House
1268 London Road
London
SW16 4ER UK

Tel: + 44 (0) 20 8679 8000
Fax: + 44 (0) 20 8679 6069
Contact: Helen Tovey

Age Concern England is the national headquarters for over 1,400 local Age Concern groups in the UK. Each group has slightly differing policies and guidelines for volunteers. Contact your local county or large town group by telephone, details available from your local telephone directory. Contact Age Concern England for a leaflet on volunteering.

Total projects worldwide: 1,400
Total UK projects: 1,400
Starting months: January–December.
Time required: 1–52 weeks.
Age requirement: 16 plus.
Causes: Elderly people.
Activities: Administration, caring (general and day), counselling, driving, fundraising, research, social work, training, visiting/befriending.
When to apply: All year.
Work alone/with others: Both.
Volunteers with disabilities: Possible.
Qualifications: Nil but references checked before volunteer can start work.
Health requirements: Nil.
Costs: Nil.
Benefits: Out-of-pocket expenses.
Certification: Certificate or reference provided.
Charity number: 261794
UK placements: *England* (throughout); *Wales* (throughout).

AGE-LINK
Suites 9/10
The Manor House
The Green
Southall
Middlesex
UB2 4BR UK

Tel: + 44 (0) 20 8571 5888
Contact: Mrs Mavis Piper

Age-Link needs volunteers in the Greater London area to help the elderly. A typical day would involve collecting an elderly person from their home, driving them to another family where they would have tea and be entertained, and then driving them home again.

Total projects worldwide: 1
Total UK projects: 1
Starting months: January–December.
Time required: 1–52 weeks.
Age requirement: 16 plus.
Causes: Elderly people.
Activities: Driving, fundraising, visiting/befriending.
When to apply: All year.
Work alone/with others: Both.
Qualifications: Nil. Drivers especially needed.
Health requirements: Nil.
Costs: Nil.
UK placements: *England* (London).

AGENTS OF DEVELOPMENT FOR THE RURAL COMMUNITY (ADRUCOM)
PO Box 324
Bolgatanga
Upper East Region
Ghana

Contact: Elias B. Ayeebo

ADRUCOM is a national organization working with a wide variety of projects, including reforestation, agriculture, forestry, agroforestry, beekeeping, vegetable farming and women's issues. Volunteers can help with the above projects, especially vegetable farming, beekeeping and agricultural work, and can stay between four weeks and six months. Training can also be provided. Volunteers are expected to pay for food.

Total projects worldwide: Many.
Total UK projects: 0
Starting months: January–December.
Time required: 1–52 weeks.
Age requirement: 17 plus.
Causes: Conservation, environmental causes.
Activities: Agriculture/farming, community work, conservation skills, forestry, gardening/horticulture.
When to apply: All year.
Work alone/with others: With others.
Qualifications: Nil.
Equipment/clothing: Suitable for outdoor work in hot weather.
Costs: Flight to Ghana and journey to the North. Cost of food.

Benefits: Accommodation.
Worldwide placements: *Africa* (Ghana).

AKLOWA – THE AFRICAN TRADITIONAL VILLAGE

Takeley House
Brewers End
Takeley
Bishop's Stortford
Hertfordshire
CM22 6QR UK

Tel: +44 (0) 1279 871062
Contact: Felix Cobbson

Aklowa needs volunteers to undertake office work, gardening or decorating in this project which has created a Ghanaian village reflecting African culture. Groups – generally from schools and holiday schemes – come to the village for half a day to dress, eat, make music and experience Ghanaian lifestyle.

Total projects worldwide: 1
Total UK projects: 1
Starting months: May–October.
Time required: 1–52 weeks.
Age requirement: 18 plus.
Causes: Heritage.
Activities: Administration, DIY, gardening/horticulture.
Work alone/with others: As part of a small team.
Volunteers with disabilities: Possible.
Qualifications: Nil.
Health requirements: Nil.
Benefits: Accommodation and food.
UK placements: *England* (Hertfordshire).

AKTION SÜHNEZEICHEN FRIEDENSDIENSTE e.V.

Augustr. 80
10117 Berlin
Germany

Tel: 00 49 30 28395 184
Fax: 00 49 30 28395 135
e-mail: asf@asf-ev.de
Contact: Mr Baldassare

Alternative address:
Coventry Cathedral International Centre
7 Priory Row
Coventry
CV1 5ES UK
Tel: +44 (0) 1203 222487
Contact: Mr Hardy Kluge

Aktion Sühnezeichen Friedensdienste (ASF) was founded in 1958 by women and men who had been active in the Protestant resistance to the Nazi regime in Germany. Presently about 150 ASF long-term volunteers (12–18 months) and about 300 ASF short-term volunteers (2–4 weeks) are working in many countries around the world. (Long-term UK volunteers are only eligible to work in the UK and Germany.) The long-term volunteers, mostly young people aged 18–27, work in various projects including (a) educational work: together with survivors of the Holocaust, at memorial centres of former concentration camps, in institutes and museums; as well as educational work in the field of human rights and anti-racism; (b) marginalized groups: refugees, homeless persons, elderly (mostly Holocaust survivors) and disabled persons, drug addicts, persons who are mentally ill, as well as in neighbourhood centres situated in poor urban areas. The short-term volunteers are active in international groups in more than 25 summer camps working in social facilities, on Jewish cemeteries and on memorial sites of former concentration camps. We want to encourage young people to overcome the feeling of powerlessness, as well as indifference and complacency, in order to contribute to a more just and peaceful world.

Total projects worldwide: 155
Total UK projects: 12
Starting months: September
Time required: 4–52 weeks.
Age requirement: 18 plus.
Causes: Children, disabled (learning), elderly people, health care/medical, human rights, poor/homeless, refugees, work camps – seasonal.
Activities: Administration, caring (general and day), community work, counselling, development issues, library/resource centres, research, summer camps, work camps – seasonal.
Vols under 26 placed each year: 145 of a total of 160.
When to apply: Before 1 March.
Work alone/with others: With other young volunteers.
Volunteers with disabilities: Possible.
Qualifications: We expect of our volunteers a certain amount of language skills (varying with countries/projects); experience in local voluntary social or political work, and above

all a great deal of motivation and energy to work with ASF and in the projects.

Health requirements: Nil.

Costs: Before starting, each volunteer must find £8 per month. Health insurance, including dental treatment, is essential and is the volunteer's responsibility. Support can be offered in single cases, if requested.

Benefits: Travel, board and lodging, pocket money.

Supervision: Every 2 weeks there is a meeting with a responsible contact person to discuss problems and requirements.

Nationalities accepted: Only limited by visa requirements.

Interview details: UK volunteers are interviewed in Coventry.

Certification: Certificate or reference provided, both from the project and from ASF.

Worldwide placements: *Europe* (Czech Republic, France, Germany, Italy, Latvia, Lithuania, Netherlands, Poland, Russia).

UK placements: *England* (Hampshire, London, West Midlands).

ALPES DE LUMIÈRE
Prieure de Salagon
Mane
04300 France

Tel: 00 33 492 75 70 50 or 75 70 54
Fax: 00 33 92 75 70 51
Contact: Laurence Michel

Alpes de Lumière organizes several camps around Provence dedicated to the restoration of historic buildings and the development of historic sites. These sites become recreational and cultural centres.

Total projects worldwide: 12
Total UK projects: 0
Starting months: June–September.
Time required: 3–52 weeks.
Age requirement: 18 plus.
Causes: Architecture, conservation, environmental causes, heritage, work camps – seasonal.
Activities: Building/construction, conservation skills, cooking, manual work, summer camps, work camps – seasonal.
Total no. of vols placed each year: 160
Vols under 26 placed each year: 160.
When to apply: As early as possible.
Work alone/with others: With others (12).
Volunteers with disabilities: Not possible.

Qualifications: Nil except ability to speak French or English and work under the sun.
Equipment/clothing: Sleeping bag, good shoes, old clothes (T-shirts and shorts), sun cream, anti-mosquito lotion.
Health requirements: No allergies.
Costs: Approximately FF600 per month plus pocket money and travel.
Benefits: Food, basic accommodation, trip around the area, free entry to museums and concerts.
Interview details: No interview necessary.
Certification: Certificate or reference provided.
Worldwide placements: *Europe* (France).

AMERICAN FARM SCHOOL – GREEK SUMMER PROGRAM
1133 Broadway @ 26th Street
New York
NY 10010
USA

Tel: 00 1 212 463 8434
Fax: 00 1 212 463 8208
e-mail: nyoffice@amerfarm.org
Contact: Mr Nicholas Apostal, Program Co-ordinator

American Farm School – Greek Summer Programme is a five week summer work and travel programme for high-school sophomores, juniors and seniors based at the American Farm School in Thessaloniki, Greece. Every year since 1970 the Farm School has brought 40 teenagers from around the USA and Europe to Greece to be a part of a once in a lifetime experience living in and travelling through one of the most ancient cultures on earth. The heart of the programme is a work project in a small village in northern Greece. Participants live with village families while they complete a much needed community improvement, such as a road or a foundation for a building. Outside of the time at the village, the group travels around the country to see the historical sights of Greece such as the monasteries of Meteora, the Oracle of Delphi and the Acropolis in Athens. In addition there are excursions to the vineyards at Porto Carras, the quiet fishing town of Nafplion, the island of Skiathos, and frequent stops at local beaches. The trip culminates with a two-day climb to the peak of Mount Olympus, home of the Greek gods. If you are interested in being a part of Greek Summer, please contact Nicholas Apostal. Join us for a volunteer experience that will change your life.

Total projects worldwide: 1
Total UK projects: 0
Starting months: June.
Time required: 5 weeks.
Age requirement: 15–18
Causes: Archaeology, poor/homeless, refugees.
Activities: Building/construction, manual work.
Vols under 26 placed each year: 40.
When to apply: All year.
Work alone/with others: With others.
Volunteers with disabilities: Not possible.
Qualifications: Nil.
Equipment/clothing: Work clothes, leather work gloves.
Health requirements: Nil.
Costs: Application fee US$500, programme fee US$2,600 plus return air fare to Greece.
Benefits: All food, lodging and travel within Greece. American Farm School provides insurance.
Training: Full construction, project, language and cultural training is provided during orientation.
Supervision: There is a programme director, three assistant directors and four counsellors throughout the trip.
Interview details: Volunteers are interviewed either locally or by telephone.
Certification: Reference on request.
Worldwide placements: *Europe* (Greece).

AMERICAN FARM SCHOOL – SUMMER INTERNATIONAL INTERNSHIP PROGRAM
1133 Broadway
New York
NY 10010
USA

Tel: 00 1 212 463 8433
Fax: 00 1 212 463 8208
e-mail: nyoffice@amerfarm.org
Contact: The Programme Co-ordinator

Every summer the American Farm School organizes an international group to help man the agricultural and maintenance programs at the school in Greece when regular staff and students are on vacation. The work involves a 35 hour week. Other activities include a

climb up Mount Olympus, trips into Thessaloniki and the islands, as well as a short stay with a family in a rural village.

Total projects worldwide: 1
Total UK projects: 0
Starting months: June, July.
Time required: 1–52 weeks.
Age requirement: 18–25
Causes: Animal welfare.
Activities: Agriculture/farming, manual work.
Vols under 26 placed each year: 30
When to apply: Any time before 30 April.
Work alone/with others: With others.
Volunteers with disabilities: Not possible.
Qualifications: College enrolment.
Equipment/clothing: Everyday warm weather work clothes.
Health requirements: Nil.
Costs: Fare to Thessaloniki.
Benefits: Accommodation, meals and a small allowance. American Farm School provides insurance.
Training: Complete job and farm training provided on the site.
Supervision: Supervised by the programme director and various farm managers.
Interview details: No interview necessary.
Worldwide placements: *Europe* (Greece).

AMERICAN HIKING SOCIETY'S VOLUNTEER VACATIONS
PO Box 20160
Washington
DC 20041-2160
USA

Tel: 00 1 301 565 6704
Fax: 00 1 301 565 6714
e-mail: info@americanhiking.com
Web: www.americanhiking.org
Contact: Shirley Hearn

For more than 20 years, American Hiking Society's Volunteer Vacations has been sending hundreds of volunteers each year into America's most special places to revitalize trails. Over the years, thousands of vacationers rake, shovel, trim, lop and chop hundreds of trail miles that, without these crews, would be unsafe for foot travel. Kicking off its third decade of caring for America's trails, AHS Volunteer Vacations will send more than 70 trail volunteer teams into America's national parks, forests and rangelands in 2001. Participants will restore deteriorating trails and build new ones while enjoying unique one or two week vacations. More than a programme that rehabilitates trails, AHS Volunteer Vacations is fostering public land stewardship and giving volunteers the opportunity to give back to the trails they love, and to have a great time doing it!

Total projects worldwide: 70
Total UK projects: 0
Starting months: January–December.
Time required: 1–52 weeks.
Age requirement: 18 plus.
Causes: Conservation, environmental causes, work camps – seasonal.
Activities: Building/construction, conservation skills, forestry, group work, manual work, outdoor skills, work camps – seasonal.
Vols under 26 placed each year: 50 of a total of 500.
When to apply: All year.
Work alone/with others: With others.
Volunteers with disabilities: Possible.
Qualifications: Nil, but international driving licence useful. Trail maintenance experience is helpful.
Equipment/clothing: List provided: must have backpack, sleeping bag and tent.
Health requirements: Able to hike at least 5 miles a day.
Costs: Travel and all expenses.
Benefits: Occasionally accommodation – usually volunteers camp with own equipment. Food usually provided. The agency hosting the trip provides insurance.
Supervision: By Federal Land Management Agency ranger.
Interview details: No interview necessary.
Worldwide placements: *North America* (USA).

AMERICAN JEWISH SOCIETY FOR SERVICE
15E 26th Street
New York
NY 10010
USA

Tel: 00 1 212 683 6178
Contact: Henry Kohn, Chairman

The American Jewish Society conducts voluntary work service camps for teenagers. Volunteers are needed to work as counsellors and to help with the camps' construction work.
Total projects worldwide: 1

Total UK projects: 0
Starting months: July.
Time required: 6–7 weeks.
Age requirement: 16–18
Causes: Work camps – seasonal.
Activities: Building/construction, counselling, manual work, work camps – seasonal.
Vols under 26 placed each year: 48.
When to apply: January–May.
Work alone/with others: With others.
Costs: US$2,500 plus pocket money and travel costs.
Benefits: Accommodation.
Interview details: Interviews take place in New York City or by telephone.
Worldwide placements: *North America* (USA).

AMIZADE
367 S. Graham Street
Pittsburgh
PA
15232 USA

Tel: 00 1 888 973 4443
Fax: 00 1 412 648 1492
e-mail: Volunteer@amizade.org
Web: http://amizade.org
Contact: Mike Sandy

Amizade is a non-profit organization dedicated to promoting volunteering and providing community service in locations throughout the world. Our programmes offer a mix of community service and recreation which provides our volunteers with the unique opportunity to participate first hand in the culture of the region where they are travelling. Past projects have included building a vocational training centre for street children on the Amazon, building additional rooms onto a health clinic in the Bolivian Andes and doing some historic preservation and environmental clean up in the Greater Yellowstone Area. Volunteers do not need any special skills, just a willingness to help.

Total projects worldwide: 5
Total UK projects: 0
Starting months: January–December.
Time required: 1–4 weeks.
Age requirement: 12 plus.
Causes: Animal welfare, architecture, children, conservation, disabled (learning and physical), elderly people, environmental causes, heritage, poor/homeless, unemployed, wildlife, young people.

Activities: Building/construction, community work, conservation skills, forestry, gardening/horticulture, manual work, sport, visiting/befriending.

Vols under 26 placed each year: 72 of a total of 120.

When to apply: At least 4 months before programme start date.

Work alone/with others: With other young people in Brazil and Bolivia.

Volunteers with disabilities: Possible.

Qualifications: Only a sense of humour.

Equipment/clothing: Varies with the programme site.

Health requirements: Volunteers must have had a physical examination during the previous 12 months.

Costs: Fees vary with each programme. Volunteers must cover their own medical and health insurance.

Benefits: Fees cover board and lodging, recreational activities and may include air fares.

Training: Volunteers are sent a volunteer pack.

Supervision: Local masons and carpenters as well as an Amizade programme director supervise the volunteers on every aspect of the programme.

Worldwide placements: *Australasia* (Australia); *North America* (USA); *South America* (Bolivia, Brazil).

AMNESTY INTERNATIONAL
99–119 Rosebery Avenue
London
EC1R 4RE UK

Tel: +44 (0) 20 7814 6200
Fax: +44 (0) 20 7833 1510
e-mail: rjones@amnesty.org.uk
Web: www.amnesty.org.uk
Contact: Rhiannon Jones, Personnel Officer

Amnesty International is an independent worldwide movement working for the release of prisoners of conscience; seeking fair and prompt trials for political prisoners; and working towards the end of torture and executions throughout the world. The UK section of Amnesty International has over 130,000 members and approximately 330 local groups throughout the UK. The section office is based in London and has a staff of 65 and many full-time and part-time volunteers. It is divided into six departments: administration and finance, campaigns, communications, marketing, deputy directorate and the directorate. Volunteers are allocated to a team and assist with clerical and administrative duties, such as word processing, filing, photocopying, sending faxes, helping with mailings and occasional special projects. Where a volunteer works depends upon a match between a current vacancy and the skills and experience of the volunteer.

Total projects worldwide: 100 plus.

Total UK projects: 100 plus.

Starting months: January–December.

Time required: 12–52 weeks (plus).

Age requirement: 16 plus.

Causes: Human rights.

Activities: Accountancy, administration, campaigning, computers, fundraising, marketing/publicity, newsletter/journalism, research.

Vols under 26 placed each year: 33 of a total of 66.

When to apply: A month before starting.

Work alone/with others: Both.

Volunteers with disabilities: Possible.

Qualifications: Computer, communication skills, campaigning/fundraising experience plus clerical, administrative skills, press/media experience all useful but not essential.

Health requirements: Nil.

Costs: Nil.

Benefits: £3.50 luncheon vouchers per day plus travel costs up to £7.50 per day reimbursed. There is general office insurance.

Supervision: All volunteers work closely with a member of staff.

Certification: Reference or certificate on request.

UK placements: *England* (London, Nottinghamshire); *Scotland* (Edinburgh, E. Lothian, W. Lothian); *Northern Ireland* (Belfast City).

ANGAIA CAMPHILL DO BRASIL
Caixa Postal 332
36.001 – 970 Juiz de Fora – MG
Brazil

Contact: The Director

Camphill Community Angaia Camphill Do Brasil is part of the worldwide Camphill movement which was founded by the Austrian medical doctor Karl König at the end of the Second World War when he was living as a refugee in Aberdeen, Scotland. The basis of work in any Camphill Community is anthroposophy by Dr Rudolf Steiner and the first memorandum by Dr König. Camphill Communities are now found all over the world and one of our main tasks is to live with and care for people with mental disabilities in a social therapeutic way which includes daily life, work, cultural activities and religious life as well as many other aspects of life.

Total projects worldwide: 1
Total UK projects: 0
Starting months: January–December.
Time required: 4–52 weeks.
Age requirement: 18 plus.
Causes: Disabled (learning and physical).
Activities: Agriculture/farming, arts/crafts, caring (residential), gardening/horticulture, manual work, outdoor skills.
When to apply: All year.
Work alone/with others: With others.
Qualifications: Nil.
Health requirements: General good health.
Costs: Travel to Brazil.
Benefits: Board and lodging.
Worldwide placements: *South America* (Brazil).

ANGLO-POLISH ACADEMIC ASSOCIATION (APASS])
93 Victoria Road
Leeds
LS6 1DR UK

Tel: +44 (0) 113 275 8121
Contact: The Honorary Secretary

Total projects worldwide: 1
Total UK projects: 0
Starting months: June.
Time required: 3–52 weeks.
Age requirement: 18–40
Causes: Teaching/assisting (secondary, mature, EFL).
Activities: Teaching.
When to apply: March–May. Send a large stamped addressed envelope and six first class postage stamps.
Work alone/with others: Both.
Volunteers with disabilities: Not possible.
Qualifications: Good spoken and written English.
Health requirements: Nil.
Costs: Travel costs, membership or

registration fees – £102 total.
Benefits: Assisted travel. Free board and lodging.
Certification: Certificate or reference provided on request.
Worldwide placements: *Europe* (Poland).

ANNÉE DIACONALE
SPJ
Rue du Champ de Mars 5
1050 Bruxelles
Belgium

Tel: 00 32 2 513 24 01
Fax: 00 32 2 511 28 90
Contact: The Director

Année Diaconale is the Belgian branch of the European Diaconal Year Network which consists of a number of national Christian-based volunteering schemes. (The British branch is Time For God.) We share common standards, and a commitment to the personal development of the volunteer through this form of work.

Total projects worldwide: 1
Total UK projects: 0
Starting months: September.
Time required: 42–52 weeks.
Age requirement: 18–25
Causes: Addicts/Ex-addicts, Aids/HIV, children, disabled (learning and physical), elderly people, offenders/ex-offenders, poor/homeless, refugees, young people.
Activities: Caring (general), community work.
Vols under 26 placed each year: 20
Work alone/with others: With others.
Qualifications: Some French, Flemish or German and respect for the aims of the scheme.
Costs: Travel to Belgium, health insurance and administration costs.
Benefits: Pocket money (£80 per month), board, lodging, laundry, travelling expenses.
Supervision: Each branch offers support to the volunteers through both personal supervision and regular residential conferences or seminars.
Worldwide placements: *Europe* (Belgium).

ANNÉE DIACONALE – STRASBOURG
8 quai Finkwiller
Strasbourg
F-67000 France
Tel: 00 33 388 35 46 76

Fax: 00 33 388 25 19 57
Contact: Claudie Harel

L'Année Diaconale is the French branch of the European Diaconal Year Network. For more details, see the entry under Année Diaconale above.

Total projects worldwide: 1
Total UK projects: 0
Starting months: September.
Time required: 45–49 weeks.
Age requirement: 18–25
Causes: Children, disabled (learning), elderly people, health care/medical, young people.
Activities: Social work.
Vols under 26 placed each year: 60
When to apply: March.
Work alone/with others: Dependent on the placement.
Volunteers with disabilities: Not possible.
Qualifications: Some ability to speak and understand French and at least 'open' to spirituality.
Health requirements: Good health essential.
Costs: Registration cost of FF250. Travel costs to the French border.
Benefits: Pocket money (FF670 per month), board and lodging.
Training: Each branch offers support to the volunteers through both personal supervision and regular residential conferences or seminars.
Interview details: Interviews take place in the UK.
Certification: Provided.
Worldwide placements: *Europe* (Belgium, France, Germany, Hungary, Italy, Spain); *North America* (USA).

ANNUNCIATION HOUSE
1003 East San Antonio
El Paso
Texas
79901 USA

Tel: 00 1 915 545 4509
Fax: 00 1 915 544 4041
Contact: Ruben Garcia or Julia Tierney

Annunciation House is an organization that operates three houses of hospitality for the homeless poor, undocumented, internal immigrants from Mexico and refugees from Central and South America. We extend to the homeless: hospitality, shelter, meals, clothing, some basic medical care and, above all, a willing ear to listen to the struggle and suffering in their lives. It is a busy and demanding work which calls for a real commitment to the people themselves. Our houses function 90 to 95% in Spanish. It is important that volunteers understand that we do this work not only because we desire to serve the poor, but because we have come to recognize our own poverty and our own desire to feel the worthiness of life. As we serve the homeless in their daily needs, so they too serve and teach us through their faith, determination, strength and especially the witness of their very lives. Volunteers with Annunciation House must be willing to live in a community made up of those whom we welcome as guests as well as volunteers. As a staff, we strive to live simply and in solidarity with the poor, remaining mindful of the gospel in our daily work. Prospective volunteers who are not of US citizenship must obtain a visa before coming to volunteer with Annunciation House.

Total projects worldwide: 3
Total UK projects: 0
Starting months: January, April, June, August, November.
Time required: 10–52 weeks (plus).
Age requirement: 20 plus.
Causes: Poor/homeless, refugees.
Activities: Accountancy, administration, building/construction, community work, computers, cooking, driving, library/resource centres, newsletter/journalism, research, social work, teaching, translating, visiting/befriending.
Vols under 26 placed each year: 9 of a total of 14.
When to apply: Any time.
Work alone/with others: With others.
Volunteers with disabilities: Not possible.
Qualifications: No dependants. If little or no knowledge of the Spanish language, a desire and commitment to learn.
Health requirements: Must be physically, mentally and emotionally healthy. Medical examination required.
Costs: Travel, visa costs and insurance.
Benefits: Board and accommodation in a shared room.
Training: We hold a week long orientation for all new volunteers shortly after they arrive. After these sessions are completed, volunteers are assigned to any one of our hospitality houses.

Supervision: Each house has a co-ordinator. This person is always available to all the volunteers in the house. The new volunteer may speak with him/her at any time.
Interview details: Prospective volunteers are sometimes interviewed over the telephone.
Certification: Reference or certificate provided.
Worldwide placements: *North America* (USA); *Central America* (Mexico).

APARE/GEC
41 Cours Jean Jaures
Avignon
84000 France

Tel: 00 33 4 90 85 51 15
Fax: 00 33 4 90 86 82 19
e-mail: gec@apare-gec.org
Contact: Pascale Reder

Groupement Européen des Campus (GEC) organizes and recruits volunteers for two activities: the European Campuses and the European Voluntary Service. The extensive network of academic workshops (campuses) is intended for all young people interested in environment and heritage. As training projects and tools of action at the service of local initiatives, they provide students with an opportunity for training and action in the real world. Under academic supervision, students, in groups of about 15, for periods of two to four weeks, study or work in support of local public or voluntary programmes. Projects are open to all young people of 18 to 25 interested in participating in a 6 to 12 months voluntary service in another country. The European Voluntary Service represents a chance to travel, discover another country and participate in a useful activity validated by a certificate from the European Commission. Evaluation sessions at the end of the project held in Avignon.

Total projects worldwide: 25–30
Total UK projects: 1 or 2
Starting months: July–October.
Time required: 3–52 weeks.
Age requirement: 18–25
Causes: Archaeology, architecture, conservation, environmental causes, heritage, wildlife, work camps – seasonal.
Activities: Campaigning, conservation skills, development issues, group work, manual work, marketing/publicity, research, scientific work, summer camps, translating, work camps – seasonal.
Vols under 26 placed each year: 45
When to apply: Mid-June at the latest.
Work alone/with others: With others.
Volunteers with disabilities: Possible.
Qualifications: A-level plus 1 year of study minimum. Language ability.
Equipment/clothing: On some projects, working clothes.
Health requirements: Nil.
Costs: Return fare home. For campuses: registration fee E70. For voluntary service: no costs.
Benefits: Board and lodging are free during campuses. Volunteers on voluntary service are given an allowance. Full insurance cover will be taken out by us for all volunteers – provided by the European Commission.
Training: Information packs and meetings.
Supervision: A person from the host organization is responsible for supervision and personal support during the project.
Interview details: No interview necessary.
Certification: Reference or certificate provided.
Worldwide placements: *Africa* (Algeria, Morocco, Tunisia); *Asia* (Lebanon); *Europe* (Austria, Belarus, Belgium, Bulgaria, Cyprus, Czech Republic, Denmark, Finland, France, Germany, Greece, Hungary, Ireland, Italy, Luxembourg, Malta, Netherlands, Norway, Poland, Portugal, Romania, Russia, Slovakia, Slovenia, Spain, Sweden, Turkey, Ukraine, Yugoslavia).
UK placements: *England* (London).

APENA
Hameau de la Pinede
Traverse Valette
13009 Marseille
France

Tel: 00 33 491 25 05 30
Contact: Jean Luc Recordon

Apena runs two children's holiday camps, one in Marseille and the other in Switzerland. Between 20 and 25 volunteers are needed for one month in the summer to act as instructors. Each instructor will be responsible for looking after a group of eight children between 6 and 15. One day off per week.

Starting months: May–August.
Time required: 4–52 weeks.
Age requirement: 18 plus.

Causes: Children.
Activities: Summer camps.
Vols under 26 placed each year: 20–25
Qualifications: Fluent French and previous experience with children.
Costs: Travel costs.
Benefits: Accommodation.
Worldwide placements: *Europe* (France, Switzerland).

APF EVASION
Association des Paralysés de France
17 Bd Auguste Blanqui
Paris
75013 France

Tel: 00 33 1 40 78 69 00
Fax: 00 33 1 40 78 69 73
e-mail: apfevasion@aol.com
Web: www.apf.asso.fr
Contact: Pierre-Philippe Audineau

APF Evasion needs volunteers to help people with physical disabilities go on collective holidays. You will visit tourist sites, go on excursions, arrange picnics and organize entertainment in the evenings. Volunteers with an offending background may be accepted.

Total projects worldwide: 1
Total UK projects: 0
Starting months: July.
Time required: 1–4 weeks.
Age requirement: 19–35
Causes: Children, disabled (physical), holidays for disabled.
Activities: Caring (residential), group work, summer camps.
Vols under 26 placed each year: 1,200 of a total of 1,800.
When to apply: Anytime before mid-July.
Work alone/with others: With others.
Volunteers with disabilities: Not possible.
Qualifications: All are welcome. We have particular need for bus drivers, lifesavers, cooks, nurses and medical students.
Health requirements: Good health and strength.
Costs: Very small.
Benefits: Travel costs within France and complete board and lodging.
Interview details: No interviews necessary.
Certification: Certificate or reference provided.
Worldwide placements: *Europe* (France).

APTIBET
London Fashion Centre
87–93 Fonthill Road
Finsbury Park
London
N4 3HT UK

Tel: +44 (0) 20 7281 8180
Fax: +44 (0) 20 7281 8280
e-mail: aptibet@gn.apc.org
Web: www.aptibet.org
Contact: Pete Crawford, Operations Director

ApTibeT (Appropriate Technology for Tibetans) was founded in 1984. Over the past 15 years, we have implemented more than 100 major development projects. Our work has focused on a number of main areas: (a) Housing. ApTibeT has started five low cost building centres (LCBCs). Almost the full range of low environmental impact construction methods are used: stabilized mud block bricks; micro-cement roofing tiles; ferro-cement. (b) Water and sanitation. Projects aim to provide skills leading to community construction of UNICEF/WHO recommended pour flush composting latrines, generally constructed in ferro-cement. We have also completed a number of large-scale water supply projects using conventional building methods. (c) Power and household fuel. We are the major user of an indigenously produced, high quality, low maintenance and low cost wind pump. In addition, we have implemented large scale biogas and improved stove design (chula) projects. (d) Solar energy. Both solar water heating systems (SWHS) and photovoltaic (PV) energy have featured in our programmes. (e) Agroforestry. We work with grassroots organizations in India, Nepal and China and are developing a project in Mongolia. Volunteers with an offending background may be accepted – each case individually assessed.

Total projects worldwide: 15
Total UK projects: 0
Starting months: January–December.
Time required: 8–52 weeks.
Age requirement: 18 plus.
Causes: Conservation, environmental causes, refugees.
Activities: Accountancy, administration, conservation skills, development issues, fundraising, international aid, marketing/publicity, newsletter/journalism, research.

Vols under 26 placed each year: 3–4 of a total of 6–8.
When to apply: All year.
Work alone/with others: Both.
Volunteers with disabilities: Only for office work in London (such as work on our web site). The office in London has full disabled access.
Qualifications: Various skills needed in many different areas of work.
Health requirements: Nil.
Costs: Nil.
Benefits: London: Travel and £6 subsistence per day. Training for long-term/specialist work. We supply statutory insurance cover.
Training: Induction.
Supervision: Volunteers have a job description detailing tasks and their manager. They also receive support sessions.
Interview details: Interviews take place in our office in London.
Certification: References provided.
Charity number: 1072962
Worldwide placements: *Asia* (China, India, Nepal).
UK placements: *England* (London).

ARBEITSKREIS FREIWILLIGE SOZIALE DIENSTE DER JUGEND
Stafflenbergstraße 76
Stuttgart
70184 Germany

Tel: 00 49 711 2159 420 417
Contact: The Bundestutor/in

Arbeitskreis Freiwillige Soziale Dienste der Jugend organizes volunteer work in the Evangelical Church of Germany. Volunteers work mostly for people who need help, for example, with ill, handicapped or old people, but also in kindergartens or homes for children and young people. Throughout the one-year programme, there are seminars and discussions led by the trained group leaders. Keeping in contact with other people through the practical work and the seminars gives a chance for each volunteer to increase their personal growth and learn through new experiences.
Starting months: August, September, October.
Time required: 52 weeks.
Age requirement: 18 plus.
Causes: Children, disabled (learning and physical), elderly people, health care/medical,

young people.
Activities: Caring (day), religion.
When to apply: One year in advance.
Qualifications: Spoken German essential.
Costs: Travel.
Benefits: Board, lodging, plus DM300 per month and insurance.
Worldwide placements: *Europe* (Germany).

ARCHAEOLOGY ABROAD
31–34 Gordon Square
London
WC1H 0PY UK

Fax: +44 (0) 20 7383 2572
e-mail: arch.abroad@ucl.ac.uk
Web: www.britarch.ac.uk/archabroad
Contact: Honorary Secretary

Archaeology Abroad does not place volunteers, but aims to provide information about archaeological projects requiring volunteers. It is the responsibility of individuals to make direct contact with project directors/organizers. Volunteers with an offending background might be accepted – check with each project director.

Total projects worldwide: 50
Total UK projects: 0
Starting months: May–October.
Time required: 2–52 weeks.
Age requirement: 18 plus.
Causes: Archaeology, heritage.
Activities: Group work, manual work, outdoor skills, technical skills.
When to apply: As soon as possible.
Work alone/with others: With others.
Volunteers with disabilities: Would need to be checked with each project director.
Qualifications: Some digs provide training but some archaeological experience preferable. Languages are a plus.
Equipment/clothing: Strong shoes, wet weather gear – otherwise according to project director.
Health requirements: Anti-tetanus advisable – otherwise depending on country.
Costs: Varies from project to project. Air fares plus local travel to/from site. Registration fees often apply. Personal and medical insurance is required, arranged by the volunteer.
Benefits: Food, accommodation (campsite sometimes) and occasionally pocket money.
Training: We recommend that those wishing to dig abroad gain some archaeological

experience/training in their own country, if possible, prior to venturing abroad.
Supervision: Varies from site to site.
Nationalities accepted: Any restrictions would need to be checked with each project director.
Interview details: Applicants are not interviewed but may need to complete a detailed application/registration form.
Certification: References or certificates not normally provided but check with the individual project director.
Worldwide placements: *Asia* (Israel); *Europe* (Belgium, France, Germany, Italy, Portugal, Spain); *North America* (USA); *Central America* (Belize); *South America* (Peru).

ARCHEOLO-J
Avenue Paul Terlinden 23
1330 Rixensart
Belgium

Tel: 00 32 2 653 8268
Fax: 00 32 2 654 1917
Contact: J. Gillet, President

Archeolo-J organizes international work camps at archaeological excavations where volunteers assist with all aspects of the excavations, digging, drawing finds and surveying the sites.

Starting months: July.
Time required: 1–3 weeks.
Age requirement: 14 plus.
Causes: Archaeology.
Activities: Manual work.
Vols under 26 placed each year: 100
When to apply: May.
Work alone/with others: With others.
Volunteers with disabilities: Not possible.
Qualifications: Able to understand French.
Equipment/clothing: Wellington boots, rain clothes, sleeping equipment and air mattress.
Health requirements: Nil.
Costs: FB8,000 – FB15,000 plus travel costs, drinks, insurance and FB150 membership fee.
Benefits: Accommodation in tents plus food plus 1 visit to the region per week.
Worldwide placements: *Europe* (Belgium).

ARMY CADET FORCE
E Block
Duke of York's Headquarters
London
SW3 4RR UK

Tel: +44 (0) 20 7730 9733

Fax: +44 (0) 20 7730 8264
e-mail: acfa@armycadets.com
Web: www.armycadets.com
Contact: Brigadier J.E. Neeve, General Secretary

Army Cadet Force offers a rewarding job giving a helping hand to young people between 13 and 18 years of age to develop their full potential. We offer all those sound military-based principles of which we are proud – and a great deal more. Emphasis is placed on looking after those from disadvantaged backgrounds. Today we continue to provide friendship, discipline, leadership, challenging outdoor activities – expeditions, survival techniques, adventurous training and sport. Volunteers with an offending background are sometimes accepted depending on the offence.

Total projects worldwide: 62–63
Total UK projects: 61
Starting months: January–December.
Time required: 1–52 weeks (plus).
Age requirement: 19–40
Causes: Disabled (learning and physical), environmental causes, inner city problems, offenders/Ex-offenders, poor/homeless, teaching/assisting (secondary), unemployed, young people.
Activities: Administration, campaigning, caring (general), community work, counselling, driving, first aid, fundraising, group work, manual work, marketing/publicity, music, outdoor skills, social work, sport, summer camps, teaching, technical skills, training, visiting/befriending.
Vols under 26 placed each year: 4,750 of a total of 7,000.
When to apply: Any time.
Work alone/with others: With others.
Volunteers with disabilities: Must be capable of undertaking some physical activity.
Qualifications: Must be British subjects.
Equipment/clothing: Provided.
Health requirements: Reasonable level of fitness.
Costs: Nil.
Benefits: Pocket money per day for up to 28 days. When on ACF business, volunteers are covered by ACF insurance.
Training: Full training is given. If the volunteer has the time he/she can do any training course we offer.
Supervision: Each 2 or 3 volunteers will have

a supervisor, always present. Monitored by senior members of ACF.

Nationalities accepted: British only.
Interview details: Interviews take place, invariably in county headquarters
Certification: Certificate or reference provided.
Charity number: 305962
Worldwide placements: *Africa* (Egypt, South Africa, Zimbabwe); *Asia* (India, Nepal, Pakistan); *Australasia* (Australia); *Europe* (Andorra, Austria, Belgium, Cyprus, Denmark, France, Germany, Greece, Ireland, Italy, Luxembourg, Netherlands, Norway, Poland, Portugal, Spain); *North America* (Canada, USA); *Central America* (Bahamas, Barbados, Bermuda, Jamaica, Trinidad and Tobago).
UK placements: *England* (throughout); *Scotland* (throughout); *Northern Ireland* (throughout); *Wales* (throughout).

ARTEMIS CLOUDFOREST PRESERVE
Apdo 937
2050 San Pedro
Montes de Oca
Costa Rica

Tel: 00 506 253 72 43
Fax: 00 506 253 72 43
Contact: Hilda M. de Pina

Artemis is a private cloudforest reserve in the Talamanca Mountains of Costa Rica. It lies at an elevation of approximately 8,800 ft and comprises 25 ha of intricate, primary forest. A cloudforest is very different from a rainforest environment. Temperatures are much lower, and the forest is often shrouded in mist. The flora and fauna, adapted to these conditions, tend to be much 'softer' than those found in the rainforest. Tree life is dominated by the towering white oak (up to 35 m high), squat and twisted laurels (sometimes 4 m in diameter), and carboniferous tree ferns. Among, and piled within, these ancient trees lies an entanglement of flowering vines, bromeliads, orchids, climbing ferns, rich mosses and velvet fungi. With such a collection of plants, there are virtually no bare surfaces at all and thus the forest is very soft to the touch. It is difficult to see mammals in the cloudforest, but this is countered by a great diversity of tropical birds (including tiny hummingbirds and the quetzal – famous in Mayan legend),

singing frogs, beautiful moths and fantastic insects – like golden beetles, violently coloured and peculiarly shaped. There are very few animals or insects which are harmful in the cloudforest. The preserve is owned by a Costa Rican/American family who are trying to protect the cloudforest and open it up to others whether they be visitors, enthusiasts, school children, etc. Thus volunteers will be needed to build a trail system and help with the reafforestation of cleared areas. Work of this kind gives volunteers the chance to learn about the cloudforest environment and simple conservation measures. The work need not be restricted to these two tasks. Volunteers of all backgrounds are welcome to share their talents with the others, whether biologists, ecologists, ornithologists, surveyors, engineers, artists, etc. Also, from time to time, maintenance work has to be done around the house, e.g. clearing property boundaries, fixing fences, simple gardening. The working day is approximately six hours long and volunteers work 20 days out of 28 (i.e. five days on, two days off) although both are flexible. People are taken on for at least one month.

Starting months: January–December.
Time required: 4–8 weeks.
Age requirement: 18–40
Causes: Conservation, environmental causes, teaching/assisting (primary, EFL), wildlife.
Activities: Conservation skills, DIY, gardening/horticulture, teaching.
Vols under 26 placed each year: 20
When to apply: All year.
Work alone/with others: With others.
Volunteers with disabilities: Not possible.
Qualifications: Nil.
Equipment/clothing: Sleeping bag, hiking and rubber boots, warm old clothes, waterproofs and work gloves.
Health requirements: Nil.
Costs: Travel, insurance and minimum US$150 per week.
Benefits: Board, lodging, laundry service, hot showers, home atmosphere.
Certification: Certificate or reference on request
Worldwide placements: *Central America* (Costa Rica).

**ASARD (ASSOCIATION FOR SOCIAL
ACTION AND RURAL DEVELOPMENT)**
AT/PO Raikia
District Phulbani
Orissa 762101
India

Tel: 00 91 6 847 64696
e-mail: asard_raikia@yahoo.com.
Contact: Sisir Kumar Parichha, Secretary

ASARD is a non-profit, non-political, non-religious organization, working for the deprived and tribal (indigenous) people of the area. Our major aim is to make people self-sufficient by developing the resources which are available to them. Ill health is a serious problem in the area largely due to illiteracy and a general lack of health education. In response to these needs, we have, since 1988, adopted a project-based comprehensive approach, tackling education, health, community organization, socio-economic development, rural technology and forestry. Many of the people are Christians, as the nearby missions play a crucial role in education. Volunteers from all over the world are needed on the work camps, where you can participate in village activities from sanitation projects, construction work, forestry and agricultural work, visiting schools and attending village meetings. Tasks are worked out upon the arrival of the volunteer, but usually last between 2–3 weeks. However, Sisir Kumar is particularly keen to host anyone interested in long-term study of development issues and would be happy to offer his experience and expertise for anyone carrying out thesis or doctoral research. Write to Sisir Kumar allowing at least six weeks for a reply or send him an e-mail.

Total projects worldwide: 3
Total UK projects: 0
Starting months: January–December.
Time required: 2–4 weeks.
Age requirement: 16–30
Causes: Children, conservation, environmental causes, poor/homeless, teaching/assisting (primary), young people.
Activities: Agriculture/farming, community work, conservation skills, fundraising, group work, international aid, newsletter/journalism, research, social work, summer camps, visiting/befriending, work camps – seasonal.

Vols under 26 placed each year: 75 of a total of 100.
When to apply: 6 weeks before wishing to start.
Work alone/with others: With others.
Volunteers with disabilities: Not possible.
Qualifications: Nil.
Equipment/clothing: Sleeping bag, raincoat (June/July), warm clothes (November/December), torch, water purification pills.
Health requirements: Nil.
Costs: Air fares and fortnightly donation of about US$100 divided as 25% administration, 25% community work, 50% board and lodging. Volunteers must arrange their insurance before arriving.
Benefits: Above donation includes basic local food, accommodation and transport to nearby villages.
Training: One day orientation briefing on camp schedule and facilities available.
Supervision: Volunteers are always accompanied by camp supervisors.
Interview details: No interview necessary.
Worldwide placements: *Asia* (India).

**ASHIANA COMMUNITY SERVICE
PROJECT**
23–25 Grantham Road
Sparkbrook
Birmingham
B11 1LU UK

Tel: +44 (0) 121 773 7061
Fax: +44 (0) 121 766 7503
Contact: Andrew Hewitt

Ashiana Community Project has four projects based in the multi-racial and inner city area of Sparkbrook which seek to respond to poverty, unemployment and racism in the district. Our guiding principles are to: respond innovatively and flexibly to the diverse needs of the community; be managed by members of the local community; provide a quality service; provide a welcoming and accessible environment to all local people; ensure equal opportunities in all aspects; work in partnership with voluntary and statutory organizations; be a non profit making organization. We aim to: provide learning opportunities which enable people to gain their personal goals and access employment; encourage community management; create opportunities for volunteering; promote health in the community; provide access to free legal and welfare advice; raise awareness of environmental issues; promote understanding of cultural diversity.

Total projects worldwide: 3
Total UK projects: 3
Starting months: January–December.
Time required: 1–52 weeks.
Age requirement: 16 plus.
Causes: Children, conservation, health care/medical, human rights, inner city problems, poor/homeless, teaching/assisting (EFL), young people.
Activities: Administration, arts/crafts, community work, computers, conservation skills, DIY, fundraising, gardening/horticulture, group work, marketing/publicity, social work, teaching, translating, visiting/befriending.
Vols under 26 placed each year: 100.
When to apply: All year.
Work alone/with others: With others.
Volunteers with disabilities: Possible, but not wheelchairs.
Costs: Contribution if possible.
Benefits: Accommodation.
UK placements: *England* (London, Manchester, West Midlands, S. Yorkshire).

ASSOCIATE MISSIONARIES OF THE ASSUMPTION
227 N. Bowman Avenue
Merion
Pennsylvania
19066 USA

Tel: 00 1 610 664 1284
Fax: 00 1 610 664 7328
e-mail: FJoseph@SJuPhil.Edu
Contact: Sr Francis Joseph RA, The Director

Associate Missionaries of the Assumption (AMA) is a lay missionary programme, sponsored by the Religious of the Assumption. AMA is a group of women and men using their gifts and skills in service with the poor. For one year, an AMA volunteer will work in a school, hospital, parish or social service agency while living simply in a faith support community.

Total projects worldwide: Varies.
Total UK projects: 3
Starting months: September.
Time required: 45–52 weeks.
Age requirement: 22 plus.

Causes: Children, disabled (learning and physical), elderly people, health care/medical, teaching/assisting (EFL), young people.
Activities: Caring (general and residential), development issues, teaching.
Vols under 26 placed each year: 22–45
When to apply: Before 1 March.
Work alone/with others: With others – community and faith based.
Qualifications: Deep faith. Graduates preferred. Previous voluntary work essential.
Health requirements: Certificate of good health – physically and psychologically.
Costs: One way fare in some cases. US$5 application costs.
Benefits: Board and lodging plus health insurance in most cases plus US$100 per month. One way fare.
Interview details: Interviews take place in our office in Merion.
Worldwide placements: *Africa* (Burkina Faso, Ivory Coast, Gambia, Ghana, Guinea, Kenya, Liberia, Malawi, Mozambique, Namibia, Nigeria, Tanzania, Uganda); *Asia* (Japan); *Europe* (France, Germany, Ireland, Italy, Lithuania, Spain); *North America* (USA); *Central America* (Mexico); *South America* (Bolivia).
UK placements: *England* (London, Suffolk, E. Sussex, W. Sussex).

ASSOCIATION DE RECHERCHES ET ÉTUDES D'HISTOIRE RURALE
Maison du Patrimonie
21190 Saint-Romain
France

Tel: 00 33 380 21 28 50
Contact: M. Serge Grappin

The Association de Recherches et Études d'Histoire Rurale is conducting a long term research project on the archaeological, ethnological and historical development of the Saint-Romain area. The work consists of digging and restoration.

Starting months: August.
Time required: 4–52 weeks.
Age requirement: 17 plus.
Causes: Archaeology, heritage.
Activities: Manual work.
Vols under 26 placed each year: 40
When to apply: Before 30 May.
Work alone/with others: Usually with others.
Costs: Pocket money, food and travel to

campsite.
Benefits: Accommodation.
Worldwide placements: *Europe* (France).

ASSOCIATION DES CHANTIERS DE JEUNES (ACJ)
BP 171
Salé – Medina
Morocco

Tel: 00 212 37 855350 [mob 066949519]
Fax: 00 212 37 855350
e-mail: acj.ong.maroc@caramail.com
Contact: Taki Abderrahmane, President

Association des Chantiers de Jeunes is a non-profit organization with 14 local projects in Morocco. The following seven goals are at the core of our work: to safeguard the environment; to integrate youth in social and cultural life; to fight illiteracy; to brighten the lives of immigrant children; to develop the rural regions; to restore monuments; to institute peace and co-operation between people of different religions, sex, colour or language. We co-operate with local and international organizations all over the world to help with development projects, to help citizens in precarious situations especially children and women in Morocco. We organize voluntary work camps during school holidays.

Total projects worldwide: Varies.
Total UK projects: Varies.
Starting months: April, July, August, December.
Time required: 1–8 weeks.
Age requirement: 16 plus.
Causes: Archaeology, children, disabled (learning and physical), elderly people, environmental causes, holidays for disabled, human rights, inner city problems, offenders/ex-offenders, poor/homeless, teaching/assisting, work camps – seasonal, young people.
Activities: Agriculture/farming, arts/crafts, building/construction, campaigning, caring (general), community work, first aid, forestry, fundraising, gardening/horticulture, group work, manual work, music, research, social work, sport, summer camps, teaching, technical skills, training, visiting/befriending, work camps – seasonal.
Vols under 26 placed each year: 100 of a total of 500.
When to apply: From 1 April.

Work alone/with others: With others.
Volunteers with disabilities: Possible.
Qualifications: Nil but English and/or French an advantage.
Equipment/clothing: Sleeping bags, musical instruments and animation equipment.
Health requirements: No volunteers with contaminating illnesses.
Costs: Travel and FF300 participation fees. Health and travel insurance are the responsibility of the volunteer.
Benefits: Lodging and food.
Training: We have information meetings about the projects. For special projects we run training sessions.
Interview details: No interviews necessary.
Certification: Written reference provided.
Worldwide placements: *Africa* (Algeria, Morocco, Tunisia); *Europe* (France).

ASSOCIATION DE TRAVAIL VOLONTAIRE ET CULTUREL
BP 4537
Casablanca
Morocco

Total projects worldwide: 1
Total UK projects: 0
Starting months: July, August.
Time required: 3–4 weeks.
Age requirement: 18–35
Causes: Work camps – seasonal.
Activities: Work camps – seasonal.
Vols under 26 placed each year: 500
Work alone/with others: With others.
Costs: Travel and pocket money.
Benefits: Board, lodging and insurance.
Worldwide placements: *Africa* (Morocco).

ASSOCIATION FOR BRAIN-DAMAGED CHILDREN AND YOUNG ADULTS
Clifton House
3 St Paul's Road
Foleshill
Coventry
CV6 5DE UK

Tel: +44 (0) 24 7666 5450
Fax: +44 (0) 24 7666 5450
Contact: Mrs E. Markey

The Association for Brain-Damaged Children and Young Adults is based at Clifton House which is situated in a residential area close to shops and bus routes, in the north of Coventry. The home is laid out on ground floor level and has been adapted as a family-type home for up to five children at any time with a wide variety of needs. The objective of the home is to care for the children in a warm and homely environment. While staying at Clifton House, children go out to their usual schools using Social Services or Education buses or taxis as if they were at home. Whilst in Clifton House, the children are also encouraged to continue their usual outside activities such as youth clubs, swimming, horse riding etc. At weekends and during school holidays the children are cared for at the home and the staff have use of their mini-bus for day trips and outings.

Total projects worldwide: 2
Total UK projects: 2
Starting months: January–December.
Time required: 1–52 weeks.
Age requirement: 18 plus.
Causes: Children, disabled (learning and physical), young people.
Activities: Arts/crafts, caring (general, day and residential), fundraising, music, social work.
When to apply: All year.
Work alone/with others: With others.
Volunteers with disabilities: Not possible.
Qualifications: Nil.
Health requirements: Nil.
Benefits: Meals on duty and free outings.
Interview details: Interviews take place at Clifton House.
Charity number: 500452
UK placements: *England* (West Midlands).

ASSOCIATION JEAN-FREDERIC OBERLIN

Foyer Les Trois Sources
1 Rue des Jardins
F-67420 Colroy-la-Roche
France

Tel: 00 33 388 97 61 09
Contact: The Director

Association Jean-Frederic Oberlin runs a small home for adults with special needs that wants to grow into a Camphill Community. For more details of Camphill Communities, see the first Camphill listing under Angaia Camphill Do Brasil, above.

Total projects worldwide: 1
Total UK projects: 0
Starting months: January–December.
Time required: 40–52 weeks.

Age requirement: 14 plus.
Causes: Disabled (learning and physical).
Activities: Agriculture/farming, arts/crafts, forestry, gardening/horticulture, group work, manual work, music, outdoor skills.
When to apply: All year.
Work alone/with others: With others.
Volunteers with disabilities: Not possible.
Qualifications: Nil.
Equipment/clothing: Nothing special – outdoor wear.
Health requirements: Nil.
Costs: Travel to Colroy-la-Roche.
Benefits: Board and lodging provided.
Worldwide placements: *Europe* (France).

ASSOCIATION LE MAT

Le Viel Audon
07120 Balazuc
France

Tel: 00 33 475 37 73 80
Contact: The Co-ordinator

Association Le Mat undertakes restoration, reconstruction, farm and agricultural activities at the village of Audon. Volunteers can choose their daily task from those offered as long as they work at least five hours per day.

Total projects worldwide: 1
Total UK projects: 0
Starting months: January–December.
Time required: 1–52 weeks.
Age requirement: 17 plus.
Causes: Architecture, conservation, environmental causes, heritage.
Activities: Agriculture/farming, conservation skills, manual work.
Vols under 26 placed each year: 300.
When to apply: All year.
Work alone/with others: With others.
Costs: Food (about £4 daily), £1 for insurance and joining fee of £5.
Benefits: Camping areas are provided and some beds are available.
Worldwide placements: *Europe* (France).

ASSOCIATION LES COMPAGNONS DU CAP

Pratcoustals
Arphy
F-30120 le Vigan
France

Tel: 00 33 467 81 82 22

Association Les Compagnons du Cap is based at Pratcoustals. This small village, abandoned by its original inhabitants more than 50 years ago, sits high above the Arphy Valley surrounded by chestnut forest. The village is brought back to life each year, thanks to the enthusiasm of many work groups. The renovation work is preparing the site to become a permanent centre with a small museum and a restaurant to go with the already existing Gite d'Etape holiday cottage and group holiday house. Work 4½ days a week, 6½ hours a day. This is varied including re-roofing with traditional canal tiles, drystone walling, rebuilding stone steps and general improvement of the surroundings. There is also the chance to do some research into the village and to produce some written documents. Activities include hiking, mountain-biking, swimming in mountain rivers, table-tennis, volley-ball, bar, music and many other choices. The quality of meals is excellent – traditional French cuisine with a healthy bias: wholemeal organic bread, yogurt, organic muesli etc. Meals are taken outside on the terrace of the village restaurant. Participation in the service is expected.

Total projects worldwide: 1
Total UK projects: 0
Starting months: July, August, September.
Time required: 2–52 weeks.
Age requirement: 18 plus.
Causes: Conservation, environmental causes, heritage.
Activities: Agriculture/farming, building/construction, conservation skills, forestry, gardening/horticulture.
Work alone/with others: With others.
Qualifications: Some knowledge of French.
Costs: FF910 per 13 days plus FF250 inscription plus insurance.
Benefits: Excellent board, dormitory/tent lodging.
Worldwide placements: Europe (France).

ASSOCIATION OF GREATER LONDON OLDER WOMEN (AGLOW)
9 Manor Gardens
London
N7 6LA UK
Tel: +44 (0) 20 7281 3485
Contact: Louie Hart, Project Worker

Starting months: April–September.

Time required: 1–52 weeks.
Age requirement: 18 plus.
Causes: Elderly people.
Activities: Administration, computers, DIY, library/resource centres, newsletter/journalism, research.
When to apply: As early as possible.
Work alone/with others: Working with staff.
Health requirements: Nil.
Benefits: Expenses reimbursed – travel and lunch.
Interview details: Interviews take place at our office.
UK placements: England (London).

ASSOCIATION OF VOLUNTEERS IN PROTECTED AREAS (ASVO)
10104-100 San Jose
Costa Rica

Tel: 00 506 57 0922
Fax: 00 506 23 6963
Contact: Karla Morales

ASVO needs volunteers to live and work with the park guards in the mountains and coastal parks of Costa Rica. The work consists of maintenance (cooking, cleaning, collecting litter, repairing buildings or trails), environmental education and general vigilance and support in case of emergency.

Starting months: January–December.
Time required: 8–52 weeks.
Age requirement: 18 plus.
Causes: Conservation, environmental causes.
Activities: Conservation skills, cooking, manual work.
When to apply: All year.
Qualifications: Fluent Spanish and ability to live in rural tropical conditions.
Costs: $350 per month contribution plus air fare.
Benefits: Transport, food, accommodation and materials.
Worldwide placements: Central America (Costa Rica).

ASSOCIATION TUNISIENNE DE L'ACTION VOLONTAIRE (ATAV)
Maison du RCD
Boulevard 9 Avril
Lakasbah
Tunis 1006
Tunisia

Tel: 00 216 1 564899

Fax: 00 216 1 573065
Contact: Hafidh Rahoui, Secretary General

ATAV arranges short-term work camps and
leadership training courses throughout
Tunisia. Work camp projects typically involve
construction and maintenance work,
providing social and medical assistance, and
the protection and conservation of the natural
environment, especially in rural areas.
Volunteers of all nationalities can participate
in the work camps that are held throughout
the summer of each year.

Total projects worldwide: 15
Total UK projects: 0
Starting months: July, August.
Time required: 1–3 weeks.
Age requirement: 18–35
Causes: Archaeology, conservation,
environmental causes, poor/homeless, work
camps – seasonal, young people.
Activities: Building/construction,
campaigning, catering, community work,
conservation skills, development issues, DIY,
gardening/horticulture, group work, manual
work, training, work camps – seasonal.
Vols under 26 placed each year: 500
When to apply: May or June.
Work alone/with others: With others.
Volunteers with disabilities: Not possible.
Qualifications: French or Arabic speaking and
open-minded.
Equipment/clothing: Suitable for outside
work.
Health requirements: Good health.
Costs: Travel to Tunisia and to the location.
Benefits: Free food and accommodation.
Interview details: No interviews necessary.
Certification: Certificate or reference
provided.
Worldwide placements: *Africa* (Tunisia).

ASSOCIATIONS DES PARALYSES DE FRANCE
17 Boulevard Auguste-Blanqui
F-75013 Paris
France

Tel: 00 33 240 78 69 00
Contact: Service Vacances

Associations des Paralyses de France needs
volunteers to help in its work with people
suffering from paralysis. Much of the work is
a matter of helping the handicapped get
around, e.g. pushing wheelchairs, etc. and

assisting the handicapped when they go on
holiday usually in specially organized groups.

Starting months: May, June, July, August.
Time required: 3–4 weeks.
Age requirement: 18 plus.
Causes: Disabled (physical), holidays for
disabled.
Activities: Caring (general).
Vols under 26 placed each year: 1,500
Work alone/with others: Both.
Qualifications: Nil but some French useful
and males especially welcome.
Benefits: Board, accommodation, expenses
and pocket money.
Worldwide placements: *Europe* (France).

ASSOCIAZIONE ITALIANA SOCI COSTRUTTORI – I.B.O.
Via Smeraldina 35
44044 Cassana
(Ferrara)
Italy

Tel: 00 39 0532 730079
Fax: 00 39 0532 736069
e-mail: i.b.o.@Fe.nettuno.it
Web: www.nettuno.it/Fiera/ibo
Contact: Dino Montanari or Angela Milan

Associazione Italiana Soci Costruttori I.B.O.
is a branch of International Building
Companions and arranges construction work
camps in Europe in the summer for all
nationalities. These last for three weeks.

Total projects worldwide: 50 (20 in Italy).
Total UK projects: 0
Starting months: June.
Time required: 3 weeks.
Age requirement: 18–19
Causes: Addicts/Ex-addicts, archaeology,
children, disabled (physical), environmental
causes, poor/homeless.
Activities: Agriculture/farming, building/
construction, cooking, manual work, work
camps – seasonal.
Vols under 26 placed each year: Majority of
2,000.
When to apply: All year.
Volunteers with disabilities: Not possible.
Qualifications: Nil.
Equipment/clothing: Working clothes,
gloves, sleeping bag, heavy shoes. No specific
equipment.
Health requirements: Nil.
Costs: Travel costs plus Euro 77 or Lire

150,000.
Benefits: Board and lodging, insurance.
Training: Any necessary training is given.
Supervision: There is a responsible supervisor in the work camp.
Interview details: No interview necessary.
Worldwide placements: *Europe* (Albania, Andorra, Armenia, Austria, Azerbaijan, Belarus, Belgium, Bosnia-Herzegovina, Bulgaria, Croatia, Cyprus, Czech Republic, Denmark, Estonia, Finland, France, Georgia, Germany, Gibraltar, Greece, Hungary, Iceland, Ireland, Italy, Latvia, Liechtenstein, Lithuania, Luxembourg, Macedonia, Malta, Moldova, Monaco, Netherlands, Norway, Poland, Portugal, Romania, Russia, San Marino, Slovakia, Slovenia, Sweden, Switzerland, Turkey, Ukraine, Vatican City, Yugoslavia).

ASTOVOCT

(Association Togolaise des Volontaires
Chrétiens au Travail)
BP 97, Route de Hanyigba
Kpalime, Kloto
Togo

Tel: 00 228 41 07 15
Fax: 00 228 41 07 15
e-mail: astovoct@yahoo.com
Contact: Komi Edem Bansah, Secretary
General

ASTOVOCT is a non-profit-making evangelistic Presbyterian organization, working towards the improvement of the standard of living in the rural areas of Togo. One hundred volunteers are recruited each year to work on short-term work camps for about one month to help with the building of health centres and schools, and also with tree planting and agricultural work. Volunteers have brainstorming sessions with local volunteers before going to a project. Longer work camps are organized all year round.

Total projects worldwide: 10
Total UK projects: 0
Starting months: January–December.
Time required: 3–52 weeks.
Age requirement: 18 plus.
Causes: Children, conservation, disabled (physical), environmental causes, health care/medical, heritage, poor/homeless, teaching/assisting (nursery, primary, secondary, mature, EFL), young people.
Activities: Agriculture/farming, arts/crafts, building/construction, campaigning, community work, computers, conservation skills, cooking, counselling, development issues, fundraising, group work, international aid, library/resource centres, manual work, music, outdoor skills, sport, summer camps, teaching, theatre/drama, training.
Vols under 26 placed each year: 72 of a total of 90.
When to apply: From May.
Work alone/with others: With others.
Qualifications: Good knowledge of French or English.
Equipment/clothing: Working shoes, mosquito net and sleeping mat.
Health requirements: Vaccination and certificate against Yellow Fever and anti-malaria pills.
Costs: Food, accommodation and travel, insurance and registration of FF1,000 per place. Volunteers must take out health insurance.
Benefits: Cultural exchange, experience in social work and working in a group.
Supervision: We have 2 camp leaders and 1 co-ordinator who supervise and direct the camp.
Interview details: Volunteers are interviewed in Togo before going to their project.
Certification: Certificate of attendance provided.
Worldwide placements: *Africa* (Togo).

ATD FOURTH WORLD

48 Addington Square
London
SE5 7LB UK

Tel: +44 (0) 20 7703 3231
Fax: +44 (0) 20 7252 4276
e-mail: atd.uk@ukonline.co.uk
Web: http://web.ukonline.co.uk/atd.uk/cover.htm
Contact: John Penet

ATD Fourth World is an international voluntary organization that works in England, Scotland and 24 countries on five continents (North and South America, Europe, Africa and Asia) and develops a human rights approach to overcoming extreme poverty. We work in partnership with the most disadvantaged, supporting their efforts in the fight against poverty and their struggle for dignity. We encourage public awareness of poverty through the publication of books and videos that tell the story of the poor and excluded through their own experience, providing them with a voice. We also periodically publish newsletters through which the experience and knowledge of the core workers can be shared with everyone. All positions are for two years except for the work camps described below. Two-week international work camps in France, Germany and the UK are organized during the summer.

Total projects worldwide: 30
Total UK projects: 3
Starting months: January–December.
Time required: 2–52 weeks (plus).
Age requirement: 18 plus.
Causes: Addicts/Ex-addicts, Aids/HIV, children, health care/medical, human rights, inner city problems, offenders/ex-offenders, poor/homeless, teaching/assisting (nursery), unemployed, work camps – seasonal, young people.
Activities: Accountancy, administration, arts/crafts, building/construction, campaigning, caring (general), catering, community work, computers, conservation skills, cooking, counselling, development issues, DIY, driving, fundraising, group work, international aid, library/resource centres, manual work, marketing/publicity, music, newsletter/journalism, outdoor skills, research, social work, sport, summer camps, teaching, technical skills, theatre/drama, training, translating, visiting/befriending, work camps – seasonal.
Vols under 26 placed each year: 10 overseas, 30 UK of a total of 40.
When to apply: All year.
Work alone/with others: With others.
Volunteers with disabilities: Possible.
Qualifications: Participation in an induction weekend in London or Surrey.
Health requirements: Nil.
Costs: Less than £50 if less than 2 weeks, £120 if 3 months or more plus travel to London.
Benefits: Coreworker volunteers: accommodation, pocket money after first month; salary and National Insurance after 1 year. Always health insurance if overseas. Friends: accommodation is offered when taking part in residential projects. No insurance cover is necessary if volunteer is British.
Training: Induction weekend (residential) at the beginning of each month. Further training (a day a week at least) for the 2 years.
Supervision: Volunteers always work as part of a team under close supervision and with close support of long-term coreworkers who have been working for many years in the organization.
Nationalities accepted: Mainly EU citizens and others who have a visa (ATD cannot help people get a visa).
Interview details: Our induction weekends act as an interview.
Certification: Reference on request.
Charity number: 271784
Worldwide placements: *Europe* (France, Germany).
UK placements: *England* (London, Surrey, W. Yorkshire); *Scotland* (Edinburgh, Glasgow City, E. Lothian, W. Lothian).

ATEJ/TURISMO ESTUDANTIL
Apartado 4586
P-4009 Porto Codex
Portugal

Atej/Turismo Estudantil needs volunteers to work on farms, archaeological digs, with the handicapped, etc., working 5–8 hours per day.

Starting months: July, August, September.
Time required: 13–50 weeks.
Age requirement: 14 plus.
Causes: Archaeology, conservation, disabled (learning and physical), environmental causes, heritage.
Activities: Agriculture/farming, building/construction, community work, conservation skills.
When to apply: Before the end of April.
Work alone/with others: Usually with others.
Qualifications: Knowledge of Spanish and English or French.
Benefits: Board and lodging.
Worldwide placements: *Europe* (Portugal).

ATLANTIS WORKING GUEST
Rolf Hofmosgate 18
0655 Oslo
Norway

Starting months: January–December.
Time required: 4–12 weeks.
Age requirement: 18–30
Causes: Animal welfare, conservation, environmental causes.

Activities: Agriculture/farming, conservation skills.
When to apply: 3–4 months before desired date of arrival.
Qualifications: Agricultural experience preferred by not essential. Fluent English.
Costs: Registration fee of NOK880, travel expenses.
Benefits: Board and lodging and pocket money (NOK600 per week).
Worldwide placements: *Europe* (Norway).

AVON WILDLIFE TRUST
The Wildlife Centre
32 Jacob's Wells Road
Bristol
BS8 1DR UK

Tel: +44 (0) 117 926 8018
Fax: +44 (0) 117 929 7273
e-mail: avonwt@cix.co.uk
Web: www.wildlifetrust.org.uk/avon
Contact: Volunteering Officer

The Avon Wildlife Trust aims to protect wildlife in our area, and to educate people about that wildlife. Volunteers are involved in all areas of the organization, from administration, looking after members to education of children, leading practical days on nature reserves, working with planning applications, surveying wildlife sites etc. Volunteers with an offending background are accepted.

Total projects worldwide: 20
Total UK projects: 20
Starting months: January–December.
Time required: 6–52 weeks (plus).
Age requirement: 16 plus.
Causes: Conservation, environmental causes, teaching (primary), wildlife.
Activities: Administration, agriculture/farming, campaigning, computers, conservation skills, driving, forestry, group work, manual work, teaching.
Vols under 26 placed each year: 11 of a total of 20.
When to apply: All year.
Work alone/with others: With other young volunteers.
Volunteers with disabilities: Possible – there are outdoor-based and office-based projects.
Qualifications: Nil.
Health requirements: Nil.
Costs: Travel.
Benefits: Reimbursement of actual travel expenses. The Trust carries public liability insurance.
Training: Job specific. Additional training is offered to longer term placements.
Supervision: Volunteer officer.
Interview details: Interviews at our office in Bristol.
Certification: Reference on request.
Charity number: 280422
UK placements: *England* (Bristol, Gloucestershire, Somerset).

B

BAND (BRISTOL ASSOCIATION FOR NEIGHBOURHOOD DAYCARE)
81 St Nicholas Road
St Paul's
Bristol
BS2 9JJ UK

Tel: +44 (0) 117 954 2128
Fax: +44 (0) 117 954 1694
e-mail: bandltd@aol.com
Contact: Paul Dielhenn, Co-ordinator

BAND was established in 1978 in response to the Finer Joint Action Committee report. This report recognized that one of the most basic needs for working or training parents is care for school age children outside school hours. Such a facility would enable parents to work or train full time thus supporting the family unit to become stable and financially independent. Formed originally by five childcare groups the number of BAND member organizations providing after-school and/or holiday services soon began to grow. Funding for a full time co-ordinator was secured in 1982 and by 1986 there were 12 BAND groups operating. Financial support from national and local government, trusts and charities allowed more staff to be employed by BAND Central. This supported the further promotion and development of new and existing groups, expansion of the range of support services offered to members and an increase in the level of networking opportunities, locally, regionally, nationally and internationally. BAND currently employs 12 staff and has 135 autonomous full or affiliated member groups, providing services to approximately 4,000 families. Full member groups are managed by voluntary committees whose members have children attending the group. Affiliated members share BAND's overall aims and operate in the field of childcare. The continued growth in member groups and the high demand for the services they offer is clear indication that affordable, accessible, good quality, neighbourhood-based childcare remains a basic need for many parents, particularly for single parent and/or low income families.

Total projects worldwide: 1
Total UK projects: 1
Starting months: January–December.
Time required: 1–52 weeks.
Age requirement: 16 plus.
Causes: Children, young people.
Activities: Arts/crafts, cooking, music, outdoor skills, theatre/drama.
Vols under 26 placed each year: All volunteers are under 25.
When to apply: Holidays – particularly summer holidays.
Work alone/with others: With others.
Volunteers with disabilities: Possible.
Qualifications: Nil but driving licence would be useful.
Health requirements: Nil.
Costs: Sometimes travel costs.
Benefits: Sometimes travel costs. Employer's and public liability insurance provided by groups.
Training: Access to BAND training programme. Groups arrange their own induction programmes.
Supervision: By senior playworker, ultimately by manager of groups.
Charity number: 1017307
UK placements: *England* (Gloucestershire, Somerset).

BAPTIST MISSIONARY SOCIETY
PO Box 49
Baptist House
Didcot
Oxfordshire
OX11 8XA UK

Tel: +44 (0) 1235 517700
Fax: +44 (0) 1235 517601
e-mail: jwilson@bms.org.uk
Contact: Julie Wilson, Manager for Volunteer Development

The Baptist Missionary Society works in partnership with Baptist churches in more than 30 countries on four continents – Africa, Asia, Latin America and Europe. We have around 200 missionaries engaged in pastoral and church planting work, engineering, teaching, agriculture, community and medical work, etc. Our aim is to enable the Baptist churches in Britain to respond to the call of God by sharing with all God's people in making known the gospel of Jesus Christ throughout the whole world, principally beyond the British Isles. The BMS Volunteer Programme runs three types of schemes: Firstly a year out programme, called Action Teams, for young people between the ages of 18–25. Six months are spent overseas and on return the team tour around the UK sharing with Baptist churches what they have learnt and experienced. Training prior to departure overseas and on their return are seen as important parts of this programme. Secondly, Summer Teams are run in the months of July and August and consist of teams going overseas for between three and six weeks. Previous teams have gone to Sao Paulo in Brazil and Prague in the Czech Republic, assisting in various social development projects and supporting the work of local missionaries. Thirdly, individual volunteers serve with BMS from between three months and two years. Volunteers are accepted with specialist and non-specialist skills, depending on the need in a particular country.

Total projects worldwide: 10
Total UK projects: 10
Starting months: July, September.
Time required: 2–52 weeks (plus).
Age requirement: 18–25
Causes: Addicts/Ex-addicts, Aids/HIV, children, elderly people, health care/medical, human rights, inner city problems, poor/homeless, refugees, teaching/assisting (nursery, primary, secondary, EFL), unemployed, work camps – seasonal, young people.
Activities: Administration, arts/crafts, building/construction, caring (general, day and residential), community work, computers, cooking, development issues, DIY, gardening/horticulture, group work, library/resource centres, manual work, music, newsletter/journalism, outdoor skills, religion, social work, sport, summer camps, teaching, technical skills, theatre/drama,

training, visiting/befriending, work camps – seasonal.

Vols under 26 placed each year: Approximately 40.

When to apply: All year but the end of February for Action Teams.

Work alone/with others: With others in a team of between 4 and 10.

Volunteers with disabilities: Dependent on the country being visited.

Qualifications: Committed Christians recommended by own church.

Health requirements: Reasonable health but really dependent on the country.

Costs: Approximately £2,900 fully inclusive (board, travel, training etc.) for year £500–£1,500 for summer.

Benefits: Medical and travel insurance is necessary and BMS arrange it.

Training: Five weeks for year teams. Weekend for summer teams. Devotional, practical and adventure training.

Supervision: Team leader appointed and pastoral contact. Missionary or other church worker oversees the team.

Nationalities accepted: No restrictions but applicants should be UK based.

Interview details: Interviews take place in Oxford for year teams and locally for summer applicants.

Certification: References available.

Charity number: 233782

Worldwide placements: *Africa* (Angola, Mauritius, South Africa, Zimbabwe); *Asia* (Bangladesh, India, Indonesia, Nepal, Sri Lanka, Thailand); *Europe* (Albania, Belgium, Czech Republic, France, Hungary, Italy, Malta, Portugal); *Central America* (Belize, El Salvador, Jamaica, Nicaragua, Trinidad and Tobago); *South America* (Brazil). UK placements: *England* (throughout); *Scotland* (throughout); *Northern Ireland* (throughout); *Wales* (throughout).

BARDOU RESTORATION PROJECT

Bardou
Mons La Trivalle
F-34390 Olargues
34390 France

Tel: 00 33 467 97 72 43

Contact: Klaus and Jean Erhardt

Bardou needs volunteers to help restore and maintain 16th century stone houses and to assist with a flock of an endangered breed of sheep in a remote mountain hamlet. 16 hours weekly participation in community projects is expected. Volunteers needed 1 March until 1 July and 15th September to 1 November. Paying guests (FF50/£5 per night) accepted for shorter stay than the four week minimum. The hamlet is easiest reached by taking the TGV (fast trains daily) from Paris to Montpellier. Outside the station (upstairs), a bus numbered 485 leaves daily at 1530 in the direction of Bedarieux-Saint Pons from the first lane outside the door. You pay the driver approximately FF70 for the fare and arrive at 1735 in Mons La Trivalle. (You must ask the driver to stop for you to get off.) From there you can call a taxi or walk the last three beautiful miles up to Bardou. (If in doubt of the way, phone 04.67.97.7243 from the coin-operated or the telecard phones near the café or church.) Bardou can be found on the detailed Michelin Map No. 83, Fold 3/4. Applicants should include such personal information as: age, sex, education, travel, practical experience, cultural hobbies and dates of availability.

Total projects worldwide: 1

Total UK projects: 0

Starting months: March–September

Time required: 4–12 weeks.

Age requirement: 20 plus.

Causes: Animal welfare, architecture, conservation, environmental causes, heritage, wildlife.

Activities: Agriculture/farming, arts/crafts, building/construction, conservation skills, forestry, manual work, music, theatre/drama.

Vols under 26 placed each year: 4

When to apply: Any time.

Work alone/with others: Both.

Volunteers with disabilities: Not possible.

Qualifications: English language, energy, attentiveness and good will.

Equipment/clothing: Recommended to bring: torch (flashlight), matches, light rain gear, sturdy shoes, alarm clock, food and sleeping bag (if possible).

Health requirements: Physically and mentally fit.

Costs: Travel costs, food and insurance.

Benefits: Free lodging (self catering house). Breakfast on work days and large meal on Sunday.

Nationalities accepted: From Australia, New Zealand, Canada, South Africa, EU and USA.

Interview details: Interviews are conducted by letter or phone.
Certification: Reference provided.
Worldwide placements: *Europe* (France).

BARNARDO'S – LEASE CHILDREN'S SERVICES
Scotch House
Tanners Lane
Barkingside
Ilford
Essex
IG6 1QG UK

Tel: +44 (0) 20 8551 0011
Fax: +44 (0) 20 8551 8267
Contact: Rob Jackson, Volunteer Co-ordinator (Children's Services)

Barnardo's, the UK's biggest and best known children's charity, works with 47,000 children, young people and families. We have 300 services which provide accommodation and support for young people who have lived in local authority homes and are leaving care; youth training; day care in deprived areas; special education for children with disabilities; and fostering and adoption. We work with those affected by poverty, Aids/HIV, homelessness and child sexual abuse. We work with children and their families and provide day care and safe play areas for under fives. All applicants are police checked.

Total projects worldwide: 37
Total UK projects: 37
Starting months: January–December.
Time required: 1–52 weeks.
Age requirement: 12 plus.
Causes: Addicts/Ex-addicts, Aids/HIV, children, disabled (learning and physical), inner city problems, offenders/ex-offenders, poor/homeless, refugees, teaching/assisting, work camps – seasonal, young people.
Activities: Accountancy, administration, agriculture/farming, arts/crafts, building/construction, campaigning, caring (general, day and residential), catering, community work, computers, conservation skills, cooking, counselling, development issues, DIY, driving, first aid, forestry, fundraising, gardening/horticulture, group work, international aid, library/resource centres, manual work, marketing/publicity, music, newsletter/journalism, outdoor skills, religion, research, scientific work, social work, sport, summer camps, teaching, technical skills, theatre/drama, training, translating, visiting/befriending, work camps – seasonal.
Vols under 26 placed each year: 10 of a total of 20,000.
When to apply: All year.
Work alone/with others: With others.
Volunteers with disabilities: Possible.
Qualifications: Nil.
Health requirements: Nil.
Costs: Normally Nil.
Benefits: Expenses reimbursed, training.
Nationalities accepted: Although we have no restrictions on nationalities of volunteers, obtaining the necessary police check from the Home Office means that we cannot normally use volunteers from overseas.
Interview details: Volunteers are interviewed at the projects in which they are to work.
Certification: Certificate or reference provided.
Charity number: 216250
UK placements: *England* (throughout); *Scotland* (throughout); *Northern Ireland* (throughout); *Wales* (throughout).

BARNARDO'S – MIDLANDS
Reception, Divisional Office
Brooklands
Great Cornbow
Halesowen
West Midlands
B6 3AB UK

Tel: +44 (0) 121 550 5271
Fax: +44 (0) 121 550 2594
Contact: Volunteer Co-ordinator

Barnardo's Midlands. For more details of Barnardo's, see Barnardo's – Lease Children's Services, above.

Total projects worldwide: Varies
Total UK projects: Varies
Starting months: January–December.
Time required: 1–52 weeks (plus).
Age requirement: 12 plus.
Causes: Children, young people.
Activities: Administration, arts/crafts, caring (general), catering, community work, DIY, driving, gardening/horticulture, group work, manual work, outdoor skills, social work, teaching, technical skills, theatre/drama, training, visiting/befriending.
Work alone/with others: Both.
Volunteers with disabilities: Depends on projects. Barnardo's Equal Opportunities

apply.
Qualifications: Nil.
Health requirements: Nil.
Costs: Nil.
Benefits: Travel and all expenses paid.
Nationalities accepted: Although we have no restrictions on nationalities of volunteers, obtaining the necessary police check from the Home Office means that we cannot normally use volunteers from overseas.
Interview details: Volunteers are interviewed at the projects in which they are to work.
UK placements: *England* (West Midlands).

BARNARDO'S – NORTH EAST
Orchard House
Fenwick Terrace
Jesmond
Newcastle upon Tyne
NE2 2JQ UK

Tel: +44 (0) 191 281 5024
Fax: +44 (0) 191 281 9840
Contact: Regional Co-ordinator

For more details of Barnardo's, see Barnardo's – Lease Children's Services, above. Barnardo's – North East was born in 1892 when the first 'Ever Open Door' house opened in Saville Row. Since then we have come a long way, meeting the ever-changing needs of children, young people and their families. We now have over 35 projects working in Tyne and Wear, Durham, Northumberland and Cleveland. We work in partnership with local authorities and many of our projects are jointly funded.

Total projects worldwide: 28
Total UK projects: 28
Starting months: January–December.
Time required: 1–52 weeks (plus).
Age requirement: 16 plus.
Causes: Addicts/Ex-addicts, Aids/HIV, children, disabled (physical), inner city problems, offenders/ex-offenders, poor/homeless, teaching (mature), unemployed, young people.
Activities: Administration, arts/crafts, caring (general), catering, community work, DIY, driving, gardening/horticulture, group work, manual work, music, outdoor skills, social work, sport, teaching, technical skills, theatre/drama, training, visiting/befriending.
Vols under 26 placed each year: 180 of a total of 300.
When to apply: All year.

Work alone/with others: Both.
Volunteers with disabilities: Depends on projects. Barnado's Equal Opportunities apply.
Qualifications: Nil.
Health requirements: Nil.
Costs: Nil.
Benefits: Travel and all expenses paid. Insurance provided for volunteers at work.
Training: Differs from project to project but training is mainly given in working with children, child protection, health and safety, equal opportunities.
Supervision: Named person at project responsible for volunteers.
Nationalities accepted: Although we have no restrictions on nationalities of volunteers, obtaining the necessary police check from the Home Office means that we cannot normally use volunteers from overseas.
Interview details: Interviews take place either at Divisional Office or at the project.
Certification: References available.
Charity number: 216250
UK placements: *England* (Co. Durham, Cumbria, Northumberland, Tyne and Wear).

BARNARDO'S – NORTH WEST
7 Lineside Close
Belle Vale
Liverpool
Merseyside
L25 2UD UK

Tel: +44 (0) 151 488 1100
Fax: +44 (0) 151 488 1101
e-mail: susan.lewis@barnardos.org.uk
Web: www.barnardos.org.uk
Contact: Susan Lewis, Regional Volunteer Co-ordinator for Children's Services

Barnardo's North West. For more details of Barnardo's, see Barnardo's – Lease Children's Services, above.

Total projects worldwide: 33
Total UK projects: 33
Starting months: January–December.
Time required: 1–52 weeks (plus).
Age requirement: 16 plus.
Causes: Aids/HIV, children, disabled (learning and physical), inner city problems, poor/homeless, young people.
Activities: Administration, arts/crafts, caring (general and day), community work, counselling, driving, fundraising, group work, music, social work, theatre/drama,

training, visiting/befriending.
Vols under 26 placed each year: Varies.
When to apply: All year.
Work alone/with others: Both.
Volunteers with disabilities: Dependent on project. Commitment to trying to ensure specific needs met.
Qualifications: None needed but any welcomed, depending on project e.g. driving licence, languages etc.
Health requirements: Nil.
Costs: Nil.
Benefits: Insurance provided by Barnardo's.
Training: Differs from project to project but training is mainly given in working with children, child protection, health and safety, equal opportunities.
Supervision: Depends on involvement; e.g. summer play schemes – daily informal supervision.
Nationalities accepted: Although we have no restrictions on nationalities of volunteers, obtaining the necessary police check from the Home Office means that we cannot normally use volunteers from overseas.
Interview details: Volunteers are interviewed at the projects in which they are to work.
Certification: Reference on request.
Charity number: 216250
UK placements: *England* (Cheshire, Cumbria, Lancashire, Manchester, Merseyside).

BARNARDO'S – NORTHERN IRELAND
Divisional Office
542/544 Upper Newtownards Road
Belfast
BT4 3HE N. Ireland

Tel: +44 (0) 28 9067 2366
Fax: +44 (0) 28 9067 2399
Contact: Mr Alun Kane, Volunteer Co-ordinator

For more details of Barnardo's, see Barnardo's – Lease Children's Services, above. Last year Barnardo's in Northern Ireland helped over 2,000 families, children and young people – 47,000 throughout all of the UK. At present Barnardo's provides 20 projects/services within Northern Ireland. Volunteers with an offending background are accepted, depending on the nature of the offences relevant to childcare work.
Total projects worldwide: 20
Total UK projects: 20
Starting months: January–December.

Time required: 2–52 weeks (plus).
Age requirement: 16 plus.
Vols under 26 placed each year: 30
When to apply: Any time but 2 months in advance of preferred start date.
Work alone/with others: Mostly with others.
Volunteers with disabilities: Possible.
Qualifications: Varies, depending on volunteer work in question.
Health requirements: There may be possible restrictions, e.g. those with chest complaints/asthma/bronchitis may not be able to work in a cystic fibrosis project.
Costs: Board and lodging.
Benefits: Out-of-pocket expenses and travel reimbursed.
Nationalities accepted: Although we have no restrictions on nationalities of volunteers, obtaining the necessary police check from the Home Office means that we cannot normally use volunteers from overseas.
Interview details: Interviews take place either at the projects or at the divisional office.
Certification: Certificate or reference provided.
UK placements: *Northern Ireland* (throughout).

BARNARDO'S – SCOTLAND
Divisional Office
235 Corstorphine Road
Edinburgh
EH12 7AR Scotland

Tel: +44 (0) 131 316 9893
Fax: +44 (0) 131 316 4008
Contact: Pat Gilmore, Personnel Secretary.

Barnardo's – Scotland: For more details of Barnardo's, see Barnardo's – Lease Children's Services, above.

Total projects worldwide: 1
Total UK projects: 1
Starting months: January–December.
Time required: 1–52 weeks (plus).
Age requirement: 16 plus.
Causes: Children, young people.
Activities: Administration, arts/crafts, caring (general), catering, community work, DIY, driving, gardening/horticulture, group work, manual work, outdoor skills, social work, teaching, technical skills, theatre/drama, training, visiting/befriending.
Vols under 26 placed each year: Varies.
When to apply: All year.
Work alone/with others: Both.

Volunteers with disabilities: Depends on project – Barnado's Equal Opportunities apply.
Qualifications: Nil.
Health requirements: Nil.
Costs: Nil.
Benefits: Travel and all expenses paid.
Nationalities accepted: Although we have no restrictions on nationalities of volunteers, obtaining the necessary police check from the Home Office means that we cannot normally use volunteers from overseas.
Interview details: Volunteers are interviewed at the projects in which they are to work.
Certification: Certificate or reference on request.
UK placements: *Scotland* (E. Lothian).

BARNARDO'S – WALES AND SOUTH WEST ENGLAND

11–15 Columbus Walk
Brigantine Place
Atlantic Wharf
Cardiff
CF1 5BZ Wales

Tel: + 44 (0) 29 2049 3387
Fax: + 44 (0) 29 2048 9802
Web: www.barnardos.org.uk
Contact: Sian Jones

For more details of Barnardo's, see Barnardo's – Lease Children's Services, above. Barnardo's Wales and South West England: during the summer months children and young people who have a learning or physical disability look forward to summer playschemes within the area in which they live. The children and young people need one-to-one care and support during this time and enjoy being involved in the events and activities we provide. The schemes are usually held in a leisure centre or community centre. The times are usually between 10 and 4 p.m. with a break for lunch, five days per week over a four week period. The work is demanding, so you need to be fairly fit and energetic; have an awareness of children and young people who have a learning or physical disability; and an awareness of their needs. We are committed to inclusion and it is essential that these play schemes include these children and young people in activities within their own community. We welcome applicants and if there is one area that you would like to be involved in please contact Sian Jones for

an informal chat. Volunteers with offending backgrounds will be assessed on an individual basis.

Total projects worldwide: 350
Total UK projects: 350
Starting months: July, August.
Time required: 4 weeks.
Age requirement: 16 plus.
Causes: Children, disabled (learning and physical), young people.
Activities: Arts/crafts, caring (day), cooking, driving, first aid, outdoor skills, sport, summer camps.
Vols under 26 placed each year: 438 of a total of 1,750.
When to apply: All year.
Work alone/with others: Both.
Volunteers with disabilities: All play schemes are within buildings accessible to volunteers and clients.
Qualifications: Nil.
Health requirements: Nil.
Costs: Nil.
Benefits: Travel, meal subsistence and all expenses paid. Full public liability insurance cover is provided for all our volunteers.
Training: Full training given before any volunteering is undertaken. There is usually an induction training given to prepare volunteers for their role and an opportunity to meet other workers and volunteers.
Supervision: Support and supervision is given to all volunteers.
Nationalities accepted: Although we have no restrictions on nationalities of volunteers, obtaining the necessary police check from the Home Office means that we cannot normally use volunteers from overseas.
Interview details: Volunteers are interviewed at the projects in which they are to work.
Certification: Certificate or reference provided.
Charity number: 216250
UK placements: *England* (Bristol, Somerset); *Wales* (throughout, except for Powys).

BARNARDO'S – YORKSHIRE

Signpost
Constance Green Centre
24 Cheapside
Wakefield
W. Yorkshire
WF1 2TF UK

Tel: + 44 (0) 1924 304100

Fax: +44 (0) 1924 304101
Web: www.barnardos.org.uk
Contact: Liz Richardson

For more details of Barnardo's, see
Barnardo's – Lease Children's Services,
above. Barnardo's – Yorkshire. Barnardo's is
an association whose inspiration and values
derive from the Christian faith. These values,
enriched and shared by many people of other
faiths and philosophies, provide the basis of
our work with children and young people,
their families and communities. Volunteers
bring a diversity of skills, experience, links
with communities, service opportunities and
funds. You increase public understanding of
our work and challenge our thinking about
the organization. Volunteers gain experience
which enhances training and work
opportunities, develops potential, increases
self-reliance and underpins a sense of worth.
Volunteers perform essential, supportive and
complementary tasks to those undertaken by
paid employees. Your role is an enriching
one: you share our concern and
understanding; you offer opportunities for
people to express their caring in a committed
and practical way. Barnardo's values
volunteering because everybody – the user of
our services, staff and volunteers – benefits.
Volunteers with an offending background
may be accepted.

Total projects worldwide: 1
Total UK projects: 1
Starting months: January–December.
Time required: 1–52 weeks (plus).
Age requirement: 16 plus.
Causes: Children, disabled (learning and
physical), holidays for disabled, offenders/ex-
offenders, poor/homeless, young people.
Activities: Driving, group work, visiting/
befriending.
Vols under 26 placed each year: 25 of a total
of 200.
When to apply: All year, particularly in
September and April.
Work alone/with others: Occasionally with
other young volunteers.
Volunteers with disabilities: Projects vary –
some are more accessible than others.
Qualifications: Individual assessment to
ascertain suitability.
Health requirements: Nil.
Costs: Nil.
Benefits: All out-of-pocket expenses met.

Nationalities accepted: Although we have no
restrictions on nationalities of volunteers,
obtaining the necessary police check from the
Home Office means that we cannot normally
use volunteers from overseas.
Interview details: All volunteers are
interviewed – each project has a screening
process for volunteers.
Certification: Certificate or reference on
request.
Charity number: 216250
UK placements: *England* (E. Yorkshire, N.
Yorkshire, S. Yorkshire, W. Yorkshire).

BEANNACHAR (CAMPHILL) LTD
Beannachar
Banchory-Devenick
Aberdeen
Aberdeenshire
AB12 5YL Scotland

Tel: +44 (0) 1224 869138
Fax: +44 (0) 1224 869250
e-mail: beannachar@talk21.com
Web: http://www.camphillsccotland.org.uk
Other Web: www.beannachar.co.uk
Contact: Elisabeth Phethean

Beannachar needs volunteers to live and work
with young adults with special needs. Work
is to be done in the kitchen, laundry, garden
and on the farm. Tasks also include making
herbal medicines and candles, weaving and
pottery.

Total projects worldwide: 1
Total UK projects: 1
Starting months: January–December.
Time required: 26–52 weeks.
Age requirement: 21 plus.
Causes: Animal welfare, disabled (learning
and physical), teaching/assisting young
people.
Activities: Agriculture/farming, arts/crafts,
building/construction, caring (general, day
and residential), catering, cooking,
gardening/horticulture, manual work, music,
outdoor skills, sport, teaching, theatre/
drama, training.
Vols under 26 placed each year: 10–12
When to apply: All year.
Work alone/with others: All live and work
together as a community.
Volunteers with disabilities: Possible.
Qualifications: Fluent English, enthusiasm
and an interest in others.
Equipment/clothing: Old clothes suitable for

gardening and walks, waterproofs and warm clothes.
Health requirements: Good health.
Costs: Nil.
Benefits: Organisation pays for day-to-day living costs plus £30 per week and insurance cover for all volunteers.
Training: Induction talks at the beginning and foundation course once weekly throughout stay.
Supervision: By house parent and experienced co-workers.
Interview details: Interviews take place, if possible, at the office in Aberdeen.
Certification: Certificate provided for full year's attendance of foundation course.
Charity number: 103915
UK placements: *Scotland* (Aberdeen City, Aberdeenshire, Angus, Argyll and Bute, Clackmannanshire, Dumfries and Galloway, Edinburgh, E. Lothian, W. Lothian, Moray, Perth and Kinross, Stirling).

BEAUFORT COMMUNITY CENTRE
Beaufort Road
Southbourne
Bournemouth
Dorset
BH6 5LB UK

Tel: +44 (0) 1202 417143
Fax: +44 (0) 1202 434203
e-mail: Beaufort@beaufort45.freeserve.co.uk
Contact: Sue Smith

The Beaufort Community Centre is an independent charity providing facilities for education, recreation and social welfare in Bournemouth. Volunteers with an offending background may be accepted.

Total projects worldwide: 1
Total UK projects: 1
Starting months: January–December.
Time required: 1–52 weeks.
Age requirement: 16 plus.
Causes: Children, elderly people, young people.
Activities: Administration, arts/crafts, caring (general and day), catering, newsletter/journalism.
Vols under 26 placed each year: 5 of a total of 40.
When to apply: All year.
Work alone/with others: With others.
Volunteers with disabilities: People with disabilities are accepted and welcomed.

Qualifications: If working with children, volunteers must be approved by Social Services.
Health requirements: Nil.
Costs: Nil.
Benefits: Travel expenses paid. The Centre holds all necessary insurances.
Training: As necessary.
Supervision: Manager and administrator give support and supervision of all staff and volunteers.
Interview details: Interviews take place at the Centre in Dorset.
Certification: Written reference if required and certificate.
Charity number: 800843
UK placements: *England* (Dorset).

BEFRIENDERS INTERNATIONAL
Room 2, Parman House
30/36 Fife Road
Kingston-upon-Thames
KT1 1SY UK

Tel: +44 (0) 20 8547 3041
Fax: +44 (0) 20 8547 3905
e-mail: fundraising@befrienders.org
Web: www.befrienders.org
Contact: Leish Mason, Fundraiser

Befrienders International is the umbrella organization of The Samaritans and has branches all over the UK and in 41 countries abroad. Volunteers are only needed for our London office.

Total projects worldwide: 1
Total UK projects: 1
Starting months: January–December.
Time required: 12–52 weeks (plus).
Age requirement: 18 plus.
Causes: Addicts/Ex-addicts, Aids/HIV, disabled (learning and physical), elderly people, health care/medical, human rights, inner city problems, offenders/ex-offenders, poor/homeless, refugees, unemployed, young people.
Activities: Administration, community work, fundraising, marketing/publicity.
When to apply: All year.
Work alone/with others: With others.
Volunteers with disabilities: No disabled access to building. (No lift or escalator.)
Qualifications: Nil.
Health requirements: Nil.
Costs: Nil.
Benefits: Reasonable travel expenses and £3

lunch substitute.
Certification: Written reference.
UK placements: *England* (London).

BELARUSSIAN ASSOCIATION OF INTERNATIONAL YOUTH WORK
220119 Belarus
P/b 64, Minsk
Belarus

Tel: 00 375 172 278183
Fax: 00 375 172 222714
Contact: Anna Dolgatcheva or Tanya Barinova

Belarussian Association of International Youth Work (ATM) is an independent NGO, which promotes voluntary work through participation in various youth exchanges: work camps, study camps, seminars and Russian language courses. It is a member of the Co-ordinating Committee for International Voluntary Service (CCIVS UNESCO), of the Belarussian Youth Council, of GATE (East–West Commission of Service Civil International), and of Mobility International. One of the basic activities of ATM is the organization of work camps and study camps (usual duration of three to four weeks) in Belarus in such different fields as: ecology and environment; work with children; work with disabled people; renovation/reconstruction/archaeology; social/youth problems; peace work. ATM is realizing the Anti-Chernobyl Project. ATM is also concerned with democracy education and is now implementing the TACIS democracy programme 'Common Power or Common Sense', and promoting by way of its work camps and study camps grassroots education regarding alternative ways of living, practical experimentation with power games and discussions concerning organizational democracy. Volunteers with an offending background are accepted. All people should apply on equal grounds through the regular application process.

Total projects worldwide: 14
Total UK projects: 0
Starting months: July–September.
Time required: 20–35 weeks.
Age requirement: 18–25
Causes: Archaeology, architecture, children, disabled (physical), environmental causes, human rights, work camps – seasonal, young people.

Activities: Administration, building/construction, community work, computers, development issues, fundraising, group work, library/resource centres, newsletter/journalism, research, social work, summer camps, technical skills, training, translating, visiting/befriending, work camps – seasonal.
Vols under 26 placed each year: 150.
When to apply: All year.
Work alone/with others: With others in groups of 10–20 people.
Volunteers with disabilities: Possible.
Qualifications: English, Russian desirable, computer skills.
Equipment/clothing: Personal computer if possible. Working clothing for work camps.
Costs: Depends on each project. Insurance needed. DM100–150 registration fee. Internal travel costs.
Benefits: Food, accommodation, cultural activities.
Interview details: Applicants are interviewed.
Certification: Certificate or reference provided.
Worldwide placements: *Europe* (Belarus).

BELGIAN EVANGELICAL MISSION
PO Box 165
Swindon
Wiltshire
SN5 6LU UK

Tel: +44 (0) 1793 882368
Fax: +44 (0) 1793 882368
e-mail: bemuk@cs.com
Web: www.B-E-M.org
Contact: Roy Saint

The Belgian Evangelical Mission (BEM) conducts summer evangelical campaigns in a number of towns and villages in both French- and Dutch-speaking Belgium. We have run short-term programmes since the 1970s. In the early days teams were involved, and still are today if there are sufficient volunteers for a given period. However, when numbers are low individuals can be accommodated, working in support of our church-planting projects and gaining experience of serving the Lord in another culture. Study days are arranged in relation to the work of the Mission.

Total projects worldwide: Up to 10
Total UK projects: 0
Starting months: June–September.
Time required: 3–52 weeks.

Age requirement: 18–30
Causes: Children, young people.
Activities: Campaigning, music, religion, sport, theatre/drama.
Vols under 26 placed each year: 5–10 of a total of 10–20.
When to apply: Preferably before May but definitely before the end of June.
Work alone/with others: With others under experienced leadership.
Volunteers with disabilities: Possible.
Qualifications: For long projects (e.g. 11–12 months) language required.
Health requirements: Reasonably fit.
Costs: £50 per week plus travel. E111 will cover basic health care. Travel insurance is recommended, payable by the volunteer.
Benefits: Accommodation.
Training: A booklet of notes and advice to volunteers is provided. A training element is incorporated into the placement.
Supervision: Volunteers are placed in teams under the supervision of permanent staff normally based locally.
Certification: Reference provided by your church.
Charity number: 249192
Worldwide placements: *Europe* (Belgium).

BENDRIGG TRUST
Bendrigg Lodge
Old Hutton
Kendal
Cumbria
LA8 0NR UK

Tel: + 44 (0) 1539 723766
Fax: + 44 (0) 1539 722446
e-mail: Bendrigg@msn.com
Web: www.bendrigg.org.uk
Contact: Mrs Sue Murphy, The Volunteer Co-ordinator

The Bendrigg Trust is a residential activity centre for disabled and disadvantaged people. We are open throughout the year and take a very wide range of groups including people with learning disabilities, physical disabilities or sensory disabilities. We also run courses for able-bodied young people who are socially disadvantaged in any way and for minority groups. We employ a team of experienced and qualified staff to run the centre and to provide the activities. However, we need extra people to help us in a voluntary capacity in all areas of our work.

The Trust uses the outdoors and the residential experience to: promote integration, encourage independence and to build self-confidence in our visitors. We also try to ensure that there are as many benefits to the volunteer as to the Bendrigg Trust. Volunteers help us in a number of ways including maintenance, grounds, catering and domestic work. We also need help for our tutorial staff in providing support for the activities we provide. These include: climbing and abseiling; canoeing, kayaking and rafting; caving; sailing; orienteering; ropes courses; aerial runway and tube-slide; arts and crafts including games and projects. We try to utilize whatever skills the volunteers have for the benefit of our visiting groups. Volunteers with an offending background are accepted providing they can be interviewed first at Bendrigg Lodge.

Total projects worldwide: 1
Total UK projects: 1
Starting months: January–December.
Time required: 1–4 weeks.
Age requirement: 16 plus.
Causes: Children, disabled (learning and physical), holidays for disabled, inner city problems, unemployed, young people.
Activities: Arts/crafts, caring (residential), catering, cooking, gardening/horticulture, group work, outdoor skills.
Vols under 26 placed each year: 120 of a total of 150.
When to apply: All year.
Work alone/with others: Both.
Volunteers with disabilities: Possible.
Qualifications: Not essential but useful.
Health requirements: Nil, but any medical condition must be declared.
Costs: Initial travel to Bendrigg.
Benefits: Board and lodging and insurance.
Supervision: At all times by qualified instructors and the volunteer co-ordinator.
Interview details: All interviews take place at Bendrigg Lodge.
Certification: Reference on request.
Charity number: 508450
UK placements: *England* (Cumbria).

BERKS, BUCKS AND OXON WILDLIFE TRUST
The Lodge
1 Armstrong Road
Littlemore
Oxford

OX4 4XT UK

Tel: +44 (0) 1865 775476
Fax: +44 (0) 1865 711301
e-mail: gillormrod@bbowt.cix.co.uk
Web: www.wildlifetrust.org.uk/
berksbucksoxon
Contact: Gill Ormrod

The Berkshire, Buckinghamshire and
Oxfordshire Wildlife Trust is an independent
registered charity and is the only voluntary
organization concerned with all aspects of
wildlife conservation in these counties. We
protect wildlife on over 90 nature reserves
and aim to involve all people – children,
adults, community groups and organizations
– in taking action for local wildlife. Modern
threats to wildlife include intensive farming,
industrial development, house and road
building, and the use of pesticides. Nature
reserves are places where wildlife – especially
rare and endangered wildlife – can be looked
after, studied and enjoyed. Our nature
reserves are carefully looked after to
encourage the survival and spread of wild
plants and animals. Every five years our
conservationists work out new action plans
for each nature reserve. The plans are
individually tailored for the particular species
that need to be protected on each site and
identify key tasks – such as clearing ponds or
creating nature trails – which are mainly
carried out by local volunteers. Regular
surveys ensure the plans are successful and
that our nature reserves continue to be havens
for local wildlife.

Total projects worldwide: Approximately 50.
Total UK projects: Approximately 50.
Starting months: January–December.
Time required: 1–52 weeks (plus).
Age requirement: 16 plus.
Causes: Conservation, environmental causes,
wildlife.
Activities: Conservation skills, forestry,
gardening/horticulture, manual work,
marketing/publicity, outdoor skills, research.
Vols under 26 placed each year: 400 of a
total of 2,000.
When to apply: All year.
Work alone/with others: With others.
Volunteers with disabilities: Not possible.
Qualifications: Nil.
Equipment/clothing: Old clothes,
waterproofs, sturdy boots. We provide safety
boots.

Health requirements: Any medical conditions
(illness, allergy or physical disability) that
may require treatment/medication or which
affects the volunteer working with machinery
must be notified to us in advance.
Costs: Travel costs to and from pick-up
points plus packed lunch.
Benefits: Tea and coffee, transport to the
worksite and insurance.
Interview details: No interview necessary.
Certification: Reference if required.
Charity number: 204330
UK placements: *England* (Berkshire,
Buckinghamshire, Oxfordshire).

BERRINGTON HALL – NATIONAL TRUST

Berrington Hall
Leominster
Herefordshire
HR6 0DW UK

Tel: +44 (0) 1568 615721
Fax: +44 (0) 1568 613263
e-mail: vbeasb@smtp.ntrust.org.uk
Contact: Yvonne Osborne

Berrington Hall is a National Trust property
which requires volunteer room stewards every
day from April to October. Also needed are
volunteer car park attendants to work on
Bank Holidays, and volunteer flower
arrangers to prepare floral displays in the
mansion. Volunteer office staff required all
year.

Total projects worldwide: 1
Total UK projects: 1
Starting months: January–December.
Time required: 1–52 weeks.
Age requirement: 16 plus.
Causes: Heritage.
Activities: Administration, community work,
computers, fundraising, gardening/
horticulture, manual work.
Vols under 26 placed each year: 1 of a total
of 100.
When to apply: All year.
Work alone/with others: Both.
Volunteers with disabilities: Possible.
Qualifications: Nil.
Health requirements: Must be fit.
Costs: Subsistence.
Benefits: Travel costs and insurance. Those
who offer 40 hours of service get a volunteer
card entitling them to free entry to National
Trust Properties in the UK and 10% discount

in the shops.
Training: Visit to property and 'job shadowing'.
Supervision: Volunteers use 'buddy' system and are supervised overall by house steward.
Interview details: Interviews take place at the property.
Certification: Reference provided.
Charity number: 205846
UK placements: *England* (Herefordshire, Worcestershire).

BETSELEM
8 Hatibonim Street
Jerusalem 92386
Israel

Tel: 00 972 2 667 271 / 667 274
Contact: Professor Uriel Procachia, Chairperson

Betselem's purpose is to document and bring to the public's and to policymakers' attention the human rights violations in the Israeli occupied territories. We collect information from various independent sources on human rights related issues in the occupied territories; follow changes in policy; and encourage and support intervention in all possible cases. We make our information available to any individual or body which wants to use it.

Starting months: January–December.
Time required: 1–52 weeks.
Age requirement: 21 plus.
Causes: Human Rights.
Activities: Newsletter/journalism, research.
Vols under 26 placed each year: Hundreds.
When to apply: All year.
Work alone/with others: With others.
Qualifications: English essential, Arabic/Hebrew useful. Human rights experience useful.
Worldwide placements: *Asia* (Israel).

BHARAT SEVAK SAMAJ (BSS)
Nehru Seva Kendra
Gugoan Bye Pass Road
Mehrauli
New Delhi 30
India

Tel: 00 91 11 6852215/6967609/6969743
Contact: The General Secretary

Bharat Sevak Samaj (BSS) runs a programme which includes child welfare centres, nursery schools, training camps for national reconstruction work, and family planning camps and clinics. The work also encompasses relief and reconstruction after natural calamities such as famine, drought, cyclones and earthquakes as well as the construction of houses for the Scheduled Caste (lowest) and tribes, and low cost latrines in villages.

Starting months: January–December.
Time required: 2–12 weeks.
Age requirement: 14 plus.
Causes: Children, conservation, environmental causes, health care/medical, poor/homeless, teaching/assisting (EFL).
Activities: Building/construction, caring (general), community work, conservation skills, development issues, group work, international aid, social work, teaching.
Vols under 26 placed each year: 50
When to apply: All year.
Qualifications: English speaking.
Costs: Total cost of travel and stay.
Worldwide placements: *Asia* (India).

BIG SWAMP WILDLIFE PARK
Prince Philip Drive
PO Box 21
Bunbury
6230 Western Australia

Tel: 00 61 8 9721 8380
Fax: 00 61 8 9721 7509
Contact: Sheri Melternick-Jones

The Big Swamp Wildlife Park is a city council owned facility established in 1986. The Park is maintained primarily by volunteers. Along with a full-time co-ordinator, two part-time animal attendants aid in the upkeep and running of the facility. Volunteers are responsible for daily kiosk operation, grounds keeping, feed preparation and enclosure maintenance. Along with core volunteers, community service personnel work for the dole participants. All contribute to the running of this unique wildlife park.
Volunteering at the Big Swamp Wildlife Park is a great opportunity to meet new people and gain valuable experience in the areas of customer relations and wildlife care.
Volunteers with an offending background are accepted but an Australian visa may prove difficult.

Total projects worldwide: 1

Total UK projects: 0
Starting months: January–December.
Time required: 12–52 weeks (plus).
Age requirement: 18 plus.
Causes: Animal welfare, children, conservation, offenders/ex-offenders, unemployed, wildlife, young people.
Activities: Building/construction, community work, conservation skills, gardening/horticulture, manual work, outdoor skills.
Vols under 26 placed each year: 90 of a total of 100.
When to apply: Approximately 1 week before starting.
Work alone/with others: With others.
Volunteers with disabilities: Suitable for some smaller projects – light gardening etc. depending on disability.
Qualifications: English-speaking and numeracy.
Equipment/clothing: Neat, tidy clothes and enclosed shoes.
Health requirements: Nil.
Costs: All costs, including own lunch, travel, accommodation etc.
Interview details: Interviews take place on location, prior to commencement.
Certification: Certificate or reference provided if it is earned.
Worldwide placements: *Australasia* (Australia).

BIRMINGHAM AND BLACK COUNTRY URBAN WILDLIFE TRUST

28 Harborne Road
Edgbaston
Birmingham
B15 3AA UK

Tel: +44 (0) 121 454 1199
Fax: +44 (0) 121 454 6556
e-mail: urbanwt@cix.co.uk
Web: www.wildlifetrust.org.uk/urbanwt
Contact: Wendy Burnett

Birmingham and Black Country Urban Wildlife Trust is an independent voluntary nature conservation organization. We are a member of the Wildlife Trusts, a national partnership of 47 county trusts. Volunteers are needed to help in the office, in the horticulture nursery, the environment education centre or to help outposted project officers. There may also be opportunities to undertake ecological survey.

Total projects worldwide: 4

Total UK projects: 4 plus office.
Starting months: January–December.
Time required: 1–52 weeks (plus).
Age requirement: 18 plus.
Causes: Conservation, environmental causes, wildlife.
Activities: Conservation Skills, gardening/horticulture, manual work, outdoor skills.
Vols under 26 placed each year: 15 of a total of 30.
When to apply: All year.
Work alone/with others: With others.
Volunteers with disabilities: Possible.
Qualifications: Practical and office skills useful. For ecological survey relevant qualifications necessary.
Equipment/clothing: Smart casual for office. Work clothes, waterproofs, stout boots for outdoor work.
Health requirements: Any medical conditions (illness, allergy or physical disability) that may require treatment/medication or which affects the volunteer working with machinery must be notified to us in advance.
Costs: Bring own packed lunch.
Benefits: Travel costs and insurance.
Training: Some in-house training if and when available and if funds allow.
Supervision: Work is undertaken under the supervision of the relevant member of staff.
Interview details: Interviews held at our office are essential.
Certification: Reference on request.
Charity number: 513615
UK placements: *England* (West Midlands).

BIRMINGHAM PHAB CAMPS

2 Lenchs Green
Edgbaston
Birmingham
B5 7PX UK

Tel: +44 (0) 121 440 5727
Web: www.bhamphabcamps.org.uk
Contact: Maxine Wallis

Birmingham PHAB Camps runs holiday camps each summer in England for equal numbers of physically disabled and able-bodied children, enabling the disabled children to integrate with their able-bodied contemporaries. There are six camps a year, three of which cater for different age groups from 8–16 years; two are run for severely multiply-disabled children of all ages; and one for young adults aged 18 to around 25.

Many children who are physically disabled have little opportunity to mix and form friendships with their peer groups, and the camps are designed to remedy this isolation and overcome prejudice. There is a wide range of activities, from swimming and discos to seaside and theme parks in which all the children take part together as equals. The camps are run entirely by unpaid volunteers. The team includes an experienced leader and a qualified nurse.

Total projects worldwide: 6
Total UK projects: 6
Starting months: July, August.
Time required: 1 week.
Age requirement: 16–30
Causes: Children, disabled (learning and physical), holidays for disabled, young people.
Activities: Arts/crafts, caring (general), driving, fundraising, music, outdoor skills, sport, summer camps, theatre/drama.
Vols under 26 placed each year: 90 of a total of 100.
When to apply: Any time but preferably around March.
Work alone/with others: With others.
Volunteers with disabilities: Possible – assessed on ability to offer something to the holiday.
Qualifications: Fluent English essential.
Health requirements: Nil.
Costs: Pocket money plus £10 for police check. We have our own personal liability insurance but we cannot insure personal belongings.
Benefits: Accommodation, food and transport between camp and Birmingham.
Training: We run a training day around the end of June where we cover all aspects of the camp and volunteers have the opportunity to meet others. Training days are given before each camp.
Supervision: Each camp is staffed by a group of volunteers of which some will be new and others experienced. These include an experienced leader and a qualified nurse.
Nationalities accepted: No restrictions but volunteers must be able to speak English.
Interview details: No interview necessary but essential that applicants attend a training day in June.
Certification: Reference on request.
Charity number: 502073
Worldwide placements: *Europe* (Ireland).

UK placements: *England* (Derbyshire, Hampshire, Shropshire, West Midlands, N. Yorkshire).

BIRMINGHAM YOUNG VOLUNTEERS
4th Floor
Smithfield House
Digbeth
Birmingham
B5 6BS UK

Tel: +44 (0) 121 622 2888
Fax: +44 (0) 121 622 3616
Contact: BYV Co-ordinator

BYV Adventure Camps exists to provide summer holidays for children and young people who otherwise would not have a holiday. All the children are referred by Social Services, schools and other agencies. Volunteers who have been involved with the Adventure Camps project for a week during the summer are encouraged to become involved with the management of the project and the planning of the holidays. There are a number of committee posts to fill, such as children's co-ordinator, volunteer co-ordinator, transport co-ordinator, training co-ordinator, trusts co-ordinator etc. These posts are taken on for the year and involve a certain number of hours' work outside committee meetings and reporting back at committee meetings.

Total projects worldwide: 2
Total UK projects: 2
Starting months: January–December.
Time required: 1–52 weeks.
Age requirement: 17 plus.
Causes: Children, young people.
Activities: Administration, arts/crafts, cooking, driving, first aid, fundraising, marketing/publicity, newsletter/journalism, outdoor skills, social work, sport, summer camps, training, visiting/befriending.
Vols under 26 placed each year: 140–160
When to apply: Before school summer holidays.
Work alone/with others: Both, but mainly with other volunteers as a team supervising children and young people.
Volunteers with disabilities: Limited access for residential centres. Camping holidays may be difficult for wheelchairs.
Qualifications: Previous experience with the young an advantage. Driving, first aid, sport, arts etc. It is essential that volunteers taking

on these posts are Birmingham based or are able to attend meetings regularly.

Equipment/clothing: Clothes suitable for camping and outdoor activities.

Health requirements: Need to know volunteers' medical condition so their needs can be assessed.

Costs: £10–£5 registration fee returnable if not placed, plus spending money.

Benefits: All costs are met during the week's camps. There are opportunities for training, both within the project and using Birmingham City Council resources related to play, youth and community work. Much of this training is free.

Nationalities accepted: No restrictions but volunteers must be Birmingham based.

Certification: Certificates provided.

UK placements: *England* (Herefordshire, Warwickshire); *Wales* (Gwynedd).

BONDWAY NIGHT SHELTER
Bondway Shelter
35–43 Bondway
London
SW8 1SJ UK

Tel: +44 (0) 20 7482 6202
Contact: Claire Simpson at CSV Tel: +44 (0) 20 7278 6601 or 0800 374991

Bondway Shelter is a 95-bed direct access hostel for homeless men aged 30 and over, many of whom have alcohol and mental health problems, plus long histories of homelessness. The Shelter offers a basic, but supportive, environment 24 hours a day, seven days a week. It is also the base for outreach work and a soup run which operates every night of the year, catering for up to 200 people sleeping rough in central London. The Shelter's philosophy places minimum demands on the residents, showing a high level of tolerance in order to discourage them from returning to the streets. There are up to 17 volunteer trainees at all times, who work a 40 hour week. Duties include: assisting residents with medication and personal hygiene, liaising with outside agencies, e.g. hospitals, DSS, dental appointments etc., booking in residents, assisting residents with welfare benefit claims, collecting and distributing the post, maintaining the security of the building, preparing the food for the soup run and being responsible for the smooth running of

it, assisting in the running of the duty office, handling enquiries etc., dealing with aggressive situations.

NB No volunteers can be recruited directly by Bondway Night Shelter. Prospective volunteers must contact:
Ms Claire Simpson
CSV
237 Pentonville Road
London
N1 9NJ UK
Tel: +44 20 7278 6601 or 0800 374991

Total projects worldwide: 6
Total UK projects: 6
Starting months: January–December.
Time required: 26–52 weeks.
Age requirement: 18 plus.
Causes: Disabled (learning), elderly people, poor/homeless, unemployed.
Activities: Administration, caring (general, day and residential), catering, counselling, driving, training, visiting/befriending.
Vols under 26 placed each year: 24
When to apply: All year.
Work alone/with others: With other young volunteers.
Volunteers with disabilities: Not possible.
Qualifications: Competent English. No previous experience needed.
Equipment/clothing: Old clothes for working.
Health requirements: We advise volunteers to have hepatitis and TB innoculations before starting.
Costs: Nil.
Benefits: Accommodation, meals on duty, travel expenses to the project and £62 per week.
Interview details: Interviews take place at the Shelter.
Certification: Reference provided.
UK placements: *England* (London).

BOOK AID INTERNATIONAL
39–41 Coldharbour Lane
London
SE5 9NR UK

Tel: +44 (0) 20 7733 3577
Contact: Nayla Islam

Book Aid International is a registered charity which supports education, training and literacy in the developing world by sending over 500,000 books overseas every year in response to urgent requests. Each year over 1.5 million books are donated; unsuitable books are sold or recycled; and funds are raised to buy books not available from donated stock.

Starting months: January–December.
Time required: 2–52 weeks (plus).
Age requirement: 16 plus.
Activities: Development issues, international aid.
When to apply: All year.
Qualifications: English speaking, basic literacy and numeracy and ability to work as part of a team.
Health requirements: Nil.
Costs: Nil.
Benefits: Travel costs within London travelcard area provided.
UK placements: *England* (London).

BOX-AID SSS (SIMPLE SUSTAINABLE SOLUTIONS)
11 Hill Top Lane
Saffron Walden
Essex
CB11 4AS UK

Tel: +44 (0) 1799 523321
Fax: +44 (0) 1799 523321
Contact: Anna Pearce

Box-Aid makes, demonstrates and cooks with solar cooking and 'Wonderboxes' at Green Fairs in the UK and also at Sunseed's desert technology centre in Spain. Volunteers of any nationality would begin by experimenting with the cookers. If keen, you can then progress to demonstrating in Spain. We are in the final stages of working out a way to help any organization in whatever way they choose, which is most likely to be to help volunteers stay at missions in any country to teach fuel-saving etc.

Starting months: January–December.
Time required: 1–52 weeks.
Age requirement: 14 plus.
Causes: Conservation, environmental causes, unemployed.
Activities: Conservation skills, cooking, development issues.
When to apply: All year.
Volunteers with disabilities: Possible.
Qualifications: An interest in cooking and practical experience of fuel-saving cooking or sewing machines.

Costs: All costs in the UK.
Benefits: Board and lodging provided in Spain.
Charity number: 1057146
Worldwide placements: *Europe* (Spain).
UK placements: *England* (Essex).

BOYS' BRIGADE, THE
Felden Lodge
Felden
Hemel Hempstead
Hertfordshire
HP3 0BL UK

Tel: +44 (0) 1442 231681
Fax: +44 (0) 1442 235391
e-mail: bbhq@boys-brigade.org.uk
Web: www.boys-brigade.org.uk
Contact: Martyn Waters

The Boys' Brigade (BB) is an interdenominational Christian-based uniformed youth organization for boys. We aim to communicate a live and meaningful Christian faith. We offer a wide-ranging and progressive programme of activities in five age groupings: Anchor Boys (5–8), a programme of games, stories, crafts and music; Juniors (8–11), a programme of physical activities, team games, arts and crafts and stories. Some of this is centred around an award scheme offering over 200 activities; Company (12–15), activities based around the headings of adventure, interests, physical, leadership and community. Participation in running the local group is encouraged; Seniors (16–19), active leadership and participation in the BB and the local church, together with work in the local community. Awards include the BB President's and Queen's badges as well as the D of E scheme. AMICUS (15–22), a pilot project working with young men and young women. Members are fully involved in the management of their local group and in determining their own programmes. Volunteers with an offending background may be accepted, subject to the provisions of the Rehabilitation of Offenders Act 1974 (Exemptions) Order 1975.

Total projects worldwide: 2,100
Total UK projects: 2,100
Starting months: January–December.
Time required: 13–52 weeks.
Age requirement: 16 plus.
Causes: Children, young people.
Activities: Administration, arts/crafts,

community work, computers, cooking, first aid, fundraising, group work, music, outdoor skills, religion, sport, summer camps, theatre/drama, training, work camps – seasonal.

Vols under 26 placed each year: 2,500 of a total of 20,000.

When to apply: All year.

Work alone/with others: As part of a team.

Volunteers with disabilities: Possible. Enquiries welcome.

Qualifications: Skills and abilities to work with children (5 plus) and young people (up to 22). Christian.

Equipment/clothing: The BB is a uniformed youth organization.

Health requirements: Nil.

Costs: Annual levy of £18 payable in December, discounts for students and those on a state retirement pension.

Benefits: Some groups are able to reimburse out-of-pocket expenses. The BB in England is a Millenium Volunteers partner, volunteers aged 16–25 may be able to claim out-of-pocket expenses and monies for training. Insurance is provided by the BB via the annual levy.

Training: A programme of training is made available to volunteers.

Supervision: Volunteers are supervised by the leader in charge of the unit. Volunteers operate within the BB code of good practice for adults working with children and young people.

Interview details: Applicants for volunteer positions are interviewed by local churches who have BB companies. Applicants are required to supply references and complete an application form.

Certification: References on request.

Charity number: 305969

UK placements: *England* (throughout, except Rutland); *Scotland* (throughout); *Northern Ireland* (throughout); *Wales* (Blaenau, Gwent, Bridgend, Caerphilly, Cardiff, Conwy, Flintshire, Monmouthshire, Neath, Port Talbot, Newport, Rhondda, Cynon, Taff, Swansea, Torfaen, Vale of Glamorgan, Wrexham).

BOYS HOPE IRELAND

Lynnwood House
Oldenway Business Park
Ballybrit
Galway

Ireland

Tel: 00 353 91 773577
Fax: 00 353 91 773580
e-mail: info@boyshope.ie
Web: www.boyshope.ie
Contact: Paul O'Callaghan

Boys Hope Ireland admits young adolescents who are unable to remain at home due to family circumstances such as illness, neglect or abuse. Boys Hope offers security and stability at its residential facility through the forming of trusting relationships between the staff and the young person. The young person is supported in continuing in an educational programme in the community, and encouraged to re-engage with the family of origin where appropriate. Boys Hope is seeking volunteers who may be college graduates of a related discipline and who are interested in broadening their experience through working with young people in a residential programme. All volunteers and staff must submit to a police check in advance of security placement.

Total projects worldwide: 28
Total UK projects: 0
Starting months: January–December.
Time required: 12–52 weeks.
Age requirement: 19 plus.
Causes: Children, teaching (primary, secondary, mature, EFL), young people.
Activities: Caring (day and residential), outdoor skills, social work, sport, teaching.
Vols under 26 placed each year: 1 of a total of 4.
When to apply: All year.
Work alone/with others: With full-time staff.
Volunteers with disabilities: Not possible.
Qualifications: Clean driving licence, experience working with young people preferred. Volunteers should be prepared to be flexible in the work of the project.
Equipment/clothing: Some sports clothes and camping gear.
Health requirements: General good health.
Costs: Travel to project.
Benefits: Health insurance, board and lodging and a small allowance. Volunteers are covered by public liability insurance which is provided by Boys Hope.
Supervision: Volunteers work alongside full-time staff.
Nationalities accepted: No restrictions although non-EU citizens will have to satisfy

immigration procedures.
Interview details: Interviews take place at the national office in Galway.
Certification: May receive written reference.
Charity number: CHY 11215
Worldwide placements: *Europe* (Ireland).

BRATHAY EXPLORATION GROUP TRUST LTD
Brathay Hall
Ambleside
Cumbria
LA22 0HP UK

Tel: +44 (0) 1539 433942
Fax: +44 (0) 1539 433942
e-mail: admin@brathayexploration.org.uk
Web: www.brathayexploration.org.uk
Contact: The Administrator

The Brathay Exploration Group was established in 1947. It is a non-profit-making voluntary organization running expeditions and courses aimed at increasing members' understanding of the natural environment and the people and cultures of the places visited. Volunteers with an offending background are accepted.

Total projects worldwide: 15
Total UK projects: 3
Starting months: April–September.
Time required: 1–5 weeks.
Age requirement: 16–25
Causes: Conservation, wildlife, young People.
Activities: Conservation skills, first aid, outdoor skills, scientific work, training.
Vols under 26 placed each year: 250
When to apply: As soon as possible.
Work alone/with others: With others.
Volunteers with disabilities: Possible.
Equipment/clothing: Group equipment only provided.
Costs: Expedition fee depending on destination, this includes comprehensive insurance cover.
Training: Most expeditions organize a training/packing weekend at our base.
Supervision: All leaders are volunteers, qualified in relation to expedition destination and activities.
Interview details: No interview necessary.
Charity number: 1061156
Worldwide placements: *Africa* (Ghana, South Africa); *Asia* (India, Malaysia, Oman); *Europe* (France, Greece, Romania); *North America* (Canada).

UK placements: *England* (Cumbria); *Scotland* (Western Isles).

BREAK
7a Church Street
Sheringham
Norfolk
NR26 8QR UK

Tel: +44 (0) 1263 822161
Fax: +44 (0) 1263 822181
e-mail: office@break-charity.demon.co.uk
Contact: Geoffrey Davison or Mrs Gray

BREAK needs volunteers to work as part of the care team and make an important contribution to the life of the centres. We assist staff in all day-to-day activities, including the personal welfare of guests and their recreational programme. The work can be both physically and emotionally demanding, requiring great patience, a strong sense of responsibility and co-operation from all staff. Candidates must be able to understand and speak English. We are not ideal for those whose main objective is to learn or greatly improve their English. Placements of between three and six months at holiday centres and up to one year for the family assessment unit and children's home. Volunteers work an average 40 hour week. Volunteers with an offending background may be accepted depending on offence.

Total projects worldwide: 6
Total UK projects: 6
Starting months: January–December.
Time required: 6–52 weeks.
Age requirement: 18–25
Causes: Children, disabled (learning and physical), holidays for disabled.
Activities: Arts/crafts, caring (day and residential).
Vols under 26 placed each year: 40
When to apply: All year.
Work alone/with others: Usually with others.
Volunteers with disabilities: Possible, if physically able e.g. to lift guest.
Qualifications: Nil.
Equipment/clothing: Casual clothing.
Health requirements: Ability to cope with physically and emotionally demanding work.
Costs: Nil, except travel costs to UK if overseas.
Benefits: Board, lodging plus £25 per week pocket money and travel to and from

placement in UK. 1 week's paid leave is given, including return travel costs to and from a destination in the UK, for each completed 4 months of service.
Interview details: Holiday applicants are not interviewed. Applicants for the residential family assessment centre will probably be interviewed.
Certification: Reference provided.
Charity number: 286650
UK placements: *England* (Norfolk).

BRECKNOCK WILDLIFE TRUST
First Floor Office
2 The Struet
Brecon
Powys
LD3 7LH UK

Tel: +44 (0) 1874 625708
Fax: +44 (0) 1874 625708
Contact: Diane Russell

The Brecknock Wildlife Trust has established a number of important nature reserves, many of them Sites of Special Scientific Interest, either by purchase or through agreement with sympathetic land owners. These reserves are managed for wildlife by the Trust's conservation volunteers, who hold regular work parties. Volunteers with an offending background may be accepted depending on the offence.

Total projects worldwide: 1
Total UK projects: 1
Starting months: January–December.
Time required: 1–52 weeks (plus).
Age requirement: 14 plus.
Causes: Animal welfare, conservation, environmental causes, teaching/assisting wildlife.
Activities: Administration, campaigning, computers, conservation skills, fundraising, library/resource centres, manual work, marketing/publicity.
Vols under 26 placed each year: 40
When to apply: All year.
Work alone/with others: Both.
Qualifications: Interpersonal and communication skills.
Health requirements: Nil.
Costs: Travel and subsistence.
Interview details: Interviews take place in the office.
Charity number: 239674
UK placements: *Wales* (Powys).

BRETHREN VOLUNTEER SERVICE
1451 Dundee Avenue
Elgin
Illinois
60120 USA

Tel: 00 1 847 742 5100
Fax: 00 1 847 742 6103
Contact: Dan McFadden, Recruitment Officer

Brethren Volunteer Service is people giving their time and skills to help a world in need. It is a way for people to work at issues greater than themselves, recognizing that their efforts may not immediately solve deep-rooted problems, but can be part of ongoing work for justice, peace, and the integrity of creation. As sponsor of the programme, the Church of the Brethren exemplifies its heritage in peacemaking and service through the goals of BVS: working for peace; advocating justice; serving basic human needs; maintaining the integrity of creation. Some volunteers engage in projects that deal with immediate needs. Others work towards changing unjust systems. Sharing God's love through acts of service, volunteers bring hope to shattered lives, offer food and shelter to those in need, and build understanding between individuals, groups, nations and humanity and the world we share. BVS seeks volunteers willing to act on their commitment and values. We challenge individuals to offer themselves, their time and their talents to work which is both difficult and demanding, rewarding and joyful.

Total projects worldwide: 100
Total UK projects: 0
Starting months: January, June, September.
Time required: 1–52 weeks (plus).
Age requirement: 20 plus.
Causes: Addicts/Ex-addicts, Aids/HIV, children, disabled (learning and physical), elderly people, environmental causes, health care/medical, human rights, inner city problems, offenders/ex-offenders, poor/homeless, refugees, teaching/assisting (nursery, primary, secondary, mature, EFL), unemployed, wildlife, work camps – seasonal, young people.
Activities: Accountancy, administration, agriculture/farming, arts/crafts, building/construction, campaigning, caring (general, day and residential), community work, computers, conservation skills, cooking, counselling, development issues, driving, first

aid, forestry, fundraising, gardening/
horticulture, group work, international aid,
library/resource centres, manual work,
marketing/publicity, music, newsletter/
journalism, outdoor skills, religion, research,
social work, sport, summer camps, teaching,
technical skills, theatre/drama, training,
translating, visiting/befriending, work camps
– seasonal.

Vols under 26 placed each year:
Approximately 100.
When to apply: Any time but at least 4–6
weeks prior to orientation.
Work alone/with others: Both.
Volunteers with disabilities: Possible.
Qualifications: Some.
Health requirements: Nil.
Costs: US$13 registration fee, return travel to
USA, some medical coverage, travel to
European interview.
Benefits: Medical insurance, board and
lodging, pocket money, annual retreat.
Training: Volunteers begin their term of
service by participating with 12–30 other
volunteers in a BVS orientation. These are
scheduled for the summer, autumn and
winter of each year.
Interview details: Europeans need to be
interviewed by the Geneva co-ordinator of
Brethren Service or by someone designated –
may be in Geneva or in the UK.
Certification: Certificate or reference on
request.
Worldwide placements: *North America*
(USA).

BRIDGE CAMPHILL COMMUNITY
Main Street
Kilcullen
Co. Kildare
Ireland

Contact: The Director

Total projects worldwide: 1
Total UK projects: 0
Starting months: January–December.
Time required: 1–52 weeks (plus).
Age requirement: 12 plus.

BRISTOL FRIENDS OF THE EARTH
10–12 Picton Street
Montpelier
Bristol
BS6 5QA UK

Tel: +44 (0) 117 942 0129

Contact: Mandy Garrett

Starting months: January–December.
Time required: 1–52 weeks (plus).
Age requirement: 12 plus.

BRISTOL LINK WITH NICARAGUA
(BLINC)
6 West Street
Old Market
Bristol
BS2 0BH UK

Tel: +44 (0) 117 941 1442
Contact: The Secretary

Bristol Link with Nicaragua was set up in
1985 to manage and develop a link with
Puerto Morazán, a fishing community of
approximately 2,000 people living on a tidal
estuary on the Pacific coast of Nicaragua.
BLINC supports a range of small
development and educational projects there,
and also organizes cultural, social and
commercial events in Bristol focusing on
Nicaragua. There are opportunities for self-
funded volunteers to work on a number of
projects in Nicaragua, including working on
a shrimp farm or iguana farm; helping in
teaching and organizing excursions at a
Montessori-style nursery school; teaching
craft and literacy skills and organizing
cultural and sports events at a community
centre; teaching English at a secondary
school; and health education work at a
health centre. In both Bristol and Nicaragua
volunteers can also do general administrative
work to support the twinning process.

Total projects worldwide: 1
Total UK projects: 1
Starting months: January–December.
Time required: 12–52 weeks.
Age requirement: 18 plus.
Causes: Health care/medical, poor/homeless,
teaching/assisting (nursery, primary,
secondary, mature, EFL).
Activities: administration, agriculture/
farming, arts/crafts, building/construction,
community work, development issues,
driving, gardening/horticulture, international
aid, manual work, outdoor skills, social
work, teaching, training, visiting/befriending.
When to apply: All year.
Qualifications: Knowledge of Spanish
essential. Experience campaigning and/or
development preferable, not essential.

Volunteers should be independent, confident, enthusiastic, with an interest in the Latin America region, good interpersonal skills and motivation.
Costs: All costs including travel, insurance, board and accommodation.
Worldwide placements: *Central America* (Nicaragua).

BRIT VALLEY PROJECT
Dorset Countryside
The Barracks
Bridport Road
Dorchester
Dorset
DT1 1RN UK

Tel: +44 (0) 1305 268731
Fax: +44 (0) 1305 266920
e-mail: dorsetcountryside@ic21.net
Contact: Jenny Penney, Countryside Ranger

Brit Valley Projects are: to conserve, sustain and enhance the special character and diversity of landscape and wild life through the Brit Valley; to improve the opportunities for informal access and recreation within the Brit Valley; to ensure the provision of interpretative and educational material and information which will lead to greater understanding and enjoyment of the countryside; to contribute to the quality of life for local people, in particular through support for community initiatives and schemes which promote sustainable tourism in the economy. Volunteers with an offending background may be accepted depending on the offence.

Total projects worldwide: 1
Total UK projects: 1
Starting months: January–December.
Time required: 1–52 weeks.
Age requirement: 16 plus.
Causes: Conservation, disabled (learning and physical), environmental causes, unemployed, wildlife, young people.
Activities: Administration, conservation skills, group work, manual work, newsletter/journalism, outdoor skills, research.
Vols under 26 placed each year: 10
When to apply: All year.
Work alone/with others: Groups.
Volunteers with disabilities: Possible.
Qualifications: Huge enthusiasm, artistic design talent and practical skills for outdoor work. Previous experience not necessary.

Equipment/clothing: Sturdy boots and old clothes plus gardening gloves if possible.
Health requirements: Nil.
Costs: Local people will be required to travel to site.
Benefits: Work experience.
Training: Under the Ranger's supervision (health and safety is a high priority).
Supervision: By Ranger.
Interview details: Interview to ascertain suitability at our office.
Certification: Reference on request.
UK placements: *England* (Dorset).

BRITAIN–TANZANIA SOCIETY
c/o 13 Highfield Drive
Uxbridge
Middlesex
UB10 8AL UK

Tel: +44 (0) 1895 235983
Contact: Trevor Jaggar, Honorary Executive Secretary

The Britain–Tanzania Society/Tanzania Development Trust (TDT) is not a volunteer-sending organization. Projects supported by TDT are normally implemented by Tanzanian nationals – our project partners working with the ultimate beneficiaries. Members of both the UK and Tanzania chapters of the Society give their services voluntarily in connection with the selection, evaluation, processing and funding of projects. We have a range of projects supported by TDT designed to relieve poverty and ignorance, to improve health and nutrition, and to promote self-reliance.

Alternative contact address:
Peter O. Park, Honorary Projects Officer
45 Highsett
Cambridge
CB2 1NZ
Tel: +44 (0) 1223 314835

Total projects worldwide: 6–10
Total UK projects: 0
Starting months: January–December.
Time required: 1–52 weeks.
Age requirement: 17 plus.
Causes: Addicts/Ex-addicts, Aids/HIV, animal welfare, archaeology, architecture, children, conservation, disabled (learning and physical), elderly people, environmental causes, health care/medical, heritage, holidays for disabled, human rights, inner

city problems, offenders/ex-offenders, poor/ homeless, refugees, teaching/assisting (nursery, primary, secondary, mature, EFL), unemployed, wildlife, work camps – seasonal, young people.
Activities: Agriculture/farming, arts/crafts, building/construction, community work, conservation skills, development issues, forestry, gardening/horticulture, library/ resource centres, scientific work, teaching, technical skills, training.
Vols under 26 placed each year: Varies.
When to apply: All year.
Work alone/with others: Both.
Volunteers with disabilities: Possible.
Qualifications: Any qualifications are a bonus.
Equipment/clothing: Depends on project.
Health requirements: Anti-malarial pills and necessary innoculations.
Costs: Depends on project – air fare to Tanzania.
Benefits: Depends on project.
Training: Varies according to project.
Supervision: Projects are normally implemented by Tanzanian nationals – our project partners working with the ultimate beneficiaries.
Charity number: 270462
Worldwide placements: *Africa* (Tanzania).

BRITISH FORCES YOUTH SERVICE
HQ Land Command
Inkerman Block, Erskine Barracks
Wilton
Salisbury
Wiltshire
SP2 0AG UK

Tel: +44 (0) 1722 436393
Fax: +44 (0) 1722 436387
Contact: CS(PM)A1

The British Forces Youth Service contributes to the welfare of service families by providing social and educational opportunities for young people aged 10 to 20.

Starting months: July.
Time required: 4–6 weeks.
Age requirement: 21 plus.
Causes: Children, young people.
Activities: Arts/crafts, community work, computers, first aid, group work, music, outdoor skills, sport, summer camps, theatre/drama, visiting/befriending.
Vols under 26 placed each year: 30

When to apply: Before 15 April.
Work alone/with others: Under supervision of a full-time youth and community worker or military personnel.
Volunteers with disabilities: Possible.
Qualifications: Single UK nationals. German language useful (Germany only), sports, first aid, arts and crafts, music and enthusiasm. A driving licence is essential in Cyprus, useful in Germany.
Costs: Nil.
Benefits: Pocket money, flights to Germany/ Cyprus, accommodation and food provided.
Training: Induction and limited on-the-job training is provided.
Supervision: By fully qualified youth workers or military personnel.
Nationalities accepted: Volunteers must be UK based and UK nationals.
Interview details: Interviews take place in the UK.
Certification: Testimonials can be provided.
Worldwide placements: *Europe* (Cyprus, Germany).

BRITISH RED CROSS – BUCKINGHAMSHIRE
123 London Road
High Wycombe
Buckinghamshire
HP11 1BY UK

Tel: +44 (0) 1494 525361
Fax: +44 (0) 1494 465649
e-mail: andrea@redcross.fsnet.co.uk
Contact: Mrs Alex Ashby, Branch Youth Officer

The Red Cross is committed to attracting young people. Our Youth Programme offers a range of training opportunities and skills designed to inspire young people to help their local communities. Young people join either as Junior Members (5–10/11 years), Youth Members (10/11–18 years), or Pioneer Members (16–25 years). You receive free training in skills such as first aid, communication (e.g. reassuring a client), public speaking, leadership and rescue techniques, with the emphasis on personal development. Red Cross Youth is not all 'blood and guts'. Other training includes nursing, child care, camping and the Duke of Edinburgh's Award Scheme to name but a few. All Red Cross branches nationwide have their own youth groups. There are 21 Youth,

Junior and Pioneer groups in Buckinghamshire. The Society attracts both individual members and school groups through our active schools programme. Volunteers with an offending background are accepted depending on the offence.

Total projects worldwide: Varies.
Total UK projects: Varies.
Starting months: January–December.
Time required: 1–52 weeks.
Age requirement: 12–25
Causes: Children, disabled (learning and physical), elderly people, health care/medical, holidays for disabled, teaching/assisting, young people.
Activities: Administration, arts/crafts, caring (general and day), community work, driving, first aid, fundraising, library/resource centres, marketing/publicity, outdoor skills, summer camps, teaching, training, visiting/befriending.
Vols under 26 placed each year: 45 of a total of 300.
When to apply: All year.
Work alone/with others: Both.
Volunteers with disabilities: Possible.
Qualifications: Nil – basic training given.
Health requirements: Nil.
Costs: Nil.
Benefits: Travel costs paid.
Interview details: Interview location depends on the project.
Certification: Certificate or reference provided.
Charity number: 220949
UK placements: *England* (Bedfordshire, Berkshire, Buckinghamshire, Essex, Hertfordshire, Kent, London, Suffolk, Surrey, E. Sussex, W. Sussex).

BRITISH YOUTH COUNCIL
2 Plough Yard
Shoreditch High Street
London
EC2A 3LP UK

Tel: +44 (0) 20 7422 8640
Fax: +44 (0) 20 7422 8646
Contact: Nicky Thomson

Although the British Youth Council does not itself provide volunteering opportunities, we will direct any person between 16 and 25 to an appropriate organization for voluntary work.
Starting months: January–December.

Time required: 1–52 weeks.
Age requirement: 16–25
Causes: Human rights, inner city problems, young people.
Activities: Accountancy, administration, agriculture/farming, arts/crafts, building/construction, campaigning, caring (general, day and residential), catering, community work, computers, conservation skills, cooking, counselling, development issues, DIY, driving, first aid, forestry, fundraising, gardening/horticulture, group work, international aid, library/resource centres, manual work, marketing/publicity, music, newsletter/journalism, outdoor skills, religion, research, scientific work, social work, sport, summer camps, teaching, technical skills, theatre/drama, training, translating, visiting/befriending, work camps – seasonal.
When to apply: All year.
Charity number: 305973
UK placements: *England* (throughout); *Scotland* (throughout); *Northern Ireland* (throughout); *Wales* (throughout).

BSES EXPEDITIONS
at The Royal Geographical Society
1 Kensington Gore
London
SW7 2AR UK

Tel: +44 (0) 20 7591 3141
Fax: +44 (0) 20 7591 3140
e-mail: bses@rgs.org
Web: www.bses.org.uk
Contact: The Executive Director

All BSES Expeditions combine adventure in wilderness and trackless areas overseas with scientific fieldwork, research and conservation. The aim is to educate and aid the self-development process of young people, principally from the UK, between 16.5 and 20 years old. Team leaders range from 25 years upwards (assistant leaders 21–24 years). Volunteers with an offending background are accepted in limited numbers.

Total projects worldwide: 5
Total UK projects: 0
Starting months: January, July, September.
Time required: 4–16 weeks.
Age requirement: 16.5 plus.
Causes: Archaeology, conservation, disabled (learning and physical), environmental causes, wildlife, young people.

Activities: Arts/crafts, community work, conservation skills, forestry, fundraising, group work, outdoor skills, research, scientific work.

Vols under 26 placed each year: Approximately 215 of a total of 270.

When to apply: Summer of the previous year. For gap year expeditions, approximately 18 months in advance.

Work alone/with others: With others.

Volunteers with disabilities: Possible, but full walking ability essential.

Qualifications: Selection by personal interview. Leaders qualified in science/adventure.

Equipment/clothing: Basic adventure clothing e.g. boots, sleeping bag etc.

Health requirements: Must be fit.

Costs: Between £2,000–£2,800. Gap expeditions between £3,000–£4,000. Comprehensive insurance cover is paid from contribution.

Benefits: Advice and assistance given with fundraising, adventure and scientific education.

Training: There is a training session, usually Easter week, at Ilkley, Yorkshire.

Supervision: Leaders and assistant leaders responsible for groups of approximately 12 people.

Interview details: Interviews take place in the London office and in the volunteers' own home areas.

Certification: Certificates or references and membership of Society.

Charity number: 802196

Worldwide placements: *Africa* (Botswana, Kenya, Lesotho, Malawi, Morocco, Namibia, Zimbabwe); *Asia* (India, Indonesia, Kyrgyzstan); *Australasia* (Australia, Papua New Guinea); *Europe* (Finland, Iceland, Norway, Russia, Sweden); *North America* (Canada, Greenland, USA); *South America* (Falkland Islands).

BTCV – HQ
36 St Mary's Street
Wallingford
Oxfordshire
OX10 0EU UK

Tel: + 44 (0) 1491 821600
Fax: + 44 (0) 1491 839646
e-mail: Information@btcv.org.uk
Web: www.btcv.org
Contact: Customer Services

BTCV (British Trust for Conservation Volunteers) is the UK's largest practical conservation charity. It enables people of all ages from all sections of the community to take action in caring for their environment in towns, cities and the countryside. Every year over 130,000 volunteers take part on conservation projects that include woodland management and tree planting, pond creation and restoration, drystone walling and footpath work. No prior experience is needed as all projects have experienced leaders. Volunteer opportunities range from day projects, both at weekends and during the week, to week-long conservation working holidays. Inexpensive training courses enable volunteers to develop new skills. BTCV runs an affiliation scheme for school, youth and community groups that are carrying out practical conservation work. All BTCV projects are organized and run from local offices throughout the country. Each office is managed by at least one fully qualified professional member of staff, but almost all of our offices rely to a greater or lesser extent on the support of VOs (Volunteer Officers). VOs run courses, working holidays and volunteer groups and provide information and advice to local communities. The role of VO varies from office to office, as does the level of responsibility. Most VOs are over 21 and are asked to commit between six months and a year to BTCV. In return BTCV makes a commitment to training and developing the skills of their VOs and will often be able to offer accommodation as well as support in claiming benefits. VOs gain experience in practical conservation, wildlife and countryside skills, organizational and publicity skills, project liaison, etc. Many VOs move on into full-time employment in the environmental sector. Volunteers with an offending background are accepted at BTCV's discretion.

Total projects worldwide: 650 plus.

Total UK projects: 500 plus.

Starting months: January–December.

Time required: 1–52 weeks (plus).

Age requirement: 16 plus.

Causes: Conservation, environmental causes, heritage, wildlife, work camps – seasonal, young people.

Activities: Agriculture/farming, building/construction, community work, conservation

skills, forestry, gardening/horticulture, group work, manual work, marketing/publicity, outdoor skills, summer camps, technical skills, training, work camps – seasonal.
Vols under 26 placed each year: 25,000 of a total of 130,000.
When to apply: All year.
Work alone/with others: With other volunteers.
Volunteers with disabilities: Varies.
Qualifications: Varies.
Equipment/clothing: Waterproofs, strong boots.
Health requirements: Tetanus vaccination.
Costs: UK conservation holidays £25-£100 depending on destination. International from £200–£1,000.
Benefits: Expenses generally paid. BTCV covers all insurance of volunteers.
Training: Training available during placement.
Supervision: By qualified leaders.
Interview details: No interview necessary.
Charity number: 261009
Worldwide placements: *Africa* (South Africa); *Asia* (Japan, Nepal, Thailand, Turkey); *Australasia* (Australia); *Europe* (Bulgaria, Estonia, France, Germany, Greece, Hungary, Iceland, Ireland, Italy, Lithuania, Norway, Poland, Portugal, Romania, Slovakia, Spain, Turkey); *North America* (Canada, USA); *Central America* (Mexico).
UK placements: *England* (throughout); *Scotland* (throughout); *Northern Ireland* (throughout); *Wales* (throughout).

BTCV – NORTH WEST REGION
Davy Hulme Water Treatment Works
Rivers Lane
Urnston
Manchester
M41 7JB UK

Tel: + 44 (0) 161 608 0498
Fax: + 44 (0) 161 608 0497
e-mail: m.desborough@btcv.org.uk
Web: www.btcv.org.uk
Contact: Maria Desborough

British Trust for Conservation Volunteers (BTCV) North West Region. For more details of BTCV, see BTCV HQ, above.

Total projects worldwide: 60–70
Total UK projects: 60–70
Starting months: January–December.
Time required: 1–52 weeks.

Age requirement: 16 plus.
Causes: Conservation, environmental causes, wildlife.
Activities: Administration, community work, computers, conservation skills, first aid, forestry.
When to apply: All year.
Work alone/with others: With others.
Volunteers with disabilities: Not possible.
Qualifications: Commitment and enthusiasm.
Equipment/clothing: Strong boots and waterproofs.
Health requirements: Nil.
Costs: Varies.
Benefits: Free training, improved employability. BTCV covers all insurance of volunteers.
Training: Training available during placement.
Supervision: By qualified leaders.
Interview details: Applicants are sometimes interviewed.
Charity number: 261009
UK placements: *England* (Cheshire, Cumbria, Lancashire, Manchester, Merseyside).

BTCV – SCOTLAND
Ballalan House
24 Allan Park
Stirling
FK8 2QG Scotland

Tel: + 44 (0) 1786 479697
Fax: + 44 (0) 1786 465359
e-mail: stirling@btcv.org.uk
Web: www.btcv.org
Contact: Peter Blackburn

British Trust for Conservation Volunteers (BTCV) Scotland is a branch of the UK's largest environmental conservation charity. (For more details of BTCV, see BTCV HQ, above.) We involve people in improving the quality of the environment through practical conservation. Volunteers on these projects carry out work such as drystone dyking, footpath construction, vegetation clearance and tree planting. Projects last between 7 and 14 days and are residential. Regular midweek groups operate in Glasgow, Edinburgh, Stirling, and Aberdeen.

Total projects worldwide: Approximately 40.
Total UK projects: Approximately 40.
Starting months: March–October.
Time required: 1–2 weeks.
Age requirement: 16 plus.

Causes: Archaeology, architecture, conservation, environmental causes, heritage, wildlife, work camps – seasonal.
Activities: Administration, building/construction, conservation skills, forestry, fundraising, gardening/horticulture, manual work, marketing/publicity, outdoor skills, technical skills, work camps – seasonal.
Vols under 26 placed each year: 6,000 of a total of 8,000.
When to apply: Any time.
Work alone/with others: With others usually.
Volunteers with disabilities: Depends on work and site. Contact BTCV for advice.
Qualifications: Nil.
Equipment/clothing: Warm, waterproof, safety boots.
Health requirements: In reasonable health.
Costs: Varies.
Benefits: Accommodation, food, insurance and training.
Training: Given on site.
Supervision: A leader and assistant leader on every project.
Interview details: No interview necessary.
Charity number: 261009
UK placements: *Scotland* (throughout).

BTCV – SOUTH EAST/LONDON REGION

80 York Way
King's Cross
London
N1 9AG UK

Tel: +44 (0) 20 7713 5328
Fax: +44 (0) 20 7278 5095
e-mail: N.Greenhalgh@btcv.org.uk
Web: www.btcv.org.uk
Contact: Nigel Greenhalgh, Regional Director

British Trust for Conservation Volunteers (BTCV) South East/London Region. For more details of BTCV, see BTCV HQ, above.

Total projects worldwide: 1,000
Total UK projects: 1,000
Starting months: January–December.
Time required: 1–52 weeks.
Age requirement: 16 plus.
Causes: Conservation, environmental causes, unemployed, wildlife, work camps – seasonal.
Activities: Building/construction, conservation skills, gardening/horticulture, manual work, outdoor skills, work camps –

seasonal.
Vols under 26 placed each year: 500 plus.
When to apply: All year.
Work alone/with others: With others.
Volunteers with disabilities: Possible.
Qualifications: Nil.
Equipment/clothing: Strong boots and waterproofs.
Health requirements: Nil, but any allergies or special medical needs should be declared.
Costs: Small contribution for accommodation (approximately £13 for weekend, £40 for week).
Benefits: Food and equipment provided. BTCV covers all insurance of volunteers.
Training: Health and Safety induction and introduction to site ecology.
Supervision: By experienced trained leaders.
Interview details: No interview necessary.
Certification: Reference or certificate on request.
Charity number: 261009
UK placements: *England* (Bedfordshire, Berkshire, Buckinghamshire, Essex, Hampshire, Isle of Wight, Kent, Lincolnshire, London, Norfolk, Northamptonshire, Oxfordshire, Surrey, E. Sussex, W. Sussex).

BTCV – SOUTH WEST AREA

7 Station Road
Hemyock
Cullompton
Devon
EX15 3SE UK

Tel: +44 (0) 1823 680061
Fax: +44 (0) 1823 680061
e-mail: M.Sibley@btcv.org.uk
Web: www.btcv.org
Contact: Miles Sibley

British Trust for Conservation Volunteers (BTCV) South West Area. For more details of BTCV, see BTCV HQ, above.

Starting months: January–December.
Time required: 1–52 weeks.
Age requirement: 16 plus.
Causes: Conservation, environmental causes, heritage, wildlife, young people.
Activities: Administration, community work, computers, conservation skills, driving, first aid, forestry, fundraising, group work, manual work, outdoor skills, technical skills, training.
Vols under 26 placed each year: 40
When to apply: As soon as possible.

Work alone/with others: Mainly with others.
Volunteers with disabilities: Possible.
Qualifications: Interest in the environment.
Health requirements: Nil.
Costs: Nil.
Benefits: Skills training, environmental education, job responsibilities to add to CV. BTCV covers all insurance of volunteers.
Training: Training available during placement.
Supervision: By qualified leaders.
Interview details: Informal interview may be required.
Certification: Reference on request.
Charity number: 261009
UK placements: *England* (Bristol, Cornwall, Devon, Dorset, Gloucestershire, Somerset, Wiltshire).

BTCV – WALES REGIONAL OFFICE
Wales Conservation Centre
Forest Farm Road
Whitchurch
Cardiff
CF14 7JJ Wales

Tel: +44 (0) 29 2052 0990
Fax: +44 (0) 29 2052 2181
e-mail: wales@btcv.org.uk
Web: www.btcv.org
Contact: Regional Administrator

British Trust for Conservation Volunteers (BTCV) Wales Regional Office. For more details of BTCV, see BTCV HQ, above.

Starting months: January–December.
Time required: 1–52 weeks.
Age requirement: 16 plus.
Causes: Conservation, disabled (learning and physical), environmental causes, heritage, inner city problems, unemployed, wildlife.
Activities: Administration, catering, community work, computers, conservation skills, driving, forestry, fundraising, group work, manual work, marketing/publicity, outdoor skills, training.
Vols under 26 placed each year: Approximately 47 of a total of 100.
When to apply: All year.
Work alone/with others: With others.
Volunteers with disabilities: Possible.
Qualifications: Interest in the environment.
Equipment/clothing: Outdoor.
Health requirements: Anti-tetanus innoculation recommended.
Costs: Varies.

Benefits: Free training, improved employability.
Training: Training available during placement.
Supervision: Qualified paid staff and volunteers.
Interview details: No interview necessary.
Certification: Reference on request.
Charity number: 261009
UK placements: *Wales* (throughout, except for Powys).

BTCV – YORKSHIRE REGION
Bridge Mill
St George's Square
Hebden Bridge
W. Yorkshire
HX7 8ET UK

Tel: +44 (0) 1422 845440
Fax: +44 (0) 1422 846453
e-mail: L.Blezard@btcv.org.uk
Web: www.btcv.org
Contact: Liz Blezard

British Trust for Conservation Volunteers (BTCV) Yorkshire Region: For more details of BTCV, see BTCV HQ, above.

Total projects worldwide: 1,500
Total UK projects: 1,500
Starting months: January–December.
Time required: 1–52 weeks (plus).
Age requirement: 16 plus.
Causes: Conservation, environmental causes, heritage, wildlife.
Activities: Administration, conservation skills, forestry, manual work, outdoor skills, scientific work.
Vols under 26 placed each year: 5,000 of a total of 10,000.
When to apply: All year.
Work alone/with others: With others.
Volunteers with disabilities: Varies.
Qualifications: Nil.
Equipment/clothing: Strong boots and waterproofs.
Health requirements: Anti-tetanus innoculation.
Costs: Travel to pick-up point.
Benefits: Expenses and insurance.
Training: BTCV provides all training where required/requested but not necessary to all volunteering opportunities.
Supervision: By qualified leaders.
Interview details: No interview necessary.
Certification: Reference on request. Specific

training courses for qualifications available
e.g. first aid.
Charity number: 261009
UK placements: *England* (E. Yorkshire,
N. Yorkshire, S. Yorkshire, W. Yorkshire).

BUNAC (BRITISH UNIVERSITIES NORTH AMERICA CLUB)
16 Bowling Green Lane
London
EC1R 0QH UK

Tel: +44 (0) 20 7251 3472
Fax: +44 (0) 20 7251 0215
e-mail: prome@bunac.org.uk
Web: www.bunac.org
Contact: General Enquiries Department

BUNAC was formed in 1962 by students
from various North American and Canadian
Clubs at UK universities. BUNAC is a non-
profit organization committed to providing
the best possible affordable opportunities in
international work and travel programmes for
students and young people around the world.
BUNAC's programmes include two fare-paid
programmes placing people either as summer-
camp counsellors (Summer Camp USA) or
kitchen and maintenance staff (KAMP) at US
and Canadian children's camps. Work
Canada and Work America offer students
and those in a gap year the opportunity to
spend either the summer or up to one year
working and travelling abroad. Work
Australia and Work New Zealand offer the
same opportunities but are open to anyone
between 18 and 25 years old (18 and 30 for
New Zealand). Opportunities are also
available for recent graduates to work in
Ghana, South Africa, Jamaica and Argentina.
Anyone wishing to apply for programmes
should contact the first enquiries department
from October onwards and request a copy of
Working Adventures Abroad.

Total projects worldwide: 12
Total UK projects: 0
Starting months: June.
Time required: 8–52 weeks.
Age requirement: 18–35
Causes: Children, disabled (learning and
physical), health care/medical, teaching/
assisting, young people.
Activities: Agriculture/farming, arts/crafts,
caring (general and residential), catering,
community work, cooking, counselling, first
aid, manual work, music, newsletter/

journalism, outdoor skills, religion, sport,
summer camps, teaching, theatre/drama.
Vols under 26 placed each year: 9,000 of a
total of 10,000.
When to apply: All year.
Work alone/with others: Both.
Volunteers with disabilities: Possible – each
individual is assessed.
Qualifications: Sporting/dramatic/arts skills
for counsellors. Catering skills for Kamp.
Health requirements: Medical for childcare/
nursing positions.
Costs: Varies with programme. All
participants must take BUNAC insurance.
Benefits: Varies with programme.
Training: Orientation before departure is
provided on all programmes.
Supervision: Depends on programme but
back-up support in each country is provided.
Nationalities accepted: Work America,
Summer Camp USA, Kamp: any nationality;
Work Canada: British or Irish nationalities;
Work Australia: British, Irish, Canadian or
Dutch nationalities; Work Jamaica: British
nationality.
Interview details: Only Counsellors are
interviewed.
Worldwide placements: *Africa* (Ghana, South
Africa); *Australasia* (Australia, New
Zealand); *North America* (Canada, USA);
Central America (Jamaica).

BUSCA (Brigada Universitaria de Servicios Comunitarios Para la Autogestion)
Jose Ma. Vigil 91 C-9
Col. Tacubaya
Mexico DF
11870 Mexico

e-mail: busca@laneta.apc.org

BUSCA (Brigada Universitaria de Servicios
Comunitarios para la Autogestion) organizes
volunteers to work with young local people
in indigenous communities in Mexico on
development projects concerned with areas
such as health, education, human rights, the
environment, community work etc.
Volunteers live and work in teams of five or
six people in hardship conditions and in a
very different culture. The minimum period
of work is seven weeks between 25 June and
20 August. Volunteers must be willing to
share and exchange experiences. They should
have initiative, as well as respect for other
lifestyles and cultures. No pocket money.

Starting months: June, July.
Time required: 5–7 weeks.
Age requirement: 18–26
Causes: Environmental causes, health care/medical, poor/homeless, teaching/assisting, young people.
Activities: Building/construction, community work, development issues, international aid, teaching.
Vols under 26 placed each year: 20
When to apply: From February to 1 May.
Qualifications: Basic knowledge of Spanish.
Costs: Travel costs to and from Mexico plus US$500 for board, lodging and transport in Mexico.
Worldwide placements: *Central America* (Mexico).

C

CAISSE POPULAIRE D'ASSURANCE-MALADIES DES TRAVAILLEURS SALARIES
BP 5698
Kinshasa
Gombe 10
Democratic Republic of Congo

Contact: Jean Pierre Longo, President

CPAMTS is a Christian medical missionary organization, a Christian health association and a voluntary health service. We collect together Christians working at all levels of professional life who believe in evangelizing life in all its fullness. We give medical and pharmaceutical assistance to needy people. We organize construction of hospitals, clinics, dispensaries and health centres, together with conferences and seminars on key medical problems.

Total projects worldwide: 6
Total UK projects: 0
Starting months: November.
Time required: 45 weeks.
Age requirement: 18–35
Causes: Addicts/Ex-addicts, Aids/HIV, children, disabled (learning and physical), elderly people, health care/medical, poor/homeless, refugees, unemployed, young people.

Activities: Building/construction, caring (general, day and residential), community work, development issues, driving, first aid, international aid, religion, social work.
Vols under 26 placed each year: 11 of a total of 15.
When to apply: May, June and July.
Work alone/with others: With others.
Volunteers with disabilities: Not possible.
Qualifications: A-levels or baccalaureat in science, nurse or doctor, social worker or interested in social work, driving licence and a knowledge of French.
Equipment/clothing: Microscope, stethoscope etc.
Health requirements: Must be in very good health.
Costs: Approximately US$2,400 to include return air fare, board and lodging etc.
Benefits: Pocket money of US$20 per day. End of placement bonus.
Interview details: No interview necessary, but we need to see a curriculum vitae and 2 passport photos.
Charity number: 677/M.J/99
Worldwide placements: *Africa* (Congo Dem. Republic).

CAMBRIDGE AIDS ACTION
Office B
Dales Brewery
Gwydir Street
Cambridge
Cambridgeshire
CB1 2LJ UK

Tel: +44 (0) 1223 508805
Fax: +44 (0) 1223 508808
Contact: Kate Ross, Manager

Cambridge AIDS Action needs volunteers who must live locally. This is a very supportive environment with lots of support networks within the organization.

Total projects worldwide: 1
Total UK projects: 1
Starting months: January–December.
Time required: 52 weeks.
Age requirement: 17 plus.
Causes: Aids/HIV, Health Care/Medical, Young People.
Activities: Administration, counselling, group work, training, visiting/befriending.
Vols under 26 placed each year: Up to 60.
When to apply: All year.
Work alone/with others: With others.

Volunteers with disabilities: Not possible.
Qualifications: Volunteers must live locally.
Health requirements: Nil.
Benefits: Local travel costs and out-of-pocket expenses reimbursed.
Certification: Reference on request.
UK placements: *England* (Cambridgeshire).

CAMBRIDGE CYRENIANS
4 Short Street
Cambridge
CB1 1LB UK

Tel: + 44 (0) 1223 712501
Fax: + 44 (0) 1223 712503
e-mail: moira@camcyrenians.fsnet.co.uk
Contact: Moira Mehrishi, Deputy Project Leader

Cambridge Cyrenians provides a range of accommodation and support services to single, homeless men and women in Cambridge. We recruit up to six full-time volunteers at any one time to live and work with residents in our community houses. Support is provided by experienced staff daytime, evenings and weekends. Volunteers are responsible for the day-to-day running of the projects and can be involved in project planning if they choose. An offending background would not necessarily be a bar to volunteering.

Total projects worldwide: 3
Total UK projects: 3
Starting months: January–December.
Time required: 26–52 weeks.
Age requirement: 18 plus.
Causes: Addicts/Ex-addicts, offenders/ex-offenders, poor/homeless, unemployed.
Activities: Caring (residential), social work.
Vols under 26 placed each year: 9–10 of a total of 10–12.
When to apply: All year.
Work alone/with others: Volunteers work with a co-volunteer and meet up with other volunteers regularly.
Volunteers with disabilities: Volunteers would need to be able to climb stairs on all the projects.
Qualifications: Good English essential.
Health requirements: General good health.
Costs: Nil. Volunteers are responsible for personal possessions insurance.
Benefits: Travel costs up to £60 to and from the project plus up to £60 for holidays. £42 per week pocket money plus an additional

£42 for each week of holidays (1 week due for 10 weeks' work) plus £10 per month leaving bonus. All bills paid, except private phone calls. We provide basic public liability insurance.
Training: There is an induction period and training is provided once on placement. We encourage potential volunteers to visit before accepting a place if this is possible.
Supervision: Volunteers have one-to-one fortnightly supervision with the deputy project leader, daily contact with several members of staff, weekly meetings with staff and can call on staff at any time day or night.
Interview details: No interview necessary, but visit if possible.
Certification: Reference on request.
Charity number: 261994
UK placements: *England* (Cambridgeshire).

CAMDEN AND WESTMINSTER CITIZEN ADVOCACY
380 Harrow Road
London
W9 2HU UK

Tel: + 44 (0) 20 7289 5051 plus minicom
Fax: + 44 (0) 20 7289 5510
e-mail: cawca@cawca.freeserve.co.uk
Contact: Joanna Bell

Camden and Westminster Citizen Advocacy needs: 1. Citizen Advocates to befriend and support people with learning difficulties. Advocates help people to express their needs, and to get the things they need. This is about civil rights, respect and empowerment. It is a one-to-one partnership done in the volunteer's free time. It involves a personal commitment. 2 Management Committee members. People with a variety of skills and backgrounds are needed to support the work of the project. Various tasks: fundraising, publicity, finance. Experience not essential. Volunteers with an offending background may be accepted depending on the offence.

Total projects worldwide: 1
Total UK projects: 1
Starting months: January–December.
Time required: 1–52 weeks (plus).
Age requirement: 21 plus.
Causes: Disabled (learning and physical), health care/medical, human rights.
Activities: Accountancy, caring (general), community work, fundraising, marketing/

publicity, visiting/befriending.
Vols under 26 placed each year: 10 of a total of 38.
When to apply: All year.
Work alone/with others: Alone but there is a support group for our volunteers.
Volunteers with disabilities: Possible.
Qualifications: Nil, experience not essential.
Health requirements: Nil.
Benefits: Out-of-pocket expenses reimbursed.
Training: 4 week preparation training (one evening per week).
Supervision: Monthly contact in person or by phone. 2-monthly support groups.
Interview details: Interviews take place in office, community or at home.
Certification: Reference on request.
Charity number: 1044286
UK placements: *England* (London).

CAMP AMERICA – CAMPOWER PROGRAMME
Dept YFB2
37a Queen's Gate
London
SW7 5HR UK

Tel: + 44 (0) 20 7581 7373
Fax: + 44 (0) 20 7581 7377
e-mail: brochure@campamerica.co.uk
Contact: Gwen Miller

Camp America is the largest of the summer camps international exchange programmes. While we do not own or operate camps, we carefully select and monitor those where we place international staff. Last year, we placed 7,500 applicants from over 20 countries. Camps vary in size and in philosophy, and are often sited in areas of outstanding natural beauty. Children are usually 6–18. As a Campower you will be working as camp support staff. Roles range from kitchen, laundry and general maintenance work to secretarial, horse/stable care and cleaning. The Campower Extended Stay option gives you the chance to work for up to 17 weeks. There is also the opportunity for Campowers to be placed in resorts or conference facilities. The Campower Programme is an ideal option if you prefer not to work directly with children. You will be working long hours, but you will receive more pocket money than general counsellors and you will have more free evenings. Brochures and application forms can be obtained at the address listed.

Volunteers with an offending background may be accepted but not with a criminal record relating to children or drugs. Records must be produced and then considered.

Total projects worldwide: 800
Total UK projects: 0
Starting months: May, June.
Time required: 9–19 weeks.
Age requirement: 18 plus.
Causes: Children, young people.
Activities: Administration, catering, cooking, DIY, driving, group work, manual work, summer camps.
Vols under 26 placed each year: 6,500 of a total of 8,000.
When to apply: October–April.
Work alone/with others: With others.
Volunteers with disabilities: Possible.
Qualifications: For the Campower Programme, you must be a student or intending to be a student in the autumn.
Health requirements: Health medical check has to be undertaken before leaving UK.
Costs: 1st deposit £40, 2nd deposit including visa/insurance fee £165.
Benefits: Free London–New York return flight, board and lodging plus up to 10 weeks independent travel. Depending on the length of placement, you can earn up to US$1,620!
Interview details: Interviews take place all over the UK and overseas.
Certification: Certificate or reference provided.
Worldwide placements: *North America* (USA).

CAMP AMERICA – COUNSELLOR PROGRAMME
37a Queen's Gate
Dept YFB1
London
SW7 5HR UK

Tel: + 44 (0) 20 7581 7373
Fax: + 44 (0) 20 7581 7377
e-mail: brochure@campamerica.co.uk
Contact: Anne Chancel

For more details of Camp America, see Camp America – Campower Programme, above. As a Camp America Counsellor, you can be working as a specialist instructor, and teach different groups of children specific skills such as sports or arts, or as a general bunk counsellor and assist in a variety of activities and be responsible for the supervisory care of a specific group of children. Within the Counsellor programme, there is an additional option: as a Special Needs Counsellor you will be working with physically and/or mentally disabled campers. These camps may include adults as well. Supervision and caring is a priority on a special needs camp. Brochures and application forms can be obtained at the above address. Volunteers with an offending background accepted but court records must be produced. We do not take people with a criminal record relating to children or drugs.

Total projects worldwide: 800
Total UK projects: 0
Starting months: May, June.
Time required: 9–19 weeks.
Age requirement: 18 plus.
Causes: Children, disabled (learning and physical), inner city problems, teaching/ assisting young people.
Activities: Arts/crafts, caring (general), catering, computers, group work, manual work, music, outdoor skills, sport, summer camps, teaching, theatre/drama.
Vols under 26 placed each year: 6,500 of a total of 8,000.
When to apply: End October previous year – end April.
Work alone/with others: With others.
Volunteers with disabilities: Generally possible especially on special disability camps.
Qualifications: Preferably sports, arts/crafts, drama etc. Special Needs Counsellors need to have prior experience with people with special needs.
Health requirements: Medical required before leaving UK.
Costs: 1st deposit £40, 2nd deposit/ insurance/visa fee £165.
Benefits: London-NY flights, board and lodging plus pocket money.
Interview details: Interviews take place all over the UK and overseas.
Certification: Certificate or reference provided.
Worldwide placements: *North America* (USA).

CAMP BEAUMONT
Linton House
164–180 Union Street
Waterloo

London
SE1 0LH UK

Tel: +44 (0) 20 7922 1234
Fax: +44 (0) 20 7928 7733
e-mail: jobs@camp-beaumont.co.uk
Contact: Sarah Goldson

Camp Beaumont runs three residential year-round centres and 12 summer camps for children. Volunteers who just want to work with children need no skills. 16–18 year olds are needed as volunteers. Telephone for a recruitment pack.

Total projects worldwide: 11
Total UK projects: 3 permanent, 8 summer
Starting months: June–August.
Time required: 1–52 weeks.
Age requirement: 16–30
Causes: Children, health care/medical, teaching/assisting (nursery, primary, secondary, EFL), work camps – seasonal, young people.
Activities: Administration, arts/crafts, caring (general, day and residential), catering, computers, cooking, DIY, driving, first aid, forestry, gardening/horticulture, group work, manual work, music, newsletter/journalism, outdoor skills, scientific work, sport, summer camps, teaching, technical skills, theatre/ drama, translating, work camps – seasonal.
Vols under 26 placed each year: 550–600
When to apply: From January.
Work alone/with others: Both.
Volunteers with disabilities: Possible.
Qualifications: Specialist skill for activity centre ideal, but not essential. Police check.
Equipment/clothing: Uniform supplied – otherwise very casual.
Health requirements: Health check.
Costs: Travel to camp.
Benefits: Board, lodging, training and living allowance. Those over 18 years are salaried employees.
Certification: Reference or certificate.
Worldwide placements: *Europe* (France).
UK placements: *England* (Berkshire, Devon, Essex, Isle of Wight, Kent, London, Norfolk, Staffordshire, Surrey).

CAMP COUNSELORS USA LTD
Green Dragon House
64–70 High Street
Croydon
Surrey
CR0 9XN UK

Tel: +44 (0) 20 8688 4051
Fax: +44 (0) 20 8681 8168
e-mail: inquiry@ccusaweusa.co.uk
Web: www.campcounselors.com
Contact: Jamie Mackler, Marketing Co-ordinator

Camp Counselors USA need counsellors to look after children (or adults with special needs if they prefer) and teach activities on summer camps in America. These activities can be general or specialized and cover a massive range from soccer to jazz dance and from orienteering to pottery. Support staff work behind the scenes running the catering, secretarial and maintenance departments of the camps. Applicants must be available for nine weeks beginning between 30 May and 30 June. Volunteers can work from 7am until 11 p.m. with free time during the day and one day off per week. Nine weeks actual work but five month visas allow plenty of time for travel. Volunteers with an offending background may be accepted depending on offence. Each application is taken on an individual basis.

Total projects worldwide: 1,000
Total UK projects: 0
Starting months: June.
Time required: 1–9 weeks.
Age requirement: 18–30
Causes: Children, disabled (learning and physical), health care/medical, holidays for disabled, inner city problems, poor/homeless, teaching/assisting (nursery, primary, secondary), work camps – seasonal, young people.
Activities: Administration, agriculture/farming, arts/crafts, caring (general, day and residential), catering, community work, computers, cooking, counselling, driving, first aid, forestry, gardening/horticulture, group work, manual work, music, newsletter/journalism, outdoor skills, religion, social work, sport, summer camps, teaching, technical skills, theatre/drama, work camps – seasonal.
Vols under 26 placed each year: 1,350, total of 1500 from UK.
When to apply: As soon as possible, but before 30 April.
Work alone/with others: Both.
Volunteers with disabilities: Possible.
Qualifications: Strong English Language. Love of children. Experience with children,

sport, art or craft, performing art, outdoor activity, catering, secretarial, maintenance is an advantage, but enthusiasm and the right attitude are more important for the job.
Health requirements: Good general health.
Costs: Total cost: £215 for insurance and registration deposits.
Benefits: Return flight to the USA, accommodation, 3 months' comprehensive insurance, travel to camp, food, J1 working visa, 24 hour emergency service whilst in the USA and pocket money up to US$750. Up to 7 weeks free time to travel around the USA at the end.
Training: Pre-departure orientation and on-the-job training.
Interview details: Interviews are conducted by a regional network of interviewers all over England and Wales.
Certification: Certificate of Achievement provided.
Worldwide placements: *North America* (USA).

CAMPAIGNERS
Campaigners House
St Mark's Close
Colney Heath
St Albans
Hertfordshire
AL4 0NQ UK

Tel: +44 (0) 1727 824065
Fax: +44 (0) 1727 825049
Contact: John Radcliffe

Campaigners was founded in 1922 by an Anglican vicar. Every group is attached to a local church. We cater for 4–18 year olds in four different groupings. We offer a weekly meeting programme for children and young people and the programme comprises anything from sports activities, Duke of Edinburgh, Bible teaching to games and refreshments.

Total projects worldwide: 250
Total UK projects: 250
Starting months: January–December.
Time required: 1–52 weeks.
Age requirement: 17 plus.
Causes: Children, disabled (learning and physical), young people.
Activities: Arts/crafts, caring (general), DIY, gardening/horticulture, manual work, music, outdoor skills, religion, sport, summer camps, teaching, theatre/drama, visiting/befriending.

When to apply: All year.
Work alone/with others: With others under supervision of trained youth workers.
Volunteers with disabilities: Possible.
Qualifications: Nil – Christians preferred.
Health requirements: Nil.
Costs: Nil.
Benefits: Training and possible summer camps.
Interview details: Interviews are conducted at Campaigner headquarters.
Certification: Certificate or reference provided if recognized course completed.
Charity number: 283171
UK placements: *England* (Bedfordshire, Berkshire, Buckinghamshire, Cambridgeshire, Cheshire, Cornwall, Derbyshire, Devon, Dorset, Essex, Gloucestershire, Hampshire, Herefordshire, Hertfordshire, Kent, Lancashire, Leicestershire, London, Manchester, Merseyside, Northamptonshire, Nottinghamshire, Shropshire, Somerset, Staffordshire, Suffolk, Surrey, E. Sussex, W. Sussex, Warwickshire, West Midlands, Wiltshire, N. Yorkshire, S. Yorkshire, W. Yorkshire); *Scotland* (throughout); *Northern Ireland* (Antrim, Armagh, Belfast City, Derry/Londonderry, Down); *Wales* (throughout).

CAMPHILL COMMUNITIES, ONTARIO

R.R. # 1
Angus
Ontario
LOM 1BO Canada

Tel: 00 1 705 424 5363
Fax: 00 1 705 424 1854
e-mail: info@camphill.on.ca
Web: www.camphill.on.ca
Contact: Co-worker Care Group, Volunteer

Camphill Communities, Ontario is one centre of the world-wide Camphill Movement. For more details of Camphill Communities, see the first Camphill listing under Angaia Camphill do Brasil, above. These communities establish a helpful and healing influence in the lives of children and adults with special needs. Camphill Nottawasaga is a rural community on 300 acres near Barrie. It comprises several homes and workshops, a large vegetable garden and a farm. Our work is to care for each other, our homes, our gardens and our land. We share this work, each one according to his wishes and capabilities. We now have a small urban centre in Barrie with a future day programme, cafe and bakery called Camphill Sofia Creek. In our houses, co-worker families and assistants live together with up to five adults with disabilities. Each family circle has a particular character depending upon its members. Out of the strong support of this family, individuals can work in the community, make friends, and find ways to contribute their talents in the wider community. The Christian festivals through the year provide the content for many social and artistic activities in the village. We encourage individual and group study, therapies, outings, recreation and hobbies. The aim of Camphill Ontario is to build a vital community life that offers each person the conditions for healing, growth and renewal. One year is the recommended length of stay. Three month summer help possible.

Total projects worldwide: 1
Total UK projects: 0
Starting months: January–December.
Time required: 12–52 weeks.
Age requirement: 19 plus.
Causes: Disabled (learning and physical).
Activities: Agriculture/farming, arts/crafts, building/construction, caring (general), community work, cooking, counselling, driving, forestry, fundraising, gardening/horticulture, manual work, music, outdoor skills, religion, social work, sport, technical skills, theatre/drama, training.
Vols under 26 placed each year: 8 or 9 of a total of 9–10.
When to apply: All year but at least 4 months before coming. (Visa takes 3 months.)
Work alone/with others: With others, generally.
Volunteers with disabilities: Not possible.
Qualifications: English speaking, being open to life. 1 year is recommended or 3 month summer stay.
Equipment/clothing: Good solid work clothes for all seasons. Winters very cold, summers hot.
Health requirements: Health insurance for the first 3 months.
Costs: Return travel fare, Hepatitis B vaccine, visa costs.
Benefits: Board, lodging, pocket money C$125 per month. Health insurance after 3 months.

Training: No pre-placement training for short-term volunteers. All volunteers have an induction training at the beginning and then a weekly orientation course.

Nationalities accepted: No restrictions with UK volunteers but Canadian immigration is tough with certain nationalities.

Certification: Certificate or reference provided.

Charity number: 0553834.56

Worldwide placements: *North America* (Canada).

CAMPHILL COMMUNITY BALLYBAY
Robb Farm
Corraskea
Co. Monaghan
Ireland

Tel: 00 353 42 974 1939
Fax: 00 353 42 974 1359
e-mail: bkonink@eircom.net
Other e-mail: camphillballybay@eircom.net
Contact: Betsie Konink, Co-worker

The Camphill Community Ballybay is part of the worldwide Camphill movement. For more details of Camphill Communites, see the first Camphill listing under Angaia Camphill do Brasil, above. Camphill Community Ballybay is a rural community which works about 20 acres of land and has different craft workshops for weaving, candle making, woodwork and basket making. Everyone lives and works together in community houses varying in size from nine to 15 people. Prospective volunteers can apply by letter.

Total projects worldwide: 1
Total UK projects: 0
Starting months: January–December.
Time required: 1–52 weeks (plus).
Age requirement: 19 plus.
Causes: Disabled (learning).
Activities: Agriculture/farming, arts/crafts, caring (general and residential), driving, group work, manual work, outdoor skills.
Vols under 26 placed each year: 5 of a total of 15.
When to apply: All year, preferably at least 6 months in advance Prospective volunteers can apply by letter.
Work alone/with others: Both.
Volunteers with disabilities: We are unable to place people with disabilities as at present we are not wheelchair friendly.

Qualifications: Nil but an open attitude to our way of life. Must be able to speak reasonable English.

Equipment/clothing: Enough clothes for a year including rainwear.

Health requirements: General good health.

Costs: Travel to Ballybay only.

Benefits: Board and lodging, insurance and about £20 pocket money per week.

Supervision: Everybody has a mentor.

Nationalities accepted: No restrictions but must be able to speak reasonable English.

Certification: Reference on request.

Worldwide placements: *Europe* (Ireland).

CAMPHILL COMMUNITY BALLYTOBIN
Callan
Co. Kilkenny
Ireland

Tel: 00 353 56 25114
Fax: 00 353 56 25849
e-mail: ballytobin@camphill.ie
Contact: Gladys Lydon

The Camphill Community Ballytobin is part of the international Camphill movement. For more details of Camphill Communities, see the first Camphill listing under Angaia Camphill do Brasil, above. Ballytobin is a small rural community caring at present for 22 children and 12 adults all with disabilities. Ballytobin has a school, a garden, a bio-dynamic farm, a weaving workshop and also offers many individual therapies, for example: music, coloured-shadow, speech therapy, eurythmy, physiotherapy and horse riding! Ballytobin was established in 1979 to provide a home and school mainly for children with exceptional needs. The community has always been open to caring for challenging, disturbed and severely handicapped children, alongside more amenable and sociable children. There are five houses. Everyone lives as an extended family, sharing in cooking, cleaning and the household tasks, with everybody contributing what he or she can. Every co-worker has a definite daily programme with main responsibilities. Some have the care of a group of children as a main task and in addition help out in the school, house or farm. Previous experience is not asked for, but willingness to do what is needed and enthusiasm to learn is essential! To live in Ballytobin presents a challenge for most people. To share one's life with children and adults with disabilities in a community setting can be demanding and tiring, especially in the beginning when there is much to learn. Yet it is intensely interesting, often humorous, good fun and is a life full of idealism. There are also 'fun things' to do together as co-workers, like singing, dancing, playing music and of course going out for entertainment too! Artistic activities are considered of great importance. Music especially has a well-established home here and if you play an instrument you must certainly bring it along. Individual creativity and initiative is particularly welcomed. Long-term volunteers beginning in August and staying for 52 weeks are needed. There are some places for short-term volunteers in the summer for only 4–6 weeks.

Total projects worldwide: 1
Total UK projects: 0
Starting months: July.
Time required: 4–52 weeks.
Age requirement: 17 plus.
Causes: Children, disabled (learning and physical), work camps – seasonal.
Activities: Caring (general and residential), gardening/horticulture, work camps – seasonal.
Vols under 26 placed each year: 20–25
When to apply: Spring.
Work alone/with others: With others.
Volunteers with disabilities: Not possible.
Qualifications: Nil but all skills welcome.
Health requirements: Good general health as work with disabled children can be demanding.
Costs: Travel to Ireland.
Benefits: Full board and lodging plus pocket money and expenses. Holidays if stay is over 12 months.
Nationalities accepted: Long-term work permits may be difficult for non-EU citizens.
Interview details: No interview necessary but we require references, etc.
Certification: Reference on request.
Charity number: 5861 Irish
Worldwide placements: *Europe* (Ireland).

CAMPHILL COMMUNITY DUNSHANE
Dunshane House
Brannockstown
Naas
Co. Kildare
Ireland

Tel: 00 353 45 483628
Fax: 00 353 45 483833
Contact: Veronika van Duin

The Dunshane Community caters for adolescents and young adults in need of special care. The community consists of three houses, which offer residential and day-care facilities for young people aged 15 to 22 years. The co-workers, their families and the residential students live together in extended families. Everybody is encouraged to take an active part in the running of the houses in order to develop a sense of independence and responsibility. An important feature of the Dunshane Community is the special interrelationship with the local people. With a Government FAS scheme in operation, and local volunteers giving their time to help out, there is a mutually beneficial exchange of support and service. (FAS is an Irish Government funded one-year work placement scheme for the long-term unemployed.)

Total projects worldwide: 1
Total UK projects: 0
Starting months: August.
Time required: 44–52 weeks (plus).
Age requirement: 21–35
Causes: Disabled (learning), teaching/assisting (secondary, mature), young people.
Activities: Agriculture/farming, arts/crafts, building/construction, caring (general and residential), catering, community work, cooking, counselling, DIY, first aid, gardening/horticulture, group work, manual work, music, outdoor skills, social work, teaching, theatre/drama, training.
Vols under 26 placed each year: 14
When to apply: May.
Work alone/with others: With others.
Volunteers with disabilities: Not possible.
Qualifications: Good will and an open mind.
Equipment/clothing: Practical wear and something for special occasions.
Health requirements: Good health in general.
Costs: Travel costs.
Benefits: Board and lodging plus a small amount of pocket money.
Interview details: If possible interviews take place at Dunshane.
Certification: Written reference.
Worldwide placements: *Europe* (Ireland).

CAMPHILL COMMUNITY KYLE
Coolagh
Callan
Co. Kilkenny
Ireland

Tel: 00 353 56 25848
Contact: The Director

Total projects worldwide: 1
Total UK projects: 0
Starting months: January–December.
Time required: 1–52 weeks (plus).
Age requirement: 12 plus.

CAMPHILL COMMUNITY THOMASTOWN
Jerpoint Barn
Thomastown
Co. Kilkenny
Ireland

Tel: 00 353 56 24844
Contact: The Director

Camphill Community Thomastown includes two places: Jerpoint, a small residential, land-based community with adults in need of special care and The Watergarden, a coffeeshop, landscaped garden and garden centre in town, open to the public. The two places which are about three miles apart work together as one. The people from Jerpoint plus a good number of local people find their daily work at The Watergarden in all the different areas, including the craft workshops which are candlemaking and papermaking at present. Living at Jerpoint Community means sharing responsibility for the challenging work that the place offers. We are 12–14 adults – some of whom are in need of special care – living in a beautiful old 'barn' in Ireland's countryside. Volunteers with an offending background may possibly be accepted – by arrangement.

Total projects worldwide: 2
Total UK projects: 0
Starting months: January–December.
Time required: 1–52 weeks (plus).
Age requirement: 18 plus.
Causes: Conservation, disabled (learning and physical), environmental causes, holidays for disabled.
Activities: Agriculture/farming, arts/crafts, caring (general, day and residential), catering, conservation skills, cooking, DIY, fundraising, gardening/horticulture, group work, manual work, music, outdoor skills, religion, social work, sport.
Vols under 26 placed each year: Varies.
When to apply: All year.
Work alone/with others: With others.
Volunteers with disabilities: Depending on disability. We need people able to do physical work and care for others.
Qualifications: Nil.
Health requirements: Nil.
Costs: Travel to Thomastown only.
Benefits: All board, lodging and approx. £20 per week pocket money.
Interview details: No interview necessary but applicants can come on a trial visit.
Worldwide placements: *Europe* (Ireland).

CAMPHILL DORFGEMEINSCHAFT HAUSENHOF
Altheim 59
D91463 Dietersheim
Germany

Tel: 00 49 9164 9984 0
Fax: 00 49 9164 9984 10
Contact: Mrs Marianne Kasjan/ Mr Konstantin Josek

The Camphill Dorfgemeinschaft Hausenhof is part of the worldwide Camphill movement. For more details of Camphill Communities, see the first Camphill listing under Angaia Camphill do Brasil, above.

Total projects worldwide: 1
Total UK projects: 0
Starting months: January–December.
Time required: 1–52 weeks (plus).
Age requirement: 18–30
Causes: Disabled (learning and physical), health care/medical.
Activities: Agriculture/farming, arts/crafts, caring (general, day and residential), catering, community work, cooking, driving, gardening/horticulture, group work, manual work, music, outdoor skills, religion, social work, sport, theatre/drama, training.
Vols under 26 placed each year: 15–20
When to apply: All year but as early as possible.
Work alone/with others: Mainly with others.
Volunteers with disabilities: Not possible.
Qualifications: Basic knowledge of German language.
Health requirements: Health or medical problems must be reported when applying.
Costs: Travel costs only.

Benefits: Board and lodging. For people staying for a year or more, small wage also.
Nationalities accepted: No restrictions providing they hold a work and residence permit.
Interview details: Applicants are interviewed where possible but written applications are also accepted.
Certification: Certificate or reference provided.
Worldwide placements: *Europe* (Germany).

CAMPHILL DORFGEMEINSCHAFT HERMANNSBERG

D88633
Heiligenberg-Hattenweiler
Germany

Tel: 00 49 7552 2601 0
Fax: 00 49 7552 2601 40
Contact: Mrs Margaret Mentzel

At Camphill Dorfgemeinschaft Hermannsberg, living together in family units with our handicapped friends is one way of getting nearer to integration. The co-workers as part of the house community are involved in the care of those in need. As we also have workshops, most of our helpers are part-time giving a helping hand in one or other of the workshops according to his/her interest and abilities. Anyone can take part in the social/cultural activities within our life. As everyone is part of the 'family', a normal work schedule is not possible. Every co-worker has a day off a week as well as any additional free time needed. In a house community there are generally 6–9 villagers (adults with learning disabilities) together with their houseparents and their children and two helpers who can be Seminarists, Praktikanten or others. We have a number of workshops: a candle workshop, a small weavery, a joinery/wood workshop, a laundry, a big paper workshop where copybooks for many Waldorf schools in Germany are produced. We also have a garden/estate group and about one mile up the road is our farm with three houses, stables, utility sheds etc. Altogether we have 13 house communities, where at present up to 100 villagers live with their houseparents/co-workers; quite a number of employed co-workers from 'outside' join us daily in the house and kitchen, in the office, in specific care for some villagers and in the workshops. We also run

a recognized seminar, training for the 'Heilerziehungspfleger', with an official State-recognized examination at the end of the four-year course.

Total projects worldwide: 1
Total UK projects: 0
Starting months: January–June, September–December.
Time required: 12–52 weeks.
Age requirement: 19–28
Causes: Disabled (learning).
Activities: Caring (residential).
When to apply: Anytime between September and end of June.
Volunteers with disabilities: Not possible.
Qualifications: EU Nationals only. Driving licence and some foundation in German are both a bonus.
Equipment/clothing: Normal winter/summer clothing required – also for outside work.
Health requirements: Must be physically, psychologically and mentally fit.
Benefits: Pocket money of DM300–350 per month. Board and lodging, health insurance and all taxes.
Nationalities accepted: Only EU nationals.
Interview details: Only those living in Germany are interviewed.
Certification: Reference on request.
Worldwide placements: *Europe* (Germany).

CAMPHILL DORFGEMEINSCHAFT SELLEN E.V

Sellen 101
D48565 Steinfurt/Burgsteinfurt
Nordrhein-Westphalen
48565 Germany

Tel: 00 49 2551 9366 0 or 35
Fax: 00 49 2551 9366 11
e-mail: Camphill-Steinfurt@t-online.de
Web: www.camphill.org.uk/diverty/germany/sellen.htm
Contact: Mrs Lieselotte Liebeck

Camphill Dorfgemeinschaft Sellen e.v. is an institution with 51 mentally disabled people. They live in seven separate houses together with their co-worker family. This co-worker family may be a couple with their own children. The volunteer workers are integrated in such a family in their daily life. The day begins with waking up the 'villagers' (disabled persons). Some of them have to be dressed, washed etc. The household eats breakfast together; then they go to work on the farm, in the garden, household, textile-workshop etc. At 12.30 p.m. everyone eats lunch together with their family. At 2.30 p.m. the work starts again and ends at 5.30 p.m. The villagers then take showers and some of them need the help of the volunteers with that. Again the supper is eaten together with the whole family. In general the volunteers plan their evenings by themselves, but they are also involved in leisure activities, for example drama, dancing, outings, music etc.

Total projects worldwide: 6
Total UK projects: 0
Starting months: May, August.
Time required: 4–52 weeks.
Age requirement: 18–30
Causes: Disabled (learning and physical), environmental causes, holidays for disabled, young people.
Activities: Agriculture/farming, arts/crafts, building/construction, caring (residential), catering, cooking, driving, forestry, gardening/horticulture, group work, manual work, music, outdoor skills, social work, sport, summer camps, theatre/drama.
Vols under 26 placed each year: 4
When to apply: 2–3 months before wishing to start.
Work alone/with others: Both.
Volunteers with disabilities: Possible.
Qualifications: Willingness to do any kind of craftwork and look after our people (washing/dressing etc).
Equipment/clothing: Working trousers and shoes.
Health requirements: A certificate for a Common Health Test is required (Gesundheits-Zeugnis).
Costs: Travel costs except in special cases.
Benefits: Board (3 meals), lodging, and DM300 per month pocket money. If volunteer is from the EU they are insured by us.
Training: One afternoon per week there is a special introductory course run by the staff especially for the volunteers to give them an understanding of our work with the disabled people.
Supervision: Supervised by trained responsible co-workers.
Nationalities accepted: Must be EU nationals unless coming only for 4 weeks and take out own insurance.
Interview details: Volunteers are interviewed

by Mrs Silvia Shin, Camphill St Albans, 50 Carlisle Avenue, St Albans, Hertfordshire AL3 5LT. Tel: +44 (0) 1727 811228 or phone Lieselotte Liebeck at 00 49 2551 936635.
Certification: Certificate or reference provided.
Charity number: VR705(E.V.)
Worldwide placements: *Europe* (Germany).

CAMPHILL FARM COMMUNITY AND CAMPHILL SCHOOL
PO Box 301
Hermanus 7200
Cape Province
South Africa

Tel: 00 27 28 3121120
Fax: 00 27 28 3123555
Contact: The Reception Group, Co-worker / Volunteer

The Camphill School is dedicated to the care of mentally handicapped children and adolescents. We provide education and training in both a residential and day setting, spanning the ages between 5 and 20, and providing for a wide range of learning difficulties, developmental handicaps and emotional disturbances. The residential children live in family groups in various houses. All of the children belong to school classes according to their age. The curriculum covers a wide range of subjects and is based on the Waldorf curriculum for normal children, but each subject is adapted to suit the specific needs of the children. This curriculum is carefully planned to assist children through their successive stages of development and hence its particular value when applied to children with handicaps. In addition to the training in basic skills, there is a good deal of artistic work such as drawing and painting, music and modelling, movement and drama. The school year starts at the beginning of January. Camphill Farm Community for mentally handicapped adults is based on the ideal of mutual care, where there is an interdependence between all members of the community. Through living and working together, the distinctions between various members of the community are replaced by an appreciation that we all depend on each other, and that each person has a particular contribution to make to the whole community. A busy working life, whether in a house, workshop or on the land, calls on everyone according to their individual capabilities. Evenings and weekends allow time for social activities and a rich cultural life. Volunteers with an offending background may be accepted, dependent on the offence.

Total projects worldwide: 1
Total UK projects: 0
Starting months: January–December.
Time required: 1–52 weeks (plus).
Age requirement: 20 plus.
Causes: Children, disabled (learning), teaching/assisting (nursery, primary, secondary).
Activities: Agriculture/farming, arts/crafts, caring (general, day and residential), cooking, fundraising, gardening/horticulture, group work, manual work, music, outdoor skills, teaching, technical skills, theatre/drama.
Vols under 26 placed each year: 6–8 of a total of 20–25.
When to apply: 6–12 months before.
Work alone/with others: Both.
Volunteers with disabilities: Not possible.
Qualifications: Must be able to speak English, otherwise only enthusiasm.
Equipment/clothing: Sufficient clothing, i.e. for work and formal occasions for at least one year.
Health requirements: Good health as our way of life is strenuous.
Costs: Medical insurance or costs, visa costs including extensions, travel costs, holiday costs.
Benefits: Board and lodging and modest pocket money.
Interview details: No interview necessary.
Certification: Reference if volunteer completes the time agreed upon.
Charity number: 78/03803/0
Worldwide placements: *Africa* (South Africa).

CAMPHILL HEIMSONDERSCHULE FÖHRENBÜHL
D88633 Heiligenberg-Steigen
Bodenseekreis
Germany

Tel: 00 49 7554 80010
Fax: 00 49 7554 8001 63
e-mail: camphill.fohrenbuhl@t-online.de
Other e-mail: foehrenbuehl@foehrenbuehl.de
Web: www.camphill.org.uk (for general information)

www. camphill.de (for German centres)
www.foehrenbuehl.de (for Föhrenbühl direct)
Contact: Richard Steel

Camphill Heimsonderschule Föhrenbühl is a school community with family-like units in which handicapped and staff live and learn together. It has a kindergarten and school with trainee course for children and young people with special needs. The Camphill movement was founded by Dr Karl König and based on the teachings of Rudolf Steiner. Applicants with an offending background may be accepted depending on the offence.

Total projects worldwide: 1
Total UK projects: 0
Starting months: January–December.
Time required: 3–52 weeks (plus).
Age requirement: 18–30
Causes: Children, disabled (learning and physical), teaching/assisting (nursery, primary, secondary), young people.
Activities: Arts/crafts, caring (general and residential), cooking, gardening/horticulture, manual work, teaching.
Vols under 26 placed each year: 18 of a total of 20.
When to apply: All year.
Work alone/with others: With others.
Volunteers with disabilities: Good movement needed for looking after children. Each case open to discussion.
Qualifications: German language (basic at least) is a help.
Health requirements: Health certificate required proving absence of contagious diseases.
Costs: Travel costs only.
Benefits: Board and lodging (single rooms usually). After 3 weeks pocket money (DM200 plus per month). Full insurance including medical insurance.
Training: A practical visit can be arranged in a Camphill Centre near to the volunteer's home.
Supervision: Volunteers work within a house community where experienced house parents are responsible. Also school work is only under guidance of responsible teacher. A contact person is always available for questions/problems.
Nationalities accepted: Applicants with EU passports, otherwise a work permit must be applied for well in advance.
Interview details: Applicants are interviewed

at the nearest Camphill Centre to their home address if this is practicable.
Certification: Reference provided.
Worldwide placements: *Europe* (Germany).

CAMPHILL IN POLAND – WÓJTÓWKA
Stójków 22
Wójtówka 1
PL-57540 Ladek Zdrój
Poland

Tel: 00 48 74 146 501
Fax: 00 48 74 141 366
Contact: Aleksandra Mossekowska

Wspolnota Wójtówka is a village community for adults with special needs, 600 m up in the mountains of SW Poland. On an abandoned farm, buildings are being restored, fields reclaimed for ecological farming and a whole new approach to the mentally handicapped person is being launched. What makes the Polish project so fascinating is that reclamation, rebuilding and ecological planning are being taken on with the help of mentally handicapped persons. This aspect of human ecology is unique for this part of the world, where in a sense the mentally handicapped were until now classified as 'non-existent'. As a result, Poland's mentally handicapped have for the past 50 years been gathered in huge institutions, some for men, others for women – 'out of sight, out of mind'. Today, Poland is taking important steps to correct all this, but progress is slow. Camphill Wójtówka lies in a narrow valley with steep, state-owned forests pressing in from both sides. The farm is long, narrow and idyllic – ten hectares, with a little brook flowing the whole of its length. In 1989 when first steps were taken to turn the former gristmill, family dwelling and cowshed into a liveable village house there was little to inspire enthusiasm with no inside water or toilet, single-glass windows and no insulation. Parts of the outside brick and stone walls were crumbling and half of the building which had once housed the mill and water-wheel was simply three storeys of empty space. Today we have ten bedrooms which house five villagers and five co-workers with their three children plus a new combined kitchen, dining and sitting room with 75 sq.m of tiled floor and a meeting room of similar size on the third floor. Everyone is a volunteer. Work camps start in late May. Longer-term volunteers may join at any time.

Total projects worldwide: 1
Total UK projects: 0
Starting months: January–December.
Time required: 2–52 weeks (plus).
Age requirement: 18–26
Causes: Disabled (learning), environmental causes, holidays for disabled, teaching (EFL), work camps – seasonal, young people.
Activities: Agriculture/farming, building/construction, community work, cooking, driving, forestry, gardening/horticulture, manual work, outdoor skills, summer camps, technical skills, work camps – seasonal.
Vols under 26 placed each year: 10–15 of a total of 10–15.
When to apply: Work camps: before 1 April. Other volunteers: All year.
Work alone/with others: With others.
Volunteers with disabilities: Not yet suitable. Wójtówka is a pioneer venture.
Qualifications: Nil but manual skill and/or basic knowledge of Polish plus int. driving licence an advantage.
Equipment/clothing: Wellingtons, waterproofs, warm clothing and general work clothing.
Health requirements: Applicants should arrange own medicinal needs and not require dental care.
Costs: All travel costs for return round trip.
Benefits: Board and lodging, pocket money for long-term volunteers.
Interview details: No interview necessary.
Certification: Certificate or reference provided.
Worldwide placements: *Europe* (Poland).

CAMPHILL LEBENSGEMEINSCHAFT KÖNIGSMÜHLE
Schöntalstr. 9
Neustadt a.d. Weinstrasse
Rheinland-Pfalz
D67434 Germany

Tel: 00 49 6321 7289 or 7295
Fax: 00 49 6321 31487
Contact: Herr Ehmcke or Herr Foskett

Camphill Lebensgemeinschaft Königsmühle is a small community (four families) with 24 young disabled adults, together with our own eight children and one or more young volunteers. We live, work and 'play' together which includes basket making, candle making, wood workshop, weavery, gardening, and grape growing. We organize concerts, plays and talks for the surrounding population.

Total projects worldwide: 1
Total UK projects: 0
Starting months: January–November.
Time required: 26–52 weeks.
Age requirement: 18–25
Causes: Disabled (learning and physical).
Activities: Caring (general, day and residential), forestry, fundraising, gardening/ horticulture, group work, manual work, music, social work, theatre/drama.
Vols under 26 placed each year: 5–6
When to apply: All year.
Work alone/with others: With others.
Volunteers with disabilities: Not possible.
Qualifications: Open-minded to new impressions.
Health requirements: Nil.
Costs: Travel costs (refunded if volunteer stays a year or more).
Benefits: Board, lodging and pocket money DM400 a month, medical insurance and state pension. We are responsible for all insurance so none is necessary.
Training: As needed.
Supervision: Trained staff always there.
Interview details: Interviews are conducted only if possible.
Certification: Written reference.
Worldwide placements: *Europe* (Germany).

CAMPHILL LIEBENFELS
Pflausach 3
A9556 Liebenfels/Kärnten
Austria

Tel: 00 43 4215 2466
Fax: 00 43 4215 246620
Contact: The Administrative Group

Camphill Liebenfels is a village community with adults with special needs.

Total projects worldwide: 1
Total UK projects: 0
Starting months: January–December.
Time required: 12–52 weeks (plus).
Age requirement: 21 plus.
Causes: Disabled (learning), holidays for disabled.
Activities: Agriculture/farming, arts/crafts, caring (residential), cooking, gardening/ horticulture, music.

Vols under 26 placed each year: 40
When to apply: All year.
Work alone/with others: Both.
Volunteers with disabilities: Possible.
Qualifications: Good German.
Health requirements: Nil but injection against tick-bites is advisable.
Costs: Travel costs and health and travel insurance.
Benefits: Board and lodging, pocket money of OS2,000 per month.
Nationalities accepted: No restrictions but EU regulations make it difficult for non-EU nationals to stay in this country for longer than 3 months.
Interview details: No interview necessary.
Certification: Certificate or reference provided.
Worldwide placements: *Europe* (Austria).

CAMPHILL RUDOLF STEINER SCHOOLS
Central Office, Murtle Estate
Murtle House
Bieldside
Aberdeen
AB15 9EP Scotland

Tel: +44 (0) 1224 867935
Fax: +44 (0) 1224 868420
e-mail: office@crss.org.uk
Contact: Mrs K. Ehlen

A Camphill Rudolf Steiner School is a residential school for children and youngsters in need of special care. We cater for a great variety of developmental, psychological, emotional and physical handicaps (ages 4–19 years). Adults (carers) and pupils live in houses, within the estate, of varying sizes and form the community. The pupils live in groups of 2–3 in one room and are looked after by houseparents, group parents, and other co-workers. The task of a group parent is to look after the physical and emotional needs of the pupils with the guidance of experienced co-workers and to create a 'home' of understanding and warmth so that teaching and development is made possible. Apart from attending to the needs of the pupil individually, group activities are carried out and the volunteer is encouraged to take an active and creative, as well as therapeutic, part in them. The pupils attend school five mornings a week, in addition to individual therapies some afternoons. There are 40 Camphill Communities in the UK and another 40 worldwide. Addresses can be obtained from Camphill Schools, Aberdeen. Enquiries should be made directly to the individual community.

Total projects worldwide: 40 plus.
Total UK projects: 40
Starting months: January, April, August, October.
Time required: 36–49 weeks.
Age requirement: 18 plus.
Causes: Children, disabled (learning and physical), teaching/assisting, young people.
Activities: Caring (general and residential), cooking, gardening/horticulture, group work, music, outdoor skills, religion, sport, summer camps, teaching, theatre/drama, training.
Vols under 26 placed each year: 60 of a total of 80.
When to apply: 8–12 weeks prior to school entry term (August, October, January, April).
Work alone/with others: With others.
Volunteers with disabilities: Possible.
Qualifications: Adequate understanding of the English language.
Equipment/clothing: For Sunday services and festivals only: girls skirts, boys no jeans.
Health requirements: Up-to-date medical health record. (No serious back problems or mental instability.)
Costs: Own travel expenses to Aberdeen.
Benefits: £30 pocket money per week Volunteers covered by our insurance except for his/her own valuables.
Training: Induction course.
Supervision: House parents and senior co-workers are on hand for guidance and supervision.
Nationalities accepted: No restrictions – only an adequate understanding of the English language.
Interview details: Volunteer applicants are interviewed where possible.
Certification: After one year a certificate is awarded stating courses attended.
Charity number: SCO 15588
Worldwide placements: *Africa* (South Africa); *Europe* (Finland, Germany, Norway, Sweden, Switzerland); *North America* (Canada, USA).
UK placements: *Scotland* (Aberdeen City, Aberdeenshire).

CAMPHILL SOLTANE
224 Nantmeal Road
Glenmoore
Pa. 19343
USA

Tel: 00 1 610 469 0933
Fax: 00 1 610 469 1054
e-mail: soltane@aol.com
Web: www.camphillsoltane.org
Contact: Annegret Goetze

Camphill Soltane is an intentional community based on the work of Rudolf Steiner. Essentially, it attempts to create a life-sharing community, work towards social renewal and practice awareness of each other's needs through a life of meaning and fulfilment together with mentally handicapped young men and women aged 18–25. Our students or companions live, learn and work in Camphill Soltane together with co-workers and their families, interns, 'practicants' and shorter term co-workers. Soltane's primary work is 'Youth Guidance' – leading the young adult with developmental disabilities towards a sense of self, a sense of interdependence, and a sense of being and participating as a contributing member in the fellowship of human kind. Life in Soltane is vigorous, diverse and rich. There is little 'private' time, yet there are great opportunities for creative initiative and full involvement by every co-worker. Co-workers meet regularly about a variety of community issues. There is a choir and there are several opportunities for adult education activities. Principally, however, the life, welfare and development of our companions is the foremost responsibility of all co-workers and involves daily direct care. With 50 acres of rolling fields, woodlands, gardens and orchards there is ample opportunity for hiking, outdoor recreational and educational activities and nature study at Soltane. Metro Philadelphia, with over four million inhabitants, is less than one hour's drive.

Total projects worldwide: 1
Total UK projects: 0
Starting months: January, September.
Time required: 12–52 weeks (plus).
Age requirement: 18–25
Causes: Disabled (learning), teaching (secondary), young people.
Activities: Agriculture/farming, caring (general and residential), community work, cooking, counselling, driving, gardening/horticulture, group work, manual work, outdoor skills.

Vols under 26 placed each year: 3–5
When to apply: By 1 May (for September start) or 1 November (for January start).
Work alone/with others: With other experienced workers.
Volunteers with disabilities: Not possible.
Qualifications: English language. Interest and commitment to community. Experience with developmental disabilities preferred.
Health requirements: Able-bodied, healthy, no major illness or disease.
Costs: Travel costs. Health insurance for first 6 months.
Benefits: Room and board and US$100 pocket money monthly. Health insurance after first 6 months.
Training: After arrival before companions return from vacation, we have orientation sessions and common planning meetings. Throughout the year each young and new co-worker has a mentor within the community.
Supervision: Co-working with house-parents and work masters.
Interview details: Interviews are conducted by mail or over the telephone.
Worldwide placements: *North America* (USA).

CAMPHILL SPECIAL SCHOOLS (BEAVER RUN)

Camphill Special Schools
Beaver Run
1784 Fairview Road
Glenmoore
Pennsylvania 19343
USA

Tel: 00 1 610 469 9236
Fax: 00 1 610 469 9758
e-mail: BvrRn@aol.com
Web: www.beaverrun.org
Contact: Anne Sproll, Applications Group

Camphill Special Schools provide extended family living in a sheltered community, education, and therapy for mentally and physically disabled children and youngsters in a wholesome, rural setting. The work is inspired by Rudolf Steiner's anthroposophy as further developed by Karl König, Camphill's founder. (The 'mother' school is in Aberdeen.) Volunteers belong to a household and assist in the daily care and training of the special needs children. Each week volunteers have one day and several evenings off. Volunteers must be willing to serve the needs of others and work co-operatively.

Total projects worldwide: 1
Total UK projects: 0
Starting months: August.
Time required: 46–50 weeks.
Age requirement: 20–28
Causes: Children, disabled (learning), teaching/assisting young people.
Activities: Arts/crafts, caring (residential), community work, cooking, driving, gardening/horticulture, group work, manual work, music, outdoor skills, social work, summer camps, teaching, theatre/drama.
Vols under 26 placed each year: 28–30 of a total of 40–60.
When to apply: 4–6 months in advance.
Work alone/with others: With others.
Volunteers with disabilities: Each case considered separately. Hilly terrain and physically demanding work.
Qualifications: Experience with children desirable. If possible volunteers should visit a Camphill Centre in the UK.
Equipment/clothing: Bring own clothing: snowy winters, hot summers.
Health requirements: Good mental and physical health, TB screening required.
Costs: Travel.
Benefits: Board, lodging plus US$135 per month pocket money, vacation stipend, medical insurance.
Training: Ongoing training on campus. Volunteers receive some training and orientation, 3–8 hours per week.
Supervision: Special education teachers for school, house-parents for the houses, therapists for therapy.
Certification: A testimonial letter after 1 year, a certificate in curative education after 3 years' training.
Worldwide placements: *North America* (USA).

CAMPHILL VILLAGE ALPHA (WESTERN CAPE)

PO Box 1451
Dassenberg 7350
Western Cape
South Africa

Tel: 00 27 21 572 2345
Fax: 00 27 21 572 2238
e-mail: info@camphill.org.za
Contact: Lee Eksteen

Camphill Village (Western Cape) is a rural

working community of 160 men, women and children. Some 90 adults, many of whom are ageing, have learning difficulties and special needs. There are 16 households where co-workers and villagers live together in group homes. We share our daily living and work with villagers. A warm and healthy home life is integral to the wellbeing of our community and all co-workers share responsibility in our homes. We employ some local people from the surrounding district. Our 240 ha property suffers from extremely poor sandy soil. We strive to work creatively with our limited resources in an attempt to bring healing to the land and increase our productivity. Land departments include farm, vegetable garden, orchards and herb growing. Our enterprises include herb processing, cosmetics, a dairy, a bakery and a basket workshop.Preference is given to those who can commit themselves for one year.

Total projects worldwide: 1
Total UK projects: 0
Starting months: January–December.
Time required: 52 weeks (plus).
Age requirement: 18–25
Causes: Disabled (learning and physical).
Activities: Agriculture/farming, arts/crafts, caring (general and residential), catering, community work, cooking, driving, first aid, gardening/horticulture, group work, manual work, outdoor skills, social work, sport, visiting/befriending.
Vols under 26 placed each year: 8
When to apply: All year.
Work alone/with others: Both.
Volunteers with disabilities: Not possible.
Qualifications: Driving licence, English, good social skills, common sense, practical nature, love for people.
Equipment/clothing: Work clothes, casual clothes and one set of informal but good clothes.
Health requirements: Need to come with health insurance.
Costs: Return ticket and travel transport costs within S. Africa. Insurance.
Benefits: R300 per month plus full board and lodging.
Training: Ongoing training. 2 hours orientation per week.
Supervision: Houseparents and work masters supervise.
Nationalities accepted: There are no restrictions on nationalities of volunteers except Africans. Due to affirmative action in South Africa, we only take Africans who are from South Africa.
Interview details: Applicants are interviewed by correspondence and possibly by other friends of Camphill in UK.
Certification: Written reference.
Worldwide placements: *Africa* (South Africa).

CAMPHILL VILLAGE COMMUNITY DUFFCARRIG
Duffcarrig
Gorey
Co. Wexford
Ireland

Tel: 00 353 55 25911
Fax: 00 353 55 25910
e-mail: duffcarrig@camphill.ie
Web: www.camphill.ie
Contact: The Admissions Group

Camphill Village Community Duffcarrig is a centre with adults (aged 20–77) who have a mental handicap. Camphill Communities can be found in many countries all over the world and are dedicated to creating a healthy social life with handicapped people of all ages. This work is based on the philosophy and insights of Rudolf Steiner, whose pupil, Dr Karl König, founded the Camphill Movement. Duffcarrig is situated on the coast of County Wexford in the sunny south-east of Ireland, five minutes walk from the sea, and is neighbour to farms and holiday homes. The nearest town, Gorey, is 3½ miles away. There is no public transport to the town, but our own vehicles make regular trips there. Dublin is only two hours away. In Duffcarrig, there are seven households, with a total population of 80. We maintain a bio-dynamic farm and garden and have workshops for weaving, pottery, basketry and laundry. Housework and estate maintenance complete our normal working situation. We prefer volunteers for a year or longer but there are some openings for 2–3 months in the summer.

Total projects worldwide: 1
Total UK projects: 0
Starting months: January–December.
Time required: 52 weeks (plus).
Age requirement: 19 plus.
Causes: Disabled (learning).
Activities: Agriculture/farming, arts/crafts, caring (residential), cooking, gardening/

horticulture, manual work, social work.
Vols under 26 placed each year: 15 of a total of 30.
When to apply: All year.
Work alone/with others: With others.
Volunteers with disabilities: Possible.
Qualifications: Good knowledge of English language is essential.
Equipment/clothing: For outside workers, wellies, rainwear etc.
Health requirements: Varies from applicant to applicant.
Costs: Travel.
Benefits: Pocket money of £25 per week, food and accommodation. Basic medical and accident insurance.
Training: Leaflet and co-worker information sheet. Visit before if wished for. Any questions answered by contact person.
Supervision: Introductory course, study groups, working together and introduction by long-term co-workers.
Interview details: Interviews are conducted by letter. 2 references and a CV must be supplied plus a police statement.
Certification: Reference provided.
Worldwide placements: *Europe* (Ireland).

CAMPHILL VILLAGE KIMBERTON HILLS, INC

PO Box 155
Kimberton
Kimberton
Pennsylvania
19442 USA

Tel: 00 1 610 935 3963
Fax: 00 1 610 935 8896 or 3963
e-mail: campkimbpf@aol.com
Web: www.camphillKimberton.org
Contact: The Personnel Forum

Camphill Village Kimberton Hills is an agricultural community based on a 430 acre estate in the rolling hills of south-east Pennsylvania. There is a total population of about 120, including some 50 adults with mental handicaps. The community raises vegetables, grains, fruits and meat, and produces milk and cheese from a small dairy herd. Their own baked goods are sold in a health food store nearby. Volunteers are required to live and work as co-workers within the community, working side by side with developmentally disabled adults. Work takes place on the farm, in the bakery, coffee shop, orchards, food processing plant, craft workshops, administrative office, and in extended family homes.

Total projects worldwide: 1
Total UK projects: 0
Starting months: January–December.
Time required: 25–52 weeks (plus).
Age requirement: 19 plus.
Causes: Conservation, disabled (learning), environmental causes, holidays for disabled, wildlife.
Activities: Agriculture/farming, arts/crafts, caring (general and residential), conservation skills, cooking, driving, gardening/horticulture, group work, manual work, music, social work, teaching, visiting/befriending.
Vols under 26 placed each year: About 20 of a total of 47.
When to apply: At least 2 months in advance of preferred starting date.
Work alone/with others: Both.
Volunteers with disabilities: Possible.
Qualifications: Enthusiasm and idealism.
Equipment/clothing: Prepared for all seasons of temperate climate: hot summers, snowy winters.
Health requirements: Must be able to work.
Costs: Travel costs.
Benefits: Board and lodging and US$100 per month pocket money. If a volunteer does not have insurance coverage, we will supply basic medical coverage.
Training: On-the-job training at work site.
Supervision: By long-term co-workers in the house and at work stations.
Interview details: Applicants from the UK are not interviewed except by correspondence or telephone.
Certification: Reference on request.
Worldwide placements: *North America* (USA).

CAMPHILL VILLAGE MINNESOTA

Box 249
Route 3
Sauk Centre
Minnesota
MN 56378 USA

Tel: 00 1 320 732 6365
Fax: 00 1 320 732 3204
e-mail: cvmn@rea-alp.com
Web: www.camphill.org
Contact: Trudy Pax

The mission of Camphill Village Minnesota is to create and sustain a community where people with and without disabilities live, work, and care for each other to foster social, cultural and agricultural renewal. This village is an intentional community of approximately 60 people, including adults with developmental disabilities. The community is based on the belief that every individual, regardless of ability, is an independent spiritual being. Developmental disabilities are treated not as illnesses, but as part of the fabric of human experience, and all members of the community are cared for in the context of a healthy home and village life. Camphill is located on a 360 acre working farm ten miles north of Sauk Centre in central Minnesota. People live together family-style in seven different homes. Everyone shares in the responsibilities of life in the community. The village has a strong agricultural component made up of farming, beekeeping and gardening. Craft work includes weaving and woodwork, as well as a bakery that provides for the needs of the village and sells in the surrounding area. Life in the village revolves around the cycles of nature, with festivals marking the changing seasons. Plays, concerts, lectures and continuing education add depth and colour to the fabric of the community.

Total projects worldwide: 1
Total UK projects: 0
Starting months: January–December.
Time required: 24–52 weeks (plus).
Age requirement: 18 plus.
Causes: Disabled (learning and physical).
Activities: Agriculture/farming, arts/crafts, caring (general), catering, community work, cooking, counselling, driving, first aid, gardening/horticulture, group work, manual work, music, outdoor skills, social work, theatre/drama.
Vols under 26 placed each year: 3 of a total of 4.
When to apply: All year.
Work alone/with others: Both.
Volunteers with disabilities: Not possible.
Qualifications: Language ability.
Equipment/clothing: Heavy winter outdoor gear if coming in winter.
Health requirements: Reasonable health is required.
Costs: Travel costs.
Benefits: Board, lodging and US$50 per month pocket money. We provide insurance and cover medical expenses for volunteers who stay at least 6 months.
Training: We would like a prospective volunteer to visit a Camphill in the UK before coming.
Supervision: We expect volunteers to be able to work independently. There is guidance of course but not always supervision.
Interview details: We ask people to visit a Camphill near them.
Certification: Reference on request.
Worldwide placements: *North America* (USA).

CAMPHILL VILLAGE TRUST (HQ)
Delrow House
Hilfield Lane
Watford
Hertfordshire
WD2 8DJ UK

Tel: +44 (0) 1923 856006
Fax: +44 (0) 1923 858035
e-mail: info@camphill.org.uk
Web: www.camphill.org.uk
Contact: The Admissions Group

Camphill Village Trust is an organization which caters for adults with special needs. Most of the centres are working communities and some of the centres also cater for people with mental health problems. We supply, where possible, the addresses of our centres abroad and also addresses of other co-workers who have worked in our centres when we have no centre abroad to contact. Volunteers with an offending background are accepted on some specific projects.

Total projects worldwide: 1
Total UK projects: 1
Starting months: January–December.
Time required: 12–52 weeks.
Age requirement: 20 plus.
Causes: Disabled (learning and physical).
Activities: Agriculture/farming, arts/crafts, caring (general), catering, cooking, gardening/horticulture, group work.
Vols under 26 placed each year: 20
When to apply: All year.
Work alone/with others: With others.
Volunteers with disabilities: Not possible.
Qualifications: Good command of English.
Health requirements: Hepatitis B innoculation recommended.
Costs: Nil except travel to and from centre.

Benefits: Board, lodging and small pocket money. Insurance provided by our organization.
Training: Provided during the volunteers' working period at our centres.
Supervision: Each volunteer has a tutor who is concerned with their progress through the stay at our centres.
Interview details: Applicants are interviewed if they apply in the UK or we suggest that they visit one of our centres local to them.
Certification: Certificate or reference provided.
Charity number: 232402
Worldwide placements: *Africa* (Botswana, South Africa); *Asia* (India); *Europe* (Austria, Denmark, Estonia, Finland, France, Germany, Ireland, Netherlands, Norway, Poland, Romania, Russia, Sweden, Switzerland); *North America* (Canada, USA).
UK placements: *England* (Bristol, Buckinghamshire, Devon, Dorset, Gloucestershire, Hampshire, Hertfordshire, Norfolk, E. Sussex, W. Sussex, West Midlands, N. Yorkshire, S. Yorkshire, W. Yorkshire); *Scotland* (Aberdeenshire, Dumfries and Galloway, Edinburgh, Highland, Perth and Kinross, Stirling); *Northern Ireland* (Down, Tyrone); *Wales* (Carmarthenshire, Pembrokeshire).

CAMPHILL VILLAGE TRUST – LOCH ARTHUR COMMUNITY
Stable Cottage
Beeswing
Dumfries
DG2 8JQ Scotland

Tel: + 44 (0) 1387 760687
Fax: + 44 (0) 1387 760618
Contact: Lana Chanarin, Admissions Officer

Work activities in the Loch Arthur Community include farming (crops, dairy, beef and sheep), gardening, estate work, creamery, bakery, weaving workshop and housework. We hope that co-workers joining us are willing and able to participate in any of these activities, depending on where the needs are in the community at the time in question. There are people in Loch Arthur who require help with personal care (bathing, dressing, eating, etc.) and co-workers joining us should be willing to be involved in such care. Our cultural activities are influenced by the Christian festivals which we celebrate and which lead us through the seasons of the year in a meaningful way. Volunteers with an offending background may be accepted depending on the nature of the offence.

Total projects worldwide: 1
Total UK projects: 1
Starting months: January–December.
Time required: 26–52 weeks (plus).
Age requirement: 18 plus.
Causes: Disabled (learning and physical), teaching/assisting.
Activities: Agriculture/farming, arts/crafts, caring (day and residential), catering, cooking, driving, gardening/horticulture, group work, music, teaching.
Vols under 26 placed each year: 13
When to apply: All year – apply at least 2 months in advance.
Work alone/with others: Both.
Volunteers with disabilities: Not possible.
Qualifications: Open mindedness and enthusiasm.
Equipment/clothing: Sufficient clothing for duration of stay remembering Scottish weather and rural setting.
Health requirements: Physically and mentally fit to be able to participate fully and assist less able members.
Costs: Travel to and from the Community.
Benefits: Board and lodging plus pocket money. British volunteers covered by our insurance.
Training: On the job.
Supervision: By long-term members of the community.
Interview details: Volunteer applicants are not necessarily interviewed – some do visit prior to placement. 2 references and a criminal record check is required.
Certification: Reference on request.
Charity number: 232402
UK placements: *Scotland* (Dumfries and Galloway).

CAMPHILL VILLAGE TRUST LTD
Gawain House
56 Welham Road, Norton
Malton
North Yorkshire
YO17 9DP UK

Tel: + 44 (0) 1653 694197
Fax: + 44 (0) 1653 600001
e-mail: andy@croftcvt.demon.co.uk
Web: www.camphill.org.uk

Contact: Andy Paton

The idea of Camphill is founded on co-workers living and working alongside people with special needs. Each individual disabled person has different needs which should be met in different ways. Camphill Village Trust Ltd was established to work with people who are mentally handicapped – and this is still its principal role today. From the outset, the intention was to do this work not as a 'job' in the usual sense of the word, but as a way of life. A community of co-workers was formed who shared all the work that had to be done: teaching, caring, household tasks, gardening. This work was used as one of the means of curative education and the children helped in this work insofar as they were able. These children, and later adolescents and adults, became members of the community where they lived, working alongside the co-workers. Mankind has struggled to find new forms of community life for centuries – now in Camphill, a new form of human co-operation is able to establish itself and flourish.

Volunteers with an offending background may be accepted with full disclosure. Each case is considered individually.

Total projects worldwide: 100
Total UK projects: 47
Starting months: January–December.
Time required: 26–52 weeks (plus).
Age requirement: 18 plus.
Causes: Disabled (learning and physical).
Activities: Administration, agriculture/farming, arts/crafts, caring (general, day and residential), catering, community work, cooking, counselling, DIY, gardening/horticulture, group work, manual work, music, outdoor skills.
Vols under 26 placed each year: 240 of a total of 300.
When to apply: All year.
Work alone/with others: With other volunteers and staff.
Volunteers with disabilities: Possible.
Qualifications: Nil, only a sense of humour.
Equipment/clothing: Varied.
Health requirements: Health record required.
Costs: Dependent on placement.
Benefits: In Britain usually Community Service Volunteer rates.
Interview details: Interviews sometimes take place at centre applied to.
Charity number: 232402

Worldwide placements: *Africa* (Botswana, South Africa); *Europe* (Austria, Denmark, Estonia, Finland, France, Germany, Ireland, Netherlands, Norway, Poland, Sweden, Switzerland); *North America* (Canada, USA); *South America* (Brazil).
UK placements: *England* (Buckinghamshire, Devon, Dorset, Gloucestershire, Hampshire, Hertfordshire, Norfolk, E. Sussex, West Midlands, N. Yorkshire, W. Yorkshire); *Scotland* (Aberdeenshire, Angus, Argyll and Bute, Dumfries and Galloway, Highland, Moray, Perth and Kinross, Stirling); *Northern Ireland* (Belfast City, Down, Tyrone); *Wales* (Carmarthenshire, Pembrokeshire).

CAMPHILL VILLAGE USA, INC

Copake
New York
12516 USA

Tel: 00 1 518 329 4851/7924
Fax: 00 1 518 329 0377
e-mail: cvvolunteer@taconic.net
Web: www.camphill.org
Contact: Penelope Roberts, Associate Director

Camphill Village USA is an intentional, international community of approximately 250 people, about 110 of whom are adults with mental disabilities. Located on 800 acres of woodland and farmland 100 miles north of New York City, the Village has a large bio-dynamic dairy farm, and gardens, seven craft shops, a production bakery, a community centre, a gift shop, a food co-op and 20 family residences in each of which life is shared by 5–7 adults with disabilities and 2–4 co-workers and their families, often with children. It is part of the wider Camphill movement based on the innovative therapeutic work of Karl König MD, and Anthroposophy, the worldview of Rudolf Steiner, Austrian philosopher 1879–1924. The Village life includes farming, gardening, craft work, a rich social and cultural life and a religious life. Co-workers live here as full-time volunteers, receiving no salary, but working in answer to the needs of others while, in return, their own needs are provided for. Through this viable alternative to the wage system it becomes possible to develop a sense of mutual responsibility and brotherhood. Camphill Village offers a three year training in social therapy and a one year introductory course beginning in September.

Total projects worldwide: 90
Total UK projects: 20
Starting months: January–December.
Time required: 13–52 weeks (plus).
Age requirement: 18 plus.
Causes: Disabled (learning and physical), work camps – seasonal.
Activities: Administration, agriculture/farming, arts/crafts, building/construction, caring (general and residential), catering, cooking, driving, forestry, gardening/horticulture, group work, manual work, music, newsletter/journalism, outdoor skills, social work, teaching, theatre/drama, training, work camps – seasonal.
Vols under 26 placed each year: 40 of a total of 80.
When to apply: All year.
Work alone/with others: Both.
Volunteers with disabilities: Possible, but volunteers must be ambulatory.
Qualifications: Willingness to learn, to help out, and to join in our way of life. Volunteers must be able to speak and understand English.
Equipment/clothing: Nil – winters are cold and summers can be hot.
Health requirements: Physically fit and well, strong and ambulatory.
Costs: Travel costs.
Benefits: Board, lodging plus US$80 per month pocket money. Medical insurance after 3 months.
Training: After arrival.
Supervision: Depends on experience. Always supervision of experienced co-workers leading to more independent responsibility if appropriate.
Nationalities accepted: No restrictions but volunteers should be able to speak and understand English.
Interview details: Interviews take place if possible at one of our 80 Camphill centres worldwide.
Certification: Certificate or reference provided.
Worldwide placements: *North America* (USA).

CAMPHILL VILLAGES (UK) – BOTTON VILLAGE

Botton Village
Danby
Whitby
N. Yorkshire

YO21 2NJ UK

Tel: + 44 (0) 1287 660871
Contact: Mrs Jane Balls, The Reception Group

Camphill Villages (UK) provides a home for mentally (and often physically) handicapped children or adults.

Total projects worldwide: 1
Total UK projects: 1
Starting months: January–December.
Time required: 4–52 weeks.
Age requirement: 20 plus.
Causes: Children, disabled (learning and physical).
Activities: Agriculture/farming, arts/crafts, caring (general and residential), gardening/horticulture, music, outdoor skills.
Vols under 26 placed each year: Approximately 30.
When to apply: All year.
Work alone/with others: Both – depending on the work.
Volunteers with disabilities: Possible, but we are a farming community where people have to be responsible for mentally-handicapped adults.
Qualifications: Social skills as well as common sense.
Equipment/clothing: Waterproofs, wellington boots, warm clothing. (N. Yorkshire Moors with unfriendly weather).
Health requirements: Nil.
Costs: Travel costs.
Benefits: Board and lodging. Pocket money when stay is longer than 4 weeks.
Interview details: No interview necessary but people can visit our community to meet us before applying.
Certification: Reference on request.
Charity number: 232402

CAPE TRIBULATION TROPICAL RESEARCH STATION

PMB 5
Cape Tribulation
Queensland
4873 Australia

Tel: 00 61 7 4098 0063
Fax: 00 61 7 4098 0063 (Ring first)
e-mail: austrop@austrop.org.au
Web: www.austrop.org.au
Contact: Hugh Spencer

The Cape Tribulation Tropical Research

Station is a research and conservation organization specializing in lowland tropical ecosystems, and has been in operation since 1988. It is independent and non-affiliated, and is funded by the not-for-profit Australian Tropical Research Foundation. Station projects: Ecology of flying foxes (fruit bats) and their relatives; productivity and pollination of cluster figs; development of techniques for assisted regeneration of rainforests; development of appropriate technology for the wet tropics; rainforest and reef conservation; plus a variety of projects by researchers outside the Station. The area has a variety of habitats from coastal reefs to tropical rainforest. Volunteers assist in research and Station activities, from radio-tracking bats to counting figs and constructing Station buildings. All volunteers are expected to actively participate in the household activities of the Station. The facilities are relatively spartan. Interns pay US$20 a day (interns are only part-time volunteers, involved in specific research projects requiring input of staff time and equipment). Students pay US$25 per day (small volunteer component, the rest is research time). How to apply: First look at the website, especially the 'What's New?' pages which are fairly regularly updated. Look at the information on the Station itself and the current conservation activities. Determine whether you want to be a volunteer, an intern or a student. Then send a brief e-mail to the director, describing your interest, likely time of visiting and a brief résumé. E-mail is about the only way in which you can be guaranteed an answer. If you apply by letter send an international reply coupon and a SAE. If you don't hear from us, contact us again. (We are a small outfit and it is easy for correspondence to get lost.) The Station relies on solar power and cannot leave the fax on. If you wish to fax, call first and ask to send a fax.

Total projects worldwide: 1
Total UK projects: 0
Starting months: January–December.
Time required: 2–12 weeks.
Age requirement: 20 plus.
Causes: Animal welfare, conservation, environmental causes, wildlife.
Activities: Conservation skills, outdoor skills, research, scientific work, technical skills.
When to apply: All year.

Qualifications: Open, flexible attitude, willing actively to contribute to even the most mundane activity.
Health requirements: Nil.
Costs: US$15 per day plus transport to and from Cape Tribulation. This is at the volunteer's expense, although every reasonable effort will be made to find cheap or free transport.
Benefits: The cost covers food (lots) plus modest accommodation.
Worldwide placements: *Australasia* (Australia).

CARE – COTTAGE AND RURAL ENTERPRISES LIMITED
9 Weir Road
Kibworth
Leicester
Leicestershire
LE8 0LQ UK

Tel: +44 (0) 116 279 3225
Fax: +44 (0) 116 279 6384
Contact: Mr John Higgins, Director of HR and QA

CARE is concerned with giving support, through the provision of residential accommodation and work facilities, to people who have a learning disability. This offers each person the opportunity to live a full and purposeful life. Volunteers with an offending background may be accepted depending upon the circumstances.

Total projects worldwide: 8 plus.
Total UK projects: 8 plus.
Starting months: January–December.
Time required: 4–52 weeks.
Age requirement: 18 plus.
Causes: Disabled (learning).
Activities: Arts/crafts, caring (general, day and residential), cooking, gardening/horticulture, visiting/befriending.
Vols under 26 placed each year: Varies.
When to apply: All year.
Work alone/with others: Volunteers provide help to staff assisting those with learning disabilities.
Volunteers with disabilities: CARE operates an Equal Opportunities policy.
Qualifications: Good Communication Skills.
Health requirements: Nil.
Costs: None.
Benefits: Board, accommodation and full insurance provided, plus £30 per week pocket

money.

Training: All volunteers go through a full induction process before commencement of any duties.

Supervision: All volunteers would have a nominated supervisor who would carry out regular supervision.

Interview details: Interviews take place in the local community.

Certification: Reference on request.

Charity number: 250058

UK placements: *England* (Devon, Kent, Lancashire, Leicestershire, Northumberland, Shropshire, W. Sussex, Wiltshire).

CARE AND RELIEF FOR THE YOUNG (CRY)
Unit 4
Stirling House
Hedge End
Southampton
Hampshire
SO30 4AA UK

Tel: +44 (0) 1489 788300
Fax: +44 (0) 1489 790750
e-mail: ukoffice@cry.org.uk
Web: www.cry.org.uk
Contact: David Farndale

Care and Relief for the Young (CRY) is a Christian charity. After the downfall of Romanian dictator Nicolae Ceausescu in December 1989, pictures that shocked the world revealed thousands of neglected and abandoned children living in appalling conditions in Romanian state orphanages. Pictures that left permanent scars in most human minds – warehouses for bodies. Many of these dispossessed children still live in stark state institutions or on the streets – inhabiting the sewers, underground heating systems and Metro service tunnels of major cities. Many are killing themselves by sniffing glue to stave off hunger pangs, others sell their bodies to the preying paedophiles for a few coins. CRY has designed and initiated a long-term childcare project – a unique working partnership with the local authorities. CRY's Casa Robin Hood project in Bucharest provides a residential home for up to 60 children in small family units; a childcare training programme for Romanian childcare workers; a vocational training programme with micro business centre and street outreach. A 'model' children's home is much needed as a catalyst for improving Romanian child care methods and policy. The long-term goal is to equip Romanian people to take responsibility themselves. Casa Robin Hood, set in 3/4 acre of grounds, has been completely refurbished at a cost of £400,000. Opportunities exist for volunteers who are able to give six months or more of their time in Romania, 'living in' at the Centre. There are occasional places on DIY work parties. You can visit our website.

Total projects worldwide: 1
Total UK projects: 1
Starting months: January–December.
Time required: 12–52 weeks (plus).
Age requirement: 21 plus.
Causes: Children, poor/homeless, teaching/assisting (EFL), work camps – seasonal, young people.
Activities: Administration, arts/crafts, caring (general and residential), community work, computers, cooking, DIY, first aid, gardening/horticulture, group work, international aid, manual work, marketing/publicity, music, newsletter/journalism, outdoor skills, religion, research, social work, summer camps, technical skills, theatre/drama, training, visiting/befriending, work camps – seasonal.
Vols under 26 placed each year: 40 of a total of 50.
When to apply: All year.
Work alone/with others: With staff/volunteers.
Volunteers with disabilities: Possible, but stairs to climb and working with ex-street children can be hard work!
Qualifications: Active Christian commitment.
Health requirements: Yes – as medical support is limited in Bucharest, we issue a detailed health form.
Costs: £180 per month of stay must be prepaid before departure, £130 of this is paid back locally. Travel (air fare approximately £250 return) plus insurance and visa.
Benefits: Costs cover just about everything; the £130 paid back is pocket money and for off-duty food. All other costs covered by the £50 we retain.
Training: All volunteers receive a comprehensive pack and cultural awareness dialogue.
Supervision: By group leaders and home director.
Interview details: Once prospective volunteers

have passed initial screening and telephone call, interviews usually take place in Southampton or Scunthorpe.
Certification: Reference or certificate provided.
Charity number: 1011513
Worldwide placements: *Europe* (Romania).
UK placements: *England* (Hampshire).

CAREFORCE
35 Elm Road
New Malden
Surrey
KT3 3HB UK

Tel: +44 (0) 20 8942 3331
Fax: +44 (0) 20 8942 3331
e-mail: enquiry@careforce.co.uk
Web: www.careforce.co.uk
Contact: The Reverend Ian Prior

Careforce serves evangelical churches and organizations by placing Christian volunteers aged 18–25 where their help is most needed in the UK and Ireland. Careforce enables volunteers to offer themselves to serve God in an area of need for a year alongside local Christians. Careforce placements include: serving with local churches; youth and schools work; evangelistic outreach; serving people who are homeless; drug/alcohol related problems; have a physical disability or learning difficulties; are from families facing difficulty; supporting the elderly. Volunteers with an offending background are accepted.

Total projects worldwide: 1
Total UK projects: 150 per year.
Starting months: September.
Time required: 44–52 weeks.
Age requirement: 18–25
Causes: Addicts/Ex-addicts, Aids/HIV, children, disabled (learning and physical), elderly people, inner city problems, offenders/ex-offenders, poor/homeless, teaching/assisting (nursery, primary, secondary), young people.
Activities: Administration, arts/crafts, caring (general, day and residential), community work, development issues, DIY, music, outdoor skills, religion, social work, sport, teaching, training, visiting/befriending.
Vols under 26 placed each year: 150
When to apply: Any time. Interviews held February–August for UK based applicants. 28 February for applicants outside the UK.
Work alone/with others: Mainly placed as

one volunteer within a team of local workers.
Volunteers with disabilities: Possible.
Qualifications: Committed Christians.
Health requirements: Nil.
Costs: Travel cost to interview. Insurance of personal possessions.
Benefits: Board and lodging, insurance (death or permanent injury, and motor where relevant) and travel plus £30 per week pocket money.
Training: Careforce holds an induction course for all volunteers at the start of year, otherwise local induction training is given by placement. Volunteers also attend two national Careforce conferences during their year.
Supervision: Each volunteer has a work supervisor on placement and an area Careforce staff worker is attached to all volunteers for the year.
Nationalities accepted: No restrictions but those from overseas need to be commended by their church leader.
Interview details: Interviews are conducted at various UK based centres.
Charity number: 279443
Worldwide placements: *Europe* (Ireland).
UK placements: *England* (throughout); *Scotland* (throughout); *Northern Ireland* (throughout); *Wales* (throughout).

CARIBBEAN VOLUNTEER EXPEDITIONS
Box 388
Corning
New York 14830
USA

Tel: 00 1 607 962 7846
Fax: 00 1 607 936 1153
e-mail: ahershcve@aol.com
Web: www.cvexp.org
Contact: Ann Hersh

Caribbean Volunteer Expeditions needs volunteers to document, measure and photograph historic buildings in the Caribbean. Throughout the Caribbean we find many deteriorated historic structures. Other historic and architecturally valuable buildings are being torn down and replaced by more modern buildings. The purpose of Caribbean Volunteer Expeditions is to record and document these buildings and structures. Our effort adds information about styles, history, and architecture of the Caribbean.

And more importantly, we hope our work will encourage the preservation of important architectural and cultural heritage.

Starting months: January–December.
Time required: 1–2 weeks.
Age requirement: 17 plus.
Causes: Architecture, heritage.
Activities: Building/construction, computers, gardening/horticulture, library/resource centres, research.
Vols under 26 placed each year: Between 20 and 80.
When to apply: All year.
Work alone/with others: With others.
Volunteers with disabilities: Possible.
Qualifications: Nil but architecture, photography, surveying, preservation are helpful.
Health requirements: Nil.
Costs: Cost per trip = US$500–US$1,500. Registration fee US$150.
Benefits: Free or very inexpensive lodging.
Interview details: No interview necessary.
Charity number: 501 c3
Worldwide placements: *Central America* (Aruba, Bahamas, Barbados, Bermuda, Costa Rica, Dominica, Montserrat, Netherlands Antilles, Puerto Rico, Saint Christopher/Nevis, Saint Lucia, Saint Vincent/Grenadines, Trinidad and Tobago, Turks and Caicos Islands, Virgin Islands); *South America* (Guyana, Suriname).

CASA GUATEMALA
c/o Caring and Sharing
Market Cottages
Market Street
Hailsham
East Sussex
BN27 2AG UK

Tel: +44 (0) 1323 846696
Contact: Michael J. Upfield

Casa Guatemala cares for malnourished, abandoned, and orphaned children, providing them with a school, medical clinic and a farm. In particular the clinic needs a qualified doctor and nurse to volunteer for a minimum of six months. The school needs 2–4 volunteers to teach English and other subjects to pupils at early secondary level. Teachers must be fluent in Spanish. Other volunteers with experience in childcare are needed to work as nannies in the orphanage. All volunteers are expected to keep an open mind and become involved in the daily life of the centre and its daily chores. Teachers and agronomists are required for a minimum of one year. Applicants must meet very strict moral criteria.

Total projects worldwide: 1
Total UK projects: 0
Starting months: January–December.
Time required: 12–52 weeks.
Age requirement: 18 plus.
Causes: Children, health care/medical, poor/homeless, teaching/assisting (EFL), young people.
Activities: Arts/crafts, caring (general), music, sport, teaching.
Vols under 26 placed each year: 100
When to apply: All year.
Work alone/with others: With others.
Volunteers with disabilities: Not possible.
Qualifications: Spanish an advantage, enthusiasm, teaching or child care qualifications.
Equipment/clothing: Tropical clothes for rainforest region plus torch and batteries.
Health requirements: Relevant vaccinations, malaria pills and water purifying pills.
Costs: All costs.
Benefits: Bed and board.
Certification: Certificate or reference on request.
Worldwide placements: *Central America* (Guatemala).

CAT SURVIVAL TRUST, THE
The Centre
Codicote Road
Welwyn
Hertfordshire
AL6 9TU UK

Tel: +44 (0) 1438 716873
Fax: +44 (0) 1438 717535
Contact: Dr Terry Moore

The Cat Survival Trust is a charity for endangered species of wild cats and their environment.

Total projects worldwide: 1
Total UK projects: 1
Starting months: January–December.
Time required: 1–52 weeks.
Age requirement: 17 plus.
Causes: Animal welfare, conservation, environmental causes, wildlife.

Activities: Administration, conservation skills, DIY, fundraising, gardening/horticulture, library/resource centres, research, teaching.
When to apply: All year.
Work alone/with others: With others.
Volunteers with disabilities: Limited access.
Qualifications: Nil.
Equipment/clothing: Outdoor clothes.
Costs: All costs including travel for Argentina.
Benefits: Accommodation, electricity, heating and basic food in UK.
Worldwide placements: *South America* (Argentina).
UK placements: *England* (Hertfordshire).

CATHEDRAL CAMPS
16 Glebe Avenue
Flitwick
Bedfordshire
MK45 1HS UK

Tel: +44 (0) 1525 716237
Fax: +44 (0) 1525 716237
e-mail: admin@cathedralcamps.org.uk
Web: www.cathedralcamps.org.uk
Contact: Mrs Shelley Bent

Cathedral Camps undertakes the conservation and restoration of cathedrals and major parish churches and their environments, including tasks that have hitherto been postponed because of a lack of resources. Volunteers are needed to work in groups of 15–25 people throughout the country.

Total projects worldwide: 24
Total UK projects: 24
Starting months: July–September.
Time required: 1–2 weeks.
Age requirement: 16–30
Causes: Conservation, heritage, work camps – seasonal.
Activities: Building/construction, conservation skills, work camps – seasonal.
Vols under 26 placed each year: 400 of a total of 500.
When to apply: February–July prior to camp starting.
Work alone/with others: With others.
Volunteers with disabilities: Possible.
Qualifications: Nil.
Equipment/clothing: All equipment provided.
Health requirements: Fit.
Costs: £55 per week towards the cost of camp, board and lodging. Travel insurance if required.

Benefits: Can be used towards Gold Duke of Edinburgh Award. The scheme is insured and volunteers are covered by public liability.
Supervision: By camp leaders and staff at the camp.
Interview details: No interview necessary but we require a reference for their first camp.
Certification: Suitable for Gold Duke of Edinburgh's Award.
Charity number: 286248
UK placements: *England* (throughout); *Scotland* (throughout); *Northern Ireland* (throughout); *Wales* (throughout).

CCM YOUTH ORGANIZATION
PO Box 19989
Dar es Salaam
Tanzania

Tel: 00 255 51 150644 / 151064
Contact: Kipepe Samson

CCM Youth Organization projects are conducted in different places, especially in cold areas of Tanzania, in mountain places. Most of our activities are picking tea, coffee, visiting potential areas etc.

Total projects worldwide: 25
Total UK projects: 0
Starting months: July–September.
Time required: 2–4 weeks.
Age requirement: 14–35
Causes: Animal welfare, archaeology, architecture, health care/medical, inner city problems, teaching/assisting (nursery, secondary, mature, EFL), unemployed, wildlife, work camps – seasonal, young people.
Activities: Agriculture/farming, arts/crafts, building/construction, community work, gardening/horticulture, group work, manual work, outdoor skills, social work, sport, summer camps, teaching, training, visiting/befriending, work camps – seasonal.
Vols under 26 placed each year: 50–100
When to apply: December/January.
Work alone/with others: With others.
Volunteers with disabilities: We are unable to place people with disabilities as most of our activities involve physical work.
Qualifications: English language essential. Any other qualifications are a bonus.
Equipment/clothing: Tanzania has equatorial and tropical climate.
Health requirements: Physically and mentally fit.

Costs: At least US$200 for registration fees. We assist with accommodation and local transport.
Benefits: Help with accommodation, medical care, health insurance and internal transport.
Training: A general introduction is given pre-placement.
Supervision: Work camp supervisors.
Worldwide placements: *Africa* (Tanzania).

CEDAM INTERNATIONAL
One Fox Road
Croton-on-Hudson
NY 10520 USA

Tel: 00 1 914 271 5365
Fax: 00 1 914 271 4723
e-mail: cedam@bestweb.net
Web: www.cedam.org
Contact: Susan Sammon, Director

Cedam International is a non-profit agency organizing marine expeditions to tropical locations such as Mexico, the Seychelles, the Galapagos, Kenya, Australia, Belize etc. Cedam International focuses principally on conservation, environmental education and marine research, with expert divers, photographers and biologists undertaking marine research activities. Volunteers can participate in these expeditions for short-term periods. Those with scuba qualifications or skills in underwater video/photography are welcome to apply, though these skills are not essential. Expeditions are made up of teams of volunteers, scientists, divers etc. and therefore a team spirit is required.

Starting months: January–December.
Time required: 1–2 weeks.
Age requirement: 12 plus.
Causes: Conservation, environmental causes, heritage.
Activities: Conservation skills, manual work, outdoor skills, sport.
Costs: US$1,500–US$4,000 depending on location.

CENTRAL COUNCIL OF PHYSICAL RECREATION
Francis House
Francis Street
London
SW1P 1DE UK

Tel: +44 (0) 20 7828 3163
Fax: +44 (0) 20 7630 8820
e-mail: rtulley@bst.org.uk
Web: www.thebritishsportstrust.org.uk
Contact: Mr R. Tulley

The Central Council of Physical Recreation (CCPR) is the parent body that represents the national governing bodies of sport in the UK. In 1981 it launched the community sports leader award (CSLA) with the aim of training volunteers to assist in the organization of safe and purposeful activities. The CCPR set up a charity 'The British Sports Trust' which now administers four sports leader awards within one scheme. Schools, colleges, local authorities, youth associations and prisons are the main users of the following awards: 1. Junior Sports Leader Award. 14 years plus. Predominantly used in schools. 2. Community Sports Leader Award. 16 years plus. 3. Basic Expedition Leader Award. 18 years plus, leadership in the outdoors. 4. Hanson Higher Leader Award. 18 years plus specializing in certain areas e.g. special needs, sports administration.

Total projects worldwide: 2,600
Total UK projects: 2,600
Starting months: January–December.
Time required: 1–52 weeks (plus).
Age requirement: 14 plus.
Causes: Children, conservation, disabled (learning and physical), elderly people, offenders/ex-offenders, teaching/assisting (nursery, primary, secondary), unemployed, young people.
Activities: Community work, conservation skills, development issues, outdoor skills, sport, summer camps, teaching.
Vols under 26 placed each year: 26,000 of a total of 48,000.
When to apply: All year.
Work alone/with others: Both.
Volunteers with disabilities: Possible.
Qualifications: Nil.
Equipment/clothing: Safe sporting clothes and footwear.
Health requirements: Nil.
Costs: Award 1: £5, Award 2: £10, Award 3: £20 and Award 4: £20. Fees include third party liability insurance for a one-year period.
Training: Strongly recommended for tutors of courses.
Supervision: As part of our courses our volunteers work with sports/youth clubs. They are supervised by the coaches/youth

workers.
Certification: Nationally recognized
certificate.
Charity number: 299810
UK placements: *England* (throughout);
Scotland (throughout); *Northern Ireland*
(throughout); *Wales* (throughout).

CENTRE 63
Old Hall Lane
Kirkby
Merseyside
L32 5TH UK

Tel: +44 (0) 151 549 1494
Contact: Dave Coates

Centre 63 was set up in 1963. Volunteers are
very welcome to work as part of a team in an
innovative go-ahead youth organization
working in a disadvantaged estate in North
Merseyside. Volunteers with an offending
background may be accepted depending on
the offence.

Total projects worldwide: 2
Total UK projects: 2
Starting months: January–December.
Time required: 1–52 weeks.
Age requirement: 18 plus.
Causes: Addicts/Ex-addicts, children, health
care/medical, inner city problems, poor/
homeless, unemployed, young people.
Activities: Administration, arts/crafts,
community work, fundraising, group work,
newsletter/journalism, outdoor skills, social
work, sport, summer camps, visiting/
befriending.
Vols under 26 placed each year: 5–10
When to apply: All year.
Work alone/with others: With others.
Volunteers with disabilities: Possible.
Qualifications: Sense of humour and good
command of English.
Health requirements: Nil.
Costs: Nil.
Benefits: Travel expenses and lunch.
Interview details: Applicants are interviewed
in Kirkby.
Certification: Certificate and reference on
request.
Charity number: 700064
UK placements: *England* (Merseyside).

CENTRE DE RESERCHES
ARCHEOLOGIQUES (CNRS)
1 Place Aristide Briand

F-92195 Meudon Cedex
France

Tel: 00 33 1 45 07 50 04
Contact: M.F. Audouze

Centre de Reserches Archeologiques needs
volunteers to help in the archaeological
excavation of an upper paleolithic settlement
in Picardy. Work eight hours a day, six days
a week.

Starting months: July.
Time required: 3–52 weeks.
Age requirement: 14 plus.
Causes: Archaeology, conservation,
environmental causes, heritage.
Activities: Conservation skills, manual work,
research, scientific work, technical skills.
Vols under 26 placed each year: 5
When to apply: All year but as early as
possible.
Work alone/with others: With others.
Qualifications: French speaking and
archaeological experience.
Benefits: Board and accommodation free.
Worldwide placements: *Europe* (France).

CENTRE FOR ALTERNATIVE
TECHNOLOGY
Machynlleth
Powys
SY20 9AZ Wales

Tel: +44 (0) 1654 702400
Fax: +44 (0) 1654 702782
e-mail: cat@gn.apc.org
Contact: Rick Dance

Centre for Alternative Technology: before you
apply, please think about why you want to
come and what we have to offer. The
Volunteer Programme is not a course, and we
do not give any formal training or
instruction. Conditions are far from
luxurious. You will have the chance to learn
and experience what we are doing through
working, talking to people, consulting
information material and the bookshop, etc.
It is very much up to you. A variety of
different work tasks are undertaken in each
volunteer week and an element of flexibility
is essential (especially dependent on the
weather!). Sometimes you may simply be
asked to help with whatever jobs are most
urgent at the time. You may imagine that we
spend all our time erecting windmills or
building solar panels, but actually most of

the work we do is pretty ordinary: digging holes and barrowing rocks about, fixing leaks, cooking, cleaning, typing, answering letters, removing slugs. No animals or illegal drugs. If bringing children, please bring a friend to look after them whilst you are working. Try to arrive on Monday, not Sunday. No work is organized for volunteers at the weekend but you may stay through until the following Monday. Travel to Machynlleth is easy by car, train, bus or thumb. From there the three mile walk to the Centre (on the Dolgellau road, A487) can be enjoyable, especially along the back road if you can find it. Buses run erratically to nearby Pantperthog Monday–Saturday. If arriving in Machynlleth in the day, call at the Centre's 'Quarry Shop' in the main street, in case anyone can give you a lift to the Centre. If stuck, telephone the Centre! Volunteers with an offending background may be accepted since we never ask in advance!

Total projects worldwide: 1
Total UK projects: 1
Starting months: March–September.
Time required: 1–2 weeks.
Age requirement: 18 plus.
Causes: Environmental causes.
Activities: Building/construction, cooking, gardening/horticulture, manual work.
Vols under 26 placed each year: 70
When to apply: As early in the year as possible.
Work alone/with others: With others.
Volunteers with disabilities: No, regrettably.
Qualifications: Nil.
Equipment/clothing: Strong work clothes, waterproof clothes, wellingtons, sleeping bag/bedding.
Health requirements: Nil.
Costs: Short-term volunteers come to help and are asked to contribute for bed and board – £5 (waged) or £4 (low-waged and claimants) per week day, and £6/£5 per weekend day.
Benefits: Shared accommodation, food, drinks, soap, shampoo, toothpaste, tampons, etc. provided.
Interview details: No interview necessary.
Certification: Arranged if requested.
Charity number: 265239
UK placements: *Wales* (Powys).

CENTRE FOR ENVIRONMENT AND DEVELOPMENT

Godicherla Post
via Payakaraopeta
Visakhapatnam District
Andhra Pradesh
531 126 India

Tel: 00 91 8854 53664
Fax: 00 91 891 563704
e-mail: vijaylaxmicead@yahoo.com
Contact: Ms G. Vijayalaxmi and Mr G.S.P. Kumar

Centre for Environment and Development (CEAD) is a women's development organization which was established by a group of educated women from remote rural areas. These women had gone through the problems/disadvantages in their area, observing the situation since childhood and they decided to form CEAD in order to take action. CEAD strives to develop issues like literacy, the rights of the girl-child, land development, watershed, animal and human health, savings, access to credit, gender balance and equality, women's rights, communication and media. CEAD's mission is to eliminate extreme poverty by empowering the rural poor women through a process of social mobilization combined with creating opportunities for self-reliance. CEAD identifies crucial development issues and evolves a strategy to build local bodies to be effective in the respective areas. Issues of local areas are identified, followed up and training programmes are held to improve planning, implementation, administration, finance, organizational and individual skills. Our objectives are to sensitize members to the issue of self-esteem and dignity of work, to eliminate the middlemen's control and to secure greater bargaining power in the market. We undertake to explore land/livestock-based activities that will generate sources of income for the people in our target areas. The Nakkapalli and Payakaraopeta areas are continuously affected by drought and Nakkapalli is one of the most backward areas in the district. People are totally landless or with marginal land. Most people migrate to other neighbouring districts in search of a livelihood. Women and children are the worst sufferers.

Total projects worldwide: 2
Total UK projects: 0

Starting months: January–December.
Time required: 2–12 weeks.
Age requirement: 15 plus.
Causes: Aids/HIV, animal welfare, children, disabled (learning and physical), elderly people, environmental causes, health care/medical, human rights, poor/homeless, teaching/assisting (nursery, primary, secondary, mature).
Activities: Community work, computers, counselling, development issues, forestry, fundraising, gardening/horticulture, group work, international aid, newsletter/journalism, outdoor skills, research, scientific work, social work, theatre/drama, training, translating.
Vols under 26 placed each year: 25–50
When to apply: All year.
Work alone/with others: With others usually.
Volunteers with disabilities: Possible.
Qualifications: Interest in working with the poorest. Experience in animal, documentation, teaching, computer education and management a bonus.
Equipment/clothing: Casual cottons during summer and light wool mix in winter.
Health requirements: Nil. CEAD will provide boiled drinking water free or bottled mineral water and soft drinks at nominal cost.
Costs: Travel, pocket money. Board and lodging for £3 a day.
Benefits: Travel costs within the project will be reimbursed. The cost of board and lodging covers unlimited amounts of tea and coffee, Indian or continental breakfast, lunch and dinner of vegetables with mutton, chicken or fish.
Interview details: No interviews necessary.
Certification: Certificate or reference on request.
Worldwide placements: *Asia* (India).

CENTRO CAMUNO DI STUDI PREISTORICI

Via Marconi 7
25044 Capo di Ponte
Brescia
Italy

Tel: 00 390 364 42091
Fax: 00 390 364 42572
e-mail: ccsp@tin.it
Web: www.globalnet.it/ccsp/ccsp.htm
Contact: Director's Office

Centro Camuno di Studi Preistorici is a research institute concentrating on the study of prehistory and primitive art, with field projects in Europe, the Near East, Asia and Africa, and run by a non-profit-making cultural association. Volunteers are needed to participate in the exploration of sites and also for assisting in laboratory, archives and library. Skilled volunteers in computer editing, graphics, topography, photography and translations are welcome. There are projects all year long in Valcamonica, Italy; from March–April in the Negev Desert, Israel; and from August–September in the Helanshan Mountains, Ningxia, China or in Oceania. For additional information visit our other website: www.rockart-ccsp.com. There is a special page on volunteering.

Total projects worldwide: 4
Total UK projects: 0
Starting months: January–December.
Time required: 12–52 weeks.
Age requirement: 18 plus.
Causes: Archaeology, heritage, work camps – seasonal.
Activities: Arts/crafts, computers, fundraising, library/resource centres, manual work, newsletter/journalism, research, scientific work, summer camps, teaching, technical skills, training, translating, work camps – seasonal.
Vols under 26 placed each year: 12 of a total of 50.
When to apply: January, April, July, October.
Work alone/with others: Both.
Volunteers with disabilities: Possible, with specific skills.
Qualifications: Deep interest in archaeology, primitive art, anthropology or history of religions.
Equipment/clothing: Casual clothes.
Health requirements: Health insurance and good health.
Costs: All, including board, lodging, local travel and insurance (health and accident).
Benefits: Knowledge and experience in prehistoric and primitive art and experience in the field.
Training: Reading a list of brochures.
Supervision: Each volunteer has a supervisor who follows up his/her work.
Interview details: Centro Camuno di Studi Preistorici.
Certification: Certificate or reference provided.

Worldwide placements: *Africa* (Egypt, Morocco); *Asia* (China, Israel, Jordan); *Australasia* (Australia, Oceania); *Europe* (Azerbaijan, France, Italy).

CENTRO DE ATENCION INTEGRAL 'PIÑA PALMERA' A.C.
Apdo Postal 109
Carretera hacia Mazunte s/n, Playa Zipolite
Pochutla
Oaxaca
70900 Mexico

Tel: 00 52 958 40342 and 43113
Fax: 00 52 958 40342 and 43113
e-mail: pinapalmera@laneta.apc.org
Web: www.laneta.apc.org/pina/
Contact: Anna Johansson de Cano and/or the Volunteer Co-ordinator

Piña Palmera is a resource and rehabilitation centre for disabled people, principally children, in a little village, Zipolite. Volunteers with some sort of medical skill, such as doctors, nurses, occupational therapists, physiotherapists, pedagogists, kindergarten teachers and psychologists are always needed. Volunteers with experience in building and construction are also badly needed after the hurricane. Help is particularly needed from March to September as this is when we generally have fewer volunteers. We work with community-based rehabilitation in surrounding communities. There is also a programme for lifeguards on the beach and we need experienced lifeguards and instructors in CPR.

Total projects worldwide: 1
Total UK projects: 0
Starting months: January–December.
Time required: 26–52 weeks.
Age requirement: 18 plus.
Causes: Children, disabled (learning and physical), health care/medical, human rights, teaching/assisting (primary), young people.
Activities: Administration, agriculture/farming, arts/crafts, building/construction, caring (general and residential), community work, computers, cooking, counselling, development issues, DIY, driving, first aid, fundraising, gardening/horticulture, group work, library/resource centres, manual work, music, newsletter/journalism, outdoor skills, social work, sport, summer camps, teaching, technical skills, theatre/drama, training, translating.

Vols under 26 placed each year: 6–12 of a total of 10–20.
When to apply: 6 months in advance.
Work alone/with others: With others.
Volunteers with disabilities: Volunteers with disabilities welcomed.
Qualifications: Fluent spoken Spanish. Medical skills plus rehabilitation experience particularly welcome.
Equipment/clothing: Very hot climate so light clothes recommended.
Health requirements: Imperative to bring all own medicines and to have appropriate vaccinations.
Costs: Travel costs, insurance (including full medical cover) and personal expenses.
Benefits: Accommodation, food and cost of visa if volunteer stays for at least 1 year.
Training: Upon arrival, volunteers go through an introduction period of about one week.
Supervision: There is a co-ordinator in each area and a co-ordinator for the volunteers.
Interview details: No interview necessary.
Certification: Reference on request.
Worldwide placements: *Central America* (Mexico).

CENTRO STUDI TERZO MONDO
Via G.B.Morgagni 39
20129 Milan
Italy

Tel: 00 390 2 2940 9041
Fax: 00 390 2 2940 9041
e-mail: melotti.uml@iol.it
Contact: The Director

Centro Studi Terzo Mondo was founded in 1962 and works on development projects in many countries throughout the developing world. We recruit approximately 25 volunteers a year to work as teachers, community development workers, doctors, nurses and project leaders. Qualifications are an asset but not always required. We do, however, expect volunteers to be motivated and committed towards their work. Volunteers are expected to work at least 36 hours a week. Volunteers with an offending background are accepted.

Total projects worldwide: 13
Total UK projects: 0
Starting months: January–December.
Time required: 2–52 weeks.
Age requirement: 18 plus.

Causes: Health care/medical, teaching/assisting.
Activities: Administration, caring (general), community work, development issues, research, teaching, training.
Vols under 26 placed each year: 25
When to apply: All year.
Work alone/with others: Both.
Qualifications: Any qualifications an asset.
Health requirements: Depending on location.
Costs: Occasionally board and lodging not provided. Travel if stay less than 6 months. Insurance.
Benefits: Usually board and accommodation plus US$100 per week. Volunteers who commit themselves for longer than 6 months will also have their travel expenses paid.
Interview details: Volunteer applicants are only interviewed in special cases and this would be in Rome or Milan, or occasionally in volunteer's town.
Worldwide placements: *Africa* (Angola, Cape Verde, Chad, Ethiopia, Mauritius, Mozambique, Tanzania); *Asia* (India, Indonesia); *Europe* (Italy); *South America* (Brazil, Ecuador, Peru).

CHALCS
Unit 16
9 Harrogate Road
Tech North
Leeds
West Yorkshire
LS7 3NB UK

Tel: +44 (0) 113 262 3892
Fax: +44 (0) 113 295 9596
e-mail: rita@Kingston44.freeserve.co.uk
Contact: Rita Kingston

CHALCS (Chapeltown and Harehills Assisted Learning Computer School) is a seven-day week school, opening evenings and weekends, to help inner city children from the areas of Chapeltown and Harehills. The school uses computers to encourage children to achieve their full educational potential, and all usual curriculum subjects are taught. The children range in age from 7 to 18, and GCSE and A-level support is also given. The school has 590 children attending each week and there is a waiting list of over 400. In addition to computer classes a basic literacy scheme is run to help children reach their correct reading age before moving on to the more advanced computer classes. This scheme is

operated by volunteers, and more are urgently needed if we are to match demand for the classes. Children here range from 6–13 and all are behind with their reading, spelling and arithmetic. Volunteers supported by a qualified teacher run classes to help children reach their correct level of literacy. These classes operate on Thursday evenings between 6.00 p.m. and 8.00 p.m. and our volunteers come from a wide range of backgrounds. Volunteers with an offending background would not be accepted if offence is connected with children.

Total projects worldwide: 1
Total UK projects: 1
Starting months: January–December.
Time required: 13–52 weeks.
Age requirement: 16 plus.
Causes: Children, inner city problems, teaching/assisting (primary, secondary).
Activities: Computers, group work, teaching.
When to apply: All year.
Work alone/with others: With others.
Volunteers with disabilities: Possible if able to read, write and help others. Disabled facilities available.
Qualifications: Interest in developing children.
Health requirements: Nil.
Costs: Nil except travel costs to the school.
Benefits: Training given. We provide insurance.
Training: On the job, and ongoing throughout the term.
Supervision: By a qualified teacher.
Interview details: All volunteers are police checked and interviewed at our address.
Certification: Reference. NVQ Level 3 accreditation available if required.
Charity number: 1001323

CHANGING WORLDS
11 Doctors Lane
Chaldon
Surrey
CR3 5AE UK

Tel: +44 (0) 1883 340960
Fax: +44 (0) 1883 330783
e-mail: welcome@changingworlds.co.uk
Web: www.changingworlds.co.uk
Contact: Roger Salwey, Director

Changing Worlds is a small organization run by a former director of another gap-year organization and an ex-VSO teacher. On offer are voluntary work assignments in

Tanzania, Zimbabwe, India and Nepal. Most of the placements involve teaching in secondary schools. We were founded to enable volunteers to gain a full understanding of the communities they will be part of and hope volunteers will forge lifelong ties with these schools and other projects. Most placements run from September and January for three or six months. Whilst in the host country, volunteers are backed up by the Changing Worlds representative who will help with any problems volunteers experience and will source suitable placements. Representatives are usually expatriates who are selected for their local knowledge and an understanding of life as a volunteer. We look for determined and adaptable volunteers who can get on with others. Basic teaching techniques are covered at the residential weekend. Most volunteers are 18–25 although older applicants are welcomed. A Changing Worlds placement can be used as part of the service section of The Duke of Edinburgh Award scheme and is well regarded by employers and universities.

Total projects worldwide: 4–6
Total UK projects: 0
Starting months: January, March, September.
Time required: 12–26 weeks.
Age requirement: 18–35
Causes: Teaching/assisting (primary, secondary), young people.
Activities: Caring (general), catering, development issues, group work, manual work, teaching, training.
Vols under 26 placed each year: 25 of a total of 30.
When to apply: Not less than 8 weeks before departure.
Work alone/with others: With others.
Volunteers with disabilities: Not possible.
Qualifications: A-levels and spoken English. Volunteers are expected to undertake some pre-departure research and have a basic understanding of the language.
Health requirements: Nil.
Costs: Prices range from £1,495 to £1,875 (which includes a 12-month open air ticket) plus insurance £130, plus subsistence £200, plus innoculations £50, plus visa £0–40 plus pocket money. We have our own comprehensive insurance package which we encourage volunteers to take out for the entire duration of their placement.
Benefits: The cost includes flight, pre-departure briefings, meeting on arrival and transport to placement, accommodation and representative.
Training: A pre-departure weekend is held when volunteers are fully briefed on the country of their destination and teaching on vocational training.
Supervision: We employ in-country representatives who welcome volunteers to the country, take them to their placements and visit them.
Nationalities accepted: No restrictions but volunteers need to speak English.
Interview details: Prospective volunteers are interviewed in Caterham, Surrey, where they take part in some team exercises. We also assess written references.
Certification: Reference on request.
Worldwide placements: *Africa* (Tanzania); *Asia* (India, Nepal).

CHANTIERS DE JEUNES PROVENCE/CÔTE D'AZUR

7 Avenue Pierre de Coubertin
La Bocca
06150 France

Tel: 00 33 4 93 47 89 69
Fax: 00 33 4 93 48 12 01
e-mail: cjpca@club-internet.fr
Web: www.club-internet.fr/perso/cjpca
Contact: Stéphane Victorion

Chantiers de Jeunes Provence/Côte D'Azur needs volunteers to take part in the restoration and environmental protection of historic monuments. Projects consist of five hours' work in the morning and organized activities such as sailing, climbing and diving in the afternoons and evenings. French camps take place on Sainte-Margerite island near Cannes, in the Alpes or in Provence. Apply with an international reply coupon and a letter written in French. There are about 14 volunteers per camp and about 20 camps in the summer. Projects in Italy run all year. Volunteers with an offending background may be accepted depending on the offence.

Total projects worldwide: 6
Total UK projects: 1
Starting months: January–December.
Time required: 1–2 weeks.
Age requirement: 14–17
Causes: Archaeology, Architecture, Conservation, Environmental Causes, Heritage, Work Camps – Seasonal, Young

People.
Activities: Arts/crafts, building/construction, catering, conservation skills, manual work, music, sport, summer camps, work camps – seasonal.
Vols under 26 placed each year: 280, all under 18 years.
When to apply: All year.
Work alone/with others: With others – about 15 teenagers.
Volunteers with disabilities: Not possible.
Qualifications: A little French speaking.
Equipment/clothing: Suitable clothes and shoes for working.
Health requirements: Normal.
Costs: Approx FF2,000.
Benefits: Food, accommodation, insurance and activities.
Supervision: 3 professionals are always with young volunteers.
Nationalities accepted: No restrictions but volunteers must speak a little French.
Certification: A certificate for living collectively and for diving sports is provided.
Worldwide placements: *Europe* (France, Italy).
UK placements: *England* (London).

CHANTIERS D'ÉTUDES MEDIEVALES
4 rue du Tonnelet Rouge
F-67000 Strasbourg
France

Tel: 00 33 3 88 37 17 20
Fax: 00 33 3 88 37 17 20
e-mail: castrum@wanadoo.fr
Web: http://perso.wanadoo.fr/castrum
Contact: Mélanie Rouviere

The aim of Chantiers d'Études Medievales is to organize voluntary work centres for youngsters. These working sites are devoted to the study and restoration of monuments or sites which date back to the Middle Ages. The working sites are open to volunteers from all countries without discrimination, who work together to carry out a manual task they think useful to society as a whole. The Association is not a travel agency. We offer you an opportunity to meet other youngsters who share your goal. Through our specific operations on historic sites, you are offered not only physical exercise but cultural enrichment as well. You have an opportunity to give new social functions to the monuments you help to save: parks, cultural

centres, recreation centres, etc. The outstanding organization of the Association enables us to welcome all volunteers, previous acquaintance being unnecessary. Our reception is friendly and simple. For the last 15 years the Association has welcomed each summer about 100 volunteers from over 20 countries who are divided into 20 or 30 member teams. Through our experience we aim to preserve this human dimension in which individuals can still learn to know and appreciate one another.

Total projects worldwide: 4
Total UK projects: 0
Starting months: July, August.
Time required: 2–52 weeks.
Age requirement: 16–30
Causes: Archaeology, architecture, environmental causes, heritage, work camps – seasonal.
Activities: Building/construction, forestry, gardening/horticulture, summer camps, work camps – seasonal.
Vols under 26 placed each year: 70 of a total of 80.
When to apply: Before April.
Work alone/with others: With others.
Volunteers with disabilities: Not possible.
Qualifications: English or French speaking, capable of hard work.
Equipment/clothing: Old strong clothes.
Health requirements: Good health.
Costs: Approximately £55 covers board and basic accommodation for 15 days.
Benefits: Your financial contribution includes insurance, meals and lodging.
Interview details: No interview necessary.
Certification: Certificate of participation at the work camp on request.
Worldwide placements: *Europe* (France).

CHANTIERS HISTOIRE ET ARCHITECTURE MEDIEVALES (CHAM)
5 et 7 rue Guilleminot
75014 Paris
France

Tel: 00 33 1 43 35 15 51
Fax: 00 33 2 43 20 46 82
Contact: Rose-Méry Lafable

Chantiers Histoire et Architecture Medievales is dedicated to the conservation and restoration of medieval buildings around France. Founded in 1980, we organize permanent or seasonal volunteer sites across the country. We welcome any motivated volunteer who wishes to participate in historical heritage rescue and restoration. Volunteers work on a specific monument daily (for about six hours a day) with breaks. Qualified supervisors and technicians are on hand to give training.

Starting months: April, July, August, October, November.
Time required: 2–52 weeks.
Age requirement: 16 plus.
Causes: Architecture, conservation, heritage.
Activities: Building/construction, conservation skills, manual work.
Vols under 26 placed each year: 540 of a total of 600.
When to apply: As early as possible.
Work alone/with others: With others.
Qualifications: Some understanding of French.
Equipment/clothing: Sleeping bags, blankets and working clothes. Mat or airbed might also be useful.
Health requirements: Good health essential.
Costs: Travel expenses plus one contribution of FF200. Also FF65 per day for board/lodging.
Interview details: No interview necessary.
Worldwide placements: *Europe* (France).

CHESHIRE AND WIRRAL FEDERATION OF YOUTH CLUBS

17 Castle Street
Chester
Cheshire
CH1 2DS UK

Tel: +44 (0) 1244 325867
Fax: +44 (0) 1244 317506
e-mail: youthfed@aol.com
Contact: David Packwood

Cheshire and Wirral Federation of Youth Clubs needs volunteers to work in various youth clubs in disadvantaged housing estates and communities and to assist with a wide ranging programme of youth activities. There are some opportunities to work with Federation HQ team; other opportunities to work with a local youth group or project. The Federation will try to match people with the appropriate placement. Much work takes place during evenings, weekends and holidays. Unless the volunteer has financial support it is best to place local young people with local projects. We now have four

volunteer development workers based in Chester, East Cheshire, Walton and Wirral. Their role is to recruit, select and induct volunteers. They will also offer training and continue mentor support. Volunteers with offending backgrounds accepted depending on the offence.

Starting months: January–December.
Time required: 1–52 weeks.
Age requirement: 14 plus.
Causes: Addicts/Ex-addicts, disabled (learning and physical), elderly people, inner city problems, offenders/ex-offenders, poor/homeless, unemployed, young people.
Activities: Administration, arts/crafts, community work, counselling, driving, fundraising, group work, music, newsletter/journalism, outdoor skills, research, social work, sport, summer camps, visiting/befriending.
Vols under 26 placed each year: 1,200 of a total of 2,000.
When to apply: All year.
Work alone/with others: With others.
Volunteers with disabilities: Possible.
Qualifications: Dependent on project – enthusiasm and energy.
Health requirements: Nil.
Costs: Board and lodging.
Benefits: Expenses reimbursed and help to find accommodation if needed. All volunteers are covered by our insurance.
Training: 6-week induction training.
Supervision: On a monthly basis by development workers.
Interview details: Interviews take place in Chester.
Certification: Youth Achievement Awards (ASDAN). The work can be linked with NVQ qualification participation 'Certificate of Achievement'.
Charity number: 506539
UK placements: *England* (Cheshire, Merseyside).

CHESHIRE WILDLIFE TRUST

Grebe House
Reaseheath
Nantwich
Cheshire
CW5 6DG UK

Tel: +44 (0) 1270 610180
Fax: +44 (0) 1270 610430
Contact: Chris Mahon, The Director

Cheshire Wildlife Trust is the region's leading environmental conservation charity, incorporating Cheshire, Warrington, Halton, Tameside, Trafford, Stockport and Wirral. We safeguard local wildlife by: encouraging practical conservation involving local members; defending plant and animal communities against development through the planning system; caring for over 40 nature reserves covering more than 250 ha, including woodland, meadows, heathland, wetland, coastal dunes and much more; campaigning for wildlife and the environment; managing the county's database of over 400 sites of biological importance; providing advice on all aspects of nature conservation to local authorities, industry and business, farming and local communities; encouraging environmental education at all levels, and through WATCH, the Trust's junior wing.

Total projects worldwide: 20
Total UK projects: 20
Starting months: January–December.
Time required: 2–52 weeks (plus).
Age requirement: 14 plus.
Causes: Conservation, environmental causes, wildlife.
Activities: Agriculture/farming, building/construction, campaigning, conservation skills, forestry, fundraising, gardening/horticulture, library/resource centres, manual work, marketing/publicity, newsletter/journalism, research, scientific work.
Vols under 26 placed each year: 20
When to apply: As early as possible.
Work alone/with others: Both.
Volunteers with disabilities: Some – mostly office based research and design.
Qualifications: Varies, depending on the job.
Equipment/clothing: Nil, providing health and safety requirements are satisfied.
Health requirements: Nil, providing health and safety regulations are satisfied.
Costs: Nil.
Benefits: Expenses for work done in work time (mileage) and some small research costs.
Interview details: Prospective volunteers are interviewed at our office in Nantwich.
Certification: Reference on request.
Charity number: 214927
UK placements: *England* (Cheshire).

CHILDREN OF THE ANDES
4 Bath Place
Rivington Street

London
EC2A 3DR UK

Tel: +44 (0) 20 7739 1328
Fax: +44 (0) 20 7739 5743
e-mail: info@children-of-the-andes.org
Web: www.children-of-the-andes.org
Contact: Jenny Townsend, Administrator/Database Manager

Children of the Andes, a British Charity founded in 1991, is dedicated to improving the lives of street children and children at risk in Colombia. We also support Colombian non-governmental organizations working for the same objectives. We raise funds and awareness, distribute grants and assess and monitor projects. Our work falls into four main categories: rescue and rehabilitation of street children; education, training and therapy for displaced children and parents who have fled from political violence; work in shanty towns to prevent children resorting to the streets; provision for health care and special needs.

Total projects worldwide: 1
Total UK projects: 1
Starting months: January–December.
Time required: 12–52 weeks.
Age requirement: 20 plus.
Causes: Children.
Activities: Administration, computers, fundraising, research, translating.
Vols under 26 placed each year: 1 or 2 of a total of 5.
When to apply: All year.
Work alone/with others: Mainly with the staff.
Volunteers with disabilities: Possible.
Qualifications: Language ability, telephone, writing, communication skills, PC skills.
Health requirements: Nil.
Costs: Nil.
Benefits: Local transport and lunch, maximum £10 per day.
Training: We give our own training.
Supervision: Volunteers are supervised.
Interview details: In our offices.
Certification: Written reference.
UK placements: *England* (London).

CHILDREN ON THE EDGE
Watersmead
Littlehampton
West Sussex
BN17 6LS UK

Tel: +44 (0) 1903 850906
Fax: +44 (0) 1903 859296
e-mail: children_on_the_edge@bigfoot.com
Web: www.cote.org.uk
Contact: Suzanne Handsford

Children on the Edge, a project of The Body Shop Foundation, is involved in the refurbishment of orphanages, the running of healthcare programmes, playschemes and community work. Qualified volunteers are needed occasionally for up to a year. There are also 2–4 week opportunities for unskilled volunteers.

Total projects worldwide: Approximately 5.
Total UK projects: 0
Starting months: January–December.
Time required: 2–52 weeks.
Age requirement: 18 plus.
Causes: Children, disabled (learning and physical), elderly people, health care/medical, poor/homeless, refugees, teaching/assisting (primary, secondary), unemployed, young people.
Activities: Administration, arts/crafts, building/construction, caring (general, day and residential), community work, cooking, first aid, fundraising, group work, international aid, outdoor skills, social work, sport, summer camps, teaching, theatre/drama, translating.
Vols under 26 placed each year: 20 of a total of 40.
When to apply: All year but beginning of January for playscheme.
Work alone/with others: With others as part of a team.
Volunteers with disabilities: Possible – depends on location and working conditions.
Qualifications: Childcare professionals, art and play therapists, nurses.
Health requirements: Good health.
Costs: Playscheme volunteers: £1,000 for air fare, travel, insurance (we arrange insurance for UK volunteers), visa, accommodation, food and equipment for children.
Benefits: Chance to help children by taking part in play, art and sports activities during the summer playscheme.
Training: Briefed with information packs and videos.
Supervision: By core team on ground who lead sessions through.
Interview details: No interview necessary. Applicants will be assessed by an application form.
Charity number: 802757R
Worldwide placements: *Asia* (Indonesia); *Europe* (Albania, Bosnia-Herzegovina, Romania, Yugoslavia).

CHILDREN'S COUNTRY HOLIDAYS FUND
42–43 Lower Marsh
Tanswell Street
London
SE1 7RG UK

Tel: +44 (0) 20 7928 6522
Fax: +44 (0) 20 7401 3961
e-mail: cchf@dircon.co.uk
Web: www.childrensholidays-cchf.org
Contact: The Camps Co-ordinator

Children's Country Holidays Fund need volunteers to supervise small groups of London children in need under the direction of a camp leader, in purpose-built accommodation for the duration of an eight-day holiday camp. Volunteers are expected to participate in and supervise the organized activities and to take an interest in the well-being and happiness of these children, aged 8–12. Volunteers with offending backgrounds may be accepted, but not if child, sex or drug related. Each case is treated individually.

Total projects worldwide: 15–20
Total UK projects: 15–20
Starting months: July, August.
Time required: 1–3 weeks.
Age requirement: 18 plus.
Causes: Children, Poor/Homeless.
Activities: Arts/crafts, outdoor skills, sport, summer camps.
Vols under 26 placed each year: 38 of a total of 75.
When to apply: January – May.
Work alone/with others: With experienced leaders.
Volunteers with disabilities: Not possible.
Qualifications: Nil.
Health requirements: Nil.
Costs: Nil. Out-of-pocket expenses are refunded.
Benefits: Free travel, insurance, board, food and training plus £15 allowance on camp.
Training: Training weekend including child protection, anti-discrimination roles and responsibilities, a day in the life of a camp, working as a team, managing difficult behaviour.

Supervision: On camp by leader and deputy.
Nationalities accepted: Only applicants who are resident in England and Wales and have been so for 5 years are accepted.
Interview details: Applicants will need to attend for separate interview and training.
Certification: Supervision meeting the day after camp finishes.
Certificate or reference on request.
Charity number: 206958
UK placements: *England* (throughout); *Wales* (throughout).

CHILDREN'S EXPRESS (CE) UK
Exmouth House
3–11 Pine Street
London
EC1R 0JH UK

Tel: + 44 (0) 20 7833 2577
Fax: + 44 (0) 20 7278 7722
e-mail:
enquiries@childrensexpress.btinternet.com
Web: www.childrens-express.org
Contact: Joan A. Speers, Development Director

Children's Express is an out-of-school programme of learning and development through journalism for children aged 8 to 18. Our aim is to give young people the power and means to express themselves publicly on vital issues that affect them, and in the process to raise their self-esteem and develop their potential. CE reporters and editors research and report stories on subjects of their choice. They also accept commissions from newspapers and magazines. CE operates like a news agency by selling their stories to local, national and regional newspapers and magazines. Children's Express targets children aged 8 to 18 from inner-city areas, working with them after school, at weekends and during the holidays. The young people are the workforce, and take responsibility not only for their stories, but the way the programme is run. It is highly participatory. Every member is required to go through a one- or two-day induction programme, run by specially trained editors (aged 14–18). The younger children, aged 8–13, are the reporters; editors are older, aged 14–18. They take responsibility for editing and overseeing the editorial activities. They work in teams of five to develop the story angle and questions. Every aspect of the story, from basic interview to impressions afterwards, is tape-recorded. Not only does this mean that the programme is open to all, regardless of academic ability, but it encourages literacy, organization and good writing. In particular it reinforces numerous aspects of the National Curriculum. The journalists take an extraordinary degree of ownership into the process, from the initial story idea right through to seeing their names on the published article. They run the reporters' and editors' boards, determine which stories to follow, initiate research and interviews and work together in teams to realize their aims. They organize and run monthly meetings, quarterly training sessions and presentations. The adults in the programme make sure the whole process works. There are no academic requirements and no discrimination against those excluded from school or with an offending background.

Total projects worldwide: 4
Total UK projects: 4
Starting months: January–December.
Time required: 1–52 weeks (plus).
Age requirement: 12–18
Causes: Children, inner city problems, young people.
Activities: Administration, computers, development issues, fundraising, group work, marketing/publicity, newsletter/journalism, research, technical skills, translating.
Vols under 26 placed each year: 150 of a total of 300.
When to apply: All year.
Work alone/with others: Mainly in teams.
Volunteers with disabilities: No wheelchair access.
Qualifications: Enthusiasm.
Health requirements: Nil.
Costs: Nil.
Benefits: Expenses paid on all assignments.
Interview details: No interview necessary but there is an application form and a day's training required (delivered by teen trainers).
Certification: Certificate for training; investigating accreditation.
Charity number: 1043300
UK placements: *England* (London, Tyne and Wear, West Midlands, S. Yorkshire).

CHILD WELFARE SCHEME
30 Spirit Quay
Wapping
London

E1W 2UT UK

Tel: + 44 (0) 20 7488 4394
Fax: + 44 (0) 20 7488 4394
e-mail: triffid@compuserve.com
other e-mail: cws@wlink.cnet.com.np
Web: www.childwelfarescheme.org
Contact: Mrs T.J.E. Beaumont

CWS concentrates on rural and urban projects in Nepal. We have built our projects together with the local village people, achieving eight daycare/health centres in remote villages and a clinic in Pokhara. We are building a college and a hostel for boys and girls, which we hope to open for street children between the ages of 14 and 22 towards the end of 2001. A full-scale drinking water project and a smokeless stove project have also been established. Two tourist hotels have been set up to cover local overhead costs in order to create local sustainability and to ensure that all donations go straight to the physical creation of each project. The main aims and objectives are: to reduce infant mortality and create awareness in local rural communities on health issues and how to prevent simple illnesses and diseases; to introduce pre-primary education in a local culturally sustainable manner; improve domestic health in the local village mud houses; to provide a free medical health service for marginalized children and youths in urban areas; to form a bridge for marginalized youths to bring them back to society; to ensure projects are culturally and sustainably sound; to ensure that all donated funds go straight to where they are intended and not on so-called 'project costs'! We particularly need doctors, medical students and nurses. All volunteers help train and assist their Nepalese colleagues. The advice and experiences of the volunteers contribute to planning current and future programmes.

Total projects worldwide: 11
Total UK projects: 0
Starting months: January–December.
Time required: 16–40 weeks.
Age requirement: 25 plus.
Causes: Children, health care/medical, poor/homeless, teaching/assisting (nursery), young people.
Activities: Agriculture/farming, caring (general), community work, counselling, development issues, first aid, research, social work, teaching, technical skills.
Vols under 26 placed each year: 1 or 2 of a total of 9.
When to apply: All year but for August or September start, apply April–June.
Work alone/with others: Sometimes alone and sometimes with other young volunteers.
Volunteers with disabilities: Depends on the disability. Nepal is mountainous and not always easily accessible.
Qualifications: Doctors, medical students, nurses and any volunteers who are independent, flexible, able to take initiative, open to other cultures.
Health requirements: Volunteers must be fit and healthy as there is usually a lot of walking involved.
Costs: Travel to Nepal. Visa costs (first 2 months US$30, for each month thereafter $50 per month). Food and lodging and other miscellaneous costs (approximately US$175 per month). Volunteers are responsible for their own insurance.
Benefits: For volunteers who commit themselves for longer than 40 weeks, we pay all visa costs, board and lodging and local travel expenses.
Training: A 2-week introduction in Nepal before starting in the field project.
Supervision: Constant monitoring is done by the INGO (CWS and CWSN) and the NGO. Depending in which department you work, 1 supervisor and 1 monitor will be in constant contact.
Interview details: Interviews usually take place in London at the Secretariat.
Certification: Certificate or reference provided.
Charity number: 1061699
Worldwide placements: *Asia* (Nepal).

CHRISTIAN APPALACHIAN PROJECT
322 Crab Orchard Street
Lancaster
KY 40446 USA

Tel: 00 1 606 792 2219
Fax: 00 1 606 792 6625
Contact: Kathy Kluesener

Have an adventure in beautiful Appalachia! Come and volunteer for a year or a summer with the Christian Appalachian Project. We are a non-profit, interdenominational, service organization that assists people in Appalachia to become self-sufficient. More specifically, we serve economically, socially, and/or physically disadvantaged people in eastern Kentucky through programmes such as child development, adult education, home repair, elderly programmes, respite care, emergency outreach, summer camps, spouse abuse shelters, teen/youth centres and many more. Our volunteers live together sharing meals, prayer, and the challenge of fighting poverty as they support each other through their strong Christian motivation to serve people. Come join other volunteers from around the country who are putting their faith into action to fulfil a dream for Appalachia! Minimum age 18 for summer but 21 years for a one-year position.

Total projects worldwide: 1
Total UK projects: 0
Starting months: January–December.
Time required: 3–52 weeks.
Age requirement: 18 plus.
Causes: Children, disabled (learning and physical), elderly people, environmental causes, holidays for disabled, human rights, poor/homeless, teaching/assisting (nursery, mature), unemployed, young people.
Activities: Arts/crafts, building/construction, caring (general, day and residential), community work, cooking, counselling, driving, group work, manual work, social work, summer camps, teaching, visiting/befriending.
Vols under 26 placed each year: About 500.
When to apply: Minimum 7 months in advance for 3–20 week position, 4 months for 1 year.
Work alone/with others: Both.
Volunteers with disabilities: Possible.
Qualifications: English language, driving licence, openminded, flexible individuals.
Equipment/clothing: Depends on the job. Usually casual or rugged clothing. Not usually dress-up clothing.
Health requirements: Depends on individual case.
Costs: Return fare to Kentucky plus visa costs. Short-term volunteers must arrange their own insurance.
Benefits: Board and lodging. Long-term (1 year) volunteers receive US$100 per month, health insurance and loan deferment information.
Interview details: Prospective volunteers are interviewed in Kentucky.
Certification: Possible certificate or reference.

Worldwide placements: *North America* (USA).

CHRISTIAN FOUNDATION FOR CHILDREN AND AGING
1 Elmwood Avenue
Kansas City,
Kansas 66103-3719
USA

Tel: 00 1 800 875 6564/1 913 384 6500
Fax: 00 1 913 384 2211
e-mail: cfca@sky.net
Contact: Volunteer Director

Christian Foundation for Children and Aging (CFCA) is a sponsorship organization run by Catholic lay people striving to fulfil the educational, nutritional, healthcare and spiritual needs of poor children and ageing people throughout the world. CFCA volunteers strive to walk with and understand the plight of the poor. Responsibilities include teaching, translating (Spanish–English), childcare, healthcare, parish work. The religious affiliation is Catholic. All projects are for a minimum of 52 weeks except for some 26-week opportunities in India.

Starting months: January–December.
Time required: 26–52 weeks (plus).
Age requirement: 21 plus.
Causes: Children, disabled (learning and physical), elderly people, health care/medical, poor/homeless, teaching/assisting (nursery, primary, secondary, mature), young people.
Activities: Administration, arts/crafts, building/construction, caring (general, day and residential), community work, computers, cooking, fundraising, gardening/horticulture, group work, social work, teaching, translating.
Vols under 26 placed each year: 100
When to apply: All year.
Work alone/with others: Work with local religious community.
Volunteers with disabilities: Possible.
Qualifications: Desire to serve and live with the poor. Previous experience useful. Spanish/Portuguese for Latin America. If volunteers are not Catholic, they must be comfortable living in Catholic religious or lay communities.
Costs: Travel, insurance and living expenses. Volunteers recruit their own sponsors.
Benefits: Board and lodging.
Interview details: Volunteer candidates are

required to go to Kansas City, Kansas, USA for an interview/orientation.
Worldwide placements: *Africa* (Madagascar, Nigeria); *Asia* (India, Philippines); *Central America* (Costa Rica, El Salvador, Guatemala, Haiti, Honduras, Mexico, Nicaragua); *South America* (Bolivia, Brazil, Chile, Colombia, Ecuador, Venezuela).

CHRISTIAN LITERATURE CRUSADE
Shawton House
792 Hagley Road West
Oldbury
West Midlands
B68 0PJ UK

Tel: +44 (0) 121 422 5755
Contact: Mrs Grant

Starting months: January–December.
Time required: 1–52 weeks (plus).
Age requirement: 18 plus.

CHRISTIAN WELFARE AND SOCIAL PROJECT ORGANIZATION
39 Soldier Street
Freetown
Sierra Leone
West Africa

Tel: 00 232 22 229779 or 224096
Fax: 00 232 22 224439
Contact: Ms Joyor Cummings

Christian Welfare and Social Project Organization was established in 1980 as a non-governmental, non-political, non-profit organization, active in the field of rural grassroot development in the different villages where education, health and other facilities are not available. We are engaged in literacy programmes caring for street children, displaced children, refugees, school drop-outs, orphans, neglected school children, and children affected by the civil war. Farming, setting up literacy classes and vocational training centres, caring for handicapped/aged/adults/youths are also all part of our remit. We set up mobile health centres in the different camps and assist children, youth/adults in each village to know more about their culture and the culture of the volunteer as well. The organization is a Christian body which offers the chance to work for God and we run a variety of pro-church programmes. One such programme, CWASRO Crusaders Sierra Leone needs committed Christians and

aims to bring together talented young Christian musicians and volunteers to work to achieve a common goal. Committed volunteers are sent to different villages where no church is located.

Total projects worldwide: Many.
Total UK projects: 0
Starting months: January–December.
Time required: 4–52 weeks.
Age requirement: 18 plus.
Causes: Animal welfare, children, disabled (learning and physical), elderly people, health care/medical, poor/homeless, refugees, teaching/assisting (primary, secondary, mature, EFL), unemployed, work camps – seasonal, young people.
Activities: Administration, agriculture/farming, arts/crafts, caring (day and residential), counselling, driving, first aid, gardening/horticulture, international aid, manual work, social work, teaching, visiting/befriending.
When to apply: All year.
Work alone/with others: Both.
Volunteers with disabilities: Not possible.
Qualifications: Nil – but any welcome.
Health requirements: Innoculations required.
Costs: Air fare to Sierra Leone and from £300 for one month to £1,900 for 1 year.
Benefits: Accommodation.
Worldwide placements: *Africa* (Sierra Leone).

CHRISTIANS ABROAD
1 Stockwell Green
London
SW9 9HP UK

Tel: +44 (0) 20 7346 5950
Fax: +44 (0) 20 7346 5955
e-mail: wse@cabroad.org.uk
Contact: Kevin Cusack

Christians Abroad is the only organization providing vocational information and advice about working in the Third World to people of any faith or none. World Service Enquiry, the information activity of Christians Abroad, has information on voluntary and paid opportunities, short or long term in aid, development and mission agencies, for both skilled/qualified and unskilled people. Our comprehensive free information guide, updated annually, is geared mainly to unskilled people without professional experience. It gives details about how to start a search for work overseas, outlines organizations with information on development issues and those international organizations recruiting volunteers, with useful addresses to contact. For those considering where and how they can best use their experience abroad, World Service Enquiry also provides one-to-one vocational guidance interviews. These provide a forum to discuss interest in working overseas and possible ways forward. For those already qualified with some work experience we publish a monthly magazine, *Opportunities Abroad*, on subscription, which contains up-to-date vacancies (overseas and in the UK) from international and UK agencies. We also hold a development worker database of skilled personnel seeking contracts overseas. This is available on the internet and allows any agency to search your personal web page. Volunteers with offending backgrounds are accepted.

Total projects worldwide: Many
Total UK projects: 0
Starting months: January–December.
Time required: 1–52 weeks (plus).
Age requirement: 16 plus.
Causes: Aids/HIV, archaeology, children, conservation, disabled (learning and physical), elderly people, environmental causes, health care/medical, heritage, holidays for disabled, human rights, inner city problems, offenders/ex-offenders, poor/homeless, refugees, teaching/assisting (nursery, primary, secondary, mature, EFL), unemployed, wildlife, work camps – seasonal, young people.
Activities: Accountancy, administration, agriculture/farming, arts/crafts, building/construction, campaigning, caring (general, day and residential), catering, community work, computers, cooking, counselling, development issues, DIY, driving, first aid, forestry, fundraising, gardening/horticulture, group work, international aid, library/resource centres, manual work, marketing/publicity, music, newsletter/journalism, outdoor skills, religion, research, scientific work, social work, sport, summer camps, teaching, technical skills, theatre/drama, training, translating, visiting/befriending, work camps – seasonal.
Vols under 26 placed each year: Many.
When to apply: Between 6 months and 1 year in advance.
Work alone/with others: Both.

Volunteers with disabilities: Generally no.
Qualifications: Language helps, especially Portuguese, French, Spanish.
Equipment/clothing: Depends on the project.
Health requirements: Good health.
Costs: Varies from £50 to £2,000 per project, plus insurance if necessary.
Benefits: Vary – accommodation usually provided plus often local salary. World Service Enquiry also provides one-to-one vocational guidance interviews.
Training: Depends on the project.
Supervision: Depends on the project.
Nationalities accepted: No restrictions generally but some organizations require volunteers to be British nationals.
Interview details: Applicants are not interviewed by Christians Abroad.
Certification: Written reference on request.
Charity number: 265867
Worldwide placements: *Africa* (Angola, Benin, Botswana, Burkina Faso, Burundi, Cameroon, Cape Verde, Central African Republic, Chad, Comoros, Congo Dem. Republic, Congo Republic, Ivory Coast, Egypt, Equatorial Guinea, Eritrea, Ethiopia, Gabon, Gambia, Ghana, Guinea, Guinea-Bissau, Kenya, Lesotho, Liberia, Libya, Madagascar, Malawi, Mali, Mauritius, Mayotte, Morocco, Mozambique, Namibia, Niger, Nigeria, Reunion, Rwanda, Saint Helena, Senegal, Sierra Leone, Somalia, South Africa, Sudan, Swaziland, Tanzania, Togo, Tunisia, Uganda, Zambia, Zimbabwe); *Asia* (Afghanistan, Bangladesh, Bhutan, Cambodia, China, India, Indonesia, Iran, Israel, Japan, Jordan, Kazakhstan, Korea (North), Korea (South), Kyrgyzstan, Laos, Lebanon, Myanmar (Burma), Nepal, Pakistan, Philippines, Sri Lanka, Syria, Taiwan, Tajikistan, Thailand, Tibet, Turkey, Turkmenistan, Uzbekistan, Vietnam, Yemen); *Australasia* (Kiribati, Micronesia, Papua New Guinea, Solomon Islands, Tuvalu, Vanuatu); *Europe* (Albania, Austria, Belgium, Bosnia-Herzegovina, Bulgaria, Croatia, Czech Republic, Estonia, France, Germany, Hungary, Italy, Latvia, Lithuania, Macedonia, Moldova, Poland, Portugal, Romania, Russia, Slovakia, Slovenia, Spain, Turkey, Ukraine, Yugoslavia); *North America* (Canada, USA); *Central America* (Antigua and Barbuda, Barbados, Belize, Costa Rica, Cuba, Dominica, Dominican Republic, El Salvador, Guatemala, Haiti, Honduras,

Mexico, Netherlands Antilles, Nicaragua, Panama, Puerto Rico, Saint Christopher/ Nevis, Saint Lucia, Saint Vincent/ Grenadines, Trinidad and Tobago, Turks and Caicos Islands, Virgin Islands); *South America* (Argentina, Bolivia, Brazil, Chile, Colombia, Ecuador, French Guiana, Guyana, Paraguay, Peru, South Georgia, Suriname, Uruguay, Venezuela).

CHRISTIANS AWARE
2 Saxby Street
Leicester
LE2 0ND UK

Tel: +44 (0) 116 254 0770
Fax: +44 (0) 116 254 0770
e-mail: barbarabutler@christiansaware.co.uk
Web: www.christiansaware.co.uk
Contact: Barbara Butler, Executive Secretary

Christians Aware is an international and educational charity. Our main aim is to develop multi-cultural understanding and friendship locally, nationally and internationally, in a spirit of sharing. Thus new energy is generated for action towards human development and justice, through conferences, work camps, international exchanges and written resources, including a range of books and the quarterly magazine. An international visits brochure lists the group visits for the next two years. There are no experts in Christians Aware. Everyone is welcome for all conferences, courses and visits. Our written resources offer insights and suggest ways forward. We are continually reminded of the advice of Ronald Wynne who has worked for many years in Botswana: 'Do not try to teach anyone anything until you have learnt something from them.' Christians Aware recognizes the importance of openness, adaptability and faith in the future. Applicants with an offending background will be assessed and interviewed.

Total projects worldwide: Varies.
Total UK projects: Varies.
Starting months: January–December.
Time required: 2–52 weeks.
Age requirement: 18 plus.
Causes: Children, conservation, environmental causes, health care/medical, human rights, refugees, teaching/assisting, work camps – seasonal, young people.
Activities: Administration, agriculture/ farming, arts/crafts, community work, computers, conservation skills, development issues, fundraising, group work, international aid, manual work, newsletter/journalism, outdoor skills, religion, social work, summer camps, work camps – seasonal.
Vols under 26 placed each year: 30 of a total of 75.
Work alone/with others: With other young volunteers.
Volunteers with disabilities: Possible.
Qualifications: Nil.
Equipment/clothing: Kit list available for the tropics.
Health requirements: Innoculations for the tropics.
Costs: Each project individually priced.
Interview details: Interviews take place in Leicester or London.
Certification: Written reference can be arranged.
Charity number: 328322
Worldwide placements: *Africa* (Kenya, Mauritius, South Africa, Tanzania, Uganda, Zimbabwe); *Asia* (Bangladesh, China, India, Japan, Sri Lanka); *South America* (Peru).
UK placements: *England* (Leicestershire, London).

CHRISTLICHER FRIEDENSDIENST DEUTSCHER ZWEIG e.v.
Rendeler Strasse 9–11
60385 Frankfurt/Main
Germany

Tel: 00 49 69 45 90 71
Fax: 00 49 69 46 12 13
Contact: Mr G. Wolf

Christlicher Friedensdienst Deutscher Zweig e.v. conducts international work camps on ecological and peace projects for volunteers. Volunteers work in children's centres, on conservation projects etc. which require light manual work and occasionally campaigning activities. Ample time is provided for the discussion of questions which arise from the work and for leisure activities. Volunteers with offending backgrounds are accepted if they accept our conditions.

Applications must not be made to Germany. Please apply only to our UK branch:

YAP/Methold House
North Street
Worthing

W. Sussex BN1 1DU
Tel: +44 (0) 1903 528619
Fax: +44 (0) 1903 528611

Starting months: June–September.
Time required: 2–3 weeks.
Age requirement: 18–26
Causes: Conservation, environmental causes.
Activities: Campaigning, conservation skills, manual work.
Vols under 26 placed each year: 200
When to apply: As early as possible.
Work alone/with others: With others.
Qualifications: Nil.
Costs: Travel.
Benefits: Board and lodging.
Interview details: No interview necessary.
Worldwide placements: *Africa* (Egypt, Ghana, Morocco, Togo, Tunisia, Zambia); *Asia* (India, Israel, Japan, Jordan, Lebanon, Syria); *Europe* (Germany, Russia); *Central America* (Cuba, Honduras, Mexico); *South America* (Peru).

CHRYSALIS YOUTH PROJECT
65a Fryston Road
Airedale
Castleford
West Yorkshire
WF10 3EW UK

Tel: +44 (0) 1977 603756
Contact: Jane Masterman

Chrysalis Youth Project was originally sponsored by The Rank Foundation. It is a community facility with a go-kart track and training centre and depends on volunteers to manage, run and organize the project. In return they will be put through an OCN accredited training. This training is to bridge the gap between leaving school and further education or employment. Volunteers with an offending background may be accepted depending on each individual case.

Total projects worldwide: 0
Total UK projects: 1
Starting months: January–December.
Time required: 1–52 weeks.
Age requirement: 16–25
Causes: Children, conservation, disabled (learning and physical), environmental causes, unemployed, young people.
Activities: Administration, caring (general), catering, community work, computers, conservation skills, driving, fundraising,
gardening/horticulture, group work, manual work, marketing/publicity, outdoor skills, social work, sport, training.
Vols under 26 placed each year: 18
When to apply: Any time.
Work alone/with others: With others.
Volunteers with disabilities: Possible.
Qualifications: Nil.
Health requirements: Nil.
Costs: Nil.
Interview details: There is an interview selection process which takes place at the office.
Certification: Certificate or reference provided.
Charity number: 1066871

CHURCH MISSION SOCIETY – ENCOUNTER
157 Waterloo Road
London
SE1 8UU UK

Tel: +44 (0) 20 7928 8681
Fax: +44 (0) 20 7401 3215
e-mail: kathy.tyson@cms-uk.org
Web: www.com-uk.org
Contact: Kathy Tyson

The Church Mission Society (CMS) is a voluntary society within the Anglican Church, established in 1799, working in partnership with Asian, African and East European churches, sending and receiving personnel to share in and learn from each other's mission. Encounter provides exciting opportunities for Christians to go as part of a group and live alongside national Christians in Asia, Africa or Eastern Europe, sharing their lifestyle, witness, worship, hopes and aspirations. Volunteers with an offending background may be accepted. Each case is assessed separately.

Total projects worldwide: 4
Total UK projects: 0
Starting months: July, August.
Time required: 3–4 weeks.
Age requirement: 18 plus.
Causes: Children, conservation, disabled (learning and physical), elderly people, inner city problems, poor/homeless, refugees, teaching/assisting (EFL), work camps – seasonal, young people.
Activities: Agriculture/farming, arts/crafts, building/construction, caring (general), community work, computers, conservation

skills, development issues, forestry, gardening/horticulture, group work, manual work, music, outdoor skills, religion, sport, summer camps, teaching, visiting/ befriending, work camps – seasonal.

Vols under 26 placed each year: 30–35 of a total of 40–50.

When to apply: Before April for summer placement.

Work alone/with others: With others.

Volunteers with disabilities: Possible, but we would not be able to place wheelchair users.

Qualifications: British residents, Christian.

Equipment/clothing: Varies according to location – kit list provided.

Health requirements: Health clearance required; innoculations vary according to location.

Costs: £600-£1,000. Help and advice on fundraising given. Volunteers must arrange and pay for insurance cover for health, accident, third party, baggage, money and cancellation.

Benefits: Training, debriefing and experienced leaders.

Training: 2 pre-placement training weekends.

Supervision: Accompanied by 2 leaders with previous overseas experience.

Nationalities accepted: British volunteers only.

Interview details: Applicants are interviewed by residential selection – location varies.

Certification: Confirmation of involvement. Group leaders may give references.

Charity number: 220297

Worldwide placements: *Africa* (Gambia, Kenya, Tunisia, Uganda); *Asia* (China, India, Lebanon, Pakistan, Philippines, Syria); *Europe* (Romania, Russia, Ukraine).

CHURCH MISSION SOCIETY – MAKE A DIFFERENCE (IN BRITAIN)

157 Waterloo Road
London
SE1 8UU UK

Tel: +44 (0) 20 7928 8681
Fax: +44 (0) 20 7401 3215
e-mail: kathy.tyson@cms-uk.org
Web: www.com-uk.org
Contact: Experience Programme Adviser

For details of the Church Mission Society (CMS) see Church Mission Society – Encounter, above. Make a Difference (In Britain) placements provide exciting opportunities to form cross-cultural relationships and grow spiritually through being involved in a parish or project in Britain. Britain Experience placements are generally in multicultural, inner city areas. Volunteers with an offending background may be accepted. Each case is assessed separately.

Total projects worldwide: 12

Total UK projects: 12

Starting months: January, September.

Time required: 28–52 weeks (plus).

Age requirement: 18–30

Causes: Children, disabled (learning and physical), elderly people, inner city problems, poor/homeless, teaching/assisting (nursery), unemployed, work camps – seasonal, young people.

Activities: Administration, caring (general), community work, driving, group work, library/resource centres, manual work, music, religion, social work, summer camps, teaching, visiting/befriending, work camps – seasonal.

Vols under 26 placed each year: 1 or 2.

When to apply: All year.

Work alone/with others: With local people.

Volunteers with disabilities: Possible.

Qualifications: British residents, Christian.

Health requirements: Nil.

Costs: All. No insurance necessary.

Benefits: Occasionally board, lodging and pocket money. Training and re-orientation courses.

Training: 10 days at CMS Training College.

Supervision: Person to whom volunteer is responsible in parish/project is identified.

Nationalities accepted: British volunteers only.

Interview details: Interviews take place in London.

Certification: Confirmation of involvement. The Local Supervisor may give references.

Charity number: 220297

UK placements: *England* (Derbyshire, Lancashire, London, Manchester, West Midlands, S. Yorkshire, W. Yorkshire).

CHURCH MISSION SOCIETY – MAKE A DIFFERENCE (OVERSEAS)

157 Waterloo Road
London
SE1 8UU UK

Tel: +44 (0) 20 7928 8681

Fax: +44 (0) 20 7401 3215
e-mail: kathy.tyson@cms-uk.org
Web: www.com-uk.org
Contact: Experience Programme Adviser

For more details of the Church Mission Society, see Church Mission Society – Encounter, above. Make a Difference (Overseas) provides challenging opportunities to form cross-cultural relationships, to grow spiritually through contact with the national church and to gain experience in Africa, Asia and Eastern Europe. Church Mission Society Make a Difference (Overseas) placements can be arranged together with a Church Mission Society British Experience placement.
Overseas locations vary each year. Volunteers with offending backgrounds may be accepted. Each case is assessed separately.

Total projects worldwide: 40
Total UK projects: 0
Starting months: January, September.
Time required: 26–52 weeks (plus).
Age requirement: 18–30
Causes: Addicts/Ex-addicts, children, disabled (learning), elderly people, environmental causes, health care/medical, inner city problems, poor/homeless, refugees, teaching/assisting (nursery, primary, secondary, EFL), unemployed, work camps – seasonal, young people.
Activities: Accountancy, administration, building/construction, caring (general and residential), community work, computers, development issues, driving, group work, library/resource centres, manual work, music, religion, social work, summer camps, teaching, translating, visiting/befriending, work camps – seasonal.
Vols under 26 placed each year: 10 of a total of 15.
When to apply: All year.
Work alone/with others: With local people.
Volunteers with disabilities: Not possible.
Qualifications: British residents, Christian, professional qualifications/experience or graduates preferred.
Health requirements: Nil.
Costs: £2,500 per annum. Volunteers must arrange and pay for insurance cover for health, accident, third party, baggage, money and cancellation.
Benefits: Training and reorientation courses. Occasionally board, lodging and pocket money.

Training: 10 days at CMS Training College.
Supervision: Person to whom responsible on location is identified.
Nationalities accepted: British volunteers only.
Interview details: Interviews take place in London.
Certification: Confirmation of involvement. Overseas supervisor may give references.
Charity number: 220297
Worldwide placements: *Africa* (Egypt, Gambia, Guinea, Kenya, South Africa, Tanzania, Uganda); *Asia* (Bangladesh, India, Japan, Nepal, Pakistan, Philippines, Taiwan); *Europe* (Czech Republic, Romania, Russia, Ukraine).

CHURCH OF ENGLAND YOUTH SERVICE
Church House
Great Smith Street
London
SW1P 3NZ UK

Tel: +44 (0) 20 7898 1509
Fax: +44 (0) 20 7233 1094
e-mail: peter@boe.demon.co.uk
Contact: Peter Ball

Church of England Youth Service ask that in the first instance enquiries should be made to the National Youth Service at Church House, as above. Depending on the time of year the enquiry is made, opportunities could be available in any part of the country.

Starting months: January–December.
Time required: 1–52 weeks.
Age requirement: 18–25
Causes: Addicts/Ex-addicts, children, disabled (learning and physical), elderly people, inner city problems, poor/homeless, teaching/assisting, unemployed, young people.
Activities: Caring (general), community work, counselling, group work, international aid, music, newsletter/journalism, religion, social work, summer camps, teaching, visiting/befriending.
When to apply: 6 months in advance.
Work alone/with others: With others.
Volunteers with disabilities: Possible.
Qualifications: Nil.
Health requirements: Nil.
Costs: Contribution if possible.
Benefits: Board and lodging usually. Opportunities to develop new skills and

experience living and working in new communities.

Certification: Reference provided.

UK placements: *England* (throughout); *Scotland* (throughout); *Northern Ireland* (throughout); *Wales* (throughout, except for Vale of Glamorgan).

CHURCH'S MINISTRY AMONG JEWISH PEOPLE, THE

30c Clarence Road
St Albans
Hertfordshire
AL1 4JJ UK

Tel: +44 (0) 1727 833114
Fax: +44 (0) 1727 848312
e-mail: enquiries@cmj.org.uk
Contact: Jeremy Purcell, Israel Volunteers

The Church's Ministry Among Jewish People has a threefold aim: evangelism – to share the gospel widely, particularly with Jewish people; encouragement – to support and encourage Jewish believers in Jesus; education – to teach the Church about its Jewish roots. In Israel we run three centres/guesthouses where Messianic congregations meet and accommodation is provided for conferences/students at Bible college. In Jerusalem we run the Anglican School and also Shoresh Tours who run study tours of Israel. CMJ workers in South Africa, Argentina, Ireland and UK work with and train churches in evangelism to Jews. The Simeon Centre in North London is the centre for a growing Messianic congregation. *Shalom* magazine is sent out from St Albans. The Bible Come to Life exhibition is a travelling exhibition which visits schools/churches during the year. Volunteers are involved in the three centres/guest houses in Israel where they help with the day to day running of the centres carrying out mainly domestic/maintenance or reception duties. Volunteers with an offending background are accepted.

Total projects worldwide: 3
Total UK projects: 0
Starting months: January–December.
Time required: 6–52 weeks.
Age requirement: 18 plus.
Activities: Administration, catering, cooking, DIY, gardening/horticulture, manual work, religion.
Vols under 26 placed each year: 60–70 of a total of 80–100.

When to apply: 3 months prior to start.
Work alone/with others: With others.
Volunteers with disabilities: Manual/domestic work so generally no. Individual enquiries always welcome.
Qualifications: Committed Christians involved in local church.
Health requirements: Nil – good health.
Costs: Travel costs plus medical insurance = £300 plus. Travel insurance optional. Voluntary church support = £45 per week.
Benefits: Board and accommodation, pocket money.
Training: When practical an orientation day is provided in St Albans or Oxford. Volunteers are placed in contact with a CMJ area representative who lives nearest to them.
Supervision: By the centre directors on a continuous basis.
Nationalities accepted: No restrictions on nationalities of volunteers but volunteers from other countries must arrange visas if necessary.
Interview details: Applicants are not interviewed but must complete a 3-page application form and supply 3 references all of which is sent to Israel.
Certification: Reference on request.
Charity number: 228519
Worldwide placements: *Africa* (Ethiopia, South Africa); *Asia* (Israel); *South America* (Argentina).

CHURCHTOWN OUTDOOR ADVENTURE CENTRE

Lanlivery
Bodmin
Cornwall
PL30 5BT UK

Tel: +44 (0) 1208 872148
Fax: +44 (0) 1208 873377
Contact: Rowena Doughty

Churchtown Outdoor Adventure Centre provides outdoor, environmental and adventurous training courses accessible to everyone, regardless of degree of special need. As well as the more traditional courses, in ecology and outdoor pursuits, a new development is the provision of personal development programmes which concentrate on personal growth, encouraging a positive image of self and promoting self-confidence. The Centre is attractively converted and well equipped with an indoor swimming pool, farm, nature reserve and attractive grounds. Sailing and canoeing take place on the nearby River Fowey and the Centre is only five miles from the coast. Ten volunteers are needed at a time to support the professional staff.

Total projects worldwide: 1
Total UK projects: 1
Starting months: January–December.
Time required: 3–52 weeks.
Age requirement: 18 plus.
Causes: Animal welfare, children, conservation, disabled (learning and physical), elderly people, environmental causes, health care/medical, holidays for disabled, teaching/assisting (nursery, primary, secondary, EFL), unemployed, wildlife, young people.
Activities: Administration, agriculture/ farming, arts/crafts, building/construction, caring (general, day and residential), catering, conservation skills, forestry, fundraising, gardening/horticulture, group work, manual work, marketing/publicity, music, outdoor skills, sport, summer camps, teaching.
Vols under 26 placed each year: 30
When to apply: All year.
Work alone/with others: With others.
Volunteers with disabilities: Possible if able to assist others with special needs. Individually assessed.
Qualifications: Enthusiasm.
Health requirements: Must be fit.
Costs: Travel costs only to and from Centre.
Benefits: Full board and lodging plus £20 per week for a stay of 3 or more weeks.
UK placements: *England* (Cornwall).

CITIES IN SCHOOLS (CiS)
60-61 Trafalgar Square
London
WC2N 5DS UK

Tel: +44 (0) 20 7839 2899
Fax: +44 (0) 20 7839 6186
Contact: The Director

CiS is an organization that helps children who have difficulties at school to build their confidence and self-image. Volunteers are needed to help such children and young people in local projects. Our projects are usually small-scale but there are larger programmes run during vacations.

Total projects worldwide: 3
Total UK projects: 3
Starting months: January–December.
Time required: 1–52 weeks.
Age requirement: 12 plus.
Causes: Children, teaching/assisting (primary, secondary), young people.
Activities: Arts/crafts, teaching, training.
When to apply: All year.
Work alone/with others: Both.
Qualifications: Free training given.
Health requirements: Nil.
Costs: Nil.
Benefits: Free training given.
Training: Free training provided.
UK placements: *England* (London); *Wales* (Newport).

CITIZENSHIP FOUNDATION, THE
Ferroners House
Shaftesbury Place
off Aldersgate Street
London
EC2Y 8AA UK

Tel: +44 (0) 20 7367 0500
Fax: +44 (0) 20 7367 0501
Contact: Fiona Hogarth

Starting months: January–December.
Time required: 1–52 weeks.
Age requirement: 14 plus.

CLUB DU VIEUX MANOIR
Siège National
10 rue de la Cossonnerie
F-75001 Paris
France

Tel: 00 33 1 45 08 80 40
Fax: 00 33 1 42 21 38 79

Club du Vieux Manoir – founded in 1953 – is a volunteer association formed of young people who want to spend some of their spare time doing rescue and restoration work (under direction) on ancient monuments and sites. On the different sites two aims are pursued: the historic monuments and places which form part of the national heritage are restored and brought to life; the participants are offered a leisure activity where they can work with their hands and at the same time learn about different techniques. The young people, divided into groups, share the day-to-day organization of the camp and site: everybody lends a hand to achieve a common objective. The monuments and sites undertaken are always open to the public.

Usually they belong to local councils or societies. Thus after the work is finished the building continues to be of use.

Office address of Secretariat-General:
Monique Dine, Directeur
Ancienne Abbaye du Moncel
60700 – Pontpoint
France
Tel: 00 33 44 72 33 98
Fax: 00 33 44 70 13 14

Total UK projects: 0
Starting months: January–December.
Time required: 1–52 weeks.
Age requirement: 15 plus.
Causes: Archaeology, architecture, conservation, heritage, work camps – seasonal.
Activities: Arts/crafts, building/construction, conservation skills, summer camps, work camps – seasonal.
Vols under 26 placed each year: 3,500 of a total of 4,670.
When to apply: All year.
Work alone/with others: With others.
Qualifications: Nil.
Equipment/clothing: Sleeping bag and camp cooking utensils.
Health requirements: Nil.
Costs: Approx £7 per day. FF90 per year in advance to cover all insurance.
Benefits: Accommodation in tents.
Training: Courses in various techniques available for youngsters from 16 years old upwards. Practical instruction given on the site.
Supervision: Group leaders, site director, technical supervision, architects, archaeologists, historians and volunteers who return regularly to the same site.
Interview details: No interview necessary.
Worldwide placements: *Europe* (France).

CLUB UNESCO AU MONDE DES LECTEUR (CUML)
BP 4671 Kinshasa 2
7 Rue Meteo No. 7
Djelo Binza (Delvaux)
Zone de Ngaliema
Kinshasa
Democratic Republic of Congo

Contact: Mr Atumanu Mbanza

CUML, founded in 1983, is a non-governmental organization concerned with voluntary services committed to improving the standard of life in Congo (ex Zaire). Its voluntary workers are active in every sphere of life: health, agriculture, the environment, social issues, education, economic and the cultural issues.

Total projects worldwide: Many.
Total UK projects: 0
Starting months: January–December.
Time required: 3–52 weeks.
Age requirement: 18–35
Causes: Children, conservation, disabled (learning and physical), elderly people, environmental causes, health care/medical, heritage, poor/homeless, refugees, teaching/assisting, young people.
Activities: Administration, agriculture/farming, arts/crafts, building/construction, caring (general), catering, community work, conservation skills, development issues, forestry, gardening/horticulture, group work, international aid, social work, teaching.
Vols under 26 placed each year: Approximately 150.
When to apply: All year.
Work alone/with others: Both.
Qualifications: Nil.
Costs: Travel and insurance.
Benefits: Food, accommodation, pocket money and some travel expenses.
Worldwide placements: *Africa* (Zambia).

COLLÈGE LYCÉE CÉVENOL INTERNATIONAL
Chambon-sur-Lignon 434000
Haute Loire
France

Tel: 00 33 4 71 59 72 52
Fax: 00 33 4 71 65 87 38
Contact: The Director

Collège Lycée Cévenol International work camp takes place in the Massif Central. The surrounding country is wooded and mountainous and provides an invigorating setting for the camp activities. The present school at Chambon-sur-Lignon has been partly built by work camps held at the site.

Starting months: July.
Time required: 3 weeks.
Age requirement: 18–30
Causes: Architecture, environmental causes.
Activities: Building/construction, manual work.

When to apply: As early as possible.
Work alone/with others: With others.
Qualifications: Nil.
Health requirements: Good.
Benefits: Accommodation, food and all other facilities. Free registration.
Interview details: No interview necessary.
Worldwide placements: *Europe* (France).

COLORADO TRAIL FOUNDATION
548 Pine Song Trail
Golden,
Colorado 80401
USA

Tel: 00 1 303 526 0809
Contact: The President of Foundation

The Colorado Trail Foundation builds and maintains a 500 mile trail across the Continental Divide which is very remote from civilization. Some crews backpack, some drive-in and others 'jeep-in'. Each crew has a trained leader. Most projects are at high altitude. Any volunteers who cannot do the physical work are put to work in the base camp.

Starting months: June–August.
Time required: 1–10 weeks.
Age requirement: 16 plus.
Causes: Conservation, environmental causes, heritage, wildlife.
Activities: Building/construction, conservation skills, forestry, manual work, outdoor skills.
Vols under 26 placed each year: 300-500
When to apply: February to May.
Work alone/with others: With others.
Qualifications: Nil.
Equipment/clothing: Tent, sleeping bag and pad, leather boots.
Health requirements: Good physical condition.
Costs: Travel, pocket money.
Benefits: Food, tools and hard hats. Leaders and base camp work 4 days a week. Time to explore.
Interview details: No interview necessary.
Worldwide placements: *North America* (USA).

COMMUNITY FOR CREATIVE NON-VIOLENCE
425 2nd Street NW
Washington

DC 20001
USA
Tel: 00 1 202 393 1909
Fax: 00 1 202 783 3254
Contact: Steve Voorhies

Starting months: January–December.
Time required: 26–52 weeks.
Age requirement: 18 plus.
Causes: Addicts/ex-addicts, health care/medical, poor/homeless.
Activities: Catering, library/resource centres, social work.
When to apply: All year.
Qualifications: Nil.
Costs: Fares, pocket money and USA visa.
Benefits: Board and dormitory accommodation.
Worldwide placements: *North America* (USA).

COMMUNITY MUSIC WALES
2 Leckwith Place
Canton
Cardiff
CF11 6QA Wales

Tel: +44 (0) 29 2038 7620
Fax: +44 (0) 29 2023 3022
e-mail: admin@comunitymusicwales.org.uk
Web: www.communitymusicwales.org.uk
Contact: Eileen Smith, Administration Director

Community Music Wales aims to make music available to people who would normally be marginalized in society, e.g. people with learning difficulties, people with physical disabilities, people with mental health problems, people from ethnic minorities, young offenders. Our aim is to create and promote music-making opportunities for people of all ages, skills and experience. We only take volunteers every six months. Volunteers with an offending background are accepted.

Total projects worldwide: 40
Total UK projects: Approximately 40.
Starting months: January–November.
Time required: 1–52 weeks.
Age requirement: 14 plus.
Causes: Disabled (learning and physical), inner city problems, offenders/ex-offenders.
Activities: Music.
Vols under 26 placed each year: 4
When to apply: All year.

Work alone/with others: With others.
Volunteers with disabilities: Possible.
Qualifications: Interest in music and working in the community.
Health requirements: Nil.
Costs: Nil.
Benefits: Expenses paid.
Training: Any needed would be carried out at headquarters.
Supervision: Full supervision at all times.
Interview details: Interviews take place at CMW's headquarters in Cardiff.
Charity number: 1009867
UK placements: *Wales* (throughout, except for Powys).

COMMUNITY PARTNERS' ASSOCIATION (COPA)

Green Banks
Old Hill
Longhope
Gloucestershire
GL17 OPF UK

Tel: +44 (0) 1452 830492
Fax: +44 (0) 1452 830492
Contact: David Wilson, International Co-ordinator

Community Partners' Association (COPA) is a small but very active charity working in poor rural villages in the Dominican Republic. In the village of La Hoya we have completed the construction of a school for approximately 400 children up to year eight and a pre-school. We have also built and maintain a rural clinic there. Nearby, Bombita is occupied entirely by very poor migrant Haitians where we have built and maintain a school for 400 children and a clinic. The aim of COPA is to provide the expertise and finance to help very poor communities to help themselves. The communities have therefore been heavily involved as volunteers in the construction. Work groups from the USA and the UK travel to the Dominican Republic for periods of two or three weeks to work alongside the local people on the building site and in the school. The COPA projects are run by two-year volunteers directed by a management team in the UK. Short-term volunteers are also welcome for periods of less than one year. The teachers are all Dominican and one of the principal roles of volunteers is to support them in the classroom and also to teach English to the older students. Volunteers help visiting work groups as translators. There is usually administrative work to be done for those with computer skills. COPA is a Christian organization and expects volunteers to work in sympathy with its aims. Applications from qualified primary teachers or qualified nurses are particularly welcome for two-year contracts.

Total projects worldwide: 4
Total UK projects: 0
Starting months: January–December, except October.
Time required: 5–52 weeks.
Age requirement: 18 plus.
Causes: Children, health care/medical, poor/homeless, teaching/assisting (nursery, primary, secondary, EFL), work camps – seasonal, young people.
Activities: Administration, building/construction, computers, development issues, teaching, translating, work camps – seasonal.
Vols under 26 placed each year: 5 of a total of 6.
When to apply: All year.
Work alone/with others: With others.
Volunteers with disabilities: Not suitable for severely disabled.
Qualifications: A-level and ability to converse in Spanish.
Health requirements: Good health essential.
Costs: Return air fare and subsistence (approximately £200 per month) for short-term volunteers. No contribution is required from 2-year volunteers. Health and travelinsurance is paid by COPA for 2-year volunteers. Short-term volunteers must provide their own health and travel insurance.
Benefits: Free accommodation, water and electricity.
Training: One-day pre-placement preparation. On-the-job training by COPA staff. Written notes also given to volunteers.
Supervision: Resident COPA staff supervise short-term volunteers.
Interview details: Interviews take place in Gloucester.
Certification: Certificate or reference provided.
Charity number: 1027117
Worldwide placements: *Central America* (Dominican Republic).

COMMUNITY SERVICE VOLUNTEERS

237 Pentonville Road

London
N1 9NJ UK

Tel: +44 (0) 20 7278 6601/free 0800 374 991
Fax: +44 (0) 20 7837 9621
e-mail: 106167.2756@compuserve.com
Web: www.csv.org.uk
Contact: Natasha Theobold

CSV invites all young people aged 16 to 35 to experience the challenge, excitement and reward of helping people in need. Each year it places 3,000 volunteers on projects throughout the UK, working with elderly or homeless people, adults or children with disabilities, learning difficulties or mental illness, and young people who are in care or in trouble. No volunteer is ever rejected. Volunteers work hard, have fun and gain valuable experience working away from home for four to twelve months. Applications are welcome throughout the year. There are specialist projects for volunteers with disabilities (physical and learning) and CSV would welcome more applications from people with disabilities. Volunteers need to be prepared to work flexible hours but not more than 40 hours per week. Specialist schemes – Local Action – cater for vulnerable people from disadvantaged backgrounds, such as substance misusers, homeless people, young people looked after by local authorities and young offenders, who may need special encouragement to volunteer. Opportunities are available for these volunteers to work part-time locally on one of many CSV Local Action schemes nationwide while receiving pro-rata weekly allowance, food, travel expenses and supervision.

Total projects worldwide: 800
Total UK projects: 800
Starting months: January–December.
Time required: 16–52 weeks.
Age requirement: 16–35
Causes: Addicts/Ex-addicts, Aids/HIV, children, disabled (learning and physical), elderly people, inner city problems, offenders/ex-offenders, poor/homeless, young people.
Activities: Administration, building/construction, caring (general, day and residential), community work, cooking, counselling, driving, group work, social work, visiting/befriending.
Vols under 26 placed each year: 2,200

When to apply: 6–8 weeks before start.
Work alone/with others: Both.
Volunteers with disabilities: Possible.
Qualifications: Nil.
Health requirements: Nil.
Costs: Nil.
Benefits: Board and lodging plus £24 per week for 40 hour week.
Training: Dependent on placement.
Supervision: Dependent on placement.
Nationalities accepted: Volunteers from outside the UK are accepted but they must pay a charge (currently £490) and satisfy UK visa requirements.
Interview details: Volunteers are interviewed at the CSV office nearest to them.
Certification: Certificate or reference provided.
Charity number: 291222
UK placements: *England* (throughout); *Scotland* (throughout); *Wales* (throughout).

COMMUNITY SERVICE VOLUNTEERS EDUCATION
237 Pentonville Road
London
N1 9NJ UK

Tel: +44 (0) 20 7643 1313
Fax: +44 (0) 20 7278 1020
Contact: Melanie Elkan

Community Service Volunteers is an organization which offers people the opportunity to play an active part in the community by volunteering. CSV Education for citizenship is a part of CSV which encourages young people to volunteer in their schools and communities and promotes the involvement of adults volunteering in schools. The scheme, known as Adults Other Than Teachers, aims to improve links between schools and the adult community. Pupils gain a great deal from the voluntary support of adults who can offer one-to-one or group-work time. Volunteers generally offer an hour a week to work with children in areas such as reading support, numeracy, sports, arts, crafts, music or leisure activities. Volunteers do not need to have any experience. They should be interested in children and able to make a commitment of at least a term. Volunteers are required to undergo a formal recruitment procedure, including a police check. Volunteers will apply to individual schools. Volunteers with an offending background may be accepted. Police check for purposes of child protection will be carried out.

Total projects worldwide: 40
Total UK projects: 40
Starting months: January–December.
Time required: 10–52 weeks (plus).
Age requirement: 18 plus.
Causes: Children, teaching/assisting (primary).
Activities: Arts/crafts, music, sport, teaching, theatre/drama, translating, visiting/befriending.
Vols under 26 placed each year: 20
When to apply: All year.
Work alone/with others: With others.
Volunteers with disabilities: Possible.
Qualifications: Nil.
Health requirements: Nil.
Costs: Travel costs – ideally volunteers will live close enough to schools to avoid travel costs.
Training: Schools will provide the necessary induction and training.
Supervision: Depending on the placement.
Interview details: You will be interviewed at the school at which you wish to volunteer.
Certification: Volunteers have options to follow recognized accredited courses.
Charity number: 291222
UK placements: *England* (London).

CONCORDIA
20–22 Heversham House
Boundary Road
Hove
East Sussex
BN3 4ET UK

Tel: +44 (0) 1273 422218
Fax: +44 (0) 1273 422218
e-mail: gwyn@concordia-iye.uk
Web: www.concordia-iye.org.uk
Contact: Gwyn Lewis, Volunteer Programme Manager

Concordia runs short-term (2–3 weeks) international volunteer projects. We also run volunteer projects in the UK for overseas volunteers and needs UK volunteers who must be aged 20 plus and have previous work camp or leadership experience, to act as project co-ordinators. Volunteers with an offending background are accepted unless they want to work on a children's camp and the offence was child related.

Total projects worldwide: 300 plus.
Total UK projects: 15 plus.
Starting months: March–October.
Time required: 2–4 weeks.
Age requirement: 17–30
Causes: Animal welfare, archaeology, children, conservation, disabled (learning and physical), elderly people, environmental causes, health care/medical, heritage, holidays for disabled, inner city problems, poor/homeless, refugees, teaching/assisting, unemployed, wildlife, work camps – seasonal, young people.
Activities: Arts/crafts, building/construction, caring (general and day), community work, conservation skills, cooking, forestry, gardening/horticulture, group work, manual work, music, social work, sport, summer camps, teaching, theatre/drama, work camps – seasonal.
Vols under 26 placed each year: 180 of a total of 200.
When to apply: As early as possible.
Work alone/with others: With others in a group of about 10-15 international volunteers.
Volunteers with disabilities: Possible unless disability seriously interferes with ability to undertake the work or where accessibility to sites is limiting. All applications treated individually.
Qualifications: Language ability for some projects.
Equipment/clothing: Sleeping bag, rollmat, strong shoes, old clothes plus work gloves.
Health requirements: Fit enough to undertake the (often physical) work required.
Costs: Registration fee £80, plus travel, insurance and membership fee of £6.50/£10. Volunteer is responsible for personal travel insurance but on many projects some insurance (accident, illness, third party) is provided.
Benefits: Board and lodging, social programme.
Supervision: Dependent on project, country etc. but usually there are 2 project co-ordinators with additional supervision during the work.
Interview details: No interview necessary.
Certification: Certificate or reference on request.
Charity number: 381668
Worldwide placements: *Africa* (Ghana, Kenya, Morocco, South Africa, Tanzania,

Tunisia, Zimbabwe); *Asia* (Bangladesh, Japan, Korea (South), Nepal, Thailand, Turkey); *Europe* (Azerbaijan, Belarus, Belgium, Bulgaria, Czech Republic, Denmark, Estonia, Finland, France, Germany, Greece, Italy, Latvia, Lithuania, Macedonia, Netherlands, Norway, Poland, Russia, Slovakia, Spain, Switzerland, Turkey, Ukraine, Yugoslavia); *North America* (Canada, USA); *South America* (Ecuador). UK placements: *England* (Derbyshire, London, Northumberland, Oxfordshire, Staffordshire, E. Sussex, W. Sussex, West Midlands); *Wales* (Bridgend, Gwynedd, Rhondda, Cynon, Taff, Vale of Glamorgan).

CONFERENCE ON TRAINING IN ARCHITECTURAL CONSERVATION (COTAC)

Room 97A, Platform 7
St Pancras Station
Euston Road
London
NW1 2QP UK

Tel: +44 (0) 20 7713 0135
Fax: +44 (0) 20 7713 0359
Contact: Mr Richard Davies, Director

The Conference on Training in Architectural Conservation (COTAC) was formed 30 years ago to initiate better eduation for architects who wished to work on the repair and conservation of historic buildings. It is now composed of representatives from the main conservation bodies, the relevant professions, the construction industry, government agencies and educational institutions. As it has evolved, COTAC works for the training of all disciplines and crafts concerned with building conservation: architects, surveyors, engineers, conservation officers, construction managers, facility managers and skilled craftsmen and women. We recognize that conservation is a theme that involves society at all levels as well as being a positive force for unity within the construction industry. We aim: to encourage a general appreciation of the benefits of skilled conservation amongst all sections of the building industry in the community; to identify and encourage the development of general and specialist training in conservation skills at professional, technical and craft levels; to foster links between centres involved in both formal training and practical conservation in the UK

and abroad; to assist in developing appropriate methods for monitoring training standards and specialist qualifications; to encourage funding for the development of courses and other training methods and to support students in the study of architectural conservation and associated craft skills.

Total projects worldwide: 7
Total UK projects: 4
Starting months: January–December.
Time required: 4–52 weeks (plus).
Age requirement: 18 plus.
Causes: Architecture, conservation, heritage, inner city problems.
Activities: Administration, arts/crafts, building/construction, computers, conservation skills, fundraising, library/resource centres.
When to apply: As soon as possible.
Work alone/with others: With a small team of consultants.
Volunteers with disabilities: Possible.
Qualifications: Reasonably literate, numerate, with common sense and application. Good competence in English essential.
Health requirements: Nil.
Costs: Nil apart from local travel.
Benefits: By negotiation, some contribution to volunteers' expenses may be possible.
Interview details: Prospective volunteers are interviewed at COTAC office.
Certification: Reference provided.
Charity number: 1036263
Worldwide placements: *Europe* (Finland, France, Hungary, Ireland, Italy, Portugal, Spain).
UK placements: *England* (London).

CONSERVATION VOLUNTEERS AUSTRALIA

Box 423
Ballarat
Victoria
3353 Australia

Tel: 00 61 3 5333 1483
Fax: 00 61 3 5333 2166
e-mail: info@conservationvolunteers.com.au
Web: www.conservationvolunteers.com.au
Contact: Executive Director

Conservation Volunteers Australia is a not-for-profit, non-political, community-based organization undertaking practical conservation projects in all states and territories. Typical projects include tree planting, erosion and salinity control; collection of native seed; habitat restoration; endangered flora/fauna survey and monitoring; noxious weed eradication; and heritage projects. Projects are supervised by CVA team leaders and take place on private land (e.g. farms); public lands (e.g. council/shire projects; rivers and creeks; coastal areas etc.) and national and state parks (sometimes including World Heritage areas). All training is provided.

Total projects worldwide: 1,500 plus.
Total UK projects: 0
Starting months: January–December.
Time required: 6–26 weeks.
Age requirement: 15 plus.
Causes: Conservation, environmental causes, heritage, wildlife, young people.
Activities: Agriculture/farming, building/construction, community work, conservation skills, forestry, gardening/horticulture, group work, manual work, outdoor skills, research, training.
Vols under 26 placed each year: 960 plus of a total of 1,200 plus.
When to apply: 4 weeks in advance (2 months preferred).
Work alone/with others: With others.
Volunteers with disabilities: Physical work and camping is entailed. Applications considered individually.
Qualifications: Ability to speak and understand English. Interest in practical conservation. No prior experience necessary.
Equipment/clothing: Strong work boots, sleeping bag, wet weather gear, sun hat. (Full list available).
Health requirements: Reasonable fitness.
Costs: AU$23 per day plus travel to starting point. Volunteers should have personal medical insurance with travel insurance and cover for personal items.
Benefits: All food, accommodation and transport whilst working with CVA.
Training: All volunteers are briefed on arrival, at the start of each week, and daily reminders are given regarding safety.
Supervision: CVA team leaders are with volunteers throughout projects. The leaders are responsible for on-site training safety, project management and volunteer welfare.
Nationalities accepted: No restrictions but must be able to understand English for safety reasons.
Interview details: No interview necessary.

Certification: Certificate or reference on request.
Worldwide placements: *Australasia* (Australia).

CONSERVATION VOLUNTEERS IRELAND
PO Box 3836
Ballsbridge
Dublin 4
Ireland

Tel: 00 353 1 6681844
Fax: 00 353 1 6681844
e-mail: Littles@indigo.ie
Contact: Melanie Hamilton, Executive Director

Conservation Volunteers Ireland is involved in many projects all over Ireland. Volunteers interested in working with CVI need no previous skills or experience, just energy and commitment.

Total projects worldwide: 20
Total UK projects: 0
Starting months: January–December.
Time required: 1 week.
Age requirement: 18 plus.
Causes: Conservation, environmental causes, heritage, wildlife.
Activities: Conservation skills, forestry, group work, outdoor skills, technical skills, training.
Vols under 26 placed each year: 20 of a total of 50.
When to apply: All year.
Work alone/with others: With others.
Volunteers with disabilities: Possible.
Qualifications: Nil.
Equipment/clothing: Wet weather clothing and strong boots.
Health requirements: Good general health.
Costs: Travel and membership. Board and lodging at a reasonable cost.
Benefits: Internal travel.
Training: An induction course is provided.
Supervision: By 2 field officers.
Certification: There is an exit interview for volunteer officers carried out by the volunteer's line manager's line manager. Certificate or reference provided.
Charity number: 10105
Worldwide placements: *Europe* (Ireland).

CONSERVATION VOLUNTEERS NORTHERN IRELAND (CVNI)

159 Ravenhill Road
Belfast
Co. Antrim
BT6 0BP N. Ireland

Tel: + 44 (0) 28 9064 5169
Fax: + 44 (0) 28 9064 4409
e-mail: cvni@cvni.org
Web: www.cvni.org.uk
Contact: Billy Belshaw, Information Officer

Conservation Volunteers Northern Ireland is part of BTCV. For more details of BTCV, see the entry under BTCV – HQ. Week-long natural breaks and weekend breaks are organized throughout the year, costing from £69 (natural breaks) and £14 for weekend breaks. BTCV is striving towards equal opportunities for all, regardless of age, class, colour, disability, employment status, ethnic or national origins, marital status, race, religious beliefs, responsibilities for children or dependents, sex, sexual orientation or unrelated criminal offences. Volunteers with an offending background are accepted but this does depend upon the type of offence and type of work.

Total projects worldwide: Hundreds
Total UK projects: Hundreds
Starting months: January–December.
Time required: 1–52 weeks (plus).
Age requirement: 16 plus.
Causes: Conservation, environmental causes, unemployed, wildlife, work camps – seasonal, young people.
Activities: Administration, arts/crafts, community work, computers, conservation skills, cooking, driving, forestry, fundraising, group work, library/resource centres, manual work, marketing/publicity, newsletter/journalism, outdoor skills, technical skills, training, work camps – seasonal.
When to apply: All year.
Work alone/with others: With others.
Volunteers with disabilities: Possible.
Qualifications: Nil.
Health requirements: Nil.
Costs: £14 for weekend breaks, from £69 for natural breaks.
Benefits: Unemployed volunteers get £2.50 per day. Unemployed can do NVQ at no cost. We provide insurance cover when working on task.
Training: Volunteers receive free training at our training centre in Clandeboye Estate.
Supervision: By trained members of staff and/or volunteer officers.
Interview details: Only applicants for volunteer officers (volunteers willing to give 6 months or more of their time) are interviewed. There is a volunteer questionnaire. Interviews would take place at the area office.
Certification: NVQ in Landscapes and Ecosystems (levels 2 and 3), Chainsaw licence, Pesticide Licence.
Charity number: 261009
UK placements: *Northern Ireland* (throughout).

CO-ORDINATING COMMITTEE FOR INTERNATIONAL VOLUNTARY SERVICE

UNESCO House
1 rue Miollis
75732 Paris Cedex 15
France

Tel: 00 33 1 45 68 49 36
Fax: 00 33 1 42 73 05 21
e-mail: ccivs@unesco.org
Web: www.unesco.org/ccivs
Contact: Simona Costanzo, Director

CCIVS was created in 1948 under the aegis of UNESCO as an international non-governmental organization responsible for the co-ordination of voluntary service world-wide. Its 142 member organizations implement voluntary programmes in the fields of environment, literacy, preservation of cultural heritage, aid to refugees, health service, emergency relief, development, social services. These programmes are generally carried out through work camps, consisting of a national or an international group working on a common project. Please note that work camps and longer-term projects are not organized directly by CCIVS, and that we do not recruit volunteers directly. These activities are carried out by CCIVS member organizations who undertake the recruitment. Our new public information centre provides information to volunteers wishing to participate in a project abroad (work camps or longer-term projects). We provide directories on voluntary work abroad (explanation of what is a work camp, how to participate, age, qualifications, expenses and useful advice) with the addresses of the organizations you need to contact, costing FF35 (US$7, 10DM, £3.50 or seven international reply coupons). Please send international reply coupons.

Starting months: January–December.
Time required: 1–52 weeks.
Age requirement: 15 plus.
Causes: Archaeology, children, conservation, disabled (learning and physical), elderly people, environmental causes, health care/medical, heritage, human rights, refugees, teaching/assisting work camps – seasonal, young people.
Activities: Administration, agriculture/farming, building/construction, campaigning, caring (general), community work, conservation skills, development issues, first aid, forestry, fundraising, group work, international aid, library/resource centres, manual work, outdoor skills, research, social work, summer camps, teaching, technical skills, training, work camps – seasonal.
Vols under 26 placed each year: 24,000 of a total of 30,000.
When to apply: All year.
Work alone/with others: Dependent on the placement.
Volunteers with disabilities: Dependent on the placement.
Qualifications: Dependent on the placement.
Equipment/clothing: Dependent on the placement.
Health requirements: Dependent on the placement.
Costs: Dependent on the placement.
Benefits: Dependent on the placement.
Training: Dependent on the placement.
Supervision: Dependent on the placement.
Interview details: Dependent on the placement.
Certification: Dependent on the placement.
Worldwide placements: *Africa* (Algeria, Benin, Botswana, Burkina Faso, Burundi, Cape Verde, Congo Republic, Ivory Coast, Ethiopia, Ghana, Kenya, Lesotho, Liberia, Libya, Mali, Mauritius, Morocco, Mozambique, Namibia, Nigeria, Reunion, Senegal, Sierra Leone, South Africa, Swaziland, Tanzania, Togo, Tunisia, Uganda, Zambia, Zimbabwe); *Asia* (Bangladesh, Cambodia, China, India, Indonesia, Israel, Japan, Korea (South), Lebanon, Malaysia, Maldives, Nepal, Pakistan, Philippines, Singapore, Sri Lanka, Taiwan, Thailand, Turkey, Vietnam); *Australasia* (Australia, New Zealand); *Europe* (Armenia, Austria, Azerbaijan, Belarus, Belgium, Bosnia-Herzegovina, Bulgaria, Croatia, Cyprus, Czech Republic, Denmark, Estonia, Finland, France, Georgia, Germany, Gibraltar, Greece, Hungary, Iceland, Ireland, Italy, Latvia, Liechtenstein, Lithuania, Malta, Netherlands, Norway, Poland, Portugal, Romania, Russia, Slovakia, Slovenia, Spain, Sweden, Switzerland, Turkey, Ukraine, Yugoslavia); *North America* (Canada, Greenland, USA); *Central America* (Costa Rica, Cuba, Dominica, El Salvador, Guadeloupe, Guatemala, Honduras, Martinique, Mexico); *South America* (Argentina, Bolivia, Brazil, Chile, Colombia, Ecuador, Peru, Uruguay, Venezuela).

CORAL CAY CONSERVATION LTD
154 Clapham Park Road
London
SW4 7DE UK

Tel: +44 (0) 20 7498 6248
Fax: +44 (0) 20 7498 8447
e-mail: information@coralcay.org
Web: www.coralcay.org
Contact: Andrea Simmons, Volunteer Recruitment Manager

Coral Cay Conservation (CCC) is seeking volunteers to assist with tropical forest and coral reef conservation projects throughout the Asia-Pacific region and in the Caribbean. Volunteers can spend from two to 12 weeks participating on expeditions, with monthly departures throughout the year. The aim of CCC expeditions is to help gather data for the protection and sustainable use of tropical resources, and to offer poverty alleviation and alternative livelihood opportunities for local communities. Current CCC projects are based in the Philippines and Honduras. No previous experience is required. Since 1986, thousands of CCC volunteers have helped establish eight new marine reserves and wildlife sanctuaries, including the Belize Barrier Reef World Heritage Site. CCC also requires volunteers to assist in a busy administration and scientific centre in London. A limited number of scholarships are awarded on a discretionary basis for volunteer staff wishing to gain industrial experience in the marine and terrestrial sciences at CCC's London offices. Presentations take place at regular pre-arranged national/international venues. Volunteers with an offending background are accepted at the discretion of CCC.

Total projects worldwide: 5
Total UK projects: 0
Starting months: January–December.
Time required: 2–12 weeks.
Age requirement: 16 plus.
Causes: Conservation, environmental causes, teaching/assisting, wildlife.
Activities: Administration, building/construction, community work, conservation skills, development issues, DIY, first aid, forestry, fundraising, group work, international aid, manual work, marketing/publicity, outdoor skills, research, scientific work, sport, teaching, technical skills, training.
Vols under 26 placed each year: 240 of a total of 400.
When to apply: 3 months in advance is advised but depending on availability of projects.
Work alone/with others: In groups.
Volunteers with disabilities: Possible, but not for severely disabled.
Qualifications: Nil.
Equipment/clothing: Own basic equipment is required.
Health requirements: Must be reasonably fit.
Costs: Overseas from £715 for 2 weeks. You are responsible for providing your own insurance cover. Comprehensive diving insurance required for marine projects.
Benefits: Free scuba training available Daily trekking on forest projects.
Training: Full expedition training is provided on site. UK pre-departure meeting to meet fellow volunteers and expedition staff. Fully accredited scientific and expedition training courses, including scuba training are given.
Supervision: Trained and experienced expedition staff.
Interview details: During presentations, full expedition briefings given which are followed by informal group interviews.
Certification: Scuba diving certification and basic Tropical Rainforest Ecology and Natural Resource Assessment Certificate. Reference on request.
Charity number: 1025534
Worldwide placements: *Asia* (Philippines); *Central America* (Honduras).

CORD – CHRISTIAN OUTREACH RELIEF AND DEVELOPMENT
1 New Street
Leamington Spa
Warwickshire
CV31 1HP UK
Tel: +44 (0) 1926 315301
Fax: +44 (0) 1926 885786
e-mail: cord_uk@compuserve.com
Contact: Mrs Kay Bugg

The aim of CORD is to demonstrate the love of Jesus by practical care of vulnerable and marginalized people, especially children, displaced communities and refugees, by: endeavouring to remain a caring organization characterised by a Christian ethos, professionalism and concern for the underprivileged; setting up operational work in areas where there are no local organizations; using professional Christian staff; giving priority to areas where there are health concerns; encouraging self-reliance and the strengthening of local structures. 'A three-stranded CORD is not easily broken' (Ecclesiastes 4 v 12). As a Christian agency, we endeavour to seek and follow God's will in our prayer and planning, in our projects and publicity. He is the central and strongest strand in all that we do. The second strand is our dedicated teams of expatriate and national staff, who often work in very difficult and isolated conditions. To keep our programmes running, CORD also needs a third strand – people like you. Without the gifts and prayers of individuals and churches throughout the country, our work would not be possible, which is why we value close relationships with our supporters. CORD's aim is that at least 90% of our annual income goes directly to our projects overseas, to support the poor and vulnerable people who need help most. Volunteers with an offending background are accepted.

Total projects worldwide: 6
Total UK projects: 0
Starting months: January–December.
Time required: 52 weeks.
Age requirement: 21 plus.
Causes: Children, health care/medical, refugees.
Activities: Accountancy, administration, building/construction, caring (residential), community work, development issues, religion, technical skills.

Vols under 26 placed each year: 1 or 2 of a total of 25 plus.
When to apply: All year.
Work alone/with others: With others.
Volunteers with disabilities: Possible.
Qualifications: Christian commitment and post-school specialized training.
Equipment/clothing: £200.
Costs: Travel to UK for overseas volunteers.
Benefits: Food and accommodation, insurance, travel plus £90 pocket money per month. We pay for insurance cover via an EMA Scheme.
Training: 1 week's in-house orientation plus occasional outside training.
Supervision: By country director of project co-ordinator.
Interview details: Interviews take place at our offices in Leamington Spa.
Charity number: 1070684
Worldwide placements: *Africa* (Mozambique, Rwanda, Tunisia); *Asia* (Cambodia, Vietnam); *Europe* (Albania).

CORNWALL WILDLIFE TRUST
Five Acres
Allet
Truro
Cornwall
TR4 9DJ UK

Tel: +44 (0) 1872 273939
Fax: +44 (0) 1872 225476
e-mail: cornwt@cix.compulink.co.uk
Web: www.wildlifetrust.org.uk/cornwall/
Contact: Gavin Henderson

Cornwall Wildlife Trust is a member of the Wildlife Trusts, a national partnership of 47 county trusts. The aims of the Trust are primarily to: promote nature conservation in the community; acquire and manage nature reserves; monitor biological and geological resources; liaise with local authorities to promote regard for nature conservation; offer practical advice on nature conservation to landowners. It is our policy to involve all sectors of the community, of all ages, backgrounds, abilities and disabilities towards these ends. Volunteers require no previous experience just lots of enthusiasm. You will receive on-the-job training in an informal atmosphere and, if you desire, can go on to participate more fully assisting with the organization and running of activities/projects. Limited opportunities may also

arise, for those with a longer-term commitment, for NVQ training to level 2 in Landscapes and Ecosystems. Volunteers with an offending background may be accepted – each case separately assessed.

Total projects worldwide: 25 plus
Total UK projects: 25 plus
Starting months: January–December.
Time required: 1–52 weeks (plus).
Age requirement: 16 plus.
Causes: Conservation, environmental causes, wildlife.
Activities: Computers, conservation skills, driving, forestry, gardening/horticulture, manual work, outdoor skills, research, scientific work, technical skills.
Vols under 26 placed each year: 75 of a total of 150.
When to apply: All year.
Work alone/with others: With others.
Volunteers with disabilities: Possible.
Qualifications: Nil but practical skills useful.
Equipment/clothing: Casual work clothes, waterproofs, stout boots. Protective safety gear is provided.
Health requirements: Any medical conditions (illness, allergy or physical disability) that may require treatment/medication or which affect the volunteer working with machinery must be notified to us in advance. Tetanus injections must be up to date.
Costs: Bring your own packed lunch.
Benefits: Out-of-pocket expenses provided. Public liability and employers liability insurance provided by us.
Training: On-the-job training provided.
Supervision: All volunteers are supported either directly by staff supervision or with experienced volunteers.
Interview details: Interviews at our office.
Certification: Reference on request.
Charity number: 214929
UK placements: *England* (Cornwall).

CORPORACIÓN PARA EL DESAROLLO DEL APRENDIZAJE (CDA)
Grajales 2561
Santiago Central
Chile

Tel: 00 56 2 689 1633
Fax: 00 56 2 671 2493
Contact: Helena Todd or Irma Almeyda

Corporación para el Desarrollo del Aprendizaje (CDA) is a foundation for the treatment and stimulation of 5–18 year olds with neuro-cognitive deficit from deprived backgrounds who also attend the normal school system. The family also receives attention. Volunteers may provide auxilliary service to the children and youths, in the preparation of didactic materials, in fund raising and organizational activities, and other suitable activities according to the talents shown on their CV.

Total projects worldwide: 15
Total UK projects: 0
Starting months: March, July.
Time required: 16–50 weeks.
Age requirement: 18–25
Causes: Children, disabled (learning and physical), elderly people, health care/medical, inner city problems, teaching/assisting (primary, secondary, EFL), young people.
Activities: Administration, caring (general), community work, computers, first aid, fundraising, group work, library/resource centres, music, newsletter/journalism, social work, teaching, technical skills, translating, visiting/befriending.
Vols under 26 placed each year: 2–4
When to apply: Up to 2 months prior to arrival.
Work alone/with others: Varies.
Volunteers with disabilities: Not possible.
Qualifications: None but Spanish useful – as are art and computer skills.
Equipment/clothing: Huge seasonal and geographical variations in climate. Sleeping bags, towels and sheets, drivers licence. English music/family photos etc.
Health requirements: We care for minor illnesses. Recommend wisdom teeth removed prior to travel. If spectactles are worn, please bring spare pair. Eat well and sensibly. Volunteers should not travel to the north of Chile into the mountain regions if there is any heart weakness. (We have no centres there but volunteers like to travel and visit.)
Costs: The volunteer has to cover everything. We do however provide very cheap board and lodging in Santiago and Illapel. We are aiming to provide the same in Magallanes and Concepcion.
Benefits: Help to find paid TEFL positions. Paid travel with CDA professionals to regions other than where volunteers are located, also for participation in some events in Santiago. Latin American fiction and professional articles on care available.

Training: 3–4 weeks at our main centre in Santiago.
Supervision: Volunteers are assigned to one therapist and have a monthly meeting with the Director.
Interview details: Applicants are interviewed only by letter and fax.
Certification: Written reference provided.
Charity number: DofL 659
Worldwide placements: *South America* (Chile).

CORPS VOLONTAIRES CONGOLAIS AU DEVELOPPEMENT (COVOCODE)

7 Rue Meteo
Quartier Kimpe, Commune de Ngaliema
Kinshasa
3410 Kin/Gombe
Democratic Republic of Congo

Fax: 00 1 770 240 2901/2902/2985
Contact: Joseph Milamba Kasongo, Executive Co-ordinator

Corps Volontaires Congolais au Developpement (COVOCODE) aims to increase the awareness of the social problems throughout the country as well as to help with the particularly deprived areas. Volunteers are needed to work on long-term projects with a minimum of a three-month commitment, and a maximum of a year.

Total projects worldwide: 1
Total UK projects: 0
Starting months: January–December.
Time required: 12–52 weeks.
Age requirement: 17–30
Causes: Aids/HIV, architecture, children, conservation, environmental causes, health care/medical, human rights, inner city problems, offenders/ex-offenders, poor/homeless, teaching/assisting (primary, secondary), work camps – seasonal, young people.
Activities: Agriculture/farming, arts/crafts, building/construction, campaigning, caring (general, day and residential), community work, computers, conservation skills, development issues, forestry, fundraising, group work, library/resource centres, manual work, newsletter/journalism, outdoor skills, religion, research, scientific work, social work, summer camps, teaching, technical skills, training, translating, visiting/befriending, work camps – seasonal.
Vols under 26 placed each year: 20 of a total

of 35.
When to apply: All year.
Work alone/with others: With others.
Volunteers with disabilities: Not possible.
Qualifications: French or English speaking.
Post A-level, International Baccaleureate or
university.
Equipment/clothing: Sunshade and umbrella
– our country is tropical! Camera and films
etc.
Health requirements: Medical certificate
confirming that the volunteer is healthy to
work in a tropical country.
Costs: Travel to Kinshasa, subsistence fees as
follows: 1–3 months US$500, 4–6 months
US$800, 7–12 months US$1,000.
Registration fee of US$150 to be paid before
arrival.
Benefits: Modest accommodation, local travel
to project and pocket money.
Certification: Certificate or reference
provided.
Charity number: 73-309

CORRYMEELA COMMUNITY
5 Drumaroan Road
Ballycastle
Co. Antrim
BT54 6QU N. Ireland

Tel: +44 (0) 28 2076 2626
Fax: +44 (0) 28 2076 2770
e-mail: ballycastle@corrymeela.org
Contact: Helen Rooney, Volunteer
Co-ordinator

Corrymeela is a dispersed Christian
community, founded in 1965, that is
committed to the healing of social, religious,
and political divisions that exist in Northern
Ireland and throughout the world.
Corrymeela seeks to offer a safe place in
which people can meet one another as they
are, and thus enable new relationships to
grow. Our work is grounded on the belief
that reconciliation is central to finding new
ways to live together, at both personal and
societal levels. Each year Corrymeela recruits
a team of ten volunteers to assist the
permanent staff in the running of the
Ballycastle centre. The commitment is usually
for one year, starting in September, with two
six-month volunteers being added in March.
Full-time volunteers form an integral part of
the Corrymeela programme. We try each year
to include people from a range of social,

religious and cultural backgrounds. Usually,
about half the team are from outside
Northern Ireland. Volunteers help with all
aspects of the work at Ballycastle, an eight-
acre residential village on the beautiful north
coast of County Antrim. The work includes
hosting groups, planning activities, cooking,
leading discussions, assisting, housekeeping,
showing visitors around, working on
reception, singing, leading worship, staffing
the tuck shop, driving (if you have a bus
driver's licence) and much more. Volunteers
have two days off in every ten days and four
weeks annual holiday. Volunteers give a great
deal of themselves, not only to fellow
members of the team but also to those who
come to the centre. At times this can lead to
long working days (up to 16 hours), and the
work is not always 'glamorous'. Corrymeela
is definitely not a place for those who seek a
regular work experience! This, together with
the tensions which will be experienced by any
small group living together in a community,
results in a way of life that is challenging,
sometimes demanding, but also unusually
rewarding and enriching. Approximately 25
volunteers are also needed during each week
of July/August for 1–3 weeks. Volunteers
with an offending background may be
accepted depending on the offence.

Total projects worldwide: 200–300
Total UK projects: 200–300
Starting months: March, July, August,
September.
Time required: 1–52 weeks.
Age requirement: 18 plus.
Causes: Children, disabled (learning and
physical), elderly people, environmental
causes, inner city problems, offenders/ex-
offenders, teaching/assisting (nursery,
primary, secondary), unemployed, young
people.
Activities: Administration, arts/crafts, caring
(general and residential), community work,
computers, cooking, counselling,
development issues, driving, fundraising,
group work, manual work, music, outdoor
skills, religion, sport, summer camps,
teaching, theatre/drama, visiting/befriending.
Vols under 26 placed each year: 180–250 of
a total of 200–300.
When to apply: March (12 month), October
(6 month).
Work alone/with others: Both.
Volunteers with disabilities: Possible.

Qualifications: Nil, but all skills helpful and valued.
Health requirements: Nil.
Costs: Travel to and from Corrymeela. Personal property insurance needs to be provided by volunteer. We provide other insurance.
Benefits: Free board and lodging.
Training: Provided at the beginning of the placement.
Supervision: Regular meetings in group, and monthly with the volunteer co-ordinator.
Interview details: Interviews normally take place in Ballycastle but elsewhere sometimes.
Certification: Reference on request.
Charity number: XN48052A
UK placements: *Northern Ireland* (Antrim).

COTSWOLD COMMUNITY, THE
Spine Road West
Ashton Keynes
Nr Swindon
Wiltshire
SN6 6QU UK

Tel: +44 (0) 1285 861239
Fax: +44 (0) 1285 860114
Contact: The Principal

The Cotswold Community is a village-type community. We cater for approximately 40 boys, in the age range 9–18, living in four separate households. Preferred age for admission is 9–12. In addition there is a school and a farm. The emphasis is on small group living as a basis for the healing culture. Most staff and their families live within the Cotswold, helping to create a village type of community. The Community caters for severely emotionally disturbed and abused boys. Their personalities are very fragile and they have few inner controls. They see the world as untrustworthy and hostile and tend to be continuously disruptive and subject to destructive outbursts of anger. These children need to incorporate a positive experience of 'parental' care to repair the damage of their negative actual experience in infancy, and early childhood. The primary task of the Cotswold Community is treatment and the cornerstone of treatment is the formation of a deep and trusting relationship between a child and a grown up. When the early emotional gaps have been filled, the child will begin to evolve.

Total projects worldwide: 1
Total UK projects: 1

Starting months: January–December.
Time required: 16–52 weeks.
Age requirement: 21–26
Causes: Children, teaching/assisting (primary, secondary), young people.
Activities: Caring (general and residential), cooking, counselling, DIY, driving, first aid, gardening/horticulture, group work, music, outdoor skills, social work, sport, teaching.
Vols under 26 placed each year: 9 of a total of 10.
When to apply: All year.
Work alone/with others: With other staff.
Volunteers with disabilities: Not possible.
Qualifications: Previous childcare experience, basic living skills. Driving/music/arts/crafts desirable.
Health requirements: Nothing that could put children at risk.
Costs: Nil.
Benefits: Board, lodging, £24 per week pocket money. Travel to and from project at beginning and end of placement.
Interview details: Interviews take place at the Cotswold Community.
Certification: Written references and testimonials.
Charity number: 215301
UK placements: *England* (Gloucestershire, Wiltshire).

COUNCIL FOR EDUCATION IN WORLD CITIZENSHIP
15 St Swithin's Lane
London
EC4N 8AL UK

Tel: +44 (0) 20 7929 5090
Fax: +44 (0) 20 7929 5091
e-mail: cewc@campus.bt.com
Contact: Mr David Pinder

Council for Education in World Citizenship needs volunteers for educational, research, office administration and computer work. Volunteers with an offending background are possibly accepted.

Total projects worldwide: 3
Total UK projects: 3
Starting months: January–December.
Time required: 6–52 weeks (plus).
Age requirement: 16 plus.
Causes: Children, environmental causes, human rights, poor/homeless, refugees, teaching/assisting (primary, secondary), young people.

Activities: Administration, community work, computers, development issues, fundraising, marketing/publicity, teaching.
Vols under 26 placed each year: 7 of a total of 30.
When to apply: All year as early as possible.
Work alone/with others: With others.
Volunteers with disabilities: Possible in the London office.
Qualifications: Strong motivation, good research, reading and writing.
Health requirements: Nil.
Costs: Nil.
Benefits: Travel costs and a small daily lunch allowance.
Interview details: Interviews usually in London.
Certification: Certificate or reference provided.
Charity number: 313176
UK placements: *England* (London); *Northern Ireland* (Belfast City); *Wales* (Cardiff, Vale of Glamorgan).

COVENANTERS

Mill House
Mill Lane
Cheadle
Cheshire
SK8 2NT UK

Tel: +44 (0) 161 428 5566
Fax: +44 (0) 161 428 2299
e-mail: covies@dial.pipex.com
Contact: Paul Wilcox

Covenanters is an evangelical organization 'Serving the Local Church' in its work with children and young people. By offering advice on mainstream resources, we help you to reach children and young people, developing and equipping them for continued Christian life and service. Covenanters helps churches by offering an age structure covering 0–20 years, providing training, support and resources for leaders and members. The Covenanter package is Bible-based, church-controlled, interdenominational, non-uniformed and flexible. Our Holidays Programme for 10–19 year olds includes opportunities for Christians aged 16 and upwards to participate as members of leadership teams. All team members attend at least one day's team preparation when they can have input into project planning. More experienced team members are invited to join

management groups. We have service opportunities for ages 16 plus through Energize Community Sports Initiative. Nine projects are based in urban priority areas. Contact us above for more information. Field Force is Covies regional development involving nine regions with between three and five areas in each throughout the UK. Each region will ultimately have a full-time manager. At present the East/West Midlands and North West regions have workers.

Total projects worldwide: 14
Total UK projects: 14
Starting months: July.
Time required: 1–4 weeks.
Age requirement: 18 plus.
Causes: Children, teaching/assisting (primary, secondary), young people.
Activities: Catering, cooking, first aid, group work, music, outdoor skills, religion, sport, summer camps, teaching, training, visiting/befriending.
Vols under 26 placed each year: 280 of a total of 2,344.
When to apply: March–May.
Work alone/with others: With others.
Volunteers with disabilities: Possible.
Qualifications: Not essential but first aid, lifesaving, catering, outdoor pursuits skills useful.
Equipment/clothing: Only for participation in outdoor pursuits.
Health requirements: Medical certificates for all projects and more required for overseas projects.
Costs: Subsistence etc. costs £85–£150 for UK and £800 including travel for overseas.
Benefits: Reductions to the costs may be made at the discretion of the leader.
Charity number: 282122
Worldwide placements: *Africa* (Zambia, Zimbabwe).
UK placements: *England* (Buckinghamshire, Cheshire, Cumbria, Gloucestershire, Hampshire, Herefordshire, Lancashire, Manchester, Merseyside, Norfolk, Shropshire, Staffordshire, Suffolk, Surrey, Warwickshire, West Midlands); *Scotland* (Angus, Argyll and Bute, Clackmannanshire, Dumfries and Galloway, Edinburgh, Fife, Glasgow City, E. Lothian, W. Lothian, Perth and Kinross, Scottish Borders, Stirling); *Wales* (Gwynedd).

CRESSET HOUSE CAMPHILL VILLAGE

PO Box 74

Halfway House
1685 Transvaal
South Africa

Contact: Ann Haberkorn or Patricia Tippett

Total projects worldwide: 1
Total UK projects: 0
Starting months: July, August.
Time required: 52 weeks (plus).
Age requirement: 19 plus.
Causes: Disabled (learning and physical), environmental causes, teaching/assisting.
Activities: Agriculture/farming, arts/crafts, caring (residential), community work, cooking, counselling, gardening/horticulture, religion, social work, sport, training.
Vols under 26 placed each year: 5–6
When to apply: February/March.
Work alone/with others: Both.
Volunteers with disabilities: Not possible.
Qualifications: Spoken English and willingness to help wherever needed (workshops, land, houses).
Equipment/clothing: Working clothes and good clothes for Sunday festivities.
Health requirements: Volunteers should be healthy – teeth in good condition.
Costs: Travel costs to and from RSA.
Benefits: Board, lodging, acute medical and dental costs, pocket money R260/month.
Interview details: Only via correspondence.
Certification: Certificate or reference provided.
Worldwide placements: *Africa* (South Africa).

CRIME CONCERN TRUST
London Office
89 Albert Embankment
London
SE1 7TS UK

Tel: +44 (0) 20 7820 6012
Fax: +44 (0) 20 7587 1617
e-mail: adrian.smith@crimeconcern-se.org.uk
Web: www.crimeconcern.org.uk
Contact: Adrian Smith, Development Officer – Volunteers

Crime Concern is a national crime prevention charity specializing in youth crime, criminality prevention, high crime neighbourhoods, women's safety, business and town centre crime, rural crime and school, hospital and passenger safety. We manage around 60 projects across England and Wales, prepare crime surveys, reports and briefings and work in partnership with local authorities, police, housing and youth agencies, businesses and parish councils.

Total projects worldwide: 60
Total UK projects: 60
Starting months: January–December.
Time required: 1–52 weeks (plus).
Age requirement: 16 plus.
Causes: Children, environmental causes, inner city problems, offenders/ex-offenders, young people.
Activities: Administration, community work, fundraising, group work, social work, sport, summer camps, visiting/befriending.
Vols under 26 placed each year: 400–500 of a total of 600–700.
When to apply: All year.
Work alone/with others: With others.
Volunteers with disabilities: Disabled volunteers welcomed.
Qualifications: Interest in community work and young people. A police check will be needed for those working with young people.
Health requirements: Nil.
Costs: Nil.
Benefits: Expenses paid. Volunteers are covered by our insurance.
Training: Training as required is provided.
Supervision: As required.
Interview details: Interview is part of the selection process.
UK placements: *England* (Bedfordshire, Bristol, Devon, Hampshire, Kent, Leicestershire, London, Manchester, Merseyside, Northumberland, Nottinghamshire, Somerset, Staffordshire, Tyne and Wear, Warwickshire, West Midlands, Wiltshire); *Wales* (Cardiff, Vale of Glamorgan).

CRISIS
First Floor
Challenger House
42 Adler Street
London
E1 1EE UK

Tel: +44 (0) 20 7655 8300
Contact: Karyn Jones, Volunteer Co-ordinator

Crisis is a grant-giving charitable trust, raising money and giving grants to projects working with homeless people. We also run the CRISIS Open Christmas, which provides food and shelter for homeless people in

London over the Christmas period.
Volunteers are needed to help with
administration, computer work,
wordprocessing, fundraising and public
relations work in the London office. Extra
volunteers are also needed to help run the
Open Christmas project.

Starting months: January–November.
Time required: 1–52 weeks (plus).
Age requirement: 16 plus.
Causes: Poor/homeless.
Activities: Administration, computers,
fundraising, marketing/publicity.
When to apply: All year.
Work alone/with others: With others.
Volunteers with disabilities: Blind, deaf and
physically disabled welcome.
Qualifications: Nil, except enthusiasm and
commitment.
Benefits: Travel expenses provided. Public
liability insurance cover is given.
UK placements: *England* (London).

CROSSLINKS
251 Lewisham Way
London
SE4 1XF UK

Tel: +44 (0) 20 8691 6111
Fax: +44 (0) 20 8694 8023
e-mail: smile@crosslinks.org
Web: www.crosslinks.org
Contact: Oliver Leonard, Volunteer
Co-ordinator

Crosslinks is an Anglican evangelical mission
agency, working worldwide in partnership
with churches and other agencies. We support
mission partners, study partners and projects
and link these with local churches in Britain
and Ireland. Our SMILE programme (Short-
term Mission Involvement, Learning and
Experience) gives you the opportunity to find
out what it is like to take God's Word to
God's world. Whether you have a week or
two, or six months, to spare, here is the
chance for you to do something really useful
for the gospel. SMILE volunteers have been
seen around the world – teaching in
Tanzania, working on holiday clubs in
Ireland, or studying wildlife in Portugal.
There is even the opportunity to teach
English in China, or to study Mandarin.
Ireland is summer holiday clubs. Portugal is
environmental work. China is language
placements. Kenya, Tanzania and Uganda are

maximum six month placements. Volunteers
with an offending background will probably
be accepted.

Total projects worldwide: 6
Total UK projects: 1
Starting months: January, July, August,
September.
Time required: 1–52 weeks.
Age requirement: 17 plus.
Causes: Children, conservation,
environmental causes, poor/homeless,
teaching/assisting (primary, secondary, EFL).
Activities: Building/construction,
conservation skills, development issues,
religion, sport, summer camps, teaching.
Vols under 26 placed each year: 45 of a total
of 50.
When to apply: All year.
Work alone/with others: With others.
Volunteers with disabilities: Possible.
Qualifications: Training in TEFL for some
placements (e.g. China).
Health requirements: Good health is
essential, particularly for Africa. Some
innoculations recommended.
Costs: For Africa: travel costs £500
approximately and subsistence £1,500 for six
months. For UK: £30 per week subsistence
plus travel. Insurance necessary for all.
Training: Comprehensive pre-departure
training is provided.
Supervision: All volunteers are placed near
long-term overseas personnel.
Interview details: Interviews take place in
London or the UK regions.
Certification: Certification or reference on
request.
Worldwide placements: *Africa* (Kenya,
Tanzania, Uganda); *Asia* (China); *Europe*
(Ireland, Portugal).
UK placements: *Northern Ireland* (Antrim).

CRUSADERS
FREEPOST 544
2 Romeland Hill
St Albans
Hertfordshire
AL3 4ET UK

Tel: +44 (0) 1727 855422
Fax: +44 (0) 1727 848518
e-mail: crusoe@crusaders.org.uk
Web: www.crusaders.org.uk
Contact: Sam Henry, CRUSOE Co-ordinator

Crusaders is an international youth

organization helping churches and volunteers reach young people with the Christian message, through youth groups, holiday programmes and overseas projects. The emphasis is on relevance and on equipping volunteers with leadership training, active teaching materials and the latest specialist youth resources, through local and national support. Committed Christians are invited to volunteer as youth leaders for new or existing youth groups, as holiday staff, for short-term service opportunities overseas or in the UK. Youth leaders: aged 21 plus. Training is given for new leaders in all the important skills. Assistant leaders: aged 17 plus, nominated by local leaders. Group helpers: aged 15–16 who have leadership potential and are beginning to assist the group appointed by local leaders. Training through new 'Into Action' programme. Holiday staff: roles include small group team leaders, speakers, catering staff, programme planners; anyone aged 17 plus, with tremendous energy and enthusiasm for young people can apply; those with gifts in specialist areas such as sports, music, etc. especially welcome. CRUSOE (Crusaders Overseas Expeditions): for any committed young Christian aged 14-22 to put faith into practice in projects during summer break. Selection weekend in February and de-brief weekend in September. Romania Project: aged 18 plus, to help Romanian Christians run holiday camps for young people. Fund Raisers and Supporters: a valuable role for volunteers. Volunteers with an offending background may be accepted depending on circumstances and subject to references.

Total projects worldwide: 511
Total UK projects: 500
Starting months: July–September.
Time required: 1–5 weeks.
Age requirement: 14 plus.
Causes: Children, holidays for disabled, poor/homeless, teaching/assisting work camps – seasonal, young people.
Activities: Administration, arts/crafts, building/construction, catering, community work, cooking, development issues, first aid, fundraising, group work, international aid, manual work, marketing/publicity, music, outdoor skills, religion, social work, summer camps, teaching, translating, work camps – seasonal.
Vols under 26 placed each year:

Approximately 100 of a total of 150.
When to apply: November–February for CRUSOE; May for Romania; all year for UK.
Work alone/with others: With others.
Volunteers with disabilities: Possible.
Qualifications: Varies according to vacancy. Sympathy with our Christian basis.
Equipment/clothing: Variable.
Health requirements: Need to have good health for heavy overseas projects.
Costs: £500-£1,400 to fund trip for CRUSOE.
Benefits: The cost covers all needs.
Training: Depends on project. Normally one weekend pre-placement training a minimum.
Supervision: Under 18s supervised by leaders.
Interview details: CRUSOE selection weekends take place in central England, Scotland and Northern Ireland.
Charity number: 223798
Worldwide placements: *Africa* (Kenya, South Africa, Tunisia, Uganda, Zambia, Zimbabwe); *Asia* (India, Philippines, Thailand); *Europe* (France, Germany, Ireland, Lithuania, Poland, Portugal, Romania, Switzerland); *Central America* (Costa Rica, El Salvador, Guatemala, Honduras, Mexico, Nicaragua, Panama); *South America* (Bolivia, Brazil, Chile).
UK placements: *England* (Bedfordshire, Berkshire, Bristol, Buckinghamshire, Cambridgeshire, Channel Islands, Cheshire, Cornwall, Cumbria, Derbyshire, Devon, Dorset, Essex, Gloucestershire, Hampshire, Hertfordshire, Isle of Man, Isle of Wight, Kent, Lancashire, Leicestershire, Lincolnshire, London, Manchester, Merseyside, Norfolk, Northamptonshire, Northumberland, Nottinghamshire, Oxfordshire, Shropshire, Somerset, Staffordshire, Suffolk, Surrey, E. Sussex, W. Sussex, Tyne and Wear, Warwickshire, West Midlands, Wiltshire, S. Yorkshire, W. Yorkshire); *Scotland* (throughout); *Northern Ireland* (throughout); *Wales* (Bridgend, Caerphilly, Cardiff, Conwy, Gwynedd, Newport, Powys, Rhondda, Cynon, Taff, Vale of Glamorgan).

CUBA SOLIDARITY CAMPAIGN (CSC), THE
Red Rose Club
129 Seven Sisters Road
London
N7 7QG UK

Tel: +44 (0) 20 7263 6452
Fax: +44 (0) 20 7561 0191
e-mail: office@cuba-solidarity.org.uk
Web: www.cuba-solidarity.org.uk
Other web: www.cubaconnect.co.uk
Contact: Rob Miller, National Co-ordinator

The Cuba Solidarity Campaign works to develop understanding of Cuba and to build support for the following positions: respect for Cuba's right to sovereignty and independence; an end to the USA's trade blockade against Cuba. Twice a year CSC sends a delegation to join groups from other European countries on an international Brigade. During their three weeks' stay, Brigadistas work with Cubans mainly on agricultural projects. Visits to schools, hospitals, factories and places of cultural and historic interest are organized as well as meetings with representatives of Cuba's mass organizations. The Brigade is an excellent opportunity to witness Cuban society at first hand. Volunteers with an offending background are accepted.

Total projects worldwide: 2
Total UK projects: 0
Starting months: July, December.
Time required: 3–52 weeks.
Age requirement: 16 plus.
Causes: Conservation, environmental causes, human rights, young people.
Activities: Agriculture/farming, building/construction, conservation skills, development issues, international aid, manual work, music, outdoor skills.
Vols under 26 placed each year: 30–40 of a total of 60–80.
When to apply: 3–4 months prior to departure.
Work alone/with others: With others.
Volunteers with disabilities: Equal Opportunity selection.
Qualifications: Wish to help Cuba and Cuban people.
Health requirements: Nil.
Costs: Travel costs and contribution to accommodation, food and local travel (£770 approximately) to be arranged by the volunteer.
Benefits: Will be able to see the real Cuba – experience of a lifetime.
Training: Participants should attend a preparation weekend in London where sessions are given on Cuban life, daily life on the Brigade, and the volunteers can get to know each other and plan solidarity action.
Supervision: During work times there is supervision to ensure safety.
Interview details: Application form.
Worldwide placements: *Central America* (Cuba).

CUMBRIA WILDLIFE TRUST
Brockhole
Windermere
Cumbria
LA23 1LJ UK

Tel: +44 (0) 15394 48280
Fax: +44 (0) 15394 48281
e-mail: cumbriawt@cix.co.uk
Web: www.wildlifetrust.org.uk/cumbria
Contact: Rachel Osborn, Environmental Awareness Project Officer

Cumbria Wildlife Trust works in partnership with landowners, local authorities, other conservation organizations and businesses to conserve wildlife everywhere in Cumbria. Through surveys and projects collects information on particular sites and species. Projects include the monitoring of butterfly populations and promoting the conservation message through major campaigns such as the National Peatland Campaign. Cumbria Wildlife Trust manages 41 nature reserves throughout Cumbria extending to over 3,000 ha. Volunteers contribute greatly to the success of the Trust and are able to help with a wide range of tasks.

Total projects worldwide: 41
Total UK projects: 41
Starting months: January–December.
Time required: 1 week.
Age requirement: 16 plus.
Activities: Administration, computers, conservation skills, forestry, fundraising, manual work, marketing/publicity, newsletter/journalism, outdoor skills, research, scientific work, teaching, training.
Vols under 26 placed each year: Less than 10.
When to apply: All year.
Work alone/with others: Both.
Volunteers with disabilities: Possible.
Qualifications: English. Practical skills/experience, first aid, computing and any other skills an advantage.
Equipment/clothing: Outdoor clothing etc. for reserve work.

Health requirements: Varies. There may be health restrictions for certain sites.
Costs: Only the volunteer's own living costs, including rent, travel etc.
Benefits: Out-of-pocket expenses.
Training: Limited on-the-job training.
Nationalities accepted: No restrictions but English speaking.
Interview details: No interview necessary.
Certification: Written reference provided.
UK placements: *England* (Cumbria).

D

DAKSHINAYAN
F-1169 Chittaranjan Park
New Delhi
110019 India

Tel: 00 91 11 6484468
Fax: 00 91 11 6484468
e-mail: sid@postone.com
Web: www.linkindia.com/dax
Contact: Siddharth Sanyal

Dakshinayan aims to promote international and intercultural understanding through the Development Education Programme. The aim of the programme is to introduce concerned and sensitive individuals to rural development projects in India so that they may gain an in-depth understanding of the myth and reality of 'Third World poverty'. The programme is not meant for 'helping the poor, underdeveloped' people living in Indian villages, but rather to participate in what is being done by grassroots development projects. The programme is open to both skilled and unskilled participants. Those who wish to join the programme should be seriously interested in visiting a rural development project and understanding the reality of rural India. It should not matter to them where they are placed nor to what work they are assigned. Dakshinayan has a policy of sending not more than two or three participants to a project at the same time. This facilitates better integration and interaction with the community and project. It also ensures that the natural rhythm of the project is not disturbed.

Total projects worldwide: 3
Total UK projects: 0
Starting months: January–December.
Time required: 4–32 weeks.
Age requirement: 18 plus.
Causes: Children, conservation, elderly people, environmental causes, health care/medical, teaching/assisting (nursery, primary, EFL), wildlife.
Activities: Administration, agriculture/farming, arts/crafts, building/construction, caring (general), community work, conservation skills, cooking, development issues, first aid, forestry, fundraising, gardening/horticulture, group work, international aid, manual work, music, newsletter/journalism, outdoor skills, social work, sport, teaching, technical skills, training, translating, visiting/befriending, work camps – seasonal.
Vols under 26 placed each year: 150 of a total of 200.
When to apply: 1 month prior to arrival.
Work alone/with others: With others.
Volunteers with disabilities: Not possible.
Qualifications: Nil.
Health requirements: Physically and mentally fit.
Costs: Registration fee of $50 plus fares plus $150 per month.
Benefits: The cost covers board and lodging.
Interview details: Prospective volunteers are screened in New Delhi before orientation.
Certification: Certificate or reference provided.
Worldwide placements: *Asia* (India).

DALE VIEW, THE
Punalal PO
Poovachal – 695 575
Thiruvananthapuram District
Kerala State
India

Tel: 00 91 471 882063 or 882163
e-mail: ducdas@md3.vsnl.net.in
Contact: Mr C. Das, The Director

'Be not weary in well doing' is the motto of The Dale View and it sums up the aim of the organization. The projects vary enormously, focusing on what is needed locally and encouraging self-help. The largest project is a pair of schools, with over 1,400 students. The fastest growing project is the Micro Credit Scheme, which encourages women to set up financial Self-Help Groups (SHGs). The Dale View loans money to the SHGs to start Income Generating Projects (IGPs). The De-Addiction Centre caters for local alcohol and substance abusers, to whom we offer a free 21-day treatment. This includes medical care, dry therapy and group and individual counselling sessions. The Dale View runs environmental projects, like our watershed scheme, the digging of community wells and latrines, and our bio-gas plant programme. We have helped over 370 local disabled people to start IGPs to give them mental satisfaction and financial independence. Other schemes include our crèche, forestry project, plant nursery, piggery and poultry unit, and training centre. Volunteers can 'shadow' the hard-working director, but they are encouraged to partake in the projects that interest them. The language barrier prevents most volunteers from working directly with the locals, but most of the staff speak basic English. The Dale View encourages all forms of support and individual sponsorship. We hope soon to set up a hospital and a special school for physically handicapped children. We are especially interested in people with expertise in these fields, although we warmly welcome all volunteers. Volunteers with offending backgrounds may be accepted. Each case individually assessed.

Total projects worldwide: 35
Total UK projects: 0
Starting months: January–December.
Time required: 3–18 weeks.
Age requirement: 16 plus.
Causes: Addicts/ex-addicts, Aids/HIV, animal welfare, children, conservation, disabled (physical), environmental causes, health care/medical, human rights, poor/homeless, teaching/assisting (nursery, primary, EFL), unemployed, work camps – seasonal, young people.
Activities: Agriculture/farming, building/construction, campaigning, caring (day and residential), community work, computers, conservation skills, cooking, counselling, development issues, first aid, forestry, fundraising, gardening/horticulture, group work, international aid, marketing/publicity, research, social work, teaching, technical skills, training, translating, visiting/befriending, work camps – seasonal.
Vols under 26 placed each year: 13 or 14 of a total of 15.

When to apply: At least a month in advance.
Work alone/with others: With local volunteers.
Volunteers with disabilities: Paths and tracks are unsuitable for wheelchairs. Others will be assessed individually.
Qualifications: Nil, but those skilled are encouraged to help in relevant projects.
Equipment/clothing: Nil, but suitable for hot temperatures.
Health requirements: Only very limited healthcare is available.
Costs: Travel to Trivandram. US$125 per month donation. Volunteers responsible for their own personal travel insurance.
Benefits: The donation (listed under costs) covers the cost of food and lodging.
Supervision: By the director and his wife.
Nationalities accepted: No restrictions providing you have necessary visas to stay in India.
Interview details: No interview but details are exchanged by post and telephone to check suitability of candidates.
Certification: Reference on request.
Charity number: 96/1978
Worldwide placements: *Asia* (India).

DANEFORD TRUST, THE
45–47 Blythe Street
London
E2 6LN UK

Tel: +44 (0) 20 7729 1928
Fax: +44 (0) 20 7729 1928
e-mail: dfdtrust@aol.com
Contact: Anthony Stevens

The Daneford Trust is a community-based organization and our priority is to increase and develop young people's activity in their local areas, both in London and in Africa, Asia and the Caribbean. We seek to work in active partnership with relevant initiatives that are being taken by organizations and individuals in local communities. Young people's work has included assisting with teaching English, youth work, office and library administration, work with people with disabilities and organizing children's summer schemes.

Total projects worldwide: 20
Total UK projects: 5
Starting months: January, April, September.
Time required: 12–52 weeks.
Age requirement: 18–25

Causes: Disabled (physical), poor/homeless, teaching/assisting (primary, secondary), young people.
Activities: Community work, teaching, training.
Vols under 26 placed each year: 20
When to apply: All year.
Work alone/with others: Both.
Qualifications: Commitment – A levels useful, English language and Bengali useful in some cases.
Costs: £1,500–£4,000 depending on placement, raised with help from Trust. Volunteers are responsible for their own insurance.
Benefits: Accommodation and small expenses provided.
Training: 2 annual seminars. Monthly briefings, various observations and workshops as required.
Supervision: From trust whilst in UK and within project overseas.
Charity number: 283962
Worldwide placements: *Africa* (Botswana, Namibia, South Africa, Zimbabwe); *Asia* (Bangladesh); *Central America* (Barbados, Jamaica, Saint Lucia, Saint Vincent/Grenadines).
UK placements: *England* (London).

DAYCARE TRUST
4 Wild Court
London
WC2B 4AU UK

Tel: +44 (0) 20 7405 5617
Fax: +44 (0) 20 7831 6632
Contact: Lucy Lloyd, Policy and Information Manager

Daycare Trust was established in 1986 to provide information on childcare services and to promote affordable, accessible, quality childcare that provides equal opportunities for all. We give free advice to parents and childcare workers, and advise and brief childcare professionals, employers, trade unions, researchers, early years workers and teachers, journalists, local authorities, TECs, politicians, policy-makers, charities and other organizations interested in childcare provision, childcare information services or family-friendly policies. Volunteers are needed to help with administrative and information work in the London office.

Total projects worldwide: 1

Total UK projects: 1
Starting months: January–December.
Time required: 4–52 weeks.
Age requirement: 16 plus.
Causes: Children.
Activities: Administration, campaigning, community work, computers, fundraising, library/resource centres, marketing/publicity, newsletter/journalism, research.
Vols under 26 placed each year: 2–3
When to apply: All year.
Work alone/with others: It varies.
Volunteers with disabilities: We are thinking of moving offices and the conditions are not yet known.
Qualifications: Graduate level.
Health requirements: Nil.
Costs: Nil.
Benefits: Travel to and from office, £1.30 towards lunch.
Interview details: Interviews are conducted at our Holborn office.
Certification: Certificate or reference provided.
UK placements: *England* (London).

DCF PREMIER WORKSHOPS TRUST
211 Wick Road
Brislington
Bristol
BS4 4HP UK

Tel: +44 (0) 117 985 1188
Fax: +44 (0) 117 985 1188
e-mail: dcfpremier@aol.com
Web: www.members.aol.com/dcfpremier
Contact: Peter Hamar, Centre Manager

DCF Premier Workshops Trust is open five days a week throughout the year providing a working environment for people with disabilities. We are a Christian charity open to all volunteers of any or no persuasion.

Total projects worldwide: 1
Total UK projects: 1
Starting months: January–December.
Time required: 1–44 weeks.
Age requirement: 16 plus.
Causes: Disabled (learning and physical).
Activities: Arts/crafts, catering, computers, cooking, fundraising, gardening/horticulture, music, newsletter/journalism, technical skills.
Vols under 26 placed each year: 3 plus.
When to apply: Any time.
Work alone/with others: With others.
Volunteers with disabilities: Possible.

Qualifications: Caring nature.
Health requirements: Nil.
Costs: All costs except free travel to Centre.
Benefits: Occasionally 2-course lunch for
£1.30, free travel to Centre.
Training: Any training which is necessary
would be given.
Supervision: At all times.
Interview details: Interviews take place at our
office.
Certification: Reference provided.
UK placements: *England* (Bristol).

DEAFBLIND UK
100 Bridge Street
Peterborough
Cambridgeshire
PE1 1DY UK

Tel: +44 (0) 1733 358100
Fax: +44 (0) 1733 358356
e-mail: Jackie@deafblnd.demon.co.uk
Contact: Lisa Bloodworth

Deafblind UK: being without both sight and
hearing is hard. It puts a great strain on
people. It makes simple things difficult and
requires a lot of determination to live life to
the full. But it does not stop people being
people. Deafblind people are not totally
different from everyone else. They have the
same sorts of needs, interests, likes, dislikes,
fears, hopes and ambitions as sighted hearing
people. They want to live their lives, make
choices, meet people and explore their
individual interests just like everybody else. If
you are reliable and have patience, you can be
a great help to deafblind people. Here are
some ideas: visit and chat; write letters; teach
a skill; read magazines and newspapers; be a
lifeline to services such as doctors, hospitals
or dentists; take a deafblind person out and
about, shopping, visiting friends, taking part
in activities; help in the Rainbow Club for
deafblind people; go on holiday with
Deafblind UK.

Total projects worldwide: 1
Total UK projects: 1
Starting months: January–December.
Time required: 1–52 weeks (plus).
Age requirement: 16 plus.
Causes: Disabled (physical), elderly people,
holidays for disabled.
Activities: Caring (general), fundraising,
visiting/befriending.
When to apply: All year.

Work alone/with others: Both.
Volunteers with disabilities: Possible.
Qualifications: Nil. Training in
communication and guiding skills is given.
Awareness training given.
Health requirements: Nil.
Costs: Nil.
Benefits: Public transport costs reimbursed.
Petrol reimbursed at 25p per mile.
Interview details: Interviews take place locally
to the volunteer.
Certification: Certificate or reference
provided.
Charity number: 802976
UK placements: *England* (throughout);
Scotland (throughout); *Northern Ireland*
(throughout); *Wales* (throughout).

DEVON WILDLIFE TRUST
Shirehampton House
35–37 St David's Hill
Exeter
Devon
EX4 4DA UK

Tel: +44 (0) 1392 279244
Fax: +44 (0) 1392 433221
Contact: Peter Folland, Community Network
Officer

Devon Wildlife Trust has opportunities for
volunteer involvement in all areas of the
Trust's work from conservation to general
office work. Volunteers play a key role and
volunteer opportunities exist especially for
environmental graduates seeking conservation
'work' experience with: estate team –
practical conservation tasks and training in a
range of skills; awareness – 'Wild Night' out!
People and wildlife skills essential. Ideal for
those interested in environmental education;
office – data entry, marketing, PR, fundraising etc. NB: Long-term placements are
sought after and limited.

Total projects worldwide: 1
Total UK projects: 1
Starting months: January–December.
Time required: 1–52 weeks (plus).
Age requirement: 18 plus.
Causes: Conservation, wildlife.
Activities: Administration, conservation skills,
fundraising, library/resource centres, manual
work, marketing/publicity, outdoor skills,
scientific work.
Vols under 26 placed each year:
Approximately 40.

When to apply: All year.

Work alone/with others: With others.

Volunteers with disabilities: Possible.

Qualifications: Conservation/wildlife/environmental interests.

Equipment/clothing: Provided if necessary for health and safety.

Health requirements: Nil.

Costs: Travel to work (or central pick-up point) only.

Benefits: Training provided.

Training: Training is provided where needed, particularly for long-term conservation work, educational activities and local group activities.

Supervision: By a designated manager, who can be a member of staff, or another volunteer.

Interview details: Selection by interview. CVs accepted. Interviews take place in the Trust HQ in Exeter.

Charity number: 213224

UK placements: *England* (Devon).

DEVON YOUTH ASSOCIATION

1b Costly Street
Ivybridge
Devon
PL21 ODB UK

Tel: +44 (0) 1752 691511
Fax: +44 (0) 1752 895411
e-mail: dya@dya.org.uk
Web: www.dya.org.uk
Contact: Tim Todd or Jo Gunner

Devon Youth Association needs volunteers to work in youth clubs, in independent projects which we sponsor and with detached youth workers working on the streets with young people. We have a special project promoting work with girls in girls' clubs, a workshop project in a deprived area, advice and information, and issue based youth work. We also have an increasing need for administrative back-up by volunteers and information dissemination by way of a newsletter which would benefit from volunteer input. Volunteers with an offending background may be accepted. We take each individual case on its merits. We have an equal opportunities policy.

Total projects worldwide: 13–14
Total UK projects: 13–14
Starting months: January–December.
Time required: 1–52 weeks.

Age requirement: 16–25

Causes: Addicts/ex-addicts, Aids/HIV, disabled (learning and physical), human rights, inner city problems, offenders/ex-offenders, poor/homeless, unemployed, young people.

Activities: Administration, arts/crafts, community work, computers, counselling, DIY, fundraising, group work, library/resource centres, marketing/publicity, music, newsletter/journalism, outdoor skills, social work, sport, summer camps, theatre/drama, training, visiting/befriending.

Vols under 26 placed each year: 65 of a total of 80.

When to apply: All year.

Work alone/with others: Possible, but no wheelchair access to our office.

Qualifications: Nil – enthusiasm and motivation. 'Hands-on' experience always a benefit.

Health requirements: Nil.

Costs: Accommodation if needed.

Benefits: Travel costs and out-of-pocket expenses.

Interview details: Interviews take place in Ivybridge, Plymouth or Exeter.

Certification: Reference provided.

Charity number: 301028

UK placements: *England* (Devon).

DEYA ARCHAEOLOGICAL MUSEUM AND RESEARCH CENTRE (DAMARC)

c/o Earthwatch Europe
57 Woodstock Road
Oxford
OX2 6HJ UK

Tel: +44 (0) 1865 318831
Fax: +44 (0) 1865 311383
e-mail: vp@earthwatch.org.uk
Web: www.earthwatch.org/europe
Contact: Sandra Winnick, Volunteer Programme Manager

Deya Archaeological Museum and Research Centre organizes prehistoric site excavation, cleaning, classifying, restoring, drawing, measuring pottery and bones, site surveying and photography combined with lectures. Live in Centre, help with chores, swim, sun and learning experience combined.

Total projects worldwide: 150
Total UK projects: 10
Starting months: January–December.
Time required: 2–6 weeks.

Age requirement: 16 plus.
Causes: Archaeology, conservation, environmental causes, heritage, work camps – seasonal.
Activities: Arts/crafts, building/construction, computers, conservation skills, library/ resource centres, manual work, outdoor skills, research, scientific work, technical skills, training, work camps – seasonal.
Vols under 26 placed each year: 22 of a total of 110.
When to apply: All year.
Work alone/with others: With others.
Volunteers with disabilities: Not possible.
Qualifications: Nil.
Equipment/clothing: Long trousers, sturdy shoes, sleeping bag and sheet.
Health requirements: Need to cope with heavy dust and lifting and carrying.
Costs: Travel, medical insurance, which must be taken out by the volunteer, plus from £995 to cover board, lodging and tuition.
Benefits: Tuition, excavation, conservation, lab experience.
Training: On-site training.
Nationalities accepted: No restrictions but must speak English and be over 16 years.
Charity number: 327017
Worldwide placements: *Europe* (Spain).

DIAKONALA ARET
Svenska kyrkans Forsamlingsnamnd
S-75170 Uppsala
Sweden

Tel: 00 46 18 16 95 00
Fax: 00 46 18 16 96 18
Contact: The Director

Diakonala Aret is the Swedish branch of the European Diaconal Year network which consists of a number of national Christian-based volunteering schemes. (The British branch is Time For God.) We share common standards, and a commitment to the personal development of the volunteer through this form of work.

Total projects worldwide: 1
Total UK projects: 0
Starting months: August.
Time required: 42–52 weeks (plus).
Age requirement: 18–25
Causes: Addicts/ex-addicts, children, elderly people, young people.
Activities: Caring (general and residential), community work, training.

When to apply: Before April.
Qualifications: Small knowledge of Swedish and active Christian church membership.
Costs: Income tax and travel to Sweden.
Benefits: Pocket money, board, lodging, health and pension insurance.
Training: Regular residential conferences or seminars.
Supervision: Personal supervision and regular residential conferences or seminars.
Worldwide placements: *Europe* (Sweden).

DIAKONI AARET
Diakonissestiftelsen
Peter Bangs Vej l
Frederiksberg
DK-2000
Denmark

Tel: 00 45 38 38 41 26
Fax: 00 45 38 87 14 93
e-mail: diakoniaaret@diakonissen.dk
Web: www.diakoniaaret@diakonissen.dk
Contact: Anne Marie Boile Nielsen

Diakoni Aaret is the Danish branch of the European Diaconal Year network which consists of a number of national evangelical Lutheran-based volunteering schemes. (The British branch is Time For God.) We share common standards, and a commitment to the personal development of the volunteer through this form of work. Support is offered to the volunteers through both personal supervision and regular residential conferences or seminars.

Total projects worldwide: 1
Total UK projects: 0
Starting months: September.
Time required: 48–49 weeks.
Age requirement: 18–25
Causes: Children, elderly people, inner city problems, poor/homeless, refugees, teaching/ assisting (nursery), young people.
Activities: Administration, campaigning, caring (general and day), computers, cooking, marketing/publicity, music, religion, social work, summer camps, teaching, training, visiting/befriending.
Vols under 26 placed each year: 50
When to apply: March–May.
Work alone/with others: Mostly alone but support by a counsellor.
Volunteers with disabilities: Possible.
Qualifications: Some Danish language.
Health requirements: Nil.

Costs: Travel to Denmark.
Benefits: Pocket money DKr1,500 per month. Board DKr 1,521 per month. Lodging plus local travel costs. We have insurance for accident at work but the volunteer must have free-time accident insurance. Common health care is provided.
Training: On arrival a week's seminar of pre-placement training is provided.
Supervision: Every volunteer has a supervisor at the placement. In January all have the possibility of evaluating at the mid-term seminar.
Nationalities accepted: No restrictions but volunteers must speak a little Danish.
Certification: Certificate or reference provided.
Worldwide placements: *Europe* (Denmark).

DIAKONISCHES JAHR

Diakonisches Werk der Pfalz
Karmeliterstrasse 20
67346 Speyer
Germany

Tel: 00 49 6232 664209
Fax: 00 49 6232 6642427
e-mail: djaus@diakonie.pfulz.de
Web: www.djia.de
Contact: Astrid Guhmann

Diakonisches Jahr is the German branch of the European Diaconal Year network which consists of a number of national Christian-based volunteering schemes. (The British branch is Time For God.) They share common standards, and a commitment to the personal development of the volunteer through this form of work, and offer support to the volunteers through both personal supervision and regular residential conferences or seminars. Placements generally include residential care projects (children, elderly, disabled, learning difficulties, sick, etc.), rehabilitation/hostel work (drug abusers, ex-offenders, homeless, refugees, etc.), community support (visiting elderly, families affected by HIV/Aids, youth work, etc.), and churches (assisting ministry teams, parish work, pastoral care, youth work, children). The degree of fluency in German determines to which type of placement a volunteer is assigned. Volunteers with an offending background may be accepted on the programme. Apply in your own country through our partner organization.

Total projects worldwide: 1
Total UK projects: 0
Starting months: August, September.
Time required: 36–52 weeks.
Age requirement: 18–27
Causes: Aids/HIV, children, disabled (learning and physical), elderly people, health care/medical, holidays for disabled, inner city problems, offenders/ex-offenders, poor/homeless, refugees, teaching/assisting (nursery), young people.
Activities: Caring (general, day and residential), community work, counselling, group work, outdoor skills, religion, social work, sport, training, visiting/befriending.
Vols under 26 placed each year: 45 of a total of 50.
When to apply: 1 January–30 April at latest.
Work alone/with others: Both.
Volunteers with disabilities: Possible.
Qualifications: A willingness to serve full-time and open to working in church-related placements. Working with children and youth requires a good level of German whilst caring for the elderly and people with special needs requires less proficiency.
Health requirements: Nil.
Costs: Travel to and from placement (paid if EVS approved).
Benefits: Pocket money, board, lodging, social insurance (includes health, pension and accident). All volunteers in Germany are covered for sickness, accident and civil liability.
Training: There are at least four 1-week residential seminars for volunteers during the year, usually in groups of 15–25. One of these is an orientation.
Supervision: In each institution, there is a named supervisor who has regular meetings with the volunteer. There are also counsellors in the regional volunteer co-ordinating organizations who visit the volunteers in the placement.
Nationalities accepted: UK, France, Denmark, Sweden, Austria, Belgium, Hungary, Estonia, Poland,the Netherlands, Italy and the USA – all countries where we have partner organizations.
Worldwide placements: *Europe* (Germany).

DISABLEMENT INFORMATION AND ADVICE LINES (DIAL UK)

St Catherine's
Tickhill Road,

Doncaster
DN4 8QN UK

Tel: + 44 (0) 1302 310123
Fax: + 44 (0) 1302 310404
e-mail: dialuk@aol.com
Web: http://members.aol.com/dialuk
Contact: Jo Vickerman, Assistant Director
(Information)

Disablement Information and Advice Lines
are local advice centres running telephone
advice lines and drop-in information centres.
There are over 100 of them across the UK.
Anyone who needs disability-related
information may use their services: people
with disabilities, their families, carers or
professionals. Volunteers with an offending
background may be accepted.

Total projects worldwide: 104
Total UK projects: 104
Starting months: January–December.
Time required: 1–52 weeks (plus).
Age requirement: 20 plus.
Causes: Disabled (learning and physical),
holidays for disabled.
Activities: Administration, campaigning,
community work, computers, counselling,
fundraising, library/resource centres, social
work, visiting/befriending.
When to apply: All year.
Work alone/with others: Both.
Volunteers with disabilities: Possible.
Qualifications: Telephone skills, computer
and word processing useful.
Health requirements: Volunteers with
disabilities sought after.
Costs: None. No extra insurance required.
All volunteers covered under public liability
via MIA.
Benefits: Travel expenses within reasonable
distances.
Training: DIAL UK induction.
Supervision: By line managers.
Interview details: Interviews take place at
local DIALS. Contact DIAL UK for details of
local DIALS.
Certification: Written references provided.
Charity number: 283937
UK placements: *England* (throughout);
Scotland (throughout); *Northern Ireland*
(throughout); *Wales* (throughout).

DISAWAY TRUST, THE
2 Charles Road
Merton Park

London
SW19 3BD UK

Tel: + 44 (0) 20 8543 3431
Fax: + 44 (0) 20 8543 3431
Contact: Roy Sheridan

The aim of the Disaway Trust is to provide
holidays for physically disabled adults who
would not be able to travel alone. Our Trust
provides a one-to-one carer for each
holidaymaker whom we try to match to a
like-minded helper. We stay in regular hotels
both at home and abroad and organize trips
out to interesting venues. Venues change
every year and are decided in the summer of
the previous year.

Total projects worldwide: 1–2
Total UK projects: 1
Starting months: March, July, September,
October.
Time required: 12 weeks.
Age requirement: 18 plus.
Causes: Disabled (physical), holidays for
disabled.
Activities: Caring (residential).
Vols under 26 placed each year: 40
When to apply: Any time after January.
Work alone/with others: Both.
Volunteers with disabilities: Only if able to
care for other physically disabled youngsters.
Qualifications: Nil, but caring attitude,
adaptable and a good sense of humour.
Health requirements: General physical health
OK.
Costs: Half cost of the holiday plus travel to
London departures.
Benefits: Board and lodging in a hotel while
on holiday.
Interview details: No interview necessary.
Certification: Reference on request.
Charity number: 282874
Worldwide placements: *North America*
(*Canada*).
UK placements: *England* (Cumbria).

DISCOVER NEPAL
GPO Box 20209
Kathmandu
Nepal

Tel: 00 977 1 416326
Fax: 00 977 1 255487
e-mail: stt@mos.com.np
Web: www.discovernepal.com.np
Other web: www.catmando.com/

discovernepal
Contact: Bijaya Pradhan, Chairman

Discover Nepal, a government-registered NGO, was established in Nepal in 1998. Our aim is to provide opportunities for the involvement of volunteers in the development process, and to contribute practically towards the socio-economic development of the country. The programme involves teaching English at a school for a period of 10–20 weeks. Apart from teaching English, in some schools volunteers are expected to help in extra-curricular activities (sports, music, art, clubs, environmental conservation etc.). Volunteers with some teaching experience or experience with children would be preferred but it is not essential.

Total projects worldwide: 3
Total UK projects: 0
Starting months: January, April, November.
Time required: 10–20 weeks.
Age requirement: 20–40
Causes: Conservation, disabled (learning and physical), environmental causes, health care/medical, holidays for disabled, refugees, teaching/assisting (nursery, primary, secondary), work camps – seasonal, young people.
Activities: Administration, campaigning, caring (residential), community work, computers, conservation skills, development issues, forestry, group work, international aid, outdoor skills, research, social work, sport, summer camps, teaching, technical skills, training, visiting/befriending, work camps – seasonal.
Vols under 26 placed each year: 15–25 of a total of 20–30.
When to apply: Two months ahead.
Work alone/with others: With other young volunteers.
Volunteers with disabilities: Not possible.
Qualifications: Minimum GCSE, good English language skills.
Equipment/clothing: Warm clothes required for winter season.
Health requirements: Yes.
Costs: £700 (US1,000) for education programme plus air fares and personal expenses. Travel/health insurance to be covered by the volunteer.
Benefits: All board and lodging at school plus 2 weeks orientation, 2 weeks lodging, 1 week trek, jungle safari and sightseeing.

Training: 2-week orientation programme.
Supervision: By authorities at place of voluntary assignment and Discover Nepal also monitors their activities.
Interview details: Prospective volunteers are not interviewed but must meet our selection criteria.
Certification: Certificate or reference provided.
Worldwide placements: *Asia* (Nepal).

DIVINE ONKAR MISSION
Unit 10 Niphon Works
43–68 Lower Villiers Street
Wolverhampton
WV2 4NA UK

Tel: +44 (0) 1902 429789
Fax: +44 (0) 1902 429789
e-mail: support@divine-onkar.org.uk
Web: www.divine-onkar.org.uk
Contact: Tersam Lal

The Divine Onkar Mission was initiated in 1991 and registered in 1992 with the Charity Commission. Our aims are the advancement of education, medical and agricultural development in Third World countries especially in India. We are currently running projects in the following areas of India: 1. Leprosy aid. We support a leper colony in Delhi, funding all costs for their treatment and rehabilitation. 2. Orphanage/boarding school. In Behar State, we are running the project for children whose parents have been victims of leprosy and other deadly diseases. 3. General hospital. We provide medical care free of charge for the poor whom we select from remote jungle areas. Some 300–400 patients are seen of whom 50–60 receive eye operations to correct cataract and other eye defects. 4. In Orissa state we are funding similar projects for children and widows. The mortality rate amongst young males is very high. A large area of land has been donated by the locals who want paid work in return for cultivating and developing the land. Volunteers with an offending background may be accepted.

Total projects worldwide: 4
Total UK projects: 1
Starting months: August, September.
Time required: 4–52 weeks.
Age requirement: 18 plus.
Causes: Animal welfare, children, disabled (physical), elderly people, health care/

medical, holidays for disabled, teaching/
assisting (nursery, primary, secondary,
mature, EFL), work camps – seasonal.
Activities: Administration, agriculture/
farming, building/construction, community
work, computers, counselling, development
issues, first aid, forestry, fundraising,
international aid, marketing/publicity, music,
newsletter/journalism, research, social work,
teaching, technical skills, theatre/drama.
Vols under 26 placed each year: 2 of a total
of 5.
When to apply: March or April.
Work alone/with others: With others.
Volunteers with disabilities: Possible for
charity shop, office work or driving.
Qualifications: Driving licence would be an
advantage but not essential.
Health requirements: Nil.
Costs: Travel to project.
Benefits: Board and lodging.
Interview details: Interview in our office in
Wolverhampton.
Certification: Certificate or reference
provided.
Charity number: 1074527
Worldwide placements: *Asia* (India).
UK placements: *England* (West Midlands).

DO DROP IN COMMUNITY PROJECT
25 Woodland Drive
Smethwick
Warley
West Midlands
B66 1JF UK

Tel: +44 (0) 121 558 6821
Fax: +44 (0) 121 558 7289
Contact: The Administrator

Do Drop In aims to be a focus for
community development on Galton Village
housing estate. It is sponsored by the
Methodist Church and enjoys active support
from local people. The playscheme is run
from several venues with local authority
funding, paid staff and resident volunteers.
Volunteers can choose to work with 3–5 year
olds, 5–8 year olds or over 8 year olds.
Volunteers with an offending background
may be accepted as long as the offence is not
with children.

Total projects worldwide: 1
Total UK projects: 1
Starting months: March, April, July, August.
Time required: 1–4 weeks.

Age requirement: 18 plus.
Causes: Children, young people.
Activities: Arts/crafts, music, outdoor skills,
sport.
Vols under 26 placed each year: 3–4
When to apply: 2 months in advance.
Work alone/with others: With others.
Volunteers with disabilities: Possible.
Qualifications: There will be a police check
before starting.
Health requirements: Nil.
Costs: Nil – but no food or accommodation
provided.
Interview details: Applicants are interviewed
at the office.
Certification: Certificate or reference
provided.
UK placements: *England* (West Midlands).

DOLPHIN RESEARCH CENTER
P O Box 522875
Marathon Shores
Monroe
33052-2875 USA

Tel: 00 1 305 289 1121
Fax: 00 1 305 743 7627
e-mail: drc-vr@dolphins.org
Web: www.dolphins.org
Contact: Merrell Williams, Volunteer
Resources

Dolphin Research Center is pleased to offer
volunteer opportunities designed for
individuals who would like to donate their
efforts to assist the various departments of
our organization. Although volunteers do not
work directly with the dolphins, participants
do encounter many unique opportunities for
learning about various aspects of the daily
operations of a marine mammal care facility.
The responsibilities typically handled by our
volunteers all represent vital aspects of our
operations. You may find yourself preparing
our dolphins' meals or caring for our family
of exotic birds. We utilize volunteers for
assistance with the public through duties
which include shadowing tour groups,
answering questions, or monitoring Swim
With The Dolphin sessions. Volunteers are
involved with facility maintenance such as
rubbish collection, recycling, painting and
landscaping projects. Volunteers also help
with administrative projects such as computer
data entry and the preparation of bulk
mailings. Our Volunteer Resources

Department is staffed throughout the year. Our non-local volunteers work 40 hours per week and a 4–8 week commitment is usually required. The centre is situated in the middle of Florida Keys. Within our Volunteer Resources Department, we offer an Intern Program. Regular internships, involving concentration in a specific department, are normally 3–4 months in length, and are offered during the summer, autumn and winter terms. We usually have more applicants than we can accept during the summer but would like more from September to May. Volunteers with an offending background may be accepted depending on the circumstances.

Total projects worldwide: 1
Total UK projects: 0
Starting months: January–December.
Time required: 4–12 weeks.
Age requirement: 18 plus.
Causes: Animal welfare, conservation, wildlife.
Activities: Conservation skills, group work, manual work.
Vols under 26 placed each year: 75 of a total of 100.
When to apply: At least 3 months before wishing to start.
Work alone/with others: With others.
Volunteers with disabilities: We are unable to place people with disabilities as tasks require mobility, many hours in the sun and occasional heavy lifting.
Qualifications: Fluent spoken English.
Equipment/clothing: Swimsuits.
Health requirements: Many activities involve manual labour – ability to lift at least 30 lbs essential.
Costs: All travel costs and living expenses plus US$35 programme fee. It is best but not essential if you are able to rent a car while here. Total costs depend on air fares and length of stay – US$1,500–$4,000.
Benefits: Programme fee entitles volunteers to 3 volunteer shirts which must be worn.
Training: On-the-job training.
Supervision: Volunteer resource staff supervise the volunteers Monday to Friday. Other staff are available to provide necessary assistance at the weekends.
Interview details: Prospective volunteers are interviewed by telephone.
Certification: Certificate or reference provided.

Worldwide placements: *North America* (USA).

DORSET ASSOCIATION FOR THE DISABLED
c/o Weymouth Outdoor Education Centre
Knightsdale Road
Weymouth
Dorset
DT4 0HS UK

Tel: +44 (0) 1305 761840 (9 a.m. 12 noon) + answerphone
Fax: +44 (0) 1305 761840
e-mail: angela.barnsley@btclick.com
Web: www.dorsetdisabled.co.uk
Contact: Angela Barnsley

The Dorset Association for the Disabled was set up to provide additional services and social amenities for disabled people, complementing and supplementing the services provided by the statutory welfare authorities. We also embrace Tapes for the Handicapped who provide talking magazines of local interest to those disabled people who unfortunately are also housebound. Branch committees run social clubs and outings and some also run handicraft groups. We provide a visiting service to housebound people and an advisory service to the disabled members and families in a wide variety of spheres. Annual holidays are organized to a number of resorts and many members treat these events as reunions with other branches. Funds are raised by branches through flag days, sales of work, coffee mornings, car boot sales, etc. and from the generosity of the public in donations and covenants. Acceptance of volunteers with an offending background would depend on the offence committed.

Total projects worldwide: A few.
Total UK projects: A few.
Starting months: May, June, September.
Time required: 1–4 weeks.
Age requirement: 18 plus.
Causes: Disabled (physical), holidays for disabled.
Activities: Caring (general).
Vols under 26 placed each year: A few of a total of 300.
When to apply: March.
Work alone/with others: With others.
Volunteers with disabilities: Possible, particularly with the office administration.

Qualifications: Nil.
Health requirements: Fit and healthy.
Costs: Travel to and from pick-up point for holiday.
Benefits: No financial support but board and lodging given on holiday.
Interview details: Interviews conducted in Weymouth, Dorset.
Certification: Certificate or reference on request.
Charity number: 202524
UK placements: *England* (Devon, Dorset, Somerset).

DORSET WILDLIFE TRUST
Brooklands Farm
Forston
Dorchester
Dorset
DT2 7AA UK

Tel: + 44 (0) 1305 264620
Fax: + 44 (0) 1305 251120
e-mail: dorsetwt@cix.compulink.co.uk
Contact: The Director

The Dorset Wildlife Trust aims to achieve now and for the future a county and, through the Wildlife Trusts, a United Kingdom, that is richer in wildlife, managed on sustainable principles. This aim will be achieved by: acquiring and managing nature reserves; acquiring data on habitats and species; promoting conservation and management of important wildlife sites by their existing landowners; influencing decisions on land use; increasing awareness of the value of wildlife. This work creates volunteering opportunities in practical estate work, recording and monitoring, formal and informal education projects for people of all ages, developing and facilitating community projects, raising awareness of the need to conserve wildlife through art, design and creative writing, raising money and membership, as well as administration and building maintenance. The more complex the task, the longer the placement should be.

Total projects worldwide: 40
Total UK projects: 40
Starting months: January–December.
Time required: 2–52 weeks.
Age requirement: 18 plus.
Causes: Conservation, environmental causes.
Activities: Administration, agriculture/farming, community work, computers, conservation skills, forestry, fundraising, library/resource centres, manual work, marketing/publicity, newsletter/journalism, outdoor skills, research, scientific work, teaching.
Vols under 26 placed each year: 400
When to apply: All year.
Work alone/with others: With others.
Volunteers with disabilities: Not at present.
Qualifications: Varies according to projects.
Equipment/clothing: Equipment supplied.
Health requirements: Varies according to projects.
Costs: Nil.
Benefits: All expenses reimbursed. Informal training; work experience, chance to help wildlife. We have public liability insurance cover.
Training: We invite placement volunteers for an informal introduction.
Supervision: Volunteers are usually assigned to one named person for supervision.
Charity number: 200222
UK placements: *England* (Dorset).

DORSET YOUTH AND COMMUNITY SERVICE
Princes House
Princes Street
Dorchester
Dorset
DT1 1TP UK

Tel: + 44 (0) 1305 225291
Fax: + 44 (0) 1305 225293
e-mail: d.m.higton@dorset-cc.gov.uk
Web: www.dorset-lea.org.uk
Contact: Derek Higton

Dorset Youth and Community Service supports young people aged 12–21 in their transition from childhood to responsible adulthood, encourages their social development and individual fulfilment, and helps them participate fully in society. Youth work in Dorset is critically informed by a set of beliefs which include a commitment to equal opportunity, and to young people as partners in learning and in decision making. We also aim to develop within young people a sense of both their rights and responsibilities as citizens. We offer a comprehensive range of flexible educational programmes and projects in which young people choose to be involved. We encourage young people to be both critical and creative in responding to their world, and widen their experiences within it. The programmes and projects also provide opportunities for relaxation, meeting friends and having fun. Youth work in Dorset complements and supports learning in school and college and contributes to social welfare and community development. We offer to all a constructive and educational use of leisure time. We help young people achieve and fulfil their potential and make choices about their lives, offering them information, advice and support. We work with other agencies to encourage society to be responsive to young people's needs, especially those young people who are vulnerable.

Total projects worldwide: 70
Total UK projects: 70
Starting months: January–December.
Time required: 12–52 weeks (plus).
Age requirement: 18–25
Causes: Young People.
Activities: Arts/crafts, community work, counselling, group work, music, social work.
Vols under 26 placed each year: 200
When to apply: All year.
Work alone/with others: Both.
Volunteers with disabilities: Possible.
Qualifications: Nil.
Health requirements: Nil.
Costs: Nil.
Benefits: Training opportunities are available. County Council provides necessary insurance.
Training: Induction process for all volunteers.
Supervision: As necessary by professionally qualified staff.
Interview details: Volunteers are interviewed at the youth centre in which they will work.
Certification: Certificate or reference provided.
UK placements: *England* (Dorset).

DUKE OF EDINBURGH'S AWARD ARTS PROJECT
Community, Learning and Leisure Service, Hammersmith and Fulham
Munster Centre
Filmer Road
London
SW6 6AS UK

Tel: +44 (0) 20 7736 0864
Fax: +44 (0) 20 7736 0103
Contact: Jo Saunders, Arts Project Co-ordinator

Following the pilot of the Duke of Edinburgh's (D of E) Award Arts Project Hammersmith and Fulham have now included it in their arts strategy for the borough. The aim of the project remains to make the Award Scheme more flexible and accessible by integrating art activities into the more traditional and sports based D of E Award Scheme. Street dance, DJ-ing, circus skills, dance, drama, photography and visual arts are used to attract and stimulate young people into participation, and through these activities to achieve D of E Awards. Schools, colleges, youth clubs and independent arts organizations all combine to provide these activities and the unit structure in which the young people operate. The project continues with participation in the Bronze and Silver levels of the Award being the most active. Voluntary involvement is available on two levels: 1. Participants (aged 14–25 years) – those young people who are volunteering their recreation time to complete D of E Awards or certificates which include a section in which they provide voluntary service to the community for a minimum of six months. 2. Leaders – people of any age who have relevant experience and/or qualifications who volunteer to lead groups of participants through specialized activities or act as the overall leader/co-ordinator of a unit of participants, which would require relevant skills of and enthusiasm for working with young people. Opportunities for training exist for leaders, which may be linked to nationally accredited qualifications. We are keen to hear from individuals with skills/experience in the arts. Volunteers with an offending background are accepted.

Total projects worldwide: 10
Total UK projects: 10
Starting months: January–April, September–December.
Time required: 24–52 weeks (plus).
Age requirement: 14–25
Causes: Disabled (learning and physical), elderly people, environmental causes, inner city problems, poor/homeless, teaching (primary), young people.
Activities: Arts/crafts, music, newsletter/journalism, outdoor skills, sport, theatre/drama.
Vols under 26 placed each year: 200
When to apply: All year. Most volunteers start at start of school year – September or October.
Work alone/with others: With others.

Volunteers with disabilities: Possible.
Qualifications: Nil.
Health requirements: Nil.
Costs: Minimal. Every effort is made to ensure that economic circumstances do not prevent participation.
Training: Volunteers who wish to participate as leaders/assistants on the Award would need to attend a training weekend (residential) paid for by us.
Supervision: Leaders are supported by borough award co-ordinators. Volunteer participants are organized into Award Units under leaders.
Interview details: No interview necessary.
Certification: On a project to project basis. Duke of Edinburgh Awards and Certificates.
UK placements: *England* (London).

DURHAM WILDLIFE TRUST
Rainton Meadows
Chilton Moore
Houghton-Le-Spring
Tyne and Wear
DH4 6PU UK

Tel: +44 (0) 191 5843112
Fax: +44 (0) 191 5843934
e-mail: kfisher@durhamwt.co.uk
Contact: Karen Fisher

Durham Wildlife Trust is a member of the Wildlife Trusts, a national partnership of 47 county trusts. For more details of the Wildlife Trusts, see the entry under Cornwall Wildlife Trust.

Total projects worldwide: 1
Total UK projects: 1
Starting months: January–November.
Time required: 1–52 weeks (plus).
Age requirement: 16 plus.
Causes: Conservation, environmental causes, unemployed, wildlife.
Activities: Community work, computers, conservation skills, driving, forestry, gardening/horticulture, group work, manual work, outdoor skills, research, scientific work, technical skills, training.
Vols under 26 placed each year: 60 of a total of 150.
When to apply: All year.
Work alone/with others: With others.
Volunteers with disabilities: Possible.
Qualifications: Nil but practical skills useful.
Equipment/clothing: Casual work clothes, waterproofs, stout boots. Protective safety gear is provided.

Health requirements: Any medical conditions (illness, allergy or physical disability) that may require treatment/medication or which affect the volunteer working with machinery must be notified to us in advance. Tetanus injections must be up to date..
Costs: Bring your own packed lunch.
Benefits: Out-of-pocket expenses. Public liability insurance taken out by us.
Training: 2–4 hour induction on health and safety issues. On the job training in an informal atmosphere.
Supervision: By our staff and other volunteers. Risk assessments carried out on site.
Interview details: Interviews at our office.
Certification: Reference on request.
UK placements: *England* (Co Durham).

E

E.I.L
287 Worcester Road
Malvern
Worcestershire
WR14 1AB UK

Tel: +44 (0) 1684 562577
Fax: +44 (0) 1684 562212
e-mail: info@eiluk.org
Contact: Karen Morris or Neil Humpage

EIL specializes in intercultural learning and education. We are part of a federation and there are partner organizations thoughout the world. The core of our work involves travelling to different countries and experiencing their cultures through homestays. Both individuals and groups ask us to arrange homestay experiences. Our volunteering opportunities, for young UK volunteers, are mainly concentrated within Europe. In 1999 we were the UK's biggest sending organization for the European Union's EVS programme (European Voluntary Service). We have contacts with many different projects throughout the European Union. It is possible to specify a country and also the type of work that you wish to do. However, the fewer restrictions that are imposed on a volunteering experience the greater the likelihood of our being able to place you. Volunteers usually go for between six months and one year. Shorter programmes, for between three weeks and three months are available for some young people. EIL has contacts with other organizations in different parts of the world, but these often have higher costs for volunteers. Volunteers with an offending background are accepted.

Total projects worldwide: Thousands.
Total UK projects: 7
Starting months: January–December.
Time required: 3–52 weeks.
Age requirement: 18–25
Causes: Children, conservation, disabled (physical), elderly people, environmental causes, health care/medical, heritage, holidays for disabled, unemployed, wildlife, young people.
Activities: Administration, arts/crafts, building/construction, campaigning, caring (general, day and residential), catering, community work, computers, conservation skills, cooking, DIY, gardening/horticulture, group work, library/resource centres, manual work, marketing/publicity, music, outdoor skills, research, social work, sport, teaching, theatre/drama, training, visiting/befriending.
Vols under 26 placed each year: 120
When to apply: All year.
Work alone/with others: With others.
Volunteers with disabilities: Possible.
Qualifications: Nil.
Health requirements: Some projects may have restrictions but not all.
Costs: Nil. All costs paid by European Union.
Benefits: Travel, board, lodging, medical insurance, pocket money (£25 per week). Medical insurance is necessary and provided by the European Union.
Training: Meeting in UK and induction in country of project.
Supervision: Personal mentor provided by project.
Nationalities accepted: Only from the EU for EVS positions.
Interview details: Interviews take place in Malvern, although interviews nearer volunteers' homes are sometimes possible.
Certification: Certificate or reference provided.
Worldwide placements: *Europe* (Austria, Belgium, Cyprus, Denmark, Finland, France, Germany, Greece, Iceland, Ireland, Italy, Netherlands, Norway, Portugal, Spain, Sweden, Switzerland).
UK placements: *England* (Hampshire, London, Merseyside).

EARTHWATCH
57 Woodstock Road
Oxford
OX2 6HJ UK

Tel: +44 (0) 1865 318831
Fax: +44 (0) 1865 311383
e-mail: vp@earthwatch.org.uk
Web: www.earthwatch.org/europe
Contact: The Volunteer Programme

Earthwatch is an international charity which sponsors environmental and cultural research by sending paying volunteers to help scientists on their expeditions around the world. The volunteers' time and money has enabled scientists on 1,800 projects in 104 countries to conduct research into a wide variety of issues, from vanishing musical traditions to global warming and dolphin intelligence. Earthwatch gives people the chance to do more than just read about the environment. Volunteers do not need any special skills, just two weeks of their time and curiosity. You are guaranteed a safe, well organized experience with like-minded people working alongside world experts. Many of the volunteers are single or have had children and are now retired.

Total projects worldwide: 120 plus.
Total UK projects: 9
Starting months: January–December.
Time required: 1–4 weeks.
Age requirement: 16 plus.
Causes: Animal welfare, archaeology, architecture, conservation, environmental causes, health care/medical, wildlife.
Activities: Computers, conservation skills, research, scientific work, technical skills.
Vols under 26 placed each year: 250 of a total of 1,000.
When to apply: All year.
Work alone/with others: With others.
Volunteers with disabilities: Possible.
Qualifications: Nil.
Equipment/clothing: Depending on project – most equipment provided.
Health requirements: Depending on project/location.
Costs: £65–£2,665 per trip plus travel costs (Optional membership £25, £15 for students). Normal travel insurance which can

be arranged by the volunteer through Earthwatch or through a travel agent.

Benefits: Small grants available from Earthwatch.

Training: All volunteers are sent a detailed project briefing explaining the aims of the project, volunteer tasks etc.

Supervision: At all times by the project staff.

Interview details: No interview necessary.

Charity number: 327017

Worldwide placements: *Africa* (Cameroon, Ghana, Kenya, Madagascar, Namibia, South Africa, Tunisia, Zambia, Zimbabwe); *Asia* (China, India, Indonesia, Israel, Japan, Malaysia, Mongolia, Nepal, Philippines, Sri Lanka); *Australasia* (Australia, New Zealand); *Europe* (Czech Republic, Hungary, Iceland, Italy, Netherlands, Romania, Russia, Spain, Turkey); *North America* (Canada, USA); *Central America* (Bahamas, Belize, Bermuda, Costa Rica, Dominica, Mexico, Puerto Rico, Trinidad and Tobago, Virgin Islands); *South America* (Argentina, Bolivia, Brazil, Chile, Ecuador, Peru, Uruguay).

UK placements: *England* (Hampshire, London, Oxfordshire, Tyne and Wear); *Scotland* (E. Ayrshire, N. Ayrshire, S. Ayrshire, Dumfries and Galloway, Inverclyde, Renfrewshire, E. Renfrewshire); *Wales* (Monmouthshire, Newport, Torfaen).

EAST SUSSEX VOLUNTARY RANGERS

ESCC Transport and Environment
Countryside Management, County Hall
St Anne's Crescent
Lewes
East Sussex
BN7 1UE UK

Tel: +44 (0) 1273 482670
Fax: +44 (0) 1273 479536
e-mail: cathy.abel@eastsussexcc.gov.uk
Web: www.eastsussexcc.gov.uk/env/cms/main.htm
Contact: Cathy Abel

The East Sussex Voluntary Ranger Service is part of the Countryside Management Group with East Sussex County Council. Come and see the beautiful East Sussex countryside and get involved in some enjoyable practical conservation work. You will have the satisfaction of making a real contribution to the environment of East Sussex with the added bonus of possible training in skills that are important to work in countryside

management. The qualification we believe is essential is enthusiasm for the work. You also need to be over 18 (younger volunteers must be accompanied by an adult). A team of volunteers is in operation with us throughout the week. You may wish to join them every day, once a week or just on those occasions when you fancy a trip into the country. A day out with the Rangers may include coppicing in the woods, building stiles on Ditchling Common, heathland management on Chailey Common or work on any of our other sites. Once you have completed and returned the application form with two passport photos, we will send you a welcome letter. You will then be free to join us whenever you like. Volunteers with an offending background are accepted in some cases.

Total projects worldwide: 1
Total UK projects: 1
Starting months: January–December.
Time required: 1 week.
Age requirement: 16 plus.
Causes: Conservation, environmental causes, heritage, wildlife.
Activities: Agriculture/farming, building/construction, conservation skills, driving, forestry, gardening/horticulture, group work, manual work, outdoor skills, technical skills, training.
Vols under 26 placed each year: 24 of a total of 40.
When to apply: All year.
Work alone/with others: With others.
Volunteers with disabilities: Possible.
Qualifications: Nil – enthusiasm and motivation.
Equipment/clothing: Sturdy boots, waterproof jacket, green clothes and a packed lunch.
Health requirements: Tetanus and Hepatitis B injections recommended.
Costs: None apart from travel from home to Lewes base.
Interview details: If an interview is required it would be at Lewes.
Certification: Certificate or reference on request.
UK placements: *England* (E. Sussex).

ECUMENICAL NETWORK FOR YOUTH ACTION

U Nas 9
CZ-147 00 Prague 4
Czech Republic

Tel: 00 420 2 472 7390
Fax: 00 420 2 472 7390
e-mail: cejenya@mbox.vol.cz
Contact: Cath Moss

Ecumenical Network for Youth Action (ENYA) is an exciting membership/partnership based movement of churches and related organizations, including youth groups, women's networks, diaconal projects, children's rights and protection activists, social movements, justice, peace, reconciliation and environmental groups, NGOs/INGOs combined with individual members from over 50 countries around the world. Volunteers with an offending background may be accepted depending on the offence and the nature of the project.

Total projects worldwide: 15–20
Total UK projects: 2
Starting months: January–December.
Time required: 2–52 weeks.
Age requirement: 15 plus.
Causes: Addicts/ex-addicts, Aids/HIV, children, human rights, inner city problems, offenders/ex-offenders, poor/homeless, refugees, unemployed, work camps – seasonal, young people.
Activities: Administration, arts/crafts, building/construction, campaigning, caring (residential), community work, computers, development issues, DIY, fundraising, group work, international aid, newsletter/journalism, outdoor skills, religion, social work, summer camps, technical skills, training, visiting/befriending, work camps – seasonal.
Vols under 26 placed each year: Approximately 45 of a total of 50.
When to apply: All year.
Work alone/with others: With others.
Volunteers with disabilities: Possible.
Qualifications: An openness to others, their cultures, traditions and religions. If working with children's projects, clearance papers from justice authorities are needed.
Equipment/clothing: Any special equipment would be provided by us.
Health requirements: Nil.
Costs: Varies depending on the placement and the length of time. Average £50 per week. Volunteers need to have their own personal and medical health insurance. Our insurance only covers emergencies.
Benefits: Depends on project. Generally volunteers are not provided with any financial benefits and need to contribute to their accommodation and food costs unless from Eastern or Central Europe.
Training: There is always an orientation meeting at the beginning of any placement and occasional evaluations throughout the placement period.
Supervision: Trained supervisors in each project placement.
Nationalities accepted: We welcome all young people and look forward to the diversity of inter-cultural exchanges.
Interview details: Interviews are in person by a member of the ENYA national committee and by telephone with the volunteer co-ordinators.
Certification: A certificate is provided and a written reference on request.
Charity number: ICO: 65998871
Worldwide placements: *Africa* (Cameroon, Congo Dem. Republic, Egypt, South Africa, Zimbabwe); *Asia* (Hong Kong, India, Israel, Pakistan, Thailand); *Australasia* (Australia, Fiji); *Europe* (Albania, Armenia, Austria, Belarus, Bulgaria, Croatia, Czech Republic, Denmark, Estonia, Finland, France, Georgia, Germany, Greece, Hungary, Ireland, Latvia, Lithuania, Malta, Moldova, Poland, Portugal, Romania, Russia, Slovakia, Slovenia, Switzerland, Ukraine, Yugoslavia); *North America* (Canada, USA); *Central America* (Antigua and Barbuda, Cuba, Jamaica); *South America* (Brazil).
UK placements: *England* (Manchester, Oxfordshire, Tyne and Wear); *Scotland* (Edinburgh, Fife, Perth and Kinross); *Northern Ireland* (Antrim, Belfast City).

EDINBURGH CYRENIANS
57 Albion Road
Edinburgh
EH7 5QY Scotland

Tel: +44 (0) 131 475 2354
Contact: Des Ryan

Edinburgh Cyrenian Trust was established in June 1968 to develop and provide services to homeless single people in Edinburgh and the Lothian Region. The Trust runs two communities for single, homeless men and women aged 18–30 years old. One is in Edinburgh and the other is the Rural Project at Humbie Holdings in West Lothian. The communities are a mix of people who are either referred to us by social workers, hospitals or other helping agencies. Volunteers live and work alongside the residents. There are 11 volunteers and 19 resident places. For residents, length of stay depends on the needs of the individual. Volunteers commit themselves to a minimum of six months. Volunteers with an offending background may be accepted dependent on type of offence and how recent. Please write to the above address to obtain an application form.

Total projects worldwide: 2
Total UK projects: 2
Starting months: January–December.
Time required: 20–52 weeks.
Age requirement: 18–30
Causes: Addicts/ex-addicts, animal welfare, offenders/ex-offenders, poor/homeless, unemployed, young people.
Activities: Agriculture/farming, arts/crafts, caring (general), community work, cooking, driving, first aid, fundraising, gardening/horticulture, group work, manual work, outdoor skills, sport, visiting/befriending.
Vols under 26 placed each year: 22
When to apply: All year.
Work alone/with others: In a team.
Volunteers with disabilities: Not possible.
Qualifications: Fluent spoken English essential.
Health requirements: Nil.
Costs: Nil.
Benefits: Lodgng plus £28 per week plus £35 clothing allowance plus holiday grant £160.
Nationalities accepted: No restrictions but must be fluent in English.
Interview details: Applicants visit the project for one week and are interviewed then.
Certification: Written reference provided.
Charity number: CR 40460
UK placements: *Scotland* (Edinburgh).

EDINBURGH MEDICAL MISSIONARY SOCIETY
7 Washington Lane
Edinburgh
EH11 2HA Scotland

Tel: +44 (0) 131 313 3828
Fax: +44 (0) 131 313 4662
e-mail: emms@btinternet.com
Web: www.emms.org
Contact: Mr Robin G.K. Arnott, Executive Director

The Edinburgh Medical Missionary Society

assists seven Christian hospitals and clinics in Africa, Asia and the Middle East to obtain volunteers for occasional support and general maintenance work. Vacancies occur regularly at any time of the year. Enquiries should be made to us.

Total projects worldwide: 6
Total UK projects: 0
Starting months: January–December.
Time required: 4–52 weeks.
Age requirement: 18 plus.
Causes: Children, disabled (learning and physical), elderly people, health care/medical, work camps – seasonal.
Activities: Administration, building/construction, caring (general), DIY, gardening/horticulture, manual work, religion, teaching, technical skills, work camps – seasonal.
Vols under 26 placed each year: 3 of a total of 10.
When to apply: Any time.
Work alone/with others: With others.
Volunteers with disabilities: Possible.
Qualifications: Nil but experience and/or skill valuable.
Equipment/clothing: Provided by the hospitals/clinics.
Health requirements: Fit and in good health.
Costs: Return travel to the country involved and possibly some accommodation costs. Insurance for travel, health, personal items etc. is the volunteer's responsibility.
Benefits: Simple accommodation and meals plus small pocket money.
Supervision: Hospital would provide this.
Interview details: No interview necessary.
Charity number: SC 015000
Worldwide placements: *Africa* (Malawi); *Asia* (India, Israel, Nepal).

EIN YAEL LIVING MUSEUM
PO Box 9679
Jerusalem 91094
Israel

Tel: 00 972 2 638421
Contact: Gershon Edelstein, Director

The Ein Yael Living Museum is situated in the Rephaim Valley of Jerusalem. The project combines experimentation in the techniques of traditional agriculture with crafts such as pottery, weaving, mosaic, basketry and construction as practised in various historical periods. The research in these fields is an attempt to understand the way ancient man interacted with his environment. Volunteers are needed for the building of workshops, to act as guides for child visitors and to help with research and archaeological excavations on the site.

Total projects worldwide: 1
Starting months: January–December.
Time required: 2–52 weeks.
Age requirement: 16 plus.
Causes: Archaeology, conservation, heritage.
Activities: Arts/crafts, building/construction, conservation skills, manual work, research.
When to apply: All year.
Qualifications: Nil.
Worldwide placements: *Asia* (Israel).

ELI SHENHAV: JNF
11 Zvi Shapira Street
Tel Aviv
Israel

Tel: 00 972 3 2561129
Contact: Eli Shenhav

Eli Shenhav needs volunteers to work on an excavation of a Roman theatre three miles from Caesarea and a Roman theatre in Shuni. Working hours are from 5.30 a.m. – noon, five days a week.

Total projects worldwide: 1
Total UK projects: 0
Starting months: July.
Time required: 152 weeks.
Age requirement: 14 plus.
Causes: Archaeology.
Vols under 26 placed each year: 17
When to apply: As early as possible.
Qualifications: Nil.
Costs: Board and accommodation at approximately £10 per day.
Worldwide placements: *Asia* (Israel).

EMMAUS HOUSE/HARLEM
PO Box 1177
New York City
New York 10035
USA

Tel: 00 1 212 410 6006
Fax: 00 1 212 410 4377
Contact: Fr David Kirk or Theodore Jackson

Emmaus House celebrated 34 years of service to the poor in 2000. Emmaus works for change in both society and church and is called the Mecca of the New Left. It became a centre for the Black Panthers. Emmaus emphasizes church as community and as a hospital for wounded humanity. Their approach to homelessness is holistic and integral. Every Emmaus community member must work six hours daily, work on education at night (literacy etc.), have therapy in this supportive community, reorientate values and seek action for social and personal change. The community is different because its structure is a circle rather than a pyramid. Social workers support rather than dominate. The homeless are involved in all decision making including hiring and firing. Emmaus seeks to make its own income through 'Emmaus works'. They live totally in dependence on God.

Total projects worldwide: 1
Total UK projects: 0
Starting months: January–December.
Time required: 1–52 weeks (plus).
Age requirement: 12 plus.
Causes: Addicts/Ex-addicts, Aids/HIV, inner city problems, offenders/ex-offenders, poor/homeless.
Activities: Caring (general and residential), computers, cooking, fundraising, group work, manual work, theatre/drama.
When to apply: All year.
Work alone/with others: With other young volunteers.
Volunteers with disabilities: Not possible.
Qualifications: Nil.
Health requirements: Should be in good health.
Costs: Fares to USA. Volunteers must have their own insurance.
Training: All volunteers are briefed in Emmaus programme.
Supervision: Volunteers usually have their own supervision.
Interview details: Prospective volunteers are only interviewed on the telephone.
Worldwide placements: *North America* (USA).

EMMAUS INTERNATIONAL
183 bis, rue Vaillant-Couturier
BP 91
94140 Alfortville
France

Tel: 00 33 1 48 93 29 50
Fax: 00 33 1 43 53 19 26
e-mail: emausint@globenet.org

Web: www.emmaus-international.org
Contact: The Secretary

The Emmaus movement started in Paris in 1949 and there are now some 357 Emmaus communities in 42 countries. These communities try to provide a meaning to life for those without one – that meaning being to help others in need. Each community is autonomous and independent of race, sex, religion, politics, age etc. Living conditions are usually simple and the work is hard. The activities of Emmaus groups all round the world are recycling, sorting and resale of second-hand items. The benefits are given to Emmaus social action. Although in Europe, Africa, Asia and the Americas, Emmaus never sends volunteers to the third world countries because they employ local people on the spot. Volunteers with offending backgrounds are accepted.

Total projects worldwide: Approximately 5.
Total UK projects: 0
Starting months: July–September.
Time required: 2–10 weeks.
Age requirement: 18 plus.
Causes: Work camps – seasonal.
Activities: Community work, manual work, summer camps, work camps – seasonal.
Vols under 26 placed each year: 400 of a total of 500.
When to apply: February / March.
Work alone/with others: With others.
Qualifications: Spoken English or language of project country.
Costs: All costs except food and accommodation. Volunteers must have E111 health insurance.
Benefits: Accommodation and food.
Training: Dependent on project.
Supervision: A responsible supervisor is in charge of volunteers and also the friends of the communities which organize the camps.
Interview details: No interview necessary.
Worldwide placements: *Europe* (Denmark, Italy, Poland, Portugal).

ENDEAVOUR TRAINING
Sheepbridge Centre
Sheepbridge Lane
Chesterfield
Derbyshire
S41 9RX UK

Tel: +44 (0) 1246 454957
Fax: +44 (0) 1246 261865

Contact: Colin Matchett

Endeavour Children's Camps offer holidays under canvas for underprivileged children. Staffed by Endeavour volunteers, each one week long, there are four planned each summer with 15 staff per camp. Other projects – environmental and community – are run by Endeavour Local Groups throughout various regions in the Midlands, North East, East and North. Volunteers with an offending background are accepted. Applicants have to become members.

Total projects worldwide: 5 plus
Total UK projects: 5 plus.
Starting months: May–September.
Time required: 1 week.
Age requirement: 16 plus.
Causes: Children, poor/homeless, young people.
Activities: Arts/crafts, community work, fundraising, group work, outdoor skills, summer camps.
Vols under 26 placed each year: 500 plus.
When to apply: As early as possible.
Work alone/with others: With others.
Volunteers with disabilities: Possible.
Qualifications: Membership of Endeavour. Caring, dependable.
Health requirements: Nil.
Costs: Membership fee £3.50–£7.50 plus Travel.
Benefits: Board and lodging.
Training: Volunteers have to participate in training and events before participating on projects with at-risk groups.
Interview details: References are checked and volunteers undergo vetting procedures before acceptance.
Certification: Certificate or reference provided.
Charity number: 275061
UK placements: *England* (Co. Durham, Derbyshire, Norfolk, Nottinghamshire, Tyne and Wear, Warwickshire, West Midlands, S. Yorkshire).

ENSEIGNANTS SANS FRONTIÈRES
7 rte de Sauvabelin
1052 Le Mont-sur-Lausanne
Vaud
Switzerland

Tel: 00 41 21 652 17 55
Fax: 00 41 21 652 17 55
Contact: Mrs Anne-Marie Baur, President

Enseignants sans Frontières (Teachers without Borders) was established as a non-profit organization in 1994 following collaboration between several Swiss and African teachers. Subsequently, further groups were established in Belgium, France, Senegal and Burkina Faso, with a view to promoting international co-operation between educators and teachers in French-speaking countries. Since 1996, we have run short term teacher training courses for volunteers in Kafountine, Senegal and Ouahigouya, Burkina Faso. Volunteers are required to work during the month of July and should be fluent in French. Further details can be obtained by contacting the President at the above address, and correspondence must be in French.

Total projects worldwide: 3
Total UK projects: 0
Starting months: July.
Time required: 15 weeks.
Age requirement: 18 plus.
Causes: Children, health care/medical, teaching/assisting (nursery, primary, mature).
Activities: Development issues, DIY, fundraising, group work, manual work, teaching, training.
Vols under 26 placed each year: 5–10 of a total of 10–20.
Work alone/with others: With others.
Qualifications: Fluent French.
Health requirements: Good health required.
Costs: Volunteers must fund their costs in full and have their own private insurance.
Interview details: Interviews are conducted.
Worldwide placements: *Africa* (Burkina Faso, Senegal); *Europe* (Switzerland).

ENVIRONMENTAL LIAISON CENTRE INTERNATIONAL
PO Box 72461
Nairobi
Kenya

Tel: 00 254 2 562022 or 576154
Fax: 00 254 2 562175
e-mail: herren@africaonline.co.ke
Web: http://info@elci.org
Contact: Barbara Gemmill

Environmental Liaison Centre International (ELCI) aims to empower grassroots environment and development organizations, and to increase NGO involvement in government environmental policy with a view to improving environmental problems. Most work is carried out in the following areas: women, environment and development, food security and forestry, energy for sustainable development, industrialization and human settlements, and international environment and economic relations. We accept volunteers who wish to learn about global environmental and development issues, giving you a chance to work on substantive projects in the secretariat's office in Nairobi.

Total projects worldwide: Many.
Total UK projects: 0
Starting months: January–December.
Time required: 20–40 weeks.
Age requirement: 20 plus.
Causes: Environmental Causes.
Activities: Computers, development issues, fundraising, group work, newsletter/journalism.
Vols under 26 placed each year: 2 of a total of 3.
When to apply: All year.
Work alone/with others: Both.
Volunteers with disabilities: Not possible.
Qualifications: Only an interest in environmental/development issues.
Health requirements: Nil.
Costs: Return travel to Nairobi. Subsistence in Nairobi approximately £20 per week (more for first week).
Interview details: Prospective volunteers are not interviewed but e-mail communication is used for screening.
Worldwide placements: *Africa* (Kenya).

ESCUELA DE ENFERMERIA – STELLA MARIS
Apartado Postal 28
Zacapu
Michoacan
CP 58670
Mexico

Tel: 00 52 436 3 1300
Contact: Christine Wilson ·

Stella Maris is a private nursing school whose student body is made up of many students from very poor areas. Volunteers are needed to help with general school maintenance and act as secretaries or, if qualified, to be teaching nurses or doctors.

Total projects worldwide: 1
Total UK projects: 0

Starting months: January–December.
Time required: 26–52 weeks.
Age requirement: 14 plus.
Activities: Training.
Vols under 26 placed each year: 1-6
When to apply: All year.
Qualifications: Preferably knowledge of
Spanish, driving licence, typing, organizing
skills.
Costs: Travel.
Benefits: Accommodation and small monthly
allowance.
Worldwide placements: *Central America*
(Mexico).

ESPACO T

Avenida de Franca 256
Centro Comercial Capitolio, Salas 5, 12, 22,
23
Porto
4050-276 Portugal

Tel: 00 351 22 830 2432
Fax: 00 351 22 830 5593
e-mail: espacot@espacot.pt
Web: www.espacot.pt
Contact: Jorge Oliveira

Espaco t (Association for Support and Social
and Community Integration) takes care of
people with multiple physical, psychological
and social problems. We provide them with
artistic activities including photography,
theatre, painting, physical education, music,
dance, tai-chi-chuan and journalism. In the
social area, Espaco t has a UNIVA (Unity of
Insertion in the Active Life) department
whose main aim is promoting employment in
areas of unemployment. We also have a
phone line which informs about Espaco t's
activities and which also supports people in
crisis and distress. About 30 volunteers are
taken on annually to help with cultural
activities. Volunteers with an offending
background are accepted.

Total projects worldwide: 1
Total UK projects: 0
Starting months: January.
Time required: 2–4 weeks.
Age requirement: 18 plus.
Causes: Addicts/ex-addicts, Aids/HIV,
disabled (learning and physical), offenders/
ex-offenders, poor/homeless, unemployed.
Activities: Arts/crafts, community work,
group work, music, newsletter/journalism,
social work, sport, theatre/drama.

Vols under 26 placed each year: 10 of a total
of 30.
When to apply: Any time.
Work alone/with others: With others.
Volunteers with disabilities: Possible.
Qualifications: Knowledge of Portuguese,
Spanish or Italian and some artistic or social
work expertise.
Health requirements: Good health essential,
both physically and mentally.
Costs: All costs.
Benefits: Insurance against work accidents is
provided by us.
Training: The team will brief the volunteer
about the Association's activities.
Supervision: By director, psychologist and the
social-cultural animator.
Interview details: Interviews are conducted
either by telephone or at the Association
offices.
Certification: Certificate or reference
provided.
Worldwide placements: *Europe* (Portugal).

ÉTUDES ET CHANTIERS (UNAREC)

3, rue des Petits Gras
Delegation Internationale UNAREC
Clermont-Ferrand
63000 France

Tel: 00 33 4 73 36 52 28
Fax: 00 33 4 73 36 46 65
Contact: François Ribaud, Colègue
international

Études et Chantiers is a non-profit and non-
governmental organization, organized locally
by regional associations and federated with a
national union (UNAREC). All associations
lead permanent actions to help deprived areas
and people with work for local communities:
120 staff and 100 volunteers lead these
projects throughout the year. In ten regions of
France and 29 countries in the world, Études
et Chantiers invites you to take part in
practical action to build and enrich
communities and the environment ('spaces of
life').

Total projects worldwide: 60
Total UK projects: 0
Starting months: June.
Time required: 2–24 weeks.
Age requirement: 14 plus.
Causes: Conservation, environmental causes,
heritage, work camps – seasonal.
Activities: Building/construction,

conservation skills, forestry, international aid, social work, work camps – seasonal.
Vols under 26 placed each year: 800
When to apply: Before end of May.
Work alone/with others: With others.
Volunteers with disabilities: Not possible.
Qualifications: Nil.
Equipment/clothing: Work clothes, sleeping bag, good shoes, boots, gloves, suncream.
Health requirements: Nil.
Costs: Registration and insurance FF600.
Travel/camp fees: 13–16 years FF2400; 17–18 years) FF900; adults over 18 Free.
Benefits: Board and lodging, leisure activities.
Interview details: No interview necessary.
Worldwide placements: *Europe* (France).

EUROPE CONSERVATION ITALY
Via del Macao
00185 Roma
Italy

Tel: 00 39 06 4741241
Fax: 00 390 06 4744671
e-mail: ecomil@imiucca.csi.unimi.it
Contact: Silvia Franco

Europe Conservation Italy is pursuing the following objectives: improving the knowledge, management and rational use of natural resources on an international level; gathering funds intended for projects of nature conservation and sustainable development in Europe and other continents; promoting Ecovoluntary programmes with the double goal of supporting conservation projects and favouring the spread of a cross-national environmental culture; carrying out programmes of environmental awareness and education.

Total projects worldwide: 6
Total UK projects: 0
Starting months: January–December.
Time required: 1–3 weeks.
Age requirement: 14 plus.
Causes: Animal welfare, conservation, environmental causes, wildlife.
Activities: Building/construction, campaigning, conservation skills, manual work, outdoor skills, research, scientific work.
When to apply: All year.
Work alone/with others: Both.
Volunteers with disabilities: Varies according to project.
Qualifications: Nil.

Health requirements: Nil.
Costs: Varies according to project (including the need for insurance).
Benefits: Varies according to project.
Training: Varies according to project.
Supervision: Varies according to project.
Interview details: Interviews for some projects are held in our offices.
Certification: Varies according to project.
Worldwide placements: *Africa* (Kenya); *Asia* (Thailand); *Europe* (Croatia, Greece, Italy, Romania); *North America* (Canada); *Central America* (Mexico).

EUROPEAN VOLUNTARY SERVICE
The British Council
10 Spring Gardens
London
SW1A 2BN UK

Tel: +44 (0) 20 7389 4030
Fax: +44 (0) 20 7389 4033
Contact: Julie Stimpson

The European Voluntary Service scheme is open to all young people with no qualification requirement. There is a very wide range of tasks and positive measures will enable disadvantaged young people to have access to the programme. Although you will have a say over your placement and type of work you must be prepared to work in any one of the fields listed. You will meet volunteers from other European countries to share experiences. You will have a rewarding experience doing something useful for other communities. You will learn a lot, at the same time helping yourself to develop as a person and to develop your future. You will learn new skills which make you more attractive to future employers. It is exciting and you will get to see places. You will be living in another country for quite a long time. You will learn about their customs and feel a sense of belonging to the European Union. You will make useful contacts for the future, even at European level, and also have an active part in discussing your role, place and responsibilities in the host project. At in-service training events you will have the chance to meet other EVS volunteers in your country and to discuss and reflect upon your experiences. You may be the only volunteer at your assignment or you may be working with a group of volunteers. But you will always be part of a team.

Total projects worldwide: 100 plus.
Total UK projects: 0
Starting months: January–December.
Time required: 26–52 weeks.
Age requirement: 18–25
Causes: Addicts/ex-addicts, Aids/HIV, animal welfare, archaeology, architecture, children, conservation, disabled (learning and physical), elderly people, environmental causes, health care/medical, heritage, holidays for disabled, human rights, inner city problems, offenders/ex-offenders, poor/homeless, refugees, unemployed, wildlife, work camps – seasonal, young people.
Activities: Accountancy, administration, agriculture/farming, arts/crafts, building/construction, campaigning, caring (general, day and residential), catering, community work, computers, conservation skills, cooking, counselling, development issues, DIY, driving, first aid, forestry, fundraising, gardening/horticulture, group work, international aid, library/resource centres, manual work, marketing/publicity, music, newsletter/journalism, outdoor skills, religion, research, scientific work, social work, sport, summer camps, teaching, technical skills, theatre/drama, training, translating, visiting/befriending, work camps – seasonal.
When to apply: All year.
Work alone/with others: Both.
Volunteers with disabilities: Possible.
Qualifications: Nil.
Equipment/clothing: Any special equipment or clothing supplied.
Health requirements: Any special health requirements for a specific project would be notified to prospective volunteer.
Costs: Nil.
Benefits: Board and lodging plus pocket money approximately £20 per week. Travel money and special equipment.
Training: You will be given preparatory training before you leave including language training and preparation for the new culture you will be living in. You will also attend an in-service training event during the course of your assignment.
Supervision: As well as a job supervisor, you will have a personal supervisor unconnected with your project whom you can turn to for personal support if needed.
Nationalities accepted: Only EU citizens.
Certification: Certificate or reference provided

– European approved certificate.
Worldwide placements: *Europe* (Austria, Belgium, Denmark, Finland, France, Germany, Greece, Iceland, Ireland, Italy, Liechtenstein, Luxembourg, Netherlands, Norway, Portugal, Spain, Sweden).

EVANGELISCHE KIRCHE IN OSTERREICH

Diakonisches Werk Österreich
Trautsongasse 8
A-1080 Wien
Austria

Tel: 00 43 1 409 80 01
Fax: 00 43 1 409 80 01 20
Contact: Mag. Margarita Hummel

Evangelische Kirche – Diakonisches Werk Österreich is the Austrian branch of the European Diaconal Year network which consists of a number of national Christian-based volunteering schemes (the British branch is Time For God). We share common standards, and a commitment to the personal development of the volunteer through this form of work.

Total projects worldwide: 5
Total UK projects: 0
Starting months: January–December.
Time required: 26–52 weeks.
Age requirement: 18–25
Causes: Children, disabled (learning), elderly people.
Activities: Caring (general, day and residential), social work.
Vols under 26 placed each year: 10–15
When to apply: Before March to start the following school year.
Work alone/with others: With others.
Volunteers with disabilities: Not possible.
Qualifications: Fluent German. Personal active Christian Faith.
Health requirements: Must be in good health.
Costs: Travel costs to the Austrian border or location of placement.
Benefits: Board and Lodging, pocket money (As2,100 per month), social insurance.
Supervision: Personal supervision and regular residential conferences or seminars.
Certification: Certificate about the duration and the location of the voluntary service.
Worldwide placements: *Europe* (Austria).

F

F. DUMASY

25 Boulevard Arago
Paris
75013 France

Total projects worldwide: 1
Total UK projects: 0
Starting months: August.
Time required: 2 weeks.
Age requirement: 18–25
Causes: Archaeology.
Activities: Manual work.
When to apply: As early as possible.
Health requirements: Anti-tetanus
vaccination.
Interview details: No interview necessary.
Worldwide placements: *Europe* (France).

FAIRBRIDGE

207 Waterloo Road
London
SE1 8XD UK

Tel: +44 (0) 20 7928 1704
Fax: +44 (0) 20 7928 6016
e-mail: info@fairbridge.org.uk
Web: www.fairbridge.org.uk
Contact: Rebecca Leete, Communications
Officer

Fairbridge works with disaffected young
people aged 14–25 in 12 of the UK's inner
cities. We offer a long-term personal
development programme which focuses on
the development of personal and social skills.
As participants progress, they also build a
balanced portfolio of secondary skills such as
independent living skills, recreation and
community skills and work-based skills.
Various vehicles are used to deliver the
programme, from challenging outdoor
activities to the arts and workplace
environments. Each young person tailors the
programme to their individual needs by
selecting from a wide range of courses and is
supported by a mentor to develop a personal
action plan. Volunteers contribute to all
aspects of programme delivery within
Fairbridge, depending on individual skills and
the needs of the particular Fairbridge team.
Responsibilities could include recruitment of
young people for the programme, project
delivery, mentoring or administrative duties.

Volunteers with an offending background will
be considered.

Total projects worldwide: 12
Total UK projects: 12
Starting months: January–December.
Time required: 4–52 weeks (plus).
Age requirement: 18 plus.
Causes: Addicts/ex-addicts, conservation,
inner city problems, offenders/ex-offenders,
poor/homeless, unemployed, young people.
Activities: Administration, community work,
conservation skills, cooking, counselling,
driving, first aid, fundraising, group work,
marketing/publicity, music, newsletter/
journalism, outdoor skills, theatre/drama,
training.
When to apply: All year.
Work alone/with others: Both.
Volunteers with disabilities: Possible.
Qualifications: Driving licence and first aid
an advantage.
Health requirements: Nil.
Costs: Nil.
Benefits: Travel, subsistence, training,
insurance.
Training: Depending on the position,
volunteers will be interviewed and expected
to participate in an induction process. A
budget is available for further training.
Supervision: Supervised by a head of
department and appraised regularly.
Interview details: Volunteer applicants are
always recruited and interviewed at the
relevant team centre (details of centres can be
obtained from Central Office).
Certification: Certificate or reference
available.
Charity number: 206807
UK placements: *England* (Bristol, Hampshire,
Kent, London, Manchester, Merseyside, Tyne
and Wear, West Midlands, N. Yorkshire);
Scotland (Edinburgh, Glasgow City); *Wales*
(Cardiff).

FAMILY INVESTMENT LTD

51 Old Dover Road
Canterbury
Kent
CT1 3DE UK

Tel: +44 (0) 1227 456963
Fax: +44 (0) 1227 456963
e-mail: FI-office@Talk21.com
Contact: Jenny Gurney, Director

Family Investment provides support for

disabled adults in their daily living. Volunteers are needed as care/support workers throughout the year to act as escorts on outings and to take part on an instructional basis in their work placements. Duty hours are from 7.30 a.m. to 10.30 p.m. but shifts no longer than eight hours. You should be motivated with a sense of humour and a realistic attitude.

Total projects worldwide: 7
Total UK projects: 7
Starting months: January–December.
Time required: 20–52 weeks (plus).
Age requirement: 18 plus.
Causes: Disabled (learning and physical), holidays for disabled.
Activities: Agriculture/farming, arts/crafts, caring (general, day and residential), catering, cooking, first aid, gardening/horticulture, group work, music, outdoor skills, training.
Vols under 26 placed each year: 2 of a total of 7.
When to apply: All year.
Work alone/with others: With others.
Volunteers with disabilities: Possible.
Qualifications: Driving licence is a help.
Equipment/clothing: Waterproof clothes if wishing to work outside alongside the learning disabled people.
Health requirements: Nil.
Costs: None.
Benefits: All meals and drinks provided as well as out-of-pocket expenses. Company has full insurance.
Training: Induction given.
Supervision: Main staff take responsibility of volunteers working with them.
Interview details: Prospective volunteers are interviewed in Canterbury.
Certification: References provided.
Charity number: 328496
UK placements: *England* (Kent).

FARM AFRICA

9–10 Southampton Place
London
WC1A 2DA UK

Tel: +44 (0) 20 7430 0440
Contact: Benjamin Janes

Farm Africa was founded in 1985 with the aim of helping small peasant farmers in Africa develop agricultural skills and techniques, increase food production and break the cycle of famine.

Total projects worldwide: 1
Starting months: February, March.
Time required: 12–52 weeks (plus).
Age requirement: 18 plus.
Causes: Poor/homeless.
Activities: Administration, computers, development issues, marketing/publicity.
When to apply: All year but November/December preferred.
Volunteers with disabilities: Possible.
Qualifications: Enthusiasm and real interest in Africa. Communication abilities.
Costs: Nil.
Benefits: Insurance and some travel expenses.
UK placements: *England* (London).

FELLOWSHIP OF RECONCILIATION (FOR)

Task Force on Latin America and Caribbean
2017 Mission Street, #305
San Francisco
CA 94110 USA

Tel: 00 1 415 495 6334
Fax: 00 1 415 495 5628
e-mail: volfor@igc.org
Web: www.forusa.org/volunteer
Contact: John Lindsay-Poland

The Fellowship of Reconciliation invites you to: join in efforts on behalf of Latin America and the Caribbean's poor majority; develop ties with groups working for nonviolent social change; contribute to intercultural understanding and respect; immerse yourself in Latin American culture; learn about the impact of US culture and politics in the region; have fun! Volunteers with an offending background are accepted.

Total projects worldwide: 12
Total UK projects: 0
Starting months: January–December.
Time required: 12–52 weeks (plus).
Age requirement: 21 plus.
Causes: Human rights, teaching/assisting.
Activities: Administration, teaching, training, translating.
Vols under 26 placed each year: Approximately 5 of a total of 10.
When to apply: All year.
Work alone/with others: With host group.
Volunteers with disabilities: Possible.
Qualifications: Fluent in Spanish.
Equipment/clothing: Bring enough for own living situation, or purchase in-country.
Health requirements: Physically and

psychologically well.
Costs: Travel, insurance, board and lodging plus US$60 registration fee.
Training: Background information is provided.
Supervision: Volunteers work with host groups – capacity for supervision varies. Often the volunteer is part of a team.
Nationalities accepted: Volunteers living or staying in the US preferred.
Interview details: Interviews take place in California or by phone.
Certification: Reference on request.
Worldwide placements: *Central America* (Mexico, Nicaragua, Panama, Puerto Rico); *South America* (Argentina, Bolivia, Chile, Ecuador, Paraguay, Peru).

FFESTINIOG RAILWAY COMPANY
Harbour Station
Porthmadog
Gwynedd
LL49 9NF N. Wales

Tel: +44 (0) 1766 512340
Fax: +44 (0) 1766 514715
e-mail: info@Festrail.demon.co.uk
Web: www.festrail.co.uk
Contact: The Volunteer Officer

The world famous Ffestiniog Railway runs from the sea at Porthmadog into the mountains of Snowdonia to Blaenau Ffestiniog. The railway was originally built to carry slate from the quarries at Blaenau Ffestiniog down to the ships at the port of Porthmadog. Originally operated by gravity and horses and then by steam, the railway now winds its way up the valley with the passengers enjoying some unique views. The railway closed down in 1946 due to the decline in the demand for slate. However, the line reopened in 1954 thanks to the time and dedication of volunteers. Volunteers still play a major role on the Ffestiniog Railway. Thousands give up their free time to come and work on the railway and give their continued support. There are many different types of jobs to do, from serving passengers on our buffet cars to working on locomotives, tracks, buildings, gardens or restoring carriages. There is always something to keep you busy.

Total projects worldwide: 1
Total UK projects: 1
Starting months: January–December.

Time required: 1–52 weeks.
Age requirement: 16 plus.
Causes: Conservation, Heritage.
Activities: Building/construction, catering, conservation skills, DIY, gardening/horticulture, group work, manual work, marketing/publicity, outdoor skills.
Vols under 26 placed each year: Approximately 500 of a total of 1,000 plus.
When to apply: As soon as possible.
Work alone/with others: With others.
Volunteers with disabilities: Please contact to discuss options.
Qualifications: Nil.
Equipment/clothing: Yes – details on application.
Health requirements: Yes – details on application.
Costs: Hostel £3.50 per night self-catering.
Benefits: Free Ffestiniog Railway travel, food and drink discounts on duty. Railway projects are covered by our company insurance.
Training: A safety induction pack is sent from 'safety critical' sections.
Supervision: Varies but normal distribution is one staff to five volunteers. On special working parties, some work is on a one-on-one basis.
Nationalities accepted: No restrictions but, for the safety of all, a good comprehension of English required.
Interview details: Applicants may be interviewed.
Certification: Reference on request.
UK placements: *Wales* (Gwynedd).

FIRST CONTACT
The Sheffield Centre
50 Cavendish Street
Sheffield
South Yorkshire
S3 7RZ UK

Tel: +44 (0) 114 272 7451
Fax: +44 (0) 114 279 5863
e-mail: ruth@word-on-the-web.co.uk
Contact: Ruth Mills, Project Administrator

First Contact is a year out scheme, which seeks to place volunteers alongside a trained Church Army evangelist. Church Army have five areas of focus, which are: children and young people, homelessness, church planting, older people, area evangelism. The mission statement of Church Army is 'Sharing Faith through Words and Action'. At First Contact we seek to share the good news of God's love as seen in Jesus Christ. Volunteers are placed in teams for a year. The work varies from place to place but generally includes: some work in schools, work with young people, involvement in a local church, music and drama where appropriate. You have two residential training conferences, expenses for which are paid by Church Army. This is a chance to reflect on some of the experiences gained during your placement, and to meet up with other First Contact volunteers in different teams. In selecting volunteers, we seek to find those whom God is calling to work alongside Church Army. We are looking for active Christian young people who are enthusiastic about their faith and interested in sharing it with others. Volunteers with an offending background might be accepted if the offence did not relate to children or young people. Each case is looked at individually.

Total projects worldwide: 6
Total UK projects: 6
Starting months: September.
Time required: 30–46 weeks.
Age requirement: 18–30
Causes: Children, elderly people, inner city problems, poor/homeless, young people.
Activities: Campaigning, community work, group work, music, religion, teaching, theatre/drama.
Vols under 26 placed each year: Approximately 24 of a total of 25.
When to apply: Before 30 April.
Work alone/with others: With others.
Volunteers with disabilities: We do not exclude disabled volunteers. If a person is selected as being called by God, we will work to place them on a suitable team.
Qualifications: An active Christian faith and a desire for others to experience relationship with Jesus.
Health requirements: Nil.
Costs: Pocket money (a small bursary is available).
Benefits: Board and lodging, travel to and from the placement each term.
Training: 2 residential training conferences and on-the-job training from a qualified Church Army evangelist.
Supervision: By line manager locally with pastoral visits from the project co-ordinators.
Interview details: Interviews take place in

Sheffield.
Certification: Reference on request.
Charity number: 226226
UK placements: *England* (throughout); *Northern Ireland* (throughout).

FLYING ANGEL CLUB
76 Queen Victoria Street
Fremantle
6160 Western Australia

Tel: 00 61 8 9335 5000
Fax: 00 61 8 9335 5321
Contact: Mr Jim Cross

Flying Angel Club is the commonly used name of the British and International Sailors' Society and The Missions to Seamen which is the Anglican Church's ministry to seafarers of all races and creeds. The people who make up the Missions to Seamen include volunteers who work in the Society's centres and those who raise funds for its work, as well as chaplains and other full-time staff.

Total projects worldwide: 1
Total UK projects: 0
Starting months: January–December.
Time required: 1–52 weeks.
Age requirement: 18 plus.
Causes: Inner city problems, poor/homeless, young people.
Activities: Administration, catering, driving, marketing/publicity, religion, social work, visiting/befriending.
Vols under 26 placed each year: 2 of a total of 20.
When to apply: All year.
Work alone/with others: Mostly with older volunteers.
Volunteers with disabilities: Not possible.
Qualifications: Ordinary driving licence and, if possible, a bus driving licence.
Health requirements: Good general health.
Costs: Travel to Fremantle, Australia.
Benefits: Subsidized board and lodging.
Worldwide placements: *Australasia* (Australia).

FOCUS (Bridge and Challenge Programmes)
Komtech House
255–257 London Road
Headington
Oxford
Oxfordshire
OX3 9EH UK

Tel: +44 (0) 1865 308488
Contact: Denise Barrows, Director

Focus (Bridge and Challenge Programmes) was set up by Cambridge students in 1988 and aims to challenge the way people see themselves, to provide opportunities for people to focus on their abilities and interests, and gain in self-confidence. We achieve our aims by running a wide variety of team-based projects, bringing together a wide range of people to understand and appreciate each other: local teenagers aged 12–16 who need a break; adults with a physical disability; adults with learning disabilities; students. We provide week-long adventure camps for an integrated group of mentally and physically handicapped adults and socially disadvantaged children. Teams of very different people are challenged to work together on activities ranging from building a medieval encampment to hot air ballooning. Progress is built on by a programme of year-round projects including weekend mini-camps and long-term team challenges. There is also a new SCOPE project, challenging teams of teenage schoolchildren to organize their own community projects.

Total projects worldwide: 10 plus.
Total UK projects: 10 plus.
Starting months: March–August.
Time required: 1–6 weeks.
Age requirement: 18 plus.
Causes: Children, disabled (learning and physical), elderly people, holidays for disabled, poor/homeless, young people.
Activities: Caring (residential), community work, first aid, fundraising, group work, outdoor skills, social work, summer camps, training.
Vols under 26 placed each year: Approximately 400.
When to apply: For Easter camps apply by March at the latest. For Summer camps apply by June at the latest.
Work alone/with others: Normally in teams.
Volunteers with disabilities: Possible
Qualifications: Willingness to work hard, help others plus make the camps FUN! Police profiling possible.
Equipment/clothing: Warm clothing and fancy dress (if possible).
Health requirements: Nil.
Costs: May include travel to/from camp sites.
Benefits: Board and lodging normally

provided on camps.
Certification: Certificate or reference on request.
Charity number: 1028637
UK placements: *England* (Cambridgeshire, Nottinghamshire, Oxfordshire).

FOOD FOR THE HUNGRY UK
44 Copperfield Road
Bassett
Southampton
Hampshire
SO16 3NX UK

Tel: +44 (0) 23 8090 2327
Fax: +44 (0) 23 8090 2327
e-mail: uk@fhi.net
Web: www.uk.fhi.net
Contact: Doug Wakeling, Executive Officer

The international partnership of Food for the Hungry, motivated by Christ's love, exists to meet both physical and spiritual hungers of the poor in Uganda. Volunteers with offending backgrounds will probably be accepted.

Total projects worldwide: 1–2
Total UK projects: 0
Starting months: August.
Time required: 3–5 weeks.
Age requirement: 19–25
Causes: Children, conservation, elderly people, health care/medical, poor/homeless, unemployed, work camps – seasonal, young people.
Activities: Agriculture/farming, building/construction, community work, conservation skills, gardening/horticulture, religion, visiting/befriending, work camps – seasonal.
Vols under 26 placed each year: Up to about 20.
When to apply: Any time before mid-March.
Work alone/with others: With leaders and field staff.
Volunteers with disabilities: Not really.
Qualifications: Christian commitment and willingness to work alongside Ugandan nationals.
Equipment/clothing: Summer clothes.
Health requirements: Travel vaccinations and anti-malarial tablets.
Costs: £900 total.
Benefits: Lodging in Uganda, training before going, debriefing on return.
Interview details: Prospective volunteers are interviewed in Bournemouth.

Charity number: 328273
Worldwide placements: *Africa* (Uganda).

FORENINGEN STAFFANSGAARDEN
Box 66
Furugatan 1
82060 Delsbo
Sweden

Tel: 00 46 653 16850
Fax: 00 46 653 10968
e-mail: staffansgarden@user.bip.net
Contact: Per Iversen

Foreningen Staffansgaarden is a community
for mentally handicapped adults in Sweden.
A volunteer can help in many ways, including
working in the bakery, the wood workshop,
the garden, weaving, farming, cooking and
cleaning or merely by participating in daily
life with the handicapped adults. Volunteers
with an offending background are accepted.

Total projects worldwide: 1
Total UK projects: 0
Starting months: January–December.
Time required: 26–52 weeks (plus).
Age requirement: 18 plus.
Causes: Disabled (learning).
Activities: Agriculture/farming, arts/crafts,
caring (general, day and residential),
community work, cooking, driving, forestry,
gardening/horticulture, group work, music,
outdoor skills, religion, social work, sport,
theatre/drama, training.
Vols under 26 placed each year: 5 of a total
of 10.
When to apply: All year.
Work alone/with others: Both.
Volunteers with disabilities: Possible, but not
for people with nervous problems.
Qualifications: Swedish speaking is a big plus
and driving licence is also preferred.
Equipment/clothing: Warm clothing for the
winter.
Health requirements: Stable mental health.
Costs: Fare to Staffansgaarden. Travel
insurance.
Benefits: Board and lodging plus pocket
money and insurance plus fare home after 6
months.
Supervision: The volunteer always has a
house parent or workshop master to help in
the daily task.
Interview details: No interview necessary.
Certification: Reference or certificate
provided.

Worldwide placements: *Europe* (Sweden).

FOREST SCHOOL CAMPS
21 Dukes Avenue
London
N10 2PS UK

Tel: +44 (0) 20 8444 8884
Fax: +44 (0) 20 8444 8884
e-mail: gil53@dial.pipex.com
Web: www.fsc.org.uk
Contact: The Secretary

Forest School Camps is a national
organization for young people which aims to
encourage the idea that socially necessary
work should be undertaken by volunteers on
behalf of the general community.

Total projects worldwide: 82
Total UK projects: 80
Starting months: March, April, May, July,
August.
Time required: 1–2 weeks.
Age requirement: 18 plus.
Causes: Children, disabled (learning and
physical), work camps – seasonal.
Activities: Arts/crafts, caring (general),
manual work, music, outdoor skills, sport,
summer camps, work camps – seasonal.
Vols under 26 placed each year: 350–400 of
a total of 750–800.
When to apply: January, February, March.
Work alone/with others: Work as part of
camping community – mostly in small
groups.
Qualifications: None but personal/
professional references requested.
Equipment/clothing: Lightweight tent if
possible.
Health requirements: Health status not
necessarily a factor unless it impairs ability to
contribute to the group.
Costs: All costs plus contribution towards
food and expenses. Insurance of personal
belongings.
Training: Weekend training near Cambridge
– one weekend must be attended before
becoming a staff member of Forest School
Camps.
Supervision: We are all volunteers. Those
more experienced guide and support those
less so.
Interview details: No interview necessary.
Worldwide placements: *Europe* (France,
Ireland).
UK placements: *England* (Berkshire,

Cornwall, Cumbria, Derbyshire, Devon, Essex, Gloucestershire, Herefordshire, Lancashire, Lincolnshire, London, Norfolk, Somerset, Staffordshire, E. Sussex, W. Sussex, Warwickshire, West Midlands, N. Yorkshire, S. Yorkshire, W. Yorkshire); *Scotland* (Scottish Borders); *Wales* (throughout).

FOUR CORNERS SCHOOL OF OUTDOOR EDUCATION
PO Box 1029
196 S. Main St (shipping orders only)
Monticello
San Juan
84535, USA

Tel: 00 1 435 587 2156
Fax: 00 1 435 587 2193
e-mail: fcs@igc.apc.org
Contact: Janet Ross, Director of the School

Four Corners School, located in a 160,000 square mile region known as the Colorado Plateau, aims to increase participants' awareness and sensitivity to the physical and cultural heritage. The school teaches outdoor skills, natural sciences and land stewardship by creating a community of individuals who share their interests through informal, relaxed, hands-on experiences. We do not expect to take volunteers for 2001 but thereafter the programme will be re-established.

Total projects worldwide: 35 plus.
Total UK projects: 0
Starting months: March–October.
Time required: 1–2 weeks.
Age requirement: 18 plus.
Causes: Archaeology, conservation, environmental causes, teaching/assisting, wildlife.
Activities: Conservation skills, manual work, outdoor skills, research, scientific work, teaching.
Vols under 26 placed each year: 60 plus.
When to apply: 60 days prior to a scheduled programme.
Work alone/with others: With others – usually 8–12 to a programme.
Volunteers with disabilities: Not possible.
Qualifications: Nil.
Equipment/clothing: Depends on time of year, location and programme.
Health requirements: Physical fitness essential.

Costs: Tuition fees, travel costs.
Benefits: Lodging, meals, transport, guides/experts, group equipment and park fees.
Interview details: No interview necessary.
Worldwide placements: *North America* (USA).

FOYER THÉRAPEUTIQUE DE RUZIÈRE
Chateau de Ruzière
F 03160 Bourbon-l'Archambault
France

Tel: 00 33 4 70 67 00 23
Contact: The Director

Foyer Thérapeutique de Ruzière is a training and social therapeutic community for adolescents and young people with special needs. It is part of the Camphill Community organization.

Total projects worldwide: 1
Starting months: January–December.
Time required: 1–52 weeks (plus).
Age requirement: 14 plus.
Causes: Disabled (learning).
When to apply: All year.
Qualifications: Nil.
Health requirements: Healthy.
Costs: Travel to the Centre.
Worldwide placements: *Europe* (France).

FRENCH ENCOUNTERS
63 Fordhouse Road
Bromsgrove
Worcestershire
B60 2LU UK

Tel: +44 (0) 1527 873645
Fax: +44 (0) 1527 832794
e-mail:
admin@frenchencounters.freeserve.co.uk
Web: www.frenchencounters.co.uk
Contact: Soula Callow and Patsy Musto

French Encounters is a small independent family company specialising in French language field trips for schools. The programme, based in two chateaux centres in Normandy, is designed to give maximum linguistic and educational benefit to children in the 10–13 age range. Some older groups, for GCSE and A-levels projected. We are looking for 'gap year' students who need to work in France, who have stamina, enthusiasm and a sense of humour and adventure. You need to be reliable, responsible and calm in crises. You would work from mid-February to mid-June as animateurs/couriers, giving commentaries, organizing activities and entertainments, and giving general assistance to the director of the programme. Volunteers with an offending background may be accepted but not racists, rapists or known drug addicts.

Total projects worldwide: 2
Total UK projects: 0
Starting months: February
Time required: 12–17 weeks.
Age requirement: 18–21
Causes: Children, teaching/assisting, young people.
Activities: Arts/crafts, first aid, group work, music, outdoor skills, sport, teaching, theatre/drama, training.
Vols under 26 placed each year: 8
When to apply: Before 25 September.
Work alone/with others: Both.
Volunteers with disabilities: Not possible.
Qualifications: A-Level French or equivalent, experience with pre-teens, enthusiasm, good general educational background.
Health requirements: Good general health, stamina and energy essential.
Costs: Nil, except personal travel for pleasure.
Benefits: Full board and lodging plus £60 per week approximately plus weekend allowance, transport to and from Normandy and comprehensive insurance.
Training: 2 weeks on-site training. Detailed handbook provided well in advance of start of season. English Speaking Board professional presentation skills training and assessment provided, first aid training also.
Supervision: Adult director in overall charge with additional supervision by owner/director.
Interview details: Interviews take place at the head office in Bromsgrove.
Certification: Reference on request.
Worldwide placements: *Europe* (France).

FRIEDENSDORF INTERNATIONAL (PEACE VILLAGE INTERNATIONAL)
Aktion Friedensdorf e.V.
Lanterstrasse 21
Dinslaken 46539
Germany

Tel: 00 49 20644974 0
Fax: 00 49 20644974 999
e-mail: info@friedensdorf.de

Web: www.friedensdorf.de
Contact: Department 0410

For 32 years Friedensdorf International has worked with wounded children from war-torn and crisis areas including Afghanistan, Vietnam, Romania, Angola, Armenia, Georgia, Kazakhstan and Tajikistan who need medical treatment in European hospitals. After appropriate treatment the children live in the Peace Village care station in Oberhausen for rehabilitation until they return to their native countries and to their families. The children range from one year up to 12 years of age. About 15 volunteers work in the Village every year. Volunteers are required all the year round to take care of the children in the Peace Village. The work includes all kind of day care occupations with those children who have already finished their treatment in hospital and need to wait for their return flight home or with children whose treatment is interrupted for a while. Duties include the preparation of meals and working in the Village's educational institution. You may also be needed to help with practical work under the janitor's guidance, which might include general repairs to the houses. Learning German is very useful. Although some of our staff members speak English, it is easier to communicate with the children in German. Nevertheless, you will also have a good time with the children without speaking German, just by using gestures or signs.

Total projects worldwide: 1
Total UK projects: 0
Starting months: January–December.
Time required: 12–52 weeks.
Age requirement: 18 plus.
Causes: Children, disabled (learning and physical), health care/medical.
Activities: Caring (general), catering, first aid.
Vols under 26 placed each year: 12 of a total of 15.
When to apply: All year (minimum period of volunteering 3 months) but as early as possible as we receive very many requests.
Qualifications: Experience in social work desirable but not essential. No special skills needed except a love for children.
Health requirements: Free from infectious illnesses. Health insurance must be valid for Germany. Several children arrive with Hepatitis A, B or C. Detailed information is

given about viruses. Each volunteer must decide whether they should be injected before arrival.
Costs: All except board and accommodation.
Benefits: Board and accommodation.
Worldwide placements: *Asia* (Tajikistan); *Europe* (Germany).

FRIENDS OF BIRZEIT UNIVERSITY
21 Collingham Road
London
SW5 0NU UK

Tel: + 44 (0) 20 7373 8414
Fax: + 44 (0) 20 7835 2088
e-mail: fobzu@arab-british.u-net.com
Contact: The Co-ordinator

Every year since the late 1970s, the Palestinian Friends of Birzeit University (BZU) has organized international 'work camps' based on its own campus which is one of the best examples of modern Arab architecture in the area. From January 1988 to April 1992 the campus was closed by Israeli military order and students were banned from the campus. However, even during this time, BZU managed to arrange work camps in off-campus locations. In August/September 1992 work camps were once again held on the university campus. Two work camps are held each summer, usually during July and August. They are two weeks long and each one accommodates 30 international volunteers, of whom half are from the UK. The camps are an opportunity for volunteers from Europe and North America to experience the local situation at first hand and to contribute to improving the local conditions of life. Tasks range from helping farmers with their harvest to building basic sanitation facilities in refugee camps. Some of the work is symbolic in nature – showing solidarity with the community – and some is much-needed support which will really benefit the local people. Whilst the work is highly rewarding, participants should be prepared for strenuous activity. In addition to the work, a wide range of visits, meetings and cultural events are arranged. The social life of the work camp is very enjoyable. The political situation sometimes makes organization of the programme difficult but alternative arrangements can usually be made. You must be aware that you are travelling to an area of unrest and must

behave accordingly. There have not, however, been any serious incidents involving volunteers attending the work camps.

Total projects worldwide: 1–2
Total UK projects: 1
Starting months: June, July.
Time required: 2 weeks.
Age requirement: 20 plus.
Causes: Children, conservation, environmental causes, human rights, poor/homeless, refugees, work camps – seasonal, young people.
Activities: Administration, agriculture/farming, building/construction, campaigning, community work, computers, conservation skills, development issues, fundraising, manual work, marketing/publicity, newsletter/journalism, translating, work camps – seasonal.
Vols under 26 placed each year: 15 of a total of 20.
When to apply: Before 22 May.
Work alone/with others: With others.
Volunteers with disabilities: Possible, but work camps include manual work.
Qualifications: Nil.
Equipment/clothing: Clothes for manual outdoor work in the heat – culturally conservative dress. No shorts.
Health requirements: Reasonably fit.
Costs: For work camps: £18 application fee, £80 registration fee to include food and accommodation £200 approximately return flight to Tel Aviv and about £3 per day for extra travel and expenses.
Benefits: Board and lodging.
Interview details: Interviews take place in London. Send an A4 stamped (31p) addressed envelope.
Certification: Certificate or reference on request.
Charity number: 279026
UK placements: *England* (London).

FRIENDS OF ISRAEL EDUCATIONAL TRUST
PO Box 7545
London
NW2 2QZ UK

Tel: + 44 (0) 20 7435 6803
Fax: + 44 (0) 20 7794 0291
e-mail: foiasg@foiasg.free-online.co.uk
Contact: John D. A. Levy

Friends of Israel Educational Trust seeks to

develop critical interest in the land, peoples and cultures of Israel. The Foundation organizes an extensive lecture programme around the UK and has created a variety of hands-on working programmes in Israel for students, academics, clergy and other selected British groups. Bridge in Britain programme is a gap year scheme. In addition we offer occasional awards to graduate students of art schools, or young Christian clergy, young farmers or young horticulturalists. These are short-term placements

Total projects worldwide: 5
Total UK projects: 0
Starting months: January, February.
Time required: 24–30 weeks.
Age requirement: 18–20
Causes: Inner City Problems, teaching/assisting (primary, secondary, EFL), work camps – seasonal, young people.
Activities: Arts/crafts, music, sport, summer camps, teaching, theatre/drama, work camps – seasonal.
Vols under 26 placed each year: 12
When to apply: By 1 July.
Work alone/with others: Both.
Volunteers with disabilities: Not possible.
Qualifications: Nil. Require talented, personable good all-rounders.
Health requirements: Good physical and mental health.
Costs: Only cost is entertainment and travel when not on our programme.
Benefits: Travel plus insurance for 6 months; 5 months board and lodging carefully planned. Free time not planned.
Training: Pre-departure briefing by Trust staff and previous volunteers.
Supervision: Avoiding suffocation, we have professional co-ordinators on every programme who take general responsibility for organizing placements and monitoring progress.
Nationalities accepted: Must be UK Nationals.
Interview details: Interviews take place in London.
Charity number: 271983
Worldwide placements: *Asia* (Israel).

FRIENDS OF LUDHIANA
Partnership House
157 Waterloo Road
London
SE1 8UU UK

Tel: +44 (0) 20 7928 1173
Fax: c/o ACO 0207 620 1070
Contact: Heather Smith

Total projects worldwide: 1
Total UK projects: 0
Starting months: January–December.
Time required: 1–52 weeks (plus).
Age requirement: 12 plus.

FRIENDS OF THE EARTH BANGLADESH – IEDS
5/12–15 Eastern View (5th Floor)
50 D.IT Extension Road
GPO Box No. 3691
Dhaka – 1000
Bangladesh

Tel: 00 880 2 835394
Fax: 00 880 2 835394
e-mail: gbs@dhaka.agri.com
Contact: Mr M.F. Chowdhury, Vice-Chairman

Friends of the Earth Bangladesh is affiliated to Friends of the Earth International (FOE). This organization has been working towards creating positive solutions to many of the environmental problems threatening this planet over the last 20 years. FOE is committed to empowering local communities and people to get actively involved in the debate to protect the environment, through environmental education, public awareness, campaigning etc. Volunteers are always needed to help with a wide variety of projects.

Total projects worldwide: Many.
Total UK projects: 0
Starting months: January–December.
Time required: 1–52 weeks.
Age requirement: 16 plus.
Causes: Children, conservation, disabled (learning and physical), environmental causes, human rights, poor/homeless, refugees, teaching/assisting (primary), unemployed, wildlife, young people.
Activities: Administration, agriculture/farming, campaigning, community work, computers, conservation skills, development issues, forestry, fundraising, international aid, library/resource centres, manual work, newsletter/journalism, research, social work, training.
Vols under 26 placed each year: Many.
When to apply: All year.

Work alone/with others: Both.
Volunteers with disabilities: Not possible.
Qualifications: Nil.
Equipment/clothing: Depends on project.
Health requirements: Innoculations required for Bangladesh.
Costs: Fares and living costs, health and travel insurance.
Training: Orientation only is required.
Supervision: Experienced group leaders (local) are present at all camps and permanent staff manage the service.
Charity number: J-01947
Worldwide placements: *Asia* (Bangladesh).

FRIENDS WEEKEND WORK CAMP PROGRAM
1515 Cherry Street
Philadelphia
PA 19102
USA

Contact: Programme Organizer

Friends Weekend Work Camp Program offers short-term projects within inner city Philadelphia which combine physical work with discussions on urban poverty.

Total projects worldwide: 1
Total UK projects: 0
Starting months: January–May, October–December.
Time required: 1–52 weeks.
Age requirement: 16 plus.
Causes: Elderly people, inner city problems.
Activities: Building/construction, community work, counselling, DIY, manual work, social work.
Vols under 26 placed each year: 200
When to apply: As early as possible.
Work alone/with others: With others.
Qualifications: Spoken English.
Costs: Donation of US$35 per weekend.
Benefits: Board and lodging.
Worldwide placements: *North America* (USA).

FRIENDSHIP CLUB NEPAL
PO Box 11276
Maharajgunj
Kathmandu
Nepal
Contact: Prakash Babu Paudel

Friendship Club Nepal is a non-profit-making organization that works towards helping the poor people in rural areas of Nepal.

Volunteers are recruited to work throughout the year for both short-term (few weeks) and long-term (few months) periods. Volunteers can assist with teaching English in schools or colleges for 3–5 hours a day, six days a week, or act as Project Visitors in rural areas to conduct research and help with community building projects. You need no special skills or experience but should have a willingness to experience very basic living conditions. In return you will have the chance to experience the real Nepal. Volunteers with an offending background must provide full details, after which each case is considered separately.

Total projects worldwide: Many.
Total UK projects: 0
Starting months: January–December.
Time required: 2–22 weeks.
Age requirement: 18 plus.
Causes: Conservation, environmental causes, health care/medical, teaching/assisting (nursery, primary, secondary, EFL), work camps – seasonal, young people.
Activities: Agriculture/farming, building/construction, conservation skills, development issues, forestry, gardening/horticulture, manual work, outdoor skills, teaching, work camps – seasonal.
Vols under 26 placed each year: Most of a total of 200.
When to apply: All year.
Work alone/with others: With others.
Volunteers with disabilities: We are unable to place people with disabilities as most work is manual in remote rural areas with no facilities for disabled people.
Qualifications: Spoken English.
Health requirements: Nil but applicants should be aware of necessary medication in local areas.
Costs: $120 registration fee plus flights and visas.
Benefits: All board and lodging provided. Medium/long-term volunteers receive pocket money too.
Certification: Certificate or reference provided.
Worldwide placements: *Asia* (Nepal).

FRONTIER
77 Leonard Street
London
EC2A 4QS UK

Tel: +44 (0) 20 7613 2422

Fax: + 44 (0) 20 7613 2992
e-mail: enquiries@frontierprojects.ac.uk
Web: www.frontier.ac.uk
Contact: Jenny Darwin

Frontier is a non-profit-making organization which brings together the conservation needs of developing countries with the commitment and enthusiasm of volunteers from around the world. At a time when ecological crises are multiplying and the resources to deal with them diminishing, the Frontier initiative brings normal people to the forefront of conservation research enabling them to become involved in vital scientific work in the field. Since Frontier's inception in 1989, well over 450,000 hours of research have been undertaken by volunteers in areas under threat in Tanzania, Madagascar, Vietnam, Uganda and Mozambique. Working alongside scientists and conservation organizations from these countries, each Frontier project represents a unique and valuable scientific investigation. Volunteers, who come from all backgrounds, spend 10 or 20 weeks implementing a research programme which draws on their strengths as an expeditionary team. Unlike other organizations, the initiative comes from the volunteers themselves – a quality we look for when recruiting them. If selected, you will be encouraged to participate in every part of the project, from data collection, surveys and communication with the local population to the collection of supplies; in short with everything involved in a practical conservation research expedition undertaken in tough and often inhospitable conditions. Indeed, the 'hands on' experience Frontier offers is such that many of our volunteers subsequently move on to work in conservation-related fields. Each Frontier project is self-funded, the expeditionary team contributing to the cost of the expedition. Frontier volunteers are expected to raise around £2,450 for 10 weeks and around £3,800 for 20 weeks which covers all in-country costs as well as pre-expedition briefings and preparation. Comprehensive advice on fund-raising is made available to all volunteers. Volunteers with an offending background may be considered.

Total projects worldwide: 5
Total UK projects: 0
Starting months: January, April, July, October.
Time required: 10–52 weeks.
Age requirement: 18 plus.
Causes: Animal welfare, conservation, environmental causes, teaching/assisting, wildlife.
Activities: Administration, building/construction, computers, conservation skills, cooking, development issues, DIY, forestry, fundraising, gardening/horticulture, group work, international aid, outdoor skills, research, scientific work, teaching, training.
Vols under 26 placed each year: 225 of a total of 250.
When to apply: All year – preferably 6 months in advance. Contact office for free information pack and application form.
Work alone/with others: With others.
Volunteers with disabilities: There may be projects for volunteers with disabilities – depends on nature of disability.
Qualifications: Nil.
Equipment/clothing: Depends on location – for hot climate for camping conditions: sleeping bag etc.
Health requirements: Reasonably fit and healthy.
Costs: Around £2,450 (10 weeks) and around £3,800 (20 weeks) plus flight and visa. Own pocket money. Minimum of full medical and third party insurance is necessary – arranged by the volunteer with our help.
Benefits: Advice given on raising funds. All volunteers qualify for BTEC in Tropical Habitat Conservation which is equivalent to an A-level.
Training: Pre-expedition health and safety, basic first aid techniques and conservation methods training is given.
Supervision: By a team of 5–6 field staff experienced in logistics, training, research and health and safety. Also a fully qualified dive officer, where appropriate.
Certification: Report and reference provided.
Worldwide placements: *Africa* (Madagascar, Tunisia, Uganda); *Asia* (Vietnam).

**FRONTIERS FOUNDATION /
OPERATION BEAVER**
2615 Danforth Avenue
Suite 203
Toronto
Ontario
M4C 1L6 Canada

Tel: 00 1 416 690 3930

Fax: 00 1 416 690 3934
e-mail: frontier@globalserve.net
Contact: The Program Co-ordinator

Frontiers Foundation is a non-profit, non-denominational voluntary service organization supporting the advancement of economically and socially disadvantaged communities in Canada and overseas through the Operation Beaver Program: voluntary service program for people from Canada and around the world, interested in volunteering their time to help others help themselves; partnership between the host communities in Canada on community-based development projects, such as building and/or renovating homes, or organising activities for local youth/children at various recreation and/or educational centres; volunteers and members of the host communities exchange and share cross-cultural information and experiences and learn from each other; host communities, families or groups actively participate in the development projects. A contractual arrangement is worked out with Frontiers Foundation defining each group's responsibilities; still others offer their skills at the national or regional levels by supporting programme development or office management. Purpose: to contribute to the relief of poverty by supporting tangible community development projects which have enduring significance; to foster understanding and sharing of culture and experience through cross-cultural exchanges between various peoples of Canada and other volunteers from around the world; to support the needs and goals identified by the requesting communities; to promote development through the hands of those people who know and understand their own needs, and those of their communities. We do not aspire to change their way of life, but to work in partnership with requesting communities. Canadian volunteers with an offending background may be accepted but not those from overseas.

Total projects worldwide: 2
Total UK projects: 0
Starting months: January, June–September.
Time required: 12–52 weeks.
Age requirement: 18 plus.
Causes: Children, poor/homeless, teaching/assisting, young people.
Activities: Building/construction, community

work, group work, outdoor skills, sport, teaching.
When to apply: At least 3 months in advance.
Work alone/with others: Both.
Volunteers with disabilities: Possible.
Qualifications: Housing construction related skills preferred but not necessary. Volunteers must be able to adapt to very primitive conditions.
Costs: Travel to Canada.
Benefits: Board, lodging, insurance, local travel and pocket money after 12 weeks.
Nationalities accepted: All nationalities welcome but sometimes we have to set a limiting quota from any one country.
Interview details: Interviews take place in Toronto and other major cities in Canada and Europe.
Certification: Certificate or reference provided upon satisfactory completion.
Charity number: 13037-3970
Worldwide placements: *North America* (Canada); *Central America* (Haiti); *South America* (Bolivia).

FULCRUM CHALLENGE
Unit 7
Luccombe Farm Business Centre
Milton Abbas
Dorset
DT11 0BD UK

Tel: +44 (0) 1258 881399
Fax: +44 (0) 1258 881300
e-mail: office@fulcrum-challenge.org
Web: www.fulcrum-challenge.org
Contact: John Hunt

Fulcrum Challenge is a new and exciting educational youth initiative for A-level, GNVQ and Scottish Highers students. Fulcrum Challenge operates in regions where British Airways are strongly represented, and schools in each area are invited to nominate students who must submit a completed application form to us. We operate in other areas with other sponsors. Only 20 places are available each Challenge. We arrange a week of director shadowing for all successful students. The group spends two weeks in a remote area of the world, living and working with local communities on environmental and cultural activities. The group must take part in an environmental project in their home area in co-operation with Countryside

Agency. All students are invited to take part in a bi-annual Leadership Conference. The five phases are designed to bring together bright young people from all backgrounds, in order to learn how to work both as a group and in other communities, develop leadership and business skills, study natural and scientific topics and develop close personal links at home and abroad.

Total projects worldwide: Up to 10.
Total UK projects: Up to 10.
Starting months: January–May, August–December.
Time required: 3–4 weeks.
Age requirement: 16–18
Causes: Children, conservation, environmental causes, heritage, poor/homeless, wildlife, young people.
Activities: Accountancy, administration, agriculture/farming, arts/crafts, building/construction, caring (general and residential), community work, computers, conservation skills, cooking, counselling, development issues, DIY, first aid, forestry, fundraising, gardening/horticulture, group work, international aid, library/resource centres, manual work, marketing/publicity, music, newsletter/journalism, outdoor skills, religion, research, scientific work, social work, sport, teaching, technical skills, theatre/drama, training, visiting/befriending.
Vols under 26 placed each year: Up to 200.
When to apply: Only through heads of school and then by invitation.
Work alone/with others: As a team.
Volunteers with disabilities: Not possible.
Qualifications: A-level, GNVQ or Scottish Highers.
Equipment/clothing: Suitable for selection, environmental, overseas programmes.
Health requirements: Must be fit and take the recommended medical treatments for the overseas phase.
Costs: £1,500 raised by their own initiative.
Benefits: Flights provided free by BA and a further £1,000 is raised by us. Insurance provided by us.
Supervision: Experienced leaders and instructors are used on all stages.
Nationalities accepted: No restrictions but you must be in the UK educational system.
Interview details: There is a three-day selection programme for candidates.
Certification: Certificate or reference provided.

Charity number: 1072830
Worldwide placements: *Africa* (Botswana, Kenya, Namibia, South Africa, Tunisia, Zimbabwe); *Asia* (Bangladesh, China, Hong Kong, India, Malaysia, Mongolia, Nepal, Oman, Philippines, Thailand, Tibet, United Arab Emirates, Vietnam); *South America* (Argentina, Guyana, Paraguay, Venezuela).
UK placements: *England* (Berkshire, Cheshire, Co. Durham, Cumbria, Dorset, Herefordshire, Kent, Lancashire, London, Manchester, Merseyside, Northumberland, Shropshire, Staffordshire, Surrey, E. Sussex, W. Sussex, Tyne and Wear, Warwickshire, West Midlands, Worcestershire, N. Yorkshire); *Scotland* (throughout); *Northern Ireland* (throughout).

FUNDACIÓN GOLONDRINAS
Avenida Isabel La Católica 1559
Quito
Ecuador

Tel: 00 593 2 226 602
e-mail: manteca@uio.satnet.net
Web: www.ecuadorexplorer.com/golondrinas
Contact: Maria-Eliza Manteca Oñate, President, or Mónica Yépez, Secretary

The Fundación Golondrinas is a privately managed, non-profit organization founded in 1991. The primary site is a small farming village in Northern Ecuador where volunteers work often alongside locals on a farm and tree nursery using the principles of permaculture. This method demonstrates the advantages of farming one area of land economically and productively for an indefinite period of time, as opposed to the 'slash and burn' techniques currently used by the locals. This is rapidly and irrevocably destroying the cloudforest, which 25 years ago covered the surrounding mountains, now bare and largely infertile. Not only are we hoping to improve the productivity of the land but our goal is to rescue the old ways of farming which the local people once used in order to maintain an aspect of their culture that is becoming lost. Volunteers are needed for a number of jobs, including planting, harvesting and general farm maintenance. You need to be willing to stay a minimum of six months to act in one of the following positions: volunteer co-ordinator, teacher of environmental sustainability with local children, scientific researcher, administrative assistant or marketing representative in the office in Quito. The contribution for those volunteers wishing to stay six months or so is negotiable. The work is interesting and diverse and gives a rare opportunity to become truly involved in Ecuadorian rural life. You may also get the chance to visit the 18,000 ha of protected virgin cloudforest, owned by the project. Here there is a cabin overlooking 40 miles of undamaged forest where a range of wildlife may be seen. Lower down in the reservation is a further site where two cabins and a tree nursery are located. This is an excellent location in which to do scientific research and studies.

Total projects worldwide: 1
Total UK projects: 0
Starting months: January–December.
Time required: 4–12 weeks.
Age requirement: 18–33
Causes: Conservation, environmental causes.
Activities: Agriculture/farming, building/construction, conservation skills, forestry, manual work, outdoor skills.
Vols under 26 placed each year:
Approximately 57 of a total of 60.
When to apply: Any time but three months in advance if possible.
Work alone/with others: With others.
Volunteers with disabilities: We are unable to place people with disabilities as the work is very physically demanding and there are no facilities for disabled.
Qualifications: Spanish is absolutely essential.
Equipment/clothing: A pair of working gloves, a penknife, insect repellent, sleeping bag, rubber boots, long trousers, long-sleeve shirt, waterproof jacket.
Health requirements: Nil, but work is physical so good health is necessary.
Costs: US$240 a month includes accommodation and food ($200 a month if more than 3 months). Health and other insurance.
Supervision: On the field supervised by 2 experienced staff. In Quito volunteers are briefed in the office.
Interview details: No interview necessary but a general briefing is given before work starts and volunteers are required to sign a statement of the rules of the foundation.
Certification: Reference or certificate on request.
Charity number: 213
Worldwide placements: *South America*

(Ecuador).

FUTURE IN OUR HANDS MOVEMENT FIOH (UK)

48 Churchwood Avenue
Swindon
Wiltshire
SN2 1NH UK

Tel: +44 (0) 1793 532353
Contact: Mike Thomas

The Future in Our Hands Movement was set up in 1974 with the aims of encouraging a simpler and more ethical lifestyle, particularly in the rich countries; and promoting an emphasis on values such as sharing, co-operation and fellowship rather than dogmatic approaches to world problems.

Total projects worldwide: 6
Total UK projects: 0
Starting months: January–December.
Time required: 2–52 weeks (plus).
Age requirement: 16 plus.
Causes: Poor/homeless.
Activities: Development issues.
Vols under 26 placed each year: 4
When to apply: At least 2 months in advance.
Qualifications: Initiative and commitment to the aims of the organization.
Costs: All costs including travel and insurance. Accommodation and food provided at small charge.
Worldwide placements: *Africa* (Cameroon, Ghana, Kenya, Uganda); *Asia* (India, Sri Lanka).

FYD (FRIENDS FOR YOUNG DEAF PEOPLE)

East Court Mansion
College Lane,
East Grinstead
West Sussex
RH19 3LT UK

Tel: +44 (0) 1342 323444 minicom +44 (0) 1342 324164
Fax: +44 (0) 1342 410232
e-mail: fyd.egho@charity.vfree.com
Web: http://fyd.org.uk

The aim of FYD is to promote an active partnership between deaf and hearing people which will enable young deaf people to develop themselves and become active members of society. FYD will work to ensure that the partnership is created through friendship. Deaf people take the lead in shared responsibility as volunteers and staff work together to achieve the aim. Positive role models are provided for both deaf and hearing people. The partnership focuses on work with young people. Deaf and hearing young people share in activities which promote effective communication and self-confidence. Deaf and hearing young people train together to develop a variety of personal, leadership and work skills. The partnership acknowledges deafness as a key issue. Deaf and hearing people can choose how they can communicate through 'total communication'. Deaf people overcome disadvantage by developing skills and hearing people become more aware so that both can be equal partners with equal opportunities. Volunteers with an offending background are accepted unless it contravenes The Children Act.

Total projects worldwide: 22
Total UK projects: 22
Starting months: January–December.
Time required: 1–52 weeks.
Age requirement: 15 plus.
Causes: Children, disabled (physical), teaching (secondary, mature), unemployed, work camps – seasonal, young people.
Activities: Administration, arts/crafts, community work, computers, counselling, development issues, driving, first aid, fundraising, group work, marketing/publicity, newsletter/journalism, outdoor skills, research, sport, summer camps, teaching, theatre/drama, training, visiting/befriending, work camps – seasonal.
Vols under 26 placed each year: 150–400 of a total of 200–500.
When to apply: All year.
Work alone/with others: With others.
Volunteers with disabilities: Possible.
Qualifications: Participation in FYD training programme preferred.
Health requirements: Nil.
Costs: Nil.
Benefits: 25p per mile or 2nd class public transport. Free accommodation and meals. Insurance.
Training: FYD training programme.
Interview details: Interviews are carried out at our training programme (7 per year) and at our Embassies (SE, NW, SW, Midlands and London).

Certification: Certificate or reference provided.
Charity number: 1045011
Worldwide placements: *Australasia* (Australia, New Zealand).
UK placements: *England* (throughout).

G

GALWAY ASSOCIATION, THE
The Halls
Quay Street
Galway
Ireland

Tel: 00 353 91 567291
Fax: 00 353 91 562379
e-mail: gcamhc@iol.ie
Web: http://homepages.iol.ie/~gcamhc
Contact: Co-ordinator of Volunteers

The Galway Association needs volunteers who share their time, energy and enthusiasm with the children and adults who use our services. No particular qualifications are required, just a willingness to make a reliable commitment. Volunteers are involved in Friendship Schemes by becoming a friend to a person with a learning disability. Volunteers provide valuable assistance with leisure pursuits such as swimming, horseriding, social outings, recreation, specific programmes and projects to mention but a few!

Total projects worldwide: 1
Total UK projects: 0
Starting months: January–December.
Time required: 12–52 weeks (plus).
Age requirement: 16 plus.
Causes: Disabled (learning).
Activities: Arts/crafts, caring (general and residential), community work, computers, gardening/horticulture, music, outdoor skills, sport.
Vols under 26 placed each year: 25 of a total of 80.
When to apply: All year.
Work alone/with others: With others.
Volunteers with disabilities: Possible.
Qualifications: Good conversational English.
Health requirements: Nil.

Costs: Travel and subsistence.
Benefits: 2 residential placements offer free board/lodging. Others give out-of-pocket expenses only. We provide all insurance.
Training: Individual induction and group training.
Supervision: By co-ordinator of volunteers plus individual staff supervisor.
Interview details: Volunteers are interviewed in Galway.
Certification: Reference provided.
Charity number: 6306
Worldwide placements: *Europe* (Ireland).

GAP ACTIVITY PROJECTS

GAP House
44 Queen's Road
Reading
Berkshire
RG1 4BB UK

Tel: +44 (0) 118 959 4914 or 956 2902 (brochures)
Fax: +44 (0) 118 957 6634
e-mail: Volunteer@gap.org.uk
apply@gap.org.uk
Web: www.gap.org.uk
Contact: Applications

GAP arranges voluntary work overseas for school-leavers taking a year out before going on to higher education, further training or employment. Work placements are all of charitable or educational value and last on average five months. This can form a core of worthwhile experience and the basis for travel in a busy year-out schedule. GAP sees the year out as the ideal opportunity for young people to broaden their experience of the world while making a personal contribution to other communities. A constructive and exciting GAP project can be undertaken for less than £1,000. A variety of voluntary work opportunities exist in over 30 countries. Projects in the UK and Ireland are only for young people from outside the UK.

Total projects worldwide: 600 plus.
Total UK projects: 0
Starting months: January–October.
Time required: 12–52 weeks.
Age requirement: 18–19
Causes: Aids/HIV, animal welfare, archaeology, children, conservation, disabled (learning and physical), elderly people, environmental causes, health care/medical, heritage, inner city problems, poor/homeless, refugees, teaching/assisting (nursery, primary, secondary, mature, EFL), wildlife, work camps – seasonal, young people.
Activities: Administration, agriculture/farming, arts/crafts, building/construction, caring (general, day and residential), community work, computers, conservation skills, cooking, driving, first aid, forestry, gardening/horticulture, group work, library/resource centres, music, outdoor skills, research, scientific work, social work, sport, summer camps, teaching, theatre/drama, visiting/befriending, work camps – seasonal.
Vols under 26 placed each year: 1,400
When to apply: Any time after GCSEs. The earlier the better.
Work alone/with others: Alone or in pairs.
Volunteers with disabilities: Possible.
Qualifications: Students in their year out between school and higher education, further training or employment.
Equipment/clothing: According to placement.
Health requirements: Volunteers may be required to produce confirmation of fitness to travel overseas. Projects in some countries require a medical examination.
Costs: £515 plus £35 registration fee plus air fare, insurance and TEFL course (if necessary).
Benefits: Board and accommodation plus pocket money in most cases. Business Partnership Scheme. GAP have own insurance cover developed specifically for our volunteers.
Training: Dependent on placement. TEFL if necessary, co-ordinated by GAP and paid for by volunteer.
Supervision: All placements chosen because they are appropriate and challenging. Hosts, whether on site or staying with a family, look after volunteers. GAP has overseas agents in the host country and a project manager who will visit at least once.
Nationalities accepted: Must hold a UK or Irish passport.
Interview details: Interviews take place in Reading, Leeds, London or a regional venue. The interview is GAP's opportunity to match candidates to projects. We have something for everyone on a year out. (Academic qualifications/predictions do not affect selection.)
Charity number: 272761
Worldwide placements: *Africa* (Lesotho,

South Africa, Swaziland, Zambia); *Asia* (China, Hong Kong, India, Israel, Japan, Macao, Malaysia, Nepal, Thailand, Vietnam); *Australasia* (Australia, Fiji, New Zealand, Tonga, Vanuatu); *Europe* (Germany, Hungary, Poland, Romania, Russia, Slovakia); *North America* (Canada, USA); *Central America* (Mexico); *South America* (Argentina, Brazil, Chile, Ecuador, Falkland Islands, Paraguay).

GAP CHALLENGE
at World Challenge Expeditions
Black Arrow House
2 Chandos Road
London
NW10 6NF UK

Tel: + 44 (0) 20 8728 7274
Fax: + 44 (0) 20 8961 1551
e-mail: welcome@world-challenge.co.uk
Web: www.gap-challenge.co.uk
Contact: Rosie Bozman

Gap Challenge is part of World Challenge Expeditions who have been providing overseas opportunities for young people for over 13 years. Applicants should have a high degree of motivation and commitment and be prepared for a challenge. Placements last three and six months. With a 12-month return flight, there is plenty of opportunity for independent travel afterwards. All applicants are required to attend a 2-day selection course. These are held throughout the year. There is also a skills training course before departure where Gap Challengers receive information and briefings from qualified staff and a chance to meet ex-Gap Challengers.

Total projects worldwide: 11
Total UK projects: 0
Starting months: January, April, September.
Time required: 12–26 weeks.
Age requirement: 18–25
Causes: Children, conservation, disabled (learning and physical), environmental causes, teaching/assisting (nursery, primary, secondary, EFL).
Activities: Caring (general and residential), community work, conservation skills, gardening/horticulture, sport, teaching.
Vols under 26 placed each year: Over 400.
When to apply: Any time up to a month before departure.
Work alone/with others: Usually in pairs or

small groups.
Volunteers with disabilities: Possible.
Qualifications: 3 A-levels or equivalent preferred for teaching posts.
Equipment/clothing: Gap Challenge provides information on suitable clothing.
Health requirements: All applicants are asked to disclose pre-existing conditions.
Costs: From £1,500–£2,800 depending on destination. Advice is given on insurance. It is up to the individual to organize insurance.
Benefits: The cost includes training, return flights and travel, in-country support and London 24-hour emergency back-up.
Training: All participants attend the skills training course before their placement.
Supervision: Every country has support from in-country representatives and there is a 24-hour emergency back-up and support from Gap Challenge Headquarters in London.
Interview details: 2-day selection courses take place at various UK locations throughout the year.
Certification: Reference on request.
Worldwide placements: *Africa* (Kenya, South Africa, Tanzania); *Asia* (India, Malaysia, Nepal); *Australasia* (Australia); *North America* (Canada); *Central America* (Belize, Costa Rica); *South America* (Ecuador, Peru).

GENCTUR (TOURISM AND TRAVEL AGENCY LTD)
Istiklal Cad.
Zambak Sok. 15/AK.5
Beyoglu
80080 Istanbul
Turkey

Tel: 00 90 212 249 25 15
Fax: 00 90 212 249 25 54
Contact: Zafer Yilmaz, Work Camps Co-ordinator

Genctur needs volunteers to take part in international work camps in small Turkish villages, involving work such as constructing schools, village centres, digging water trenches, forestry etc. Study tours, camp tours, and special interest tours are all arranged.

Total projects worldwide: 25–40
Total UK projects: 0
Starting months: July–September.
Time required: 2–6 weeks.
Age requirement: 18–35
Causes: Environmental causes, teaching/

assisting (primary, secondary), work camps – seasonal.

Activities: Agriculture/farming, arts/crafts, building/construction, community work, counselling, forestry, manual work, summer camps, teaching, work camps – seasonal.
Vols under 26 placed each year: 300
When to apply: April–September.
Work alone/with others: With others.
Volunteers with disabilities: Not possible.
Qualifications: Nil.
Equipment/clothing: Additional information is supplied to the applicants.
Health requirements: Nil.
Costs: All costs plus £35 registration fee.
Benefits: Board and lodging.
Interview details: No interview necessary.
Certification: Certificate or reference provided on request.
Worldwide placements: *Asia* (Turkey); *Europe* (Turkey).

GENESIS II CLOUDFOREST PRESERVE
Apartado 655
7050 Cartago
Costa Rica

Tel: 00 506 381 0739
Fax: 00 506 551 0070
e-mail: volunteer@yellowweb.co.cr
Contact: Co-owner

Genesis II Cloudforest Preserve is a privately owned cloudforest at the 7,500 ft/2,360 m level in the Talamanca Mountains of central Costa Rica. From its inception it has been intended and operated as a preserve for academic research and recreational (non-hunting) pleasure. Within its 95 acre boundaries can be found up to 120 species of birds plus many types of ferns, orchids, fungi, and its major tree: the towering white oak. While the terrain is quite rugged, the forest is very benign: no known very venomous reptiles, plants or insects and the climate is generally best described as 'moistly soft'. There are two distinct seasons here. January to May is our dry season (summer). June to December is our wet or rainy season (winter). At most times during the year, the early mornings are clear and sunny. However, during the wet season it clouds over by 9–10 a.m. and usually rains by noon. Occasionally during this season, we may experience several continuous days of cloud and drizzle; depressing but not serious. If you choose to come during the wet season you should be prepared to work in cool, rainy conditions. To provide access to the forest for the birdwatchers, ornithologists and naturalists, we have provided a small, first class trail system of about three km. Each unit is 29 days long with a week separation between each. Opportunities now exist for volunteers to stay for more than one unit (but this should be agreed to before coming). We also can accept students on placement as part of their degree programme (with formal agreement from their supervisor and department). Cost in these situations is similar to regular volunteers. Volunteers with an offending background who are motivated may be accepted. This can be a very testing experience. We need volunteers who are totally willing – no rebels.

Total projects worldwide: 1
Total UK projects: 0
Starting months: January–October.
Time required: 4–52 weeks.
Age requirement: 21 plus.
Causes: Conservation, environmental causes, work camps – seasonal.
Activities: Building/construction, conservation skills, forestry, manual work, outdoor skills, work camps – seasonal.
Vols under 26 placed each year: 57 of a total of 60.
When to apply: All year.
Work alone/with others: Mostly with others.
Volunteers with disabilities: Not possible.
Qualifications: Willingness and a preference for studying environment and conservation. Camping/hiking/surveying skills.
Equipment/clothing: List of equipment supplied.
Health requirements: No vegans. Prefer non-smokers.
Costs: US$600 for room, board and laundry. Other costs are volunteer's responsibility, e.g. travel, insurance, pocket money.
Benefits: Board, lodging and laundry.
Interview details: No interview necessary.
Certification: Certificate or reference provided.
Worldwide placements: *Central America* (Costa Rica).

GIRLS VENTURE CORPS AIR CADETS
Redhill Aerodrome
Kings Mill Lane
South Nutfield

Redhill
Surrey
RH1 5JY UK

Tel: +44 (0) 1737 823345
Fax: +44 (0) 1737 823345
Web: www.gvcac.org.uk
Contact: Mrs M. Rowland

The Girls Venture Corps Air Cadets is a voluntary uniformed youth organization for girls between the ages of 11 and 20 years. It offers a challenging and worthwhile programme, introducing its members to a wide range of activities which help to give them a wider outlook and a greater sense of purpose. Great emphasis is placed upon leadership and initiative training, and camps and courses for this purpose are held annually. The Corps makes a great contribution to the community. Members help either individually or as a group on various community projects and service to others plays an important part in a cadet's training. Because of its origins, the Corps is slanted towards 'air-mindedness' and is unique among youth organizations in offering air experience flights arranged with flying clubs. Solo Flying Scholarships are awarded when funds permit. We seek co-operation with local authorities, schools, employers and all concerned with the welfare of youth.

Total projects worldwide: 60
Total UK projects: 60
Starting months: January–December.
Time required: 1–52 weeks.
Age requirement: 18 plus.
Causes: Young people.
Activities: Administration, arts/crafts, catering, community work, cooking, driving, first aid, fundraising, group work, newsletter/journalism, outdoor skills, sport, summer camps, training.
Vols under 26 placed each year: Approximately 52 of a total of 260.
When to apply: All year.
Work alone/with others: Both.
Volunteers with disabilities: Possible.
Qualifications: Only enthusiasm.
Equipment/clothing: Depends on activities pursued.
Health requirements: For flying, yes.
Costs: Travel costs. The cost could be any amount depending on project/commitment.
Benefits: Travel costs might be paid by the region. All members and helpers are insured.

Training: Training is provided in units.
Supervision: At unit, region and national levels.
Interview details: Interviews take place either at local, regional or national level, depending on type of project.
Certification: Certificates or references issued to successful volunteers.
Charity number: 306109
UK placements: *England* (Cambridgeshire, Co. Durham, Essex, Hampshire, Isle of Wight, Kent, Leicestershire, London, Norfolk, Nottinghamshire, Somerset, Staffordshire, Suffolk, Surrey, E. Sussex, Tyne and Wear, West Midlands, S. Yorkshire).

GLAMORGAN WILDLIFE TRUST
Fountain Road
Tondu
Bridgend
CF32 0EH UK

Tel: +44 (0) 1656 724100
Fax: +44 (0) 1656 729880
Contact: Nigel Ajax-Lewis

Glamorgan Wildlife Trust is a member of the Wildlife Trusts, a national partnership of 47 county trusts. For more details of the Wildlife Trusts, see the entry under Cornwall Wildlife Trust.

Total projects worldwide: 46
Total UK projects: 46
Starting months: January–December.
Time required: 1–52 weeks (plus).
Age requirement: 16 plus.
Causes: Conservation, environmental causes, wildlife.
Activities: Computers, conservation skills, driving, forestry, gardening/horticulture, manual work, outdoor skills, research, scientific work, technical skills.
Vols under 26 placed each year: 50 of a total of 250.
When to apply: All year.
Work alone/with others: With others.
Volunteers with disabilities: Possible.
Qualifications: Nil.
Equipment/clothing: Casual work clothes, waterproofs, stout boots. Protective safety gear is provided.
Health requirements: Any medical conditions (illness, allergy or physical disability) that may require treatment/medication or which affect the volunteer working with machinery must be notified to us in advance. Tetanus

injections must be up to date.
Costs: Bring your own packed lunch.
Benefits: Negotiable.
Training: You will receive on-the-job training in an informal atmosphere.
Interview details: Interviews at our office.
Certification: Reference on request.
Charity number: 200653
UK placements: *Wales* (Cardiff, Neath Port Talbot, Newport, Rhondda, Cynon, Taff, Vale of Glamorgan).

GLASGOW SIMON COMMUNITY

Maryhill Women's Project
9 Caldercuilt Road
Maryhill
Glasgow
G20 0AE Scotland

Tel: +44 (0) 141 946 2053
Fax: +44 (0) 141 424 3149
Contact: Susan Breen, Volunteer Co-ordinator

Glasgow Simon Community has vacancies for volunteers as and when people leave. One project manager, three senior staff workers and five volunteers are needed to work with women who have been long-term homeless. This involves group work, counselling and generally addressing the needs of the community. The Centre is situated in a six-bedroomed house in Glasgow. Volunteers with an offending background may be accepted but a decision would be made after full disclosure of facts.

Total projects worldwide: 1
Total UK projects: 1
Starting months: January–December.
Time required: 26–52 weeks.
Age requirement: 19 plus.
Causes: Addicts/Ex-addicts, health care/medical, poor/homeless.
Activities: Accountancy, administration, caring (general and residential), catering, community work, cooking, counselling, group work, social work, visiting/befriending.
Vols under 26 placed each year: 12
When to apply: Apply 3–6 months in advance.
Work alone/with others: With others.
Volunteers with disabilities: Possible, but not suitable for wheelchair access.
Qualifications: Nil.
Health requirements: Medical certificate

required.
Costs: Nil.
Benefits: £48 per week plus board and lodging and travel expenses paid.
Nationalities accepted: No restrictions but recruitment is within the UK only.
Interview details: Interviews take place mainly at Maryhill Women's Project, Glasgow. Prospective volunteers are invited to spend 3 days with the Community before joining it.
Certification: Reference provided.
Charity number: CR4 1110
UK placements: *Scotland* (Glasgow City).

GLENCREE PEACE AND RECONCILIATION CENTRE

Glencree
Enniskerry
Co. Wicklow
Ireland

Tel: 00 353 2829711 / 2766025
Fax: 00 353 276085
e-mail: info@glencree.cfr.ie
Web: www.glencree.cfr.ie
Contact: Naoise Kelly, Centre Manager

Glencree is a unique organization in the Republic of Ireland, dedicated to peace-building, offering secluded facilities and programme resources to political, religious, youth and community groups. We provide facilities devoted to peace-building and reconciliation within the island of Ireland, between Britain and Ireland, and beyond. The resources of the Centre are available to all sides involved in the conflict; to all individuals and groups who wish to work for peace in an atmosphere which is welcoming and inclusive; and to the victims of the conflict who face the huge challenge of coming to terms with their loss and suffering. Glencree is helped and supported by ten international volunteers and a small core of professional staff. Volunteers with an offending background may be accepted, depending on the offence. Each case can be discussed individually.

Total projects worldwide: 1
Total UK projects: 0
Starting months: January–December.
Time required: 2–12 weeks.
Age requirement: 18 plus.
Causes: Work camps – seasonal.
Activities: Catering, cooking, gardening/horticulture, manual work, work camps –

seasonal.

Vols under 26 placed each year: 15 of a total of 20.

When to apply: All year.

Volunteers with disabilities: Possible.

Qualifications: Nil.

Equipment/clothing: Old clothes for manual/gardening work.

Health requirements: Nil.

Costs: Travel and approximately £25 per day food and accommodation. Personal insurance is necessary.

Supervision: Volunteers will work alongside Glencree Volunteers under management supervision.

Interview details: No interview necessary.

Certification: Certificate or reference provided.

Worldwide placements: *Europe* (Ireland).

GLOBAL CITIZENS NETWORK

130 N. Howell Street
St Paul
Minnesota
55104 USA

Tel: 00 1 651 644 0960
e-mail: gcn@mtn.org
Web: www.globalcitizens.org
Contact: Kim Regnier, Program Director

Global Citizens Network (GCN) seeks to create a network of people who are committed to the shared values of peace, justice, tolerance, cross-cultural understanding and global co-operation; to the preservation of indigenous cultures, traditions and ecologies; and to the enhancement of the quality of life around the world. We send small teams of volunteers to rural communities around the world where you can immerse yourself in the daily life of the community. Trips last one, two or three weeks, depending on the site, and each team is led by a trained GCN team leader. The team works on projects initiated by people in the local community, for the benefit of the community. Such projects could include setting up a library, teaching business skills, building a health clinic, or planting trees to reforest a village. A unique and integral component of your experience includes daily activities of cross-cultural learning. You may test your skills at making tortillas, visit a nearby tea factory or the family farm, learn a local dance and discover the history and rich traditions of the area. People of all ages, backgrounds and experiences travel with GCN. Families are welcome to join our teams. Although there is really no typical day on a Global Citizens Network trip, volunteers stay in local homes or as a group in a community centre. Meals are either eaten together with your host family or communally prepared and shared with your project hosts. After breakfast, you join your team along with community members to work together on projects under the direction of the local leadership. As a volunteer, you immerse yourself in the more relaxed pace and adjust to life in a developing community. During the afternoon, you either continue working on a project or may participate in an activity which promotes cross-cultural understanding. Each evening you will join other team members and the team leader to go over the day's events and talk about what you have learned.

Total projects worldwide: 6
Total UK projects: 0
Starting months: January–December.
Time required: 1–3 weeks.
Age requirement: 18 plus.
Causes: Children, conservation, environmental causes, health care/medical, teaching/assisting, young people.
Activities: Building/construction, community work, conservation skills, cooking, development issues, group work, manual work, outdoor skills, teaching, visiting/befriending.
Vols under 26 placed each year: 25 of a total of 100.
When to apply: 2–4 months before the trip or until teams are full.
Work alone/with others: With others.
Volunteers with disabilities: Possible.
Qualifications: Nil – only an open mind and sensitivity to new cultures.
Equipment/clothing: Dependent on site – very casual dress since most projects generally involve manual labour.
Health requirements: Must be in good health. Some sites are very rural and remote – no water, electricity etc.
Costs: Program costs range from US$600–$1,650. Air fare additional. Insurance is optional, although we strongly recommend travel insurance.
Benefits: Costs include board, lodging, local transport, orientation materials and a

donation to project.

Training: Orientation manual sent out pre-trip and in-country orientation meetings on site.

Supervision: A trained team leader accompanies each team of volunteers.

Interview details: No interview necessary.

Worldwide placements: *Africa* (Kenya); *Asia* (Nepal); *North America* (USA); *Central America* (Guatemala).

GLOBAL EDUCATION: INTERNATIONAL CO-OP THAILAND

20298 Kennedy Road
Caledon
Ontario
LON 1CO Canada

Tel: 00 1 519 942 2490
Fax: 00 1 519 940 0960
e-mail: experience@globaled1.com
Web: www.globaled1.com
Contact: Bruce L. Taylor, Director

Global Education: International Co-op Thailand: exotic Thailand! An 'edventure' in community service – in elementary schools, hospitals/clinics, anti-prostitution centres, etc., combined with total cultural immersion as you homestay with Thai host families! The two different placements are: 1. Community service placements in such fields as medicine, social work, ecology, archaeology, refugees, education, gender issues, tribal projects, etc. 2. Elementary school placements in urban, rural and tribal schools in north-western Thailand. Trek in the mountains, build a tribal school, live in a rural village, work in urban slums, tour ancient sites, study in Buddhist temples, work on the 'King's Royal Projects' – together, the adventure and opportunity of a lifetime! Limited enrolment of 15–20 select participants per departure. Our programme was started in 1994 and is recognized by the Thailand Ministry of Education. Endorsed by universities and industries, academic credits are possible. This is a unique combination of academics, cultural immersion, community service, foreign language study, homestay in a Thai home, travel in northern Thailand ... and of course the friendships and memories of a lifetime!

Total projects worldwide: 1
Total UK projects: 0
Starting months: February, July, September.

Time required: 6–20 weeks.

Age requirement: 16 plus.

Causes: Addicts/ex-addicts, archaeology, children, conservation, disabled (learning and physical), environmental causes, health care/medical, human rights, inner city problems, poor/homeless, refugees, teaching/assisting (nursery, primary, secondary), unemployed, wildlife, young people.

Activities: Agriculture/farming, building/construction, community work, computers, conservation skills, cooking, counselling, development issues, forestry, gardening/horticulture, group work, international aid, manual work, newsletter/journalism, outdoor skills, religion, scientific work, social work, sport, summer camps, teaching, theatre/drama.

Vols under 26 placed each year: 30–40

When to apply: All year.

Work alone/with others: With others.

Volunteers with disabilities: Not possible.

Qualifications: Overall maturity, independence, adaptability, cultural sensitivity, teamwork skills, enthusiasm and commitment to making a difference in the world.

Equipment/clothing: Tropical weight clothes.

Health requirements: Innoculations required.

Costs: £2,595 for the two 6–8 week programmes: or Term Co-op and Summer Co-op. £2,797 for the 20-week programme: or Semester Co-op. Plus medical examination, innoculations, visas and spending money.

Benefits: Cost includes air fares, excursions, train fares, Thai language and culture studies, trekking to and living in a tribal village, all board and accommodation, guest lectures, medical insurance and flight cancellation. A final 2-day retreat is held in Thailand.

Training: Language, culture and socio-economic analysis training is provided in Thailand for 2–3 weeks.

Supervision: The Thailand programme co-ordinator (full time) monitors volunteers regularly. Volunteers are also assigned 2 supervisors at their Co-op placement, e.g. school.

Interview details: Prospective volunteers are interviewed in London.

Certification: A plaque, a reference letter and certificate is awarded on completion of the project.

Worldwide placements: *Asia* (Thailand).

GLOBAL HANDS, NEPAL
PO Box 489
Zero k.m.
Pokhara
Kaski
Nepal

Tel: 00 972 61 30266
e-mail: insight@clcexp.mos.com.np
Contact: Naresh M. Shrestha

The Kingdom of Nepal which is situated in the lap of Central Himalaya with a rich cultural heritage, is a land of ancient history and colourful cultures. Insight Nepal (see later entry) was established as an institution with a view to introducing the diverse geographical and cultural environment of Nepal to the participants, and to foster an awareness and cultural understanding. Global Hands is a short-term volunteer programme which is designed for those people who want to come to Nepal with a desire to explore, experience and discover a unique way of life. The main objective of this programme is to provide opportunities to those who have limited time and budget, but are keenly interested in gaining experiences by sharing their ideas and skills with local community service groups, and to reach the people who are in need.

Total projects worldwide: 1
Total UK projects: 0
Starting months: January–December.
Time required: 4–6 weeks.
Age requirement: 18 plus.
Causes: Children, disabled (physical), health care/medical, poor/homeless, teaching/assisting (nursery, primary, secondary, mature, EFL).
Activities: Administration, community work, computers, development issues, first aid, fundraising, social work, sport, teaching, technical skills, training, visiting/befriending.
Vols under 26 placed each year: 20
When to apply: 8 weeks in advance.
Work alone/with others: Alone or in pairs.
Qualifications: Minimum A-level. Flexibility and willingness to be immersed in another culture.
Health requirements: Immunisation against certain diseases.
Costs: US$30 application fee plus US$400 programme fee plus visa fee plus return travel. Programme fee includes a 3-day orientation training.
Benefits: The cost covers accommodation, 2 meals a day and a 3-day orientation training.
Worldwide placements: *Asia* (India, Nepal).

GLOBAL OUTREACH MISSION UK
108 Sweetbriar Lane
Exeter
Devon
EX1 3AR UK

Tel: +44 (0) 1392 259673
Fax: +44 (0) 1392 491176
Contact: Reverend David T. Cole, UK Director

The Board of Directors of Global Outreach Mission have adopted an approach that involves a diversified plan using various means of communicating the Gospel of Jesus Christ. The name of our Mission – Global Outreach – was adopted because it most accurately describes our expanded goal of making the salvation message known throughout the world. The challenges and opportunities are great. We find that God is moving in a marvellous way across the earth. Committed Christian workers are needed to respond. Global Outreach is evangelical in every way. Our sole concern is with the propagation of the gospel of the grace of God as revealed in the Holy Scriptures. Our primary objective is to be evangelistic in the winning of souls for Christ. We are interdenominational in our fellowship.

Total projects worldwide: Many.
Total UK projects: Many.
Starting months: January–December.
Time required: 1–52 weeks.
Age requirement: 18 plus.
Causes: Children, disabled (learning and physical), elderly people, health care/medical, refugees, young people.
Activities: Counselling, music, religion.
Vols under 26 placed each year: Varies.
When to apply: All year.
Work alone/with others: With others.
Volunteers with disabilities: Possible.
Qualifications: Nil.
Health requirements: Nil.
Costs: Travel and some living costs.
Interview details: Interviews take place in Exeter.
Certification: Written reference if required.
Charity number: 281583
Worldwide placements: *Africa* (Congo Republic, Egypt, Ghana, South Africa); *Asia* (Bangladesh, India, Jordan, Korea (South),

Philippines); *Australasia* (Australia); *Europe* (Austria, Belgium, Denmark, France, Germany, Greece, Ireland, Netherlands, Russia, Spain, Sweden, Ukraine, Yugoslavia); *North America* (Canada, USA); *Central America* (Bahamas, Guatemala, Haiti, Honduras, Mexico, Netherlands Antilles); *South America* (Bolivia, Brazil, Peru). UK placements: *England* (throughout); *Scotland* (throughout); *Northern Ireland* (throughout); *Wales* (throughout).

GLOBAL VISION INTERNATIONAL
Amwell Farm House
Nomansland
Wheathampstead
St Albans
Hertfordshire
AL4 8EJ UK

Tel: + 44 (0) 1582 831300
Fax: + 44 (0) 1582 831302
e-mail: GVIenquiries@aol.com
Web: www.gvi.co.uk
Contact: Richard Walton

Global Vision International (GVI), is a non-political, non-religious organization, specializing in providing travel and voluntary work experience opportunities overseas. Since its formation in 1999, we have sent almost one hundred volunteers on overseas expeditions. Through our alliance with aid reliant environmental organizations throughout the world, GVI volunteers fulfil a critical void in the fields of environmental research, conservation, education and community development. Dedicated GVI volunteers acquire and then use their expertise and skills to reach mission goals, which ultimately contribute to GVI's aim of aiding and promoting global sustainable development. We welcome individuals from a wide variety of backgrounds. No previous experience is necessary to participate in a GVI expedition, but you will need to be: enthusiastic; committed to our aims and projects; respectful of the culture, environment and communities of the host country; over 18 years old; of a reasonable physical fitness (and able to swim over 400 m for marine projects); and have a basic understanding of English. This is not a holiday. It will require your hard work and devotion and make demands on your patience and sense of humour. There will, however,

be ample opportunity for you to relax, enjoy the unique surroundings and above all, have a lot of fun. Look up our website containing the expedition photo library, past volunteers' comments and real-time project news.

Total projects worldwide: 3
Total UK projects: 0
Starting months: January–November.
Time required: 4–52 weeks.
Age requirement: 18 plus.
Causes: Children, conservation, environmental causes, teaching/assisting (primary), wildlife, young people.
Activities: Campaigning, community work, conservation skills, development issues, first aid, fundraising, group work, international aid, manual work, marketing/publicity, outdoor skills, research, scientific work, social work, sport, teaching, technical skills, training.
Vols under 26 placed each year: 75 of a total of 100.
When to apply: As early as possible.
Work alone/with others: With others.
Volunteers with disabilities: Possible.
Qualifications: Spoken English – any other qualifications are an added bonus.
Equipment/clothing: Specific clothing required: volunteers will receive detailed information pack.
Health requirements: General medical prior to departure plus relevant immunisation.
Costs: From £2,150: 10 week project, from £900: 5 week project, plus flights (fundraising possible).
Benefits: The cost covers subsistence, accommodation, expedition equipment, training plus pre-expedition training.
Training: All necessary science training on site. Resources provided in UK one month before expedition departs.
Supervision: 3 members of permanent staff.
Interview details: There is an informal selection process involving interview.
Certification: Certificate or reference provided.
Worldwide placements: *Africa* (Malawi, South Africa); *Asia* (Korea (South)); *Australasia* (Australia); *North America* (USA); *Central America* (Honduras).

GLOBAL VOLUNTEERS
375 E. Little Canada Road
St Paul
MN 55117

USA

Tel: 00 1 651 407 6100
Fax: 00 1 651 482 0915
e-mail: email@globalvolunteers.org
Web: www.globalvolunteers.org
Contact: Volunteer Co-ordinators

Global Volunteers sends teams of volunteers to live and work with local people on human and economic development projects identified by the community as important to their long-term development. In this way, the volunteers' energy, creativity and labour are put to use and at the same time they gain a genuine, first-hand understanding of how other people live day to day. Our 16 years of experience enable us to offer you: genuine opportunities to serve; immediate acceptance by host communities; continuity of programme from year to year; experienced team leaders and programme consultants; informed insight into other cultures; the joy of travelling and working with a team of like-minded people.

Total projects worldwide: 20
Total UK projects: 0
Starting months: January–December.
Time required: 1–3 weeks.
Age requirement: 18 plus.
Causes: Children, conservation, environmental causes, health care/medical, heritage, human rights, poor/homeless, teaching/assisting (primary, secondary, mature, EFL), young people.
Activities: Agriculture/farming, building/construction, caring (general, day and residential), community work, computers, conservation skills, development issues, gardening/horticulture, group work, international aid, manual work, summer camps, teaching, technical skills, training.
Vols under 26 placed each year: 600 of a total of 6,000.
When to apply: All year.
Work alone/with others: Others in a team.
Volunteers with disabilities: Possible.
Qualifications: Nil.
Equipment/clothing: No special requirements.
Health requirements: Good physical and mental health.
Costs: All costs (2000 costs ranged from US$450 to US$2,395 excluding air fares).
Benefits: Accommodation, food, ground transport, project materials and team leader.

Emergency medical evacuation insurance is included in the programme fee. All other insurance should be provided by the volunteer.
Training: Orientation training is provided for the team on site as well as a pre-trip volunteer booklet and teaching manual (for teaching sites).
Supervision: Volunteers serve as a team with an experienced team leader in charge. Volunteers under 18 are supervised by their guardian.
Interview details: No interview necessary.
Worldwide placements: *Africa* (Ghana, Tanzania); *Asia* (China, India, Indonesia, Turkey, Vietnam); *Australasia* (Oceania); *Europe* (Greece, Ireland, Italy, Poland, Romania, Spain); *North America* (USA); *Central America* (Costa Rica, Jamaica, Mexico); *South America* (Ecuador).

GLOUCESTERSHIRE WILDLIFE TRUST
Dulverton Building
Robinswood Hill Country Park
Reservoir Road
Gloucester
GL4 6SX UK

Tel: +44 (0) 1452 383333
Fax: +44 (0) 1452 383334
e-mail: gmcg@cix.comulink.co.uk
Contact: Peter Smith, Marketing Officer

The Gloucestershire Wildlife Trust was formed in 1961 by local people, including Sir Peter Scott, who wanted a better future for the county's wildlife. A variety of programmes and initiatives have been developed to help achieve the Trust's aim of caring for the wildlife and wild places of Gloucestershire. The Trust is a registered independent charity. It has a membership of over 6,100 people with more than 500 active volunteers and 15 corporate partners from the world of industry and commerce. The Trust manages 82 nature reserves in Gloucestershire which are homes to the county's rarest flora and fauna. Most of the reserves are open to the public or by permit. The Trust employs a small professional staff which carries out the increasingly technical work associated with conserving wildlife in the face of growing economic and demographic pressures. The Trust is run by a Council elected annually by the members. The Conservation Centre is the hub of all Trust activities providing information, advice, education and a huge range of environmental and wildlife materials, activities etc. in the Wildlife Shop. Events and talks are held for people of all ages and last year 3,500 school children took part in the Trust's Learning for Life education programme. The Trust's vision is to continue to use its knowledge and expertise to help the people and organizations of Gloucestershire to enjoy, understand and take action to protect the wildlife and habitats of town and countryside. Volunteers with an offending background may be accepted; each case is reviewed separately.

Total projects worldwide: 1
Total UK projects: 1
Starting months: January–December.
Time required: 1–52 weeks (plus).
Age requirement: 16 plus.
Causes: Children, conservation, environmental causes, heritage, teaching/assisting (primary), wildlife.
Activities: Administration, building/construction, campaigning, conservation skills, forestry, fundraising, library/resource centres, manual work, marketing/publicity, newsletter/journalism, outdoor skills, research, scientific work, teaching.
Vols under 26 placed each year: 10
When to apply: All year.
Work alone/with others: Either.
Volunteers with disabilities: Possible for office based work.
Qualifications: We will endeavour to find work suitable to your level of training, experience and aspirations.
Equipment/clothing: For outdoor practical conservation work, footwear, waterproofs etc.
Health requirements: Nil.
Costs: Nil.
Benefits: All out-of-pocket expenses.
Interview details: An informal interview is held to assess what work or training options volunteers can do.
Certification: NVQs can be taken, therefore certificate or reference provided.
Charity number: 232580
UK placements: *England* (Gloucestershire).

GOAL
PO Box 2876
London
W1A 5QX UK

Tel: +44 (0) 20 7631 3196
Fax: +44 (0) 20 7631 3197
e-mail: goaluk@lineone.net
Web: www.goal.ie
Contact: Cathy Kataria, Administrator

GOAL is an international relief and development agency, dedicated to the objective of alleviating the suffering of the poorest of the poor in the Third World. The organization was founded in 1977 by a sports journalist John O'Shea and four of his friends. GOAL believes that every human being has a right to the fundamentals of life, i.e. food, water, shelter, literacy and medical attention. We are non-denominational and non-political and our resources are targeted at the most vulnerable in the developing world. GOAL has responded to every major natural and man-made disaster and catastrophe over the past 21 years. At present GOAL is operational in 14 countries, while we provide financial support to a whole range of indigenous groups and missionaries who share our philosophy in many other deprived countries. Since our inception GOAL has sent in excess of 650 volunteers to work in Third World regions while £60 million has been spent by the agency, reaching those in greatest need. GOAL has managed to keep administration costs to a minimum – under 5% over the last 21 years. The organization is directly accountable to the Irish taxpayer and is audited each year by Arthur Andersen and Company. In addition to emergency relief and development activities our work is very heavily centred on street children. In our efforts to assist the poor, we receive support from, among others, the governments of Ireland, the UK, the USA, Holland and Sweden as well as from the EU, the UN and the general public. Host countries insist on police records for visa purposes.

Total projects worldwide: 50
Total UK projects: 0
Starting months: January–December.
Time required: 1–52 weeks (plus).
Age requirement: 21 plus.
Causes: Aids/HIV, children, disabled (learning and physical), health care/medical, human rights, poor/homeless, refugees, teaching/assisting (primary).
Activities: Accountancy, administration, building/construction, catering, community work, development issues, first aid,

fundraising, international aid, newsletter/
journalism, sport, teaching.
Vols under 26 placed each year: 4–5
When to apply: Any time.
Work alone/with others: With others.
Volunteers with disabilities: Possible.
Qualifications: Mainly medical staff, nurses,
midwives, doctors, administrators,
accountants. Languages: French and
Portuguese.
Health requirements: Medical examination
prior to being recruited.
Costs: Nil.
Benefits: Subsistence while abroad, small
holiday allowance, travel to and from
destination.
Interview details: Interviews take place in
London or Dublin.
Certification: Reference on request.
Charity number: 1002941
Worldwide placements: *Africa* (Angola,
Ethiopia, Kenya, Mozambique, Sierra Leone,
Swaziland, Uganda); *Asia* (India, Philippines,
Vietnam); *Europe* (Bosnia-Herzegovina,
Yugoslavia); *Central America* (Honduras).

GOODWILL CHILDREN'S HOMES
63 Denford Road
Ringstead
Northants
NN14 4DF UK

Tel: +44 (0) 1933 461799
Fax: +44 (0) 1933 461799
Contact: Peter Davis

Goodwill Children's Homes does not rely on
a volunteer workforce in the running of the
homes, staffing its schools or within the
Trade Training project, but does welcome
applications from people able to offer a
practical skill or interest that can be shared
with our Indian staff. The children greatly
benefit by contact with visitors and are keen
to practise their English. Visitors can also
contribute to the programme of recreational
activities in the evenings and at weekends. We
hope that visitors will be inspired to sponsor
a child when they have seen the work being
done and will want to share the experience
with others by fund-raising on their return,
giving a few talks to schools and
organizations. A visit can offer a chance to
see life in rural areas of South India by being
part of the community. This gives an
opportunity to appreciate a very different
culture, social structure and the effects of
poverty and is found by our visitors to be an
experience very useful in future training and
employment. It is also possible for small
groups from secondary schools and colleges
to visit to undertake a specific project.

Total projects worldwide: 7
Total UK projects: 0
Starting months: January–December.
Time required: 1–16 weeks.
Age requirement: 16 plus.
Causes: Children, teaching/assisting young
people.
Activities: Administration, agriculture/
farming, arts/crafts, computers, DIY, first aid,
fundraising, gardening/horticulture, music,
outdoor skills, teaching, technical skills.
Vols under 26 placed each year: 15 of a total
of 20.
When to apply: All year.
Work alone/with others: With others.
Volunteers with disabilities: Not possible.
Health requirements: Robust health essential.
Costs: Air fare plus £5 per day living
expenses. Insurance is the responsibility of
volunteer.
Benefits: Travel, Third World perspective.
Training: Leaflet/discussion by phone/
meeting if required/contact with previous
volunteers.
Supervision: Help and supervision provided
by local Indian staff – all speak good
English.
Charity number: 270403
Worldwide placements: *Asia* (India).

GRAIL, THE
125 Waxwell Lane
Pinner
Middlesex
HA5 3ER UK

Tel: +44 (0) 20 8866 2195/0505
Fax: +44 (0) 20 8866 1408
e-mail: grailcentre@compuserve.com
Contact: Ms J. O'Dowd

The Grail Volunteer Programme has been
running for more than 20 years. It arose out
of an idea to recruit from friends and
contacts of the resident community at The
Grail Centre, but international listing has
increasingly drawn people worldwide. The
Grail is not a high profile charity but has an
international network of contacts through its
publishing, women's groups and conferences.

The centre, a listed building with extensions, circa 1600, set in 10 acres of wooded garden is less than 45 minutes from central London. At the heart of the organization is a permanent community of Christian women. The focus is non-denominational, open, offering short- and long-term hospitality, courses and workshops designed to heal and restore people caught up in the pressures of life today. Prospective volunteers write a letter enclosing stamped envelope or international reply coupon. UK applicants may visit if they wish. Vegetarians catered for, but not dietary preferences.

Total projects worldwide: 1
Total UK projects: 1
Starting months: January–December.
Time required: 12–52 weeks.
Age requirement: 20 plus.
Causes: Conservation, elderly people, environmental causes, human rights, young people.
Activities: Administration, arts/crafts, caring (general), catering, computers, conservation skills, cooking, DIY, driving, fundraising, gardening/horticulture, group work, library/resource centres, manual work, music, newsletter/journalism, outdoor skills.
Vols under 26 placed each year: 6 or 7 of a total of 9 or 10.
When to apply: 4–6 months prior to arrival.
Work alone/with others: Both.
Volunteers with disabilities: Not possible.
Qualifications: Basic spoken English, positive attitude.
Equipment/clothing: No.
Health requirements: Good health.
Costs: Travel to and from Pinner plus any home visits or holidays plus insurance.
Benefits: Board, lodging plus £18.50 pocket money per week. 1 English lesson per week plus occasional bonuses. Accident insurance cover for those resident provided by us.
Training: In-service training only.
Supervision: Paid staff employed.
Nationalities accepted: Applicants of all nationalities are free to apply but it is increasingly difficult for some foreign nationals to gain entry.
Certification: Reference if requested.
Charity number: 221076
UK placements: *England* (London).

GRANGEMOCKLER CAMPHILL COMMUNITY

Temple Michael
Carrick-on-Suir
Co. Tipperary
Ireland

Tel: 00 353 51 647202
Fax: 00 353 51 647253
Contact: Astrid Teppan

Grangemockler Camphill Community is part of the developing international Camphill movement. Founded in 1940, much of the inspiration came from and continues to be found in the teachings of Rudolf Steiner. Camphill Communities offer those in need of special care – children, adolescents and adults – a sheltered environment in which their education, therapeutic and social needs can be met. There are about 40 people living in four houses in our community. For the majority of us this is our home, where we will probably live for several years, or perhaps even for our lifetime. For those of you coming to stay with us for some time it is an opportunity for new experiences. A basic principle of the community is that no one gets paid for their work – each person gives the benefits of their work to the community, and lives through the work of others. For those of you staying with us for more than a few weeks, your material needs will be met by the community. Our lives are not governed by rules, but everyone is expected to take as full a part as possible in all realms of our lives. This includes cooking, gardening, folkdancing, milking, eurythmy, cleaning, film shows, weaving, cutting toe nails, meetings, mucking out pigs, celebrating festivals etc. Everyone has a day off each week. This could be accurately termed a 'personal day'. Camphill is not a job but a way of life and as such goes on 24 hours a day, seven days a week. We recognize, however, that we need time for ourselves and that this is not always easy to find, unless it is written into our timetable. Weekends are not days off but time we can use to meet each other in different ways. Our care for those people with special needs does not extend only into the working realm. To go for a walk or to play a game together on a Saturday afternoon is all part of our lives.
Total projects worldwide: 1
Total UK projects: 0

Starting months: January–December.
Time required: 1–52 weeks (plus).
Age requirement: 18 plus.
Causes: Disabled (learning).
Activities: Agriculture/farming, arts/crafts, building/construction, caring (general, day and residential), catering, cooking, first aid, forestry, gardening/horticulture, group work, manual work, music, sport, theatre/drama.
Vols under 26 placed each year: 8 of a total of 16.
When to apply: All year.
Work alone/with others: With others.
Volunteers with disabilities: Possible.
Qualifications: Nil.
Equipment/clothing: Wellies amd a raincoat.
Health requirements: Nil.
Costs: Return travel costs to community if stay is short. Insurance (by E111 or arranged on arrival).
Benefits: Trust money available if staying more than one month.
Training: An introductory course held here.
Supervision: Human interest by people living here.
Interview details: No interview necessary but long-term applicants will be asked for a short handwritten CV, 2 referees and a police check.
Certification: Reference on request.
Worldwide placements: *Europe* (Ireland).

GREAT GEORGES PROJECT – THE BLACKIE

The Blackie
Great George Street
Liverpool
L1 5EW UK

Tel: +44 (0) 151 709 5109
Fax: +44 (0) 151 709 4822
Contact: The Duty Officer

Great Georges Project (The Blackie) is a centre for experimental work in the arts, sport, games and education of today. First started as an arts centre or artists' studio, the basic principle is the provision of creative opportunities for all. The Blackie – 'A bridge across troubled waters ... linking artists and communities' – was founded in 1968. And what might have seemed almost fortuitous at that time can now be seen as essential ingredients in determining the character of Britain's first community arts project. The proximity of the Blackie to Britain's oldest established African-Caribbean community – and to Europe's oldest Chinatown – has meant that cultural diversity is celebrated as a natural phenomenon. The siting of the Blackie adjoining a residential neighbourhood and yet close to the city centre has meant that both residents and visitors to the city find it accessible, and it is natural that playgroups and community enterprises should take their place alongside concerts and exhibitions.

Total projects worldwide: 1
Total UK projects: 1
Starting months: January–December.
Time required: 4–52 weeks.
Age requirement: 18 plus.
Causes: Addicts/ex-addicts, children, inner city problems, offenders/ex-offenders, poor/homeless, teaching/assisting young people.
Activities: Administration, arts/crafts, cooking, DIY, fundraising, gardening/horticulture, newsletter/journalism, sport, teaching, theatre/drama, visiting/befriending.
Vols under 26 placed each year: 55–80 of a total of 60–100.
When to apply: All year.
Work alone/with others: With others.
Volunteers with disabilities: Welcome, but notice required.
Qualifications: Huge sense of humour, working knowledge of English.
Equipment/clothing: Sleeping bag, jeans, tough shoes and clothes.
Health requirements: Nil.
Costs: £17.50 per week.
Benefits: Board and Lodging.
Certification: Reference provided.
Charity number: 9018509
UK placements: *England* (Merseyside).

GREEK DANCES THEATRE

8 Scholiou Street
Plaka
Athens
GR-10558 Greece

Tel: 00 30 1 3244395
Fax: 00 30 1 3246921
e-mail: grdance@hol.gr
Web: http//:users.hol.gr/~grdance
Contact: Adamantia Angel

The Dora Stratou Greek Dances Theatre was established in 1953 as The Living Museum of Greek Dance. This is a non-profit institution subsidized by the Ministry of Culture and the National Tourist

Organization: daily performances in its 1,000-seat garden theatre on Philopappou Hill, opposite the Acropolis; an ensemble of 80 dancers, musicians and folk singers; a collection of 2,500 village-made costumes, jewels and other works of folk art, worn on stage; courses, lectures and workshops on dance and folk culture; field research programmes in dance ethnography and dance sociology; study group, courses and workshops on Ancient Greek dance; archives of dance books, field recordings, films; series of records, cassettes, videocassettes and books on dance in Greek, English and other languages; costume copies made to order.

Total projects worldwide: 5
Total UK projects: 0
Starting months: January–December.
Time required: 4–10 weeks.
Age requirement: 16 plus.
Causes: Heritage, teaching/assisting (primary, secondary, EFL), young people.
Activities: Arts/crafts, computers, library/resource centres, music, newsletter/journalism, research, summer camps, teaching, theatre/drama, translating.
Vols under 26 placed each year: 10 of a total of 15.
When to apply: All year.
Work alone/with others: With others.
Volunteers with disabilities: Only for costume maintenance.
Qualifications: Nil.
Health requirements: Nil.
Costs: Travel to Athens and subsistence.
Interview details: No interview necessary.
Certification: Certificate or reference provided.
Worldwide placements: *Europe* (Greece).

GREENFORCE

11–15 Betterton Street
Covent Garden
London
WC2H 9BP UK

Tel: +44 (0) 20 7470 8888
Fax: +44 (0) 20 7470 8889
e-mail: greenforce@btinternet.com
Web: www.greenforce.org
Contact: Mark Watts, Managing Director

'Work on the wild side!' Greenforce needs volunteers to work with host country students side by side on environmental biodiversity and marine surveys throughout the world.

Full training provided in the UK then at the host country university, prior to leaving on the expedition. All locations are very remote and are typically the first survey of an area – come to live in the Amazon, Zambia, Borneo, Fiji or the Bahamas. Paid staff positions are first offered to suitable ex-volunteers. On each expedition, one person is chosen to stay on for the next expedition, free. You are chosen by the staff on your expedition. All staff are eligible after one year for funding to the equivalent of the fees for a UK MSc or alternative. So a Greenforce expedition can be an incredible experience and also, if you wish, the start to a career in conservation. Projects range from animal tracking in Africa, setting up Fiji's first marine park to working on the only European project of this type in the Amazon. Contact us for the latest projects. Enthusiasm, a sense of humour and the ability to cope with basic conditions are more important than experience or exam results. Free BSAC dive training provided. Staff ratio of four to one in the field. The Royal Geographical Society's YET Code of Practice and the UNESCO Scientific Guidelines are adhered to. Satellite phone back-up and air ambulances are provided which ensure volunteers enjoy this incredible experience. Come to one of the monthly open evenings in Covent Garden where slides and videos explain each project. Check out our website for further details. Volunteers with an offending background may be accepted.

Total projects worldwide: 20
Total UK projects: 0
Starting months: January, April, July, October.
Time required: 10–52 weeks (plus).
Age requirement: 18 plus.
Causes: Animal welfare, children, conservation, environmental causes, wildlife, work camps -- seasonal, young people.
Activities: Building/construction, community work, conservation skills, development issues, forestry, group work, international aid, manual work, outdoor skills, research, scientific work, social work, teaching, training, visiting/befriending, work camps -- seasonal.
Vols under 26 placed each year: 180–200 of a total of 250.
When to apply: Up to 2 months before departure.

Work alone/with others: With others.
Volunteers with disabilities: Please call for exact project location and discuss disability.
Qualifications: Enthusiasm.
Equipment/clothing: Kit list provided.
Health requirements: Subject to our doctor and insurance approval.
Costs: £2,200 for 3 months plus one free expedition per team.
Benefits: Start a career in conservation. The cost includes internal flights, board, lodging, UK training weekend, visa, medical insurance. We provide £1million medical insurance per volunteer. Volunteer can provide own baggage cover.
Training: Distance learning packs, UK training weekend, lectures in host country university. Dr or MSc level of training staff in field. Medical, scientific and survival training are also provided. Free traineeship programme and staff MSc funding.
Supervision: One full-time member of staff per 4 volunteers. Therefore, assuming there are 15 on camp, there are 4 members of staff.
Interview details: Interviews are held once a month in Covent Garden.
Certification: Certificate or reference provided.
Charity number: 3321466
Worldwide placements: *Africa* (Uganda, Zambia); *Asia* (Brunei, India, Malaysia); *Australasia* (Fiji); *Central America* (Bahamas); *South America* (Peru).

GREENHILL YMCA NATIONAL CENTRE
Donard Park
Newcastle
Co. Down
BT33 0GR N. Ireland

Tel: +44 (0) 28 4372 3172
Fax: +44 (0) 28 4372 6009
e-mail: tim@ymca-ire.dnet.co.net
Contact: Ken Byatt

The Greenhill YMCA National Centre is an outdoor education centre which needs volunteers to act as domestic staff and cooks, instructors in outdoor pursuits such as canoeing, hill walking, archery, etc., and tutors in personal development. An interest in community relations would be an advantage. Applicants complete an applications form with photo. All suitable applicants will have to have two references taken up and undergo police vetting for criminal record and offences towards children.

Total projects worldwide: 1
Total UK projects: 1
Starting months: June, September.
Time required: 8–52 weeks.
Age requirement: 18–40
Causes: Children, human rights, inner city problems, offenders/ex-offenders, teaching/assisting (primary, secondary), unemployed, work camps – seasonal, young people.
Activities: Administration, arts/crafts, caring (general), catering, community work, computers, cooking, driving, first aid, gardening/horticulture, group work, manual work, music, outdoor skills, religion, social work, sport, summer camps, teaching, technical skills, work camps – seasonal.
Vols under 26 placed each year: 11 of a total of 14.
When to apply: As early as possible.
Work alone/with others: Both.
Volunteers with disabilities: Possible.
Qualifications: Group/youth work, social work, outdoor pursuits experience welcomed. This is a Christian centre and welcome applications from those who agree with or are not opposed to the Christian faith.
Equipment/clothing: Personal clothing.
Health requirements: Physically and mentally fit.
Costs: Return travel to centre.
Benefits: Board, lodging and pocket money of £18 per week. The Centre has public liability and employer's liability insurance.
Training: One week local orientation after specialist training as assistant instructor.
Supervision: Day to day – senior instructor, overall – programme manager.
Interview details: Overseas volunteers are not interviewed but you must include a police character reference when returning your application. Only long-term Irish volunteers are interviewed.
Certification: Reference on requeste.
Charity number: XN 45820
UK placements: *Northern Ireland* (Down).

GREENPEACE
Canonbury Villas
London
N1 2PN UK

Tel: +44 (0) 20 7865 8100
Fax: +44 (0) 20 7865 8200
e-mail: andrew.sturley@uk.greenpeace.org

Web: www.greenpeace.org.uk
Contact: Andrew Sturley, Personnel Administrator

Greenpeace sometimes needs volunteers to help with office duties which are mainly routine.

Total projects worldwide: Many.
Total UK projects: Many.
Starting months: January–December.
Time required: 12–52 weeks.
Age requirement: 18 plus.
Causes: Conservation, environmental causes.
Activities: Administration, computers, conservation skills, fundraising, marketing/publicity, research.
When to apply: All year.
Work alone/with others: With others.
Volunteers with disabilities: Possible.
Qualifications: Office experience.
Equipment/clothing: Depends on the job.
Health requirements: Nil.
Costs: Nil.
Benefits: Reimburse travel expenses and lunch costs.
Training: Induction by manager on site.
Supervision: Each volunteer is placed with a supervisor (manager) who is responsible for inducting and designating work to the volunteer.
Interview details: At our head office.
Certification: Reference on request.
UK placements: *England* (London).

GROUNDWORK

85–87 Cornwall Street
Birmingham
B3 3BY UK

Tel: +44 (0) 121 236 8565
Fax: +44 (0) 121 236 7356
e-mail: dpeace@groundwork.org.uk
Web: www.groundwork.org.uk
Contact: Dawn Peace, Operations Co-ordinator

Groundwork is a leading environmental regeneration charity making sustainable development a reality in the UK's poorest neighbourhoods. We work in partnership with local people, local authorities and businesses to bring about economic and social regeneration by improving the local environment. From small community projects to major national programmes, Groundwork uses the environment as a means of engaging and motivating local people to improve their quality of life. Groundwork is a federation of over 40 Groundwork Trusts, each a partnership between the public, private and voluntary sectors and each delivering holistic solutions to the challenges faced by poor communities. Volunteers with an offending background may be accepted depending on the nature of the offence and support required by that individual.

Total projects worldwide: 44
Total UK projects: 44
Starting months: January–December.
Time required: 1–52 weeks.
Age requirement: 16–25
Causes: Children, conservation, environmental causes, inner city problems, unemployed, wildlife, young people.
Activities: Administration, agriculture/farming, arts/crafts, community work, computers, conservation skills, driving, fundraising, gardening/horticulture, group work, manual work, marketing/publicity, music, newsletter/journalism, outdoor skills, research, summer camps, technical skills, theatre/drama, training.
Vols under 26 placed each year: 16,000 of a total of 40,000.
When to apply: All year.
Work alone/with others: With others.
Volunteers with disabilities: Possible.
Qualifications: Enthusiasm, motivation and an ability to get on with people.
Equipment/clothing: Normally supplied.
Health requirements: Depends on the project.
Costs: Travel to local office.
Benefits: Travel and subsistence allowance normally offered.
Training: Dependent on the project.
Supervision: Dependent on the project.
Interview details: Interviews take place at local offices where volunteers are to be placed.
Certification: Reference on request.
Charity number: 291558
UK placements: *England* (Cheshire, Cornwall, Co. Durham, Cumbria, Derbyshire, Devon, Hertfordshire, Kent, Lancashire, Leicestershire, Lincolnshire, London, Manchester, Merseyside, Nottinghamshire, Staffordshire, Surrey, Tyne and Wear, West Midlands, E. Yorkshire, N. Yorkshire, S. Yorkshire, W. Yorkshire); *Northern Ireland* (Belfast City, Derry/Londonderry, Down); *Wales* (Bridgend,

Caerphilly, Merthyr Tydfil, Rhondda, Cynon, Taff, Wrexham).

GROUNDWORK (IRELAND)
107 Lower Baggot Street
Dublin 2
Ireland

Tel: 00 353 1 6768588
Fax: 00 353 1 6768601
e-mail: grndwork@iwt.ie
Web: http://homepage.eircom.net/
~groundwork
Contact: Barbara Henderson

Groundwork Ireland's primary aim is to carry out important nature conservation projects in Ireland which would otherwise not be done, and thereby to facilitate persons wishing to make a practical voluntary contribution to nature conservation in Ireland. Groundwork's aim is essentially to act as a bridge between the many people who want to work for conservation and the many conservation tasks that urgently need to be carried out. Secondary aims of Groundwork are to facilitate international cultural exchange by recruiting volunteers from outside Ireland and to increase the volunteers' appreciation of the importance of nature conservation and of the areas in which they are working.

Total projects worldwide: 2
Total UK projects: 0
Starting months: June.
Time required: 1–2 weeks.
Age requirement: 17 plus.
Causes: Conservation, environmental causes, work camps – seasonal.
Activities: Conservation skills, group work, manual work, work camps – seasonal.
Vols under 26 placed each year: 160 of a total of 200.
When to apply: April/May onwards.
Work alone/with others: With others.
Volunteers with disabilities: Not possible.
Qualifications: Nil.
Equipment/clothing: Waterproof boots and clothing.
Health requirements: Volunteers MUST be in good health and free from serious medical conditions.
Costs: £20 registration fee for 1 week, £30 for 2 weeks.
Benefits: Board and lodging. We provide insurance. Volunteers should bring Form E111 (health insurance).

Training: On evening of arrival volunteers are given a talk and shown a video of work practices.
Supervision: 2 leaders for each work camp and 2 supervisors.
Interview details: No interview necessary.
Certification: Reference or certificate provided.
Worldwide placements: *Europe* (Ireland).

GROUPE ARCHEOLOGIQUE DU MESMONTOIS
Mairie de Malain
21410 Pont de Pany
France

Tel: 00 33 3 80 30 05 20 or 00 33 3 80 23 66 08
Fax: 00 33 3 80 75 13 48
e-mail: louisroussel@hotmail.com
Contact: M. Roussel

Groupe Archeologique du Mesmontois undertakes archaeological digs and restoration work. Volunteers are needed to help with tasks which include sketching, photographing the finds, model making and restoration.

Total projects worldwide: 2
Total UK projects: 0
Starting months: July
Time required: 1–8 weeks.
Age requirement: 17 plus.
Causes: Archaeology, architecture, conservation, environmental causes, heritage.
Activities: Arts/crafts, building/construction, conservation skills, cooking, library/resource centres, manual work, research, scientific work, technical skills.
Vols under 26 placed each year: 24 of a total of 30.
When to apply: Before May.
Work alone/with others: With others.
Volunteers with disabilities: Not possible.
Qualifications: Care and patience.
Equipment/clothing: Sleeping bag.
Health requirements: Anti-tetanus innoculation.
Costs: FF100 per week (£10 per week approximately) towards board and lodging.
Benefits: Board and lodging.
Interview details: No interview necessary.
Certification: Certificate or reference provided.
Worldwide placements: *Africa* (Algeria, Congo Republic, Egypt, Morocco, Tunisia); *Asia* (Hong Kong, Japan); *Australasia*

(Australia); *Europe* (Austria, Belgium, Czech Republic, Denmark, Finland, France, Germany, Hungary, Ireland, Italy, Luxembourg, Netherlands, Poland, Portugal, Romania, Slovakia, Spain, Sweden, Switzerland, Ukraine, Yugoslavia); *North America* (Canada, USA); *Central America* (Guadeloupe, Martinique); *South America* (Argentina, Chile).

GRUPPI ARCHEOLOGICI D'ITALIA
via Tacito 41
I-00193 Rome
Italy

Tel: 00 390 6 6874028
Fax: 00 390 6 6896981

Gruppi Archeologici D'Italia needs volunteers to work on archaeological excavations in Italy. Six hours' work per day, six days per week. Placements involve lectures and excursions.

Total projects worldwide: 1
Total UK projects: 0
Starting months: January–December.
Time required: 2–52 weeks.
Age requirement: 16 plus.
Causes: Archaeology.
Vols under 26 placed each year: 1,000
When to apply: 15 June.
Work alone/with others: With others.
Qualifications: Previous archaeological experience desirable.
Costs: 400,000–500,000 Lire for 2 weeks board and accommodation plus fares.
Worldwide placements: *Europe* (Italy).

GRUPPO VOLUNTARI DELLA SVIZZERA ITALIANA
CP 12
Arbedo
CH-6517 Switzerland

Tel: 00 41 91 857 4520 / 79 354 0161
Fax: 00 41 91 692 7272
e-mail: fmari@vtx.ch
Contact: Mari Federico

Gruppo Voluntari Della Svizzera Italiana takes 15 volunteers per camp to take part in work camps helping mountain communities, clearing woods etc. Four hours' work per day.

Total projects worldwide: 8
Total UK projects: 0

Starting months: June–September.
Time required: 1–16 weeks.
Age requirement: 18 plus.
Causes: Conservation, elderly people, environmental causes.
Activities: Agriculture/farming, community work, conservation skills, driving, gardening/horticulture.
Vols under 26 placed each year: 6 of a total of 60.
When to apply: As early as possible.
Work alone/with others: With others.
Volunteers with disabilities: Not possible.
Qualifications: Spoken Italian, German, French, English or Spanish.
Health requirements: Nil.
Costs: £2.50 approximately per day to cover board and accommodation plus travel costs and out-of-hours activities. Insurance is volunteer's responsibility.
Nationalities accepted: There may be restrictions on nationalities of volunteers.
Interview details: Interviews take place in Switzerland, Mexico, Honduras or Brazil. Certification: Certificate or reference provided.
Worldwide placements: *Europe* (Hungary, Switzerland); *Central America* (Honduras, Mexico).

GSM – GENÇLIK SERVISLERI MERKEZI/YOUTH SERVICES CENTRE
Beyindir Sok 45/9
Kizilay-Ankara
06650 Turkey

Tel: 00 90 312 417 1124/417 2991
Fax: 00 90 312 425 8192
e-mail: gsmser@superonline.com
Web: www.gsm-youth.org
Contact: Ertugrul Senoglu, General Co-ordinator

GSM has been organising activities for young people at national and international levels since 1985. The main areas in which GSM specialize are international voluntary work camps, international youth camps and international youth exchange projects. Our main objectives are: to strengthen youth power against the dangers of war, social and racial discrimination and for peace; to contribute to young people's social, cultural and artistic development and to promote development of common understanding, friendship and solidarity among young people; to encourage young people to participate in administration, planning and production to give them an awareness of the democratic life thereby to contributing to the enrichment of the democratic culture in our country; to develop international friendship and to promote cultural exchanges among young people by making contacts with youth organizations; to sensitize young people towards their social and natural environment and to contribute to and widen the preservation of natural environment; GSM has a very democratic structure related to our aims, so is open to the participation of young people from various backgrounds. There are five people who have been working formally in GSM. In addition, there are more than 25 young people who are students in different universities in Ankara and work voluntarily in GSM throughout the year.

Total projects worldwide: 30
Total UK projects: 3
Starting months: July–September.
Time required: 2 weeks.
Age requirement: 18–28
Causes: Archaeology, architecture, conservation, environmental causes, work camps – seasonal, young people.
Activities: Conservation skills, summer camps, visiting/befriending, work camps – seasonal.
Vols under 26 placed each year: 470 of a total of 550.
When to apply: 1 October – 15 June.
Work alone/with others: With others.
Qualifications: English is essential.
Equipment/clothing: Sleeping bags, swim wear etc.
Health requirements: Nil – small health insurance is provided.
Costs: Registration fee plus travel. Volunteers should take out more substantial health and accident insurance in their own countries.
Benefits: All board and lodging and sightseeing tours.
Supervision: During working hours supervisors will be with the volunteers.
Interview details: Interviews for those going abroad from Turkey take place in our office.
Certification: Reference on request.
Worldwide placements: *Africa* (Morocco); *Australasia* (Australia); *Europe* (Austria, Belarus, Belgium, Bosnia-Herzegovina, Bulgaria, Croatia, Czech Republic, Denmark, Estonia, Finland, France, Germany, Ireland,

Italy, Netherlands, Norway, Poland, Portugal, Romania, Russia, Slovakia, Spain, Sweden, Switzerland, Turkey).
UK placements: *England* (London, Manchester, Oxfordshire, West Midlands).

GUATEMALA ACCOMPANIMENT GROUP
1A Waterlow Road
Archway
London
N19 5NJ UK

Tel: +44 (0) 20 7281 4052
Fax: +44 (0) 20 7281 4052
Contact: Chris Baird, UK Co-ordinator

The Guatemala Accompaniment Group (GAG) was founded at the beginning of 1995 in response to the increasing demand from communities of internally displaced people and returning refugees in Guatemala for international volunteers to live with them as accompaniers. The presence of international accompaniers is intended to enhance the security of communities and to deter possible aggression and violence against them. Accompaniers monitor and observe human rights in the accompanied communities and produce and disseminate information about the human rights situation. Each accompanier, depending on their own personal skills and experience, can become involved in different ways in the life of the community (e.g. administrative or technical support, participation in agricultural or other community work, etc.). Some accompaniers have contributed their skills in the field of education or health care, or in assisting the community to develop other such projects. However, the manner in which this is done should always be carefully considered so as to avoid creating dependency, or creating expectations that cannot be fulfilled. This role must always be negotiated with the community, taking into account the established methods of decision-making there. Accompaniers are under no obligation to work during their stay in a community, but they should show a willingness to get involved in the daily life of the people they are living with. Aims and Objectives of GAG: to provide physical accompaniment to returning refugees, CPR communities and other members of the displaced population of Guatemala in order to contribute to their safe resettlement and secure living conditions; to raise awareness in the UK about the displaced communities and so to help ensure that the Guatemalan government and army are aware that international attention is being focused upon their situation.

Total projects worldwide: 1
Total UK projects: 0
Starting months: January–December.
Time required: 6–52 weeks.
Age requirement: 18 plus.
Causes: Human rights, refugees.
Vols under 26 placed each year: As many as possible.
When to apply: As soon as possible.
Work alone/with others: Both.
Volunteers with disabilities: Possible. Volunteers need to be able to use very rudimentary Third World transport.
Qualifications: Sufficient Spanish to be able to communicate at a 'reasonable' level.
Equipment/clothing: Sturdy footwear, mosquito net.
Health requirements: Will need course of innoculations.
Costs: All costs including travel insurance plus return flight. Local transport and food there. Approximately £1,300 for 3 months.
Interview details: Volunteers are interviewed in London.
Certification: Reference provided.
Worldwide placements: *Central America* (Guatemala).

GUIDE ASSOCIATION, THE
17–19 Buckingham Palace Road
London
SW1W 0PT UK

Tel: +44 (0) 20 7834 6242
Fax: +44 (0) 20 7828 8317
e-mail: chq@guides.org.uk
Contact: Linda Crichton

The Guide Association, as part of a worldwide movement, enables girls and young women to fulfil their potential and to take an active and responsible role in society through a distinctive, stimulating and enjoyable programme of activities delivered by trained volunteer leaders. Our vision is to be recognized as the leading organization for girls and women and to widen and increase our membership. Guiding is about enjoyment, challenge and excitement for girls and young women from 5 to 25. It provides an opportunity to make friends, enjoy activities and achieve whatever a girl's abilities might be. Events and activities take place across the UK and there are a growing number of opportunities for international expeditions and activities.

Total projects worldwide: Many.
Total UK projects: Many.
Starting months: January–December.
Time required: 1–52 weeks (plus).
Age requirement: 12 plus.
Causes: Young people.
Activities: Arts/crafts, community work, first aid, fundraising, group work, music, outdoor skills, summer camps, theatre/drama, training.
Vols under 26 placed each year: 22,000 of a total of 661,000.
When to apply: All year.
Work alone/with others: Both.
Volunteers with disabilities: Possible.
Qualifications: Nil.
Equipment/clothing: Uniform.
Health requirements: Nil.
Costs: Membership subscription.
Benefits: Most expenses such as travel, accommodation etc. are reclaimable. We provide insurance cover for approved projects.
Training: Varies according to project.
Supervision: By other volunteers through our established structures and under the guidance of approved policies such as 'Safe From Harm'.
Certification: Certificate or reference provided.
Charity number: 306016
Worldwide placements: *Africa* (Egypt, Ethiopia, Ghana, Malawi, Tanzania, Tunisia, Uganda, Zimbabwe); *Asia* (Bahrain, Brunei, China, Indonesia, Japan, Kuwait, Malaysia, Nepal, Oman, Pakistan, Qatar, Saudi Arabia, Singapore, Taiwan, Turkey, United Arab Emirates); *Europe* (Belgium, Cyprus, Czech Republic, France, Germany, Greece, Italy, Luxembourg, Netherlands, Norway, Poland, Portugal, Romania, Russia, Spain, Switzerland, Turkey); *North America* (USA); *South America* (Brazil).
UK placements: *England* (throughout); *Scotland* (throughout); *Northern Ireland* (throughout); *Wales* (throughout).

GUIDE DOGS FOR THE BLIND ASSOCIATION – HOLIDAYS
Shap Road
Kendal
Cumbria
LA9 6NZ UK

Tel: +44 (0) 1539 735080
Fax: +44 (0) 1539 735567
e-mail: holidays@gdba.org.uk
Web: www.gdba.org.uk
Contact: Heather Rothwell

The Guide Dogs for the Blind Association (GDBA) – Holidays department runs activity and hobby holidays for blind people, in many cases providing opportunities and experiences that are outside the scope of their everyday lives. A sighted guide is needed on a one-to-one basis for each visually impaired person on almost all occasions. We would be very grateful to hear from anyone who would be prepared to help. The activities themselves vary considerably and are based both in Britain and abroad. They vary from sunbathing in Tenerife to sightseeing in Jerusalem, from ballroom dancing courses in Chester to riding a tandem in the Cotswolds. Sighted holiday guides have to work reasonably hard – it's not a cheap holiday. The most important attributes for a guide are, perhaps, common sense and the ability to communicate. Days can be long and demanding and often start with assisting at breakfast and continue through to the social activities in the evening. We need sighted holiday guides of all ages. In return for the help and assistance, costs are subsidized. If you feel you can spare a little time to help others, if you would like to see a brochure or want to discuss the idea, please telephone the above number.

Total projects worldwide: Approximately 100 a year.
Total UK projects: Approximately 70 a year.
Starting months: January–December.
Time required: 1–3 weeks.
Age requirement: 18 plus.
Causes: Holidays for disabled, work camps – seasonal.
Activities: Caring (general, day and residential), cooking, driving, group work, music, outdoor skills, sport, summer camps, theatre/drama, training, visiting/befriending, work camps – seasonal.
Vols under 26 placed each year: 100 of a total of 1,000.
When to apply: All year.
Work alone/with others: With others.
Volunteers with disabilities: Possible.
Qualifications: Not necessary though all skills can be helpful.
Health requirements: Good general health.
Costs: Dependent on the project but club membership required for volunteers: £18 over 18. Insurance is included in our subsidzied cost to the sighted guide.
Benefits: Dependent on the project.
Training: One-day training course as available, video guidance, leaflet guidance, telephone guidance if required.
Supervision: A group leader suitably qualified for the activity accompanies all groups.
Interview details: No interview necessary but a written reference is required.
Certification: Reference provided.
Worldwide placements: *Africa* (Egypt); *Asia* (China, Hong Kong, Israel, Jordan, Nepal, Singapore, Sri Lanka, Thailand); *Europe* (Andorra, Austria, Cyprus, France, Greece, Italy, Malta, Norway, Portugal, Spain); *North America* (USA).
UK placements: *England* (throughout); *Scotland* (throughout); *Northern Ireland* (throughout); *Wales* (throughout).

GWENT WILDLIFE TRUST
16 White Swan Court
Church Street
Monmouth
Gwent
NP5 3BR UK

Tel: +44 (0) 1600 715501
Fax: +44 (0) 1600 715832
Contact: The Director

Gwent Wildlife Trust is a member of the Wildlife Trusts, a national partnership of 47 County Trusts. For more details of Wildlife Trusts, see the entry under Cornwall Wildlife Trust.

Total projects worldwide: Varies.
Total UK projects: Varies.
Starting months: January–December.
Time required: 1–52 weeks (plus).
Age requirement: 16 plus.
Causes: Conservation, environmental causes, wildlife.
Activities: Computers, conservation skills, driving, forestry, gardening/horticulture, manual work, outdoor skills, scientific work,

technical skills.
Vols under 26 placed each year: Varies.
When to apply: All year.
Work alone/with others: With others.
Volunteers with disabilities: Possible.
Qualifications: Nil.
Equipment/clothing: Outdoor clothes.
Health requirements: Anti-tetanus immunisation. Any medical conditions (illness, allergy or physical disability) that may require treatment/medication or which affect the volunteer working with machinery must be notified to us in advance.
Costs: Bring your own packed lunch.
Benefits: Out-of-pocket expenses.
Training: Volunteers receive on-the-job training in an informal atmosphere.
Interview details: Interviews at our office.
Certification: Reference on request.
UK placements: *Wales* (Caerphilly, Monmouthshire, Newport, Torfaen).

H

HABITAT FOR HUMANITY INTERNATIONAL
Human Resources Department
121 Habitat Street
Americus
Georgia 31709-3498
USA

Tel: 00 1 912 924 6935
Fax: 00 1 912 924 0641
e-mail: VSD@Habitat.org
Web: www.Habitat.org
Contact: Volunteer Co-ordinator

Habitat for Humanity International is a movement of individuals and groups working in partnership to build houses with those who otherwise would be unable to afford decent shelter. Habitat partners volunteer their construction and administrative skills with the vision of eliminating poverty housing from the face of the earth. Three-month internship programme available any time within the year. Apply by sending résumé and cover letter and write/e-mail for an application form.

Total projects worldwide: 2000 plus.

Total UK projects: 3
Starting months: January–December.
Time required: 1–52 weeks (plus).
Age requirement: 18 plus.
Causes: Architecture, children, teaching/assisting (nursery), work camps – seasonal, young people.
Activities: Accountancy, administration, building/construction, computers, DIY, group work, marketing/publicity, newsletter/journalism, research, summer camps, teaching, technical skills, training, work camps – seasonal.
Vols under 26 placed each year: 210 of a total of approximately 300.
When to apply: All year.
Work alone/with others: With others.
Volunteers with disabilities: Possible.
Qualifications: Driver's licence is a plus. Degree not mandatory but preferred. Must obtain B-1 visa.
Health requirements: Depends on job/work environment.
Costs: Travel costs to and from Habitat.
Benefits: Housing and US$75 per week (grocery allowance). $600 per year insurance provided. We recommend that volunteers carry their own insurance.
Training: Training is on the job.
Supervision: By managers at all levels.
Interview details: We conduct interviews by telephone before accepting applicants.
Certification: Reference or certificate provided.
Worldwide placements: *North America* (USA).

HAIFA UNIVERSITY, DEPT OF ARCHAEOLOGY
Mount Carmel 31905
Israel

Contact: Dr Adam Zertal

Haifa University, Department of Archaeology: El Ahwat, one of the most recent and surprising discoveries in the field of biblical archaeology in Israel, is situated on a high hill overlooking the Mediterranean coast, about 12 km east of Caesarea. The site was discovered in 1992, being excavated since 1993. The site is a large fortified town enclosed by a stone-built city wall 5–6 m wide. The lines of the wall are wavy in design, having 10–12 tower-like projections along its perimeter. The area within the town is divided into four quarters by dividing walls two m wide. According to the pottery found, the site was founded near the end of the 13th century BC. It was a short-lived site – only 50 years – and then abandoned, never to be settled again. In 1995 indications were revealed which connected the site to the big island of Sardinia in the western Mediterranean. Architectural elements of the Nuragic culture of Sardinia were unearthed in the site, and there is a possibility to connect the place with the Shardana, one of the well-known tribes among the sea peoples. These were tribes who attacked the empires of the late Bronze Age in the Mediterranean and destroyed them. Working days: Sunday to Thursday. Work starts at noon on Sunday.

Total projects worldwide: 1
Total UK projects: 0
Starting months: July.
Time required: 1–4 weeks.
Age requirement: 16 plus.
Causes: Archaeology.
Activities: Scientific work.
Vols under 26 placed each year: 20
When to apply: Before 1 June.
Work alone/with others: With others.
Volunteers with disabilities: Possible.
Qualifications: Nil.
Equipment/clothing: Hat, high boots, anti-sun cream, simple clothing for a hot summer.
Health requirements: Good general health.
Costs: Travel to Israel and US$200 per week in the dig, includes everything.
Benefits: Meals are served in the kibbutz dining room. Participants will have free use of the kibbutz swimming pool. Each weekday afternoon there a free guided tour by bus to sites and places of interest in the area (Caesarea, Megiddo etc).
Certification: Certificate or reference provided.
Worldwide placements: *Asia* (Israel).

HAMPSHIRE AND ISLE OF WIGHT WILDLIFE TRUST
8 Romsey Road
Eastleigh
Hampshire
SO50 9AL UK

Tel: + 44 (0) 23 8061 3636 / 613737
Fax: + 44 (0) 23 8061 2233
Contact: Annette Forrest, Members Officer

Hampshire and Isle of Wight Wildlife Trust

invites prospective volunteers to contact the Volunteers Officer for further discussion.

Total projects worldwide: Varies.
Total UK projects: Varies.
Starting months: January–December.
Time required: 1–52 weeks (plus).
Age requirement: 16 plus.
Causes: Conservation, environmental causes, wildlife.
Activities: Administration, computers, conservation skills, driving, forestry, fundraising, gardening/horticulture, manual work, marketing/publicity, outdoor skills, research, scientific work, technical skills.
Vols under 26 placed each year: Hundreds.
When to apply: All year.
Work alone/with others: With others.
Volunteers with disabilities: Possible.
Qualifications: Nil.
Equipment/clothing: Casual work clothes, waterproofs, stout boots for outdoor work. Protective safety gear is provided.
Health requirements: Anti-tetanus innoculation recommended.
Costs: Bring your own packed lunch.
Benefits: Members officer will provide information on expenses. Trust has £5 million public liability insurance.
Training: Some training, dependent upon task.
Supervision: Senior volunteer or staff.
Certification: Reference on request.
UK placements: *England* (Hampshire, Isle of Wight).

HAMPTON HOUSE
Tonmead Road
Lumbertubs
Northampton
Northants
NN3 8JX UK

Tel: + 44 (0) 1604 403733
Fax: + 44 (0) 1604 413832
Contact: Colin Knowlton, Service Manager

Hampton House is a residential service, part of SCOPE. (SCOPE is the organization for people with cerebral palsy.)

Total projects worldwide: 1
Total UK projects: 1
Starting months: January–December.
Time required: 26–52 weeks (plus).
Age requirement: 16–25
Causes: Disabled (learning and physical).

Activities: Arts/crafts, caring (day and residential), computers, DIY, gardening/horticulture, music.
Vols under 26 placed each year: 36
When to apply: All year.
Work alone/with others: Both.
Volunteers with disabilities: Possible.
Qualifications: Some practical skills and ability in DIY and gardening.
Health requirements: Nil, other than fitness to undertake the work required.
Costs: Nil.
Benefits: Travel costs in the UK to and from placement paid. Meals plus pocket money up to £23 per week.
Interview details: Interviews take place at Hampton House.
Certification: Reference on request.
Charity number: 208231
UK placements: *England* (Northamptonshire).

HAND-IN-HAND
3 Beechcroft Road
London
E18 1LA UK

Tel: +44 (0) 20 8530 8220
Fax: +44 (0) 20 8518 8832
e-mail: hand-in-hand@tesco.net
Web: www.handinhand.8m.com
Contact: Juliet Jayson, Project Worker

Hand-in-Hand is a national network of Jewish volunteers, aged 14–17, involved in a variety of projects working with both Jewish and non-Jewish charities. Supported by a grant from the National Lottery, Hand-in-Hand is one of the services offered by the Jewish Lads and Girls Brigade to young people. Volunteers work individually or in groups in a variety of placements – befriending, running camps and activities, newsletter design, campaigning, working with disabled people, gardening, website design, entertainment and peer education projects – among other things. You would be encouraged to select activities which interest you and match the amount of time commitment you are prepared to make.

Total projects worldwide: 12
Total UK projects: 12
Starting months: January–December.
Time required: 1–5 weeks.
Age requirement: 14–17
Causes: Animal Welfare, children, disabled

(learning and physical), elderly people, poor/homeless.
Activities: Administration, arts/crafts, campaigning, caring (general), community work, computers, fundraising, gardening/horticulture, group work, music, newsletter/journalism, outdoor skills, religion, sport, summer camps, theatre/drama, visiting/befriending.
Vols under 26 placed each year: 50 of a total of 100.
When to apply: All year.
Work alone/with others: With others.
Volunteers with disabilities: Possible.
Qualifications: Nil.
Health requirements: Nil.
Costs: Nil.
Benefits: We provide insurance.
Training: Whatever is necessary.
Supervision: Adult supervision.
Nationalities accepted: No restrictions but all volunteers must be Jewish.
Interview details: Prospective volunteers are interviewed at home.
Certification: Reference on request.
Charity number: 286950
UK placements: *England* (Essex, Hertfordshire, London, Manchester).

HCJB UK
131 Grattan Road
Bradford
W. Yorkshire
BD1 2HS UK

Tel: +44 (0) 1274 721 810
Fax: +44 (0) 1274 741302
e-mail: brapley@uk.hcjb.org
Contact: Beryl Rapley, Secretary

HCJB UK is a Christian missionary organization. Volunteers with an offending background are accepted depending upon the individual case.

Total projects worldwide: Several.
Total UK projects: 1
Starting months: January–December.
Time required: 8–13 weeks.
Age requirement: 18 plus.
Causes: Health care/medical, young people.
Activities: International aid, religion, scientific work, technical skills, training.
Vols under 26 placed each year: Several.
When to apply: 1 January for summer, any time for others.
Work alone/with others: Usually with

others.

Volunteers with disabilities: Possible, but most projects entail physical work.

Qualifications: Spanish desirable. We expect all applicants to be sympathetic to and in agreement with our Christian beliefs.

Equipment/clothing: Nurses' uniforms.

Health requirements: Some vaccinations required.

Costs: All costs including travel and maintenance.

Benefits: Opportunity to gain experience in your specialism in a Latin American environment; experience of working in a Christian missionary organization.

Interview details: Interviews take place in Bradford.

Certification: Certificate or reference on request.

Charity number: 263449

Worldwide placements: *South America* (Ecuador).

UK placements: *England* (W. Yorkshire).

HEADWAY – NATIONAL HEAD INJURIES ASSOCIATION
7 King Edward Court
King Edward Street
Nottingham
Nottinghamshire
NG1 1EW UK

Tel: + 44 (0) 1159 240800
Fax: + 44 (0) 1159 240432
Contact: Ian Garrow

Headway, the National Head Injuries Association, was founded in response to these special needs and aims: to increase public awareness and understanding of head injury; to participate in activities that will reduce the incidence of head injury; to provide information and support for people with head injury, their families and carers; to promote co-ordinated multi-disciplinary approaches to head injury screening, acute care, assessment, rehabilitation and community re-entry, with clear accountability at all stages; to assist people with head injury to return to community living, including access to appropriate accommodation, social outlets and productive activity. Every year one million people in Britain attend hospitals with head injuries. Many of these people are left with a wide range of serious physical or psychological disabilities, often both. These long-standing disabilities result in considerable social and emotional problems for head injured people and their families. Volunteers with offending backgrounds are accepted with certain caveats.

Total projects worldwide: 140
Total UK projects: 140
Starting months: January–December.
Time required: 1–52 weeks.
Age requirement: 14 plus.
Causes: Children, disabled (learning and physical).
Activities: Administration, caring (day), community work, computers, fundraising.
When to apply: All year.
Work alone/with others: With others.
Volunteers with disabilities: Possible.
Qualifications: Dependent on nature of voluntary activity.
Health requirements: Good health.
Benefits: Travel expenses and subsistence.
Interview details: Interviews normally take place at the location where the applicant will assist.
Certification: Internal certificate provided.
Charity number: 1025852
UK placements: *England* (Bedfordshire, Berkshire, Buckinghamshire, Cambridgeshire, Devon, Dorset, Essex, Gloucestershire, Hampshire, Herefordshire, Kent, Leicestershire, London, Merseyside, Norfolk, Northamptonshire, Nottinghamshire, Oxfordshire, Shropshire, Somerset, Staffordshire, Suffolk, E. Sussex, West Midlands, Wiltshire, Worcestershire, W. Yorkshire); *Scotland* (Dumfries and Galloway, Edinburgh, E. Lothian, W. Lothian); *Wales* (Cardiff, Vale of Glamorgan).

HEALTH PROJECTS ABROAD
PO Box 24
Bakewell
Derbyshire
DE45 1ZW UK

Tel: + 44 (0) 1629 640053
Fax: + 44 (0) 1629 640054
e-mail: info@hpauk.org
Web: www.hpauk.org
Contact: Volunteer Programme Administrator

Volunteer in Africa! Health Projects Abroad (HPA) offers places for young people to spend three months living and working alongside local people in rural Africa. You have the unique chance to become part of a community-initiated project, such as helping to build school classrooms, water facilities or a health dispensary. Tasks on site are mainly unskilled and labour intensive – enthusiasm and motivation count. This programme is a great opportunity to experience another culture at first hand. In Tanzania, volunteers work on a village building project, alongside people from the host community and local craftsmen. Although the work is physical, anyone with a reasonable level of fitness will find it manageable – the pace of life in Tanzania is much slower than in the UK! The programme encourages interaction with the host community both on and off the work-site. Life in the villages is basic – volunteers live under canvas and cook on open stoves, collecting their own water from village sources. Volunteers are encouraged to learn KiSwahili, the national language of Tanzania, to help them get more out of their stay. Language training is provided in the package. You are asked to raise £3,000 (including flights) before departure to cover costs of taking part. A chunk of this money is transferred directly to the overseas programmes, ensuring that the communities can continue to be supported through HPA's educational activities in the long term. The first of the two training weekends deals with fundraising in great detail, and gives loads of help and ideas on where to find the money. Fundraising is a challenge, but not impossible!

Total projects worldwide: 6
Total UK projects: 0
Starting months: April, June, August.
Time required: 12–52 weeks.
Age requirement: 17–28
Activities: Building/construction, community work, development issues, fundraising, group work, manual work, outdoor skills.
Vols under 26 placed each year: Approximately 100 of a total of 140.
When to apply: All year. Write, e-mail or phone for latest details.
Work alone/with others: With others.
Volunteers with disabilities: Please telephone to discuss.
Qualifications: Nil. 2 preparation weekends provided before departure.
Equipment/clothing: Sleeping bag, rucksack or similar.
Health requirements: Must have medical

approval of individual's GP and necessary vaccinations.
Costs: £3,000 covers flights, training, insurance, accommodation, food, full support in-country and major contribution to development programmes.
Benefits: Chance to be part of a long-term sustainable development programme. Fundraising support and access to returned volunteers. Opportunity to travel independently at end of the project. Language training is provided. Further opportunities to remain involved on return to UK with our nationally-recognized training programme.
Training: HPA run two excellent training weekends for volunteers before departure.
Supervision: There is plenty of back-up and support from HPA's in-country staff, and a UK medic and engineer are with the group the whole time.
Interview details: Places on the programme are offered after a selection weekend held in Derbyshire.
Charity number: 1060753
Worldwide placements: *Africa* (Tanzania).

HEIMSONDERSCHULE BRUCKFELDEN
Adalbert Stifter Weg 3
Bruckfelden/Frickingen
D-88699 Frickingen
Germany

Tel: 00 49 7554 8173
Fax: 00 49 7554 8178
Contact: Ulrich Becker

Heimsonderschule Bruckfelden is a boarding school community for adolescents with special needs e.g. mental handicap, emotional maladjustment etc. The youngsters attend lessons here in formal, craft and garden education. They also live alongside staff and their families in house communities. Projects include helping either in the house, school or workshop or with land or estate work. Volunteer helpers come from various countries and local schools. We would be happy to integrate a number of British volunteers within our work.

Total projects worldwide: 12
Total UK projects: 0
Starting months: January, April, August, September.
Time required: 2–6 weeks.
Age requirement: 16–25
Causes: Disabled (learning), work camps –

seasonal, young people.
Activities: Agriculture/farming, caring
(general), community work, cooking,
forestry, summer camps, work camps –
seasonal.
Vols under 26 placed each year: 20
When to apply: As early as possible.
Work alone/with others: Generally groups,
occasionally alone.
Volunteers with disabilities: Not possible.
Qualifications: Nil.
Health requirements: There are some
restrictions.
Costs: Travel costs only.
Benefits: Board and lodging.
Nationalities accepted: Only those with valid
visas should apply.
Interview details: Written application only.
Certification: Certificate or reference
provided.
Worldwide placements: *Europe* (Germany).

HELP
(**Humanitarian Educational Long Term
Projects**)
60 The Pleasance
Edinburgh
EH8 9TJ Scotland

Tel: +44 (0) 131 556 9497
Fax: +44 (0) 131 650 6383
e-mail: 9627860@sms.ed.ac.uk
Web: www.eusa.ed.ac.uk/societies/help
Contact: Sarah Beslee or Jonathan Crampin

HELP was founded in 1990 by students of
Edinburgh University. It is a registered
charity sending out volunteers who are
young, unskilled yet enthusiastic, all over the
world during the summer months. You will
work on projects initiated and managed by
the host community and therefore there is no
attempt to impose our plans and objectives
on projects we assist.

Total projects worldwide: 15–20
Total UK projects: 0
Starting months: July, August, September.
Time required: 4–6 weeks.
Age requirement: 18–25
Causes: Children, conservation,
environmental causes, teaching/assisting
(EFL), work camps – seasonal.
Activities: Building/construction, community
work, conservation skills, development issues,
forestry, fundraising, group work,
international aid, manual work, outdoor

skills, social work, summer camps, teaching,
work camps – seasonal.
Vols under 26 placed each year: 150–200
When to apply: By end of January with SAE.
Work alone/with others: With others.
Volunteers with disabilities: Unsuitable as all
projects involve manual work.
Qualifications: None specific but enthusiasm,
adaptability essential. Volunteers must also
be enterprising.
Health requirements: Nil.
Costs: Approximately £210 board and
lodging plus air fare, insurance, own money
= £600 plus. There is a special 'building site'
insurance arranged by HELP and offered to
the volunteer at £50 for 3 months cover.
Benefits: Advice on fundraising, travel,
medical care, equipment. Discounts on
medical supplies, travel and camping items.
Training: Aids awareness programme for
African camps plus voluntary Kiswahili
lessons.
Supervision: Co-ordinator in overall control
of project but supervision usually by same
aged peer only with more experience.
Interview details: Applicants may be
interviewed in Edinburgh.
Certification: Reference on request.
Worldwide placements: *Africa* (Malawi,
Mozambique, South Africa, Tanzania,
Uganda, Zambia, Zimbabwe); *Asia* (India,
Nepal, Pakistan, Philippines); *Central
America* (Mexico); *South America* (Bolivia,
Ecuador, Peru).

HELP THE AGED
16–18 St James' Walk
Clerkenwell Green
London
EC1R 0BE UK

Tel: +44 (0) 20 7253 0253
Fax: +44 (0) 20 7608 3911
Contact: Shelley Woollands

Each Help The Aged shop has one or two
paid shop managers and a team of volunteer
helpers. We are always looking for people
who can spare a morning from 9.00 a.m. to
1.00 p.m., afternoon from 12.50 p.m. to
5.00 p.m. or a full day each week to work in
their local shop. You can become involved in
all aspects of shop work from sorting and
pricing stock to window dressing, operating
the till and serving customers. Facilities are
provided for making tea and coffee.

Volunteers with an offending background may be accepted. It would be left to the Area Manager's decision.

Total projects worldwide: 350
Total UK projects: 350
Starting months: January–December.
Time required: 2–52 weeks.
Age requirement: 16 plus.
Causes: Elderly people.
Activities: Fundraising.
When to apply: All year.
Work alone/with others: With others.
Volunteers with disabilities: Possible.
Qualifications: Nil.
Health requirements: Nil.
Costs: Travel costs.
Benefits: Full training.
Training: We will train you in all aspects of shop work and in Help The Aged's work.
Interview details: Interviews take place at the shop.
Certification: Reference provided.
Charity number: 272786
UK placements: *England* (throughout); *Scotland* (Edinburgh, E. Lothian, W. Lothian); *Northern Ireland* (throughout); *Wales* (Conwy).

HELP THE HANDICAPPED HOLIDAY FUND
147a Camden Road
Tunbridge Wells
Kent
TN1 2RA UK

Tel: +44 (0) 1892 547474
Fax: +44 (0) 1892 524703
e-mail: 3hfund@dial pipex com.
Contact: Peggy King, The Holiday Organizer

Help The Handicapped Holiday Fund specializes in holidays for physically disabled peole and respite for their carers. Volunteers are required to help care for the disabled guests on the holidays with full back-up of a leader and nurse on each holiday. Holidays are for one week. Portugal, Torquay and Norfolk venues are for the elderly; Cyprus, Cornwall adventure holiday and canal boats on the Norfolk Broads for the younger age group. Volunteers with an offending background are accepted.

Total projects worldwide: 10
Total UK projects: 10
Starting months: April–September.

Time required: 1 week.
Age requirement: 18 plus.
Causes: Disabled (physical), holidays for disabled.
Activities: Caring (general).
Vols under 26 placed each year: 50 of a total of 100.
When to apply: As early as possible.
Work alone/with others: Generally with others – always with a back-up.
Costs: Pocket money and personal expenses.
Benefits: Board, accommodation and travel from Tunbridge Wells.
Interview details: No interview necessary.
Charity number: 286306
Worldwide placements: *Europe* (Cyprus, Portugal).
UK placements: *England* (Cornwall, Devon, Norfolk).

HENSHAW'S SOCIETY FOR THE BLIND
John Derby House
88–92 Talbot Road
Old Trafford
Manchester
M16 0GS UK

Tel: +44 (0) 161 872 1234
Contact: Mrs Linda Norbury

Henshaw's Society for the Blind is a registered charity providing a wide range of residential, nursing, education, training, leisure and community care services for people of all ages who are blind or partially sighted across northern England and Wales.

Total projects worldwide: 1
Total UK projects: 1
Starting months: January–December, except October.
Time required: 1–52 weeks (plus).
Age requirement: 18 plus.
Causes: Children, disabled (physical), young people.
Activities: Administration, caring (day), visiting/befriending.
When to apply: All year.
UK placements: *England* (Cheshire, Manchester).

HEREFORDSHIRE NATURE TRUST
Lower House Farm
Ledbury Road
Tupsley
Hereford
HR1 1UT UK

Tel: +44 (0) 1432 356872
Fax: +44 (0) 1432 275489
Contact: Sarah Davies, Conservation
Programmes Manager

For well over 30 years, the Herefordshire
Nature Trust, a registered charity, has been
playing a key role in protecting the heritage
and conserving the wildlife of our county. We
own and manage over 46 nature reserves.
These encompass the best of the county's
natural heritage and include sites that date
back to Saxon times and beyond, like Lea
and Pagets Wood, home of the endangered
dormouse, and the flood-plain hay meadows
of the lower Lugg valley, one of the few
remaining places where the fritillary still
grows. We carry out surveys of the wildlife of
the county. We influence land use by giving
advice on conservation to statutory bodies,
landowners and all with an interest in the
countryside. We encourage a wider
understanding of nature conservation by
education and publicity and place special
importance on our WATCH groups for
children. Despite the Trust's work and
despite increasing interest in conservation and
a national commitment to conserving
biodiversity, many habitats are still under
threat; hedgerows are still being destroyed;
and a recent survey by the Trust has shown
that 70% of the county's herb-rich grasslands
have been lost in the last 15 years.

Total projects worldwide: Varies.
Total UK projects: Varies.
Starting months: January–December, except
October.
Time required: 1–52 weeks (plus).
Age requirement: 16 plus.
Causes: Conservation, environmental causes,
wildlife.
Activities: Conservation skills, outdoor skills,
scientific work.
Vols under 26 placed each year: 2 of a total
of 15.
When to apply: All year.
Work alone/with others: Both.
Volunteers with disabilities: Possible.
Qualifications: None.
Equipment/clothing: Safety clothing
provided.
Health requirements: Some restrictions when
using machinery.
Costs: Nil.
Benefits: Travel costs and NVQs.

Interview details: Interviews take place at
Herefordshire Nature Trust offices.
Certification: NVQs provided.
Charity number: 220173
UK placements: England (Herefordshire).

HERTFORDSHIRE ACTION ON DISABILITY

The Woodside Centre
The Commons
Welwyn Garden City
Hertfordshire
AL7 4DD UK

Tel: +44 (0) 1707 324581
Fax: +44 (0) 1707 371297
e-mail: herts_action@dis.pipex.com
Web: www.hertsaction.dial.pipex.com
Contact: Mrs A. Waterfield, Chief Executive

For over 30 years Hertfordshire Action on
Disability (HAD) has aimed to meet the
needs of the disabled in Hertfordshire with
services including financial support,
counselling, equipment exhibitions and hire,
and driving instruction in a fully adapted car.
The association also has its own hotel at
Clacton-on-Sea. About 100 volunteers are
needed annually to assist disabled people on
holiday for two-week periods from March to
November. Free return coach travel is
provided from the Woodside Centre to
Clacton. Further details (an information pack
and Holiday Fact Sheets 1–10) can be
obtained by sending a 75p postage stamp to
the above address. Volunteers are also needed
at the Woodside Centre for general office
duties and meeting and greeting disabled
people coming for assistance.Volunteers with
an offending background may be accepted.

Total projects worldwide: Numerous.
Total UK projects: Numerous.
Starting months: January–November.
Time required: 2–52 weeks (plus).
Age requirement: 18 plus.
Causes: Disabled (physical), elderly people,
holidays for disabled.
Activities: Administration, caring (general
and residential), fundraising, library/resource
centres.
Vols under 26 placed each year: Few of a
total of 300.
When to apply: As early as possible.
Work alone/with others: With others.
Volunteers with disabilities: Possible.
Qualifications: Nil.

Health requirements: Nil.
Costs: Nil.
Benefits: Travel and board if volunteering for hotel in Clacton. We have public liability insurance.
Training: Induction plus how we expect our guests to be treated.
Supervision: By hotel manager and assistant manager.
Interview details: Interviews take place at the Woodside Centre and at Clacton.
Certification: Reference or certificate provided.
Charity number: 1059015

HERTFORDSHIRE AND MIDDLESEX WILDLIFE TRUST
Grebe House
St Michael's Street
St Albans
Hertfordshire
AL3 4SN UK

Tel: +44 (0) 1727 858901
Fax: +44 (0) 1727 854542
Contact: The Director

Hertfordshire and Middlesex Wildlife Trust is a member of the Wildlife Trusts, a national partnership of 47 county trusts. For more details of the Wildlife Trusts, see the entry under Cornwall Wildlife Trust.

Total projects worldwide: 1
Total UK projects: 1
Starting months: January–December.
Time required: 1–52 weeks (plus).
Age requirement: 12 plus.
Causes: Conservation, environmental causes, wildlife.
Activities: Conservation skills.
When to apply: All year.
Work alone/with others: Both.
Qualifications: Nil.
Equipment/clothing: Casual Work clothes, waterproofs, stout boots for outdoor work. Protective safety gear is provided.
Health requirements: Anti-tetanus innoculation recommended.
Costs: Bring your own packed lunch.
Benefits: Out-of-pocket expenses.
UK placements: *England* (Hertfordshire).

HOGGANVIK LANDSBY
N-4210 Vikedal
Norway
Tel: 00 47 53 760 274

Fax: 00 47 53 760 408
Contact: Medarbeider Ansvarlig

Hogganvik Landsby is a Camphill village community with adults. Volunteers with an offending background are not ususaly accepted but each case is considered individually.

Total projects worldwide: 1
Total UK projects: 0
Starting months: January–December.
Time required: 12–52 weeks (plus).
Age requirement: 19 plus.
Causes: Disabled (learning).
Activities: Agriculture/farming, arts/crafts, caring (residential), forestry, gardening/horticulture.
Vols under 26 placed each year: 5 of a total of 6.
When to apply: In good time.
Work alone/with others: With others.
Volunteers with disabilities: Possible.
Qualifications: It is not always easy for people to learn Norwegian which is a necessity for a longer stay.
Equipment/clothing: Outside workclothes, free time clothes and some clothes which are respectable.
Health requirements: TB free and an openness about health problems.
Costs: Travel.
Benefits: Board, lodging and modest pocket money.
Interview details: No interview necessary.
Certification: Standard Reference provided.
Worldwide placements: *Europe* (Norway).

HOLIDAYS FOR THE DISABLED
Flat 4
62 Stuart Park
Edinburgh
EH12 8YE UK

Tel: +44 (0) 131 339 8866
e-mail: AliWalker1@aol.com
Contact: Alison Walker

Holidays for the Disabled recruits volunteers annually to help with holidays for the disabled. A large-scale annual holiday for all ages of physically handicapped people is provided. We run a wide range of interesting holidays in the UK and abroad. In addition to holidays at fixed locations there are boating and camping trips. Activities on the holidays include discotheques, swimming, horse riding, wheelchair sports, barbecues and banquets.

Total projects worldwide: 1
Total UK projects: 1
Starting months: May–September.
Time required: 1–2 weeks.
Age requirement: 18–35
Causes: Disabled (physical), holidays for disabled.
Activities: Caring (general), first aid, gardening/horticulture, manual work, music, outdoor skills, social work, sport, summer camps.
When to apply: All year.
Work alone/with others: Both.
Qualifications: Nil.
Equipment/clothing: Outdoor holiday clothes.
Health requirements: Healthy and strong.
Costs: Helpers are asked for contribution of 40% of overseas holidays and 25% of UK holidays. This can be anything from £50–£300 depending on the location.
UK placements: *Scotland* (Edinburgh, E. Lothian, W. Lothian).

HOME FARM TRUST, THE
Merchants House
Wapping Road,
Bristol
BS1 4RW UK

Tel: + 44 (0) 117 927 3746
Fax: + 44 (0) 117 922 5938
e-mail: personnel@hft.org.uk
Web: www.hft.org.uk
Contact: Suzi Walton, Fund Development and Marketing Manager

The Home Farm Trust (HFT) is a national charity and leading provider of care, opportunities and quality of life within the community for people with a learning disability. Our commitment and expertise mean that people, no matter what their disability, are helped to develop their potential. Established in 1962, we now provides services for over 800 people, an advocacy project, supported employment services and a carer support service offering support and guidance to thousands of families with a member waiting for a place within the Trust. Our approach to care is centred on the needs and wishes of the people we are here to help. We give people a say in the kind of home they want, the

activities, training and work they pursue and help them achieve greater levels of independence. People can be helped to acquire new skills and improve their self-confidence and are encouraged to participate in the community through work and college placements. Families also play a very valuable role within HFT's philosophy, supporting our work. The demands on us and our services have never been greater. Most of our funding is through statutory grants and fees, but we rely upon voluntary income in order to maintain the highest quality of care and services and to provide future scheme development.

Total projects worldwide: 15
Total UK projects: 15
Starting months: January–November.
Time required: 1–52 weeks (plus).
Age requirement: 18 plus.
Causes: Disabled (learning).
Activities: Agriculture/farming, arts/crafts, caring (general, day and residential), computers, counselling, development issues, DIY, fundraising, gardening/horticulture, music, outdoor skills, training, visiting/befriending.
When to apply: All year.
Work alone/with others: With others.
Volunteers with disabilities: Possible.
Qualifications: HFT requires a police check on all volunteers.
Health requirements: Nil, but a risk assessment of the placement would be carried out.
Costs: All own costs including travel and board.
Benefits: Subsistence plus some travel costs would be paid whilst travelling with residents. Volunteers are covered for public liability and employer's liability as though they were employees.
Training: Depends on the placement.
Supervision: By relevant staff.
Interview details: Interviews take place at the project/shop/office.
Certification: Written reference provided.
Charity number: 313069
UK placements: *England* (Bedfordshire, Cheshire, Cornwall, Derbyshire, Devon, Essex, Gloucestershire, Herefordshire, Hertfordshire, Kent, Lancashire, London, Manchester, Merseyside, Nottinghamshire, Oxfordshire, Staffordshire, Suffolk, Surrey, Warwickshire, N. Yorkshire, S. Yorkshire,

W. Yorkshire).

HOPE AND HOMES FOR CHILDREN
East Clyffe
Salisbury
Wiltshire
SP3 4LZ UK

Tel: +44 (0) 1722 790111
Fax: +44 (0) 1722 790024
e-mail: HHC@hopeandhomes.org
Web: www.hopeandhomes.org
Contact: Mrs Caroline Cook, Founder/Director

Hope and Homes for Children was started and is run by Colonel Mark Cook OBE and his wife Caroline. Our aim is 'To give hope to children who have nowhere to live, due to war or disaster, by providing them with a home'. The aims are very clear and very specific: to provide homes for orphaned children in areas afflicted by war or disaster; to support the economies of these areas by using local builders and resources; to ensure that our homes are run and maintained by people in the country concerned, respecting local customs and traditions; to insist that the homes are for children of any race, colour or creed. This is a cornerstone of our activities, and we will only embark on projects where this philosophy will be respected.

Total projects worldwide: 13
Total UK projects: 0
Starting months: January–December.
Time required: 24–52 weeks.
Age requirement: 25 plus.
Causes: Children, poor/homeless, refugees, teaching/assisting (nursery, primary, EFL), young people.
Activities: Administration, arts/crafts, caring (general), computers, cooking, group work, international aid, music, sport, teaching.
Vols under 26 placed each year: 1 of a total of 8.
When to apply: Any time – normally six months to one year before but sometimes we need volunteers quite urgently.
Work alone/with others: In pairs and with/alongside local staff.
Volunteers with disabilities: Not possible.
Qualifications: Must love children and have infinite patience. Must have some sort of childcare qualification.
Health requirements: Must be fit.
Costs: £250–£650. Volunteers would

normally fundraise for their required money. Insurance depending on country, is provided by the volunteer.
Benefits: Accommodation, return flight and insurance.
Supervision: By project director in country.
Interview details: Interviews take place at our office in Salisbury.
Certification: Reference or certificate provided.
Charity number: 1040534
Worldwide placements: *Europe* (Albania, Bosnia-Herzegovina, Croatia, Romania).

HOPE UK
25F Copperfield Street
London
SE1 0EN UK

Tel: +44 (0) 20 7928 0848
Fax: +44 (0) 20 7401 3477
e-mail: Sarah@HopeUK.org
Contact: Sarah Brighton

Hope UK needs volunteers to become our local representatives by being involved in alcohol and other drug-related education which involves working with young people and children. This is mostly preventative work and takes at least six months to train. Volunteers with an offending background may be accepted.

Total projects worldwide: Varies.
Total UK projects: Varies.
Starting months: January–December.
Time required: 26–52 weeks (plus).
Age requirement: 18 plus.
Causes: Addicts/ex-addicts, children, conservation, health care/medical, inner city problems, offenders/ex-offenders, teaching/assisting (nursery, primary), young people.
Activities: Caring (general), conservation skills, fundraising, group work, summer camps, teaching, theatre/drama, training.
Vols under 26 placed each year: Varies.
Work alone/with others: Both.
Volunteers with disabilities: Possible.
Qualifications: Nil, but we are a Christian organization.
Health requirements: Nil.
Costs: Volunteers need own car insurance if using for Hope UK business.
Benefits: Training, support, expenses all provided. Public liability and personal accident covered by Hope UK.
Training: A training course accredited by

Open College Network Group or individual face-to-face meetings and sessions.
Supervision: Training co-ordinator, 2 regional representatives, part-time office support and volunteers assigned to member of staff.
Interview details: Interviews take place either at our head office or at an appropriate place near where the applicant lives.
Certification: Reference or certificate provided.
Charity number: 1044475
UK placements: *England* (throughout); *Scotland* (throughout); *Northern Ireland* (throughout); *Wales* (throughout).

HUMAN RIGHTS WATCH
33 Islington High Street
London
N1 9LH UK

Tel: +44 (0) 20 7713 1995
Fax: +44 (0) 20 7713 1800
e-mail: hrwuk@hrw.org
Web: www.hrw.org
Contact: Ms Rachael Noronha, Office Manager

Human Rights Watch conducts regular systematic investigations into human rights abuses in countries all over the world. Volunteers are needed in the office helping out with basic and administrative office tasks.

Total projects worldwide: 1
Total UK projects: 1
Starting months: January–December.
Time required: 4–52 weeks.
Age requirement: 18–30
Causes: Human Rights.
Activities: Administration.
Vols under 26 placed each year: 3 of a total of 4.
When to apply: All year.
Work alone/with others: Alone.
Volunteers with disabilities: Possible.
Qualifications: Basic office skills, word processing etc.
Health requirements: Nil.
Costs: Nil.
Benefits: Travel expenses (within limits) refunded. Basic liability is covered in our insurance.
Certification: Reference on request.
UK placements: *England* (London).

HUMAN SERVICE ALLIANCE (HSA)
3983 Old Greensboro Road
Winston-Salem
North Carolina
27101 USA

Tel: 00 1 910 761 8745
Fax: 00 1 910 722 7882
Contact: Margaret Perkins, Volunteer Co-oordinator

Human Service Alliance (HSA) represents an idea whose time has come: the idea that ordinary human beings, with jobs and families, can do extraordinary things when they work together as a group in service to others. We are a non-profit organization composed completely of volunteers – there is no paid staff whatsoever – providing all services at no charge. HSA represents a reproducible model based on principles and methods that can be taught to people of goodwill throughout the community and the world. You are invited to come and be a part of this unique group expression of love in action. At HSA, volunteers experience the joy of service and the virtually unlimited possibilities for renewal and growth which open up to us when we give of ourselves in service to others. HSA is funded through a variety of sources such as individual donors, churches, clubs and businesses as well as foundation grants. There is no government or religious affiliation. We welcome people of all faiths who are responding to the call of serving others. We offer a full-time, live-in volunteer programme. While HSA has four operational projects, the Care for the Terminally Ill Project (CTI) represents an attempt to respond creatively to the diverse experiences of death. The Center for the Care of the Terminally Ill offers a homelike setting where the 'guests' live out their last days in a loving and supportive environment. Round-the-clock care is provided by trained volunteers from all over the world. People from every walk of life – male, female, young and old come to volunteer at the Center. Many come from across the US and around the world. Everyone contributes in a number of ways. In addition to direct care of clients, there are numerous opportunities for working with your hands under the guidance of skilled professionals – gardening, grounds maintenance, carpentry and general upkeep of the facilities. While providing valuable service to others, you can discover many opportunities for learning hands-on skills. No prior special training is required. Of course, if someone has had prior training or experience, their skills are most welcome.

Total projects worldwide: 4
Total UK projects: 0
Starting months: January–December.
Time required: 2–52 weeks.
Age requirement: 16 plus.
Causes: Aids/HIV, children, disabled (learning and physical), elderly people, health care/medical.
Activities: Administration, building/construction, caring (general, day and residential), computers, cooking, gardening/horticulture, manual work.
Vols under 26 placed each year: 20–25
When to apply: All year – application process takes 4–6 wks.
Work alone/with others: With others.
Volunteers with disabilities: Not possible.
Qualifications: Must speak fluent English.
Health requirements: Nil.
Costs: Air fares, travel, insurance, pocket money and all expenses.
Benefits: Volunteers who commit to a specific period of time of service (minimum of two weeks) receive meals and a place to stay at the HSA facility at no charge. Applicants must arrange insurance themselves.
Training: Excellent training is provided to all who volunteer.
Supervision: Excellent supervision is provided to all who volunteer.
Interview details: Applicants for volunteer projects are interviewed by telephone.
Worldwide placements: *North America* (USA).

I

IFJUSAGI IRODA/WWOOF
Godollo ATE
2103 Prater Karoly u. 1
Hungary

Tel: 00 36 28 310 200
Fax: 00 36 28 310 804

Ifjusagi Iroda/WWOOF places volunteer

farm workers on organic farms and gardens in Hungary. Work can include weeding, animal husbandry and helping with the harvest. 8–10 hours' work per day, five days per week.

Total projects worldwide: 1
Total UK projects: 0
Starting months: April–October.
Time required: 2–52 weeks.
Age requirement: 14 plus.
Causes: Animal welfare, conservation, environmental causes.
Activities: Agriculture/farming, conservation skills, gardening/horticulture.
When to apply: As early as possible.
Work alone/with others: Generally with others.
Qualifications: English or German speakers. Knowledge of Russian useful.
Health requirements: Anti-tetanus injection.
Benefits: Food and accommodation but no pocket money.
Worldwide placements: *Europe* (Hungary).

IJGD (INTERNATIONALE JUGENDGEMEINSCHAFT DIENSTE EV)
Kaiserstrasse 43
D-53113 Bonn
Germany

Tel: 00 49 228 2280011
Fax: 00 49 228 2280024
e-mail: ijgd@comlink.org
Web: www.ijgd.de
Contact: The Secretary General

The IJGD needs volunteers to work on summer projects such as environmental protection, the restoration of educational centres, and to assist with city fringe recreational activities. 30 hours' work per week.

Total projects worldwide: 12
Total UK projects: 0
Starting months: June–September.
Time required: 3–52 weeks.
Age requirement: 16–25
Causes: Archaeology, conservation, elderly people, environmental causes, work camps – seasonal.
Activities: Arts/crafts, building/construction, conservation skills, forestry, gardening/horticulture, manual work, social work, work camps – seasonal.
Vols under 26 placed each year: 6000

When to apply: As soon as possible.
Work alone/with others: With others.
Qualifications: Knowledge of German only required on social projects.
Costs: Travel expenses. For health, third party, accidents (emergency treatment), volunteers should have E111 personal insurance.
Benefits: Free board and accommodation and insurance.
Supervision: By group leaders and work instructors.
Interview details: No interview necessary.
Worldwide placements: *Africa* (Morocco, Sierra Leone, Togo, Tunisia, Zimbabwe); *Asia* (India, Indonesia, Japan, Korea (South), Nepal); *Europe* (Armenia, Belarus, Belgium, Bulgaria, Czech Republic, Denmark, Estonia, Finland, France, Germany, Greece, Italy, Lithuania, Netherlands, Poland, Russia, Slovakia, Spain, Turkey, Ukraine); *North America* (USA); *Central America* (Mexico).

ILOS-TANZANIA
Oysterbay
Karume Road
PO Box 6995
Dar es Salaam
Tanzania

Tel: 00 255 022 245 1079
Fax: 00 255 022 211 2572
e-mail: ilos-tz@cc.udsm.ac.tz
Contact: Mr Stan Tinsh Bash, Executive Director

ILOS is a non-government organization which deals with 'education for human development without borders'. It was established in 1989 with its main office in Dar es Salaam. From here it runs other centres countrywide including Dar es Salaam, Zanzibar, Arusha, Mwanza, Kagera, Kigoma, Iringa and Morogoro. The education programmes range from kindergarten, primary, secondary to adult education. We offer language training and translation programmes to adults, organizations and various diplomatic missions such as UNDP, USAID, UNHCR, UNICEF, NORAD, SIDA, WHO. The languages are English, French, German, Spanish, Italian, Portuguese, Arabic, Kiswahili, Japanese and any other according to demand. The main aim on language training is to bring the world to work closely together without any language barriers.

Moreover, ILOS is the authorized examination centre for Cambridge University in Tanzania. We run student exchange programmes with some schools in UK, France, USA, Switzerland, Germany and Japan. ILOS formal programmes are meant to promote education for girls, especially those orphaned by HIV/Aids. These children are exempted from paying school fees in order that they may study at ILOS English Medium Nursery Schools countrywide, ILOS Primary School in Zanzibar and ILOS Secondary School in Dar es Salaam. ILOS was (1994–6) an implementing partner with UNHCR running the education programmes for refugee children in northern Tanzania. Presently we are engaged in rehabilitation programmes for the areas most affected by refugee influx. These programmes include: renewable energy, environment, water supply and sanitation, health care and counselling, women empowerment, promotion of handcraft and heritage, education on HIV/Aids and agriculture. Volunteers are placed in schools or in one of the integrated community service programmes. In order to make these programmes sustainable, we also need volunteers with fundraising skills and computer skills to assist in the management.

Total projects worldwide: 5
Total UK projects: 0
Starting months: January, February.
Time required: 12–52 weeks.
Age requirement: 22 plus.
Causes: Aids/HIV, architecture, children, conservation, environmental causes, health care/medical, heritage, poor/homeless, refugees, teaching/assisting (nursery, primary, secondary, mature, EFL), work camps – seasonal, young people.
Activities: Administration, agriculture/farming, arts/crafts, community work, computers, conservation skills, cooking, counselling, development issues, first aid, fundraising, gardening/horticulture, international aid, library/resource centres, manual work, marketing/publicity, music, outdoor skills, scientific work, social work, sport, summer camps, teaching, technical skills, theatre/drama, training, translating, work camps – seasonal.
Vols under 26 placed each year: 4 of a total of 10.
When to apply: September–November.
Work alone/with others: With other young

volunteers.
Volunteers with disabilities: Not possible.
Qualifications: Driving licence, language ability. Teachers need a first degree in order to obtain a work permit. Other community services volunteers need a diploma/qualification in the relevant field.
Equipment/clothing: Formal clothing during work sessions, casual clothing during free time.
Health requirements: Should be physically fit.
Costs: Return air fare, health, travel and personal insurance.
Benefits: $100 per month for meals and other needs. Accommodation.
Training: Swahili and cultural orientation training provided.
Supervision: Volunteers are paired to local staff and programme head i.e. headmistress, field officer, co-ordinator etc.
Interview details: Interviews are by telephone or special arrangement in the UK or USA.
Certification: Certificate of Service provided.
Charity number: S.16350
Worldwide placements: *Africa* (Tanzania).

IMPERIAL CANCER RESEARCH FUND
7400 The Quorum
Oxford Business Park North
Garsington Road
Oxford
OX4 2JZ UK

Tel: +44 (0) 1823 669468
Fax: +44 (0) 1823 669468
e-mail: Dawn.harrison@icrf.icnet.uk
Web: www.Dawn.harrison@icrf.icnet.uk
Contact: Dawn Harrison, Area Fundraising Manager

The Imperial Cancer Research Fund is dedicated to the prevention, treatment and cure of all forms of cancer, whilst relying almost entirely on voluntary contributions. Volunteers are needed to help in all kinds of administrative and fund raising activities.

Total projects worldwide: Varies.
Total UK projects: Varies.
Starting months: January–December.
Time required: 1–52 weeks (plus).
Age requirement: 18 plus.
Causes: Health care/medical.
Activities: Administration, campaigning, computers, fundraising.
Vols under 26 placed each year: Too many to count.

When to apply: All year.
Work alone/with others: Both.
Volunteers with disabilities: Possible.
Qualifications: Nil.
Health requirements: Nil.
Costs: Nil. We provide third party and public liability insurance but volunteers taking part in events should provide their own insurance.
Training: Provided for voluntary work in the regional offices.
Supervision: At all times.
Charity number: 209631
UK placements: *England* (throughout); *Scotland* (throughout); *Wales* (throughout).

INDEPENDENT LIVING ALTERNATIVES
Trafalgar House
Grenville Place
London
NW7 3SA UK

Tel: +44 (0) 20 8906 9265
Fax: +44 (0) 20 8906 9265
e-mail: ila@cwcom.net
Web: www.ILA.mcmail.com
Contact: Tracey Jannaway

Independent Living Alternatives is a voluntary organization managed by people with disabilities. We aim to facilitate freedom in living for people with physical disabilities in the London boroughs. We recruit full-time volunteers to enable people who require physical support to be independent in the community to take full control of their own lives. We recruit and place voluntary personal care assistants to provide support, such as cooking, cleaning, driving, etc., on a one-to-one basis through a philosophy of equality and interdependency. We need full-time volunteers, who have four months to spare, to provide physical support to people with physical disabilities in the London area. In return you would receive £63.50 per week living expenses and free accommodation (no bills). No experience is necessary. You would receive support as and when required and be able to participate in the running of the organization and to attend workshops on volunteering issues. We also provide support, advocacy and advice to disabled people and campaign to raise the awareness of disability issues around independent living. We produce the publications *A Strategy for Independent Living in London* and *Independent Living Through Personal Assistance*. Volunteers with an offending background will be accepted depending on when, where, how etc.

Total projects worldwide: 20
Total UK projects: 20
Starting months: January–December.
Time required: 21–52 weeks.
Age requirement: 18 plus.
Causes: Disabled (physical).
Activities: Caring (general), counselling, driving, social work.
Vols under 26 placed each year: 25–35 of a total of 50.
When to apply: All year.
Work alone/with others: Alone but live with others in time off.
Volunteers with disabilities: Possible.
Qualifications: Driving licence useful and English essential but no experience necessary.
Health requirements: Nil.
Costs: No direct costs, but enquire. ILA insurance covers UK nationals, volunteers from overseas must take out health and travel insurance. Employer's liability insurance is paid by us.
Benefits: Accommodation plus £63.50 per week plus expenses.
Training: On-site with service user. All training is provided to new volunteers.
Supervision: On demand by phone/in person/internet. Regular volunteer meetings.
Interview details: Interviews are conducted in ILA London office – can be by phone if neccesary.
Certification: Reference provided.
Charity number: 802198
UK placements: *England* (Essex, London).

INDEPENDENT LIVING, LEWISHAM SOCIAL CARE AND HEALTH
Lewisham Social Care and Health
Louise House
Dartmouth Road
Forest Hill
London
SE23 3HZ UK

Tel: +44 (0) 20 8314 7239
Fax: +44 (0) 20 8314 3014
e-mail: kensmith@lewisham.gov.uk
Contact: Kenneth Smith, Project Supervisor

Independent Living enables severely disabled people to hold on to their civil rights. Volunteer helpers help this process by being the arms and legs of the person they are assisting. Each disabled person (ILS user) has two or three volunteers working directly for him or her. Assistance with bodily functions, e.g. eating, toileting, bathing, is usually required but the volunteers can also help to facilitate social activity. Volunteers can find their experience is of value in getting paid work in the caring professions and, importantly, teaches them that people are disabled by their environment rather than by their impairment. Volunteers with an offending background are accepted – police checks made anyway. We will try to sponsor visas or work permits if required by UK government. Preferred minimum placement is six months. Placements can be extended up to two years.

Total projects worldwide: 3
Total UK projects: 3
Starting months: January–December.
Time required: 26–52 weeks (plus).
Age requirement: 17 plus.
Causes: Disabled (physical), human rights.
Activities: Caring (general), community work, cooking.
Vols under 26 placed each year: 11 of a total of 12.
When to apply: All year.
Work alone/with others: On own but as part of a team of 2 or 3.
Volunteers with disabilities: Possible, depending on ability.
Qualifications: Nil.
Health requirements: Must be capable of lifting without harming user or themself.
Costs: Nil.
Benefits: Accommodation, £23 pocket money plus £37 food per week plus £15 per month clothing/leisure. All bills paid including free local telephone calls. Insurance cover provided by disabled person's household insurance policy.
Training: By disabled person being assisted.
Supervision: Support available from Lewisham Social Care and Health.
Interview details: Interviews are conducted in London office – can be by phone if neccesary.
Certification: Reference provided.
UK placements: *England* (London).

INDIA DEVELOPMENT GROUP (UK) LTD
68 Downlands Road
Purley
Surrey

CR8 4JF UK

Tel: +44 (0) 20 8668 3161
Fax: +44 (0) 20 8660 8541
e-mail: idguk@clara.co.uk
Web: www.welcome.to/idg
Contact: Mr Surur Hoda

The India Development Group (UK) Ltd (IDG) aims to alleviate rural poverty in India by trying to enhance personal income through village-based mini industries, using appropriate and sustainable forms of technology. To this end IDG (UK) Ltd has helped to set up two associate organizations in India: (a) The Appropriate Technology Development Association (ATDA – founded in 1975) is a research and implementation agency; (b) The Schumacher Institute of Appropriate Technology (SIAT – founded in 1988) provides training in equipment using such technology and other service areas identified from the greatest needs as rural people, such as social forestry, weaving, primary health care etc. The IDG (India chapter) is currently carrying out the women's empowerment project funded by National Lotteries Charities Board.

Total projects worldwide: 5
Total UK projects: 0
Starting months: January–December.
Time required: 12–52 weeks (plus).
Age requirement: 18 plus.
Causes: Aids/HIV, environmental causes, health care/medical, human rights, poor/homeless, teaching/assisting (nursery, primary, secondary), unemployed, young people.
Activities: Agriculture/farming, building/construction, community work, development issues, first aid, forestry, fundraising, social work, teaching, technical skills, training.
Vols under 26 placed each year: Varies.
When to apply: All year.
Work alone/with others: With others or alone, depending on project.
Volunteers with disabilities: Not possible.
Qualifications: Preferably at least A level. Specialist/vocational qualifications and skills relevant to projects preferred.
Equipment/clothing: May be specific to project.
Health requirements: In good health.
Costs: Approximately £110 per month plus air fare to India, visas, innoculations, personal insurance etc.

Benefits: Friendly project teams, secure living environment, meeting other volunteers, experiencing different culture, learning new language etc.
Training: General briefing.
Supervision: Supervisors/project team are provided in the area of specialization.
Interview details: Interviews take place at our office in England.
Certification: Reference if requested.
Charity number: 291167
Worldwide placements: *Asia* (India).

INDIAN VOLUNTEERS FOR COMMUNITY SERVICE (IVCS)

12 Eastleigh Avenue
Harrow
Middlesex
HA2 0UF UK

Tel: +44 (0) 20 8864 4740
e-mail: enquiries@ivcs.org.uk
Web: www.ivcs.org.uk
Contact: General Secretary

The Indian Volunteers for Community Service programme is intended for members of IVCS over the age of 18 who are interested in going to India but want to be more than just tourists. It gives them an opportunity to meet rural Indians and learn about their culture. Under this scheme, project visitors can spend up to six months living in a rural development project in India, experiencing life in the local community and participating in rural development work.

Total projects worldwide: 22
Total UK projects: 0
Starting months: January–March, September–November.
Time required: 3–26 weeks.
Age requirement: 18 plus.
Causes: Children, health care/medical, poor/homeless, teaching/assisting (nursery, primary, secondary, EFL).
Activities: Administration, agriculture/farming, arts/crafts, computers, development issues, fundraising, gardening/horticulture, group work, library/resource centres, music, newsletter/journalism, research, teaching, technical skills.
Vols under 26 placed each year: 39 of a total of 50.
When to apply: 4 months before intended departure date.
Work alone/with others: Both.

Volunteers with disabilities: Not possible.
Qualifications: Nil.
Health requirements: Innoculations necessary.
Costs: Travel and personal expenses, plus
membership £15. Orientation in UK plus 3
weeks' orientation in India £160. Further
stays at projects in India £3 a day board and
lodging. Travel insurance.
Benefits: Opportunity to absorb the culture
of India.
Training: Orientation day (London) and 3
weeks orientation in India.
Supervision: Project staff supervise volunteers
during 3 week orientation.
Interview details: Prospective volunteers are
interviewed in London and must attend an
orientation day in London.
Certification: Certificate or reference
provided.
Charity number: 285872
Worldwide placements: *Asia* (India).
UK placements: *England* (London).

INFORMATION FOR ACTION
PO Box 1040
West Leederville
Western Australia 6901

Tel: 00 61 8 9228 0395
e-mail: rowland@informaction.org
Web: www.informaction.org
Contact: Dr Rowland Benjamin

Informaction is a free automated lobbying
service for anyone interested in the
environment. The website enables people to
contact their leaders (governments and
companies worldwide) easily and quickly and
ask them to respect the environment. The
work volunteers do on the website depends
on their level of skill and interest in the
environment. It may include scanning; word
processing; programming; data entry; creating
animations; creating sound files; searching the
net, our own database, CD Roms, telephone
directory or local library for politicians, or
company directors' contact details. We are
currently engaged in increasing our subjects,
letters and contacts; writing an environment
awareness game/quiz for kids; linking with
like-minded groups; advertising; and
maintaining the website. Our goal is basically
to increase lobbying pressure on the world's
leaders, support direct action and provide
ideas for individual change.

Total projects worldwide: 1

Total UK projects: 0
Starting months: January–December.
Time required: 2–50 weeks.
Age requirement: 20 plus.
Causes: Conservation, environmental causes,
wildlife.
Activities: Administration, campaigning,
computers, conservation skills, library/
resource centres, newsletter/journalism,
research, scientific work.
Vols under 26 placed each year: 1 of a total
of 10.
When to apply: All year.
Work alone/with others: Both.
Volunteers with disabilities: Not possible.
Qualifications: Basic computer skills.
Health requirements: Alert and intelligent.
Costs: Travel, accommodation, food.
Interview details: Prospective volunteers are
only interviewed by telephone or e-mail.
Certification: Certificate or reference provided
on request.
Worldwide placements: *Australasia*
(Australia).

INNER CITIES YOUNG PEOPLE'S PROJECT
15 St Mary's Walk
Lambeth
London
SE11 4UA UK

Tel: +44 (0) 20 7582 7231
Fax: +44 (0) 20 7582 7231
e-mail: mth.icypp@talk21.com
Contact: Martin Hine, The Director

Among its activities, the Inner Cities Young
People's Project organizes volunteers to help
with Inner City Play Scheme. These schemes
are designed to provide meaningful activities
for inner city children during the long
summer holiday.

Total projects worldwide: 20
Total UK projects: 20
Starting months: July, August.
Time required: 1–5 weeks.
Age requirement: 16–25
Causes: Children, inner city problems,
teaching/assisting (nursery, primary), young
people.
Activities: Arts/crafts, community work,
teaching.
Vols under 26 placed each year: 200
When to apply: As early as possible but
generally by 15 June.

Work alone/with others: With others.
Volunteers with disabilities: Possible.
Qualifications: Sporting skills are often useful.
Health requirements: Nil.
Costs: Travel and pocket money only.
Benefits: Financial help with travelling available when necessary. We have full insurance cover.
Training: This is provided by the holiday projects themselves.
Supervision: Provided by the project youth workers/leaders.
Certification: Certificate or reference provided sometimes.
UK placements: *England* (Bristol, London, Manchester, Merseyside).

INNISFREE VILLAGE
5505 Walnut Level Road
Crozet
Virginia 22932
USA

Tel: 00 1 804 823 5400
Fax: 00 1 804 823 5027
e-mail: innisfreevillage@prodigy.net
Web: www.avenue.org/innisfree/
Contact: Nancy Chappell

Innisfree Village is a life-sharing community with adults who have mental disabilities and the volunteers who come from all over the world to share a year of their lives with us. Volunteers also work in our weavery, woodshop, bakery, kitchen and gardens.

Total projects worldwide: 1
Total UK projects: 0
Starting months: January–December.
Time required: 1–52 weeks.
Age requirement: 21 plus.
Causes: Disabled (learning and physical), health care/medical, teaching/assisting work camps – seasonal.
Activities: Agriculture/farming, arts/crafts, caring (residential), cooking, driving, gardening/horticulture, group work, sport, teaching, training, work camps – seasonal.
Vols under 26 placed each year: 9 of a total of 15.
When to apply: All year.
Work alone/with others: With others.
Volunteers with disabilities: Difficult.
Qualifications: Related experience or college graduates, fluent English, patience, good sense of humour.

Health requirements: Chest X-ray to prove free from TB.
Costs: Travel costs return to USA.
Benefits: Board/lodging,US$215 per month, medical insurance (not pre-existing conditions), 15 days' holiday. We provide medical insurance for all volunteers staying more than 6 months.
Training: One month orientation.
Supervision: After one month volunteers are working in teams of 2–4. Support by long-term staff at all times.
Interview details: No interview necessary – there is a one month trial period.
Certification: Reference on request after 1 year's voluntary work.
Worldwide placements: *North America* (USA).

INSIGHT NEPAL
PO Box 489
Zero K.M.
Pokhara
Kaski
Nepal

Tel: 00 977 61 30266
e-mail: insight@mos.com.np
Web: www.south-asia.com/insight
Contact: Naresh M. Shrestha, Director

Insight Nepal was established not only to introduce participants to Nepal's diverse geographical and cultural environment, but also to establish and foster an awareness and understanding of cultural differences through experience. This placement scheme is designed to leave the participant with more than photographs. The participant will experience new skills, confidence and perspectives to create a new way of viewing the world by participating in a variety of programmes that are offered. Placement for Volunteer Service Work is one of these programmes. The main objective of this programme is to provide various opportunities to those who are keenly interested in gaining experience in a new and different world by contributing their time and skills to benefit worthwhile community service groups throughout the Kingdom. Insight Nepal believes that serving mankind is one of the most worthwhile experiences a person can have. Our other objective is to help those who are looking for an opportunity to reach people and community groups who are in need of their skills. Furthermore, it will provide for those who are also interested in experiencing new social and cultural aspects of urban and rural life in Nepal.

Total projects worldwide: 1
Total UK projects: 0
Starting months: January–December.
Time required: 12–16 weeks.
Age requirement: 18 plus.
Causes: Children, disabled (physical), environmental causes, health care/medical, teaching/assisting (nursery, primary, secondary, mature, EFL).
Activities: Administration, agriculture/farming, community work, computers, counselling, development issues, fundraising, music, outdoor skills, research, social work, sport, teaching, technical skills, training.
Vols under 26 placed each year: 30 of a total of 50.
When to apply: Up to 8 weeks in advance.
Work alone/with others: Alone or in pairs.
Volunteers with disabilities: Possible.
Qualifications: Educated to A- level. Working experience is desirable. Volunteers should be flexible and willing to immerse themselves in another culture.
Equipment/clothing: Dependent on work placement.
Health requirements: Physically fit and immunized against certain diseases (refer to your GP).
Costs: US$800 programme fee plus US$30 application fee plus visa fee plus fares. Volunteers are responsible for insurance.
Benefits: Half board accommodation. 1 week language/cultural training. 1 week village trip. 3-day jungle safari.
Training: Nepali language training, cross-cultural orientation, Nepali home-stay and lectures about Nepal.
Supervision: Insight Nepal organize supervision of volunteers during placement period, as and when necessary.
Interview details: Interview not necessary.
Certification: Reference from the volunteer's placement.
Worldwide placements: *Asia* (Nepal).

INSTITUT D'HISTOIRE
Université du Mans
Avenue O. Messiaen
Le Mans
F-72017 France

Tel: 00 33 2 43 83 31 64
Fax: 00 33 2 43 83 31 44
Contact: Annie Renoux

Institut d'Histoire needs volunteers to assist on archaeological digs: eight hour day, five and a half day week.

Total projects worldwide: 1
Starting months: July.
Time required: 3–52 weeks.
Age requirement: 18 plus.
Causes: Archaeology, heritage.
Activities: Manual work, technical skills.
Vols under 26 placed each year: 20
When to apply: April.
Work alone/with others: With others.
Qualifications: Knowledge of French or English.
Health requirements: Good health.
Benefits: Board and lodging provided free.
Worldwide placements: *Europe* (France).

INSTITUTE OF CULTURAL AFFAIRS, THE
P O Box 71
Manchester
M15 5BE UK

e-mail: vsp-yfb@ica-uk.org.uk
Web: www.ica-uk.org.uk
Contact: The VSP Co-ordinator

The Volunteer Service Programme of the Institute of Cultural Affairs (ICA) is a highly participatory programme for all those interested in volunteering overseas. It offers short courses for the orientation, training and preparation of volunteers, and a small number of placements each year, with local development organizations worldwide, on projects that emphasize community participation and self-help initiative. The programme has trained and placed over 300 UK volunteers since 1981. It is now run in the UK and the Netherlands by a network of returned volunteers.

Total projects worldwide: 50
Total UK projects: 0
Starting months: January–December.
Time required: 39–52 weeks.
Age requirement: 18 plus.
Causes: Aids/HIV, children, conservation, elderly people, environmental causes, health care/medical, human rights, inner city problems, poor/homeless, refugees, teaching/

assisting (nursery, primary, mature, EFL), unemployed, young people.
Activities: Accountancy, administration, agriculture/farming, arts/crafts, campaigning, community work, computers, conservation skills, development issues, driving, forestry, fundraising, gardening/horticulture, group work, international aid, library/resource centres, marketing/publicity, newsletter/journalism, research, social work, teaching, technical skills, theatre/drama, training, translating.
Vols under 26 placed each year: 10 of a total of 16.
When to apply: Before July each year.
Work alone/with others: With host organizations.
Volunteers with disabilities: Possible.
Qualifications: Nil.
Health requirements: Nil.
Costs: Variable according to placement. Generally £2,000–£4,000 total including training, travel, insurance etc.
Benefits: Scholarships of up to £500 available.
Training: Orientation weekend and foundation course. Required pre-departure training takes place only between May and October.
Supervision: Dependent on placement.
Interview details: Volunteer orientation weekends in the UK in May, June and July.
Certification: Certificate or reference provided – after completed training.
Charity number: 293086
Worldwide placements: *Africa* (Burkina Faso, Cameroon, Ivory Coast, Egypt, Gambia, Ghana, Kenya, Mali, Mauritania, Namibia, Nigeria, Reunion, Senegal, South Africa, Tanzania, Uganda, Zambia, Zimbabwe); *Asia* (Bangladesh, Cambodia, China, Hong Kong, India, Indonesia, Japan, Jordan, Korea (South), Lebanon, Malaysia, Nepal, Pakistan, Philippines, Sri Lanka, Taiwan, Thailand); *Australasia* (Australia); *Europe* (Belgium, Bosnia-Herzegovina, Croatia, Netherlands, Portugal, Russia); *North America* (Canada, USA); *Central America* (Belize, Costa Rica, El Salvador, Guatemala, Honduras, Mexico, Netherlands Antilles, Nicaragua); *South America* (Brazil, Chile, Colombia, Ecuador, Peru, Suriname, Venezuela).

INSTITUTE OF SOCIAL ECOLOGY AND TOURISM
Baikalskaya Str.279
Irkutsk
664050 Russia

Tel: 00 3952 259 215 or 430 417
e-mail: bienru@bbc.ru
Contact: Alexander Vlassov, Vice-Director

Institute of Social Ecology and Tourism runs international ecological work camps on the shores of Lake Baikal and welcomes volunteers of all nationalities. Each work camp runs for two weeks between 1 May and 3 October. We hope to see you on the shores of Lake Baikal this summer. There is something for everyone to enjoy in the region. We can arrange a visa for you within three days. It will be valid for three weeks and costs US$10. If you wish to stay longer it is possible to extend your visa.

Total projects worldwide: 1
Total UK projects: 0
Starting months: May–September.
Time required: 2–8 weeks.
Age requirement: 17 plus.
Causes: Conservation, environmental causes.
Activities: Agriculture/farming, building/construction, conservation skills, forestry, gardening/horticulture, group work, international aid, manual work, outdoor skills, summer camps, work camps – seasonal.
When to apply: All year.
Work alone/with others: With others.
Qualifications: Nil.
Health requirements: Good health.
Costs: US$200 per work camp of 2 weeks. Thereafter each week costs US$70. Return travel from your country to Irkutsk. Travel insruance is advisable.
Benefits: All transfers, accommodation in the camp, full board, guide service.
Interview details: No interview necessary.
Worldwide placements: *Europe* (Russia).

INSTITUTO DA JUVENTUDE
Av. da Liberdade 194
6th Floor
1250 Lisboa
Portugal

Tel: 00 351 213 179200 or 170200 or 536947
e-mail: carlos.rapoula@ipj.pt

Contact: Mr Carlos Rapoula

Instituto da Juventude organizes around 37 international work camps each summer. Volunteers are needed to assist with construction and reconstruction work, protection of the natural environment and the protection and restoration of Portugal's cultural heritage.

Total projects worldwide: 1
Total UK projects: 0
Starting months: April–August.
Time required: 2–52 weeks.
Age requirement: 18 plus.
Causes: Conservation, environmental causes, heritage, work camps – seasonal.
Activities: Building/construction, conservation skills, manual work, work camps – seasonal.
Vols under 26 placed each year: 740
When to apply: February or March.
Work alone/with others: With others.
Qualifications: Nil.
Benefits: Board and lodging.
Worldwide placements: *Europe* (Portugal).

INTEGRATED SOCIAL DEVELOPMENT EFFORT (ISDE)
House #485
Road #01, Block-B, Chandgoan R/A
Chittagong – 4212
Bangladesh

Tel: 00 880 31 671727
Fax: 00 880 31 671727
e-mail: isde@ctg.dolphi.net
Contact: S. M. Nazer Hossain, Director

ISDE was established by some like-minded young people of Cox's Bazar in 1987 as a private, non-profit, non-governmental voluntary, development organization to fight illiteracy, ignorance, poverty and hunger and to improve the health of people in the community. Initially it was a local voluntary youth organization but after the devastating cyclone of 1991 ISDE participated in rescue, relief and rehabilitation for the victims with the support of a number of national and international organizations. Resulting from that, it has developed into a professional development organization to serve the poorest of the poor. We are involved in: Micro-Credit for income and employment generation; Non-Formal Education Program: this is responsible for a large increase in the literacy rate in the operational areas; Community-based Primary Health Care Program: for preventative and curative maternal and child health service in 5000 households; Participatory Social Forestry Program: For this coastal disaster-prone zone of the country, social forestation is most important; Nutrition Education and Homestead Gardening Program: 90 village nurseries for year-round vegetable production; Safe Water Supply and Sanitation Programme; Disaster Preparedness and Response Program; Coastal Embankment Maintenance Program; NGO Networking and Partnership Program: to build better understanding on gender, environment and human rights; Tribal Community Development Program: to develop the indigenous tribal ethnic community; Human Rights and Legal Education Program; Coastal Fisheries Community Development; STD/HIV Prevention and Education; Fisheries and Livestock Development Program; Regenerative Agriculture Program; Rural Volunteer Program; Action Against Child and Women Trafficking; Disability and Development Program.

Total projects worldwide: 10
Total UK projects: 0
Starting months: January–December.
Time required: 2–52 weeks.
Age requirement: 20–38
Vols under 26 placed each year: 8 of a total of 20.
When to apply: All year.
Work alone/with others: With others.
Volunteers with disabilities: Disabled volunteers can work in the office, training at the training venue etc and can also work with people with disabilities. ISDE has ongoing programmes for the welfare of disabled people at Moheshkali Island at Cox's Bazar.
Qualifications: None required but any specialization or skill in relevant fields are welcomed and encouraged.
Equipment/clothing: Blanket and personal clothing is required.
Health requirements: Malaria prophylactics and usual travel pills.
Costs: All travel costs. Registration fees of US$40. Food costs. Insurance.
Benefits: Accommodation, local travel costs, cooking facilities.
Training: ISDE provides basic orientation in Bangla language and local culture.

Supervision: The Director is the overall supervisor. Team managers of each project supervise the volunteer.
Nationalities accepted: All nationalities except Israelis.
Interview details: No interview necessary – but CVs are required before a volunteer is accepted.
Certification: Certificate provided.
Charity number: FDR-803
Worldwide placements: *Asia* (Bangladesh).

INTER-ACTION TRUST
HMS President (1918)
Victoria Embankment
London
EC4Y 0HJ UK

Tel: +44 (0) 20 7583 2652
Fax: +44 (0) 20 7583 2840
Contact: Charlotte

Inter-Action Trust is an educational charity which trains inner city and deprived young people in media, computer and office skills.

Total projects worldwide: 1
Total UK projects: 1
Starting months: January–December.
Time required: 1–52 weeks.
Age requirement: 16 plus.
Causes: Inner city problems, young people.
Activities: Administration, manual work, training.
When to apply: All year.
Work alone/with others: With others.
Volunteers with disabilities: Not possible.
Qualifications: Nil.
Health requirements: Nil.
Costs: Nil.
Benefits: Expenses and lunch allowance.
Certification: Reference provided.
UK placements: *England* (London).

INTERCULTURAL YOUTH EXCHANGE
Latin American House
Kingsgate Place
London
NW6 4TA UK

Tel: +44 (0) 20 7681 0983
Fax: +44 (0) 20 7681 0983
e-mail: admin@icye.co.uk
Web: www.icye.co.uk
Contact: Co-ordinator

ICYE (Intercultural Youth Exchange) is an international organization established in 1949 and made up of autonomous national committees in Africa, Latin America, Europe and Asia. Its aims are to break down the barriers that exist between people of different cultures, faiths, ethnic groups and nationalities and to raise awareness of social and environmental issues at home and abroad. Approximately 600 young people around the world take part every year. The programme offers the opportunity for young people to live in another country and to be involved in voluntary social work. Work includes projects dealing with drug rehabilitation, protection of street children, rural and health development, work with the disabled, environmental education, childcare, women's groups, museums and many more. Volunteers with an offending background are considered.

Total projects worldwide: 600
Total UK projects: 0
Starting months: January, July.
Time required: 26–52 weeks.
Age requirement: 18–30
Causes: Addicts/ex-addicts, Aids/HIV, children, conservation, disabled (learning and physical), elderly people, environmental causes, health care/medical, human rights, poor/homeless, refugees, teaching/assisting (nursery, primary, secondary, EFL), young people.
Activities: Administration, agriculture/farming, arts/crafts, caring (general, day and residential), community work, conservation skills, development issues, fundraising, group work, international aid, newsletter/journalism, outdoor skills, social work, teaching, training, translating.
Vols under 26 placed each year: 20 of a total of 25.
When to apply: Before 1 March (late applications accepted).
Work alone/with others: With others.
Volunteers with disabilities: In some countries only. Early application required. Bring assistant if required.
Qualifications: Maturity and flexibility.
Health requirements: Nil.
Costs: £2,850–£3,150 for outside Europe. Free within Europe. Participants may want to arrange insurance for personal belongings.
Benefits: The cost covers preparation, seminars, flight, health and third party liability insurance, board, lodging and pocket money.

Training: Preparation weekend in UK before departure and orientation and language course upon arrival in host country.
Supervision: Volunteers normally have a supervisor at project plus a mentor/contact person from our partner organization in host country.
Nationalities accepted: No restriction for overseas non-European programme. For European progamme the volunteer has to be a national of a European Economic Area country.
Interview details: Open days and interviews arranged in London on a regular basis.
Certification: Certificate or reference provided.
Charity number: 1039310
Worldwide placements: *Africa* (Ghana, Kenya, Nigeria); *Asia* (India, Japan, Korea (South), Nepal, Taiwan); *Australasia* (New Zealand); *Europe* (Austria, Belgium, Denmark, Finland, France, Germany, Iceland, Italy, Poland, Spain, Sweden, Switzerland); *Central America* (Costa Rica, Honduras, Mexico); *South America* (Bolivia, Brazil, Colombia).

INTERNASJONAL DUGNAD
Nordahl Brunsgate 22
0165 Oslo
Norway

Tel: 00 47 22113123
Fax: 00 47 22207119
e-mail: idnorway@os.telia.no

Internasjonal Dugnad organizes work camps for volunteers in Norway. NB All volunteers must apply through:
The Regional Co-ordinator
International Voluntary Service (IVS – South)
Old Hall
East Bergholt
Nr Colchester
Essex CO7 6TQ UK

Tel: +44 (0) 206 298215
Fax: +44 (0) 206 299043
e-mail: ivs@ivsgbsouth.demon.co.uk

Total projects worldwide: 1
Total UK projects: 0
Starting months: January–December.
Time required: 1–16 weeks.
Age requirement: 17 plus.
Causes: Conservation, environmental causes, heritage, work camps – seasonal.

Activities: Conservation skills, group work, manual work, outdoor skills, technical skills, work camps – seasonal.
When to apply: All year.
Work alone/with others: With others.
Qualifications: Nil.
Health requirements: Nil.
Costs: Fares to Norway. Own insurance.
Interview details: Apply to Steve Davies at IVS-South for details.
Worldwide placements: *Europe* (Norway).

INTERNATIONAL CHINA CONCERN
PO Box 265
Tai Po Post Office
Tai Po
Hong Kong

Tel: 00 852 26625103
Fax: 00 852 26625738
e-mail: ICC_HK@compuserve.com
Web: www.ICC-HK.com
Contact: Ramona Bauman, HK Director

International China Concern was begun in January 1993 after the executive director, Mr David J. Gotts, travelled to an orphanage in Southern China to see the conditions that many of China's orphans are living in. At that time it was known that there were few organizations involved in relief work with Chinese orphans and so it was decided that an organization would be set up to encourage those in the West and those in Asia to support these needy children. Initially the main work of ICC was to organize teams of lay and professional people, such as doctors, nurses, physiotherapists and occupational therapists, to visit orphanages in China and to be involved in the rehabilitation of disabled children and also train local workers. This work continues and international teams travel to the orphanages in China every few months. ICC also acts as a channel through which finances, medicines, clothing and rehabilitation equipment can be given to China's orphanages. Much has been done in the last few years. ICC has two other main areas of focus. The first area is to provide rehabilitation services to the mentally and physically disabled orphans in China. In January 1997 Oasis House was established as a joint venture with the Changsha No. 1 Welfare Center in Changsha, Hunan, China. This is a residential rehabilitation, nursing and training centre providing care for 40 of the most needy orphans within the Welfare Center. ICC recently completed successful negotiations with the government in Guanzi Province, China to open a residential school and vocational training centre for physically disabled orphans.

Total projects worldwide: 4
Total UK projects: 0
Starting months: January–December.
Time required: 2–52 weeks.
Age requirement: 16 plus.
Causes: Children, disabled (learning and physical), health care/medical, holidays for disabled, poor/homeless, teaching/assisting (nursery, primary, secondary), work camps – seasonal, young people.
Activities: Accountancy, administration, caring (general, day and residential), computers, development issues, fundraising, group work, music, outdoor skills, religion, social work, summer camps, teaching, technical skills, training, translating.
Vols under 26 placed each year: 60 of a total of 150.
When to apply: Up to 1 month before start date.
Work alone/with others: With others.
Volunteers with disabilities: Possible, each considered individually.
Qualifications: Christian Commitment.
Health requirements: Health form to be completed with application.
Costs: Short term (16 days) £550 (excluding flight to HK). Medium/long term budgets available. All volunteers are expected to be self-financing.
Interview details: Only medium and long term volunteers are interviewed at our UK office: PO Box Ashington, NE63 8YH. Tel/Fax +44 0 1670-505622
e-mail: office@icc-uk2000.freeserve.co.uk.
Certification: Certificate or reference provided.
Charity number: 1068349
Worldwide placements: *Asia* (China, Hong Kong).

INTERNATIONAL ECOLOGICAL CAMP
PO Box 52
665718 Bratski-18
Irkutsk Region
Russia

Tel: 00 3953 364301
Fax: 00 3953 451579

e-mail: tatyana@bratsk.esir.ru
Contact: Belyakova Lyudmila, Director

International Ecological Camp organizes voluntary service work camps and cultural programmes in Siberia which give volunteers the opportunity to come to the heart of Russia and learn the legends, ideas and priorities of the Russians; the reality behind the news stories. Free time is spent swimming in nearby lakes, enjoying the campfire and the forest, sightseeing and experiencing local culture. Food is either cooked by the group or enjoyed at a local café. Each work camp lasts for one month and accommodates 30 people. Travel either by plane Moscow-Bratsk or by plane Moscow-Irkutsk and then train to Bratsk.

Total projects worldwide: 1
Starting months: June–August.
Time required: 4–12 weeks.
Age requirement: 19 plus.
Causes: Environmental causes, heritage, teaching/assisting (EFL).
Activities: Teaching.
Vols under 26 placed each year: 80
When to apply: All year.
Work alone/with others: With others.
Volunteers with disabilities: Work camp not accessible to wheelchairs.
Qualifications: Volunteer workers none. Volunteer leaders needed to lead the work camps must be fluent in Russian, interested in or experienced with the Russian language and culture and they must be TEFL qualified.
Costs: $240 per 4-week work camp. Return travel.
Benefits: Volunteers are met at the airport or at the train station. Accommodation and meals provided.
Worldwide placements: *Europe* (Russia).

INTERNATIONAL EXCHANGE CENTER
35 Ivor Place
London
NW1 6EA UK

Tel: +44 (0) 20 7724 4493
Contact: Patricia Santoriello

International Exchange Center needs camp leaders/sports instructors to work in children's summer camps on the Baltic Sea, and in other locations looking after children aged 8–15 years.

Total projects worldwide: 1

Starting months: July, August.
Time required: 4–12 weeks.
Age requirement: 18–40
Causes: Children, young people.
Activities: Arts/crafts, music, sport, summer camps, translating.
Vols under 26 placed each year: 20
When to apply: 2 months in advance.
Work alone/with others: With others.
Volunteers with disabilities: Not possible.
Qualifications: Energetic and friendly. Basic knowledge of local language helpful.
Health requirements: Some camps require medical certificate.
Costs: Application fee $50 plus cost of travel to camp.
Benefits: Board, lodging and pocket money equal to local counsellors.
Interview details: No interview necessary.
Worldwide placements: *Europe* (Latvia, Lithuania, Russia, Ukraine).

INTERNATIONAL OTTER SURVIVAL FUND

Broadford
Isle of Skye
IV9 9AQ UK

Tel: +44 (0) 1471 822487
Fax: +44 (0) 1471 822487
e-mail: iosf@otter.org
Web: www.otter.org
Contact: Grace Yoxon, Director

The International Otter Survival Fund (IOSF) is the only organization in the world dedicated to the conservation of all 13 species of otter. If you wish to volunteer, contact us for details of our ongoing research projects into the behaviour of otters on the Isle of Skye and elsewhere in the Hebrides.

Total projects worldwide: 4
Total UK projects: 4
Starting months: May–September.
Time required: 1 week.
Age requirement: 17 plus.
Causes: Animal welfare, wildlife.
Activities: Outdoor skills, scientific work.
Vols under 26 placed each year: 10 of a total of 60.
When to apply: Any time.
Work alone/with others: Both.
Volunteers with disabilities: Not possible.
Qualifications: Nil.
Equipment/clothing: No technical equipment but outdoor and walking gear.

Health requirements: Good level of fitness required. Projects require walking over rough ground.
Costs: Varies, from £185.
Benefits: We are responsible for insurance.
Training: Provided.
Supervision: All are supervised.
Interview details: No interview necessary.
Charity number: SCO03875
UK placements: *Scotland* (Western Isles).

INTERNATIONAL PRIMATE PROTECTION LEAGUE, THE

116 Judd Street
London
WC1H 9NS UK

Tel: +44 (0) 20 7837 7227
Fax: +44 (0) 20 7278 3317
e-mail: enquiries@ippl-uk.org
Web: www.ippl-uk.org
Contact: Mr S. Brend

The International Primate Protection League (IPPL) campaigns for the conservation and welfare of all primates. IPPL recruits volunteer staff to assist on conservation projects overseas and at animal sanctuaries in the UK. We look for mature, practical people who are committed to ensuring the well-being of the animals in their care and to the achievement of long-term conservation goals. Volunteers with an offending background may be accepted.

Total projects worldwide: 4
Total UK projects: 3
Starting months: January–December.
Time required: 4–52 weeks.
Age requirement: 24 plus.
Causes: Conservation, wildlife.
Activities: Building/construction, conservation skills, DIY, manual work, research.
Vols under 26 placed each year: 3–4 of a total of 8.
When to apply: All year.
Work alone/with others: With others.
Volunteers with disabilities: Not possible.
Qualifications: Driving licence. Practical experience in DIY, mechanical and/or animal care.
Equipment/clothing: Full briefing on acceptance.
Health requirements: Medical insurance essential for overseas placements. Rabies vaccination advised.

Costs: Membership £7 per year. Subsistence overseas £750 per year. Travel costs. Medical insurance provided by the volunteer.
Benefits: Travel may be subsidized. Overseas sanctuaries offer board and lodging.
Training: For animal care volunteers, prior training at a UK sanctuary is arranged.
Supervision: By experienced adult project manager.
Interview details: Mandatory interviews are held in our London office.
Certification: Written reference provided.
Charity number: 272723
Worldwide placements: *Africa* (Cameroon, Kenya, Nigeria).
UK placements: *England* (Surrey, West Midlands).

INTERNATIONAL VOLUNTARY SERVICE (IVS – N. IRELAND)
122 Great Victoria Street
Belfast
Co. Antrim
BT2 7BG N. Ireland

Tel: +44 (0) 28 9023 8147
Fax: +44 (0) 28 9024 4356
e-mail: ivsni@dnet.co.uk
Web: www.ivsni.dnet.co.uk
Contact: Colin McKinty, The Co-ordinator

The primary object of IVS–NI is to afford opportunities by which men and women, in a spirit of friendship, international understanding and voluntary discipline, without regard to their race, religion, creed or politics are encouraged, and enabled to give to the community, either individually or in groups, effective voluntary service. IVS–NI is a membership organization and that means that our members – participants who have been involved in any or all of the activities, or those who agree with our aims – dictate the work and the direction that IVS–NI takes. Our membership therefore is vital, not only because it lets us know that the work we are involved in is relevant and worthwhile. As a member of IVS–NI, you would have the opportunity to have your say in the future of IVS–NI. Even if you only sympathize with our aims, and do not wish to participate in activities, your support would be welcome. Please note that work in Croatia and Bosnia is not work camps but work with refugees. The minimum age for Africa and Asia is 21. Volunteers with an offending background are accepted.

Total projects worldwide: 400–500
Total UK projects: Approximately 100.
Starting months: January–December.
Time required: 2–52 weeks.
Age requirement: 18 plus.
Causes: Archaeology, architecture, children, conservation, disabled (learning and physical), elderly people, environmental causes, heritage, holidays for disabled, human rights, inner city problems, offenders/ex-offenders, poor/homeless, refugees, teaching/assisting (nursery, primary), unemployed, wildlife, work camps – seasonal, young people.
Activities: Administration, building/construction, campaigning, caring (general), catering, conservation skills, development issues, fundraising, gardening/horticulture, manual work, summer camps, teaching, training, work camps – seasonal.
Vols under 26 placed each year: Approximately 75 of a total of 100.
When to apply: May onwards for work camps.
Work alone/with others: Normally in an international group.
Volunteers with disabilities: Possible.
Qualifications: Nil.
Equipment/clothing: Dependent on work.
Health requirements: Nil.
Costs: Travel costs; registration fee; membership. Apply to branch in own country.
Benefits: International work camps: board and lodging. Long and medium term: board, lodging plus pocket money. Insurance cover is provided during the volunteer's time at the work camp.
Training: Interview plus preparation day detailing issues that are relevant to inter-cultural exchanges.
Supervision: Work camp leader at project.
Interview details: Interviews may be held, depending on the project. If so, in Belfast.
Charity number: 48740
Worldwide placements: *Africa* (Algeria, Ghana, Morocco, Namibia, Senegal, Sierra Leone, Swaziland, Tanzania, Togo, Tunisia, Uganda, Zimbabwe); *Asia* (Bangladesh, India, Japan, Kazakhstan, Korea (South), Lebanon, Malaysia, Mongolia, Nepal, Sri Lanka, Thailand, Turkey); *Australasia* (Australia); *Europe* (Armenia, Austria, Azerbaijan, Belarus, Belgium, Bosnia-

Herzegovina, Bulgaria, Croatia, Czech Republic, Denmark, Estonia, Finland, France, Georgia, Germany, Gibraltar, Greece, Hungary, Iceland, Ireland, Italy, Latvia, Lithuania, Macedonia, Netherlands, Norway, Poland, Portugal, Romania, Russia, Slovakia, Slovenia, Spain, Sweden, Switzerland, Turkey, Ukraine, Yugoslavia); *North America* (Canada, Greenland, USA).
UK placements: *Northern Ireland* (throughout).

INTERNATIONAL VOLUNTARY SERVICE (IVS – North)
Castlehill House
21 Otley Road
Leeds
West Yorkshire
LS6 3AA UK

Tel: +44 (0) 113 230 4600
Fax: +44 (0) 113 230 4610
e-mail: ivsgbn@ivsgbn.demon.co.uk
Web: www.ivsgbn.demon.co.uk
Contact: Col Collier, Regional Co-ordinator

International Voluntary Service works for peace, justice and international understanding through voluntary work. It brings together groups of international volunteers to work on projects of importance to community groups. Volunteers live and work together. Accommodation can be basic and the volunteers live communally, sharing the cooking and household tasks of the camp. In many work camps volunteers are working alongside local volunteers. Summer programmes last for between 2 and 4 weeks. Medium and long-term opportunities are for 3-plus months. Volunteers with an offending background are accepted but they need to inform the placement officer when applying.

Total projects worldwide: 750 plus.
Total UK projects: 40
Starting months: January–December.
Time required: 2–14 weeks.
Age requirement: 16 plus.
Causes: Children, conservation, disabled (physical), elderly people, environmental causes, poor/homeless, refugees, work camps – seasonal.
Activities: Administration, arts/crafts, building/construction, caring (general), conservation skills, development issues, fundraising, gardening/horticulture, manual work, theatre/drama, visiting/befriending, work camps – seasonal.
Vols under 26 placed each year: 280 plus of a total of 400 plus.
When to apply: As soon as possible after listing is available. Early April for summer placements. Any time for medium and long term placements.
Work alone/with others: With others.
Volunteers with disabilities: Welcome but no access for office work.
Qualifications: Nil.
Equipment/clothing: Work clothes and sleeping bag.
Health requirements: Volunteers with a disability need to inform placement officer when applying.
Costs: Membership of IVS, placement fee, travel to project and pocket money. Volunteer must insure their own belongings and take out additional travel insurance.
Benefits: Basic accommodation and food supplied. Basic accident, medical insurance is provided. Follow-up weekend on return.
Training: Preparation days before leaving for project.
Supervision: By professional workers. No supervision in leisure time.
Interview details: Volunteers may be required to attend orientation for certain locations.
Certification: References on request.
Charity number: 275424
Worldwide placements: *Africa* (Morocco, Tunisia); *Asia* (Japan, Lebanon, Turkey); *Australasia* (Australia); *Europe* (Albania, Armenia, Austria, Azerbaijan, Belarus, Belgium, Bosnia-Herzegovina, Bulgaria, Croatia, Czech Republic, Denmark, Estonia, Finland, France, Georgia, Germany, Gibraltar, Greece, Hungary, Iceland, Ireland, Italy, Latvia, Liechtenstein, Lithuania, Luxembourg, Macedonia, Malta, Moldova, Netherlands, Norway, Poland, Portugal, Romania, Russia, Slovakia, Slovenia, Spain, Sweden, Switzerland, Turkey, Ukraine, Yugoslavia); *North America* (Greenland, USA).
UK placements: *England* (throughout); *Scotland* (throughout, except for Orkney Islands); *Northern Ireland* (throughout); *Wales* (throughout).

INTERNATIONAL VOLUNTARY SERVICE (IVS – SCOTLAND)
7 Upper Bow
Edinburgh

EH1 2JN Scotland

Tel: +44 (0) 131 226 6722
Fax: +44 (0) 131 226 6723
e-mail: ivs@ivsgbscot.demon.co.uk
Web: www.ivsgbn.demon.co.uk
Contact: Neil Harrower, Scottish Co-ordinator

IVS is a voluntary organization that exists to provide opportunities for voluntary work for all people, both in this country and abroad, in the belief that this will further international understanding and lead to a more just and peaceful world. IVS–Scotland is the Scottish branch of Service Civil International, a worldwide organization with groups in over 30 countries.

Total projects worldwide: 750
Total UK projects: 45
Starting months: January–December.
Time required: 1–4 weeks.
Age requirement: 16 plus.
Causes: Children, conservation, disabled (learning and physical), environmental causes, holidays for disabled, human rights, inner city problems, poor/homeless, refugees, work camps – seasonal, young people.
Activities: Administration, agriculture/farming, arts/crafts, building/construction, campaigning, caring (general, day and residential), community work, conservation skills, development issues, forestry, fundraising, gardening/horticulture, group work, international aid, manual work, marketing/publicity, music, newsletter/journalism, outdoor skills, social work, sport, summer camps, work camps – seasonal.
Vols under 26 placed each year: 320 of a total of 400.
When to apply: All year.
Work alone/with others: With others.
Volunteers with disabilities: Possible, each case treated individually.
Qualifications: Nil unless specified for special projects.
Equipment/clothing: Sleeping bag and working clothes.
Health requirements: Existing medical conditions may not be covered by our insurance.
Costs: All travel, registration and membership fees of £40–£120 per work camp. Must provide own travel insurance if outside the UK. IVS has an insurance which acts as

supplementary cover if necessary.
Benefits: Board, lodging and insurance cover supplied, and also various social outings.
Training: Preparation days/weekends are optional.
Supervision: Supervision of work provided at all projects.
Interview details: No interview necessary.
Certification: Certificate or reference provided on request.
Charity number: 275424
Worldwide placements: *Africa* (Morocco, Tunisia); *Asia* (Japan, Turkey); *Australasia* (Australia); *Europe* (Albania, Armenia, Austria, Azerbaijan, Belarus, Belgium, Bosnia-Herzegovina, Bulgaria, Croatia, Cyprus, Czech Republic, Denmark, Estonia, Finland, France, Georgia, Germany, Gibraltar, Greece, Hungary, Iceland, Ireland, Italy, Latvia, Liechtenstein, Lithuania, Luxembourg, Macedonia, Malta, Moldova, Netherlands, Norway, Poland, Portugal, Romania, Russia, Slovakia, Slovenia, Spain, Sweden, Switzerland, Turkey, Ukraine, Yugoslavia); *North America* (Canada, Greenland, Saint Pierre-Miquelon, USA).
UK placements: *England* (throughout); *Scotland* (throughout); *Northern Ireland* (throughout); *Wales* (throughout).

INTERNATIONAL VOLUNTARY SERVICE (IVS – South)
Old Hall
East Bergholt
Nr Colchester
CO7 6TQ UK

Tel: +44 (0) 1206 298215
Fax: +44 (0) 1206 299043
e-mail: ivs@ivsgbsouth.demon.co.uk
Contact: Regional Co-ordinator

IVS aims to promote peace, justice and international understanding through voluntary work. IVS is the British branch of Service Civil International (SCI), a worldwide organization with branches in over 30 countries. Our main activity is the organization of work camps. Work camps help to support communities by bringing volunteers to work on useful projects. At the same time they offer opportunities to meet new people, learn new skills and have fun. Each work camp is different, but what they all have in common is that volunteers live and work together in an international group, learning about others' lifestyle and cultures. This experience can have a great impact on people, and influence the rest of their lives. The work varies enormously and can include any of the following: campaigning on issues related to the third world, racism and peace education; working with people with disabilities, children or elderly people in their homes, at day centres or on holiday; ecological and environmental work; women only camps; artistic and cultural camps. Where and when? The length of a work camp can range between two and four weeks. In return for the work, volunteers receive basic food and accommodation free. The work camp group will normally be made up of between six and 20 volunteers from almost as many countries. The volunteers will live and work together sharing the organization of work and domestic arrangements such as cooking and cleaning. Work camps take place wherever there is a project that can benefit from the assistance of volunteers. Most work camps run between June and September and details of these are provided in our summer work camp listing. Other camps take place throughout the year. Volunteers with an offending background are accepted if referred.

Total projects worldwide: 700
Total UK projects: 40
Starting months: January–December.
Time required: 2–21 weeks.
Age requirement: 18 plus.
Causes: Children, conservation, disabled (learning and physical), elderly people, environmental causes, inner city problems, poor/homeless, refugees, work camps – seasonal, young people.
Activities: Administration, arts/crafts, building/construction, campaigning, caring (general), community work, conservation skills, development issues, fundraising, gardening/horticulture, group work, international aid, manual work, outdoor skills, social work, visiting/befriending, work camps – seasonal.
Vols under 26 placed each year: 300
When to apply: All year but for Summer programme from 1 April.
Work alone/with others: With others.
Volunteers with disabilities: Possible.
Qualifications: Nil.
Health requirements: Nil.
Costs: Dependent on type of work – travel to work camp.

Benefits: Board and lodging.
Interview details: No interviews take place.
Certification: No certificate or reference provided.
Charity number: 275424
Worldwide placements: *Africa* (Algeria, Morocco, Tunisia); *Asia* (Japan, Turkey); *Australasia* (Australia); *Europe* (Albania, Armenia, Austria, Azerbaijan, Belarus, Belgium, Bosnia-Herzegovina, Bulgaria, Croatia, Czech Republic, Denmark, Estonia, Finland, France, Georgia, Germany, Gibraltar, Greece, Hungary, Iceland, Ireland, Italy, Latvia, Liechtenstein, Lithuania, Luxembourg, Macedonia, Malta, Moldova, Netherlands, Norway, Poland, Romania, Russia, Slovakia, Slovenia, Spain, Sweden, Switzerland, Turkey, Ukraine, Yugoslavia); *North America* (Canada, Greenland, Saint Pierre-Miquelon, USA).
UK placements: *England* (throughout); *Scotland* (throughout); *Northern Ireland* (throughout); *Wales* (throughout).

INTERNATIONAL VOLUNTEER PROGRAM

210 Post Street
Suite #502
San Francisco
94108 USA

Tel: 00 1 415 477 3667
Fax: 00 1 415 477 3669
e-mail: rjewell@ivpsf.com
Web: www.ivpsf.com
Contact: Rebecca Jewell, Program Director

The International Volunteer Program is a unique project that aims at promoting voluntary work in Europe and the United States. For six weeks volunteers learn how others live and view the world. La Société Française de Bienfaisance Mutuelle instituted the International Volunteer Program in 1991 with the assistance and co-operation of the French Consulate in San Francisco, the University of California at Irvine and le Comité des Jumelages de Troyes. The International Volunteer Program links cultural frontiers by allowing visitors to act as important volunteers and colleagues. This complete cultural immersion helps to open new horizons and foster philanthropy on both community and global levels. In Europe and in the United States, the International Volunteer Program has facilitated this first-hand cultural understanding for hundreds of volunteers and provided volunteer staffing for more than 100 not-for-profit organizations. Volunteers with an offending background may be accepted if they are eligible for a visa.

Total projects worldwide: 10
Total UK projects: 0
Starting months: July.
Time required: 6 weeks.
Age requirement: 18 plus.
Causes: Addicts/ex-addicts, Aids/HIV, animal welfare, children, conservation, disabled (learning and physical), elderly people, environmental causes, health care/medical, holidays for disabled, human rights, inner city problems, poor/homeless, refugees, work camps – seasonal, young people.
Activities: Arts/crafts, building/construction, caring (residential), cooking, counselling, development issues, first aid, gardening/horticulture, group work, international aid, music, outdoor skills, social work, summer camps, theatre/drama, translating, work camps – seasonal.
Vols under 26 placed each year: 19 of a total of 20.
When to apply: Before 25 April.
Work alone/with others: Usually with other young volunteers, when available.
Volunteers with disabilities: Possible.
Qualifications: Volunteers interested in going to France must be proficient in French.
Equipment/clothing: Dependent on the placement. Clothing requirements will be notified at the same time as the placement information is provided.
Health requirements: Nil.
Costs: £845 [or US$1500 or Euro1350] plus personal expenses e.g. stamps, phone calls and independent travel. Volunteers should take out additional medical insurance prior to departure for the US.
Benefits: The cost covers return ticket from London to San Francisco or Los Angeles, transport to the placement and room and board for the six weeks.
Supervision: By staff of the host agency.
Interview details: Interviews by telephone. Those wishing to go to France are interviewed in French.
Certification: Reference or certificate on request.
Worldwide placements: *Europe* (France); *North America* (USA).

INTERNATIONALE BEGEGNUNG IN GEMEINSCHAFTSDIENSTEN e.V.
Schlosserstrasse 28
Stuttgart
D-70180 Germany

Tel: 00 49 711 6491128
Fax: 00 49 711 6409867
e-mail: IBG-work camps@t-online.de
Contact: Christoph Meder or Alejandro Garcia

Internationale Begegnung in Gemeinschaftsdiensten needs volunteers to attend international youth work camps in Germany. Projects include restoring an old castle, environmental protection, children's playschemes, arts and remedial projects. Each work camp consists of a group of about 15 people aged 18–30 from all over the world. Opportunities are available in Africa, the Americas, Asia and many other countries in Europe for non-British nationals. Our current programme will be sent on receipt of two international reply coupons. Besides work camps we have long-term stays up to one year as well.

Total projects worldwide: 4
Total UK projects: 0
Starting months: June–September.
Time required: 1–52 weeks.
Age requirement: 18–27
Causes: Archaeology, children, conservation, disabled (learning and physical), elderly people, environmental causes, holidays for disabled, inner city problems, poor/homeless, refugees, teaching/assisting (primary, EFL), unemployed, wildlife, work camps – seasonal, young people.
Activities: Agriculture/farming, arts/crafts, building/construction, community work, computers, conservation skills, forestry, gardening/horticulture, manual work, music, social work, theatre/drama, work camps – seasonal.
Vols under 26 placed each year: 400
When to apply: April–July.
Work alone/with others: Group of 10–20 international people.
Volunteers with disabilities: Not possible.
Qualifications: Nil.
Equipment/clothing: Working clothes/boots/sleeping bag.
Health requirements: Nil.
Costs: DM250 registration fee plus travel costs and insurance.

Benefits: Board and lodging and parts of leisure activities.
Interview details: No interview necessary.
Certification:
Certificate or reference provided on request.
Worldwide placements: *Europe* (Germany).

INTERNATIONALER BAUORDEN – DEUTSCHER ZWEIG
Postfach 14 38
Liebigstr 23
D-67551 Worms
Germany

Tel: 00 49 62 41 37900 and 37901
Fax: 00 49 62 41 37902
e-mail: bauorden@t-online.de
Web: http://home.t-online.de/home/ibo-d/
Contact: Roswitha Lameli

Internationaler Bauorden – Deutscher Zweig (IBO) was founded in 1953. It aims to realize more justice by building international friendships and social work camps. IBO's motto is 'we help build'. We help through building and renovation works on homes for children, orphans, the elderly, people with disabilities and by building meeting centres for young people. IBO concentrates on people in need of help. The volunteers work on the sites for up to eight hours a day, 40 hours a week. The groups are international.

Total projects worldwide: 60
Total UK projects: 0
Starting months: June–October.
Time required: 3–4 weeks.
Age requirement: 18–25
Causes: Children, disabled (learning and physical), elderly people, holidays for disabled, poor/homeless, refugees, work camps – seasonal, young people.
Activities: Building/construction, manual work, work camps – seasonal.
Vols under 26 placed each year: 120
When to apply: As early as possible.
Work alone/with others: With others.
Volunteers with disabilities: Not possible.
Qualifications: Nil.
Equipment/clothing: Working clothes, closed shoes.
Health requirements: Nil.
Costs: Travel costs to the camp. Health and accident insurance is the responsibility of the volunteer.
Benefits: Board and lodging.
Supervision: On the project by the responsible person.
Certification: Certificate or reference provided on request.
Worldwide placements: *Europe* (Austria, Belarus, Belgium, Croatia, Czech Republic, Denmark, France, Germany, Greece, Hungary, Italy, Lithuania, Moldova, Netherlands, Poland, Portugal, Romania, Russia, Slovakia, Spain, Ukraine).

INTERNATIONALER BUND e.V.
Freiwilliges Soziales Jahr
Rathenauplatz 2
60313 Frankfurt am Main
Germany

Tel: 00 49 69 28 21 71
Fax: 00 49 69 91 39 63 65
e-mail: ibfsj.ffm@t-online.de
Web: www.internationaler-bund.de
Contact: Mr Winfried A. Burkard

Internationaler Bund can offer you work in the Federal Republic of Germany. You can work as a volunteer in a hospital, residential home for the aged or a home for handicapped people. As a volunteer you will assist the staff in all duties which can be performed by non-skilled volunteers: washing the patients, helping them to get dressed and to take their meals, running of errands etc. You'll be fully integrated into the work-flow.Like the rest of the staff, you will be required to work 38.5 hours per week, including some weekends. Your work may be early or late day shift. After six months service you are entitled to two weeks leave. Programmes start in early April and September and you can stay for a period of six or 12 months. In individual cases, exceptions to this schedule may be agreed upon. During your stay you will be given the opportunity to get to know both the country and its people and to extend your knowledge of the German language. When applying please send an application sheet, handwritten curriculum vitae, three photos, medical certificate, certificate giving evidence of your knowledge of German and last school leaving certificate.

Total projects worldwide: 25
Total UK projects: 0
Starting months: April, September.
Time required: 26–52 weeks.
Age requirement: 16–27
Causes: Disabled (learning and physical),

elderly people, health care/medical.
Activities: Caring (general).
Vols under 26 placed each year: 120
When to apply: All year.
Work alone/with others: With others.
Volunteers with disabilities: Not possible.
Qualifications: Some knowledge of German.
Costs: Travel. Full insurance is necessary. The contributions for health, pension, unemployment and accident insurance will be paid by the organizer.
Benefits: DM265 per month plus board and accommodation.
Training: Learning by doing. With other volunteers, particularly Germans, you will attend day or weekend seminars in order to exchange experiences and to discuss a number of related subjects.
Supervision: By full-time staff colleague.
Interview details: An interview will be held in Frankfurt or London prior to your acceptance.
Certification: Certificate or reference provided.
Worldwide placements: *Europe* (Germany).

INTERSERVE
On Track Programme
325 Kennington Road
London
SE11 4QH UK

Tel: +44 (0) 20 7735 8227
Fax: +44 (0) 20 7587 5362
e-mail: ontrack@isewi.globalnet.co.uk
Contact: Dave Taylor

Interserve is an international, interdenominational, evangelical Christian fellowship of about 450 committed Christians who have a desire to share their faith, as well as their skills, in another culture. Interserve's long-term partners work in the countries of Asia, the Gulf, the Middle East, and North Africa, undertaking a range of roles. On Track enables short-term volunteers to assist, or work alongside partners already in place. On Track is a short-term service programme run by Interserve and has two aims: to encourage an interest in cross-cultural Christian service overseas; to provide an opportunity for Christians to experience living, working, and sharing their faith in a cross-cultural environment. Open to those aged 18 years and over, On Track has a variety of programmes including School

Leavers, Summer Vacation Programme, Student Electives, New Graduates, and Professional/Skilled Workers. Programmes vary in length from two to 12 months and examples of the type of activities undertaken range from teaching, including TEFL, to health, development, administration, engineering and care work. Volunteers with an offending background may be accepted – each application is assessed on an individual basis.

Total projects worldwide: 200
Total UK projects: 0
Starting months: January–December.
Time required: 9–52 weeks.
Age requirement: 18 plus.
Causes: Addicts/ex-addicts, Aids/HIV, children, conservation, disabled (learning and physical), elderly people, health care/medical, inner city problems, poor/homeless, refugees, teaching/assisting (nursery, primary, secondary, mature, EFL), unemployed, young people.
Activities: Accountancy, administration, agriculture/farming, arts/crafts, building/construction, caring (general, day and residential), catering, community work, computers, conservation skills, counselling, development issues, first aid, forestry, gardening/horticulture, international aid, marketing/publicity, newsletter/journalism, religion, social work, teaching, technical skills.
When to apply: 5 months prior to intended departure date.
Work alone/with others: Both.
Volunteers with disabilities: Applicants assessed individually. Due to the nature of overseas travel, volunteers should be fit/healthy/mobile and able to cope on their own.
Qualifications: Dependent on the placement. UK residents only.
Equipment/clothing: Dependent on the placement.
Health requirements: Good health and able to cope with overseas travel and life.
Costs: Volunteers are responsible for all expenses/costs which vary and include £10 application fee, £50 for weekend training, £50 placement fee plus £15 per month after the first 3 months.
Benefits: Pastoral care.
Nationalities accepted: UK residents only.
Interview details: Prospective volunteers are

interviewed in London.
Charity number: 2789773
Worldwide placements: *Africa* (Egypt); *Asia* (Afghanistan, Bahrain, Bangladesh, China, India, Jordan, Kyrgyzstan, Lebanon, Mongolia, Nepal, Oman, Pakistan, Turkey, Yemen); *Europe* (Turkey).

INVOLVEMENT CORPS INC.
15515 Sunset Blvd Suite 108
Pacific Palisades
CA 90272
USA

Tel: 00 1 310 459 1022
Fax: 00 1 310 459 1022
Contact: Ms Ellen Linsley

Involvement Corps Inc. exists to give people the opportunity to participate in volunteer activities related to conservation, environmental research, archaeology, history or social welfare.

Total projects worldwide: 1
Starting months: January–December.
Time required: 2–12 weeks.
Age requirement: 14 plus.
Causes: Archaeology, conservation, environmental causes.
Activities: Conservation skills, social work.
When to apply: All year.
Costs: Some placements cost £34 per week for accommodation; admininstration fee £130 travel costs.
Worldwide placements: *Asia* (India); *Australasia* (Australia, Fiji, New Zealand); *Europe* (Germany); *North America* (USA).

INVOLVEMENT VOLUNTEERS
PO Box 218
Port Melbourne
Victoria
3207 Australia

Tel: 00 61 3 9646 5504 or 9392
Fax: 00 61 3 9646 5504
e-mail: ivimel@iaccess.com.au
Contact: Mr Tim B. Cox, The Director

Involvement Volunteers is a registered, not-for-profit organization, that creates programmes of suitable, unpaid, individual volunteer placements related to the natural environment and social service within the community. Volunteers participate as individuals or in groups or in teams around the world, around the calendar. Placements are available in a wide variety of situations, i.e. National Parks, and bird observatories; private landholdings and flora and fauna reserves; community based social service organizations for the benefit of both young and old as well as physically or medically disadvantaged people. Volunteers are required to speak and understand the English language for safety reasons. Volunteers gain valuable experience arranging their own visas as required; locally purchasing their air tickets and suitable travel insurance with some advice to suit their travel and volunteering programme. Involvement Volunteers meets the volunteers on arrival at Melbourne International airport, provides hostel type accommodation, advice and introduction to banking, taxation (for those with working holiday visas) and a mail base for volunteers. The IV volunteers have access to discounted coach travel, scuba diving courses and snorkelling on the Great Barrier Reef, coastal sailing and sail training, sea kayaking and special inland trips.

Total projects worldwide: Hundreds
Total UK projects: 5
Starting months: January–December.
Time required: 2–52 weeks.
Age requirement: 17 plus.
Causes: Animal welfare, archaeology, architecture, children, conservation, disabled (learning and physical), elderly people, health care/medical, heritage, holidays for disabled, refugees, teaching/assisting (nursery, primary, secondary, mature, efl), wildlife, work camps – seasonal.
Activities: Administration, agriculture/farming, arts/crafts, building/construction, caring (general and residential), computers, conservation skills, DIY, driving, first aid, forestry, gardening/horticulture, library/resource centres, manual work, marketing/publicity, music, newsletter/journalism, outdoor skills, research, scientific work, social work, sport, summer camps, teaching, training, translating, work camps – seasonal.
Vols under 26 placed each year: 600
When to apply: As early as possible.
Work alone/with others: Both.
Volunteers with disabilities: Generally not.
Qualifications: Must speak and understand English. Specific qualifications and potential interest are not necessary except in specific cases e.g. Teaching.
Equipment/clothing: Sleeping bag, removable

washable inner sheet bag, towel, long-sleeved shirts, trousers, shorts, sun hat, cool and wet weather gear plus strong walking or working boots. Backpack with overnight bag for spares in case of misplaced backpack while travelling.

Health requirements: As suitable for the site.

Costs: Application fee £80, programme fee £150, individual placement fee £25, group placement £75–£125. Volunteers must arrange their own insurance.

Benefits: Opportunities to travel and explore as individuals or in group or team activities while gaining practical and cultural experience related to activities in life while assisting others in need of assistance.

Supervision: Placement hosts or very little supervision.

Interview details: No interview necessary.

Certification: Certificate or reference provided on request.

Worldwide placements: *Africa* (Ghana, Kenya, South Africa); *Asia* (India, Lebanon, Malaysia, Thailand, Vietnam); *Australasia* (Australia, Fiji, New Zealand, Papua New Guinea); *Europe* (Estonia, Finland, Germany, Greece, Italy, Latvia, Spain); *North America* (USA); *Central America* (Barbados, Dominica, Mexico); *South America* (Argentina, Ecuador, Venezuela).

INVOLVEMENT VOLUNTEERS – DEUTSCHLAND

Naturbadstr. 50
D-91056 Erlangen
Germany

Tel: 00 49 9135 8075
Fax: 00 49 9135 8075
e-mail: ivde2@t-online.de
Contact: Marion Mayer, Chairman.

Involvement Volunteers – Deutschland is the European office of Involvement Volunteers which is based in Australia. It enables people to participate in voluntary activities related to conservation. An updated task list can be received via e-mail all year through. Volunteers with an offending background are accepted.

Total projects worldwide: 200
Total UK projects: 0
Starting months: January–December.
Time required: 2–52 weeks.
Age requirement: 17–35
Causes: Animal welfare, archaeology, architecture, children, conservation, disabled (learning and physical), elderly people, environmental causes, health care/medical, heritage, inner city problems, poor/homeless, refugees, teaching/assisting (nursery, primary, EFL), wildlife, work camps – seasonal, young people.

Activities: Administration, agriculture/ farming, building/construction, caring (general, day and residential), community work, conservation skills, development issues, forestry, gardening/horticulture, group work, manual work, outdoor skills, research, scientific work, social work, summer camps, teaching, work camps – seasonal.

Vols under 26 placed each year: 500

When to apply: 2–3 months in advance of departure.

Work alone/with others: Both, depending on preference and availability.

Volunteers with disabilities: There may be projects for volunteers with disabilities for some placements. Contact IV Melbourne, see last entry for details.

Qualifications: Nil for most placements, sometimes special skill is requested by host.

Health requirements: Nil.

Costs: DM230 initial fee plus A$340 confirmation fee for IV Australia plus travel plus A$60.

Benefits: 90% free board and lodging. Others pay A$10-50 per week.

Interview details: No interview necessary. A CV and detailed questions concerning planned travel route are basis for schedule.

Certification: Certificate or reference provided on request.

Charity number: VR1246

Worldwide placements: *Africa* (Ghana, Kenya, South Africa); *Asia* (India, Indonesia, Lebanon, Malaysia, Sri Lanka, Thailand); *Australasia* (Australia, Fiji, New Zealand, Papua New Guinea); *Europe* (Austria, Estonia, Finland, Germany, Greece, Italy, Latvia, Lithuania, Spain); *North America* (USA).

UK placements: *England* (London).

INVOLVEMENT VOLUNTEERS UNITED KINGDOM (IVUK)

7 Bushmead Avenue
Kingskerswell
Nr Newton Abbot
Devon
TQ12 5EN UK

Tel: +44 (0) 1803 872594
e-mail: IVUK@hotmail.com
Web: www.volunteering.org.au
Contact: Mrs Ratcliffe

Involvement Volunteers United Kingdom has the following UK placements: Conservation UK1001 – IVP assist with the operation of a recycling scheme which was set up by two university graduates who now operate it as their business in a local government area. Two plus weeks. Social Service UK1003 – IIVP or SIVP. A respite care and holiday centre for 60 people with physical disabilities (so their carers can have a short holiday). Volunteers live in, assist full-time staff with care and companionship of disabled guests who are happy to enjoy a holiday themselves. Volunteers take the disabled people to visit interesting places. Having just arrived in the UK, IV volunteers from overseas meet interesting people from many parts of the country, who can tell them what to see and where to go. Two plus weeks. Farm Work – Sheffield. Rural dairy farm and horse stables approximately 30 minutes from town. Live with family and help with day-to-day operations. Farm Work – Wales. A typical Welsh farm of 40 ha with a traditional mix of sheep, cattle and ponies, dogs, cats, etc. There is a small riding/pony trekking centre during summer months.

Total projects worldwide: Hundreds
Total UK projects: 4
Starting months: January–December.
Time required: 2–14 weeks.
Age requirement: 18 plus.
Causes: Animal welfare, archaeology, architecture, children, conservation, disabled (learning and physical), elderly people, environmental causes, heritage, holidays for disabled, teaching/assisting (nursery, primary, secondary, mature, EFL), wildlife, work camps – seasonal, young people.
Activities: Agriculture/farming, building/construction, caring (general, day and residential), catering, community work, conservation skills, cooking, DIY, forestry, group work, international aid, manual work, outdoor skills, social work, summer camps, teaching, technical skills, training, visiting/befriending, work camps – seasonal.
Vols under 26 placed each year: 2 or 3 of a total of 30 from UK.
When to apply: As soon as possible.

Work alone/with others: With others.
Volunteers with disabilities: Possible.
Qualifications: No qualifications needed but any will help. Teaching needs TEFL course.
Equipment/clothing: Dependent on placement.
Health requirements: Travelling vaccinations.
Costs: Registration fee £80, and programme fee of £90 for a single placement, £130 for more than one placement and a placement fee of £25 for each placement. Travel costs. Volunteers must provide their own insurance.
Benefits: Board and lodging usually paid unless volunteering in a poor country.
Training: Training is provided by placement.
Supervision: Placement provides supervision.
Interview details: No interview necessary – volunteers have to send a CV with registration form.
Certification: Reference or certificate depending on placement.
Worldwide placements: *Africa* (Ghana, Kenya, South Africa); *Asia* (India, Lebanon, Malaysia, Thailand, Vietnam); *Australasia* (Australia, Fiji, New Zealand, Papua New Guinea); *Europe* (Estonia, Finland, Germany, Greece, Italy, Latvia, Spain); *North America* (USA); *Central America* (Barbados, Dominica, Mexico); *South America* (Argentina, Ecuador, Venezuela).
UK placements: *England* (Kent, Surrey, S. Yorkshire); *Wales* (Pembrokeshire).

IONA COMMUNITY, THE

Iona Abbey
Isle of Iona
Argyll
PA76 6SN Scotland

Tel: +44 (0) 1681 700404
Fax: +44 (0) 1681 700460 or 603
e-mail: ionacomm@iona.org.uk
Web: www.iona.org.uk
Contact: The Staff Co-ordinator

The Iona Community is an ecumenical Christian Community, founded in 1938 by the late George MacLeod (Very Rev. Lord MacLeod of Fuinary) and committed to seeking new ways of living the Gospel in today's world. The Iona Community maintains three centres on Iona and Mull: Iona Abbey and the MacLeod Centre on Iona, and Camas Adventure Centre on the Ross of Mull. The islands' work focuses around welcoming guests to join in the common life of work, worship and recreation. There is a resident group living and working all year round on Iona, but the Centres can only run with the support of the volunteers from the beginning of March to the end of October. There are up to 35 volunteers here at any one time coming for six or more weeks at a time. Types of jobs on offer: kitchen assistant, housekeeping assistant, general assistant, children's worker, abbey assistant, driver, shop assistant, office assistant, gardener and maintenance assistant. Posts for Camas Adventure Camp include cook, programme workers (outdoors), gardener and general assistant. Volunteers with an offending background accepted.

Total projects worldwide: 3
Total UK projects: 3
Starting months: March–October.
Time required: 6–14 weeks.
Age requirement: 18 plus.
Causes: Addicts/ex-addicts, Aids/HIV, children, disabled (learning and physical), elderly people, holidays for disabled, human rights, inner city problems, offenders/ex-offenders, poor/homeless, teaching/assisting (nursery, primary, secondary, mature), work camps – seasonal, young people.
Activities: Administration, arts/crafts, caring (general), catering, cooking, driving, first aid, gardening/horticulture, manual work, outdoor skills, religion, summer camps, teaching, work camps – seasonal.
Vols under 26 placed each year: 26 of a total of 35.
When to apply: Previous Autumn.
Work alone/with others: With others.
Volunteers with disabilities: Possible, but there are access difficulties.
Qualifications: Drivers must be 25 or over. We require commitment to community life and to exploring/being open to Christian faith.
Health requirements: Nil.
Costs: All paid by Iona Community.
Benefits: Travel expenses within Britain, board, lodging and weekly allowance. Voluntary staff are insured for accidents at work.
Supervision: Volunteers work as part of a team and have regular team meetings and reflection sessions with their line manager.
Interview details: No interview necessary.
Certification: Reference on request.
Charity number: SCO03794

UK placements: *Scotland* (Argyll and Bute).

IRISH WILD BIRD CONSERVANCY
Ruttledge House
8 Longford Place,
Monkstown
Co. Dublin
Ireland
Tel: 00 353 1 280 4322
Fax: 00 353 1 284 4407
e-mail: bird@indigo.ie
Web: www.birdwatchireland.ie
Contact: Ashling Talent

Irish Wild Bird Conservancy undertakes reserve management, species protection and environmental surveys and research in the Republic of Ireland.

Total projects worldwide: 1
Total UK projects: 0
Starting months: January–December.
Time required: 1–12 weeks.
Age requirement: 16 plus.
Causes: Wildlife.
Activities: Administration, manual work, outdoor skills, research, scientific work.
Vols under 26 placed each year: 10
When to apply: All year.
Work alone/with others: Both.
Qualifications: No qualification necessary but any are a bonus.
Health requirements: Nil.
Costs: No direct costs but volunteers must find their own board and lodging. Volunteers must arrange their own insurance.
Benefits: Accommodation in caravans or camp sites.
Training: Training given if required.
Interview details: Interviews take place either at Ruttledge House or at the project.
Worldwide placements: *Europe* (Ireland).

IRONBRIDGE GORGE MUSEUMS, THE
The Wharfage
Ironbridge
Telford
Shropshire
TF8 7AW UK

Tel: +44 (0) 1952 583003
Fax: +44 (0) 1952 588016
e-mail: info@ironbridge.org.uk
Web: www.ironbridge.org.uk
Contact: Lisa Wood

The Ironbridge Gorge Museums require

volunteers to help with a huge variety of activities in all the different sections of the Museums. Most opportunities are with the Blists Hill Open Air Museum. Demonstrators, clad in Victorian style costume, are required to work in exhibits.

Total projects worldwide: 1
Total UK projects: 1
Starting months: January–December.
Time required: 2–52 weeks.
Age requirement: 16 plus.
Causes: Animal welfare, children, heritage, young people.
Activities: Arts/crafts, gardening/horticulture, manual work, research, theatre/drama.
Vols under 26 placed each year: 20 of a total of 60.
When to apply: January for main season, but all year for general volunteering.
Work alone/with others: Normally with others.
Volunteers with disabilities: Disabled volunteers accepted.
Qualifications: Good spoken English.
Equipment/clothing: Sensible black/dark shoes/boots.
Health requirements: Nil.
Costs: All expenses.
Benefits: Training, costume and equipment provided, lunch vouchers and free entry to other museums. We provide all insurance for all inducted volunteers.
Training: Induction training and hands-on training is carried out in house.
Supervision: Volunteers are never expected to work alone. They have a staff mentor, volunteer co-ordinator plus duty officer on hand 7 days a week.
Interview details: Wherever possible we have an informal meeting to assess suitability.
Charity number: 503717-R
UK placements: *England* (Shropshire).

I-TO-I INTERNATIONAL PROJECTS
1 Cottage Road
Headingley
Leeds
LS6 4DD UK

Tel: +44 (0) 870 333 2332
Fax: +44 (0) 113 274 6923
e-mail: info@i-to-i.com
Web: www.i-to-i.com
Contact: The i Venture Co-ordinator

i-to-i International Projects Ltd organizes intensive TEFL courses: 20 hour (one weekend) TEFL courses at venues nation-wide which give you an i-to-i TEFL certificate. Refreshments provided. Extensive guidance on work opportunities abroad. 20 hour optional home study grammar module available. Fees: £195 waged, £175 unwaged. i-Venture organizes 1. Voluntary projects operated by i-to-i. Volunteers work on school projects teaching English in Sri Lanka, India, Russia, Thailand, Nepal, China, Ghana, Uganda, Costa Rica and Bolivia. Placements are flexible and last for 1–9 months. TEFL training is provided in the UK before departure. Field staff, board and lodging included in most circumstances. 2. Conservation projects and working holidays in Australia, Costa Rica, Ecuador, Ghana, India, Thailand and Sri Lanka. Board and lodging, in-country orientation and fun-in-the-sun fully guaranteed. Age range: 18 plus. Costs for two months from £595. Deposit must be sent with application form. On application we send you a large amount of information about our projects and TEFL course and invite candidates to an afternoon briefing session in London or Leeds. A further £300 interim payment must be received by us before the TEFL course weekend or a month after applying – whichever is soonest. Volunteers with an offending background are accepted.

Total projects worldwide: 300
Total UK projects: 0
Starting months: January–December.
Time required: 2–52 weeks.
Age requirement: 17 plus.
Causes: Conservation, environmental causes, teaching/assisting (EFL), wildlife, young people.
Activities: Agriculture/farming, conservation skills, teaching.
Vols under 26 placed each year: 300 of a total of 500.
When to apply: All year.
Work alone/with others: Both.
Volunteers with disabilities: We are unable to place people with disabilities.
Qualifications: i-to-i TEFL course which is 2 days in the UK. Fluent English speakers.
Health requirements: Good health.
Costs: For 3 months from £995. Volunteers are expected to organize insurance. No volunteer can go abroad without adequate

insurance. Detailed guidance is given on which cover is necessary.

Benefits: For the fee volunteers are guaranteed (in most circumstances) food, accommodation, 15 hrs teaching per week, support from UK and weekend TEFL training in UK prior to departure and in-country support.

Training: TEFL training weekend, country briefing afternoon and Venture Pack – a comprehensive pack on how to survive abroad.

Supervision: Co-ordinators abroad, in the capital (generally) look after welfare of volunteers. They pick up from airport and visit during volunteer's stay.

Nationalities accepted: No restrictions but must be fluent English speakers.

Interview details: Interviews are held once a month in Leeds and London.

Certification: Certificate or reference provided on request.

Worldwide placements: *Africa* (Ghana, Uganda); *Asia* (China, India, Nepal, Sri Lanka, Thailand); *Australasia* (Australia); *Europe* (Russia); *Central America* (Costa Rica); *South America* (Bolivia, Ecuador).

J

JACOB'S WELL
Smile Siret Scheme
57 Cherry Garth
Beverley
E. Yorkshire
HU17 0EP UK

Tel: + 44 (0) 1482 881478
Fax: + 44 (0) 1482 865452
e-mail: 100575,2205@compuserve.com
Contact: Mrs Agnes Perry, The Secretary

Jacob's Well Appeal is a Christian charity which was founded in 1982 to send medical aid to Poland. The work in Romania is almost entirely based in the Neuropsychiatric Hospital in Siret which contains some 500 children of all ages. It is understaffed with local women working as carers for the children. The culture, attitudes and eating patterns are all very different to those in England. Siret is very remote and modern facilities such as telephones, transport, water supply and indoor toilets are scarce and unreliable. The climate is continental with wide temperature swings. Many young people have made a valuable contribution with the children during a gap year before or after university.

Total projects worldwide: 1
Total UK projects: 0
Starting months: January–December.
Time required: 4–13 weeks.
Age requirement: 18 plus.
Causes: Children, disabled (learning and physical).
Activities: Caring (general).
Vols under 26 placed each year: 60
When to apply: At least 6 months in advance.
Work alone/with others: With others.
Volunteers with disabilities: Not really, there are many steps for those working in the hospital.
Qualifications: Not essential but physiotherapists, nurses, teachers for special needs have priority.
Health requirements: Fit and healthy.
Costs: £10–£15 per week – local family accommodation plus travel expenses (approximately £250).
Interview details: Volunteers are mostly interviewed in Beverley, E. Yorkshire, occasionally in London.
Certification: Certificate or reference on request.
Charity number: 515235
Worldwide placements: *Europe* (Romania).

JATUN SACHA
Eugenio de Santillán
N34-248 y Maurian
Quito
Ecuador

Tel: 00 593 2 432 246
Fax: 00 593 2 453 583
e-mail: volunteer@jatunsacha.org
Contact: Gabriela Cadena

Jatun Sacha was created in 1989 in order to conserve areas of Ecuador that were not being protected by the government at that time. We mainly work towards environmental issues but have also some community extension programmes with the communities in the surrounding areas.

Total projects worldwide: 3
Starting months: January–December.
Time required: 2–30 weeks.
Age requirement: 16 plus.
Causes: Conservation, environmental causes, teaching (EFL), wildlife.
Activities: Agriculture/farming, community work, conservation skills, gardening/ horticulture, manual work, research, scientific work, teaching.
Vols under 26 placed each year: 300 of a total of 400.
When to apply: 2 months in advance.
Volunteers with disabilities: Not possible.
Qualifications: Basic Spanish is recommended.
Equipment/clothing: Rubber boots, torch, rain gear, bathing suit, mosquito repellent, sun protection cream.
Health requirements: Innoculations.
Costs: Application fee US$30, reserve fee US$200 (includes 3 meals a day and lodging), Travel to Reserve US$10 (one way). International insurance is required – arranged by the volunteer.
Benefits: Board and lodging included in the reserve fee.
Training: In Quito volunteers receive information regarding our organization, activities and purposes.
Supervision: Each reserve has a director, administrator and volunteer co-ordinator. There is also a central volunteer co-ordinator for the three reserves.
Interview details: No interview necessary, just e-mail or telephone.
Certification: We give a certificate which indicates that the person has worked with us in conservation.
Worldwide placements: *South America* (Ecuador).

JESUIT VOLUNTEER COMMUNITY: BRITAIN
23 New Mount Street
Manchester
M4 4DF UK

Tel: +44 (0) 161 832 6888
Fax: +44 (0) 161 832 6958
e-mail: Staff@jvc.u-net.com
Web: www.jesuitvolunteers-uk.org
Contact: The Administrator

The Jesuit Volunteer Community: Britain (JVC) is a registered charity, part of the Trust for Roman Catholic Purposes. We exist to offer young people, aged between 18 and 35, a one-year developmental programme.

In offering this programme, JVC aims to enable young people to become more reflective, grow in self-awareness, develop a greater understanding of the needs of others (particularly those who are marginalized in Britain today) in order to promote Christian values. This aim is achieved through four core experiential themes: living in community; working in areas of social need; leading a simple lifestyle; integrating life and faith within a Christian context. During the year volunteers work in placements such as homeless hostels, alcohol and drug dependency units, local community schemes, Citizens Advice Bureaux, victim support schemes, centres of mental and physical disability, centres for victims of Aids.

We ask for a commitment to exploring the above four values, for which we supply resources and information, and a series of residential events throughout the year. Volunteers with offending backgrounds are accepted.

Total projects worldwide: 13
Total UK projects: 4
Starting months: September.
Time required: 47 weeks.
Age requirement: 18–35
Causes: Addicts/ex-addicts, Aids/HIV, children, disabled (learning and physical), elderly people, human rights, inner city problems, offenders/ex-offenders, poor/ homeless, refugees, unemployed, young people.
Activities: Administration, arts/crafts, campaigning, caring (general and day), community work, computers, development issues, driving, fundraising, group work, library/resource centres, outdoor skills, religion, research, social work, sport, training, visiting/befriending.
Vols under 26 placed each year: 18 of a total of 25.
When to apply: January–July.
Work alone/with others: With others.
Volunteers with disabilities: Not possible.
Qualifications: Nil.
Health requirements: JVC cannot accept anyone with a personal history of problem alcohol or drug use unless he/she has completed rehabilitation or ceased drug or alcohol misuse for a minimum of two years.

Costs: Travel to JVC Interview, placement interview and orientation at beginning of the year. Insurance (cover is provided at work only for work-related claims).
Benefits: Self-catering accommodation, £55 per week pocket money and some travel costs. A 4-day residential evaluation and a follow-up weekend 6 months later.
Training: A 5-day residential orientation.
Supervision: Each volunteer has a work supervisor with a supervision session at least once a month. JVC provides supervision of the programme overall.
Interview details: A residential interview takes place in Manchester.
Certification: Certificate provided.
Charity number: 230165
Worldwide placements: *Europe* (Austria, Belgium, Bosnia-Herzegovina, Croatia, France, Germany, Hungary, Ireland, Poland, Slovakia, Spain, Switzerland).
UK placements: *England* (Manchester, Merseyside, West Midlands); *Scotland* (Glasgow City).

JEUNESSE EN MISSION
Kpalime
Kloto
40 Togo

Tel: 00 228 47 10 12
Fax: 00 228 47 10 12
Contact: Yawo Selom Hadzi

Jeunesse en Mission works in three main areas: Evangelism: organizing Christian summer camps; Formation: preparing and equipping the young in different Mission schools; Aid: helping at times of natural catastrophes and crisis. Volunteers with an offending background are accepted – we believe that God changes people.

Total projects worldwide: 2
Total UK projects: 0
Starting months: July, August.
Time required: 1–4 weeks.
Age requirement: 16 plus.
Causes: Conservation, health care/medical, teaching (EFL), work camps – seasonal, young people.
Activities: Arts/crafts, building/construction, community work, computers, conservation skills, first aid, fundraising, gardening/horticulture, group work, manual work, outdoor skills, religion, summer camps, teaching, translating, work camps – seasonal.

Vols under 26 placed each year: 50 of a total of 60.
When to apply: Before the end of June.
Work alone/with others: With others.
Volunteers with disabilities: Not possible.
Qualifications: Driving licence if possible and a little French.
Equipment/clothing: Everyday clothes for hot and cold temperatures.
Health requirements: Necessary vaccinations and anti-malarial prophylactic.
Costs: Travel, cost of living and registration fee.
Benefits: A small present as a memoir at the end of the placement.
Interview details: No interview necessary.
Certification: Written reference on request.

JEUNESSE ET CO-OPERATION
BP 19
Safi
46000 Morocco

Tel: 00 212 4 62 85 45
Fax: 00 212 4 61 00 03
Contact: Nabil Mouaddin

Jeunesse et Co-operation organizes international work camps lasting three weeks where the young of the world meet to do voluntary work. The work may be building or repairing a public building, or may be helping to supply water to a rural community or poor quarter. There are also some limited opportunities to work with children.

Total projects worldwide: 3
Total UK projects: 0
Starting months: May–August.
Time required: 3–4 weeks.
Age requirement: 18 plus.
Causes: Archaeology, children, conservation, disabled (learning and physical), elderly people, environmental causes, work camps – seasonal, young people.
Activities: Arts/crafts, building/construction, campaigning, conservation skills, cooking, gardening/horticulture, group work, manual work, music, social work, sport, summer camps, training, visiting/befriending, work camps – seasonal.
Vols under 26 placed each year: 40
When to apply: May.
Work alone/with others: With others.
Volunteers with disabilities: Possible.
Qualifications: Nil – just willingness and eagerness to be a volunteer.

Equipment/clothing: Sleeping bag and hat.
Health requirements: Nil but no one with serious health conditions.
Costs: Travel plus 1,000 Dirhanes inscription covers cost of excursions at weekends.
Benefits: Board and lodging.
Certification: Certificate or reference provided.
Worldwide placements: *Africa* (Morocco).

JEWISH CARE
Stuart Young House
221 Golders Green Road
London
NW11 9DQ UK

Tel: +44 (0) 20 8922 2407
Fax: +44 (0) 20 8922 2401
e-mail: jover@jcare.org
Contact: Juliette Overlander, Training and Development Officer

Jewish Care is the Jewish community's largest welfare charity. In total we provide support for over 5,000 elderly, physically disabled, mentally ill and visually impaired people and their families Volunteer projects for young people include a summer experience programme for sixth formers, a student work placement programme and a gap year programme. During the course of the year, student volunteers of 16 – 18 years are warmly welcomed to our team of volunteers. They work with our resources, befriending members and running small groups. In addition young people visit elderly, lonely and isolated people living on their own.

Total projects worldwide: Varies.
Total UK projects: Varies.
Starting months: January–December.
Time required: 1–52 weeks.
Age requirement: 16 plus.
Causes: Disabled (learning and physical), elderly people.
Activities: Arts/crafts, caring (general), community work, group work, music, visiting/befriending.
Vols under 26 placed each year: 100 of a total of 2,500.
When to apply: All year.
Work alone/with others: Both.
Volunteers with disabilities: Possible.
Qualifications: Nil.
Health requirements: Nil.
Costs: Nil.
Benefits: Travel expenses reimbursed. We are responsible for providing insurance.
Training: 'Introduction to Jewish Care' training day.
Supervision: All volunteers know who to contact if needed. They are each allocated a volunteer co-ordinator.
Interview details: Interviews take place at Head Office in Golders Green.
Certification: Certificate or reference provided for students.
Charity number: 802559
UK placements: *England* (Essex, London, E. Sussex).

JEWISH LADS' AND GIRLS' BRIGADE
3 Beechcroft Road
London
E18 1LA UK

Tel: +44 (0) 20 8989 5743/8990
Fax: +44 (0) 20 8518 8832
e-mail: office@jlgb.org
Web: www.jlgb.org
Contact: Richard Weber

Jewish Lads' and Girls' Brigade runs local groups and national one-week summer camps for children aged 8–11 and 11–16. Volunteers are needed to help run activities or look after the general welfare of the young people and to organize voluntary service projects and other activities all year. We also organize weekend activities and courses throughout the year. The JLGB is the only Jewish operating authority for the Duke of Edinburgh's Award, which is also offered to pupils in Jewish and State schools throughout the UK, as part of our 'Outreach Kiruv Project'. Young people working for the Award, or taking part in any other activities organized by 'Outreach', are not required to join the uniformed JLGB. The JLGB's National Lottery-funded project, 'Hand-in-Hand', offers the opportunity for 14-17 year olds to volunteer in their local community.

Total projects worldwide: 1
Total UK projects: 1
Starting months: January–December.
Time required: 1–52 weeks.
Age requirement: 18 plus.
Causes: Children, disabled (learning), work camps – seasonal.
Activities: Administration, arts/crafts, computers, first aid, fundraising, group work, marketing/publicity, music, newsletter/journalism, outdoor skills, social work,

sport, summer camps, theatre/drama, training.
When to apply: Any time.
Work alone/with others: With others.
Volunteers with disabilities: Possible.
Qualifications: Nil – references checked.
Health requirements: Medical form to be completed.
Costs: Contribution towards the camps and other activities.
Benefits: Food, accommodation as appropriate.
Interview details: Interviews take place in London and in provincial centres.
Certification: Reference on request.
Charity number: 286950
UK placements: *England* (Berkshire, Cheshire, Dorset, Essex, Hertfordshire, London, Manchester, Merseyside, Nottinghamshire, Surrey, E. Sussex, West Midlands); *Scotland* (Glasgow City); *Wales* (Cardiff).

JOHN MUIR AWARD
41 Commercial Street
Edinburgh
EH6 6SD Scotland

Tel: +44 (0) 131 624 7220
Fax: +44 (0) 131 624 7220
e-mail: johnmuiraward@jmt.org
Web: www.jmt.org
Contact: David Picken

The John Muir Award encourages young and old to 'Discover, Explore and Conserve' a wild place. There are also courses on environmental youthwork. John Muir, born in 1838 in the small Scottish port of Dunbar, emigrated with his family as a child to the USA. In his adopted homeland he became a founding father of the world conservation movement, and devoted his life to safeguarding the world's landscapes for future generations. Since 1983, the John Muir Trust, guided by Muir's charge to 'do something for wildness and make the mountains glad', has dedicated itself to making Muir's message a reality within the United Kingdom. By acquiring and sensitively managing key wild areas, the Trust sets out to show that the damage inflicted on the wild over the centuries can be repaired; that the land can be conserved on a sustainable basis for the human, animal, and plant communities which share it; and the great spiritual qualities of wilderness, of tranquillity and solitude, can be preserved as a legacy for those to come.

Total projects worldwide: 2
Total UK projects: Varies.
Starting months: January–December.
Time required: 1 weeks.
Age requirement: 14 plus.
Causes: Conservation, environmental causes, heritage, unemployed, work camps – seasonal, young people.
Activities: Arts/crafts, conservation skills, forestry, group work, manual work, outdoor skills, summer camps, training, work camps – seasonal.
Vols under 26 placed each year: 500 of a total of 1,000.
When to apply: All year.
Work alone/with others: With others.
Volunteers with disabilities: Possible. Learning disability welcomed.
Qualifications: No previous skills – ability to work in a group.
Equipment/clothing: Boots/wellies, warm old clothes and waterproofs.
Health requirements: Some sites are remote, require long walk-in, isolated.
Costs: Approximately £100 for one week's residential placement. Personal insurance.
Benefits: Discovering and exploring wild places and conserving them. General liability insurance covered by us.
Training: Yes, standard courses.
Supervision: Structured support and supervision.
Interview details: Applicants are interviewed in Edinburgh.
Certification: John Muir Award.
Charity number: CR 42964
Worldwide placements: *North America* (USA).
UK placements: *England* (Cumbria); *Scotland* (throughout); *Wales* (throughout).

JOINT ASSISTANCE CENTRE
G17/3 DLF Qutab Enclave Phase 1
Gurgaon
122002 Haryana
India

Tel: 00 91 11 835 2141
Fax: 00 91 11 463 2517
Contact: The Convenor

The international volunteer programmes of JAC are intended to provide opportunities for visiting friends from abroad to see India and learn about its people and their concerns while travelling. Programmes run all year round in different parts of the country. An individual schedule is devised for each person or group to meet their needs. Arrangements have to be made at least 30 days in advance of arrival in India in order to plan properly. Volunteers working with children will be placed in one location at a school or a home for children for a period of three months or longer. These volunteers should be prepared to learn some basic Hindi language preferably starting before they leave for India. Participation in work camps in Indian villages: these programmes involve work with villagers on such activities as sanitation projects, building construction, plant nurseries and other agricultural work, literacy and women's welfare, health projects including use of local herbal medicine, environmental awareness campaign etc. (1-4 weeks). Working with children in schools and orphanages (12 weeks minimum). Helping in JAC office in New Delhi doing office work, and research for cultural exchange, disaster preparedness and other programmes. Preparing and attending conferences on development, disasters and environmental issues. Taking part in environmentally oriented treks in the Himalayan area. Participation in yoga, meditation and natural health care training programme. Participation in individually designed projects based on special skills involving a long-term commitment in such areas as medicine, journalism and engineering.

Total projects worldwide: 1
Starting months: January–December.
Time required: 4–26 weeks.
Age requirement: 18 plus.
Causes: Children, conservation, elderly people, environmental causes, health care/medical, poor/homeless, teaching/assisting (nursery, primary, secondary, EFL), work camps – seasonal, young people.
Activities: Administration, agriculture/farming, arts/crafts, building/construction, caring (general and day), community work, conservation skills, forestry, fundraising, group work, international aid, manual work, marketing/publicity, social work, summer camps, teaching, training, work camps – seasonal.
When to apply: At least 3 months in

advance.
Qualifications: Personal faith in God.
Health requirements: Vegetarian, no alcohol, tobacco or drugs allowed.
Costs: £75 per month plus travel, insurance and pocket money. Registration fee £15.
Benefits: The cost includes food, accommodation and administrtion fee.
Worldwide placements: *Asia* (India).

JOINT STOCK COMPANY MINTA
Perkuno al 4
3000 Kaunas
Lithuania

Tel: 00 370 720 2560
Fax: 00 370 720 8321
Contact: Saulius Zobernis

Joint Stock Company Minta needs the following: Teaching assistants to work as group leaders in children's summer camps from 20 June – 31 August. Work six days per week. Minimum age 20; Volunteers to take part in international work camps. Recent projects have included archaeological digs and tree planting. Work five hours per day, six days per week. From 1 June–30 September.

Total projects worldwide: 1
Total UK projects: 0
Starting months: June.
Time required: 2–52 weeks.
Age requirement: 16 plus.
Causes: Archaeology, children, conservation, teaching/assisting (EFL), young people.
Activities: Building/construction, conservation skills, forestry, teaching.
Vols under 26 placed each year: Up to 500.
Qualifications: Previous experience of working with children an advantage.
Costs: Registration and placement fees.
Benefits: Wages by arrangement for teaching assistants. Pocket money of up to £65 per month for volunteers.
Worldwide placements: *Europe* (Lithuania).

JOSSÅSEN LANDSBY
N 7550 Hommelvik
Norway

Tel: 00 47 73 9799900
Fax: 00 47 73 978840
Contact: Birgit Hammer or Thomas Bresges

Jossåsen Landsby is a Camphill Village Community with adults. The purpose of the Trust is to create working communities where people who are mentally and physically handicapped, working together with workshop leaders, volunteers and houseparents, can find satisfaction in purposeful work in the security of a family setting. In this village, 40 km east of Trondheim, about 55 people live in five family units. There is a weavery where we also spin, a book workshop, a wood workshop, a farm with gardening in the summer and work in the forest in the winter. We also have cows, sheep, chickens etc. Like all Camphill Communities Jossåsen functions on a voluntary non-salary basis. Experience has shown that volunteer work is most valuable if you stay long enough to give you the opportunity to share in the responsibilities of living and working with people who are handicapped. Therefore it is recommended that volunteers come to Jossåsen for one year or longer. However, exceptions are made for working holidays in the summer. Bear in mind that the Norwegian climate needs warm clothing for the winter and boots etc. but in the summer it can be warm. The habitual use of drugs and alcohol is not in harmony with life in a Camphill Community. We do not want private TV either, because it may have a negative influence on the common activities we try to create together. Life in the Community can provide many lasting rewards for anyone who is willing to approach that life with goodwill, a degree of tolerance and openhearted interest and enthusiasm. People with offending backgrounds may be accepted but the 'issue' must be made clear beforehand so that we can talk openly about it. We cannot accept everybody but we are willing to consider each case separately.

Total projects worldwide: 1
Total UK projects: 0
Starting months: January–December.
Time required: 25–52 weeks.
Age requirement: 18 plus.
Causes: Disabled (learning and physical), elderly people.
Activities: Agriculture/farming, arts/crafts, building/construction, caring (general and day), catering, community work, cooking, forestry, gardening/horticulture, manual work, music, sport, theatre/drama.
Vols under 26 placed each year: 5–8
When to apply: All year.
Work alone/with others: Both.

Volunteers with disabilities: We are unable to place people with disabilities as we live in rough surroundings and have much snow in winter.
Qualifications: None specifically but volunteers must have an interest in anthroposophy.
Equipment/clothing: Warm clothes.
Health requirements: Normal health is enough.
Costs: Travel.
Benefits: Board and lodging and NKr 1,500 per month pocket money.
Training: Introduction training course.
Interview details: Volunteers are interviewed by phone and letter.
Certification: Certificate or reference provided.
Worldwide placements: *Europe* (Norway).

JUBILEE OUTREACH YORKSHIRE
4 Jubilee Way
Windhill
Shipley
W. Yorkshire
BD18 1QG UK

Tel: +44 (0) 1274 531999
Fax: +44 (0) 1274 531396
e-mail: joy@jiffytrucks.co.uk
Web: www.all-saints-halifax.org.uk/joy
Contact: Dr Kathy Tedd

JOY have been sending urgent supplies and teams of volunteers to help the needy of Romania since the beginning of 1990. From the very beginning we realized the problems of aid going on to the black market and so have only used tried and trusted contacts. So, although we have greatly improved the living conditions in many orphanages by renovation, our aim is to support the struggling families, and keep the children of the poorest families with their parents, by providing essential aid through Christian doctors and pastors. While Western European aid pours into the orphanages which the state already subsidizes, there is little or no help for the families struggling to stay together. JOY aims to try to stem the flow of children into the orphanages from families unable to cope.

Total projects worldwide: 3
Total UK projects: 0
Starting months: March.
Time required: 2–52 weeks (plus).

Age requirement: 18 plus.
Causes: Children, disabled (learning and physical), work camps – seasonal, young people.
Activities: Building/construction, caring (day), DIY, driving, fundraising, international aid, manual work, music, religion, summer camps, work camps – seasonal.
Vols under 26 placed each year: Approximately 20 of a total of 60.
When to apply: Any time.
Work alone/with others: Always in a team.
Volunteers with disabilities: Generally not suitable – travel overland in a 7-ton truck.
Qualifications: Drivers need to be 25 with clean licence and truck/van driving experience. For projects, practical building skills ideal.
Equipment/clothing: Dependent on the project.
Health requirements: Must have had triple antigen vaccine as a baby and be up to date with tetanus and polio.
Costs: Minimum £350 for 2 weeks.
Benefits: The cost covers travel, board and insurance.
Supervision: By the team leader.
Interview details: Interviews take place at the office in Shipley, W. Yorkshire.
Certification: Reference on request.
Charity number: 1004231
Worldwide placements: *Europe* (Romania).
UK placements: *England* (W. Yorkshire).

JUBILEE PARTNERS
Box 68
Comer
GA 30629
USA

Tel: 00 1 706 783 5131
Fax: 00 1 706 783 5134
e-mail: jubileep@igc.apc.org
Contact: Robbie Buller, Volunteer Co-ordinator

Jubilee Partners is a Christian community dedicated to serving poor and oppressed people. The community's work includes several areas of service: resettling refugees, peace-making, fund raising for Nicaraguan amputees and working against the death penalty. Volunteers with an offending background are considered and sometimes accepted.

Total projects worldwide: 1

Total UK projects: 0
Starting months: January, June, September.
Time required: 12–28 weeks.
Age requirement: 19 plus.
Causes: Children, human rights, offenders/ex-offenders, poor/homeless, refugees, teaching/assisting (EFL).
Activities: Administration, building/construction, caring (general), driving, fundraising, gardening/horticulture, library/resource centres, manual work, religion, teaching, visiting/befriending.
Vols under 26 placed each year: 20 of a total of 30.
When to apply: Preferably 6 months prior to start of terms.
Work alone/with others: With others.
Volunteers with disabilities: Only in rare circumstances.
Qualifications: Nil. Construction/maintenance skills welcomed.
Health requirements: Must be able to do physical work.
Costs: Transport and insurance. Volunteer is required to obtain all insurances necessary to travel to the US. Jubilee does not cover health insurance while at Jubilee.
Benefits: Board, accommodation and community allowance of US$10 per week.
Training: One week of orientation and teacher training provided upon arrival.
Supervision: Volunteer is expected to be a self-starter and to work with the minimum of supervision. Some work is individual, some done in groups. There is a work supervisor, a teaching supervisor, and a volunteer programme supervisor at Jubilee.
Interview details: No interview necessary.
Certification: References provided on request.
Worldwide placements: *North America* (USA).

K

KAIROS DWELLING
2945 Gull Road
Kalamazoo
Michigan
MI 49048 USA

Tel: 00 1 616 381 3688

Fax: 00 1 616 388 8016
e-mail: kairosdwelling1@juno.com
Contact: Sr Maureen Merry, Director

Kairos Dwelling is an ecumenically sponsored home that provides physical care, emotional support and spiritual sustenance for terminally ill persons and their loved ones in a loving and compassionate environment. When people are living with a terminal disease, it is important to have fewer distressing symptoms, the security of a caring environment and the assurance that they and their families will not be abandoned. The guest's psychological comfort will arise from arranging for special activities of interest as well as periods of peaceful withdrawal, as determined by the guest's physical state of care. It is our expectation that the guest's physical comfort will come under the direction of the pain control management of local hospices, agencies and physicians. As an ecumenical endeavour, we value the importance of the spiritual journey in one's life. Spiritual support will come from the guest's personal preference of how his or her needs are to be met. It is our hope that support from all faith communities will be available as the needs arise. The environment will be a home setting with an extended family of volunteers whose main focus is unconditional love and compassionate service. Kairos Dwelling is a home that can accommodate four guests. It is not a hospice, nursing home or assisted living facility. Room, meals and 24 hour nursing care will be provided by trained volunteers at no charge. Priority will be given to those in the greatest need.

Total projects worldwide: 1
Total UK projects: 0
Starting months: January–December.
Time required: 1–52 weeks (plus).
Age requirement: 20 plus.
Causes: Elderly people, health care/medical.
Activities: Caring (general and residential), cooking, group work.
Vols under 26 placed each year: 15 of a total of 100.
When to apply: All year.
Work alone/with others: With others at times.
Volunteers with disabilities: Possible, but volunteers need to give 'hands on' care to the terminally ill.

Qualifications: Communication skills, listening, bending, stretching, working on feet, having compassion and presence.
Health requirements: No contagious illness and able to do normal activities of daily living with ease.
Costs: All travel costs, health and general insurances, expenses and spending money.
Benefits: We provide housing and meals.
Training: 16 hours of training given.
Supervision: Direct supervision by the Director of Voluntary Co-ordination with case managing by hospice organization.
Nationalities accepted: No restrictions but it is important to speak and understand English well.
Interview details: Telephone or personal interviews.
Certification: Written reference on request.
Worldwide placements: *North America* (USA).

KENT KIDS MILES OF SMILES

Footprints
Stodmarsh Road
Canterbury
Kent
CT3 4AP UK

Tel: +44 (0) 1227 780796
Fax: +44 (0) 1227 764480
e-mail: admin@footprints-holidays.org.uk
Web: www.miles-of-smiles.org.uk
Contact: Linda George, Care Manager

The aim of Kent Kids Miles of Smiles as stated in the charity's deed trust is 'to generally assist in the well-being, comfort and happiness of sick and disabled children and to establish and run a holiday centre in the Kent area'. We hope that we are able to raise awareness in people that a sick and/or disabled child is no different to any other child in the fact that when on holiday they like to participate in all the activities enjoyed by able children and we are here to enable this. We accommodate seven children (between the ages of 3 and 15 inclusive) per week and the week's fun includes visits to local attractions (we have our own minibus) and also activities in the house and gardens at Footprints.

Total projects worldwide: 1
Total UK projects: 1
Starting months: January–December.
Time required: 1–12 weeks.

Age requirement: 16 plus.
Causes: Children, disabled (physical),
holidays for disabled.
Activities: Caring (general, day and
residential).
Vols under 26 placed each year: Most of a
total of 60.
When to apply: All year but as early as
possible as police checks are essential.
Work alone/with others: With others.
Volunteers with disabilities: Not possible.
Qualifications: Nil.
Health requirements: Must be fit and healthy.
Costs: Incidental expenses.
Benefits: Accommodation. All necessary
insurance is our responsibility.
Training: All necessary training, e.g. lifting
of children, will be given on site at induction
meetings. These take place before
commencement of voluntary time.
Supervision: Regular supervision sessions
during the week.
Interview details: Prospective volunteers are
interviewed at Footprints.
Certification: Written reference on request.
Charity number: 1018320
UK placements: *England* (Kent).

KENT TRUST FOR NATURE CONSERVATION
Tyland Barn
Sandling
Maidstone
Kent
ME14 3BD UK

Tel: +44 (0) 1622 662012
Fax: +44 (0) 1622 671390
Contact: The Director

Kent Trust for Nature Conservation is a
member of the Wildlife Trusts, a national
partnership of 47 County Trusts. For more
details of the Wildlife Trusts, see the entry
under Cornwall Wildlife Trust.

Total projects worldwide: 1
Total UK projects: 1
Starting months: January–December.
Time required: 1–52 weeks (plus).
Age requirement: 12 plus.
Causes: Conservation, environmental causes,
wildlife.
Activities: Conservation skills.
Work alone/with others: With others.
Qualifications: Nil.
Health requirements: Anti-tetanus

innoculation recommended.
Costs: Nil.
Training: On the job training given.
UK placements: *England* (Kent).

KENYA VOLUNTARY DEVELOPMENT ASSOCIATION
PO Box 48902
Nairobi
Kenya

Tel: 00 254 2 225379 or 247393
Fax: 00 254 2 225379
e-mail: kvda@wamadev.africaonline.com
Contact: The Director

Kenya Voluntary Development Association
needs volunteers to work on projects in
villages aimed at improving amenities in
Kenya's rural and needy areas, working
alongside members of the local community.
The work may involve digging foundations,
building, making building blocks, roofing,
environmental projects etc. Volunteers with
an offending background are accepted.

Total projects worldwide: 12
Total UK projects: 0
Starting months: February, April, July,
August, October, December.
Time required: 2–3 weeks.
Age requirement: 17 plus.
Causes: Conservation, poor/homeless, work
camps – seasonal.
Activities: Building/construction,
conservation skills, work camps – seasonal.
Vols under 26 placed each year: 170 of a
total of 200 plus.
When to apply: Ideally 8 weeks in advance
but any time before starting.
Work alone/with others: With others.
Volunteers with disabilities: Possible.
Qualifications: Nil.
Equipment/clothing: Strong work boots,
sleeping bag or blanket, mosquito net, mug,
plate, spoon, fork, knife, malaria tablets,
clothes for working in, toilet paper and any
other necessary personal effects.
Health requirements: Malaria pills and any
other innoculations etc.
Costs: Registration fee of $200 for one camp,
$300 for consecutive camps. Travel. All
insurance.
Benefits: Food and very basic accommodation
(classroom).
Training: Our volunteers are not given pre-
training as such but they are given orientation

which includes demonstration of what to do and what to expect.

Supervision: Camps are led by camp facilitator and the project officer keeps on checking.

Interview details: No interview necessary.

Certification: Certificate or reference provided.

Worldwide placements: *Africa* (Kenya).

KIBBUTZ REPRESENTATIVES
1a Accommodation Road
London
NW11 8ED UK

Tel: +44 (0) 20 8458 9235
Fax: +44 (0) 20 8455 7930
e-mail: enquiries@kibbutz.org.uk
Contact: Volunteer Co-ordinator

Kibbutz Representatives needs volunteers to work on kibbutzim to help the community as a whole, but also to experience the alternative lifestyle. They may be working anywhere – agriculture, industry or services.

Total projects worldwide: 1
Total UK projects: 0
Starting months: January–December.
Time required: 8–24 weeks.
Age requirement: 18–32
Causes: Animal welfare, children, conservation, elderly people, work camps – seasonal, young people.
Activities: Agriculture/farming, catering, community work, conservation skills, cooking, forestry, gardening/horticulture, group work, manual work.
Vols under 26 placed each year: 2,500 of a total of 3,000.
When to apply: For July and August it is essential to apply before Easter. For the rest of the year, 5–6 weeks in advance.
Work alone/with others: Both but mainly with others.
Volunteers with disabilities: Not possible.
Qualifications: Nil.
Health requirements: Volunteers must be physically and mentally healthy, free from chronic conditions.
Costs: Travel package cost and insurance.
Benefits: Board, lodging, leisure facilities, occasional excursions round country plus an allowance.
Interview details: Interviews take place in London or Manchester.
Certification: Certificate or reference provided

on request.
Charity number: 294564
Worldwide placements: *Asia* (Israel).

KIDS' CAMPS: CAMPS FOR STUDENTS WITH AN INTELLECTUAL DISABILITY INC.
PO Box 170
Leederville
6065 Western Australia

Tel: 00 61 8 9420 7247
Fax: 00 61 8 9420 7248
Contact: Kathy Christoffeloz

Kids' Camps Inc. provides residential camps for school-aged children (6–18 years) who live at home and are walking unassisted, i.e. no wheelchairs, and who have an intellectual disability (Downs syndrome, autism etc.). Camps are for two days or six days. Volunteer camp leaders care for up to three children, taking responsibility for their safety, welfare, personal hygiene etc. and also encouraging them to join in recreational activities in the programme. One or two paid staff supervise the group, supporting, assisting, advising and co-ordinating the volunteer staff. Qualities needed to be a volunteer leader are: genuine liking for children; sense of responsibility and understanding of duty of care issues in the daily care of children; good communication skills with kids, other leaders and staff; sense of humour, patience and ability to have fun; initiative as necessary. A booklet, *An Introduction to Volunteering with Kids Camps* is available plus orientation and information sessions. Feedback is encouraged by Kids' Camps during camps. Volunteers with an offending background would not be accepted if the charges are associated with abuse/assault or serious injury or children.

Total projects worldwide: 1
Total UK projects: 0
Starting months: January–December.
Time required: 1–52 weeks (plus).
Age requirement: 18 plus.
Causes: Children, disabled (learning), holidays for disabled.
Activities: Caring (residential), summer camps, visiting/befriending.
Vols under 26 placed each year: 120 of a total of 130.
When to apply: All year. *Extra location information.*

Work alone/with others: With others.
Volunteers with disabilities: Only if physically fit and have intellectual comprehension of duty of care, communication etc.
Qualifications: Good English speaking skills.
Health requirements: General good health and fitness.
Costs: Travel to camp.
Benefits: Accommodation, food and entertainment. Post-camp social event. Insurance provided by us for any costs not covered under Medicare.
Training: Interview and pre-camp orientation, 4–6 hours.
Supervision: Paid experienced staff offer support, assistance, advice to volunteers.
Interview details: Interviews take place in the Kids' Camps office in West Perth, W. Australia.
Certification: Certificate provided and reference.
Worldwide placements: Australasia (Australia).

KIDS' CLUBS NETWORK
Bellerive House
3 Muirfield Crescent
London
E14 9SZ UK

Tel: +44 (0) 20 7512 2112
Fax: +44 (0) 20 7512 2010
Contact: Anne Longfield

Kids' Clubs Network provides play and care opportunities for primary school-age children before and after school during term time and all day long during school holidays. Children are collected from school at the end of the day by playworkers, escorted safely to the club where they are offered tea and play activities until they are collected by parents. Whilst at the club children are able to enjoy a range of activities including arts and crafts, sports and games, drama, music, books and trips out. Kids' Club Network is the national organization for out-of-school care and can give details of local clubs. Volunteers' records will be checked by the police including for all spent convictions.

Total projects worldwide: 3,400
Total UK projects: 3,400
Starting months: January–December.
Time required: 1–52 weeks.
Age requirement: 16 plus.

Causes: Children, Teaching/assisting (primary).
Activities: Arts/crafts, caring (general and day), community work, fundraising, marketing/publicity, outdoor skills, sport, summer camps, teaching.
When to apply: All year.
Work alone/with others: Both.
Volunteers with disabilities: Possible.
Qualifications: Sensitivity, judgement, energy, arts, crafts, sports.
Health requirements: Check locally.
Costs: Out-of-pocket expenses usually.
Benefits: Dependent on the club.
Training: Dependent on each particular club.
Supervision: Dependent on the club.
Interview details: Each club interviews its own applicants.
Charity number: 288285
UK placements: England (throughout); Scotland (throughout); Northern Ireland (throughout); Wales (throughout).

KINGS CROSS – BRUNSWICK NEIGHBOURHOOD ASSOCIATION
Marchmont Community Centre
62 Marchmont Street
London
WC1N 1AB UK

Tel: +44 (0) 20 7278 5635
Contact: Linda Saltwell

Kings Cross Brunswick Neighbourhood Association is involved in a volunteer pool called South Camden Volunteers Project.

Total projects worldwide: 1
Total UK projects: 1
Starting months: January–December.
Time required: 1–52 weeks.
Age requirement: 14 plus.
Causes: Elderly People.
Activities: Arts/crafts, campaigning, driving, gardening/horticulture, training.
When to apply: All year.
Interview details: Interviews take place at the office in London.
Charity number: 1001872
UK placements: England (London).

KOINONIA PARTNERS
1324 Georgia Highway 49 South
Americus
Georgia 31709
USA

Tel: 00 1 912 924 0391
Fax: 00 1 912 924 6504
e-mail: koinonia@habitat.org
Contact: The Volunteer Co-ordinator

Koinonia Partners is a non-profit Christian organization working in the rural south of the USA to attack poverty and racism from every angle. Koinonia attempts to promote self-sufficiency for low-income neighbourhoods and to fight inequality in this region. Koinonia operates a large farm and bakery under predominantly African American management. All income from the operation is used to fund community organizing, youth education, and housing. We are trying to make our neighbourhood a model of a self-sufficient, inter-racial, empowered community. Volunteers support our full-time staff in many different areas: the farm, garden, youth programme, office, child development centre, maintenance, bakery and products business. Volunteers also share four weekly study sessions that focus on justice, racism, environmentalism, community, and issues of faith. Koinonia supports volunteers with housing, fresh garden and farm produce, access to field trips, social events, and transport.

Total projects worldwide: 1
Total UK projects: 0
Starting months: January, February, June, September.
Time required: 1–52 weeks (plus).
Age requirement: 21 plus.
Causes: Children, conservation, disabled (physical), elderly people, environmental causes, poor/homeless, teaching/assisting young people.
Activities: Administration, agriculture/farming, building/construction, conservation skills, cooking, development issues, forestry, fundraising, gardening/horticulture, manual work, outdoor skills, religion, summer camps, teaching, visiting/befriending.
Vols under 26 placed each year: 30
When to apply: As early as possible.
Work alone/with others: With others.
Volunteers with disabilities: There is office, youth, farm and garden work. We have no disabled volunteers.
Qualifications: Willing to explore the Christian faith and life. Applicants must speak English and volunteers must obtain a tourist visa.

Equipment/clothing: Clothing only.
Health requirements: Good to excellent health.
Costs: Tourist visa and travel expenses.
Benefits: Board, lodging and a stipend for food and extra costs.
Nationalities accepted: No restrictions but all applicants must speak English.
Interview details: No interview necessary.
Worldwide placements: *North America* (USA).

KRISTOFFERTUNET
Hans Collins vej 5
N 7053 Ranheim
Norway

Tel: 00 47 73 901500
Fax: 00 47 73 916885
Contact: Daan Ente

Kristoffertunet is a little Camphill community situated near Trondheim. We try to re-socialize drug-addicts after they have been for 18 months on a farm community nearby. Most of our 'patients' are mentally handicapped adults (eight persons). We live together with our children in three big houses which were built by the Germans during the Second World War. There is a big garden, some cows, hens and a fjord horse. In wintertime there is a little carpenter's workshop. Volunteers with an offending background are accepted.

Total projects worldwide: 1
Total UK projects: 0
Starting months: January–December.
Time required: 3–52 weeks (plus).
Age requirement: 18 plus.
Causes: Addicts/Ex-addicts, disabled (learning).
Activities: Agriculture/farming, building/construction, caring (general), cooking, gardening/horticulture.
Vols under 26 placed each year: 2
When to apply: Any time.
Work alone/with others: Both.
Volunteers with disabilities: Possible.
Qualifications: Nil.
Health requirements: Nil.
Costs: Travel.
Benefits: Board, lodging and pocket money.
Interview details: No interview necessary.
Certification: Certificate or reference on request.
Worldwide placements: *Europe* (Norway).

L

LA RIOBE
53 avenue Pasteur
93260 Les Lilas
France
Tel: 00 33 1 48 97 07 83 (7pm 9pm)
Contact: Ms Geneviève Gleyze

La Riobe organizes in August an archaeological dig, on a Gallo-Roman site 72 km east of Paris. The work to be done includes digging, cleaning and restoring the finds and making an inventory on computer of the finds and scientific research.

Total projects worldwide: 1
Total UK projects: 0
Starting months: August.
Time required: 2–4 weeks.
Age requirement: 18 plus.
Causes: Archaeology.
Activities: Manual work, research.
Vols under 26 placed each year: 20
When to apply: As early as possible.
Qualifications: Adequate French to be understood.
Equipment/clothing: Sleeping bag, working clothes, sun hat, rainwear.
Health requirements: Proof of anti-tetanus injection.
Costs: FF220 for inscription and insurance and FF55 per day for food.
Interview details: No interview necessary.
Worldwide placements: *Europe* (France).

LA SABRANENQUE
Centre International
Rue de la Tour de L'Oume,
F-30290 Saint Victor la Coste
France

Tel: 00 33 4 66 50 05 05
Fax: 00 33 4 66 50 12 48
e-mail: info@sabranenque.com
Web: www.sabranenque.com
Contact: Marc Simon

La Sabranenque volunteer restoration projects offer the opportunity to become directly and actively involved in the preservation and reconstruction of monuments dating often to the Middle Ages. Volunteers learn traditional construction techniques on-the-job from experienced technicians, experience daily life in Mediterranean villages, and share in a multicultural project with participants coming from a variety of countries and backgrounds.

Total projects worldwide: 3
Total UK projects: 0
Starting months: June–August.
Time required: 2–52 weeks.
Age requirement: 18 plus.
Causes: Architecture, conservation, heritage.
Activities: Building/construction, conservation skills.
Vols under 26 placed each year: 75 of a total of 150.
When to apply: Any time.
Work alone/with others: With others.
Volunteers with disabilities: Not possible.
Qualifications: Nil.
Health requirements: Nil.
Costs: Approximately £80 per week for food and accommodation in France. £180 for 3 week project including food and accommodation in Italy.
Benefits: Board and lodging.
Training: On site.
Supervision: Our team of experienced restoration technicians.
Interview details: No interview necessary.
Certification: Certificate or reference provided on request.
Worldwide placements: *Europe* (France, Italy).

LABO ANTHROPOLOGIE
UPR
403 du CNRS
Campus de Beaulieu
F-35042 Rennes Cedex
France

Tel: 00 33 2 99 28 61 09
Contact: Dr J.L. Monnier

Labo Anthropologie needs volunteers to take part in archaeological digs in the summer to work from 0830–1200 and 1400–1800, five and a half days a week.

Total projects worldwide: 1
Total UK projects: 0
Starting months: May–August.
Time required: 1–52 weeks.
Age requirement: 18 plus.
Causes: Archaeology, heritage.
Vols under 26 placed each year: 60
When to apply: As early as possible.
Qualifications: Genuine interest in prehistoric

archaeology. No language necessary.
Equipment/clothing: Camping equipment.
Benefits: Board provided.
Worldwide placements: *Europe* (France).

LAKE DISTRICT ART GALLERY AND MUSEUM TRUST
Abbot Hall Art Gallery
Kendal
Cumbria
LA9 5AL UK

Tel: +44 (0) 1539 722464
Fax: +44 (0) 1539 722494
Contact: Mr Edward King

Lake District Art Gallery and Museum Trust needs volunteer research assistants, reception staff, events helpers and coffee shop staff to work in the Kendal Museum, Abbot Hall Art Gallery and the Museum of Lakeland Life and Industry. Hours are from 9 a.m. to 5 p.m. Monday to Friday and weekends in July, August and September or at any time during the year subject to availability. Although we welcome volunteers for at least a week, we prefer a minimum stay of three months.

Total projects worldwide: 3
Total UK projects: 3
Starting months: July–September.
Time required: 1–12 weeks.
Age requirement: 18 plus.
Causes: Heritage.
Activities: Administration, research.
When to apply: As early as possible.
Work alone/with others: Both.
Qualifications: Graduates or undergraduates wishing to gain museum experience.
Health requirements: Nil.
Costs: Nil.
Benefits: Accommodation may be available free of charge.
Training: Induction will be given.
Interview details: All applicants should be available for interview in Kendal.
UK placements: *England* (Cumbria).

LANCASHIRE WILDLIFE TRUST
Cuerden Park Wildlife Centre
Shady Lane
Bamber Bridge
Preston
Lancashire
PR5 6AU UK

Tel: +44 (0) 1772 324129
Fax: +44 (0) 1772 628849
e-mail: rwebb@lancswt.cix.co.uk
Web: www.wildlifetrust.org.uk/lancashire
Contact: Mr Ronnie Webb

Lancashire Wildlife Trust is the leading regional charity committed to the protection and promotion of all native wildlife within the 'old' county of Lancashire. Lancashire's magnificent coastline, fells and river valleys form a region rich in diversity. From the splendour of our wading birds, badgers, barn owls and dragonflies to the estuaries, woods, meadows and wetlands where they live – the Trust is working on their behalf.

Total projects worldwide: 1
Total UK projects: 1
Starting months: January–December.
Time required: 6–52 weeks (plus).
Age requirement: 16 plus.
Causes: Conservation, environmental causes, wildlife.
Activities: Community work, conservation skills, forestry, fundraising, outdoor skills.
Vols under 26 placed each year: 60 of a total of 200.
When to apply: All year.
Work alone/with others: With others.
Volunteers with disabilities: Possible.
Qualifications: Nil.
Equipment/clothing: Outdoor practical work would require suitable clothing, boots etc.
Health requirements: Nil – any medical problems must be disclosed in case some areas of work are unsuitable.
Costs: Travel costs and subsistence.
Interview details: Prospective volunteers are interviewed either at our main office, Bolton office or at our larger reserves.
Certification: Reference on request.
Charity number: 229325
UK placements: *England* (Lancashire, Manchester, Merseyside).

LAND USE VOLUNTEERS
Horticultural Therapy Resource Centre
Geoffrey Udall Building
Trunkwell Park
Beech Hill
Reading
RG7 2AT UK

Tel: +44 (0) 118 988 5688
Fax: +44 (0) 118 988 5677
e-mail: hort_therapy@compuserve.com

Contact: John Dowsett

Horticultural Therapy is a charity that helps people with disabilities to enjoy and benefit from gardening, horticulture and agriculture. Its volunteer service, Land Use Volunteers, posts people who have training or experience in horticulture to projects run by a variety of other organizations. Volunteers with an offending background may be accepted depending on circumstances.

Total projects worldwide: Hundreds.
Total UK projects: Hundreds.
Starting months: January–December.
Time required: 40–52 weeks (plus).
Age requirement: 22 plus.
Causes: Addicts/Ex-addicts, Aids/HIV, conservation, disabled (learning and physical), elderly people, environmental causes, health care/medical, inner city problems, offenders/ex-offenders, poor/homeless, refugees, teaching/assisting unemployed, wildlife, young people.
Activities: Agriculture/farming, caring (general, day and residential), community work, conservation skills, counselling, development issues, forestry, fundraising, gardening/horticulture, manual work, outdoor skills, social work, teaching, technical skills.
Vols under 26 placed each year: 1–2 of a total of 7.
When to apply: All year.
Work alone/with others: Both.
Volunteers with disabilities: Possible.
Qualifications: Qualifications and/or experience in horticulture, agriculture, conservation, environment. Driving licence useful. Empathy with people with disabilities.
Health requirements: Nil.
Costs: Travel cost for interview.
Benefits: Board, lodging paid plus initial travel plus pocket money.
Interview details: Interviews take place in Coventry, London, Reading or by arrangement.
Certification: Certificate or reference on request.
Charity number: 277570
UK placements: *England* (Bedfordshire, Berkshire, Bristol, Buckinghamshire, Cambridgeshire, Channel Islands, Cheshire, Derbyshire, Devon, Dorset, Essex, Gloucestershire, Hampshire, Herefordshire, Hertfordshire, Isle of Man, Kent, Lancashire, Leicestershire, Lincolnshire, London, Manchester, Merseyside, Norfolk, Northamptonshire, Nottinghamshire, Oxfordshire, Rutland, Shropshire, Somerset, Staffordshire, Suffolk, Surrey, E. Sussex, W. Sussex, Warwickshire, West Midlands, Wiltshire, Worcestershire, E. Yorkshire, S. Yorkshire, W. Yorkshire).

LANKA JATHIKA SARVODAYA SHRAMADANA SANGAMAYA (INC)
Damsak Mandira
98 Rawatawatte Road
Moratuwa
Sri Lanka

Tel: 00 94 1 647159, 655255
Fax: 00 94 1 656512
e-mail: sarsed@lanka.ccom.lk
Web: www.sarvodaya.org
Contact: Dr Vinya Ariyaratne, Executive Director

Lanka Jathika Sarvodaya Shramadana Sangamaya was founded in 1958. The movement is a large non-governmental people's self-development effort covering nearly 8,000 villages, providing the possibility of realizing the well-being of all, be they human beings, animals or plants. It also creates awareness among deprived communities and mobilizes latent human and material potential for the satisfaction of basic human needs in a manner that ensures sustainable development and develops strategies and implements action programmes. Services of the volunteers are taken on the availability of vacancies in the fields of agriculture, bio-diversity and environment, appropriate technology, information technology, economic activities, health care, pre-school activities and legal aid programmes based at grass-roots level to satisfy the basic human needs and gradually work upwards to national and international levels. Applicants should have an awareness of their responsibility to improve human conditions wherever needed and an ability to work in sometimes difficult circumstances. They should also have a commitment to the promotion of peace and international understanding that leads to the equitable distribution of the world's resources according to need. Services of volunteers are initially taken for six months or less and on the performance of work, extensions are granted. Volunteers with an offending background may be accepted depending on the nature of the offence.

Total projects worldwide: 1
Total UK projects: 0
Starting months: January–December.
Time required: 4–52 weeks.
Age requirement: 21–35
Causes: Children, disabled (learning and physical), elderly people, health care/medical, human rights, refugees, teaching/assisting (nursery, mature).
Activities: Agriculture/farming, building/construction, community work, computers, first aid, fundraising, gardening/horticulture, marketing/publicity, newsletter/journalism, research, social work, teaching, technical skills.
Vols under 26 placed each year: 25 of a total of 30.
When to apply: 6 months in advance.
Work alone/with others: With others.
Qualifications: No special skills required and academic qualifications are optional.
Health requirements: Good health.
Costs: Rs900 per day (including accommodation but excluding meals); plus travel, medical and insurance costs. Medical insurance is necessary and the responsibility of the volunteer.
Training: Basic local language training and prior visits to the projects and programme sites.
Supervision: By the person in charge of the project/programme as and when necessary.
Certification: Certificate or reference provided.
Worldwide placements: *Asia* (Sri Lanka).

L'ARCHE – KILKENNY
Fair Green Lane
Callan
Co. Kilkenny
Ireland

Tel: 00 353 0 56 25628
Fax: 00 353 (0) 56 25957
e-mail: larche@iol.ie
Contact: The Assistants Co-ordinator, Director

L'Arche – Kilkenny provides residential care for adults with learning disabilities. L'Arche communities are places where people with and without learning disabilities live and work together in a simple way, to build community in the spirit of Jesus – places which offer a way of life that is not competitive nor dependent on material success and intellectual achievement – places that heal rather than divide. L'Arche communities provide a family atmosphere within small homes that are well integrated into the local neighbourhood. L'Arche workshops provide different kinds of work where each person can find fulfilment and opportunity for growth. L'Arche's spiritual life is particularly important, and all homes offer a life of prayer which members can share as they wish. L'Arche is a Christian community, ecumenical in spirit, striving to live a life of simplicity in the spirit of the Gospels. September start is preferred but other months are possible.

Total projects worldwide: 1
Total UK projects: 0
Starting months: January–December.
Time required: 8–52 weeks (plus).
Age requirement: 18 plus.
Causes: Disabled (learning).
Activities: Arts/crafts, caring (general, day and residential), community work, cooking, driving, gardening/horticulture.
Vols under 26 placed each year: 7 of a total of 10.
When to apply: All year.
Work alone/with others: With others.
Volunteers with disabilities: Sometimes.
Qualifications: Reasonably fluent in spoken English.
Health requirements: Hepatitis B and HIV negative documentation.
Costs: Travel to Kilkenny.
Benefits: Board, lodging and pocket money of approximately IR£180 per month. We provide insurance cover.
Supervision: Volunteers are accountable to their house leader/work leader and director.
Nationalities accepted: No restrictions but volunteers need a reasonable fluency in spoken English.
Interview details: No interview necessary – correspondence and references on paper.
Charity number: 7979
Worldwide placements: *Europe* (Ireland).

L'ARCHE MOBILE
151-A South Ann Street
Mobile
Alabama
AL 36604 USA

Tel: 00 1 334 438 2094
Fax: 00 1 334 438 2094 plus 433 5835
e-mail: larchmob@ACAN.net
Web: www.acan.net/7larchmob/
Contact: Martin E. O'Malley

L'Arche Mobile needs volunteers annually to live, work and share their lives with people with intellectual disabilities. Duties include sharing life with people as well as sharing all the daily tasks of making a home together, cooking, cleaning, yardwork, repairs etc.

Total projects worldwide: 1
Total UK projects: 0
Starting months: January–December.
Time required: 12–52 weeks.
Age requirement: 18 plus.
Causes: Disabled (learning and physical), elderly people.
Activities: Caring (general and residential), community work, cooking, DIY, driving, group work, manual work, visiting/befriending.
Vols under 26 placed each year: 3 of a total of 15.
When to apply: All year.
Work alone/with others: With others.
Volunteers with disabilities: Possible.
Qualifications: A desire to live in a community. English speaking.
Equipment/clothing: Just cotton to help with the humidity.
Health requirements: Capable of some lifting work.
Costs: Travel to and from L'Arch Mobile, medical and dental insurance for first 4 months.
Benefits: Board and lodging. Pocket money after 1 month, health insurance after 4 months if committed to 6 months. Usually there is a celebration in the house where the volunteer lived to say farewell.
Supervision: Orientation, regular meetings with the head of house, regular meetings with the assistant director. Team meetings. Assistant meetings. Evaluations after 1st and 3rd month trial and annually.
Interview details: Interviews are conducted on site.
Certification: Certificate or reference on request.
Worldwide placements: *North America* (USA).

L'ARCHE – UK
10 Briggate
Silsden
Keighley
West Yorkshire
BD20 9JT UK

Tel: +44 (0) 1535 656186
Fax: +44 (0) 1535 656426
e-mail: info@larche.org.uk
Web: www.larche.org.uk
Contact: John Peet, General Secretary

L'Arche – UK provides residential care for adults with learning disabilities. For more details of L'Arche, see L'Arche – Kilkenny, above.

Total projects worldwide: 100 plus
Total UK projects: 8
Starting months: January–December.
Time required: 8–52 weeks (plus).
Age requirement: 18 plus.
Causes: Disabled (learning).
Activities: Arts/crafts, caring (general, day and residential), community work, cooking, gardening/horticulture, group work, religion, social work.
Vols under 26 placed each year: 60–70
When to apply: As early as possible.
Work alone/with others: With others.
Volunteers with disabilities: We are unable to accept volunteers who cannot perform all duties independently.
Qualifications: Nil.
Health requirements: In good health physically, mentally and emotionally to cope with the demands of caring duties.
Costs: Travel and personal expenses.
Benefits: Board and lodging (negotiable with community) plus pocket money. Personal effects are insured but items of value are not. Separate personal cover should be taken out for these.
Training: Continuing programme.
Supervision: Each volunteer is assigned a personal mentor and is supervised regularly by the community leader.
Interview details: Process which involves correspondence and references on paper and a trial period.
Certification: References on requested.
Charity number: 264166
Worldwide placements: *Africa* (Burkina Faso, Ivory Coast, Zimbabwe); *Asia* (India, Japan, Philippines); *Australasia* (Australia, New Zealand); *Europe* (Belgium, Denmark,

France, Germany, Hungary, Ireland, Italy, Netherlands, Poland, Slovenia, Spain, Switzerland); *North America* (Canada, USA); *Central America* (Dominican Republic, Haiti, Honduras, Mexico); *South America* (Brazil). **UK placements:** *England* (Kent, Lancashire, London, Merseyside, W. Sussex); *Scotland* (Edinburgh, Highland); *Wales* (Powys).

LASALLIAN DEVELOPING WORLD PROJECTS
405 Beulah Hill
London
SE19 3HB UK

Tel: +44 (0) 20 8670 1612
Fax: +44 (0) 20 8761 7357
e-mail: ldwpuk@hotmail.com
Web: www.dlsnet.demon.co.uk
Contact: John Deeney, FSC, Director

Lasallian Developing World Projects provides opportunities for young people to give personal and practical service to the educationally deprived in developing countries. Projects normally involve building, instruction and social contact. Teams of up to 12 people work to develop school or youth facilities, usually in rural or small town areas. Volunteers fund themselves and make a small contribution towards the cost of building materials. We are a Christian organization but also work with and for those who profess other faiths.

Total projects worldwide: 4–5
Total UK projects: 0
Starting months: July.
Time required: 5 weeks.
Age requirement: 18 plus.
Causes: Children, teaching/assisting (primary, secondary, EFL), work camps – seasonal, young people.
Activities: Building/construction, cooking, development issues, fundraising, group work, international aid, manual work, teaching, work camps – seasonal.
Vols under 26 placed each year: 42 of a total of 50.
When to apply: April–May of the previous year.
Work alone/with others: With others.
Volunteers with disabilities: Not possible.
Qualifications: No skills specified.
Health requirements: Must be able to work in a tropical climate.
Costs: Total cost £1,200.

Benefits: The cost includes travel, insurance, food, lodging, training plus contribution to project materials.
Training: 3-day sessions prior to departure.
Supervision: Experienced group leaders. Local co-ordinators advise.
Nationalities accepted: No restrictions but volunteers need to be eligible for a visa in the country of placement.
Interview details: Prospective volunteers are interviewed in London, the North of England or Glasgow.
Certification: Certificate or reference provided.
Charity number: 232632
Worldwide placements: *Africa* (Ethiopia, Ghana, Kenya, Mozambique, Uganda); *Asia* (Philippines, Sri Lanka).

LATIN LINK
Short Term Experience Projects (Step/Stride)
175 Tower Bridge Road
London
SE1 2AB UK

Tel: +44 (0) 20 7939 9000
Fax: +44 (0) 20 7939 9015
e-mail: step.uk@latinlink.org
stride.uk@latinlink.org
Web: www.latinlink.org
Contact: Jo Hassoun or Laurence East

Latin Link Step projects aim to give young people the chance to live and work alongside a Latin American church community and help out in a basic building programme. In 2000 we had Steppers working on ten different projects, building orphanages, classrooms for local schools and church community centres amongst other things. In 2001 we continue our programme working in Bolivia, Brazil, Ecuador, Peru, Argentina and Mexico. There are two types of projects. Summer Projects run for four to eight weeks from mid-July until early September and usually take place in all the countries mentioned above. Spring Projects run for four months from the middle of March until mid-July. On these projects there is the option to stay on for a further seven weeks and join a summer project in the same country. Stride placements are for a minimum of six months and a maximum of two years. Candidates are placed on individual projects which match their particular skills and gifts. Stride volunteers depart for Latin America in

September each year.

Total projects worldwide: 12–15
Total UK projects: 0
Starting months: March, July, August,
September.
Time required: 4–52 weeks (plus).
Age requirement: 17 plus.
Causes: Aids/HIV, children, disabled
(learning and physical), elderly people, health
care/medical, inner city problems, offenders/
ex-offenders, poor/homeless, refugees,
teaching/assisting (nursery, primary,
secondary, EFL), young people.
Activities: Accountancy, administration, arts/
crafts, building/construction, caring
(general), community work, DIY, group
work, international aid, manual work,
music, religion, social work, teaching,
theatre/drama, translating.
Vols under 26 placed each year: 80–120 of a
total of 100–150.
When to apply: Spring: October–December.
Summer: February–May. Stride: January–
April.
Work alone/with others: Both.
Volunteers with disabilities: Possible.
Qualifications: Christian commitment.
Spanish or Portuguese is helpful but not
essential.
Equipment/clothing: Equipment list
provided.
Health requirements: Each volunteer must
prove medical fitness to Latin Link's
consultant.
Costs: Minimum £1,320. Step and Stride
have their own insurance policy to cover
volunteers while in Latin America.
Training: Step: a training weekend plus
written briefing materials. Team leaders have
an additional 2-day training course.
Stride: a 4-day orientation course in early
September.
Supervision: Teams and individuals are
supervised by local Latin Link workers and
local Christian leaders.
Interview details: Individual interviews at our
selection day.
Charity number: 1020826
Worldwide placements: *Central America*
(Costa Rica, Honduras, Mexico, Nicaragua);
South America (Argentina, Bolivia, Brazil,
Colombia, Ecuador, Peru).

LEBENSGEMEINSCHAFT ALT SCHÖNOW
Alt Schönow 5-7a
D-14165 Berlin (Zehlendorf)
Germany

Tel: 00 49 30 815 46 78
Contact: The Director

Lebensgemeinschaft alt Schönow is an urban
adult Camphill community.

Total projects worldwide: 1
Total UK projects: 0
Starting months: January–December.
Time required: 1–52 weeks.
Age requirement: 18 plus.
Causes: Disabled (learning).
Activities: Agriculture/farming, arts/crafts,
caring (general and residential), community
work, cooking, gardening/horticulture,
music, outdoor skills.
When to apply: All year.
Work alone/with others: With others.
Worldwide placements: *Europe* (Germany).

LEE ABBEY COMMUNITY
Lee Abbey
Lynton
Devon
EX35 6JJ UK

Tel: + 44 (0) 1598 752621
Fax: + 44 (0) 1598 752619
e-mail: Personnel@leeabbey.org.uk
Contact: Personnel

Lee Abbey is a Christian holiday and
conference centre run by a community
working for the renewal and refreshment of
the church. The Community has a branch in
London which is a hostel for international
students. Other branches are in Knowle West
(Bristol), Aston (Birmingham) and Blackburn.
These communities help in urban priority
areas. Volunteers with an offending
background for minor offences will be
considered.

Total projects worldwide: 1
Total UK projects: 1
Starting months: January–December.
Time required: 1–52 weeks (plus).
Age requirement: 18 plus.
Causes: Children, inner city problems, young
people.
Activities: Accountancy, administration,
agriculture/farming, catering, computers,

cooking, forestry, gardening/horticulture, manual work, marketing/publicity, outdoor skills, religion, summer camps.

Vols under 26 placed each year: 32 of a total of 80.

When to apply: All year.

Work alone/with others: With others.

Volunteers with disabilities: Not possible.

Qualifications: Nil but agricultural or catering experience useful.

Health requirements: Good, physically and mentally.

Costs: Travel expenses to Lee Abbey – no other costs.

Benefits: Board and lodging plus allowance. Each volunteer is covered by insurance for most items and we provide life insurance up to £2,000.

Supervision: Each person is on a team and is supported by a team leader. We also supply pastoral support.

Interview details: Interviews take place at Lynton, Devon.

Certification: Reference on request.

Charity number: 227322

UK placements: *England* (Devon, Lancashire, London, West Midlands).

LEICESTER CHILDREN'S HOLIDAY CENTRE

Quebec Road
Mablethorpe
Lincolnshire
LN12 1QX UK

Tel: +44 (0) 1507 472444
Fax: +44 (0) 1507 472444
e-mail: helen@lanzetta.freeserve.co.uk
Contact: Mrs Eagle-Lanzetta

Leicester Children's Holiday Centre provides summer holidays for groups of 30 girls and 30 boys from socially deprived backgrounds in the Leicester area. The two-week camps are held from May through to the end of August each year. We prefer people who are able to work the whole season, or stay at least one month. Volunteers are expected to work a six-day week on our outdoor programme of activities. Proof of no convictions required for all volunteers.

Total projects worldwide: 1
Total UK projects: 1
Starting months: May–August.
Time required: 4–16 weeks.
Age requirement: 18–35

Causes: Children.

Activities: Caring (general), catering, first aid, music, sport, summer camps, theatre/drama.

Vols under 26 placed each year: 14–18 of a total of 16–20.

When to apply: 1 January with sae.

Work alone/with others: As a team.

Volunteers with disabilities: Not possible.

Qualifications: Spoken English, plus Certificate of Good Conduct if position offered.

Health requirements: Must be fit.

Costs: Travel costs. Volunteers from outside the UK are responsible for organizing and paying for any necessary health insurance.

Benefits: Board, accommodation (shared room with one other) and national minimum wage based on 48 hours per week less deductions for food and accommodation.

Training: We provide a 2-week on-site training programme for volunteers based on the NVQ with a certificate.

Supervision: By senior staff members at the start.

Nationalities accepted: No restrictions but must be able to speak English.

Interview details: Interviews take place at the Centre in Mablethorpe, Lincolnshire or by telephone for overseas volunteers.

Certification: 2 references provided on request. NVQ certificate.

Charity number: 217976

UK placements: *England* (Lincolnshire).

LEONARD CHESHIRE

30 Millbank
London
SW1P 4QD UK

Tel: +44 (0) 20 7802 8200
Fax: +44 (0) 20 7802 8250
Contact: John Hedderman

Leonard Cheshire provides a range of high-quality services to people with physical and learning disabilities, people with mental health problems, and support for their carers. In the United Kingdom it has more than 80 homes, as well as a range of other services including day services and services for people living in their own homes. In addition there are 200 projects in a further 50 countries throughout the world. Volunteers are required to assist with the day-to-day personal care of disabled residents – tasks such as getting up, shaving, bathing, toileting, feeding and going to bed. They may also be asked to help in a wide variety of other ways. Examples include writing letters, taking residents shopping, helping them with hobbies, driving the home's or residents' transport if qualified to do so and accompanying residents on outings or holidays.

Total projects worldwide: 86
Total UK projects: 86
Starting months: January–December.
Time required: 12–52 weeks.
Age requirement: 18 plus.
Causes: Disabled (learning and physical), elderly people.
Activities: Caring (general and day), cooking, social work.
Vols under 26 placed each year: 100
When to apply: All year.
Work alone/with others: With others.
Volunteers with disabilities: Possible.
Qualifications: Good spoken English, willing to work hard with understanding and dedication.
Health requirements: Nil.
Costs: Travel costs.
Benefits: Board, lodging plus £29.50 per week pocket money.
Certification: Reference provided.
UK placements: *England* (throughout); *Scotland* (Dumfries and Galloway, Edinburgh, Fife, Highland, E. Lothian, W. Lothian); *Northern Ireland* (Armagh, Belfast City, Derry/Londonderry); *Wales* (Cardiff, Conwy, Monmouthshire, Newport, Pembrokeshire, Torfaen).

LEPROSY MISSION, THE

80 Windmill Road
Brentford
Middlesex
TW8 0QH UK

Tel: +44 (0) 20 8569 7292
Fax: +44 (0) 20 8569 7808
e-mail: friends@tlmint.org
Contact: Personnel Support Administrator

The Leprosy Mission or TLM is an international Christian charity working in over 30 countries of the developing world. Since its beginnings in 1874, TLM has been seeking to relieve the terrible suffering of people affected by leprosy through treatment, acceptance and prayer. Today leprosy can be cured with multidrug therapy or MDT, and deformities can be prevented with early treatment. The challenge facing TLM is to reach the many untreated sufferers with help – about 600,000 new cases of leprosy develop each year – and to care for people with or at risk of deformity – numbering over four million worldwide. TLM's aim is to minister in the name of Jesus Christ to the physical, mental and spiritual needs of leprosy sufferers; to assist in their rehabilitation; and to work towards the eradication of the disease. To this end we work in partnership with churches, governments and other charities around the world, depending on the prayer and finances of our Christian supporters. Volunteers with an offending background may be accepted – each person is assessed individually.

Total projects worldwide: Numerous
Total UK projects: 0
Starting months: January–December.
Time required: 8–12 weeks.
Age requirement: 20–30
Causes: Health care/medical.
Activities: Community work, religion.
Vols under 26 placed each year: 9 of a total of 12.
When to apply: At least 9 months in advance.
Work alone/with others: With trained personnel.
Volunteers with disabilities: Possible.
Qualifications: Fourth-year medical students plus nurses, physiotherapists, OTs, chiropodists. Christian commitment.
Equipment/clothing: Dependent on country.
Health requirements: Good health.
Costs: Travel expenses.
Benefits: Board and lodging.
Interview details: Interviews are conducted in Peterborough, Stirling (Scotland), Belfast (N.Ireland).
Certification: A letter is provided.
Charity number: 211432
Worldwide placements: *Africa* (Niger, Nigeria, Uganda); *Asia* (India, Nepal, Thailand).

LES AMIS DE LA TERRE – BENIN

BP 03-1162
Cotonou
Benin

Tel: 00 229 302105
Fax: 00 229 302205

e-mail: dasven.foe@bow.intnet.bj
Contact: Venance Dassi

Les Amis de la Terre is the Benin office of
Friends of the Earth, an organization which,
for the past 20 years, has been working
towards creating positive solutions to many of
the environmental problems threatening this
planet. FOE is committed to empowering
local communities and people to get actively
involved in the debate to protect the
environment through environmental
education, public awareness, campaigning
and so on. Volunteers are always needed to
help with a wide variety of projects.

Total projects worldwide: 1
Total UK projects: 0
Starting months: January–December.
Time required: 1–52 weeks (plus).
Age requirement: 12 plus.
Causes: Conservation, environmental causes,
heritage.
Activities: Conservation skills, forestry,
international aid, manual work, outdoor
skills.
Worldwide placements: *Africa* (Benin).

LES AMIS DE LA TERRE – BURKINA FASO
01 BP 5648
Ouagadougou
Burkina Faso

Tel: 00 226 306936
Contact: The Director

Les Amis de la Terre is the Burkina Faso
office of Friends of the Earth. For more
details of FOE, see Les Amis de la Terre –
Benin, above.

Total projects worldwide: 1
Total UK projects: 0
Starting months: January–December.
Time required: 1–52 weeks (plus).
Age requirement: 12 plus.
Causes: Conservation, environmental causes,
heritage.
Activities: Conservation skills, forestry,
international aid, outdoor skills.
Worldwide placements: *Africa* (Burkina
Faso).

LES AMIS DE LA TERRE – TOGO
Mensah Franco Todzro
BP 20 190 'Caisse'
Lomé

Togo
Tel: 00 228 221 731
Fax: 00 228 221 732
e-mail: foetogo@cafe.tg
Contact: The Director

Les Amis de la Terre is the Togo office of
Friends of the Earth. For more details of
FOE, see Les Amis de la Terre – Benin,
above.

Total projects worldwide: 1
Total UK projects: 0
Starting months: January–December.
Time required: 1–52 weeks (plus).
Age requirement: 12 plus.
Causes: Environmental causes, heritage.
Activities: Forestry, international aid, manual
work, outdoor skills.
Worldwide placements: *Africa* (Togo).

LES DEUX MOULINS
Gontard
Dauphin,
04300 Forcalquier
France

Les Deux Moulins needs volunteers to
construct new buildings and improve existing
amenities at this holiday centre built by and
for young people of all nationalities.
Although volunteers are unpaid, the work is
by no means rigid or exacting.

Total projects worldwide: 1
Total UK projects: 0
Starting months: January–December.
Time required: 1–52 weeks.
Age requirement: 18 plus.
Activities: Building/Construction.
When to apply: All year.
Costs: Part of costs of board and
accommodation.
Worldwide placements: *Europe* (France).

LESBIAN AND GAY YOUTH MOVEMENT
BM/GYM
London
WC1N 3XX UK

Tel: +44 (0) 20 8317 9690

Total projects worldwide: 1
Total UK projects: 0
Starting months: January–December.
Time required: 1–52 weeks.
Age requirement: 14 plus.

LESOTHO WORK CAMPS ASSOCIATION
PO Box 6
Maseru – 100
Lesotho

Contact: Kay Masitha

Lesotho Work Camps Association organizes volunteers to take part in voluntary work camps in co-operation with local communities involving manual work including building, installing water supplies, constructing roads, planting trees, soil conservation etc. The camps consist of groups of up to 25 people, mainly students, from Lesotho and abroad. A leader and a work supervisor are appointed on each camp but decisions are made communally. Eight hours work per day, five days per week.

Total projects worldwide: 1
Total UK projects: 0
Starting months: January, June, July, December.
Time required: 4–52 weeks.
Age requirement: 14 plus.
Causes: Conservation, poor/homeless.
Activities: Building/construction, conservation skills, forestry.
When to apply: October for winter, April for summer.
Benefits: Free food and accommodation provided.
Worldwide placements: *Africa* (Lesotho).

LINCOLNSHIRE WILDLIFE TRUST
Banovallum House
Manor House Street
Horncastle
Lincolnshire
LN9 5HF UK

Tel: +44 (0) 1507 526667
Fax: +44 (0) 1507 525732
e-mail: lincstrust@cix.compulink.co.uk
Contact: Dave Bromwich, Roger Parsons or Mary Edwards

The Lincolnshire Wildlife Trust, formed in 1948, is a charity dedicated to safeguarding the countryside and wildlife of the historic county. It is one of a network of Wildlife Trusts that together form the largest voluntary organization in the UK devoted to all aspects of wildlife protection. The Lincolnshire Trust is the largest voluntary organization in the county with over 11,000 members. Its junior wing is the Wildlife Watch Club which provides environmental activities for children aged between 8 and 15 years. The activities and policies of the Trust are based on its extensive records of plants and animals and of the wild places in Lincolnshire where they occur. In 1996 this data was used to compile a special report on the state of the county's wildlife habitats and endangered species. The Trust's 106 nature reserves provide the most tangible and best-known results of its work. They are enjoyed by perhaps half a million people each year. To achieve its objectives the Trust relies heavily on the commitment and support of members. Much of the work is undertaken by volunteers with the support of field staff and a small administrative staff at the headquarters office. Many hundreds of volunteers work for the Trust in activities as diverse as running sales points, managing nature reserves, conducting surveys of plants and animals. fundraising and checking planning lists.

Total projects worldwide: 105
Total UK projects: 105
Starting months: January–December.
Time required: 1–52 weeks (plus).
Age requirement: 16 plus.
Causes: Conservation, environmental causes, wildlife.
Activities: Computers, conservation skills, driving, forestry, gardening/horticulture, manual work, outdoor skills, research, scientific work, teaching.
Vols under 26 placed each year: 100–200 of a total of 1,000.
When to apply: All year.
Work alone/with others: With others.
Volunteers with disabilities: Possible.
Qualifications: Nil but any are a bonus.
Equipment/clothing: Sensible outdoor clothes.
Health requirements: General good health.
Costs: Nil.
Benefits: Improvement to CVs and good preparation for college. Volunteers are covered by the Trist's insurance.
Supervision: By trained staff.
Certification: Reference on request.
Charity number: 218895
UK placements: *England* (Lincolnshire).

LINK OVERSEAS EXCHANGE
25 Perth Road
Dundee

DD1 4LN Scotland

Tel: +44 (0) 1382 203192
Fax: +44 (0) 1382 226087
e-mail: vgreaves@linkoverseas.org.uk
Web: www.linkoverseas.org.uk
Contact: Mrs Vicky Greaves

Link Overseas Exchange was established in 1991 and has since sent over 200 volunteers overseas. This year we expect to send up to 60 volunteers to a range of projects in India, Nepal and Sri Lanka. Link volunteers primarily help to teach and develop young people's English speaking skills, working at grass-roots level in schools or community projects. A particular feature of Link's programme is its unique culture-to-culture approach and its emphasis on bringing communities together through greater understanding both here in the UK and overseas. Link volunteers have the opportunity to become completely integrated into local culture providing a unique insight into a different way of life. If volunteers are prepared to commit themselves fully the benefits from their time overseas are considerable. Most volunteers gain considerably in maturity and confidence and their experience often gives them greater direction and purpose in later life. The time overseas will be fascinating, challenging and exciting, both whilst working in the placement and during the plentiful opportunities the schedule allows for travelling. If our programme sounds interesting why not drop us a line and we will send you an application form and more information. Volunteers with an offending background may be accepted depending on circumstances.

Total projects worldwide: 20
Total UK projects: 0
Starting months: February, August.
Time required: 20–26 weeks.
Age requirement: 17–25
Causes: Children, elderly people, human rights, inner city problems, poor/homeless, refugees, teaching/assisting (nursery, primary, secondary, EFL), unemployed, young people.
Activities: Arts/crafts, caring (day), community work, computers, development issues, music, outdoor skills, social work, sport, teaching, theatre/drama, visiting/befriending.
Vols under 26 placed each year: 50–60.

When to apply: August–February.
Work alone/with others: In pairs.
Volunteers with disabilities: All applications considered.
Qualifications: Nil.
Health requirements: Medical advice available about immunizations required.
Costs: £1,800 to include flights, visas, food and accommodation, insurance, pre-departure training, UK back-up and overseas support.
Benefits: Valuable plus practical experience proven to enhance academic and career prospects. 6 months comprehensive insurance cover provided by Link.
Training: All Link volunteers attend a 4-day residential preparation course in order to prepare them as fully as possible for the experience ahead.
Supervision: Whilst overseas, volunteers are supported by a network of Link representatives and receive a visit by a UK-based Link representative once during their stay.
Interview details: Interviews are conducted at regular selection days in Scotland for groups of 6–8 candidates.
Certification: Certificate or reference provided.
Charity number: SCO 22028
Worldwide placements: *Asia* (India, Nepal, Sri Lanka).

LISLE INC.
900 County Road # 269
Leander
TX 78641
USA

Tel: 00 1 512 259 7621
Fax: 00 1 512 259 0392
e-mail: orlisle@utnet.utoledo.edu
Web: www.lisle.utoledo.edu.
Contact: Mark Kinney

Lisle broadens global awareness and increases appreciation of cultures through programmes which bring together persons of diverse religions, cultural, social, political and racial backgrounds, to interact, and to consider reflectively their experience. While on field assignments, small groups go out for several days for varied assignments with sponsoring agencies. Volunteers with an offending background are accepted.

Total projects worldwide: 3
Total UK projects: 0

Starting months: March, June, July.
Time required: 2–4 weeks.
Age requirement: 17 plus.
Causes: Children, conservation, environmental causes, health care/medical, heritage, human rights, work camps – seasonal, young people.
Activities: Agriculture/farming, arts/crafts, building/construction, caring (general), community work, conservation skills, gardening/horticulture, manual work, visiting/befriending.
Vols under 26 placed each year: Varies.
When to apply: Before 1 April.
Work alone/with others: With others.
Volunteers with disabilities: Possible.
Qualifications: Nil.
Equipment/clothing: Dependent on location.
Health requirements: Nil.
Costs: Air fare to programme plus programme fee which covers board and lodging.
Benefits: Learn about other cultures by actually living and participating in that culture.
Interview details: No interview necessary.
Worldwide placements: *Asia* (India, Malaysia); *Europe* (Poland, Turkey); *Central America* (Costa Rica).

LITTLE BROTHERS (FRIENDS OF THE ELDERLY)

25 Bolton Street
Dublin 1
Ireland

Tel: 00 353 1 873 1855
Fax: 00 353 1 873 1617
e-mail: ireland@little-brothers.org
Web: www.petits-freres.org
Contact: Niamh Macken, Co-ordinator

Little Brothers works for the elderly to alleviate loneliness and isolation by providing friendship, social contact and opportunities for participating in community activities. Each year Little Brothers takes a group of elderly on holiday to France and also to various parts of Ireland for short breaks. As many of our elderly have little variety in their lives, a holiday can do wonders for their physical and mental well-being.

Total projects worldwide: 1
Total UK projects: 0
Starting months: January–December.
Time required: 26–52 weeks.

Age requirement: 18 plus.
Causes: Disabled (learning), elderly people, holidays for disabled.
Activities: Caring (general), catering, community work, computers, cooking, social work, theatre/drama, visiting/befriending.
Vols under 26 placed each year: 35 of a total of 120.
When to apply: All year.
Work alone/with others: With others.
Volunteers with disabilities: Possible, but our work can be very physical.
Qualifications: Good working fluency in spoken and written English. Love for the elderly.
Health requirements: Nil.
Costs: Return travel to Ireland.
Benefits: Living allowance (for food) and free accommodation. We provide public liability insurance.
Training: On-the-spot training.
Supervision: By their co-ordinator and the Board.
Interview details: Interviews are held by telephone. An international application form is available. Two referees are required.
Certification: Written reference provided.
Charity number: CHY 12003
Worldwide placements: *Europe* (Ireland).

LITTLE CHILDREN OF THE WORLD

361 County Road 475
Etowah
Tennessee
37331 USA

Tel: 00 1 423 263 2303
Fax: 00 1 423 263 2303
e-mail: lcotw@tds.net
Web: www.littlechildren.org
Contact: Dr Doug Elwood, International Director

Little Children of the World is a non-profit international and interdenominational Christian service organization dedicated to creating caring communities for the world's homeless or neglected children. As a volunteer with LCW you can use your creativity to benefit children who are victims of poverty and neglect, of whom there are more than 150 million worldwide. They are God's children too and desperately need our help. Child advocacy is a new worldwide mission frontier, but so far a neglected one. Here is an opportunity to invest a portion of your life in helping to rescue children from the dire effects of poverty, neglect and abuse. As an LCW volunteer you can serve for as long a period as you like (at least one month) and you can serve in whatever capacity best suits your own personality, talents and training. You can do what you do best, and do it for a worthy cause. Serving the needs of the poor is, in fact, what Christian service is all about.

Total projects worldwide: 1
Total UK projects: 0
Starting months: January–December.
Time required: 4–52 weeks (plus).
Age requirement: 18 plus.
Causes: Children, disabled (learning and physical), poor/homeless.
Activities: Arts/crafts, caring (general and day), community work, development issues, group work, international aid, music, outdoor skills, social work, teaching.
Vols under 26 placed each year: 15–24 of a total of 25–40.
When to apply: All year.
Work alone/with others: Yes.
Volunteers with disabilities: We are unable to place people with disabilities as we have a programme for children with a disability.
Qualifications: We are flexible but applicants must be at least 18 years old.
Equipment/clothing: Nothing special but we do ask that volunteers dress modestly.
Health requirements: Must be free of any communicable diseases.
Costs: Travel costs, food, all necessary insurance. We ask for a donation of US$10 per week for use of dormitory.
Benefits: International experience.
Training: Orientation is by website and handbook.
Supervision: Volunteers are assigned to local staff for supervision.
Interview details: No interview necessary – communications are by e-mail or regular post.
Certification: Reference provided.
Worldwide placements: *Asia* (Philippines).

LITTLE JOHN'S HOUSE
2 The Square
Merton
Okehampton
Devon
EX20 3EE UK

Tel: +44 (0) 1805 603623
Fax: +44 (0) 1805 603623
e-mail: zliviu@globalnet.co.uk
Web: http://freespace.virgin.net/little.johns
Contact: John and Tilly Kimber

Little John's House (previously Orphan Aid – Romania) has the sole objective of relieving the suffering of sick and handicapped children in Romania; improving their living standards and bringing love and purpose into their lives. Little John's House provides a secure home for up to eight children with special needs and operates as a centre for respite care, serving the communities of Cisnadioara, Cisnadie and Sibiu. The main activity involves a Summer School which, between the months of June and September, receives up to 150 children of mixed abilities who are unable to attend any schooling and who are often 'imprisoned' in a single room (their home) for months on end!

Total projects worldwide: 1
Total UK projects: 0
Starting months: January–December.
Time required: 2–52 weeks.
Age requirement: 18 plus.
Causes: Children, disabled (learning and physical), health care/medical.
Activities: Administration, arts/crafts, building/construction, caring (general), cooking, DIY, international aid, manual work, music.
Vols under 26 placed each year: 35 of a total of 70.
When to apply: All year.
Work alone/with others: With others.
Volunteers with disabilities: Possible.
Qualifications: Those with and without qualifications and special needs teachers, nursery nurses, play specialists and any who feel they can cope with disabled children, to provide a fun time of working in music, art, drama, etc.
Health requirements: Innoculations before leaving.
Costs: Air fare to Romania plus contribution to food. Full travel insurance.
Benefits: Accommodation.
Training: Clear guidelines are sent to each volunteer detailing the work required and expected standard of behaviour.
Supervision: By resident English director.
Charity number: 1002714
Worldwide placements: *Europe* (Romania).

LIVERPOOL CHILDREN'S HOLIDAY ORGANISATION (LCHO)
Wellington Road School
Wellington Road
Dingle
Liverpool
L8 4TX UK

Tel: +44 (0) 151 727 7330
Contact: The Director

LCHO provides residential holidays for Merseyside children who would not normally get a holiday away from home. Volunteers are needed to act as supervisors and will be responsible for a small group of children 24 hours a day. Applicants must be over 18 and fit.

Total projects worldwide: 1
Total UK projects: 1
Starting months: July, August.
Time required: 2–6 weeks.
Age requirement: 18 plus.
Causes: Children, poor/homeless, young people.
Activities: Arts/crafts, community work, driving, group work, manual work, music, outdoor skills, sport, summer camps, theatre/drama.
When to apply: January–March.
Work alone/with others: Both.
Volunteers with disabilities: Not possible.
Qualifications: Must be fit and UK resident. Qualified first-aiders and mini-bus drivers are also needed.
Equipment/clothing: Outdoor clothes.
Health requirements: Fit and healthy.
Benefits: Accommodation provided and expenses paid.
Training: Volunteers must complete a week-long residential training course run by LCHO.
Interview details: Prior to working on the holidays, volunteers must be interviewed.
UK placements: *England* (Merseyside).

LIVERPOOL METHODIST DISTRICT EDUCATION AND YOUTH COMMITTEE
c/o 7 Rutherford Road
Liverpool
L18 0HJ UK

Contact: Mrs Alison Wilkinson, Training Development Officer

Liverpool Methodist District Education and Youth Committee is part of the Methodist Youth Work in Britain and included within the Methodist Youth Service, MAYC (Methodist Association of Youth Clubs). Since its inception in 1945, the seven guiding principles of MAYC have provided a reference point for all its groups. They are: 1. create a group; 2. grow real people; 3. encourage a sense of belonging; 4. work towards wholeness; 5. go for the best; 6. live on a large map; 7. take your place in the church. The Liverpool Methodist District includes all Methodist churches in Merseyside, the Warrington, Widnes and Ellesmere Port areas of Cheshire, West Lancashire and part of the Borough of Wigan. The majority of churches provide activities for young people, which may be uniformed organizations, youth clubs or youth fellowships, run entirely by volunteers. Some churches, usually in areas of special need, have set up community projects and employ professional staff in response to local needs. Most of these projects include services to children and young people. There is usually provision for senior citizens as well. Particular issues are addressed by some of these projects, including racism, substance abuse and the needs of young single parents. National and district structures provide support, advice and training for the local units. There are opportunities for young people to become involved in action projects, sports, youth exchanges, pilgrimages and major events, such as the annual MAYC London Weekend, which attracts up to 10,000 participants each year. Churches are being encouraged to give young people a 'voice' and to allow them to take responsibility alongside adult members. Volunteers with an offending background may be accepted. Checks are required and local project's church council decides.

Total projects worldwide: Approximately 8.
Total UK projects: Approximately 8.
Starting months: January–December.
Time required: 1–52 weeks.
Age requirement: 16–30
Causes: Children, elderly people, inner city problems, poor/homeless, unemployed, young people.
Activities: Arts/crafts, caring (general, day and residential), community work, computers, cooking, fundraising, group work, manual work, music, newsletter/journalism, outdoor skills, religion, research, sport, summer camps.

Vols under 26 placed each year: Very many.
When to apply: All year.
Work alone/with others: With others.
Volunteers with disabilities: Possible.
Qualifications: Vary according to the job to be done.
Health requirements: Nil.
Costs: Nil.
Benefits: All expenses reimbursed. In some cases accommodation can be arranged.
Interview details: Prospective volunteers are interviewed at location where they will work.
Certification: Certificate or reference can be arranged.
UK placements: *England* (Cheshire, Lancashire, Merseyside).

LIVING OPTIONS
Forum
Stirling Road
Chichester
West Sussex
PO19 2EU UK

Tel: +44 (0) 1243 672989
Fax: +44 (0) 1243 672989
Contact: Cindy Curtis, Project Manager

Living Options is a registered national charity whose aims are to provide opportunities for young people who are physically disabled to live in small groups in the community. A volunteer may be asked to: (a) assist in meeting the more personal needs of the disabled person, such as washing, bathing, toileting, dressing, etc as appropriate; (b) accompany students to lectures and on other outings of both an academic and social nature; (c) assist with the domestic tasks of the project, such as cooking, cleaning, washing of clothes etc.; (d) seek to improve self-awareness and knowledge of the needs of people who are disabled, by personal experience, reading, attending training courses (if available) and discussion of these; (e) attend, and be prepared to contribute to project meetings. Working hours are determined by the project manager, who reserves the right to vary them according to the needs of the residents. A rota is arranged and displayed on the project notice board. From time to time you may be asked to attend a project meeting when off duty. It is vital to the smooth running of the project that these meetings are attended by all residents and volunteers. Volunteers with an offending background are accepted.

Total projects worldwide: 3
Total UK projects: 3
Starting months: January–December.
Time required: 16–52 weeks.
Age requirement: 18–30
Causes: Disabled (physical).
Activities: Arts/crafts, caring (general and residential), cooking, group work, music.
Vols under 26 placed each year: 30
When to apply: All year.
Work alone/with others: With other volunteers under supervision of Manager.
Volunteers with disabilities: Volunteers care for profoundly disabled young people. They need to be able to lift with hoists. Training is given.
Qualifications: Nil.
Health requirements: Nil.
Costs: Nil. We insure volunteers for public liability insurance. Volunteers are responsible for insuring their own property if they so wish.
Benefits: Board, lodging plus personal allowance. CSV rates plus some travel expenses.
Training: Monthly training courses on a variety of subjects are held in project.
Supervision: Volunteer and house meetings.
Interview details: No interview necessary.
Certification: Certificate provided if they take part in courses.
Charity number: 299206
UK placements: *England* (W. Sussex).

LLANELLI CENTRE PROJECT
2 Station Road
Llanelli
Carmarthenshire
SA15 1AB Wales

Tel: +44 (0) 1554 771595
Contact: Mrs Averill Rees

The Llanelli Centre Project is an independent charity-funded youth organization which opened in 1989. It aims to meet the needs of young people. It is open seven days a week, usually from 10.00am – 10.00pm and employs four full-time workers as well as students in training and volunteers. Activities are used as a basis for building up better relationships with young people, and there is a focus on empowerment to help them gain control over their own lives. We run an advocacy and information service with young people dealing with issues such as: homelessness, drugs misuse, alcohol misuse, unplanned pregnancy, contraception, relationship difficulties (peers, parents, school, police etc.) and basic skills training. We are currently developing a motor project with the help of National Lottery funding. Other services provided are opportunities for young people to repay their offences by voluntary special activity orders and community service orders. All volunteers are accepted subject to police checks. Restrictions are on those with offences against children.

Total projects worldwide: 1
Total UK projects: 1
Starting months: January–December.
Time required: 1–52 weeks.
Age requirement: 16–30
Causes: Addicts/Ex-addicts, children, health care/medical, offenders/ex-offenders, poor/homeless, teaching/assisting, unemployed, young people.
Activities: Administration, arts/crafts, building/construction, computers, cooking, counselling, DIY, driving, fundraising, group work, music, outdoor skills, social work, sport, visiting/befriending.
Vols under 26 placed each year: 16 of a total of 20.
When to apply: As soon as possible.
Work alone/with others: With others.
Volunteers with disabilities: Possible.
Qualifications: References and police clearance.
Health requirements: Nil.
Costs: Nil. Public liability insurance covered by us.
Training: Induction training, introduction to staff team, members, policies, procedures etc.
Supervision: Volunteers always work under the supervision of a qualified worker.
Interview details: Interviews take place at the Llanelli Centre Project (by appointment please).
Certification: Reference provided.
Charity number: 1002011
UK placements: *Wales* (Carmarthenshire).

LONDON CHILDREN'S CAMP
The Hollies
London Road
Kessingland
Suffolk
NR33 7PQ UK

Tel: +44 (0) 1502 740255
Contact: Alec Gair

London Children's Camp provides summer camping holidays at the permanent camp site it owns at Kessingland on the Suffolk coast for underprivileged children of mixed sex in the age range of 10–13 and of a diversity of ethnic origin and cultures. Volunteers, working as a team, are responsible for the welfare of up to 60 children per camp, a camp normally being 10–12 days duration in July to August each summer. There are about 15 volunteers per camp. Most have specific responsibility for a group of five or six children. A manager and deputy manager, termed 'Organizer and Deputy Organizer' are in overall charge. As a volunteer you will be expected to: provide for the physical and emotional welfare of a tent of five or six children, run and invent activities of all kinds, be available to the children 16 to 17 hours a day, and help with all that is involved with the general day-to-day operation of the camp. You will need to be energetic, innovative, very tolerant, confident and assertive in the presence of the children, have the patience to listen and the wit to understand, and all this while maintaining a cheery disposition and a beaming smile. Volunteers must be able to function in a non-sexist, non-racist and a generally non-oppressive manner. As the volunteers will have substantial contact and involvement with children careful checks via reference, local Social Services, the Departments of Education/Social Service and the police are undertaken to ensure their suitability for work with children.

Total projects worldwide: 1
Total UK projects: 1
Starting months: July, August.
Time required: 2–35 weeks.
Age requirement: 18 plus.
Causes: Children.
Activities: Arts/crafts, music, sport, summer camps.
Vols under 26 placed each year: 30–50
When to apply: March.
Work alone/with others: With others.
Volunteers with disabilities: Not possible.
Qualifications: Nil but interest in sport/music/art and crafts very helpful.
Health requirements: Nil, but applicants subject to vetting process via police, social

services.
Benefits: Travel to compulsory training weekend, board/lodging at camp plus small allowance for travel plus pocket money.
Certification: Reference is possible.
UK placements: *England* (Suffolk).

LONDON CITY MISSION

175 Tower Bridge Road
London
SE1 2AH UK

Tel: +44 (0) 20 7407 7585
Fax: +44 (0) 20 7603 6711
e-mail: lcm.uk@btinternet.com
Web: www.lcm.org.uk
Contact: Phil Moore, Special Projects Department, Youth Co-ordinator

London City Mission has a varied programme of voluntary work within the Greater London and inner city areas which includes Christian community work, open-air meetings, door-to-door visits, working with homeless people, running youth camps and children's clubs.

Total projects worldwide: 6
Total UK projects: 6
Starting months: August, September.
Time required: 1–52 weeks.
Age requirement: 18–30
Causes: Children, elderly people, inner city problems, poor/homeless, teaching (EFL), young people.
Activities: Caring (general and day), community work, religion.
Vols under 26 placed each year: Almost all of a total of 150.
When to apply: By 1 July.
Work alone/with others: With others and full-time staff.
Volunteers with disabilities: Possible.
Qualifications: Committed Christians with membership of an evangelical church.
Health requirements: Good health required.
Costs: Donation (if possible) towards board and lodging.
Benefits: Board and lodging. (Pocket money and travel for long-term placement). Full insurance cover provided by us.
Training: Continuous training on the job.
Supervision: By full-time long-term staff.
Interview details: One formal and one informal.
Certification: Certificate or reference provided.

Charity number: 247186
UK placements: *England* (London).

LONDON WILDLIFE TRUST

Harling House
47-51 Great Suffolk Street
London
SE1 0BS UK

Tel: +44 (0) 20 7261 0447
Fax: +44 (0) 20 7261 0538
e-mail: londonwt@cix.co.uk
Web: www.wildlifetrust.org.uk/london
Contact: Emma Robertshaw

London Wildlife Trust looks after 60 nature reserves and raises awareness of nature conservation issues in London. The Trust achieves this through: community involvement: we organize over 600 free events every year. Land management: workdays on our reserves often appeal to volunteers. Effective communication: we provide a popular wildlife information service. Education – our education work is targeted at all ages. Campaigning: the London Wildlife Trust speaks up for wildlife whenever it is under threat in London.

Total projects worldwide: 6
Total UK projects: 6
Starting months: January–December.
Time required: 1–52 weeks (plus).
Age requirement: 14 plus.
Causes: Conservation, environmental causes, wildlife, young people.
Activities: Campaigning, conservation skills, gardening/horticulture, group work, outdoor skills.
When to apply: All year.
Work alone/with others: Both.
Volunteers with disabilities: Possible.
Qualifications: Nil.
Equipment/clothing: Robust outdoor clothing.
Health requirements: Nil.
Costs: Nil.
Benefits: Transport costs. The Trust fully insures all its volunteers.
Supervision: By nature reserve officers/staff. If tools are being used there will be a health and safety talk.
Interview details: Interviews take place at the site/nature reserve in question.
Charity number: 283895
UK placements: *England* (London).

LOS NIÑOS
9765 Marconi Drive
Suite 105
San Ysidro
CA 92173
USA

Tel: 00 1 619 426 9110
Contact: The Office Manager

Los Niños is a charitable organization founded to provide food, clothing, shelter, education and affection for children in orphanages and poor communities in the Mexican border cities of Tijuana and Mexicali. Volunteers assist by undertaking jobs in education, nutrition, construction, as youth consellors or in other areas of community development.

Total projects worldwide: 1
Total UK projects: 0
Starting months: January–December.
Time required: 1–6 weeks.
Age requirement: 16 plus.
Causes: Children, poor/homeless, teaching/assisting.
Activities: Caring (general), counselling, teaching.
Vols under 26 placed each year: 1,200
When to apply: All year.
Qualifications: Fluent in Spanish.
Equipment/clothing: Visa to cross US/Mexican border daily.
Costs: Programme fee to include board and lodging.
Worldwide placements: *North America* (USA); *Central America* (Mexico).

LOTHLORIEN (ROKPA TRUST)
Corsock
Castle Douglas
Kirkcudbrightshire
DG7 3DR Scotland

Tel: + 44 (0) 1644 440602
Contact: Project Manager

Lothlorien is a supportive community for people with mental health problems which was founded in 1978. It consists of a large log house with 14 bedrooms and communal living areas. It is set in 17 acres of grounds which include organic vegetable gardens, woodland, workshops and outbuildings. In 1989, Rokpa Trust took over the running of Lothlorien. The guiding principles of the community are hospitality, care and respect

for the person, and a belief that the potential of the individual can be encouraged through a communal life in which all have a contribution to make. Since 1992 Lothlorien has had government funding to employ a manager, support worker and garden co-ordinator. They provide a continuity of support to the community which normally consists of between six to eight residents and four volunteers. Lothlorien is a working community, with an emphasis on people participating to the best of their abilities. In the spring and summer the vegetable garden is the major focus. However, all year round cooking, domestic chores and house maintenance are all essential to the smooth running of the community. Overall, as well as offering the positive experience that living with a group brings, Lothlorien also affords the opportunity to develop practical life skills which enable people to move on to independent living with confidence.

Total projects worldwide: 1
Total UK projects: 1
Starting months: January–December.
Time required: 26–52 weeks.
Age requirement: 21 plus.
Causes: Health care/medical.
Activities: Building/construction, caring (residential), gardening/horticulture, manual work.
Vols under 26 placed each year: 4
When to apply: All year.
Work alone/with others: With others.
Volunteers with disabilities: Possible.
Qualifications: Nil but important to have an interest in the welfare of others.
Costs: Travel costs.
Benefits: Board and lodging plus £25 per week.
Interview details: Interviews take place at the project.
Certification: Written reference provided.
UK placements: *Scotland* (Dumfries and Galloway).

LOUIS ROUSSEL
52 rue des Forges
F-21000 Dijon
France

Contact: M. Roussel

Louis Roussel recruits volunteers to work on an archaeological dig involving a medieval chateau and a Gallo-Roman site near Dijon in July and August. In addition to digging, the jobs to be done include photographing and sketching the finds, model making and restoration. Eight hours work per day, five days per week.

Total projects worldwide: 1
Total UK projects: 0
Starting months: July, August.
Time required: 1–52 weeks.
Age requirement: 17 plus.
Causes: Archaeology, conservation, heritage.
Activities: Conservation skills.
Vols under 26 placed each year: 10
Qualifications: Experience in digging, photography, sketching, model making or restoration an advantage.
Benefits: Free accommodation provided.
Worldwide placements: *Europe* (France).

L'OUVRE-TETE
Les Maurels
Pierrerue
F-04300 France

Tel: 00 33 4 92 75 10 65
Contact: Remy Garnier

L'Ouvre-Tete (or Open Head) is the continuing project to renovate a 16th century farmhouse in the heart of Provence. The project is run by a French/English team. German is also spoken. The association has received the following categories of people: professionals – builders, electricians, plumbers, carpenters; talented artists – musicians, painters, sculptors (volunteers – no financial participation) selected on portfolio; students and young people 18–35; helpers who join in the day to day activities of L'Ouvre-Tete (building, caring for people and animals, horses). All have the chance also to go on horse treks/excursions. Mornings are for working, afternoons are free for study and leisure. Evening horse riding plus social time. French lessons.

Total projects worldwide: 1
Total UK projects: 0
Starting months: April, June–September.
Time required: 2–4 weeks.
Age requirement: 16–30
Causes: Animal welfare, architecture, conservation, teaching/assisting, young people.
Activities: Building/construction, caring (general), catering, conservation skills, cooking, gardening/horticulture, group work, manual work, outdoor skills, religion, social work, sport, teaching, theatre/drama.
Vols under 26 placed each year: 50
When to apply: At least 1 month before arrival date.
Work alone/with others: In a group or paired with professionals (e.g. carpenter).
Volunteers with disabilities: Not for wheelchairs – but other individual requests discussed.
Qualifications: Adaptable to group life with foreigners. Particular skills welcome: see notes.
Health requirements: Must be reasonably fit.
Costs: FF100 per day for food and accommodation plus travel and insurance costs.
Benefits: Free horse riding when possible. Regular French lessons, excursions, swimming.
Certification: Reference on request plus certificate may be awarded on successful completion.
Worldwide placements: *Europe* (France).

LOWER LEA PROJECT
The Lock Office
Gillender Street
Bromley-by-Bow
London
E3 3JY UK

Tel: +44 (0) 20 7515 3337
Fax: +44 (0) 20 7515 3338
e-mail: lowerlea@netscapeonline.co.uk
Contact: Marketing Officer

Lower Lea Project is an environmental organization working to improve the environment of the Lower Lea Valley in East London, through practical projects with volunteers, environmental education with schools, community development, leisure and recreation. Our programme includes conservation work on riverside areas, planting and looking after trees, clearing vegetation, creating new wildlife habitat as well as building footpaths, steps and terracing steep slopes. We also run a river maintenance team who clear rubbish from the tidal waterways of the Lea, using a variety of tools and purpose-built boats. They also remove debris from mudbanks and the riverbed, and plant reedbeds for wildlife. We welcome volunteers in this programme, during the week and on some weekends, with a minimum commitment of just one day to see if it suits you. Longer term placements are welcomed. Volunteers can learn conservation skills and how to operate boats and equipment, as well as achieving the satisfaction of having helped improve the 'urban countryside'.

Total projects worldwide: 1
Total UK projects: 1
Starting months: January–December.
Time required: 1–52 weeks.
Age requirement: 14 plus.
Causes: Conservation, environmental causes, wildlife.
Activities: Community work, conservation skills, manual work, outdoor skills, scientific work, training.
Vols under 26 placed each year: Approximately 15 of a total of 150.
When to apply: All year.
Work alone/with others: With others.
Volunteers with disabilities: Possible.
Qualifications: Nil.
Equipment/clothing: Old clothes, strong footwear.
Health requirements: Clean bill of health.
Costs: Subsistence.
Benefits: Chance to learn conservation skills and make a difference to the environment. We provide public liability and personal accident insurance cover which covers all volunteers under our supervision.
Training: On-the-job training.
Supervision: By a member of staff.
Charity number: 1075368
UK placements: *England* (London).

LUBBOCK LAKE LANDMARK
The Musuem of Texas Tech. University
Box 43191
Lubbock
Texas 79409-3191
USA

Tel: 00 1 806 742 1117(Landmark), 00 1 806 742 2479
Fax: 00 1 806 742 1136
e-mail: lubbock.lake@.ttu.edu
Web: www.ttu.edu/~museum/111/field.html
Contact: Dr Eileen Johnson, Director

The Lubbock Lake National Historic and State Archaeological Landmark is an archaeological preserve on the outskirts of Lubbock, Texas. Located in a meander of an ancient valley, Yellowhouse Draw, the preserve contains a well-stratified concurrent cultural, faunal and geological record that spans the past 12,000 years. Over 100 archaeological activity areas have been excavated from five major stratagraphic units, representing all of the major time periods of North American archaeology. The programme is aimed at the excavation and interpretation of data and requires the assistance of 50 volunteers a year. Volunteers are needed to work in the field and laboratory. Crew members come for a 6–9 week period and are expected to help with daily kitchen and camp chores, including cooking duties. The Lubbock Lake Landmark is open to the public on a daily basis, through exhibits in the Interpretative Center and guided tours of the excavation areas. Volunteers have the opportunity to assist with special programmes and tours for the public.

Total projects worldwide: 1
Total UK projects: 0
Starting months: June, July.
Time required: 6–12 weeks.
Age requirement: 18 plus.
Causes: Archaeology, heritage.
Activities: Cooking, manual work, outdoor skills, research, scientific work.
Vols under 26 placed each year: 25 of a total of 50.
When to apply: By 1 June.
Work alone/with others: With others.
Qualifications: Fluent English; no experience required – willingness to learn and work as team player.
Equipment/clothing: All supplied except hand tools.
Costs: Travel to Lubbock Lake, international health/accident insurance, local transport, personal costs and supplies.
Benefits: Board/lodging in 6-person wooden-floored tents, major equipment and field supplies.
Supervision: In the field the crew chief provides supervision. In the lab, lab assistant provides daily supervision.
Interview details: No interview necessary.
Worldwide placements: *North America* (USA).

M

MAGNET YOUNG ADULT CENTRE

81a Hill Street
Newry
Co. Down
BT34 1DG N. Ireland

Tel: +44 (0) 28 3026 9070
Fax: +44 (0) 28 3026 8132
e-mail: colette@magnet-centre.fsnet.co.uk
Contact: Colette Ross, Project Manager

Magnet Young Adult Centre is a registered charity group who provide facilities primarily, but not exclusively, for 16–25 year olds from Newry and the surrounding rural areas in a neutral and non-alcoholic environment. The Centre is managed by a voluntary group of 16–25 year olds who represent various youth groups, schools and training schemes along with a team of paid and voluntary staff. Our facilities include: social area with coffee bar; rehearsal space for musicians; guitar, bass, drum and keyboard lessons; young women's/ girls' groups; young men's group; live music; youth information centre; drama; Duke of Edinburgh Award Scheme; art projects; creative writing; study space; computer and photocopying services; and lots more! Depending on the time of year, the Centre also runs outdoor activities; pottery classes; personal development courses; live music events; festival/street entertainment; workshops on a wide range of issues (e.g. drugs, community relations, sex education); European youth exchanges; and, entertainment nights with table quizzes, videos, etc.

Total projects worldwide: 1
Total UK projects: 1
Starting months: January–December.
Time required: 8–52 weeks.
Age requirement: 16 plus.
Causes: Unemployed, young people.
Activities: Administration, arts/crafts, community work, computers, fundraising, group work, music, theatre/drama, training.
Vols under 26 placed each year: 12 of a total of 20.
When to apply: All year.
Work alone/with others: With others.
Volunteers with disabilities: Possible.
Qualifications: Interest in the area of work.

Health requirements: Nil.
Costs: Meals, travel and accommodation.
Benefits: Experience, training and accreditation where possible. Employer's liability insurance provided by either placement agency or by us.
Training: Discussion to determine suitability of placement and role of volunteer. Induction is usually completed within 2 days of starting.
Supervision: Regular contact with supervisor on a daily basis with formal supervision at least once a month depending on time commitment.
Charity number: XO/284/91
UK placements: *Northern Ireland* (Down).

MAISON EMMANUEL

156 Chemin Beaulne
Val-Morin
Quebec
JOT 2RO Canada

Tel: 00 1 819 322 3718
Fax: 00 1 819 322 6930
e-mail: m.emmanuel@polyinter.ca
Contact: Eileen Lutgendorf

At Maison Emmanuel we strive towards creating relationships based on the essential aspects of being human. The values upheld in a healthy, social environment are self-awareness, self-development, dignity, respect, and the realization of one's potential. Maison Emmanuel is modelled on the Camphill Communities existing worldwide. Camphill is inspired by the educator Rudolf Steiner and the paediatrician Karl Koenig and recognizes the spiritual uniqueness of each human being regardless of disability and religious or racial background. There are approximately 90 of these Communities, recognized by governments as viable alternatives to institutional care. Maison Emmanuel is located in a beautiful rural setting on 35 acres, in the heart of the Laurentian mountains, surrounded by forests, lakes and rivers, one hour north of Montreal. With up to 24 people in need of special care and approximately as many co-workers, we live in four residences. House-parents, their children, and a team of young committed volunteers are the basis of the family-like setting in each home. The rhythmic structure of daily work in the houses, the school, the workshops, the garden and the small farm create the warm supportive environment that is the foundation of community living. Sharing meals, seasonal festivals, plays, birthday celebrations and special outings helps to create bonds of friendship and responsibility. The basic needs of house-parents and co-workers are looked after by the community. Dedication to provide for the 'needs of others' becomes their way of life.

Total projects worldwide: 1
Total UK projects: 0
Starting months: January–December.
Time required: 48–52 weeks (plus).
Age requirement: 21 plus.
Causes: Disabled (learning and physical), holidays for disabled, work camps – seasonal.
Activities: Agriculture/farming, arts/crafts, caring (general and residential), cooking, driving, gardening/horticulture, group work, manual work, music, newsletter/journalism, summer camps, theatre/drama, work camps – seasonal.
Vols under 26 placed each year: 10 of a total of 25.
When to apply: All year.
Work alone/with others: With others.
Volunteers with disabilities: Possible – most of our homes are wheelchair accessible.
Qualifications: French is an asset.
Equipment/clothing: Warm clothes for our winters, and work clothes.
Health requirements: Doctor's certificate of good health.
Costs: Travel costs.
Benefits: Pocket money of C$150 per month plus C$50 per month vacation/travel alowance. Health insurance is provided.
Training: First aid – crisis intervention, working with the physically disabled.
Supervision: Each house has an experienced person in a supervisory position.
Interview details: No interviews but 3 written letters of reference are required.
Certification: Written reference provided.
Charity number: 1/9028850R
Worldwide placements: *North America* (Canada).

MALTA YOUTH HOSTELS ASSOCIATION
MYHA Head Office
17 Triq Tal-Borg
Pawla PLA 06
Malta

Tel: 00 356 693957
Fax: 00 356 693957
Contact: Work camp Organizer

The Malta Youth Hostels Association (MYHA) promotes international understanding by providing shelter for needy persons. To keep costs low the MYHA operates an all-the-year-round work camp where dedicated persons offer between three and ten hours every day in unpaid work which is connected with youth hostels, the MYHA HQ, youth centres and other philanthropic organizations. Please send three International Reply Coupons (obtainable from the Post Office) for details and an application form.

Total projects worldwide: 1
Total UK projects: 0
Starting months: January–December.
Time required: 2–12 weeks.
Age requirement: 16–30
Causes: Poor/homeless, work camps – seasonal, young people.
Activities: Administration, building/construction, computers, DIY, fundraising, gardening/horticulture, manual work, research, social work, visiting/befriending, work camps – seasonal.
Vols under 26 placed each year: Up to 5
When to apply: 3 plus months before start of work camp.
Work alone/with others: Both.
Volunteers with disabilities: Possible.
Qualifications: Volunteers must understand English and have a lot of goodwill and generosity.
Equipment/clothing: Work clothes which might get dusty or paint-stained.
Health requirements: Physically fit and psychologically secure.
Costs: Application fee £12 (non-returnable). Deposit (£33) – returnable on successful completion. Travel to Malta.
Benefits: Free accommodation and breakfast – no remuneration.
Interview details: No interview necessary.
Certification: After 1 month possible shortlisting for CCIVS/UNESCO certificate. (3 awarded annually).
Worldwide placements: *Europe* (Malta).

MANCHESTER YOUTH AND COMMUNITY SERVICE
122a-124a Sale Road

Northern Moor
Wythenshawe
Manchester
M23 0BX UK

Tel: +44 (0) 161 945 1032
Contact: Jennie Henry

Manchester Youth and Community Service, MYCS, is an independent, voluntary sector organization. With offices based in Wythenshawe, MYCS provides a range of services and activities which target teenaged girls and young women, women and children in the Wythenshawe areas. We were first established in 1966 following a major conference the previous year to address the needs of young people in relation to the wider communities of Manchester. Initially set up to co-ordinate and match young people's volunteering interests with community needs (e.g. environmental projects; practical support for the elderly; schools and hospitals), MYCS has moved on to develop youth and community projects which focus on personal development through education, informal and formal. MYCS's youth projects are currently made up of: three Young Women's groups which meet on a regular, weekly basis during term time; a programme of outdoor activities during the summer break; 'G' ForCE 2000 (Girls for Community Enterprise), a project to support and develop young enterprise, employment and education, including the training of up to six local people as youth and community workers; Community Gap Scheme – a full-time volunteering scheme to develop youth leadership through volunteering targeted at 18–24 year olds and lasting 6–9 months. Volunteers receive the Rank Volunteer Award and can study towards the Certificate in Foundation Studies in Informal and Community Education, worth 60 CATs and now recognized as a professional qualification. Volunteers with an offending background may be accepted dependent on the offence and designated work.

Total projects worldwide: 1
Total UK projects: 1
Starting months: January–December.
Time required: 12–52 weeks (plus).
Age requirement: 18–25
Causes: Children, unemployed, young people.
Activities: Administration, arts/crafts, community work, computers, cooking, DIY,

fundraising, gardening/horticulture, group work, library/resource centres, marketing/publicity, music, newsletter/journalism, outdoor skills, research, sport, theatre/drama.
Vols under 26 placed each year: 5–10
When to apply: January.
Work alone/with others: With others.
Volunteers with disabilities: Possible.
Qualifications: Must be able to satisfy criminal and health checks.
Health requirements: Must be able to satisfy health checks.
Costs: Daily subsistence and travel to and from office base.
Benefits: Assistance may be given determined by availability of funding.
Interview details: Interviews take place at office base.
Certification: Certificate or reference provided.
UK placements: *England* (Manchester).

MANIC DEPRESSION FELLOWSHIP
8–10 High Street
Kingston-upon-Thames
Surrey
KT1 1EY UK

Tel: +44 (0) 20 8974 6550
Contact: Michelle Rowett

Manic Depression Fellowship was set up in 1983 to help people with manic depression, their relatives, friends and others who care through the establishment of self-help groups; to educate the public and caring professions through the provision of information; and to encourage research for the better treatment of manic depression. Volunteers support the work of the administrative staff in head office. This can involve telephone work, wordprocessing, preparing letters and filing. Volunteers should already have some basic office experience and skills, and be willing to undertake a variety of tasks as part of a team.

Total projects worldwide: 1
Total UK projects: 1
Starting months: January–December.
Time required: 4–52 weeks (plus).
Age requirement: 16 plus.
Causes: Health care/medical.
Activities: Administration.
When to apply: Three months in advance.
Qualifications: Basic office skills and

experience; an understanding of mental illness.

Benefits: Travelcard expenses within London reimbursed.

UK placements: *England* (Surrey).

MANSFIELD OUTDOOR CENTRE
Manor Road
Lambourne End
Romford
Essex
RM4 1NB UK
Tel: +44 (0) 20 8500 3047
Fax: +44 (0) 20 8559 8481
Contact: Sarah Campling

Mansfield Outdoor Centre supports people of all ages and backgrounds, particularly those who are most vulnerable. We encourage everyone to take responsibility for their own physical, spiritual and psychological health so that they can make a full contribution to society and benefit from its rewards. The Outdoor Centre promotes the well-being of the people of Newham and other surrounding areas by a wide variety of programmes. The Centre offers a range of training programmes to groups of young people or adults using an outdoor environment and a variety of activities. Safe opportunities for: working as a member of a team; achieving personal goals; gaining self-respect; taking responsibility for your actions. A working farm: introduction to a variety of animals; hands-on experience caring for them; fears overcome and confidence gained; environmental awareness widened. Working with special needs: mental health problems (all ages); physical difficulties (especially wheelchairs); emotional and behavioural challenges. Facilities and activities available include: climbing wall, rope courses; swimming pool and access to lake; orienteering in Hainault Forest; canoeing and dinghy sailing; archery and problem solving exercises. Volunteers are required to help with all the above. Daily volunteers needed all year.

Volunteers with an offending background are accepted provided that the offence is not one which would cause a danger to the young people we work with.

Total projects worldwide: 0
Total UK projects: 20
Starting months: January–December.

Time required: 2–6 weeks.
Age requirement: 18–40
Causes: Addicts/Ex-addicts, Aids/HIV, animal welfare, children, conservation, disabled (learning and physical), environmental causes, human rights, inner city problems, offenders/ex-offenders, poor/homeless, refugees, teaching/assisting (primary, secondary, mature), unemployed, wildlife, work camps – seasonal, young people.
Activities: Agriculture/farming, conservation skills, DIY, first aid, gardening/horticulture, group work, manual work, outdoor skills, religion, social work, sport, summer camps, teaching, training, work camps – seasonal.
Vols under 26 placed each year: 8 of a total of 10.
When to apply: All year.
Work alone/with others: With others.
Volunteers with disabilities: Not possible.
Qualifications: A need to speak English.
Equipment/clothing: Old clothes, all specialist equipment is provided.
Health requirements: The work demands that volunteers are fit and healthy.
Costs: Residential facilities are only available from end of June to beginning September Otherwise no costs.
Benefits: £20 per week. Food allowance for summer camp volunteers. Travel costs within England at start and finish.
Interview details: If possible we invite prospective volunteers to come and see our site and the work we do before they work for us.
Certification: Certificate or reference provided on request.
Charity number: 220085
UK placements: *England* (Essex).

MARIANIST VOLUNTARY SERVICE COMMUNITIES (MVSC)
PO Box 9224
Wright Bros. Branch
Dayton
Ohio
OH 45409 USA

Tel: 00 1 513 229 4630
Fax: 00 1 513 229 2772
e-mail: mvsc@saber.udayton.edu
Contact: Laura Libertore

Total projects worldwide: 1
Total UK projects: 0

Starting months: January–December.
Time required: 1–52 weeks (plus).
Age requirement: 12 plus.

MARIE CURIE CANCER CARE
28 Belgrave Square
London
SW1X 8QG UK

Tel: +44 (0) 20 7235 3325
Fax: +44 (0) 20 7823 2380
Contact: Mrs Jean Peel or Mrs Gayle
Richards

Marie Curie Cancer Care is the only major
charity in the UK to provide practical nursing
care, throughout the day or overnight, for
cancer patients in the comfortable and
familiar surroundings of their own homes.
Marie Curie Cancer Care has 5,000 nurses
across the UK who offer not only expert
nursing support but also respite for the
patients' families by giving them the
opportunity of a good night's sleep, secure in
the knowledge that their loved ones are being
cared for by professionals. Marie Curie
Cancer Care is also the largest provider of
hospice beds, outside the NHS, with 11
Marie Curie hospice centres in the UK
dedicated to the specialist care of cancer
patients. Last year Marie Curie Cancer Care
helped a total of 22,500 people with cancer.
Volunteers are needed to work fundraising
and in the shops. For fundraising contact
Mrs Jean Peel at the above London address
and telephone number. For working in
shops, contact Mrs Gayle Richards at Unit 1,
Cheney Manor Industrial Estate, Swindon
SN2 2YX. Tel: +44 (0) 1793 863400, Fax:
+44 (0) 1793 430008. Volunteers with an
offending background may be accepted. Each
applicant would be assessed in relation to the
job description.

Total projects worldwide: 100
Total UK projects: Over 100.
Starting months: January–December.
Time required: 1–52 weeks.
Age requirement: 16 plus.
Causes: Health care/medical.
Activities: Administration, Fundraising.
When to apply: All year.
Work alone/with others: With others.
Volunteers with disabilities: Possible.
Costs: Travel, meals etc.
Benefits: Experience only.
Interview details: Interviews take place either

at 17 Grosvenor Crescent, London, or the
relevant registered office.
UK placements: *England* (throughout);
Scotland (throughout); *Northern Ireland*
(throughout); *Wales* (throughout).

MARINE CONSERVATION SOCIETY
(MCS)
9 Gloucester Road
Ross-on-Wye
Herefordshire
HR9 5BU UK

Tel: +44 (0) 1989 5660178
Fax: +44 (0) 1989 567815
Contact: Pam Bridgewater

Marine Conservation Society has volunteer
opportunities, for a minimum of one week,
available occasionally for those with marine
science qualifications.

Total projects worldwide: 1
Total UK projects: 1
Starting months: January–December.
Time required: 1–52 weeks.
Age requirement: 20 plus.
When to apply: All year.
Work alone/with others: With others.
Volunteers with disabilities: Not possible.
Qualifications: Marine science qualifications –
at or post university.
Costs: All costs including accommodation.
Worldwide placements: *Africa* (Egypt).
UK placements: *England* (Cornwall,
Cumbria, Devon, Dorset, Essex, Hampshire,
Isle of Man, Kent, Leicestershire,
Lincolnshire, Merseyside, Norfolk, Somerset,
Suffolk, E. Sussex, W. Sussex, Tyne and
Wear, N. Yorkshire); *Scotland* (throughout);
Wales (Anglesey, Bridgend, Cardiff,
Carmarthenshire, Ceredigion, Conwy,
Denbighshire, Flintshire, Gwynedd,
Monmouthshire, Neath Port Talbot,
Newport, Pembrokeshire, Swansea, Vale of
Glamorgan).

MARITIME VOLUNTEER SERVICE
202 Lambeth Road
London
SE1 7JW UK

Tel: +44 (0) 20 7928 8100
Fax: +44 (0) 20 7401 2537
Contact: The Secretary, MVS HQ

Maritime Volunteer Service (MVS): in recent
years many people from our island nation

have looked on with disquiet and a feeling of helplessness as the Royal Navy, its reserve forces and the British merchant fleet have declined substantially in size. One group of volunteers has acted to redress this trend. The MVS, founded in 1994, is a team of men and women who are determined to maintain, foster and pass on to the next generation that rich vein of maritime skills which underpins our national way of life. Members of the MVS come from a wide variety of backgrounds, ranging from former members of the Royal Navy and its reserves through merchant seafarers to ordinary citizens with no more than a keenness to learn about the sea and its ways. The MVS has already established itself with nearly fifty units around the coast of the United Kingdom. Their purpose is to provide a nucleus of trained people to support existing naval and civil authorities when needed and in so doing to advance the awareness of the local community of the importance of maritime skills and knowledge. The MVS has gained the recognition of the Royal Navy, a tribute to the important role it plays in the education and training of young people in nautical skills. Close association between the navy and the MVS is seen as contributing to the government's 'New Deal' initiative by enriching the pool of training opportunity in the community and helping young people to get jobs.

Total projects worldwide: 1
Total UK projects: 1
Starting months: January–December.
Time required: 1–52 weeks (plus).
Age requirement: 18 plus.
Causes: Environmental causes, unemployed, work camps – seasonal, young people.
Activities: Accountancy, administration, catering, cooking, driving, first aid, fundraising, newsletter/journalism, outdoor skills, sport, technical skills, training.
Vols under 26 placed each year: 500–600 of a total of 1,000.
When to apply: All year.
Work alone/with others: Work in units.
Volunteers with disabilities: Shore support only.
Qualifications: Nil – MVS provides qualifications.
Equipment/clothing: MVS is a uniformed service.
Health requirements: Medical certificate

required for afloat.
Costs: HQ membership £15 a year, local £50 approximately subject to unit. Public liability and public accident insurance included in annual subscription.
Nationalities accepted: British volunteers only.
Interview details: Prospective volunteers are interviewed by their local unit.
Certification: Recognized qualifications: RYA/MSA/VQ.
Charity number: 1048454
UK placements: *England* (Cornwall, Co. Durham, Cumbria, Devon, Dorset, Essex, Gloucestershire, Hampshire, Kent, Lancashire, Lincolnshire, Merseyside, Norfolk, Northumberland, Somerset, Suffolk, E. Sussex, W. Sussex, N. Yorkshire); *Scotland* (throughout); *Wales* (throughout, except for Powys).

MARLBOROUGH BRANDT GROUP
1A London Road
Marlborough
Wiltshire
SN8 1PH UK

Tel: +44 (0) 1672 514078
Fax: +44 (0) 1672 514922
Contact: Mrs Anita Bew

One of the aims of the Marlborough Brandt Group is to increase understanding between different cultures by maintaining a link with a community in a developing country. For the last 14 years there has been a constant flow of people in both directions between Marlborough in Wiltshire and Gunjur, a village of about 12,500 people in the Gambia, West Africa. The Gambia is one of the world's poorest nations, and is a predominantly Muslim country, so the way of life there is very different from our own. Every year at least two Gambians come to Marlborough for three months to gain experience in a particular field, staying with local families. At the same time, two young people, usually in their gap year after taking A-levels, go to Gunjur for a similar period of time to work as teaching assistants alongside a Gambian teacher in a specific project. They stay in family compounds and live as Gambians. They are expected to pay £40 per month for accommodation with a Gambian family. For this they can expect a small house, all food and washing and we recommend them to raise £1,500 for the three months. This includes air fares, insurance and other personal expenses. Going to Gunjur provides a unique opportunity to experience African life from the inside, in an environment where you have plenty of friends from the day you arrive. Our volunteers are profoundly affected by the experience, and many become involved in development issues in later life.

Total projects worldwide: 1
Total UK projects: 0
Starting months: September.
Time required: 12 weeks.
Age requirement: 18 plus.
Causes: Teaching/assisting (secondary), young people.
Activities: Community work, development issues, gardening/horticulture, library/resource centres, sport, teaching.
Vols under 26 placed each year: 2 of a total of 4.
When to apply: By 1 January.
Work alone/with others: As a group.
Volunteers with disabilities: Conditions fairly tough but possible depending on disability.
Qualifications: A-level preferred in at least one of: English, Maths, Science, French, Art.
Health requirements: Good general health important as medical facilities limited.
Costs: Administration fee £200; air fare plus insurance approximately £800. About £1,500 covers all including £130 charged for the induction and Mandinka lessons on arrival. Medical insurance is necessary and the volunteer's responsibility.
Benefits: Food, accommodation.
Training: We provide an induction programme in Marlborough for a weekend.
Supervision: Volunteers are supervised in the school in which they work and the responsibility of TARUD, our partner organization in the Gambia.
Nationalities accepted: No restrictions but school leavers only from the UK.
Interview details: There is a preliminary briefing in December before starting, followed by interviews. Interviews are held in Marlborough.
Certification: Reference on request.
Charity number: 1001398
Worldwide placements: *Africa* (Gambia).

MAYC
2 Chester House
Pages Lane,
Muswell Hill
London
N10 1PR UK

Tel: +44 (0) 20 8444 9845
Contact: Fleur Anderson

Total projects worldwide: 1
Starting months: January–December.
Time required: 1–52 weeks (plus).
Age requirement: 12 plus.

MEDICAL AID FOR PALESTINIANS
33a Islington Park Street
London
N1 1QB UK

Tel: +44 (0) 20 7226 4114
Fax: +44 (0) 20 7226 0880
Contact: Overseas Postings Officer

Medical Aid for Palestinians need qualified and experienced medical volunteers to come and share their skills with Palestinian colleagues.

Total projects worldwide: Varies.
Total UK projects: 0
Starting months: January–December.
Time required: 26–52 weeks.
Age requirement: 22 plus.
Causes: Health care/medical.
Activities: Development issues, training.
Vols under 26 placed each year: 25
When to apply: 2–3 months in advance.
Work alone/with others: With others.
Volunteers with disabilities: Possible, depending on project and practicalities.
Qualifications: Medical/nursing qualifications and 2 years' experience.
Health requirements: Nil.
Costs: Nil.
Benefits: Accommodation and living allowance plus health insurance and travel plus grant paid in UK.
Certification: Certificate or reference provided.
Worldwide placements: *Africa* (Egypt); *Asia* (Jordan, Lebanon).

MENCAP'S HOLIDAY SERVICE
Optimum House
Clippers Quay
Salford Quays
M5 2XP UK

Tel: +44 (0) 161 888 1200
Fax: +44 (0) 161 888 1210
Contact: The Holidays Administrator

Mencap's Holiday Service provides an annual programme of accompanied holidays throughout England, Wales and abroad for adults with learning disabilities. This ranges from special care holidays for people with profound and multiple disabilities to activity, guesthouse holidays and holiday villas abroad for the more able. We are looking for volunteers to help and support the guests on these holidays. The voluntary work involves being responsible for the personal care of each guest, including washing, dressing and feeding. Also essential tasks such as stimulating and interesting them in activities, communicating and being a friend. Duties shared on a rota basis may also include catering and cleaning. Volunteers must have energy, enthusiasm and an interest in people with a learning disability. No experience necessary as you will have the support and direction of experienced leaders. Maximum 14 hours work per day for 1–2 weeks.

Total projects worldwide: 45
Total UK projects: 40
Starting months: January–December.
Time required: 1–2 weeks.
Age requirement: 18 plus.
Causes: Children, disabled (learning and physical), holidays for disabled.
Activities: Arts/crafts, caring (general), catering, driving, first aid, music, outdoor skills, sport, summer camps.
Vols under 26 placed each year: 170
When to apply: All year.
Work alone/with others: With others.
Volunteers with disabilities: Possible.
Qualifications: Nil.
Health requirements: Nil.
Costs: Nil.
Benefits: Board, lodging and £25 towards travelling costs. Mencap has public liability insurance.
Training: First night meeting – 'on the job'.
Supervision: Two volunteer co-leaders with much experience supervise the volunteers.
Certification: Certificate or reference provided.
Charity number: 222377
Worldwide placements: *Europe* (Portugal, Spain); *North America* (USA).
UK placements: *England* (Cheshire, Cumbria,

Devon, Dorset, Essex, Gloucestershire, Hampshire, Hertfordshire, Kent, Lancashire, Lincolnshire, Merseyside, Nottinghamshire, Suffolk, W. Sussex, N. Yorkshire); *Wales* (Powys).

METHODIST CHURCH – NORTH LANCASHIRE DISTRICT, THE
8 Church Brow
Walton Le Dale
Preston
Lancashire
PR5 4BB UK

Tel: +44 (0) 1772 824956
Contact: Trevor Cook

Total projects worldwide: 1
Total UK projects: 1
Starting months: January–December.
Time required: 1–52 weeks.
Age requirement: 14 plus.

MID-AFRICA MINISTRY (CMS)
Youth Office
Partnership House
157 Waterloo Road
London
SE1 8UU UK

Tel: +44 (0) 20 7261 1370
Fax: +44 (0) 20 7401 2910
e-mail:
mid_africa_ministry@compuserve.com
Contact: The General Secretary

Mid-Africa Ministry (MAM) works in partnership with the Anglican Church in Rwanda, Burundi, South West Uganda and Eastern Congo. From time to time, the overseas Church requests short-term assistance or is able to accommodate offers from those who are unable to go overseas for as long as two years or who wish to test whether they are being called to Africa longer-term or who are over 65. The minimum period of time for such service is usually six months although three months is sufficient for some medical assignments; an academic year is often the requirement for teaching posts. Medicine and teaching are the most common disciplines. Offers of service need to be on a self-funded basis although MAM does have a discretionary fund and is happy to help those volunteers unable to raise all their funds. Volunteers usually live in difficult or basic conditions which is part of the 'culture shock'. Accommodation, water and electricity supply (if any!), food, health facilities, leisure activities can all be guaranteed to be very different from back home but so also can the compensations be similarly guaranteed. Volunteers are expected to be involved in the life and worship of the local Anglican Church where they work overseas; there is a requirement of obedience to the local Anglican Church and its decisions. Whilst MAM is not the employer, volunteers are expected to follow its advice, requests and decisions. MAM office has a wide range of suitable AV material and literature which is readily available for loan.

Total projects worldwide: Many.
Total UK projects: 0
Starting months: January–December.
Time required: 4–52 weeks (plus).
Age requirement: 18 plus.
Causes: Health care/medical, teaching/ assisting (primary, secondary, EFL), young people.
Activities: Accountancy, administration, agriculture/farming, building/construction, caring (general), catering, community work, computers, library/resource centres, music, religion, social work, sport, teaching, technical skills, theatre/drama, training, visiting/befriending, work camps – seasonal.
Vols under 26 placed each year: 20
When to apply: All year. For summer camps by 1 March.
Work alone/with others: With others.
Volunteers with disabilities: Possible, but most work is rather remote with basic facilities.
Qualifications: Professional skills required and also some without professional qualifications.
Equipment/clothing: Yes, if medical placement.
Health requirements: Satisfactory medical examination for tropical countries.
Costs: Air fare £600–£1,000; subsistence £150 a month; medical and travel insurance £120 a year.
Benefits: Discretionary fund available. Most volunteers. are self-funded or funded by churches etc.
Training: One week orientation in Britain.
Supervision: Under the care of the diocesan bishop of the area.
Nationalities accepted: No restrictions but UK based volunteers are generally required.

Interview details: Prospective volunteers are interviewed, usually in the London office.
Certification: Reference on request.
Charity number: 220297
Worldwide placements: *Africa* (Burundi, Congo Dem Republic, Rwanda, Uganda).

MIKKELSHOJ
Ravnsbjerg Forte 3
Skovby
DK 6500 Vojens
Denmark

Tel: 00 45 74 575912
Contact: The Director

MIKKELSHOJ is a small rurally situated training centre for youngsters.

Total projects worldwide: 1
Total UK projects: 0
Starting months: January–December.
Time required: 1–52 weeks.
Age requirement: 14 plus.
Causes: Disabled (learning), young people.
Worldwide placements: *Europe* (Denmark).

MILTON KEYNES RESOURCE CENTRE
1 Fletchers Mews
Neath Hill
Milton Keynes
Buckinghamshire
MK14 6HW UK

Tel: +44 (0) 1908 660364
Fax: +44 (0) 1908 662212
Contact: Matthew Keen

Milton Keynes Resource Centre is a day training centre covering IT, core skills, art, relaxation, DT and printing and we conform to the Scope Mission Statement: Scope exists to provide support and services for people with cerebral palsy and their families. Volunteers with an offending background may be accepted if they are an exception under the Rehabilitation Act 1974.

Total projects worldwide: 1
Total UK projects: 1
Starting months: January–December.
Time required: 1–52 weeks (plus).
Age requirement: 16 plus.
Causes: Disabled (physical).
Activities: Administration, arts/crafts, caring (day), computers, cooking, gardening/ horticulture, training.
Vols under 26 placed each year: 16–18

When to apply: All year.
Work alone/with others: With others.
Volunteers with disabilities: Possible, although some projects (gardening) may require manual work.
Qualifications: Nil.
Health requirements: Nil.
Costs: Nil.
Benefits: Reasonable travel costs.
Interview details: Prospective volunteers are interviewed at the Centre.
UK placements: *England* (Buckinghamshire).

MINISTRY OF YOUTH AND SPORTS, ENUGU STATE, NIGERIA
No 7
Edem Close
New Haven
Enugu
Nigeria

Tel: 00 234 42 458079
Fax: 00 234 42 456232
Contact: Dr Ifeanyi Nwobodo

Over 100 youth organizations scattered all over the 17 local government areas of Enugu State are affiliated to the Youth and Sports Ministry and they require voluntary help of various sorts. Some pilot projects of the Ministry are the Rangers Youth Development Programme, the Agwu Games Village, the club land and playground/pitches with tracks. Volunteers with an offending background are accepted.

Total projects worldwide: 100
Total UK projects: 0
Starting months: January–December.
Time required: 30–52 weeks.
Age requirement: 16–25
Causes: Addicts/Ex-addicts, children, disabled (physical), elderly people, health care/medical, holidays for disabled, offenders/ex-offenders, poor/homeless, teaching/assisting, unemployed, work camps – seasonal, young people.
Activities: Arts/crafts, building/construction, campaigning, caring (general), community work, counselling, development issues, international aid, outdoor skills, religion, research, scientific work, social work, sport, summer camps, technical skills, training, work camps – seasonal.
Vols under 26 placed each year: 500,000
When to apply: August.
Work alone/with others: With others.

Volunteers with disabilities: Possible.
Qualifications: At least GCSE.
Health requirements: Nil.
Costs: Travel costs, subsistence, insurance.
Training: Awgu Youth Village is used for orientation.
Supervision: Officials of the Youth Ministry in Enugu organize the supervision. We encourage volunteers to become self-reliant in their area of interest.
Interview details: Interviews are conducted in the Ministry.
Certification: Certificate or reference provided.
Worldwide placements: *Africa* (Nigeria).

MINORITY RIGHTS GROUP INTERNATIONAL
International Secretariat
379 Brixton Road
London
SW9 7DE UK

Tel: +44 (0) 20 7978 9498
Contact: The Director

Total projects worldwide: 1
Total UK projects: 0
Starting months: January–December.
Time required: 16–52 weeks.
Age requirement: 18 plus.

MISSION AVIATION FELLOWSHIP
Ingles Manor
Castle Hill Avenue
Folkestone
Kent
CT20 2TN UK

Tel: +44 (0) 1303 850950
Fax: +44 (0) 1303 852800
e-mail: maf-uk-hq@maf.org
Contact: Dave Barker, Youth Department Manager

Total projects worldwide: 1
Starting months: January–December.
Time required: 1–52 weeks (plus).
Age requirement: 12 plus.

MISSION RAINFOREST FOUNDATION
The Centre
Codicote Road
Welwyn
Hertfordshire
AL6 9TU UK

Tel: +44 (0) 1438 716873 or 716478

Contact: Dr Terry Moore

Total projects worldwide: 1
Total UK projects: 1
Starting months: January–December.
Time required: 1–52 weeks.
Age requirement: 16 plus.
Causes: Conservation, human rights.
Activities: Administration, campaigning, computers, conservation skills, development issues, fundraising, library/resource centres, research, scientific work, technical skills, translating.
Volunteers with disabilities: Possible.
Qualifications: Nil.
Benefits: Accommodation electricity and basic food provided.
UK placements: *England* (Hertfordshire).

MISSION VOLUNTEERS USA AND INTERNATIONAL

The Presbyterian Church (USA)
100 Witherspoon Street
Louisville
Kentucky 40202-1396
USA

Total projects worldwide: 1
Total UK projects: 0
Starting months: January–December.
Time required: 1–52 weeks (plus).
Age requirement: 12 plus.

MISSIONARY CENACLE VOLUNTEERS

PO Box 35105
Cleveland
Ohio
44135-0105 USA

Tel: 00 1 800 221 5740
Fax: 00 1 216 671 2320
e-mail: cenaclevol@aol.com
Web: www.tmc3.org
Contact: Shaun Witmer, Director

Since 1916, the Missionary Cenacle Volunteers have been 'Helping Catholics Become Apostles' through faith-based voluntary service, for long-term (nearly one year or more, for 21-plus year olds) and summer (18-plus year olds) service terms. Our volunteers serve throughout the US and (if Spanish speaking) in Central America. Volunteers work on our missions with Missionary Cenacle Family members and others, while participating in community life and an active prayer life. The Missionary

Cenacle Family is a Catholic missionary family devoted to fostering the vocation of the laity to become apostles, by growing spiritually while serving God and others among the spiritually abandoned and materially poor in such ministries as: parish/youth ministry, health care, education, social work and other ministries including teaching, building maintenance, cooking, religious education, clerical/office work, child care, teacher's aide, working with elderly, homeless, and persons with physical and developmental disabilities. Our Trinita summer family programme lies in the beautiful mountains of western Connecticut. For 2–6 weeks, we need young and adult Catholics (couples included) to share their gifts of faith, fellowship, music, arts and crafts, laughter, and recreation to provide a rewarding faith experience for disadvantaged inner-city families from New York, New Jersey, Connecticut and Pennsylvania. For long-term service you will receive housing, food, health insurance and a small monthly stipend for personal expenses. Room and board is provided for our summer sites. All applicants go through a background check and criminal history search.

Total projects worldwide: 20–25
Total UK projects: 0
Starting months: January–December.
Time required: 3–52 weeks (plus).
Age requirement: 18 plus.
Causes: Children, Disabled (learning and physical), Elderly People, Health Care/Medical, Inner City Problems, Offenders/ex-offenders, Poor/Homeless, Refugees, Teaching/assisting (primary), Young People.
Activities: Administration, arts/crafts, caring (general and residential), community work, computers, cooking, counselling, driving, group work, manual work, music, religion, social work, sport, summer camps, teaching, training, translating, visiting/befriending.
Vols under 26 placed each year: 20–25 long-term, 50 summer camp of a total of 75.
When to apply: February–May and year round.
Work alone/with others: Both.
Volunteers with disabilities: Possible.
Qualifications: Summer: ability to work with youth. Long-term: college degree, driving licence, comfortable working at Roman Catholic Church sites.
Equipment/clothing: Clothing based on local

climate/weather.

Health requirements: Some sites require physical ability to do manual work or heavy lifting.

Costs: Return travel to site in USA or Central America plus personal expenses.

Benefits: Board and lodging for short and long-term volunteers. Long term also offers pocket money. A mid-year volunteer retreat is offered to allow for a look ahead to plan for the end of the year. Basic health care coverage is provided by the host agency work site.

Training: A one-week programme orientation and varying on-site training depending on work site.

Supervision: Supervisors are provided at every work site to assist, orient and train volunteers in their work.

Interview details: All volunteers are interviewed in person when possible, but at least by phone when necessary.

Certification: Reference on request.

Worldwide placements: *North America* (USA); *Central America* (Costa Rica, Mexico, Puerto Rico).

MITRANIKETAN
Mitraniketan PO
Thiruvananthapuram
Vellanad
Kerala
695-543 India

Tel: 00 91 472 882045
Fax: 00 91 472 882015
Contact: K. Viswanathan, Director

Mitraniketan is well-known in India and abroad as a Kerala-based voluntary non-governmental organisation that has pioneered people-centred holistic rural development for improving the quality of life and living of village communities. It strives to promote rural development with a human face. Mitraniketan has a resident community engaged in a variety of development activities. It has an unmistakable international presence in a Kerala-setting and promotes a lifestyle that is essentially spartan. It is an education-based community which imparts community-based education which is participative by nature and emphasizes dignity of labour. It promotes sustainable agriculture and farming practices that are environment and farmer friendly. A variety of vocations for rural

employment are promoted at Mitraniketan, with efficiency-additions through appropriate science and technology inputs. Mitraniketan also strives to promote and enhance rural human resource development capabilities that can foster a participative culture and work ethic. It seeks to blend tradition with modernity and indigenous knowledge systems with other knowledge systems. In its development update and innovative endeavours, a like-minded fraternity resident in and outside Mitraniketan lends devoted support.

Total projects worldwide: 1
Total UK projects: 0
Starting months: January–December.
Time required: 1–52 weeks.
Age requirement: 18 plus.
Causes: Animal welfare, children, disabled (learning), environmental causes, health care/medical, teaching/assisting (nursery, primary, secondary, mature, EFL), young people.
Activities: Agriculture/farming, building/construction, fundraising, gardening/horticulture, international aid, library/resource centres, manual work, marketing/publicity, sport, teaching.
Vols under 26 placed each year: 55 of a total of 100.
When to apply: All year.
Work alone/with others: With others.
Volunteers with disabilities: Possible, such as teaching and health care activities.
Qualifications: English language and special skills for some projects – for other projects no skills required.
Health requirements: Nil.
Costs: Rs200 (US$5) per day for board and lodging for first 5 days. Thereafter Rs150 per day. Travel to India. The volunteer must make his/her own insurance arrangements.
Benefits: The cost covers board and lodging.
Training: One-day campus tour and orientation.
Supervision: By volunteers' co-ordinator.
Interview details: There are no interviews but bio-data is checked.
Certification: Certificate or reference provided.
Charity number: 11 of 1967
Worldwide placements: *Asia* (India).

MOKOLODI NATURE RESERVE
PO Box 170
Gaborone

Botswana

Tel: 00 267 561955 / 6
Fax: 00 267 313973
e-mail: mokolodi@info.bw
Contact: 'Puso' J.R.B. Kirby, Park Manager

The Mokolodi Nature Reserve lies in the heart of Botswana bush but only 14 km from the capital Gabarone. The Reserve is 6,300 acres with the recent acquisition of a further 3,700 acres. It is now in its sixth year of existence and almost fully stocked with a varied population of species indigenous to SE Botswana. The two founding pillars of the reserve are the reintroduction of indigenous species and environmental education. For the latter an education centre has been established, using the 'outdoor classroom', to instill in children from all over Botswana a love of nature and an understanding of the importance of conserving wildlife for Botswana and the world. Last year 9,000 children visited the Centre. One day these children will have the vote. Mokolodi is home to over a third of Botswana's white rhino population, and has a breeding programme aimed at the eventual reintroduction of the species to all parts of Botswana. The reserve has one of only two wild animal orphanages in the country and is home to Botswana's only Cheetah Transit Station, created in order to relocate 'problem' cheetahs brought in from private game farms and cattle ranches. A joint venture with the Serendib Orphanage cares for four young orphan elephants, who are being trained in an educational project firstly to disprove the long-standing myth that it is impossible to train African elephants, and secondly, to show young people the potential value of these beasts both in tourism and otherwise. Volunteers are needed to help in all areas. We are currently trying to raise funds to build volunteer accommodation. This will house 12 volunteers. Volunteers with an offending background might be accepted depending on the offence.

Total projects worldwide: 5
Total UK projects: 0
Starting months: January–December.
Time required: 12–52 weeks (plus).
Age requirement: 21 plus.
Causes: Animal welfare, archaeology, architecture, children, conservation, environmental causes, teaching/assisting (nursery, primary, secondary, mature), wildlife, work camps – seasonal.
Activities: Accountancy, administration, arts/crafts, building/construction, caring (general), catering, community work, computers, conservation skills, development issues, driving, first aid, forestry, fundraising, gardening/horticulture, group work, international aid, library/resource centres, manual work, marketing/publicity, music, newsletter/journalism, outdoor skills, research, scientific work, summer camps, teaching, technical skills, theatre/drama, training, work camps – seasonal.
Vols under 26 placed each year: Approximately 6 of a total of 12.
When to apply: All year.
Work alone/with others: Both.
Volunteers with disabilities: Possible.
Qualifications: University degree preferable but otherwise people with specific skills and experience.
Equipment/clothing: Volunteers are required to purchase uniform, approximately P700 (£120).
Health requirements: Good health. Government requirements can be obtained from the Botswana Embassy.
Costs: Return travel costs plus registration/subsistence cost of £100 per month. Essential full medical and travel insurance is the responsibility of the volunteer.
Benefits: The cost covers monthly allowance for subsistance.
Supervision: By senior management.
Interview details: Prospective volunteers are interviewed mostly by e-mail.
Certification: Certificate or reference provided.
Worldwide placements: *Africa* (Botswana).

MONKEY SANCTUARY, THE

Looe
Cornwall
PL13 1NZ UK

Tel: +44 (0) 1503 262532
e-mail: info@monkeysanctuary.org
Web: www.monkeysanctuary.org
Contact: Hanneke van Ormondt, Volunteer Co-ordinator

The Monkey Sanctuary is the home of a socially natural colony of woolly monkeys. It was established in 1964 and has received worldwide recognition as the first place where this beautiful species of monkey survived and bred outside its own habitat in the South American rainforests. All of the monkeys in the colony have been born at the Sanctuary and among them are a few who belong to the fifth generation. They form a stable group with natural kinship bonds and a dominance hierarchy based on responsible leadership. Over the course of a year the Sanctuary receives several dozen people for voluntary work, with up to four or five at any one time. Volunteers stay for periods of two to four weeks and in exchange for their help they live in with the Sanctuary team. We hope volunteers will come because they share our concern for animal welfare, conservation and a need to continue questioning people's attitude to other animals. Volunteers help in various ways, making and serving teas for the visitors, serving in the Sanctuary shop and kiosk, preparing monkey foods (a main volunteer responsibility year round), domestic help, gardening, sweeping paths and public areas and general maintenance. Volunteers with an offending background accepted.

Total projects worldwide: 1
Total UK projects: 1
Starting months: January–December.
Time required: 2–4 weeks.
Age requirement: 18 plus.
Causes: Animal welfare, conservation, environmental causes, wildlife.
Activities: Building/construction, conservation skills, DIY, gardening/horticulture, manual work.
Vols under 26 placed each year: 100 of a total of 120.
When to apply: 3 plus months in advance of preferred stay.
Work alone/with others: Both.
Volunteers with disabilities: Good vision and hearing essential. For safety all workers must be alert and quick.
Qualifications: No qualifications are needed but relevant skills welcomed. Interest in animal welfare and conservation essential. Speak and understand a high degree of English.
Health requirements: Only if it may cause possible problem with safety around the monkeys.
Costs: Travel costs plus £25 per week board and lodging is payable on confirmation of a place. If you cannot meet the weekly charge, please do not be shy to contact us anyway as we may be able to work something out.
Benefits: The cost contribution provides all board (vegetarian) and lodging.
Supervision: Volunteers work closely with Sanctuary keepers but will not be supervised during many aspects of their work.
Nationalities accepted: No restrictions but all volunteers must speak and understand a high degree of English.
Interview details: No interview necessary.
Certification: Written reference on request.
Charity number: 1038022
UK placements: *England* (Cornwall).

MONTGOMERYSHIRE WILDLIFE TRUST

Collott House
20 Severn Street
Welshpool
Powys
SY21 7AD UK

Tel: + 44 (0) 1938 555654
Fax: + 44 (0) 1938 556161
Contact: The Director

Montgomeryshire Wildlife Trust is a member of the Wildlife Trusts, a national partnership of 47 county trusts. For more details of the Wildlife Trusts, see the entry under Cornwall Wildlife Trust.

Total projects worldwide: 1
Total UK projects: 1
Starting months: January–December.
Time required: 1–52 weeks (plus).
Age requirement: 12 plus.
Causes: Conservation, environmental causes, wildlife.
Activities: Conservation skills.
Work alone/with others: Both.
Qualifications: Nil.
Equipment/clothing: Casual work clothes, waterproofs, stout boots for outdoor work. Protective safety gear is provided.
Health requirements: Anti-tetanus innoculation required.
Costs: Nil.
Benefits: Out-of-pocket expenses. Volunteers are covered by the Trust's insurance.
UK placements: *Wales* (Powys).

MOST

Service Civil International Slovenia
Breg 12 – PP 279
61000 Ljubljana
Slovenia

Tel: 00 386 61 125 8076 or 8067

MOST organizes 23 international work camps mostly ecologically orientated, although some projects are with Croatian and Bosnian refugees as well as children and handicapped people. Applicants can apply directly to above address or through International Voluntary Service in England.

Total projects worldwide: 1
Total UK projects: 0
Starting months: July–September.
Time required: 2–12 weeks.
Age requirement: 18 plus.
Causes: Children, conservation, disabled (learning and physical), elderly people, environmental causes, refugees.
Activities: Building/construction, conservation skills, DIY, gardening/horticulture, marketing/publicity, religion, summer camps.
Vols under 26 placed each year: 400
When to apply: As early as possible.
Costs: All expenses except accommodation and food.
Benefits: Accommodation and food provided.
Worldwide placements: *Europe* (Slovenia).

MOTSE WA BADIRI CAMPHILL
PO Box 2224
Gaborone
Botswana

Contact: The Director

Total projects worldwide: 1
Total UK projects: 0
Starting months: January–December.
Time required: 1–52 weeks (plus).
Age requirement: 12 plus.

MOUNT KAILASH SCHOOL CHARITABLE TRUST
5 Trewirgie Road
Redruth
Cornwall
TR15 2SX UK

Tel: +44 (0) 1209 218200
e-mail: mountkailashschool@hotmail.com
Contact: Ms Karenza Jago

Mount Kailash School is for the education of poor and needy Tibetan refugees and Nepalese children. At present there are 190 children, 12 classrooms, 30 staff and ever expanding facilities. One of the very important aims and objectives of the school is to preserve the ancient Tibetan and Nepalese cultures where there is an emphasis on drama and dance. Volunteers are desperately needed to help at all levels of everyday life as well as helping/teaching the children. Experience with children aged 3–16 and teaching is preferred. In September 1996 the first two students from Mount Kailash School started attending a college of education in the west of England, prior to going to university in the United Kingdom. (They both were top-scoring in their application tests.) One now is in the second year of a midwifery course at Bournemouth University, the other studies civil engineering at Nottingham University.

Alternative address:
Jane Osborne-Fellows
White Lodge
Shortlanesend
Truro
Cornwall
TR4 9DU UK

Total projects worldwide: 1
Total UK projects: 0
Starting months: January–December.
Time required: 4–20 weeks.
Age requirement: 18 plus.
Causes: Children, health care/medical, poor/homeless, refugees, teaching/assisting (nursery, primary, secondary, EFL), young people.
Activities: Arts/crafts, caring (general and residential), computers, development issues, first aid, fundraising, gardening/horticulture, group work, international aid, outdoor skills, social work, sport, teaching, technical skills, theatre/drama.
Vols under 26 placed each year: Approximately 8 of a total of approximately 10.
When to apply: Any time, 3 months in advance. School year starts mid-February.
Work alone/with others: Both.
Volunteers with disabilities: Possible.
Qualifications: A-levels or above. Also urgent places for qualified English or Science teachers for 1 year.
Equipment/clothing: Modest clothing – also suitable clothing for climatic changes.
Health requirements: Good health needed.
Costs: Travel, insurance, visa, airport tax and general spending money.

Benefits: Board/lodging provided. Qualified teachers get approximately £30 per month plus board, lodging.
Supervision: Volunteers are given duties by the school principal.
Interview details: Interviews take place in Redruth, Cornwall..
Charity number: 1015291

MOUVEMENT TWIZA
BP 77
Rue Chiguer Hamadi No. 23
Hay Es-Salam
Khemisset
15000 Morocco

Tel: 00 212 7 55 30 68
Fax: 00 212 7 55 73 15
Contact: Lahcen Azaddou

Mouvement Twiza organizes summer work camps for volunteers to participate in a range of socio-cultural activities including work in the slums and in schools and construction work. Volunteers with an offending background are accepted.

Total projects worldwide: 5
Total UK projects: 0
Starting months: July–September.
Time required: 3–4 weeks.
Age requirement: 18–35
Causes: Aids/HIV, archaeology, architecture, children, conservation, disabled (learning), environmental causes, inner city problems, poor/homeless, teaching/assisting (mature, EFL), unemployed, work camps – seasonal, young people.
Activities: Accountancy, administration, building/construction, campaigning, caring (day), community work, computers, conservation skills, cooking, development issues, first aid, forestry, gardening/horticulture, group work, international aid, library/resource centres, manual work, newsletter/journalism, outdoor skills, research, social work, summer camps, teaching, training, translating, visiting/befriending, work camps – seasonal.
Vols under 26 placed each year: 500
When to apply: April/May.
Work alone/with others: With others.
Volunteers with disabilities: Not possible.
Qualifications: None is necessary, although any qualifications are welcomed.
Equipment/clothing: Working clothes.
Health requirements: Healthy.

Costs: Living allowance.
Benefits: Accommodation and food.
Interview details: No interviews but an introductory round table meeting aimed at introducing volunteers to each other and the presentation of the organized work.
Certification: Certificate or reference provided.
Worldwide placements: *Africa* (Morocco).

MUSEUM NATIONAL D'HISTOIRE NATURELLE
Lab. de Prehistoire
1 rue Rene Panhard,
F-75013 Paris
France

Tel: 00 33 1 43 31 62 91
Fax: 00 33 1 43 31 22 79
Contact: Professor Henry de Lumley, Director

Museum National D'Histoire Naturelle organizes volunteers to take part in archaeological digs in France working eight and a half hours per day, six days per week.

Total projects worldwide: 1
Total UK projects: 0
Starting months: March, April, June, July, August.
Time required: 2–13 weeks.
Age requirement: 18 plus.
Causes: Archaeology.
Activities: Research, scientific work.
Vols under 26 placed each year: 10–80 per site.
When to apply: From February.
Work alone/with others: With others.
Volunteers with disabilities: Not possible.
Qualifications: Students or researchers in prehistory, archaeology or natural science.
Equipment/clothing: Nil except Mont Bego where warm clothes and camping equipment are needed.
Health requirements: Good health need for Bego.
Costs: Travel costs. No remuneration.
Benefits: Subsistence.
Interview details: No interview necessary.
Certification: Certificate or reference on request.
Worldwide placements: *Europe* (France).

MUSLIM AID
PO Box 3
London
N7 8LR UK

Tel: +44 (0) 20 7387 7171
Fax: +44 (0) 20 7387 7474
e-mail: info@muslimaid.org.uk
Web: www.muslimaid.org.uk
Contact: Mr E. Mohammed, Co-ordinator

Muslim Aid, founded in 1985 in the shadow of the raging famine in Ethiopia, has extended its humanitarian work to over 44 countries in Aisa, Africa, Middle East and Europe. It reached out to the most vulnerable, poverty stricken and desperate people and provided them the basic necessities of life – food, shelter, medicine, clean water and skills to earn a living. Besides emergency relief, Muslim Aid aims to provide short and long-term programmes to help people out of the poverty trap and thus give them dignity and self-respect.

Total projects worldwide: 1
Total UK projects: 0
Starting months: January–December.
Time required: 1–52 weeks (plus).
Age requirement: 12 plus.
Activities: Administration, campaigning, computers, fundraising, international aid, marketing/publicity, translating.
Vols under 26 placed each year: 12 of a total of 20.
When to apply: All year.
Work alone/with others: Sometimes with other young volunteers.
Volunteers with disabilities: Possible.
Qualifications: Nil.
Health requirements: Nil.
Costs: Travel costs.
Charity number: 295224

MYLLYLAHDE YHTEISO
Palomaa
SF 16800 Koski HL
Finland

Tel: 00 358 18 7641 944
Contact: The Director

Myllylahde Yhteiso is a Camphill community with adults with special needs.

Total projects worldwide: 1
Total UK projects: 0
Starting months: January–December.
Time required: 1–52 weeks.
Age requirement: 14 plus.
Causes: Disabled (learning).
Worldwide placements: *Europe* (Finland).

N

NABC – CLUBS FOR YOUNG PEOPLE
371 Kennington Lane
London
SE11 5QY UK

Tel: +44 (0) 20 7793 0787
Fax: +44 (0) 20 7820 9815
e-mail: office@nabc-cyp.org.uk
Contact: Euan Eddie

NABC-CYP is an association of about 2,000 clubs for young people throughout the UK, which provides informal educational training and leisure-time activities for young people aged between 8 and 25. It is one of the largest and most influential parts of the voluntary youth service.

Total projects worldwide: 2,000
Total UK projects: 2,000
Starting months: January–December.
Time required: 1 week.
Age requirement: 18 plus.
Causes: Children, disabled (learning and physical), environmental causes, human rights, inner city problems, unemployed, work camps – seasonal, young people.
Activities: Arts/crafts, community work, counselling, development issues, first aid, fundraising, group work, newsletter/ journalism, sport, summer camps, theatre/drama, training, work camps – seasonal.
Vols under 26 placed each year: 10,000 of a total of 23,000.
When to apply: All year.
Work alone/with others: With others.
Volunteers with disabilities: Possible.
Qualifications: Driving licence useful but not essential. Sports qualifications very useful.
Health requirements: Nil.
Costs: Limited – every attempt would be made to minimize costs.
Benefits: Reasonable expenses, travel, board, lodging etc.
Certification: Certificate of participation provided.
UK placements: *England* (throughout); *Scotland* (throughout); *Northern Ireland* (throughout); *Wales* (throughout).

NANSEN HIGHLAND
Redcastle Station
Muir-of-Ord

Ross-shire
IV6 7RX Scotland

Tel: +44 (0) 1463 871255
Fax: +44 (0) 1463 870258
e-mail: Nansen@highlandhq.freeserve.co.uk
Web: www.nansenhighland.sagehost.co.uk
Contact: Bart Lafere, Director

Nansen Highland is a non-governmental
organization and registered charity, motivated
in its aims by the humanitarian and
adventurous deeds of the explorer Fridtjof
Nansen. Much of its work is concerned with
helping young people with emotional and
behavioural difficulties to gain greater control
over their own lives and contribute more
positively to others. It runs a youth training
project at Redcastle Station. Volunteers are
required to live and work with youth
trainees. Responsibilities may include work
on the nature trail; restoration and general
maintenance work; or teaching office skills,
library skills, car mechanics, domestic work
and basic life skills such as reading and
writing. There may also be duties related to
the general administration of the project and
meetings with external bodies. Placements are
considered after receiving clean police check
and application form.

Total projects worldwide: 2
Total UK projects: 2
Starting months: January–December.
Time required: 26–52 weeks.
Age requirement: 21 plus.
Causes: Children, conservation, disabled
(learning and physical), environmental
causes, holidays for disabled, inner city
problems, offenders/ex-offenders, teaching/
assisting (mature), work camps – seasonal,
young people.
Activities: Administration, arts/crafts,
building/construction, caring (general, day
and residential), catering, computers,
conservation skills, cooking, counselling,
DIY, driving, first aid, group work, manual
work, music, outdoor skills, social work,
sport, teaching, technical skills, theatre/
drama, training, work camps – seasonal.
Vols under 26 placed each year: 1 of a total
of 3.
When to apply: All year – 2–3 months in
advance.
Work alone/with others: Both.
Volunteers with disabilities: Possible, but
physically disabled persons have no access to

residential centre.
Qualifications: Experience teaching young
people with special needs, outdoor education,
farmwork or conservation desirable. Ability
to motivate young people and fit in with the
community. Good spoken English, clean
driving licence preferred, social work
qualification.
Health requirements: Good mental and
physical health.
Costs: Travel and insurance costs.
Benefits: Board and lodging. We insure
against public liability.
Training: Full induction given.
Supervision: By the management.
Interview details: Prospective volunteers are
interviewed in person or on the telephone.
Police check is made.
Certification: Certificate or reference
provided.
Charity number: SCO28479
UK placements: *Scotland* (Highland).

NATIONAL ASSOCIATION OF CITIZENS ADVICE BUREAUX

Myddelton House
115–123 Pentonville Road
London
N1 9LZ UK

Tel: +44 (0) 20 7833 7136
Fax: +44 (0) 20 7833 4371
Web: www.nacab.org.uk

Applicants should contact the Citizens Advice
Bureaux via *Thompsons Local Directory* or
local telephone directory for details of nearest
bureau or via the NACAB website which
gives details on volunteering. Volunteers with
offending background accepted.

Total projects worldwide: 758
Total UK projects: 758
Starting months: January–December.
Time required: 1–52 weeks.
Age requirement: 16 plus.
Causes: Addicts/Ex-addicts, Aids/HIV,
children, disabled (learning and physical),
elderly people, health care/medical, human
rights, inner city problems, offenders/ex-
offenders, poor/homeless, refugees, teaching/
assisting (secondary), unemployed, young
people.
Activities: Administration, campaigning,
community work, computers, fundraising,
group work, library/resource centres,
marketing/publicity, teaching, technical

skills, training, translating.
Vols under 26 placed each year: 20,000
When to apply: All year.
Work alone/with others: With others.
Volunteers with disabilities: Possible.
Qualifications: Numeracy and literacy.
Health requirements: Nil.
Benefits: Out of pocket expenses. Some group insurance provided by NACAB (accident, public liability) – all other insurance should be arranged locally.
Training: All volunteers must complete CAB Basic Training Programme.
Supervision: Arranged locally with CAB manager.
Interview details: Interviews take place at the individual bureau.
Certification: Certificate or reference provided on completion.
Charity number: 279057
UK placements: *England* (throughout); *Scotland* (throughout); *Northern Ireland* (throughout); *Wales* (throughout).

NATIONAL ASSOCIATION OF RACIAL EQUALITY COUNCILS
8–16 Coronet Street
London
N1 6HD UK

Tel: +44 (0) 20 7739 6658

Total projects worldwide: 1
Total UK projects: 1
Starting months: January–December.
Time required: 1–52 weeks.
Age requirement: 14 plus.

NATIONAL ASSOCIATION OF TOY AND LEISURE LIBRARIES
68 Churchway
London
NW1 1LT UK

Tel: +44 (0) 20 7387 9592
Contact: Catherine Farrell

Total projects worldwide: 1
Total UK projects: 1
Starting months: January–December.
Time required: 1–52 weeks.
Age requirement: 14 plus.

NATIONAL ASSOCIATION OF YOUTH THEATRES
Unit 1304
The Custard Factory

Gibb Street
Birmingham
B9 4AA UK

Tel: +44 (0) 121 608 2111

Total projects worldwide: 1
Total UK projects: 1
Starting months: January–December.
Time required: 1–52 weeks.
Age requirement: 14 plus.

NATIONAL ASTHMA CAMPAIGN AND NATIONAL ECZEMA SOCIETY
PEAK
Providence House
Providence Place
London
N1 0NT UK

Tel: +44 (0) 20 7226 2260 x 316
Fax: +44 (0) 20 7704 0740
e-mail: mfantom@aol.com
Contact: Michael Fantom, Holiday Project Manager

The National Asthma Campaign and the National Eczema Society ask: Would you like to go windsurfing, canoeing, ice-skating and ten-pin bowling? Try your hand at jewellery making, T-shirt designing and modelling? Do you have any spare time this summer? Do you enjoy working with children and young people? Have you a sense of humour? The National Asthma Campaign and the National Eczema Society run unique holidays (PEAK) in specialized centres giving children, teenagers and young adults (age range 6–30 years) with asthma and/or eczema the chance to enjoy adventurous and social activities with their peers. For many it is the first time away from home and the holidays give them an opportunity to develop new skills, self-confidence and experience some independence. All holidays are staffed by volunteers. Staff are drawn from a wide background: some are doctors and nurses, others have personal experience of eczema or asthma; some have a background in sports or childcare; others wish to learn some new skills. Leaders take responsibility for a group of four or five children who share a room. During the day you will work with another member of staff and a group of youngsters, supporting and encouraging them through a range of activities. Participation is a vital part of the week. Activities are led by qualified instructors who do the teaching but in the evening staff work together to provide a range of social activities. In this way PEAK holidays provide an understanding environment with sympathetic, approachable staff where children, teenagers, and young adults alike can relax, have fun and enjoy themselves. The gains and rewards from volunteering for a project like this are tremendous and clearly difficult to explain. PEAK is looking for applicants with maturity combined with a sense of humour and fun, able to supervise and support children and teenagers.

Total projects worldwide: 7
Total UK projects: 7
Starting months: March, April, July, August.
Time required: 1–3 weeks.
Age requirement: 18 plus.
Causes: Children, health care/medical, holidays for disabled, young people.
Activities: Caring (general and residential), group work, sport, summer camps.
Vols under 26 placed each year: 55 of a total of 90.
When to apply: September to March/April.
Work alone/with others: With others.
Volunteers with disabilities: Possible.
Qualifications: Ability to get on with others in a group environment and lots of energy!
Health requirements: Reasonably good health.
Costs: Nil.
Benefits: All travel expenses, board and lodging and training weekend.
Certification: Reference on request.
UK placements: *England* (Buckinghamshire, Cumbria, Essex, Northamptonshire, Nottinghamshire, Suffolk); *Scotland* (Edinburgh, E. Lothian, W. Lothian).

NATIONAL AUTISTIC SOCIETY, THE
4th Floor, Castle Heights
72 Maid Marian Way
Nottingham
Nottinghamshire
NG1 6BJ UK

Tel: +44 (0) 115 9113369
Fax: +44 (0) 115 9113362
e-mail: volunteers@nas.org.uk
Contact: Claire Rintoul

The National Autistic Society's Volunteering Network is currently setting up befriending schemes throughout the UK. Volunteers over

the age of 18 are welcome to apply. Training, support and accreditation opportunities are offered to all befrienders. Outside the Volunteering Network, there are limited opportunities for volunteers to work on special projects with children with autism. Most of this work is in special schools. Some offices and units may also be able to accommodate volunteers.

Total projects worldwide: 16
Total UK projects: 16
Starting months: January–December.
Time required: 25–52 weeks.
Age requirement: 18 plus.
Causes: Children, disabled (learning).
Activities: Administration, visiting/befriending.
Vols under 26 placed each year: 45 of a total of 150.
When to apply: All year.
Work alone/with others: With others.
Volunteers with disabilities: Possible.
Qualifications: Nil.
Health requirements: Nil.
Costs: Nil.
Benefits: Travel expenses reimbursed. We provide employer's liability and public liability insurance.
Training: Training provided for Befrienders occurs once or twice a year and is compulsory before a volunteer can become a Befriender.
Supervision: 6-weekly support meeting, annual appraisal, telephone support, supervision from co-ordinator.
Certification: Reference on request.
Charity number: 269425
UK placements: *England* (Bedfordshire, Berkshire, Cheshire, Cumbria, Essex, Isle of Wight, Leicestershire, London, Manchester, Nottinghamshire, Surrey); *Scotland* (Glasgow City); *Northern Ireland* (Belfast City); *Wales* (Cardiff, Vale of Glamorgan).

NATIONAL FEDERATION OF 18 PLUS GROUPS OF GREAT BRITAIN
8–10 Church Street
Newent
Gloucestershire
GL18 1PP UK

Tel: +44 (0) 1531 821210
Fax: +44 (0) 1531 821474
Web: www.eng.warwick.ac.uk/18 plus

You can get out of 18 Plus what you put into

it and what better way than to get involved in the running of your group. 18 Plus is run by its members for its members so you have a say in what you want to do. A wide range of training is available to every member and topics including self-confidence, self-development and team skills are taught by highly experienced tutors. Our courses have also been used externally to train the staff of various companies but while this can cost hundreds of pounds to the employer, we charge our members a very minimal fee, if anything at all, for exactly the same content. With the new skills and experience gained many of our members have furthered their career prospects. Joining 18 Plus opens you up to a multitude of different opportunities, friendships, sports, trips and holidays, nightlife, charity and community work. Volunteers with an offending background are accepted.

Total projects worldwide: 1
Total UK projects: 1
Starting months: January–December.
Time required: 1–52 weeks.
Age requirement: 18–36
Causes: Conservation, disabled (learning and physical), elderly people, environmental causes, heritage, holidays for disabled, poor/homeless, wildlife, young people.
Activities: Accountancy, administration, arts/crafts, campaigning, community work, computers, conservation skills, counselling, development issues, first aid, fundraising, group work, library/resource centres, marketing/publicity, music, newsletter/journalism, outdoor skills, research, sport, summer camps, training, visiting/befriending.
Vols under 26 placed each year: 800 of a total of approximately 1,400.
When to apply: All year.
Work alone/with others: With others.
Volunteers with disabilities: Possible.
Qualifications: Nil.
Health requirements: Nil.
Costs: Not more than £20.
Interview details: No interview necessary.
Certification: 18 Plus has an awards Scheme.
UK placements: *England* (throughout); *Scotland* (throughout); *Northern Ireland* (throughout); *Wales* (throughout).

NATIONAL FEDERATION OF CITY FARMS

The Green House
Hereford Street
Bedminster
Bristol
BS3 4NA UK

Tel: + 44 (0) 117 923 1800
Fax: + 44 (0) 1017 923 1900
e-mail: 102404.14@compuserve.com
Contact: Karen Morris

The National Federation of City Farms (NFCF) was established in 1980 to provide support, advice and information for its members. NFCF have developed a youth programme. There are up to 2,000 young people who volunteer on city farms and gardens throughout the UK. The NFCF does not place volunteers directly, but will put people in touch with their nearest city farm or garden. City farms and gardens are all very different. They vary in size from a quarter of an acre to 90 acres. Some have extensive community buildings as well as farm buildings, many specialize in rare breeds of animals and poultry, some have riding stables, others are adventure playgrounds with areas for gardens or animals. Young people volunteer in many ways. Activities include helping to run summer playschemes, sporting activities if projects have a sports pitch, help with fundraising, showing animals, animal care, conservation, supporting people with learning difficulties, horticulture. There are many different things happening at city farms and gardens which means that there is a variety of ways to become involved as a volunteer. We have contacts with the European Federation of City Farms which supports 880 farms in nine countries, and if young people are interested they should contact us and we will put them in touch with European contacts.

Total projects worldwide: 75
Total UK projects: 65
Starting months: January–December.
Time required: 1–52 weeks.
Age requirement: 14 plus.
Causes: Animal welfare, architecture, children, conservation, disabled (learning and physical), elderly people, environmental causes, inner city problems, unemployed, wildlife, young people.
Activities: Accountancy, administration, agriculture/farming, arts/crafts, building/construction, community work, computers, conservation skills, forestry, fundraising,

gardening/horticulture, group work, manual work, marketing/publicity, newsletter/ journalism, outdoor skills, sport, teaching.
Vols under 26 placed each year: Up to 2,000.
When to apply: All year.
Work alone/with others: With others.
Volunteers with disabilities: Possible.
Qualifications: Nil.
Equipment/clothing: Provided if needed.
Health requirements: Nil.
Costs: Nil.
Benefits: Expenses usually covered.
Certification: Possibly NVQ.
Worldwide placements: *Europe* (Belgium, Denmark, France, Germany, Netherlands, Norway, Spain, Sweden).
UK placements: *England* (Cambridgeshire, Essex, Hampshire, Kent, Lancashire, Leicestershire, Lincolnshire, London, Manchester, Merseyside, Norfolk, Nottinghamshire, Oxfordshire, Tyne and Wear, West Midlands, N. Yorkshire, S. Yorkshire, W. Yorkshire); *Scotland* (Edinburgh, Glasgow City); *Northern Ireland* (Armagh, Derry/Londonderry); *Wales* (Cardiff).

NATIONAL FEDERATION OF GATEWAY CLUBS
123 Golden Lane
London
EC1Y ORT UK

Tel: +44 (0) 20 7454 0454
Fax: +44 (0) 20 7697 5598
Contact: Penny Mendonça

Gateway is a youth and community organization promoting leisure, recreation and social educational opportunities for people who happen to have a mental handicap. It was founded by MENCAP in 1966 and deals with all aspects of leisure. Throughout the country there are over 700 clubs all offering a variety of services to varying age groups. Examples of these are junior clubs, 14–25 youth groups and groups for older members. Each club tailors its programme of activities to suit the interests and abilities of its members. Clubs offer people a sense of belonging, the opportunity to learn new skills, make choices, take responsibilities but above all have fun. A Gateway group acts as a bridge into the community giving individuals and groups the

confidence to participate in community activities in the same way as any other member of society does. Membership is open to all approved and properly constituted groups. Most important of all, the Federation aims to increase public awareness of the needs of people with mental handicap and to ensure that they gain equal entitlement to community facilities. Volunteers with an offending background may be accepted but not if it is abuse, sexual, physical or emotional.

Total projects worldwide: 700
Total UK projects: 700
Starting months: January–December.
Time required: 1–52 weeks.
Age requirement: 14 plus.
Causes: Children, disabled (learning), young people.
Activities: Arts/crafts, caring (general and day), community work, driving, music, sport, theatre/drama.
Vols under 26 placed each year: Hundreds.
When to apply: All year.
Work alone/with others: With others.
Volunteers with disabilities: Possible.
Qualifications: Nil but references checked.
Health requirements: Nil.
Costs: Nil except expenses.
Benefits: Affiliated clubs can benefit from a number of services provided through the Federation, including insurance cover for members, volunteers and leaders.
Interview details: Applicants are interviewed, generally at the placement site.
Certification: Certificate or reference on request.
UK placements: *England* (throughout); *Northern Ireland* (throughout); *Wales* (throughout).

NATIONAL INVENTORY OF WAR MEMORIALS
Imperial War Museum
Lambeth Road
London
SE1 6HZ UK

Tel: +44 (0) 20 7416 5281
Fax: +44 (0) 20 7416 5379
e-mail: memorials@iwm.org.uk
Contact: Ms Jane Armer, Project Assistant

The National Inventory of War Memorials was initiated in 1989 by the Imperial War Museum and the Royal Commission on

Historical Monuments of England to create an archive holding information on the estimated 60,000 war memorials in the British Isles. Prior to this, there had been no centralized information on war memorials. The archive covers every conceivable type of memorial, from the frequently-seen community crosses to buildings, lych gates, gardens, hospitals, organs, chapels, windows, etc. All wars are covered, from the Roman occupation to the Gulf War, although, of course, great impetus was given to the construction of memorials by the Great War, largely because of the policy of not re-patriating bodies. Indeed, the building of so many memorials in the 1920s has been described as the largest public art project in history. We have a standard recording form which our fieldworkers use to collate the information. The type of information sought includes details of the exact location, the conflicts it commemorates, the date of its unveiling, its type and materials, dimensions, details of artists or manufacturers, its condition and other background areas of interest. Unfortunately, much of this information is frequently unavailable and we take the general view that any information, even incomplete, is better than none. Essential, however, is the type of memorial and its exact position, ideally with a photograph. So far, with the help of local volunteers, we have records of about 30,000 memorials, half of which have been put on to a computer database.

Total projects worldwide: Many.
Total UK projects: Many.
Starting months: January–December.
Time required: 1–52 weeks (plus).
Age requirement: 16–25
Causes: Heritage.
Activities: Outdoor skills, research.
Vols under 26 placed each year: About 70.
When to apply: All year.
Volunteers with disabilities: Possible, but volunteers need to travel around and gain access to many buildings.
Qualifications: Basic research skills.
Health requirements: Nil.
Costs: Research expenses.
Benefits: Sometimes, at our discretion, we reimburse photographic costs and other expenses.
Training: We do provide notes on how to fill out the form and give general information

and lists of memorials we have records for.
Supervision: We have regional co-ordinators.
Interview details: No interview necessary.
Certification: Written reference provided.
UK placements: *England* (Bedfordshire, Berkshire, Bristol, Cambridgeshire, Channel Islands, Cheshire, Cornwall, Co. Durham, Derbyshire, Devon, Dorset, Essex, Gloucestershire, Hampshire, Hertfordshire, Isle of Man, Isle of Wight, Kent, Lancashire, Leicestershire, Lincolnshire, Manchester, Merseyside, Norfolk, Northamptonshire, Nottinghamshire, Rutland, Shropshire, Somerset, Staffordshire, Surrey, E. Sussex, W. Sussex, Tyne and Wear, Warwickshire, West Midlands, Wiltshire, E. Yorkshire, N. Yorkshire, S. Yorkshire, W. Yorkshire); *Wales* (throughout).

NATIONAL TRUST, THE

Working Holidays
PO Box 39
Bromley
Kent
BR1 8XL UK

Tel: +44 (0) 20 8315 1111
e-mail: xeaajt@smtp.ntrust.org.uk
Web: www.nationaltrust.org.uk/volunteers
Contact: Working Holidays

The National Trust has special projects, not only in general countryside conservation, but also construction, archaeology, botany, working with a group from another country and short breaks.

Total projects worldwide: 400
Total UK projects: 400
Starting months: January–December.
Time required: 1–52 weeks.
Age requirement: 17 plus.
Causes: Conservation, environmental causes, wildlife, work camps – seasonal.
Activities: Building/construction, conservation skills, forestry, gardening/horticulture, manual work, work camps – seasonal.
Vols under 26 placed each year: 2,000 of a total of 4,000.
When to apply: All year.
Work alone/with others: With others.
Volunteers with disabilities: Not possible.
Qualifications: Enthusiasm only.
Equipment/clothing: Stout footwear, waterproofs and sleeping bag.
Health requirements: Physically fit.

Costs: Approximately £45-£90 per week.
Travel and pocket money not included.
Benefits: Accommodation, all meals.
Admission card (1 year) to National Trust
properties after 40 hours voluntary work.
Public liability insurance is provided by the
National Trust. Comprehensive insurance
package available as optional extra.
Training: Support literature is provided.
Supervision: By qualified National Trust
Wardens.
Interview details: No interview necessary.
Charity number: 205846
UK placements: *England* (throughout);
Northern Ireland (throughout); *Wales*
(throughout).

NATUUR 2000
Bervoetstraat 33
B-2000 Antwerpen
Belgium

Tel: 00 32 3 231 26 04
Fax: 00 32 3 233 64 99
e-mail: n2000@net4all.be
Contact: Julius Smeyers

Natuur 2000 organizes nature study and
nature conservation activities for young
people aged between 8 and 25 including
birdwatching camps, management of nature
reserves, etc. We also run an environmental
information centre for young people.

Total projects worldwide: 10
Total UK projects: 0
Starting months: June–September.
Time required: 2–4 weeks.
Age requirement: 16–23
Causes: Conservation, environmental causes,
work camps – seasonal, young people.
Activities: Administration, computers,
conservation skills, cooking, driving, library/
resource centres, newsletter/journalism,
scientific work, summer camps, work camps
– seasonal.
Vols under 26 placed each year: 20
When to apply: Before 15 May.
Work alone/with others: With others.
Volunteers with disabilities: Not possible.
Qualifications: Experience in field biology –
environmental conservation.
Equipment/clothing: Usually rucksack,
sleeping bag, isomat, boots, eating and
washing gear.
Health requirements: Medical papers
required.

Costs: Travel to/from Belgium, participation
fee and insurance.
Benefits: Accommodation, food.
Certification: Certificate or reference on
request.
Worldwide placements: *Europe* (Belgium).

NAUTICAL TRAINING CORPS
39 Chesham Road
Brighton
East Sussex
BN22 1NB UK

Tel: +44 (0) 1273 676836
Fax: +44 (0) 1273 625066
e-mail: NauticalTrainingCorps@bigfoot.con
Contact: Mrs Grace Nash

Nautical Training Corps trains young people,
with and without disabilities, in nautical
disciplines including rifle shooting, bands,
boatwork, adventure activities and all other
aspects of naval life.

Total projects worldwide: 5
Total UK projects: 5
Starting months: January–December.
Time required: 3–52 weeks.
Age requirement: 18 plus.
Causes: Children, disabled (learning and
physical), young people.
Activities: Sport, teaching, technical skills.
When to apply: All year.
Work alone/with others: With others.
Volunteers with disabilities: Possible.
Qualifications: Nautical youth work or
business experience.
Health requirements: Nil.
Costs: Nil.
Benefits: Travel expenses.
Charity number: 306084
UK placements: *England* (Hampshire,
London, Surrey, E. Sussex, W. Sussex).

NCH ACTION FOR CHILDREN
85 Highbury Park
London
N5 1UD UK

Tel: +44 (0) 20 7226 2033
Fax: +44 (0) 20 7226 2537
Contact: Jacqueline Wiltshire

Total projects worldwide: 1
Starting months: January–December.
Time required: 1–52 weeks.
Age requirement: 14 plus.

NEIGE ET MERVEILLES

F-06430 St Dalmas de Tende
France

Tel: 00 33 4 93 04 62 40
Fax: 00 33 4 93 04 88 58
Contact: Recruitment Department

Neige et Merveilles need volunteers to take part in international work camps which take place between May and September, working six hours per day, five days per week.

Total projects worldwide: 1
Total UK projects: 0
Starting months: May.
Time required: 2–24 weeks.
Age requirement: 18 plus.
Causes: Children, teaching/assisting (primary, secondary, mature), work camps – seasonal.
Activities: Forestry, group work, manual work, summer camps, teaching, training, work camps – seasonal.
Vols under 26 placed each year: 4
When to apply: All year.
Work alone/with others: With others.
Qualifications: Nil.
Equipment/clothing: For mountains and outside work.
Costs: Insurance costs approximately £40 and travel.
Worldwide placements: *Europe* (France).

NES AMMIM (COMMUNAL VILLAGE IN ISRAEL)

68 Melbourn Road
Royston
Hertfordshire
SG8 7DG UK

Tel: +44 (0) 1763 230210
Fax: +44 (0) 1763 230210
e-mail:
pjennings@royston1999.freeserve.co.uk
Contact: Peter Jennings

Nes Ammim is an international Christian community in Israel's Northwest Galilee. We aim to contribute to the creation of a new relationship between Jews and Christians following centuries of alienation and ignorance. The name Nes Ammim means 'a banner to or for the nations' and is taken from two quotations in the Book of Isaiah (11:10 and 62:10). We recently celebrated our silver jubilee as a community after being established in the 1960s by a group of Christians who had lived through the horrors of the Second World War and the Nazi Holocaust in continental Europe. Nes Ammim is the product of a dream – a dream of a radically new and positive relationship between Christians and Jews based upon mutual trust and respect. This excludes any thought of missionary activity directed at the Jewish people. The founders of Nes Ammim believe that such a relationship is not only possible, but absolutely essential. Surrounded by Jewish kibbutzim and Muslim and Druze villages, Nes Ammim is an ecumenical Christian community whose members and volunteers represent a broad spectrum of Protestant tradition. We are a learning, serving, working and worshipping community. Our main commercial business is to grow roses for export. We grow avocados too and share in the tourist industry with our guesthouse and youth hostel. We run an annual work and information programme for young European students and put very special demands upon our residents who need to be mature 'card-carrying Christians'. We emphasize the word 'mature' because in the settlement there are Christians from many denominations and any volunteer needs a fairly wide range of biblical scholarship and post-Reformation church history in Europe.

Total projects worldwide: 1
Total UK projects: 0
Starting months: January–December.
Time required: 26–52 weeks.
Age requirement: 21–30
Causes: Work camps – seasonal.
Activities: Administration, building/construction, DIY, gardening/horticulture, marketing/publicity, religion, work camps – seasonal.
Vols under 26 placed each year: 9 of a total of 20.
When to apply: 1 year in advance.
Work alone/with others: With others.
Volunteers with disabilities: Not possible.
Qualifications: Broad Christian theological awareness.
Equipment/clothing: Dress as for a sunny English summer!
Health requirements: Medical/dental certificates needed.
Costs: Costs of travel to the village in Israel.
Benefits: Board, lodging and pocket money. We provide insurance cover.

Training: Training is provided on arrival when assignment takes place.
Supervision: By professional workers/leaders in various assignments.
Nationalities accepted: No restrictions but Israeli visas must be obtained.
Interview details: Interviews generally by telephone but, if requested, take place in Royston, Herts.
Worldwide placements: *Asia* (Israel).

NETWORK DRUGS ADVICE PROJECT'S (YOUTH AWARENESS PROGRAMME)
Abbey House
361 Barking Road
Plaistow
London
E13 8EE UK

Tel: + 44 (0) 20 7474 2222
Fax: + 44 (0) 20 7473 5399
e-mail: admin@ndap.demon.co.uk
Contact: Danny Rider, Training Officer

Network Drugs Advice Project's (NDAP's) Youth Awareness Programme (YAP) is a specialist comprehensive drugs service for young people. YAP provides: drug education in schools and other settings; counselling for drug users under 25 years of age, with a focus on under 16s; literature, CDs and other drugs information resources for young people; an on-site service for 'raves'; a range of diversionary projects including graffiti and music; outreach work. Volunteers are involved in all aspects of our work except counselling. You would be encouraged to contribute to and develop areas of work in which you are interested with the support of project workers. Volunteers with an offending background would be accepted provided that the offences would not pose a risk to work with young people.

Total projects worldwide: 5
Total UK projects: 5
Starting months: January–December.
Time required: 26–52 weeks (plus).
Age requirement: 16–25
Causes: Addicts/Ex-addicts, children, disabled (learning), health care/medical, offenders/ex-offenders, teaching (primary, secondary), young people.
Activities: Campaigning, community work, first aid, group work, teaching, theatre/drama, training.
Vols under 26 placed each year: 200

When to apply: All year.
Work alone/with others: With others.
Volunteers with disabilities: Possible, but some of our premises lack suitable physical access for wheelchairs.
Qualifications: LOCF plus NVQ.
Health requirements: Current users of illegal drugs are not accepted. Ex-users are encouraged to take part.
Costs: Nil except travel to work on unauthorized business.
Benefits: Travel and training are paid for by us. The training is accredited and many volunteers go on to paid employment in a related area of work.
Training: Volunteers are required to undertake extensive training.
Interview details: Prospective volunteers are interviewed at project offices in each area of activity.
Certification: Certificate or reference provided on successful completion of training.
Charity number: 803244
UK placements: *England* (London).

NEVE SHALOM/WAHAT AL-SALAM
Doar Na Shimshon 00761
Israel

Tel: 00 972 2 912222
Contact: Volunteer Organizer

Neve Shalom/Wahat al-Salam was founded in 1972. It is a co-operative village of Jews and Palestinian Arabs of Israeli citizenship. Members are demonstrating the possibility of coexistence by developing a community based on mutual acceptance, respect and co-operation on a daily basis whilst each individual remains faithful to his/her own cultural, national and religious identity. Limited number of places for volunteers wishing to live and work in the community. Work may involve general maintenance around the village, looking after children in the kindergarten and nursery or helping out at the community's guesthouse.

Total projects worldwide: 1
Total UK projects: 0
Starting months: January–December.
Time required: 26–52 weeks.
Age requirement: 16 plus.
Causes: Children.
Activities: Administration, agriculture/farming, building/construction, caring (general), DIY, gardening/horticulture.

Vols under 26 placed each year: 5
When to apply: 6–12 months in advance.
Work alone/with others: With others.
Volunteers with disabilities: Possible.
Qualifications: At least a basic knowledge of English, Arabic or Hebrew.
Costs: Travel and insurance.
Benefits: Board, accommodation and approximately £30 per month pocket money.
Worldwide placements: *Asia* (Israel).

NEW TESTAMENT CHURCH OF GOD

Main House
Overstone Park
Overstone
Northampton
NN6 OAD UK

Tel: +44 (0) 1604 492671
Contact: The Reverend Carver Anderson

Total projects worldwide: 1
Starting months: January–December.
Time required: 1–52 weeks.
Age requirement: 14 plus.

NEW ZEALAND CONSERVANCY TRUST

Karuna Falls
RD4 Coromandel
New Zealand

Tel: 00 64 7 866 6735
e-mail: networkers@eartheal.org.nz
Web: www.eartheal.org.nz
Contact: Bryan Innes, Trustee

The focus of New Zealand Conservancy Trust is on the benefit to the volunteers. Our specific interest is in promotion of the learning of sustainable living skills. We teach permaculture design. We also teach teaching skills to environmentalists. We arrange educational/study opportunities for travellers to New Zealand. These can be in the form of volunteering, paid courses or a combination of the two. E-mail contact works best for us. Prospective volunteers tell us of their experience and interests. We suggest a programme. It is fine-tuned through negotiation. Fixed and variable costs can then be quoted. Examples of programmes of past volunteers: primary school, secondary school teaching/assisting; special education service psychological assistance; marine laboratory assistance; organic farming internship; landscape architecture internship.

Total projects worldwide: Varies
Total UK projects: 0
Starting months: January–December.
Time required: 4–52 weeks.
Age requirement: 18 plus.
Causes: Architecture, children, conservation, environmental causes, teaching/assisting (nursery, primary, secondary), wildlife.
Activities: Administration, agriculture/farming, arts/crafts, building/construction, campaigning, community work, computers, conservation skills, cooking, DIY, forestry, gardening/horticulture, group work, library/resource centres, manual work, marketing/publicity, music, outdoor skills, research, teaching, technical skills.
Vols under 26 placed each year: approx. 13 of a total of 15.
When to apply: All year.
Work alone/with others: Both.
Volunteers with disabilities: Possible.
Qualifications: Must be able to communicate in English, be independent and self-responsible.
Equipment/clothing: Dependent on programme.
Health requirements: Dependent on programme.
Costs: Set-up fee NZ$675. All travel costs. Board costs (NZ$150 per week) usually provided free. The volunteer is responsible for health and belongings insurance.
Benefits: Dependent on programme – usually free board and accommodation, sometimes other benefits.
Training: Depends on the programme – usually consistent with prior experience.
Supervision: Volunteers are always supervised, given more responsibility and independence as they show ability to handle it.
Certification: Certificate or reference provided on request.
Worldwide placements: *Australasia* (New Zealand).

NICARAGUA SOLIDARITY CAMPAIGN

129 Seven Sisters Road
London
N7 7QG UK

Tel: +44 (0) 20 7272 9619
Fax: +44 (0) 20 7277 5476
e-mail: nsc@gn.apc.org
Contact: Helen Yuill

The NSC organizes work brigades to do environmental work in Nicaragua. There are two brigades per year in summer. Volunteers with an offending background are accepted.

Total projects worldwide: 1
Total UK projects: 0
Starting months: July, August.
Time required: 4 weeks.
Age requirement: 18 plus.
Causes: Conservation, environmental causes, human rights.
Activities: Community work, conservation skills, development issues, international aid, manual work.
Vols under 26 placed each year: 13 of a total of 25.
When to apply: 3 months before departure.
Work alone/with others: With others.
Volunteers with disabilities: Possible.
Qualifications: Fit and adaptable – no specialist skills required.
Costs: £1,100 includes air fares, living expenses and transport.
Interview details: Interviews are conducted as near as possible to where applicants live.
Worldwide placements: *Central America* (Nicaragua).

NICARAGUA – UNITED STATES FRIENDSHIP OFFICE
225 Pennsylvania Avenue, SE
3rd Floor
Washington
DC 20003
USA

Tel: 00 1 202 546 0915
Fax: 00 1 202 546 0935
Contact: Stephen Poethke

Nicaragua – United States Friendship Office is a support group for other organizations which operate in solidarity with Nicaragua. Our Technical Assistance programme, organized in conjunction with FUNDECI, enables people to do voluntary work in Nicaragua. Volunteers with particular skills will be assigned to a Nicaraguan community or project in those skill areas. Almost all skills are needed.

Total projects worldwide: 1
Total UK projects: 0
Starting months: January–December.
Time required: 4–52 weeks.
Age requirement: 14 plus.

Activities: Development issues, international aid, technical skills.
Vols under 26 placed each year: 75
When to apply: All year.
Work alone/with others: With others.
Qualifications: Any technical skills and none.
Costs: Programme fee of US$300 plus monthly expenses of US$400.
Benefits: The cost covers basic expenses plus room and partial board with Nicaraguan family.
Worldwide placements: *Central America* (Nicaragua).

NICHS
547 Antrim Road
Belfast
Antrim
BT15 3BU N. Ireland

Tel: +44 (0) 28 9037 0373
Fax: +44 (0) 28 9078 1161
e-mail: nichs@bass.almac.co.uk
Contact: Paddy Doherty

NICHS is a community relations youth organization which exists to provide opportunities for young people and to promote understanding and an acceptance of cultural difference between divided and segregated communities in Northern Ireland. The organization achieves its aims by working with young people, in particular from socially disadvantaged and deprived backgrounds, through various programmes. NICHS was established in 1972 by a group of seminarians in Liverpool. Its original objectives were to provide a holiday for young Protestants and Catholics who were directly caught up in and lived in the areas worst hit by the extreme violence which was affecting Northern Ireland at that time. Since these early days NICHS has grown and developed to become a professional youth organization working with approximately 500 young people per year. NICHS has a limited number of places for volunteers from outside Northern Ireland to assist in the implementation of residentials for young people during August. In order to prepare for the residentials, you must attend an induction event, usually held in Northern Ireland and in the north of England. Volunteers with criminal records are considered on merits and nature of offence.

Total projects worldwide: 4

Total UK projects: 4
Starting months: August.
Time required: 2–52 weeks (plus).
Age requirement: 18 plus.
Causes: Children, young people.
Activities: Arts/crafts, caring (residential), catering, community work, cooking, driving, first aid, group work, music, outdoor skills, sport, summer camps.
Vols under 26 placed each year: 50–70 of a total of 60–80.
When to apply: January.
Work alone/with others: With others.
Volunteers with disabilities: Possible, but centres used by NICHS at present are not wheelchair friendly.
Qualifications: No specific skills or qualifications necessary, experience desirable. Most of our volunteers are from N. Ireland.
Health requirements: Nil but individuals need to be generally fit and active.
Costs: Nil except travel to N. Ireland.
Benefits: Volunteers can claim half of all travel to a maximum of £50. Board plus lodging provided free. We provide public liability insurance for all volunteers.
Training: Volunteers must attend and successfully complete an induction event which deals with policy issues, child care issues and good practice in youth work, among other things.
Supervision: By either staff or more experienced co-ordinating volunteers.
Interview details: Interviews take place at various locations throughout the UK..
Certification: Reference provided.
Charity number: XN48644
Worldwide placements: *Europe* (Ireland).
UK placements: *Northern Ireland* (Belfast City, Down).

NIGHTINGALES CHILDREN'S PROJECT

Meriden Lodge
11 Colin Road, Preston
Paignton
Devon
TQ3 2NR UK

Tel: +44 (0) 1803 527233
Fax: +44 (0) 1803 527233
Contact: Reg and Julia Bale, UK Co-ordinators

Nightingales Children's Project was set up by David Savage from Torbay, South Devon in 1992. He went to Romania to work in an orphanage where he found babies and children with no nappies, no bathrooms, no comforts. Since that time the organization has helped David to build bathrooms and toilets, have the orphanage fully decorated and equipped and sent a continuous stream of volunteers to love, help and stimulate the children with play and learning. Some of the children were HIV positive and David realized a special need for these children, who were not accepted for education by state schools. Nightingales raised £20,000 to have a small boarding school built in the grounds of the orphanage and 23 children live and are taught there in a loving family atmosphere. They will stay there until they die. Volunteers work mainly in the orphanage but do have contact with the HIV children. The school has also opened its door to 40 children of some of the most poverty stricken families in Cernavoda. They have a hot meal and some schooling every day. Volunteers work in teams of two. There is an apartment where you would stay, up to ten at a time, so you have to mix well. You also have to be dedicated and work very hard. You have to take it in turns to do house duties e.g. cleaning and cooking for everyone. Volunteers stay for a minimum of one month but can stay longer. All in all, the work is hard but very rewarding. Volunteers with an offending background may occasionally be accepted, depending on the offence. Please send A5 stamped addressed envelope for information and application form.

Total projects worldwide: 1
Total UK projects: 0
Starting months: January–December.
Time required: 4–12 weeks.
Age requirement: 18 plus.
Causes: Aids/HIV, Children, Disabled (learning and physical), Teaching/assisting (nursery).
Activities: Arts/crafts, caring (day), music, teaching.
Vols under 26 placed each year: 70 of a total of 100.
When to apply: 9 months before required placement.
Work alone/with others: With others.
Volunteers with disabilities: We are unable to place people with disabilities as we have accommodation on 3rd floor (no lift) and orphanage/school is quite a strenuous walk.
Qualifications: A love and understanding of

children – some with HIV and special needs.
Health requirements: Various medical tests
required and Hepatitis A and B, polio,
tetanus innoculations etc.
Costs: Flight Gatwick–Bucharest
approximately £250, Transfers £25, food and
accommodation £2.50 per day.
Benefits: Accommodation and food provided
for £2.50 per day. Personal insurance can be
arranged.
Supervision: Resident director and volunteer
supervisor in Cernavoda.
Nationalities accepted: No restrictions but
volunteers have to be interviewed in the UK.
Interview details: Interviews take place with
the nearest regional co-ordinator to the
applicant. All interviews are conducted in the
UK.
Certification: Two references provided.
Charity number: 1047698
Worldwide placements: *Europe* (Romania).

NORFOLK WILDLIFE TRUST
72 Cathedral Close
Norwich
Norfolk
NR1 4DF UK

Tel: +44 (0) 1603 625540
Fax: +44 (0) 1603 630593
Contact: The Director

Norfolk Wildlife Trust is a member of the
Wildlife Trusts, a national partnership of 47
county trusts. For more details of the Wildlife
Trusts, see the entry under Cornwall Wildlife
Trusts.

Total projects worldwide: 1
Total UK projects: 1
Starting months: January–December.
Time required: 1–52 weeks (plus).
Age requirement: 12 plus.
Work alone/with others: Both.
Qualifications: Nil.
Equipment/clothing: Casual work clothes,
waterproofs, stout boots for outdoor work.
Protective safety gear is provided.
Health requirements: Anti-tetanus
innoculation recommended.
Costs: Nil.
Benefits: Out-of-pocket expenses. Volunteers
are covered by the Trust's insurance.

NORTHUMBERLAND WILDLIFE TRUST
The Garden House
St Nicholas Park
Jubilee Road
Newcastle upon Tyne
NE3 3XT UK

Tel: +44 (0) 191 284 6884
Fax: +44 (0) 191 284 6794
Contact: David Stewart

Northumberland Wildlife Trust uses
approximately 750 active volunteers per year.
Projects include: species surveying: otters, red
squirrels, water voles; botanical surveying;
ornithological surveying; practical
conservation tasks; otters and rivers project;
school workshops; community composting
and recycling; environmental education.

Total projects worldwide: 1
Total UK projects: 1
Starting months: January–December.
Time required: 1–52 weeks (plus).
Age requirement: 16 plus.
Causes: Children, conservation,
environmental causes, wildlife.
Activities: Administration, computers,
conservation skills, fundraising, manual
work, marketing/publicity, newsletter/
journalism, outdoor skills, scientific work.
Vols under 26 placed each year: 750
When to apply: All year.
Work alone/with others: With others.
Volunteers with disabilities: Possible.
Qualifications: Nil.
Equipment/clothing: Outdoor clothes.
Health requirements: Nil.
Costs: Nil.
Benefits: Out-of-pocket expenses. Volunteers
are covered by the Trust's insurance.
Charity number: 221819
UK placements: *England* (Northumberland,
Tyne and Wear).

NORWOOD RAVENSWOOD
Broadway House
80–82 The Broadway
Stanmore
Middlesex
HA7 4HB UK

Tel: +44 (0) 20 8954 4555
Fax: +44 (0) 20 8420 6800
e-mail: norwoodravenswood@nwrw.org
Contact: Sue Soloway or Carole Levy,
Volunteer Co-ordinators

Norwood Ravenswood provides a
comprehensive range of professional childcare
services for Jewish children and their families,

and also adults with learning difficulties. We act as the authoritative voice of child care in the Jewish community, offering services which are sensitive to religious, cultural, linguistic and racial issues. We seek men and women to work closely with our professional staff, helping families and adults with learning disabilities with their day-to-day problems, as a vital part of our services. We provide support, monitoring and training; drive and escort children to and from therapy; help children in schools and nurseries; work at the Norwood Family Centre and Buckets and Spades Lodge; assist parents of children with special needs after school and in the holidays; raise funds, send out appeals, distribute collection boxes; join one of our outings groups; work in a residential home for adults with learning difficulties; work in Unity, a youth club for children and adolescents, 5–18, with learning disabilities.

Total projects worldwide: 1
Total UK projects: 1
Starting months: July, August.
Time required: 4–6 weeks.
Age requirement: 16 plus.
Causes: Children, disabled (learning and physical), teaching/assisting (nursery, primary).
Activities: Caring (day and residential), driving, fundraising, marketing/publicity, summer camps, visiting/befriending.
Vols under 26 placed each year: 60 of a total of 600.
When to apply: May/June.
Work alone/with others: With others.
Volunteers with disabilities: Not possible.
Qualifications: Driving licence useful.
Equipment/clothing: Modest dress for ladies in accordance with religious ethics, i.e. skirt and covered arms.
Health requirements: Nil.
Costs: Nil.
Benefits: Travel expenses paid. We have public liability insurance.
Supervision: By volunteer co-ordinators and by staff at Resources where volunteers are helping.
Interview details: Interviews take place at our office.
Charity number: 1059050
UK placements: *England* (Essex, London).

NOTHELFERGEMEINSCHAFT DER FREUNDE eV (NdF)

Fuggerstr. 3
D-52351 Düren
Germany

Tel: 00 49 2421 76569
Fax: 00 49 2421 76468
e-mail: NDF-DN@t-online.de
Web: www.nothelfer.org.de
Contact: Gerhard Fleming

Nothelfergemeinschaft der Freunde ev organizes volunteers for spring and summer work camps. The work may involve building, gardening or social work and learning German in one camp. There are between 10 and 20 participants at each work camp, 35 hours per week approximately.

Total projects worldwide: Approximately 10.
Total UK projects: 0
Starting months: May–September.
Time required: 4–12 weeks.
Age requirement: 18–26
Causes: Conservation, disabled (learning), elderly people, environmental causes, work camps – seasonal.
Activities: Agriculture/farming, building/construction, caring (general), conservation skills, gardening/horticulture, manual work, social work, work camps – seasonal.
Vols under 26 placed each year: 120
When to apply: March/April.
Work alone/with others: With others.
Volunteers with disabilities: Not possible.
Qualifications: Spoken English or German, friendly attitude, open mind and willingness to work.
Equipment/clothing: Working clothes e.g. old jeans and shoes.
Health requirements: Good health and good physical constitution.
Costs: Return travel fares and pocket money. Participation fee: about 70E or DM140.
Benefits: Board, accommodation and sick/liability/accident insurance. DM50 towards travel on completion.
Supervision: Dependent on the work camp.
Interview details: No interview necessary.
Worldwide placements: *Europe* (Germany).

NOTTINGHAMSHIRE WILDLIFE TRUST

310 Sneinton Dale
Nottingham
NG3 7DN UK

Tel: +44 (0) 115 9588242
Fax: +44 (0) 115 9243175
Contact: The Director

Nottinghamshire Wildlife Trust is a member of the Wildlife Trusts, a national partnership of 47 county trusts. For more details of the Wildlife Trusts, see the entury under Cornwall Wildlife Trust.

Total projects worldwide: 1
Total UK projects: 1
Starting months: January–December.
Time required: 1–52 weeks (plus).
Age requirement: 12 plus.
Causes: Environmental causes, wildlife.
Work alone/with others: Both.
Qualifications: Nil.
Equipment/clothing: Casual work clothes, waterproofs, stout boots for outdoor work. Protective safety gear is provided.
Health requirements: Anti-tetanus insurance recommended.
Costs: Nil.
Benefits: Out-of-pocket expenses. Volunteers are covered by the Trust's insurance.
UK placements: *England* (Nottinghamshire).

NOUVELLE PLANÈTE
Chemin de la Forêt
CH-1042 Assens
Switzerland

Tel: 00 41 21 881 23 80
Fax: 00 41 21 882 10 54
e-mail: info@nouvelle-planete.ch
Web: www.nouvelle-planete.ch
Contact: Philippe Randin

Nouvelle Planète is a non-profit organization founded on Albert Schweitzer's example and ethics. We work with local communities and organizations. We support definite projects which are run by dynamic partners without government intermediaries. The main regions of activity are: environmental protection, appropriate technology and social work (for women, street children, leprosy patients etc.). One of our principal goals is to set up direct relations between northern and southern groups, villages and schools. We organize youth camps each year in southern countries. The groups of 20 volunteers work on particular projects with groups of local young people for 3–4 weeks in July and August. Individuals in the group and the group collectively must organize fundraising activities prior to departure to fund project costs and travel. Volunteers with an offending background may be accepted if they co-operate with the preparation activities during the previous six months.

Total projects worldwide: 15
Total UK projects: 0
Starting months: July.
Time required: 3–4 weeks.
Age requirement: 17–30
Causes: Children, disabled (physical), environmental causes, poor/homeless, work camps – seasonal, young people.
Activities: Agriculture/farming, community work, forestry, fundraising, group work, manual work, summer camps, work camps – seasonal.
Vols under 26 placed each year: 245 of a total of 400.
When to apply: October before following July departure.
Work alone/with others: With others.
Volunteers with disabilities: Not possible.
Qualifications: English-speaking for the projects in India and Philippines. French for others.
Health requirements: Nil.
Costs: Travel costs. Everyone is responsible for their own insurance. We ask for worldwide insurance.
Benefits: Board and lodging plus local transport costs.
Training: For the 6 months preceding departure, the groups meet regularly.
Supervision: By someone from Nouvelle Planète.
Nationalities accepted: Volunteers must live in Switzerland or Europe.
Interview details: No interview necessary.
Certification: Certificate or reference provided on request.
Worldwide placements: *Africa* (Burkina Faso, Gabon, Madagascar); *Asia* (India, Philippines, Vietnam).

NOVALIS HOUSE
PO Box 267
Halfway House
1685 Transvaal
South Africa

Contact: The Director

Total projects worldwide: 1
Total UK projects: 0
Starting months: January–December.

Time required: 1–52 weeks (plus).
Age requirement: 12 plus.

O

OASIS TRUST
115 Southwark Bridge Road
London
SE1 0AX UK

Tel: + 44 (0) 20 7450 9000
Fax: + 44 (0) 20 7450 9001
e-mail: OasisTrust@compuserve.com
Web: www.oasisteams.org
Contact: Becca Gibson

Oasis is an innovative organization working in partnership in 12 countries, across four continents, to deliver global, community, youth and church action initiatives that tackle social issues that matter. Built on a Christian foundation, it operates regardless of race, religion or creed. One in 12 people in Zimbabwe will be an AIDS orphan by 2005. Oasis Global Action supports and operates projects in 12 countries on four continents working with some of the world's poorest children. In the UK over 1,600 sleep rough on the streets every night. Oasis Community Action works with the homeless and excluded. Each week approximately 240 young people stop going to church. Oasis Youth Action exists to inspire the leaders of tomorrow and young people of today. Less than 8% of people in the UK go to church. Oasis Church Action believes the future of the church is your responsibility. Volunteers with an offending background may be accepted depending on the offence.

Total projects worldwide: 6
Total UK projects: 3
Starting months: July, September, October.
Time required: 2–43 weeks.
Age requirement: 16–30
Causes: Children, elderly people, health care/ medical, inner city problems, poor/homeless, teaching/assisting, young people.
Activities: Administration, arts/crafts, caring (general), community work, counselling, fundraising, group work, manual work, music, religion, sport, teaching, technical skills, theatre/drama, training, visiting/ befriending.
Vols under 26 placed each year: 280 of a total of approximately 310.
When to apply: Between September and end of June.
Work alone/with others: Both – dependent on the project.
Volunteers with disabilities: Possible.
Qualifications: Christian commitment. For overseas placements some languages may be required.
Health requirements: Nil.
Costs: Dependent on project.
Benefits: Board and lodging, pocket money on some projects, travel to overseas placements. Volunteers will be advised on insurance by project staff. For overseas projects, insurance is arranged by Oasis staff.
Training: All volunteers are trained before going to their placement. This is generally in the form of residential training and can last from a few days to two weeks. On some projects volunteers also receive ongoing training during the duration of their project.
Supervision: By Oasis staff who will meet volunteers on a regular basis, and by someone in their placement.
Interview details: Applicants are interviewed at various selection/interview weekends in London.
Certification: Certificate or reference provided.
Charity number: 1026487
Worldwide placements: *Africa* (Kenya, Mozambique, South Africa, Tanzania, Uganda, Zimbabwe); *Asia* (India); *Europe* (France, Germany, Portugal, Romania); *South America* (Brazil, Peru).
UK placements: *England* (London, Manchester); *Scotland* (Glasgow City).

OCKENDEN INTERNATIONAL
Kilmore House
20 Prior Road
Camberley
Surrey
GU15 1DQ UK

Tel: + 44 (0) 1276 709709
Fax: + 44 (0) 1276 709707
Contact: Mrs Mary Dixon

Ockenden International is a charity registered in 1955, providing support for refugees, displaced people and the disadvantaged both at home and overseas. In the UK this consists of the provision of a home for the physically and/or mentally disabled.

Total projects worldwide: 1
Total UK projects: 1
Starting months: January–December.
Time required: 52 weeks (plus).
Age requirement: 18 plus.
Causes: Disabled (learning and physical), refugees, young people.
Activities: Administration, arts/crafts, caring (day and residential), catering, community work, cooking, DIY, driving, fundraising, gardening/horticulture, group work.
Vols under 26 placed each year: 1–6 of a total of 6.
When to apply: All year.
Work alone/with others: With others.
Volunteers with disabilities: Possible.
Qualifications: English speaking and reading. Driving licence useful.
Health requirements: Nil.
Costs: Nil.
Benefits: Up to £30 per week for reasonable expenses. Board and accommodation provided on site free. 23 days holiday per year or pro rata. We cover insurance while volunteers are on our premises.
Training: Induction course.
Supervision: Senior care supervision.
Interview details: Wherever possible, volunteers are interviewed at Kilmore.
Certification: Reference on request.
Charity number: 10533720
UK placements: *England* (Surrey).

OLEN SAFTERIET
Post boks 143
N 5580 Olen
Norway

Tel: 00 47 73 978 840
Fax: 00 47 73 978 840
Contact: The Director

Olen Safteriet is a small urban Camphill community. Sheltered workplaces: juice, health food shop etc.

Total projects worldwide: 1
Total UK projects: 0
Starting months: January–December.
Time required: 52 weeks (plus).
Age requirement: 14 plus.
Causes: Disabled (learning).
Worldwide placements: *Europe* (Norway).

ONE-TO-ONE
404 Camden Road
London
N7 OSJ UK

Tel: +44 (0) 20 7538 4321
Contact: The Administrator

One-to-One is a friendship development scheme for people with learning difficulties. Volunteers are recruited in the role of companion, enabler, friend or advocate and to form a bridge between them and their local community to enable them to gain access to leisure and social activities.

Total projects worldwide: 4
Total UK projects: 4
Starting months: January–December.
Time required: 26–52 weeks.
Age requirement: 17 plus.
Causes: Disabled (learning).
Activities: Cooking, driving, gardening/horticulture, music, visiting/befriending.
When to apply: All year.
Work alone/with others: Alone.
Volunteers with disabilities: Possible.
Qualifications: Nil but repared to undergo training programme.
Health requirements: Nil.
Costs: Nil.
Benefits: Out-of-pocket expenses provided.
Certification: Certificate or reference provided.
UK placements: *England* (London, Surrey).

OPERATION MOBILISATION – SUMMER CHALLENGE
Quinta
Weston Rhyn
Oswestry
SY10 7LT UK

Tel: +44 (0) 1691 773388
Contact: Chris Papworth

Total projects worldwide: 1
Total UK projects: 1
Starting months: January–December.
Time required: 3 weeks.
Age requirement: 17 plus.

OPERATION NEW WORLD
4 Eccleston Square
London
SW1V 1NP UK

Tel: +44 (0) 20 7931 8177
Fax: +44 (0) 20 7931 9589
Contact: Anne Leonard, Chairman

The Operation New World programme aims to motivate and train unemployed young people so that they are able to get out of 'Benefits' and into worthwhile jobs. Since we began in 1995, over 90% of the trainees found jobs or took up full-time education shortly afterwards. The beneficiaries are unemployed young people from all parts of the UK, from a variety of disadvantaged backgrounds. Most are disadvantaged by poverty and are from broken homes with a pattern of drifting from one temporary address to another. Some need help urgently in order to get restarted and avoid drifting into drink or drug related problems. They may have lost their first job or have never had a job because they lack the motivation or qualifications to do something permanent. They are coaxed into volunteering for the Operation New World programme because it offers a fresh start in life allied to environmental issues which are of great interest to this age group. Part 1: Once trainees enrol on a part-time study course, we provide residential outdoor training which aims to bond participants into a self-support group so that they help each other to stay on-course. This is achieved through teamwork, solving problems together and learning practical skills such as first aid, map reading, navigation and verbal presentation. Part 2: This is followed by a 12-week part-time course at a supporting college in numeracy and computer skills; practical environmental studies and personal development. Part 3: Once trainees have completed Parts 1 and 2, they qualify for two weeks' residential fieldwork in a remote destination, usually a nature reserve in Europe or in the UK. This is an intensive experience requiring discipline and hard work and is what makes the whole scheme work. Each day starts at 6 a.m. with classes and conservation work until dark, then lectures, presentations and written reports in the evening. Trainees practise presentation skills to help in job interviews, each giving a verbal report of his/her work at the end of each day. There are no luxuries. Everyone takes turns to prepare food, chop wood and perform other duties for the rest of the group. This experience provides young people with new skills and gives them a support group they did not have before. The increase in their self-respect empowers them to take a new course in life and become more active members of society and their positive response is reflected in the outstanding results achieved so far. Volunteers with an offending background are accepted.

Total projects worldwide: 3
Total UK projects: 3
Starting months: February, October, November.
Time required: 14–16 weeks.
Age requirement: 18–25
Causes: Conservation, environmental causes, poor/homeless, unemployed, wildlife, young people.
Activities: Conservation skills, first aid, forestry, outdoor skills.
Vols under 26 placed each year: 60
When to apply: All year.
Work alone/with others: With others.
Volunteers with disabilities: This project is not suitable for people with disabilities.
Qualifications: GCSEs.
Equipment/clothing: Outdoor clothing.
Health requirements: Applicants must be able to carry out fieldwork. May entail difficult walking conditions.
Costs: None (apart from UK travel to college or airport).
Benefits: UK expenses covered by benefits. Travel to foreign location. BTec certificate in Environmental Studies. No insurance cover necessary.
Training: BTec Certificate in Environmental Studies.
Supervision: Qualified college lecturers and TA/Regular army volunteers.
Nationalities accepted: UK and possibly EC.
Interview details: Interview takes place at the Outdoor Training Camp.
Certification: BTec Certificate.
Worldwide placements: *Europe* (France, Spain, Sweden).
UK placements: *England* (Surrey).

ÖSTERREICHISCHER BAUORDER
Postfach 186
Hornesgasse 3
1031 Wien
Austria

Tel: 00 43 222 713 52 54
Fax: 00 43 222 713 81 18
Contact: The Secretary

Every year Österreichischer Bauorder organizes around 15 projects in Austria with aims such as building homes and community centres for the handicapped, the poor, the young and the old, or constructing sports fields etc.

Total projects worldwide: 15
Total UK projects: 0
Starting months: June, July, August.
Time required: 34 weeks.
Age requirement: 18 plus.
Activities: Building/construction, community work, manual work.
Vols under 26 placed each year: 250
When to apply: As early as possible.
Work alone/with others: With others.
Qualifications: Basic knowledge of German.
Benefits: Board, lodging and insurance.
Worldwide placements: *Europe* (Austria).

OUTREACH INTERNATIONAL
Bartletts Farm
Hayes Road
Compton Dundon
Somerset
TA11 6PF UK

Tel: +44 (0) 1458 274957
Fax: +44 (0) 1458 274957
e-mail: outmex@aol.com
Web: www.outreachinternational.co.uk
Contact: James Chapman

Outreach International is an educational trust that gives school leavers, undergraduates and volunteers with at least three months of time, the opportunity to work abroad at a carefully selected project for their gap year. Volunteers make meaningful contributions to these projects at the same time as enjoying the excitement and adventure of working in challenging environments. There are a number of projects in rural Mexico that need to be filled. They incorporate conservation, ecological research, teaching or community and social work with the indigenous Huicholi people and a dance and drama project on the coast. We also have a small number of placements for volunteers interested in cultural art and design and environmental journalism. They are located in culturally fascinating communities in the mountains and coastal regions of Jalisco Province. Volunteers will form an integral part of this community and will be given every opportunity to learn Spanish. Projects last for

between three and nine months after which there will be an opportunity to travel or participate in an Outreach International expedition for a short period of time with fellow volunteers in Mexico. We also have orphanage projects in Kenya and Cambodia. We have a number of sponsors and offer all successful applicants assistance with their fund raising. Volunteers with an offending background may possibly be accepted.

Total projects worldwide: 50
Total UK projects: 0
Starting months: January, June, September.
Time required: 12–50 weeks.
Age requirement: 18 plus.
Causes: Children, conservation, environmental causes, poor/homeless, teaching/assisting (primary, secondary, mature, EFL), wildlife, young people.
Activities: Agriculture/farming, arts/crafts, conservation skills, development issues, research, scientific work, teaching.
Vols under 26 placed each year: 40 of a total of 50.
When to apply: March for September departure, July for January departure.
Work alone/with others: With others.
Volunteers with disabilities: Not possible.
Qualifications: Nil.
Health requirements: Nil.
Costs: £2,925. Sponsorship available.
Benefits: Travel, all board and lodging, insurance, Spanish language training, project training, 10-day expedition. We pay for all public liability and health insurance.
Training: There will be a briefing course in England prior to departure. On arrival in Mexico a fortnight will be spent attending a training programme and intensive Spanish course run by the full-time Mexico representative, based in Puerto Vallarta.
Supervision: Full-time representative in Mexico. Full time project managers.
Nationalities accepted: EU only.
Interview details: Interviews take place near the applicant's home town.
Certification: Certificate or reference provided.
Worldwide placements: *Africa* (Kenya); *Asia* (Cambodia); *Central America* (Mexico).

OXFAM
62 Cotham Hill
Bristol
BS6 6JX UK

Tel: +44 (0) 1179 734335
Fax: +44 (0) 1179 731449
e-mail: mbmclaughl@oxfam.org.uk
Contact: Mandi Boyd McLaughlin

Oxfam was founded in 1942 and is now one of the largest agencies working with development issues around the world. Our work overseas has two dimensions: as well as being able to respond to emergencies, Oxfam works with local people in their quest for basic rights – health, education, a decent standard of living, etc. We fund numerous small-scale projects, which are usually the initiative of the local people – real grass-roots development. In the UK and Ireland, work is constantly going on in the fields of campaigning and public education, raising awareness and raising issues with influential people. Most of the money needed to fund all this work is raised by volunteers and the famous Oxfam shops provide most of this money, as well as giving the volunteer useful skills and experience in the workplace. As the majority of these shops are run entirely by volunteers, positions of responsibility are shared among volunteers and so opportunities can exist, for the right person, to make a substantial contribution to shop management. Volunteers with a prison record are accepted.

Total projects worldwide: 800
Total UK projects: 800
Starting months: January–December.
Time required: 1–52 weeks.
Age requirement: 14 plus.
Causes: Animal welfare, children, disabled (physical), elderly people, environmental causes, health care/medical, human rights, poor/homeless, refugees.
Activities: Accountancy, administration, development issues, driving, fundraising, marketing/publicity, technical skills, training.
Vols under 26 placed each year: 2,000 of a total of 27,000.
When to apply: All year.
Work alone/with others: With others.
Volunteers with disabilities: Possible, some shops have restricted access.
Qualifications: Generally nil but required for training, driving etc.
Health requirements: Nil.
Costs: Nil – expenses can be reimbursed.
Benefits: Travel expenses can be reimbursed. Oxfam's insurance policy covers volunteers whilst on Oxfam premises.
Training: Pre-placement and on-the-job training is provided as necessary.
Supervision: As appropriate.
Nationalities accepted: We welcome volunteers from all ethnic backgrounds and nationalities.
Interview details: Interviews at the shop or locally.
Certification: Reference on request.
Charity number: 202918
UK placements: *England* (throughout); *Scotland* (throughout); *Northern Ireland* (throughout); *Wales* (throughout).

OXFORD KILBURN CLUB
45 Denmark Road
Kilburn
London
NW6 5BP UK

Tel: +44 (0) 20 7624 6292
Fax: +44 (0) 20 7624 6292
e-mail: ok_club@compuserve.com
Contact: J. Douglas, Y.W. Manager

Oxford Kilburn Club operates under a charity named the Oxford Boys' Club Trust. The club aims to meet the spiritual, physical, social, educational and recreational needs of young people and their families living in the area. The volunteer's job is to assist in all areas of the club which aims to help children and young people in this neighbourhood. You may be required to do any number of activities from attending club nights, visiting children in their homes, organizing small after-school clubs for junior children, giving support to children with special needs, participating in club holidays, organizing activities and relating to individuals in the 8–18 years age group. The club is run by Christians and one of its aims is to present the gospel of Jesus Christ to the children in the area.

Total projects worldwide: 1
Total UK projects: 1
Starting months: September.
Time required: 1–52 weeks (plus).
Age requirement: 18–29
Causes: Children, inner city problems, refugees, teaching/assisting young people.
Activities: Administration, arts/crafts, community work, cooking, DIY, fundraising, music, religion, social work, sport, summer camps, theatre/drama.

Vols under 26 placed each year: About 3.
When to apply: By March for September start.
Work alone/with others: Both but mostly with others.
Volunteers with disabilities: Possible.
Qualifications: Enthusiasm, commitment and Christianity.
Equipment/clothing: Casual and sporting clothes and equipment.
Health requirements: Nil.
Benefits: Board and lodging, travel costs and pocket money (£25 per week) plus food. We provide employer's liability insurance.
Training: Induction training covering basic health and safety, youth work, induction to organization policy and procedure etc.
Supervision: By senior youth worker, meet fortnightly.
Interview details: Interviews take place at the Oxford Kilburn Club.
Certification: Written reference on request.
Charity number: 306108
UK placements: *England* (London).

P

PACT CENTRE FOR YOUTH LTD
The Firehouse
21 Gordon Street
Paisley
Renfrewshire
PA1 1XD Scotland

Tel: +44 (0) 141 849 1149 or +44 (0) 141 884 8199
Fax: +44 (0) 141 849 1149
Contact: David Palmer

PACT is Paisley Action of Churches Together. The Youth Section has taken over the Old Fire Station and is transforming it into a Centre for Youth to serve the town of Paisley and the surrounding district. There will be a wide variety of facilities and amenities open to all young people whatever their background, creed, etc. The centre is served by full-time and part-time employed and voluntary staff. On the ground floor there is a Youth Centre with an emphasis on a discotheque/live bands arena, alcohol-free bar and cafe. The centre will encourage young people in personal (health, fitness and employment potential) and social development and focus on training in the arts and performing arts. First Floor will have a Youth Advice Centre, a point of first reference for any young person who will be put in touch with the particular resource needed. Also on this floor there will be accommodation for homeless young people.

Total projects worldwide: 1
Total UK projects: 1
Starting months: January–December.
Time required: 1–52 weeks (plus).
Age requirement: 18–35
Causes: Addicts/Ex-addicts, children, disabled (learning and physical), inner city problems, offenders/ex-offenders, unemployed, young people.
Activities: Arts/crafts, counselling, fundraising, group work, library/resource centres, music, newsletter/journalism, sport, technical skills.
Vols under 26 placed each year: 5–10
When to apply: Any time.
Work alone/with others: With others.
Volunteers with disabilities: Possible.
Qualifications: Nil.
Health requirements: Nil.
Costs: Travel only.
Interview details: Interviews take place at the Firehouse.
Certification: Certificate or reference provided.
Charity number: SCO24331
UK placements: *Scotland* (Glasgow City).

PADDINGTON ARTS
32 Woodfield Road
London
W9 2BE UK

Tel: +44 (0) 20 7286 2722
Fax: +44 (0) 20 7286 0654
e-mail: steve@padarts.idps.co.uk
Contact: Steve Shaw, Director

Paddington Arts started in 1983, under the umbrella of the Paddington Farm Trust – a community organization committed to bridging the gap between city and country life, and now the proud owner of a residential centre and 42 acre farm in Somerset. Trips to the farm have played a key part in our development, not only because of the burst of energy and creativity unleashed by going out of one's usual environment, but because our early trips provided the ideas and experiences for a children's television series, *Running Loose*, which was a popular hit with young people, and helped us set up regular dance and drama workshops in London, which have been running ever since. In 1992 we were able to acquire our own building in the area. This has enabled us to develop other workshops, such as video, scriptwriting, music and design, as well as providing us with much needed office equipment and rehearsal space. In 1997 we redeveloped our building to include a dance/drama studio, a video edit suite and a gallery/exhibition space. Volunteers with an offending background are accepted.

Total projects worldwide: 1
Total UK projects: 1
Starting months: January, April, May, September, October.
Time required: 1–52 weeks.
Age requirement: 15 plus.
Causes: Children, disabled (learning and physical), unemployed, young people.
Activities: Arts/crafts, marketing/publicity, newsletter/journalism, theatre/drama, training.
Vols under 26 placed each year: 12 of a total of 20.
When to apply: All year.
Work alone/with others: With others.
Volunteers with disabilities: There may be projects for volunteers with disabilities.
Qualifications: Nil.
Health requirements: Nil.
Costs: Nil.
Benefits: Travel expenses. We have public/employer's liability insurance.
Training: Provided as necessary.
Supervision: Supervision is given.
Interview details: Interviews take place at Paddington Arts.
Certification: Certificate or reference on request.
Charity number: 298879
UK placements: *England* (London).

PAHKLA CAMPHILLI KÜLA
Prillimae
Rapla Maakond,
Eesti EE 79702
Estonia

Tel: 00 372 48 34430
Fax: 00 372 48 97231

Contact: The Director

Pahkla Camphilli Küla is a Camphill land-based rural community for adults with special needs.

Total projects worldwide: 1
Total UK projects: 0
Starting months: January–December.
Time required: 1–52 weeks.
Age requirement: 20 plus.
Causes: Disabled (learning).
Activities: Agriculture/farming, arts/crafts, caring (general), cooking, driving, gardening/horticulture, group work, manual work, outdoor skills, social work.
Vols under 26 placed each year: 2
When to apply: All year.
Work alone/with others: With others.
Volunteers with disabilities: Not possible.
Qualifications: Nil.
Equipment/clothing: Normal everyday clothes for Estonian climate.
Health requirements: Nil.
Costs: Return travel to Estonia. Travel insurance.
Benefits: Board and lodging.
Supervision: We expect independent people who can do work responsibly after being introduced to it.
Certification: Certificate or reference on request.
Worldwide placements: *Europe* (Estonia).

PAPUA NEW GUINEA CHURCH PARTNERSHIP
Partnership House
157 Waterloo Road
London
SE1 8XA UK

Tel: +44 (0) 20 7928 8681
Contact: The Director

Total projects worldwide: 1
Total UK projects: 0
Starting months: January–December.
Time required: 26–52 weeks.
Age requirement: 20 plus.
Causes: Teaching/assisting.
Activities: Teaching.
Worldwide placements: *Australasia* (Papua New Guinea).

PARADISE HOUSE ASSOCIATION LTD
Paradise House
Painswick

Gloucestershire
GL6 6TN UK

Tel: +44 (0) 1452 813276
Fax: +44 (0) 1452 812969
Contact: Mavis Mandel

Paradise is a Christian Community based on the insights and philosophy of Rudolf Steiner. We care for a total of 27 adults with learning disabilities (mental handicaps). Food is largely vegetarian, most of it organically grown. A detailed and comprehensive leaflet is available to enquirers.

Total projects worldwide: 1
Total UK projects: 1
Starting months: July.
Time required: 1–52 weeks.
Age requirement: 18–30
Causes: Disabled (learning).
Activities: Agriculture/farming, arts/crafts, caring (residential), catering, gardening/horticulture.
Vols under 26 placed each year: 10
When to apply: All year.
Work alone/with others: Varies.
Volunteers with disabilities: Not possible.
Qualifications: Must speak good English (residents are mentally handicapped).
Health requirements: Must be healthy and prepared to help where necessary.
Costs: Return fare from destination to Paradise House.
Benefits: Board and Lodging plus £30 per week.
Nationalities accepted: No restrictions but volunteers are expected to join in the life of a Christian community.
Interview details: Application forms and 2 references followed by interviews.
Certification: Written reference provided.
Charity number: 263293
UK placements: *England* (Gloucestershire).

PARTNERSHIP FOR SERVICE – LEARNING, THE
815 Second Avenue
Suite 315
New York
NY 10017
USA

Tel: 00 1 212 986 0989
Fax: 00 1 212 986 5039
e-mail: pslny@aol.com
Web: www.ipsl.org

The Partnership for Service-Learning, founded in 1982, is an incorporated not-for-profit consortium of colleges, universities, service agencies and related organizations united to foster and develop programmes linking community service and academic study. We hold that the joining of study and service: is a powerful means of learning; addresses human needs that would otherwise remain unmet; promotes intercultural/international literacy; advances the personal growth of students as members of the community; gives expression to the obligation of public and community service by educated people; sets academic institutions in right relationship to the larger society. We design and administer off-campus programmes combining service and academic study open to all qualified students and recent graduates for the semester, year, summer or January intersession overseas or in North Dakota (with Native Americans). We are governed by an International Board of Trustees including college presidents, deans and the executives of national education and service organizations. We also advise on the development of service-learning, making known the opportunities and experience of service-learning through research and publications, and hold international conferences open to college and university personnel, service agency supervisors and students, and attended by our directors from the various programme locations. Since 1982 nearly 4,000 students from over 300 colleges and universities have participated in our programs for academic credit recognized by the students' home institutions.

Total projects worldwide: 1
Starting months: January–December.
Time required: 26–52 weeks.
Age requirement: 18 plus.
Causes: Addicts/Ex-addicts, Aids/HIV, children, disabled (learning and physical), elderly people, health care/medical, holidays for disabled, inner city problems, offenders/ex-offenders, poor/homeless, refugees, teaching/assisting (nursery, primary, secondary, mature, EFL), unemployed, young people.
Activities: Arts/crafts, caring (general, day and residential), community work, development issues, fundraising, music, sport, teaching, theatre/drama.
When to apply: All year.

Volunteers with disabilities: Possible.
Qualifications: One year's study of relevant language for Mexico, Ecuador and France.
Costs: $3,000 plus insurance, travel expenses and spending money.
Benefits: The cost covers board and accommodation plus support and study expenses.
Worldwide placements: *Asia* (India, Israel, Philippines); *Europe* (Czech Republic, France); *North America* (USA); *Central America* (Jamaica, Mexico); *South America* (Ecuador).
UK placements: *England* (throughout); *Scotland* (throughout); *Northern Ireland* (throughout); *Wales* (throughout).

PASCHIM BANGA SAMAJ SEVA SAMITY
191 Chittatanjan Avenue
Calcutta
700 007 India

Contact: The Treasurer

Total projects worldwide: 1
Total UK projects: 0
Starting months: January, February, June, July, October, November, December.
Time required: 3–4 weeks.
Age requirement: 16 plus.
Causes: Health Care/Medical.
Vols under 26 placed each year: 300
Qualifications: English speaking.
Worldwide placements: *Asia* (India).

PAX CHRISTI
St Joseph's
Watford Way
London
N4 4TY UK

Tel: +44 (0) 20 8203 4884
Contact: Pete Dunn, Work camp Organizer

Pax Christi organizes volunteers to work in an international team to provide hospitality and support for young people and children at summer camps.

Total projects worldwide: 5
Total UK projects: 4
Starting months: July, August.
Time required: 3–4 weeks.
Age requirement: 19–30
Causes: Children, young people.
Activities: Arts/crafts, community work, cooking, driving, music, outdoor skills, sport, summer camps, theatre/drama.

When to apply: From February.
Work alone/with others: With others.
Volunteers with disabilities: Possible.
Qualifications: References checked.
Health requirements: Nil.
Costs: Own travel costs to either London or Northern Ireland plus £5 registration fee.
Benefits: Board and lodging provided.
Interview details: No interview necessary.
UK placements: *England* (London); *Northern Ireland* (Belfast City, Tyrone).

PENNINE CAMPHILL COMMUNITY
Boyne Hill
Chapelthorpe
Wakefield
West Yorkshire
WF4 3JH UK

Tel: +44 (0) 1924 255281
Fax: +44 (0) 1924 240257
e-mail: student@pennine.org.uk
Web: www.pennine.org.uk
Contact: Steve Hopewell

Pennine Camphill Community offers further education and training for young people with learning difficulties or disabilities. Pennine is part of the Camphill Movement founded in 1939 in Scotland by Dr Karl König. Since then over 80 centres in 17 countries have been established providing schooling, further education and working communities for adults. We are approximately 24 co-workers and their families. There is always a strong international element with co-workers coming from many different countries. About half of the co-workers live at the Pennine on a permanent basis and half have come for a year or more to help. There are no separate staff rooms apart from your own room. Co-workers and students take meals together in the houses. Some will have helped with the growing of the produce, cooking the meal or perhaps just laying the tables. Personal preferences and experiences are obviously taken into account when arranging activities but an underlying strength of the co-worker group is the wish to help the needs of those we care for. Working at the Pennine is more a way of life and living with and sharing in interests with the students often blurs what is free time and what is work. It is a common wish that we live in a community where each works towards a common aim, to help each other's potential and awaken a sense of responsibility and interest in the world and for each other. Volunteers with an offending background may be accepted in special circumstances.

Total projects worldwide: 1
Total UK projects: 1
Starting months: January–December.
Time required: 26–52 weeks.
Age requirement: 18 plus.
Causes: Disabled (learning), teaching/assisting (mature), young people.
Activities: Agriculture/farming, arts/crafts, building/construction, caring (general), catering, cooking, DIY, gardening/horticulture, manual work, outdoor skills, teaching, training.
Vols under 26 placed each year: 2–3 of a total of 15–20.
When to apply: All year.
Work alone/with others: With others.
Volunteers with disabilities: Please enquire.
Qualifications: Nil.
Health requirements: Nil.
Costs: Initial travel to Wakefield. Medical insurance is not provided other than local services.
Benefits: Board and lodging plus £25 per week with additional holiday money.
Training: Brochures and information provided. Visits welcomed or contact with people who have volunteered in the past. An induction programme covering working essentials and our core philosophy.
Supervision: Supervision and assistance is always available.
Interview details: Prospective volunteers are interviewed at the Pennine Community, Wakefield.
Certification: Certificate or reference on request.
Charity number: 274192
UK placements: *England* (W. Yorkshire).

PENSEE ET CHANTIERS
BP 1423
Rabat R P
Morocco

Tel: 00 212 7 73 44 59
Contact: The President

Total projects worldwide: 1
Total UK projects: 0
Starting months: August.
Time required: 3 weeks.
Age requirement: 18 plus.

Causes: Work camps – seasonal.
Activities: Building/construction, forestry, gardening/horticulture, manual work, work camps – seasonal.
Costs: £30 registration fee, provide own meals and pay for own travel expenses.
Benefits: Sleeping bags and tools for the projects provided.

PEOPLE FIRST
Instrument House
207–215 King's Cross Road
London
WC1X 9DB UK

Tel: +44 (0) 20 7713 6400
Fax: +44 (0) 20 7833 1880
Contact: Director

People First is a self-advocacy organization run for and by people with learning difficulties. At a national level we provide support, information, advice and training on issues relating to people with learning difficulties and promote the use of accessible information. The staff and volunteers at People First are currently involved in London-based self-advocacy projects and a number of campaigns for the rights of people with learning difficulties, for example: Benefits, Fair Justice and the All Party Disablement Group. People First also inputs into the Disability Rights Task Force and the Department of Health Advisory Group. For more information about People First publications and membership please send an SAE to the above address. There is a small membership fee.

Total projects worldwide: 160
Total UK projects: 160
Starting months: January–December.
Time required: 1–52 weeks.
Age requirement: 18 plus.
Causes: Disabled (learning), young people.
Activities: Administration, campaigning, library/resource centres, research, training.
Vols under 26 placed each year: Approximately 5 of a total of 30.
When to apply: All year.
Work alone/with others: With others.
Volunteers with disabilities: Possible.
Qualifications: Nil.
Health requirements: Nil.
Costs: Nil.
Benefits: Expenses paid, training, insurance.
Training: Induction and on-the-job training.

Supervision: Provided.
Charity number: 1057354
UK placements: *England* (London).

PETADISTS COMMUNITY ORGANISATION

37 Pentland House
Stamford Hill
London
N16 6RP UK

Tel: + 44 (0) 20 8802 4987
Contact: Mr Peter Amadi

Total projects worldwide: 1
Total UK projects: 1
Starting months: January–December.
Time required: 8–20 weeks.
Age requirement: 17 plus.
Causes: Conservation, environmental causes, health care/medical, human rights, inner city problems, poor/homeless, refugees, teaching (primary, secondary, mature, EFL), unemployed, wildlife, young people.
Activities: Accountancy, administration, agriculture/farming, building/construction, community work, computers, conservation skills, counselling, development issues, fundraising, group work, international aid, marketing/publicity, music, newsletter/journalism, sport, teaching, training, visiting/befriending, work camps – seasonal.
Vols under 26 placed each year: 30 of a total of 50.
When to apply: All year.
Work alone/with others: With others.
Volunteers with disabilities: Possible.
Qualifications: Computer literacy skills.
Health requirements: Nil.
Costs: Travel to West Africa.
Benefits: Accommodation provided. Enugu State Government is responsible for providing insurance.
Training: Induction on the project, way of life of the people, cultural differences etc.
Supervision: Provided both from London and locally in the country.
Interview details: Interviews take place in London.
Certification: Certificate or reference provided.
Charity number: 1017691
Worldwide placements: *Africa* (Cameroon, Gambia, Ghana, Nigeria).
UK placements: *England* (London).

PGL TRAVEL

Alton Court
Penyard Lane,
Ross-on-Wye
Herefordshire
HR9 5GL UK

Tel: + 44 (0) 1989 767833
Fax: + 44 (0) 1989 768769
e-mail: personnel@pgl.co.uk
Web: www.pgl.co.uk
Contact: Personnel Department

PGL Travel is a children's activity holiday company with residential centres in the UK, France and Spain. We cater for school groups and individual youngsters during vacation time. Volunteers with an offending background may be accepted – each case will be judged on its merits.

Total projects worldwide: 29
Total UK projects: 19
Starting months: February–October.
Time required: 6–37 weeks.
Age requirement: 18 plus.
Causes: Children, young people.
Activities: Administration, agriculture/farming, caring (general), catering, computers, cooking, driving, first aid, manual work, outdoor skills, sport, summer camps, theatre/drama, training, work camps – seasonal.
Vols under 26 placed each year: 2,250 of a total of 2,500.
When to apply: From September.
Work alone/with others: Both.
Volunteers with disabilities: Possible.
Qualifications: Varies according to job.
Equipment/clothing: Supplied.
Health requirements: Nil.
Costs: Occasionally, travel to project.
Benefits: Food, accommodation plus approximately £50 per week. Travel in Europe normally provided too. Employer's and public liability insurance is provided, as well as medical insurance for employees working overseas.
Training: Full training will be provided for all positions.
Supervision: Staff report to a line manager.
Nationalities accepted: Applications will only be accepted from candidates with a legal right to work in the UK (i.e. EU and Commonwealth).
Interview details: Applicants are not generally interviewed but will be expected to complete

a probationary period.
Certification: Training/qualifications gained
are certificated.
Worldwide placements: *Europe* (France,
Spain).
UK placements: *England* (Devon,
Herefordshire, Isle of Wight, Lancashire,
Oxfordshire, Shropshire, Surrey, W. Sussex,
Worcestershire); *Scotland* (Perth and Kinross);
Wales (Powys).

PHAB ENGLAND
Summit House
Wandle Road
Croydon
Surrey
CRO 1DF UK

Tel: +44 (0) 20 8667 9443
Contact: Philip Lockwood

PHAB England exists to integrate people with
and without physical disabilities. We have
300 or so clubs throughout the country who
meet on a regular basis. Local volunteers are
always welcome. Volunteers with an
offending background are accepted.

Total projects worldwide: 5
Total UK projects: 5
Starting months: January–December.
Time required: 1–52 weeks.
Age requirement: 16 plus.
Causes: Children, disabled (physical),
holidays for disabled, young people.
Activities: Administration, driving,
newsletter/journalism, outdoor skills.
Vols under 26 placed each year: 20
When to apply: All year.
Work alone/with others: With others.
Volunteers with disabilities: Possible.
Qualifications: Driving licence.
Health requirements: Nil.
Costs: Travel costs.
Benefits: Financial assistance in respect of
holidays is provided.
Interview details: Interviews are conducted
local to the project, i.e. all over England.
Certification: Written reference provided.
Charity number: 283931
UK placements: *England* (throughout).

PHAB Northampton
Bushland Road
Headlands
Northampton
Northamptonshire

NN3 2HP UK

Tel: +44 (0) 1604 405693

Total projects worldwide: 0
Total UK projects: 1
Starting months: January–December.
Time required: 1–52 weeks.
Age requirement: 16 plus.
Causes: Children, disabled (physical), young
people.
Activities: Administration, driving,
newsletter/journalism, outdoor skills.
When to apply: All year.
Volunteers with disabilities: Possible.
UK placements: *England*
(Northamptonshire).

PHAB SW
PO Box 282
Taunton
Somerset
TA1 3YX UK

Tel: +44 (0) 1823 251004

PHAB SW promotes and encourages people
with and without physical disabilities to come
together on equal terms, to achieve complete
integration within the wider community.
PHAB organizes: clubs which belong to and
are run by disabled and abled bodied people;
area, divisional, and national structures for
support, development, training, events;
training through working with PHAB in the
community through workshops and
conferences; special emphasis on work with
children and young people, through junior
PHAB clubs; residential holidays; links and
exchanges with similar groups; an
information service for booklets, films and
speakers.

Total projects worldwide: 1
Total UK projects: 1
Starting months: January–December.
Time required: 1–52 weeks.
Age requirement: 17 plus.
Causes: Children, disabled (physical), elderly
people, young people.
Activities: Administration, arts/crafts,
driving, group work, newsletter/journalism,
outdoor skills.
Vols under 26 placed each year: 30% of
total.
When to apply: All year.
Work alone/with others: Both.
Volunteers with disabilities: Possible.

Training: All junior holidays have a training day/weekend.
Supervision: By a group leader, administrator of the project and medical appointee.
Benefits: We provide insurance.
Interview details: Applicants are interviewed somewhere convenient to the volunteer.
UK placements: *England* (Cornwall, Devon, Dorset, Gloucestershire, Hampshire, Isle of Wight, Somerset, Wiltshire).

PHOENIX YCP LTD
16 Alexander Square
Lurgan,
Craigavon
Co. Armagh
N. Ireland

Tel: +44 (0) 28 3832 7614
Fax: +44 (0) 28 3832 7614
Contact: Pearl Snowden

Phoenix YCP organizes cross community youth work with children aged between 7 and 13 years such as indoor/outdoor games, drama, music, art/crafts, environmental work, discussion groups, swimming, day trips, residentials.

Total projects worldwide: 1
Total UK projects: 1
Starting months: July, August.
Time required: 4–52 weeks.
Age requirement: 18 plus.
Causes: Children.
Activities: Arts/crafts, music, sport, summer camps, theatre/drama.
Vols under 26 placed each year: 40
When to apply: Between 1 September and 30 April.
Work alone/with others: With others.
Volunteers with disabilities: Possible.
Qualifications: Must have previous experience working with children.
Costs: Travel expenses plus £50 for board, lodging and a social programme.
Interview details: No interview necessary.
Charity number: XN 75547
UK placements: *Northern Ireland* (Armagh).

PLAN INTERNATIONAL
5–6 Underhill Street
Camden
London
NW1 7HS UK

Tel: +44 (0) 20 7485 6612
Fax: +44 (0) 20 7485 2107
e-mail: mail@plan-international.org.uk
Web: www.plan-international.org.uk
Contact: Jan Cameron, Volunteer Co-ordinator

Plan International is a child sponsorship charity helping to create lasting improvements in the lives of children, their families and communities in the developing world. Our projects include immunization, education, sanitation, agro-forestation, Aids awareness, credit schemes and improving farming techniques. Although our work is centred abroad, our volunteers in the UK help with administration in various departments including finance, enrolment, marketing and communications. Please feel free to ring for further details. Volunteers with an offending background may be accepted – each case would be considered separately.

Total projects worldwide: 1
Total UK projects: 1
Starting months: January–December.
Time required: 2–52 weeks.
Age requirement: 16 plus.
Causes: Aids/HIV, children, environmental causes, teaching/assisting.
Activities: Computers, development issues.
Vols under 26 placed each year: 35 of a total of 100.
When to apply: All year.
Work alone/with others: With others.
Volunteers with disabilities: Not possible.
Qualifications: Nil.
Health requirements: Nil.
Costs: Nil.
Benefits: Travel reimbursed up to £5 per day. £2.50 per day for lunch if more than 5 hours worked. We have suitable insurance.
Supervision: 2 members of staff look after the volunteers full time.
Interview details: Interviews take place in our London office.
Certification: Written reference provided.
Charity number: 276035
UK placements: *England* (London).

PLENTY INTERNATIONAL
PO Box 394
Summertown
Tennessee 38483
USA

Tel: 00 1 615 964 4864
Fax: 00 1 931 964 4864

Plenty is a non-governmental relief and development organization that works with native peoples from Central and South America and Africa, as well as within the US. Projects can range from community agriculture in S. Dakota to building facilities for eco-tourism in Belize. The organization publishes a quarterly bulletin, with up-to-date details of projects and endeavours which may be subscribed to by sending $10 to the above address.

Total projects worldwide: 1
Total UK projects: 0
Starting months: January–December.
Time required: 1–52 weeks.
Age requirement: 14 plus.
Activities: Building/construction, development issues, fundraising, gardening/horticulture, international aid.
When to apply: All year.
Costs: All expenses and costs including travel, accommodation rental etc.
Worldwide placements: *Africa* (Algeria, Angola, Benin, Botswana, Burkina Faso, Burundi, Cameroon, Cape Verde, Central African Republic, Chad, Comoros, Congo Dem. Republic, Congo Republic, Ivory Coast, Djibouti, Egypt, Equatorial Guinea, Eritrea, Ethiopia, Gabon, Gambia, Ghana, Guinea, Guinea-Bissau, Kenya, Lesotho, Liberia, Libya, Madagascar, Malawi, Mali, Mauritania, Mauritius, Mayotte, Morocco, Mozambique, Namibia, Niger, Nigeria, Reunion, Rwanda, Saint Helena, São Tomé and Principe, Senegal, Seychelles, Sierra Leone, Somalia, South Africa, Sudan, Swaziland, Tanzania, Togo, Tunisia, Uganda, Zambia, Zimbabwe); *North America* (USA); *Central America* (Belize, Costa Rica, Cuba, El Salvador, Guatemala, Mexico, Nicaragua, Panama, Puerto Rico); *South America* (Argentina, Bolivia, Brazil, Chile, Colombia, Ecuador, Falkland Islands, French Guiana, Guyana, Paraguay, Peru, South Georgia, Suriname, Uruguay, Venezuela).

POOLE HOSPITAL NHS TRUST PLAYCLUB
Poole Hospital NHS Trust
Longfleet Road
Poole
Dorset
BH15 2JB UK

Tel: +44 (0) 1202 665511 ext 2331
Contact: Mrs Carol Somers

Poole Hospital NHS Trust Playclub is registered with Social Services for 30 places. It is open to children aged 5–14 years and is held Monday–Friday during half terms and school holidays. The aim of the Playclub is to provide a structured day for the children, in a safe environment, and activities include outings, games, cooking, art and crafts. All volunteers will be required to be police and health checked by Social Services. Volunteers with an offending background may be accepted depending on offence.

Total projects worldwide: 1
Total UK projects: 1
Starting months: February, March, April, July, August, October, December.
Time required: 1–6 weeks.
Age requirement: 17 plus.
Causes: Children.
Activities: Arts/crafts, cooking, first aid, group work, music, outdoor skills, sport, theatre/drama.
Vols under 26 placed each year: 2
When to apply: 6 weeks before starting.
Work alone/with others: With qualified staff.
Volunteers with disabilities: Possible.
Qualifications: Previous experience working with children desirable but not essential.
Equipment/clothing: Indoor shoe wear.
Health requirements: Need to be health checked/cleared by Social Services.
Costs: Travel to and from Playclub, meals whilst there.
Nationalities accepted: Volunteers from outside the EU must have a work permit.
Interview details: Interviews take place in the hospital.
Certification: Certificate or reference on request.
UK placements: *England* (Dorset).

POWER – THE INTERNATIONAL LIMB PROJECT
14 Western Road
Henley-on-Thames
Oxon
RG9 1JL UK

Tel: +44 (0) 1491 579065
Fax: +44 (0) 1491 578088
e-mail: power@sarhodg.demon.co.uk
Contact: Mrs Sarah Hodge

Power's mission is to establish sustainable services providing high quality artificial limbs to victims of conflict to restore their mobility, self-respect and quality of life, and to give first-class professional training in prosthetics and orthotics in low-income countries. Power is a small organization set up in 1994. We are a member of the British Overseas NGOs for Development (BOND), The UK Working Group on Landmines, The International Campaign to Ban Landmines and the UK/EC NGO Network. We exist to help all who are motor-disabled and disadvantaged by so being. At present the only voluntary opportunities we have are short term in the UK or for very experienced people overseas. However, applications from well-motivated people are always welcome, particularly if you are able to meet some expenses yourself.

Total projects worldwide: 2
Total UK projects: 1
Starting months: January–December.
Time required: 13–52 weeks.
Age requirement: 18 plus.
Causes: Disabled (physical).
Activities: Accountancy, administration, computers, development issues, social work.
Vols under 26 placed each year: Varies.
When to apply: All year.
Volunteers with disabilities: Possible.
Qualifications: 'A' level abilities. Computer literacy.
Health requirements: Must be in good health.
Costs: Travel – return air fares. Insurance.
Benefits: Board and lodging. Pocket money.
Supervision: By country director or administrator.
Interview details: Prospective volunteers are interviewed in Henley-on-Thames.
Certification: Certificate or reference provided.
Charity number: 1059996
Worldwide placements: *Africa* (Mozambique); *Asia* (Laos).
UK placements: *England* (Oxfordshire).

PRINCE'S TRUST, THE
18 Park Square East
London
NW1 4LH UK

Tel: + 44 (0) 20 7543 1365
Fax: + 44 (0) 20 7543 1315
e-mail: kimfowle@princes-trust.org.uk
Web: www.princes-trust.org.uk

Contact: Kim Fowler

More than 1.5 million young people in the UK are finding life particularly tough, facing problems like poverty, unemployment, discrimination, underachievement, family breakdown, homelessness and personal crisis. The European Programme aims to help them regain self-esteem, confidence, motivation and skills through the development of European projects and grant giving. Go and Help grants enable less confident young people to take the opportunity to go to another European country and take part in voluntary projects run by other not-for-profit organizations. This provides a structured experience with the challenge of intercultural learning. Volunteers with an offending background are encouraged.

Total projects worldwide: 1
Total UK projects: 0
Starting months: January–December.
Time required: 2–24 weeks.
Age requirement: 18–25
Causes: Addicts/ex-addicts, Aids/HIV, animal welfare, archaeology, architecture, children, conservation, disabled (learning and physical), elderly people, environmental causes, health care/medical, heritage, holidays for disabled, human rights, inner city problems, offenders/ex-offenders, poor/homeless, refugees, teaching/assisting (nursery), unemployed, wildlife, work camps – seasonal, young people.
Activities: Agriculture/farming, arts/crafts, building/construction, caring (general, day and residential), community work, conservation skills, DIY, forestry, gardening/horticulture, manual work, music, outdoor skills, social work, summer camps, teaching, theatre/drama, work camps – seasonal.
Vols under 26 placed each year: 100–200
When to apply: All year.
Work alone/with others: With others.
Volunteers with disabilities: All applications are welcome.
Qualifications: Applications encouraged from those with no or few academic qualifications.
Health requirements: Nil.
Costs: Nil. Volunteers are responsible for travel insurance and E111 forms.
Benefits: The Go and Help grants cover travel and living costs up to a maximum of £450 including a cheap flight.
Supervision: This varies on different camps

but there is supervision on all camps including team leaders.

Nationalities accepted: Must be resident in the UK.

Interview details: Prospective volunteers are interviewed by a local assessor.

Certification: Certificate or reference provided.

Charity number: 1018177

Worldwide placements: *Europe* (Albania, Andorra, Armenia, Austria, Azerbaijan, Belarus, Belgium, Bosnia-Herzegovina, Bulgaria, Croatia, Cyprus, Czech Republic, Denmark, Estonia, Finland, France, Georgia, Germany, Gibraltar, Greece, Hungary, Iceland, Ireland, Italy, Latvia, Liechtenstein, Lithuania, Luxembourg, Macedonia, Malta, Moldova, Monaco, Netherlands, Norway, Poland, Portugal, Romania, Russia, San Marino, Slovakia, Slovenia, Spain, Sweden, Switzerland, Turkey, Ukraine, Yugoslavia).

PRINCESS MARINA CENTRE
Chalfont Road
Seer Green
Nr Beaconsfield
Buckinghamshire
HP10 2QR UK

Tel: +44 (0) 1494 874231
Fax: +44 (0) 1494 871001
Contact: John Inker, Manager

Princess Marina Centre (PMC) is a residential centre which is part of Scope Eastern Region. Scope exists to provide support and services for people with cerebral palsy and their families. The ongoing volunteer projects at PMC are designed to support staff already working with individuals to give greater scope for widening opportunities. Volunteers provide escorts to a range of social and educational venues, world of work initiatives, therapy clases etc. We also have opportunities for those wishing to use DIY or gardening skills on our large site. Our arts and crafts staff/tutors are always short of assistance. People with an offending background may be accepted depending on the offence.

Total projects worldwide: 1
Total UK projects: 1
Starting months: January–December.
Time required: 4–26 weeks.
Age requirement: 16 plus.
Causes: Disabled (physical).
Activities: Arts/crafts, caring (residential),

DIY, driving, gardening/horticulture, visiting/befriending.

Vols under 26 placed each year: 30
When to apply: All year.
Work alone/with others: Both.
Volunteers with disabilities: Not possible.
Qualifications: Driving licence an advantage.
Health requirements: Good health.
Costs: Travel to and from the Centre.
Benefits: CSV's receive £23 per week plus full board, students receive £50 per week plus full board.
Interview details: Interviews take place at the Centre.
Certification: Written reference provided.
Charity number: 208231
UK placements: *England* (Buckinghamshire).

PRO INTERNATIONAL
Bahnhofstrasse 26 A
D-35037 Marburg/L
Germany

Tel: 00 49 6421 65277
Fax: 00 49 6421 64407
Contact: Gerd Pause

Following the concept of 'Peace through Friendship' Pro International organizes international vacation work camps. On these camps, 10 to 15 volunteers from different countries participate. They work about five hours a day on public or social projects and spend their time together.

Total projects worldwide: 15
Total UK projects: 0
Starting months: March, April, June, July, August.
Time required: 3–52 weeks.
Age requirement: 16 plus.
Causes: Conservation, environmental causes.
Activities: Conservation skills, social work.
Vols under 26 placed each year: 500
When to apply: As early as possible.
Work alone/with others: With others.
Costs: Travel and approximately £40 to cover administration.
Benefits: Food and accommodation.
Worldwide placements: *Europe* (Germany).

PROGRAM-BELL PRIVATE SCHOOL OF ENGLISH
61-701 Poznan
ul Fredry 7, pok.22-26
Poland

Tel: 00 48 61 536 972
Fax: 00 48 61 530 612
Contact: Kataryna Lisiewicz

Program-Bell Private School of English programme needs teachers of English to teach groups of 10–12 children and teenagers for three hours per day; and supervisors to organize activities and look after children at language camps. Duties include being responsible for the children 24 hours a day.

Total projects worldwide: 10–12
Total UK projects: 0
Starting months: July, August.
Time required: 2–9 weeks.
Age requirement: 22 plus.
Causes: Children, teaching/assisting (EFL).
Activities: Summer camps, teaching.
Vols under 26 placed each year: 12–14
When to apply: By 15 April.
Work alone/with others: Both.
Volunteers with disabilities: We are unable to place people with disabilities as a lot of movement is required.
Qualifications: TEFL preferred and experience of working with children.
Equipment/clothing: Summer clothing including a sweater; teaching materials.
Health requirements: Health certificate from family doctor required.
Costs: Travel costs.
Benefits: Full board and lodging. Wages by arrangement.
Interview details: Applicants are usually interviewed in London.
Certification: References provided.
Worldwide placements: *Europe* (Poland).

PROJECT 67 LTD
10 Hatton Garden
London
EC1N 8AH UK

Tel: +44 (0) 20 7831 7626
Fax: +44 (0) 20 7404 5588

Over the last 29 years, Project 67 has arranged working holidays for over 40,000 travellers to Israel. At our offices in Central London you can view our informative video and meet our teams of experts, or simply phone for advice. On arrival in Israel you are in the safe hands of our Tel Aviv office. They arrange your placement on Kibbutz or Moshav, offer additional information and can book onward travel to other countries. A

Kibbutz is a co-operative village with up to 2,000 permanent residents, where means of production is owned by the community and private property is limited to personal possessions. All income generated by the Kibbutz is ploughed back into the community. Work is varied and often includes farming, market gardening, light industry, cooking, cleaning and laundry. Most work takes place in the morning due to the daytime heat. Each kibbutz has a swimming pool, sports facilities and social activities (some may only be seasonal). The minimum period of work is eight weeks and prices are available on request. A Moshav is a farming community where the families work within a co-operative framework, with up to 200 families on each moshav, all members owning their own house and land. Working for a single family, the work tends to be agricultural and is more demanding than kibbutz work, though more money is paid to the volunteer. Hours of work are eight hours a day, six days a week. Accommodation generally sleep 2–3 in a room. Age restrictions are 18–32 Kibbutz, 20–35 Moshav. Volunteers with an offending background may be accepted depending on the nature/severity of the offence.

Total projects worldwide: Up to 300
Total UK projects: 0
Starting months: January–December.
Time required: 8–24 weeks.
Age requirement: 18–35
Causes: Work Camps – Seasonal, young people.
Activities: Agriculture/farming, building/construction, caring (general), catering, community work, driving, fundraising, gardening/horticulture, group work, manual work, outdoor skills, teaching, work camps – seasonal.
Vols under 26 placed each year: 2,000 plus.
When to apply: As soon as possible.
Work alone/with others: With others.
Volunteers with disabilities: Possible, providing disability does not restrict manual labour.
Qualifications: Nil.
Health requirements: Medical questionnaire completed and signed by GP.
Costs: From £259 – covers return flight and registration. Must also have insurance cover.
Benefits: Full board and lodging plus allowance.

Nationalities accepted: No restrictions providing volunteers are able to obtain a visa for Israel.
Interview details: Interviews may be required for Moshav work and these take place in our London office.
Certification: References available from placements.
Worldwide placements: *Asia* (Israel).

PROJECT 2001
RSA
9 John Adam Street
London
WC2N 6EZ UK

Tel: + 44 (0) 20 7930 5115
Contact: Julie Croft

Total projects worldwide: 1
Starting months: January–December.
Time required: 1–52 weeks (plus).
Age requirement: 12 plus.

PROJECT TRUST
Hebridean Centre
Isle of Coll
Argyll
PA78 6TE Scotland

Tel: + 44 (0) 1879 230 444
Fax: + 44 (0) 1879 230 357
e-mail: info@projecttrust.org.uk
Web: www.projecttrust.org.uk
Contact: The Director

Project Trust sends school leavers from the United Kingdom overseas as volunteers for twelve months. Since 1967 it has sent over 4,000 volunteers to 53 different countries. Project Trust aims to give young people a better understanding of the world outside Europe through living and working overseas. We offer a year's placement to young people who at the time of application are in full-time secondary education and are between 17 and 19 years at the time of going overseas. Projects fall into the following categories: English language assistants – schools, colleges and universities; care work – helping in children's homes, with the disabled or homeless; assisting in health and community development projects – in hospitals or with aid organizations; education projects – teaching or assisting in primary and secondary schools; outdoor activity projects – in Outward Bound Schools.

Total projects worldwide: Approximately 95.
Total UK projects: 0
Starting months: August, September.
Time required: 50–52 weeks.
Age requirement: 17–19
Causes: Children, conservation, disabled (learning and physical), health care/medical, poor/homeless, refugees, teaching/assisting (nursery, primary, secondary, mature, EFL), wildlife, young people.
Activities: Arts/crafts, building/construction, caring (general and residential), community work, computers, conservation skills, development issues, newsletter/journalism, outdoor skills, social work, sport, teaching.
Vols under 26 placed each year: 200
When to apply: 6–18 months before departure date.
Work alone/with others: Normally in pairs.
Qualifications: Applicants must be taking 3 A-levels, Highers or equivalent qualifications, EU passport holders only.
Health requirements: Fit and healthy.
Costs: £3,550 for 2002 school leavers. This covers travel, selection, training, insurance abroad, subsistence.
Benefits: Food/lodging/insurance, travel from UK to project and £40 per month pocket money. Medical insurance is provided by Project Trust. Residential 3-day courses provided free on return.
Training: One week's residential training – mainly run by returned volunteers.
Supervision: Local representative in every country – close relationship with a personal desk officer based in the UK who makes 1 visit a year.
Nationalities accepted: EU passport holders only.
Interview details: Interviews initially take place in volunteers' local area and then on a 5-day selection course on the Isle of Coll.
Certification: Certificate provided and reference on request.
Charity number: 306088
Worldwide placements: *Africa* (Botswana, Egypt, Lesotho, Malawi, Namibia, South Africa, Swaziland, Uganda, Zimbabwe); *Asia* (China, Hong Kong, Japan, Jordan, Korea (South), Malaysia, Pakistan, Sri Lanka, Taiwan, Vietnam); *Central America* (Cuba, Dominican Republic, Honduras); *South America* (Chile, Guyana, Paraguay, Peru).

PROYECTO AMBIENTAL TENERIFE
c/o 59 St Martins Lane
Covent Garden
London
WC2N 4JS UK

Tel: +44 (0) 20 7240 6604
Fax: +44 (0) 20 7240 5795
e-mail: edb@huron.ac.uk
Web: www.interbook.net/personal/delfinc
Contact: Ed Bentham

Proyecto Ambiental Tenerife provides low cost volunteer opportunities working at grass-roots level in the areas of conservation, community development and alternative technologies. Main project areas: 1. Tenerife: whale and dolphin conservation – 300 volunteers from across Europe staying for 2–6 weeks and working as naturalist guides on research projects, running educational workshops, training workshops, exhibitions, environmental awareness campaigns, public art projects and courses/conferences. Aim of project: to develop Tenerife as a model of responsible whale watching as an example to the world, as a major platform for raising public awareness of cetacean conservation issues, and as an alternative way of life to whale hunting communities. 2. Cuba: solar energy/organic farming/community development – 12 project areas with individuals able to participate in groups between June and October. Groups will finance the project that they participate in and will work on the project, learn about Cuba and have free time to explore. Project areas: solar energy, city farms, organic farming, natural history, music, fishing (community project), education, pollution and waste management, third age.
Application details from website or send 31p stamped self-addressed A4 envelope to London office.

Total projects worldwide: 10
Total UK projects: 0
Starting months: January–December.
Time required: 1–4 weeks.
Age requirement: 17 plus.
Causes: Animal welfare, children, conservation, environmental causes, heritage, human rights, poor/homeless, teaching/assisting, wildlife, young people.
Activities: Arts/crafts, building/construction, campaigning, community work, computers, conservation skills, development issues, DIY, fundraising, gardening/horticulture, group work, outdoor skills, scientific work, teaching, training.
Vols under 26 placed each year: 500–600
When to apply: All year.
Work alone/with others: In groups.
Volunteers with disabilities: Not possible.
Qualifications: Nil.
Equipment/clothing: Dependent on location – very simple lifestyle with lots of outdoor activities.
Health requirements: Nil.
Costs: £85 per week covers accommodation, half board and funds the projects.
Benefits: Projects are self-funding. We can recommend organizations that might give support.
Certification: Certificate or reference provided.
Charity number: 38394227
Worldwide placements: *Africa* (Ghana); *Asia* (Bangladesh, Nepal, Sri Lanka, Turkey, Vietnam); *Europe* (Spain, Turkey); *Central America* (Costa Rica, Cuba); *South America* (Brazil).

PSYCHIATRIC REHABILITATION ASSOCIATION
Bayford Mews
Bayford Street
London
SW2 2DE UK

Tel: +44 (0) 20 8985 3570
Fax: +44 (0) 20 8986 1334
Contact: Mirella Manni, Deputy Director

The Psychiatric Rehabilitation Association has pioneered a comprehensive range of rehabilitation and after-care projects for the mentally ill since the Association was formed at the time of the Mental Health Act. Current projects include day centres, industrial education units, evening groups, group home accommodation, an evening restaurant club, shopwork training experience and various other activities. PRA evening centres were set up in response to a need for discharged patients to expand their social lives and leisure activities in a relaxed and friendly climate. Social isolation is a frequent consequence of mental illness, and is not conducive to recovery. Meeting with others, sharing experiences, and making plans for the future is an important rehabilitative facility appreciated by those who participate in the groups. Those attending have a history of chronic schizophrenia or depressive illness. Hospitals, social services and GPs refer patients and ex-patients whom they consider would benefit from this support. There is also a substantial element of self-referral. The Association is currently seeking additional volunteers for the teams working in these groups and day centres. There are no specific qualifications required to be a volunteer, although you should be a caring person with common sense, stability, stamina and patience. You should have the ability to share creative ideas and an enthusiasm for the enjoyment afforded by life outside the institution. Availability of volunteers will vary. However, we would ask that volunteers honour any commitment made to the Association and, if this is not possible, that enough notice is given to allow alternative arrangements to be made. Regrettably, we are unable to refund expenses. However, we offer the opportunity to work directly with people sufffering and recovering from mental illness. Volunteers with an offending background may be accepted depending on the offence.

Total projects worldwide: 22
Total UK projects: 22
Starting months: January–December.
Time required: 42–52 weeks (plus).
Age requirement: 25 plus.
Causes: Disabled (learning), elderly people, health care/medical, holidays for disabled, unemployed.
Activities: Arts/crafts, campaigning, caring (general and day), catering, computers, cooking, development issues, DIY, fundraising, gardening/horticulture, group work, manual work, music, outdoor skills, sport, teaching, training, translating.
Vols under 26 placed each year: 15
When to apply: All year.
Work alone/with others: Both. Volunteer work is supervised by the Groupworker.
Volunteers with disabilities: Possible, but not all projects are suitable for wheelchairs.
Qualifications: Adequate spoken English essential. A-level or equivalent preferred but not essential.
Health requirements: Nil, but no contagious diseases.
Benefits: Reimbursement of costs incurred while taking part in a specific project.
Training: In-house theoretical training.
Interview details: Volunteers are interviewed

at head office and references are requested.
Certification: On completion of theory and practical work, a certificate is issued. References on request.
Charity number: 292944
UK placements: *England* (London).

Q

QUAKER VOLUNTARY ACTION (QVA)
Friends Meeting House
6 Mount Street
Manchester
M2 5NS UK

Tel: 00 161 860 6707
e-mail: qva@quakervolaction.freeserve.co.uk
Contact: Sue Dixon

Quakers are a religious movement who believe that there is something of God in everyone. Religion for them is the way you live your life. This is manifested in many social and political concerns. Since the 17th century Quakers have involved themselves in humanitarian causes, endeavouring to identify the causes of conflict, oppression and inequality. In place of conflict, we try to foster understanding between individuals and nations and a respect for life. You do not have to be a Quaker to be a QVA volunteer, in fact, most volunteers are not. QVA projects are for groups of about 8–15 volunteers from different backgrounds, nationalities, cultures and abilities living and working together on a project (for 1–4 weeks or longer) which aims to meet a community need. The location of projects varies each season. We accept volunteers with an offending background.

Total projects worldwide: Hundreds
Total UK projects: 10
Starting months: June, July, August, September.
Time required: 1–4 weeks.
Age requirement: 18 plus.
Causes: Children, conservation, disabled (learning and physical), elderly people, environmental causes, holidays for disabled, inner city problems, offenders/ex-offenders, poor/homeless, unemployed, work camps –

seasonal.
Activities: Arts/crafts, building/construction, caring (general, day and residential), community work, conservation skills, cooking, gardening/horticulture, group work, manual work, social work, theatre/drama, visiting/befriending, work camps – seasonal.
Vols under 26 placed each year: 140 of a total of 250.
When to apply: April–June for summer.
Work alone/with others: With others.
Volunteers with disabilities: Possible.
Qualifications: Dependent on project.
Equipment/clothing: Sleeping bag.
Health requirements: No.
Costs: Registration fee £24–£47 for UK projects, £43–£72 for projects abroad. Travel plus pocket money.
Benefits: Accommodation and food.
Interview details: No interview necessary.
Certification: Reference provided.
Charity number: 237698
Worldwide placements: *Africa* (Morocco, South Africa); *Asia* (Japan, Turkey); *Europe* (Belarus, Belgium, Bulgaria, Czech Republic, Denmark, Estonia, Finland, France, Germany, Greece, Hungary, Ireland, Italy, Netherlands, Poland, Slovakia, Spain, Turkey); *North America* (Canada, Greenland, Saint Pierre-Miquelon, USA); *Central America* (Mexico).
UK placements: *England* (throughout); *Scotland* (throughout); *Northern Ireland* (throughout); *Wales* (throughout).

QUEST OVERSEAS
32 Clapham Mansions
Nightingale Lane
London
SW4 9AQ UK

Tel: +44 (0) 20 8673 3313
Fax: +44 (0) 20 8673 7623
e-mail: emailus@questoverseas.com
Web: www.questoverseas.com
Contact: Michael Amphlet, Director

Quest Overseas is a small organization providing an all-encompassing three month experience in South America or Southern Africa. We are a young and dedicated team of travel addicts who are intent on making your gap year the most fulfilling experience you can hope for. We have been running successful projects and expeditions overseas for over five years for small teams of up to 16 gap year students with departures from December through to April and with a summer expedition leaving every July. Apply early to secure a place on the project of your choice. Three month expeditions to South America – combine learning or improving your Spanish for three weeks on a 'one-to-one' tuition course in Quito, Ecuador, with a month working on a community project (looking after children in Peru) or on one of two conservation projects (in the heart of the Amazon Rainforest or in 15,000 acres of prime Ecuadorian Cloud Forest) before completing a mind-blowing and challenging six-week expedition through Peru, Bolivia and Chile. Alternatively, in Southern Africa – spend six weeks working with local communities and game reserves in Swaziland, undertaking ecological surveys, trail building and conservation work before an adventurous six-week expedition through Mozambique, Botswana and Zambia. Only gap year students between school and university. Students receive a fund-raising pack and year-round advice and support in raising the necessary funds. Students need to be responsible, motivated and get on well with others whilst having a good understanding of the word fun. We are a Founder Member of the Year Out Group.

Total projects worldwide: 7
Total UK projects: 0
Starting months: January–April, July.
Time required: 13 weeks.
Age requirement: 18–20
Causes: Children, conservation, environmental causes, teaching/assisting (nursery, primary), wildlife.
Activities: Arts/crafts, building/construction, community work, conservation skills, forestry, group work, manual work, music, outdoor skills, sport, teaching.
Vols under 26 placed each year: 112
When to apply: 3–18 months prior to departure. Early application recommended.
Work alone/with others: With others.
Volunteers with disabilities: Not possible.
Qualifications: A-levels – confirmed place / deferred entry to university.
Equipment/clothing: Rucksack, sleeping bag, walking boots.
Health requirements: Volunteers must not suffer from any significant medical problems.
Costs: £3,350–£3,510 plus international

flights, insurance (full insurance is necessary provided by the volunteer but we give strongly recommended guidelines) and pocket money.
Benefits: The cost covers everything.
Training: A 3-day first aid and expedition training weekend is held 3 months prior to departure.
Supervision: Project leader accompanies volunteers for the entire 13 weeks and is joined for the 6-week expedition by a highly qualified experienced expedition leader.
Interview details: Selection interview in London or Cambridge, followed by preparation and expedition training weekend for successful applicants.
Certification: A reunion party is held annually. Reference provided.
Worldwide placements: *Africa* (Botswana, Mozambique, South Africa, Swaziland, Zambia); *South America* (Bolivia, Chile, Ecuador, Peru).

QUIT
Victory House
170 Tottenham Court Road
London
W1P 0HA UK

Tel: +44 (0) 20 7388 5775

Quit is the UK's only charity whose main aim is to offer practical help to people who want to stop smoking. We run a telephone helpline and offer down-to-earth advice about stopping smoking for good. Volunteers are required to help with administration and fund-raising.

Total projects worldwide: 1
Total UK projects: 1
Starting months: January–December.
Time required: 4–52 weeks (plus).
Age requirement: 18 plus.
Causes: Addicts/ex-addicts.
Activities: Administration, computers, fundraising.
Vols under 26 placed each year: 2–5
When to apply: All year.
Volunteers with disabilities: Possible.
Qualifications: Good administration and word processing skills.
Costs: Nil.
Benefits: Travel expenses reimbursed.
UK placements: *England* (London).

R

R. IRRIBARRIA
Centre Archeologique
20 rue de la Mairie
Muides sur Loire
41500 France

Tel: 00 33 2 54 87 03 33

Total projects worldwide: 1
Total UK projects: 0
Starting months: July–September.
Time required: 1–52 weeks.
Age requirement: 18 plus.
Causes: Archaeology.
Qualifications: Experience preferred.
Health requirements: Anti-tetanus vaccination.
Worldwide placements: *Europe* (France).

RADNORSHIRE WILDLIFE TRUST
Warwick House
High Street
Llandrindod Wells
Powys
LD1 6AG UK

Tel: +44 (0) 1597 823298
Fax: +44 (0) 1597 824812
Contact: The Director

Radnorshire Wildlife Trust is a member of the Wildlife Trusts, a national partnership of 47 county trusts. For more details of the Wildlife Trusts, see the entry under Cornwall Wildlife Trust.

Total projects worldwide: 1
Total UK projects: 1
Starting months: January–December.
Time required: 1–52 weeks (plus).
Age requirement: 12 plus.
Causes: Environmental Causes.
Work alone/with others: Both.
Qualifications: Nil.
Equipment/clothing: Casual work clothes, waterproofs, stout boots for outdoor work. Protective safety gear is provided.
Health requirements: Anti-tetanus innoculations recommended.
Costs: Nil.
Benefits: Out-of-pocket expenses. Volunteers are covered by the Trust's insurance.
UK placements: *Wales* (Powys).

RAINFOREST CONCERN
27 Lansdowne Crescent
London
W11 2NS UK

Tel: +44 (0) 20 7229 2093
Fax: +44 (0) 20 7221 4094
e-mail: rainforest@gn.apc.org
Web: www.rainforest.org.uk
Contact: Helen Brown

The main objective of Rainforest Concern is to protect threatened rainforests and the vast biodiversity of life they contain. We assist the communities living close to our projects by promoting health and environmental education programmes and encourage alternative forms of income generation to take the emphasis away from slash and burn agriculture. We also encourage research programmes to investigate the biological value of tropical forests and have a research station based at the reserve in Ecuador which caters for under- and post-graduate studies. We invite volunteers to become involved with our work either in London or on our projects in Ecuador and Costa Rica. In Ecuador we have a volunteer programme which runs all year round and involves an element of research or physical labour such as trail maintenance, reforestation and organic horticulture depending on the time of year and projects being undertaken at that time. The cost reduces to US$15 per day if you stay for six weeks or more. The other project where we regularly take on volunteers for short periods (as little as two weeks) is in Costa Rica. Here we have a coastal reserve with the chief purpose of protecting the leatherback turtle. The work includes protecting the beach from poachers, monitoring and tagging turtles and clearing trails. However this opportunity is only available for the egg-laying season between the last week March and the first week of July of each year.

Total projects worldwide: 6
Total UK projects: 0
Starting months: January–December.
Time required: 1–52 weeks (plus).
Age requirement: 18 plus.
Causes: Animal welfare, children, conservation, environmental causes, teaching (EFL), wildlife.
Activities: Conservation skills, forestry, gardening/horticulture, group work, international aid, manual work, outdoor skills, scientific work, translating.
Vols under 26 placed each year: 50 plus of a total of 100 plus.
When to apply: All year.
Work alone/with others: Both.
Volunteers with disabilities: Possible, but the work is very physical and there is limited supervision.
Qualifications: Nil but biologists and geologists are particularly welcome.
Equipment/clothing: Please contact us for the kit list.
Health requirements: Reasonable level of fitness required.
Costs: Ecuador US$8 per night, Costa Rica US$100 per week towards food and accommodation. Travel. Personal insurance must be taken out.
Benefits: Costs include all accommodation and 3 substantial meals a day.
Supervision: Minimal.
Interview details: Informal phone interview and CV.
Certification: The charity has a rainforest sponsorship programme which awards certificates.
Charity number: 1028947
Worldwide placements: *Asia* (Sri Lanka); *Central America* (Costa Rica); *South America* (Ecuador).

RALEIGH INTERNATIONAL
Raleigh House
27 Parsons Green Lane
London
SW6 4HZ UK

Tel: +44 (0) 20 7371 8585
Fax: +44 (0) 20 7371 5116
e-mail: info@raleigh.org.uk web
Web: www.raleigh.org.uk
Contact: Information Officer

Raleigh International is a charity which aims to develop young people through challenging community and environmental projects on expeditions around the world. Projects range from building health posts in the Mayan communities of Belize or school building with Save the Children Fund in Uganda to conservation work in the National Parks of Namibia or glacier studies in southern Chile. Adventurous projects are also undertaken, such as scuba diving on the coral reefs of Belize, trekking above the snow line in Chile, and kayaking on seas or lakes. Volunteers are then asked to fundraise £2,995 on behalf of Raleigh. Fundraising support is provided in the form of centrally organized national fundraising events, fundraising training and lots of advice and ideas. Contact our Information Officer for an information pack. Volunteers with an offending background are accepted.

Total projects worldwide: 10
Total UK projects: Varies
Starting months: January–October.
Time required: 10–14 weeks.
Age requirement: 17–25
Causes: Conservation, environmental causes, health care/medical, wildlife, young people.
Activities: Administration, building/construction, caring (general), community work, conservation skills, development issues, DIY, fundraising, group work, outdoor skills, scientific work.
Vols under 26 placed each year: 1,000
When to apply: All year – at least 6 months ahead.
Work alone/with others: With others.
Volunteers with disabilities: Possible – physical disabilities only.
Qualifications: Comprehend English, swim 200 m.
Equipment/clothing: Varies, depending on destination.
Health requirements: Individually assessed.
Costs: £2,995 (support network to help fundraise) assessment weekend £20.
Benefits: Development of communication, teamwork, leadership and problem solving skills. Increased self-confidence and adaptability.
Interview details: No formal interview. Applicants attend an assessment weekend where their teamwork skills, adaptability and motivation are put to the test.
Certification: Certificate or reference provided.
Charity number: 1047653
Worldwide placements: *Africa* (Ghana, Namibia); *Asia* (Brunei, China, Malaysia, Oman); *Central America* (Belize); *South America* (Chile).

RATHBONE
4th Floor, Churchgate House
56 Oxford Street
Manchester
M1 6EU UK

Tel: +44 (0) 161 236 5358
Fax: +44 (0) 161 238 6356
e-mail: advice@rathbone-ci.co.uk
Contact: Special education advice line

Rathbone works to improve opportunities for people who have limited access to services, many of whom have moderate learning difficulties and other special needs. Our clients are mainly young people and adults trying to achieve independence, either through first-time employment or through newly acquired living skills. Rathbone presents opportunity in the form of stepping stones which people can choose at different stages in their lives to suit their individual needs. We also have a special education advice line which takes on volunteers to man our freephone service. The line advises parents of children with special needs on educational issues and procedures. We also take on administration volunteers to aid with office work.

Total projects worldwide: 70
Total UK projects: Approximately 70.
Starting months: January–December.
Time required: 4–52 weeks (plus).
Age requirement: 16 plus.
Causes: Children, disabled (learning and physical), offenders/ex-offenders, teaching/assisting (EFL), young people.
Activities: Administration, caring (general and residential), community work, computers, counselling, fundraising, group work, marketing/publicity, teaching, training, visiting/befriending.
Vols under 26 placed each year: 3–4 of a total of 15–20.
When to apply: All year.
Work alone/with others: With others.
Volunteers with disabilities: Possible.
Qualifications: Nil.
Health requirements: Nil.
Costs: Nil.
Benefits: Travel expenses paid. We provide insurance.
Training: 5-day training on education law and listening skills.
Supervision: Volunteers are paired with a more experienced volunteer.
Interview details: Interviews take place in various locations.
Certification: Certificate or reference provided.
Charity number: 287120

UK placements: *England* (Berkshire, Buckinghamshire, Cumbria, Derbyshire, Hertfordshire, Leicestershire, London, Manchester, Merseyside, Northamptonshire, Nottinghamshire, Shropshire, Surrey, Tyne and Wear, Warwickshire, West Midlands, S. Yorkshire, W. Yorkshire); *Scotland* (E. Ayrshire, N. Ayrshire, S. Ayrshire, E. Dunbartonshire, W. Dunbartonshire, Edinburgh, Fife, Glasgow City, Highland, E. Lothian, W. Lothian, Perth and Kinross, Stirling); *Wales* (Bridgend, Caerphilly, Cardiff, Carmarthenshire, Monmouthshire, Newport, Pembrokeshire, Rhondda, Cynon, Taff, Torfaen, Vale of Glamorgan).

RED CROSS VOLUNTARY SOCIAL YEAR
Youth and Schools Unit
British Red Cross Society
9 Grosvenor Crescent
London
SW1X 7EJ UK

Tel: +44 (0) 20 7201 5179
Fax: +44 (0) 20 7235 7447
e-mail: ksheldon@redcross.org.uk
Contact: Karen Sheldon, International Volunteering Co-ordinator

German Red Cross Voluntary Social Year: Over the last 35 years, thousands of 16–27 year olds in Germany have taken part in a national volunteering scheme enabling them to 'give' a year's service in a social setting. The German Red Cross is one of the largest 'agents' of this scheme and is now looking for British young people to take part. You should be over 18 and interested in spending a year in Germany working in social settings such as hospitals, special schools and services for elderly or disabled people, as part of the 'Voluntary Social Year' scheme. Duties may include care services such as washing, dressing, toileting etc., medical services such as taking blood pressure, changing dressings etc. and social services such as befriending, playing games, reading or going for walks with patients/clients. Successful applicants will have the opportunity to: gain challenging and recognized work experience; experience a different country, culture and language; meet new people; discover new talents and skills. Volunteers with an offending background would need to be individually assessed (depending on project).

Total projects worldwide: Varies.

Total UK projects: 30
Starting months: August, September, October.
Time required: 26–52 weeks.
Age requirement: 18–26
Causes: Addicts/ex-addicts, Aids/HIV, children, disabled (learning and physical), elderly people, health care/medical, refugees, teaching/assisting (nursery).
Activities: Administration, arts/crafts, caring (general, day and residential), community work, cooking, first aid, group work, music, outdoor skills, social work, sport, teaching, training, visiting/befriending.
Vols under 26 placed each year: 1300 (mainly Germans).
When to apply: By mid-February at the latest.
Work alone/with others: With others.
Volunteers with disabilities: Possible, but wheelchair access may be a problem.
Qualifications: Working knowledge of German and an interest in care/social work.
Health requirements: Nil.
Costs: Nil, but personal effects insurance must be organized by the volunteer.
Benefits: Board, lodging, pocket money, health cover and insurance covered by the project.
Training: Written information is given. 1 day pre-departure training, 25 seminar days during year and in-house training in most project.
Supervision: Allocated contact person in host project, Red Cross group leader in region. Regular contact.
Nationalities accepted: No restrictions but easier if UK resident.
Interview details: Prospective volunteers are interviewed in London, Liverpool or Glasgow.
Certification: Certificate or reference provided.
Worldwide placements: *Europe* (Germany).
UK placements: *England* (Kent, Lancashire, Merseyside).

REFUGEE COUNCIL, THE
3 Bondway
London
SW8 1SJ UK

Tel: +44 (0) 20 7820 3112
Fax: +44 (0) 20 7820 3118
Contact: Philippa Stonebridge, Volunteer Co-ordinator

The Refugee Council is a charity which gives practical support to refugees and promotes their rights in Britain and abroad. It acts as a representative for many different agencies and organizations involved in refugee issues. Its members and associate members include international development agencies, refugee service providers, regional refugee organizations, as well as a large number of local refugee community groups. The practical help we give includes: advice and information to individual refugees and to other advisers, support to refugee community organizations, and training for jobs. We play a central role in representing refugees' interests to governments and policy-makers, and we provide a forum for organizations involved with refugees to meet and formulate policy and advocacy on refugee issues. The work of the Refugee Council is currently delivered through three divisions whose respective directors report to the Refugee Council's Chief Executive: The Operations Group; The Communications Group; The Support Services Group.

Total projects worldwide: 1
Total UK projects: 1
Starting months: January–December.
Time required: 12–52 weeks.
Age requirement: 18 plus.
Causes: Human Rights, poor/homeless, refugees, teaching (EFL).
Activities: Administration, campaigning, cooking, driving, research, teaching, translating, visiting/befriending.
Vols under 26 placed each year: 15 of a total of 100.
When to apply: As soon as possible.
Work alone/with others: Varies.
Volunteers with disabilities: Possible.
Qualifications: Some desirable but none essential.
Health requirements: Varies according to placement.
Costs: Travel and subsistence. We cover insurance.
Training: Half-day induction currently.
Supervision: Volunteers are assigned a supervisor. Amount of supervision depends on placement.
Certification: Reference provided.
Charity number: 1014576
UK placements: *England* (London).

REFUGEE TRUST
4 Dublin Road
Stillorgan
Co. Dublin
Ireland

Tel: 00 353 1 283 4256
Fax: 00 353 1 283 5155
e-mail: Refugee-Trust@Club.ie
Contact: Robert Donnelly, Programme Manager

Total projects worldwide: 1
Starting months: January–December.
Time required: 1–52 weeks (plus).
Age requirement: 12 plus.

RELIEF FUND FOR ROMANIA
PO Box 2122
London
W1A 2ZX UK

Tel: +44 (0) 20 7437 6978
Fax: +44 (0) 20 7494 1740
Contact: Edward Parry

Relief Fund for Romania: almost all volunteers are needed in UK charity shops, very few are sent to Romania. The minimum age depends on maturity assessed at interview. Volunteers with an offending background are considered.

Total projects worldwide: Varies.
Total UK projects: Varies.
Starting months: January–December.
Time required: 1–52 weeks.
Age requirement: 18 plus.
Causes: Children, poor/homeless.
Activities: International aid.
Interview details: Interviews take place at charity shops – usually SE England.
Charity number: 1046737
Worldwide placements: *Europe* (Romania).
UK placements: *England* (London).

RESULTS EDUCATION
13 Dormer Place
Leamington Spa
Warwickshire
CV32 5AA UK

Tel: +44 (0) 1926 435430
Fax: +44 (0) 1926 435110
e-mail: results@gn.apc.org
Contact: Sheila Davie, National Director

Results Education is an international campaign group working to end hunger and poverty. Our volunteers educate themselves on development issues and then act to educate the public, the media and specifically politicians as to the possibility of ending poverty within our lifetimes. By developing relationships with their MPs, MEPs and the media, our volunteers seek to generate the political will to end poverty throughout the world. Each month Results organizes a telephone conference call with a development expert providing our volunteers with ongoing access to up-to-date development information. This knowledge is then transformed into action by our 18 volunteer groups throughout the UK with the support of our head office in Leamington Spa. We are continually seeking to expand our work and take on new volunteers in all parts of the country. Similarly, volunteers living in the Leamington area may like to consider providing administrative assistance in our head office. Joining Results provides a framework within which you can channel your concerns for those living in poverty in a focused and positive way.

Total projects worldwide: 20
Total UK projects: 20
Starting months: January–December.
Time required: 16–52 weeks (plus).
Age requirement: 18–25
Causes: Aids/HIV, children, health care/medical, human rights, poor/homeless, young people.
Activities: Campaigning, development issues, fundraising, group work, international aid.
Vols under 26 placed each year: Approximately 6 of a total of 70–100.
When to apply: All year.
Work alone/with others: With others.
Volunteers with disabilities: Possible.
Qualifications: Nil.
Health requirements: Nil.
Training: Coaching and skills training will be given to enable the volunteer to develop the necessary skills to fulfil the tasks and responsibilities. Reading material also provided.
Supervision: By Results staff.
Nationalities accepted: No restrictions but must be official residents or able to reside in the UK.
Interview details: Prospective volunteers are interviewed in person at the National Office.
Certification: Certificate or reference provided.

Worldwide placements: *Asia* (Japan); *Australasia* (Australia); *Europe* (Germany); *North America* (Canada, USA); *Central America* (Mexico).
UK placements: *England* (Berkshire, Buckinghamshire, Cheshire, Dorset, Essex, London, Manchester, Nottinghamshire, E. Sussex, Warwickshire, West Midlands, N. Yorkshire, S. Yorkshire, W. Yorkshire); *Scotland* (Edinburgh, E. Lothian, W. Lothian, Scottish Borders); *Wales* (Blaenau Gwent).

RICHMOND FELLOWSHIP
80 Holloway Road
London
N7 8JG UK

Tel: +44 (0) 20 7697 3310
e-mail: Anthony.Campbell@richmondfellowship.org.uk
Web: www.richmondfellowship.org.uk
Contact: Anthony Campbell, Personnel Department

The Richmond Fellowship has worked in the field of mental health since 1959. We run more than 150 community-based projects in the UK working with people of all ages. The projects include intensive rehabilitation programmes, supported housing projects, group homes and workshops for people with mental health problems, schizophrenia, addiction and emotional problems. Work in the projects focuses on helping residents to regain personal stability, the ability to make good relationships and to find and keep a job. We also run our own college and provide a comprehensive range of training options for our own staff and for people involved in mental health work. Volunteers are needed to work within some of the projects, supervised by project staff, assisting the residents and helping in the day-to-day running of the house. As well as assisting with the basic necessities of life, you may also become involved in activities such as gardening, cooking, art, music, drama and sport. Whilst we recognize the important role played by our volunteers, not all of our projects are able to accept volunteers.

Total projects worldwide: 150
Total UK projects: 150
Starting months: January–December.
Time required: 1–52 weeks (plus).
Age requirement: 18 plus.

Causes: Addicts/ex-addicts, disabled (learning).
Activities: Arts/crafts, caring (day), community work, cooking, driving, fundraising, gardening/horticulture, group work, music, sport, theatre/drama, training.
Vols under 26 placed each year: 100
When to apply: All year.
Benefits: Reasonable expenses reimbursed. We provide insurance cover under a public liability policy. There is no personal accident insurance cover.
Training: On-the-job training is provided plus in-house training courses.
Supervision: Supervision meeting every 2 weeks.
Charity number: 200453
UK placements: *England* (Bedfordshire, Berkshire, Bristol, Cambridgeshire, Channel Islands, Cheshire, Cornwall, Co. Durham, Devon, Dorset, Essex, Herefordshire, Hertfordshire, Isle of Man, Kent, Lancashire, Leicestershire, Lincolnshire, London, Manchester, Merseyside, Northamptonshire, Northumberland, Nottinghamshire, Oxfordshire, Rutland, Staffordshire, Suffolk, Surrey, E. Sussex, W. Sussex, Tyne and Wear, Warwickshire, West Midlands, Wiltshire, Worcestershire, E. Yorkshire, N. Yorkshire, S. Yorkshire, W. Yorkshire).

RIDING FOR THE DISABLED ASSOCIATION

Avenue R
National Agricultural Centre
Kenilworth
Warwickshire
CV8 2LY UK

Tel: +44 (0) 24 7669 6510
Fax: +44 (0) 24 7669 6532
Contact: Mrs Val David

Voluntary work may be available at the ten Riding for the Disabled Association centres around Britain in the counties indicated though accommodation is limited. There are also about 16 holidays per year from 4–7 days in duration which need volunteers. Positions are quickly filled so apply early.

Total projects worldwide: 15 holidays. 12 centres.
Total UK projects: 15 holidays. 12 centres.
Starting months: January–December.
Time required: 1–52 weeks.
Age requirement: 17 plus.

Causes: Children, disabled (learning and physical), young people.
Activities: Caring (general and day), outdoor skills, sport, summer camps.
When to apply: As early as possible.
Work alone/with others: With others.
Volunteers with disabilities: Not possible.
Qualifications: Experience with disabled and horses. First aid etc. an advantage.
Equipment/clothing: Outdoor clothes.
Health requirements: Nil.
Costs: Holidays: travel costs only (but not to and from the venue). Centres: accommodation (except Conwy and Derbyshire) and sometimes contribution to board.
Benefits: Board and lodging on holidays.
UK placements: *England* (Berkshire, Derbyshire, Essex, Gloucestershire, Herefordshire, Kent, Surrey, Warwickshire, W. Yorkshire); *Scotland* (E. Ayrshire, N. Ayrshire, S. Ayrshire, Glasgow City, N. Lanarkshire, S. Lanarkshire, E. Renfrewshire); *Wales* (Conwy).

RIGHT HAND TRUST

Gelligason
Llanfair Caereinion
Powys
SY21 9HE Wales

Tel: +44 (0) 1938 810215
Fax: +44 (0) 1938 810215
e-mail: RightHandTrust@compuserve.com
Web: www.righthandtrust.org.uk
Contact: Mark Wright, Director

The Right Hand Trust offers placements in Africa and sometimes in the Windward Islands as guests of the local Anglican Church. The purpose of the placements is to enable the volunteers to integrate into the local community as much as possible. In doing this you will benefit from a cross-cultural experience in a Christian environment. Activities in the placement are usually centred around teaching at a local school although the volunteers in recent years have been involved in a wide range of other activities with the church and community as their focus. The volunteers have a lifestyle as close to that of the host community as possible. Applicants are welcome from every Christian denomination and no particular level of commitment is expected, though communicant status in a home church is encouraged. This away year enables volunteers to grow in the faith. The Trust publishes a news sheet – the *Bush Telegraph* – available to all enquirers (please send an A4 SAE – 44p). The view of the great majority of those who have participated in the project is that they have had a life-enriching, perhaps life-changing experience which they will value for a long time. Most believe that they have received more than they could give. There is an opportunity to meet returned volunteers and to find out more about us. Write for details!

Total projects worldwide: 8
Total UK projects: 0
Starting months: January.
Time required: 32 weeks.
Age requirement: 18–30
Causes: Aids/HIV, children, health care/medical, poor/homeless, refugees, teaching/assisting (nursery, primary, secondary, EFL), unemployed, young people.
Activities: Administration, building/construction, community work, DIY, library/resource centres, music, religion, social work, sport, teaching, technical skills, theatre/drama, training, visiting/befriending.
Vols under 26 placed each year: 60
When to apply: Before 1 July (late entrants possible until 20 August).
Work alone/with others: In pairs.
Volunteers with disabilities: Not possible.
Qualifications: A-levels or vocational training (low-tech). Christian commitment.
Equipment/clothing: Nothing expensive.
Health requirements: No known medical problems. Full range of preventative injections.
Costs: Approximately £2,500 for flights, accommodation, insurance, training etc. plus cost of food (£1–£2 per day).
Benefits: Free accommodation (basic). EMA Policy via Banner provided by the Trust as part of the package.
Training: A 5-day induction in July, a placements weekend in September, and a week-long cross-cultural training course in December or early January. This is followed by a short acclimatization course in January upon arrival abroad.
Supervision: Local representative and host diocese.
Interview details: Interviews take place at our Headquarters in Powys during a Glimpse of Africa weekend – normally the last weekend of each month.

Certification: Written reference on request.
Charity number: 1014934
Worldwide placements: *Africa* (Gambia, Kenya, Malawi, Namibia, Saint Helena, Swaziland, Uganda, Zambia, Zimbabwe); *Central America* (Grenada, Saint Vincent/Grenadines).

RITCHIE RUSSELL HOUSE YOUNG DISABLED UNIT

The Churchill Hospital
Headington,
Oxford
OX3 7LJ UK

Tel: +44 (0) 1865 225482
Fax: +44 (0) 1865 225484
Contact: Mrs Barbara Martin, Voluntary Services Organizer

The Ritchie Russell House Young Disabled Unit cares for disabled people aged between 16 and 65. Ritchie Russell House is a purpose-built unit in the grounds of the Churchill Hospital. It is for the care and welfare of physically disabled people and those with a degenerative illness. The aims of the unit are to encourage self-sufficiency and to foster interests among the clients; to forge links between them, their relatives and friends, volunteers, community workers and other clients; to work together for social interaction and life-enhancing activities, so as to improve their opportunities and welfare.

Total projects worldwide: 1
Total UK projects: 1
Starting months: January–December.
Time required: 1–52 weeks.
Age requirement: 17 plus.
Causes: Disabled (physical), health care/medical, holidays for disabled.
Activities: Caring (general and day), computers, cooking, fundraising, gardening/horticulture.
Vols under 26 placed each year: 1 or 2 of a total of 40 plus.
When to apply: All year.
Work alone/with others: Both.
Volunteers with disabilities: Not possible.
Qualifications: Excellent communication skills, initiative, sensitivity to caring needs.
Equipment/clothing: Flat shoes. Aprons provided if needed.
Health requirements: Usually none but medical details must be submitted.
Costs: Find own accommodation and possible

contribution if carers go on holiday.
Benefits: Rewarding and satisfying. We have employer's liability insurance.
Training: Induction is provided.
Supervision: Voluntary services organizer available 9–12, five days a week.
Interview details: Interviews take place at Ritchie Russell House, Oxford.
Certification: Written reference on request.
Charity number: 278109
UK placements: *England* (Oxfordshire).

ROSSY CENTRE FOR HUMAN RIGHTS AND DEVELOPMENT

Divine Abosso House
Ikot-Ekpene Road, Km1, PO Box 287
Ohokobe Noume, Ibeku
Umuahia
Abia State
Nigeria

Contact: Mrs Rosemary Chi Okpara, President

Rossy Centre for Human Rights and Development has as its aims: 1. to promote community project initiative; 2. to facilitate the advancement and development of the community through voluntary efforts; 3. to spread to the general public knowledge about voluntary efforts and to devise workable strategies to achieve our aims; 4. to make the community a better place to live; 5. to empower the community youths, women and development union towards the development of their community through their voluntary efforts; 6. to educate the people that hospitals, schools, market stalls, water, electricity and other social amenities can be provided through their voluntary efforts; 7. to teach that life and property of the community can be protected by forming youthful vigilante groups to take care of the security aspect of the people. We work with community youth organizations, a service corp for young graduates, town union (ruling body of every community), schools and training centres.

Total projects worldwide: 6
Total UK projects: 0
Starting months: February.
Time required: 39–52 weeks.
Age requirement: 18 plus.
Causes: Aids/HIV, children, disabled (learning and physical), elderly people, health care/medical, human rights, offenders/ex-offenders, poor/homeless, refugees, unemployed, young people.
Activities: Community work, computers, counselling, development issues, first aid, library/resource centres, manual work, music, newsletter/journalism, outdoor skills, religion, research, social work, technical skills, training.
Vols under 26 placed each year: 253 of a total of 370.
When to apply: Before the third week of January.
Work alone/with others: With others.
Volunteers with disabilities: Not possible.
Qualifications: No qualifications necessary but any skilled volunteers very welcome.
Equipment/clothing: Yes – further details from the organization.
Health requirements: There may be some restrictions.
Costs: Membership fee £2. Travel costs £1,689. Subsistence £250.
Benefits: Board and lodging.
Training: We train unskilled volunteers and brief all as necessary about the projects and how best to do them.
Supervision: Each project has a co-ordinator and supervisor who supervise volunteers and ensure the quality of the job.
Nationalities accepted: No restrictions providing volunteers have required travelling/residential documents.
Interview details: Interviews take place at our headquarters in Nigeria.
Charity number: 022325
Worldwide placements: *Africa* (Nigeria).

ROYAL BRITISH LEGION

38 Duxbury Road
Leicester
LE5 3LQ UK

Tel: +44 (0) 116 274 3171

Total projects worldwide: 1
Total UK projects: 1
Starting months: January–December.
Time required: 1–52 weeks.
Age requirement: 14 plus.

ROYAL NATIONAL INSTITUTE FOR THE BLIND

224 Great Portland Street
London
W1N 6AA UK

Tel: +44 (0) 20 7388 1266

Contact: Katie Maeda

Total projects worldwide: 1
Total UK projects: 1
Starting months: January–December.
Time required: 1–52 weeks.
Age requirement: 14 plus.

ROYAL SOCIETY FOR THE PROTECTION OF BIRDS
Volunteer Unit
The Lodge
Sandy
Bedfordshire
SG19 2DL UK

Tel: +44 (0) 1767 680551
Fax: +44 (0) 1767 692365
e-mail: volunteers@rspb.org.uk
Web: www.rspb.org.uk
Contact: Voluntary Wardening Co-ordinator

RSPB volunteers interested in natural history and ornithology are needed for a variety of conservation-related tasks on bird reserves throughout the UK.

Total projects worldwide: 32
Total UK projects: 32
Starting months: January–December.
Time required: 1–52 weeks.
Age requirement: 16 plus.
Causes: Conservation, environmental causes, wildlife.
Activities: Agriculture/farming, building/construction, conservation skills, gardening/horticulture, manual work, outdoor skills, scientific work.
Vols under 26 placed each year: 650 of a total of 800.
When to apply: All year – write for a pack.
Work alone/with others: With others.
Volunteers with disabilities: Possible.
Qualifications: If volunteers are from outside the UK, minimum age is 18.
Equipment/clothing: Waterproof clothing, wellington boots, old clothes, sleeping bags.
Health requirements: Nil.
Costs: Food, pocket money and travel to the reserve. Insurance for personal possessions is responsibility of volunteer.
Benefits: Accommodation.
Supervision: By reserve staff.
Interview details: For long-term placements only.
Certification: Certificate or reference provided for specific requests.

UK placements: *England* (Bedfordshire, Berkshire, Bristol, Buckinghamshire, Cambridgeshire, Channel Islands, Cheshire, Cornwall, Co. Durham, Derbyshire, Devon, Essex, Gloucestershire, Hampshire, Herefordshire, Hertfordshire, Isle of Man, Isle of Wight, Leicestershire, Lincolnshire, London, Manchester, Merseyside, Northamptonshire, Northumberland, Nottinghamshire, Oxfordshire, Rutland, Shropshire, Somerset, Surrey, E. Sussex, W. Sussex, Tyne and Wear, Warwickshire, West Midlands, Wiltshire, Worcestershire, E. Yorkshire, N. Yorkshire, S. Yorkshire); *Scotland* (Argyll and Bute, E. Ayrshire, N. Ayrshire, S. Ayrshire, Clackmannanshire, Dumfries and Galloway, E. Dunbartonshire, W. Dunbartonshire, Falkirk, Fife, Inverclyde, N. Lanarkshire, S. Lanarkshire, E. Lothian, W. Lothian, Midlothian, Renfrewshire, E. Renfrewshire, Scottish Borders, Stirling, Western Isles); *Wales* (Bridgend, Caerphilly, Cardiff, Carmarthenshire, Conwy, Merthyr Tydfil, Monmouthshire, Neath Port Talbot, Newport, Rhondda, Cynon, Taff, Swansea, Torfaen, Vale of Glamorgan).

RURAL ORGANISATION FOR SOCIAL ELEVATION (ROSE)
Sonargon
P O Kanda
Uttar Pradesh
263631 India

Tel: 00 91 5963 22131
Fax: 00 91 5963 22131
e-mail: hansi@origin8.demon.co.uk
Web: www.origin8.demon.co.uk/hansi.html
Contact: Mr Jeevan Lal Verma

ROSE began life in 1981, fuelled by the determination of a local man, Jeevan Lal Verma, to try to tackle the many problems he saw being experienced in his local community. Starting initially with a school, to provide education to the children of the more deprived families in the area, the organization soon expanded, developing its Ghandian aims of promoting equality for men and women of differing castes in order to raise the quality of life for all. In 1988 the organization began to receive volunteers who have provided their skills and services and in return benefited from the cultural experience of immersion in rural Indian life. Volunteers are treated as family members and help in the fields and with various household tasks as well as teaching English every morning to the children who now come to school at Mr Verma's house. Project work is continually being devised and is implemented when funds allow. Volunteer involvement in planning and management is welcome from those skilled in relevant areas. Currently ROSE is seeking to complete repairs to local homes damaged in an earthquake in March 1999; continue with the construction of an earthquake-proof house for a local family; repair/replace a water pipeline supplying the local hospital; expand and develop the tree nursery (to counter de-forestation in the area); and to complete the construction of an outhouse for the cattle. However, each year the monsoon brings with it no shortage of project work in an area prone to landslides at this time of year. As a non-governmental organization (NGO) the key problem has always been funding and volunteer work can involve fundraising whilst staying here (by letter) and some volunteers have chosen to continue this work after returning home. The main challenge for young volunteers is the journey from Delhi to ROSE. Please contact Hansi, PO Box 521, Hove, E. Sussex BN3 6HY for more information.

Total projects worldwide: 1
Total UK projects: 0
Starting months: January–December.
Time required: 2–26 weeks.
Age requirement: 16 plus.
Causes: Children, conservation, environmental causes, health care/medical, poor/homeless, teaching/assisting (nursery, primary, EFL), work camps – seasonal.
Activities: Administration, agriculture/farming, arts/crafts, building/construction, campaigning, catering, community work, conservation skills, cooking, development issues, DIY, first aid, forestry, fundraising, gardening/horticulture, group work, international aid, manual work, marketing/publicity, newsletter/journalism, outdoor skills, social work, teaching, work camps – seasonal.
Vols under 26 placed each year: 30–35 of a total of 35–40.
When to apply: All year.
Work alone/with others: Sometimes with others depending when other young volunteers arrive.
Volunteers with disabilities: Very unlikely –

definite problems for people with impaired mobility.
Qualifications: Spoken English essential. Some Hindi helpful. Flexibility and resilient sense of humour!.
Equipment/clothing: Clothes must cover upper arms and legs. Sturdy footwear and sandals. Warm clothes for winter. Sleeping bag, insect repellent, torch, candles, 2 padlocks, hat or head scarf, first aid kit, umbrella (useful for sun and rain).
Health requirements: Must be fit and in good health.
Costs: Registration: R700 (£10), board and lodging R210 (£3) rupees per day. Volunteers should provide their own general travel insurance.
Training: Help and advice are always available from Mr Verma and care is taken to allow volunteers time to adjust.
Supervision: Mr Verma is always on hand. Any tasks or project work undertaken will be under his supervision.
Interview details: There is no interview but a current CV required.
Certification: Reference on request.
Charity number: 1098
Worldwide placements: *Asia* (India).

S

SALISBURY CHOICES PROJECT
Greencroft House
42–46 Salt Lane
Salisbury
Wiltshire
SP1 1EJ UK

Contact: Sue Harper

Total projects worldwide: 1
Total UK projects: 1
Starting months: January–December.
Time required: 1–52 weeks (plus).
Age requirement: 12 plus.

SALMON YOUTH CENTRE, THE
43 Old Jamaica Road
Bermondsey
London
SE16 4TE UK

Tel: +44 (0) 20 7237 3788
Fax: +44 (0) 20 7252 0285
Contact: Pete Devlin, Senior Youth Worker

The Salmon Youth Centre exists to meet the physical, social, intellectual, emotional and spiritual needs of the young people in Bermondsey. Our hope is that the young people will recognize and respond to the Christian faith, which is the basis of all the work, and which we believe is the ultimate answer to their needs.

Total projects worldwide: 1
Total UK projects: 1
Starting months: January–December, except September.
Time required: 1–52 weeks.
Age requirement: 12 plus.
Causes: Children, young people.
Activities: Administration, community work, marketing/publicity, religion, sport, summer camps.
Vols under 26 placed each year: 15
When to apply: All year.
Work alone/with others: With others.
Volunteers with disabilities: Not possible.
Qualifications: Nil.
Equipment/clothing: Casual clothes.
Health requirements: Nil.
Costs: Nil.
Benefits: Full-time volunteers are given board, lodging and some travel costs.
Interview details: Interviews take place at the Centre.
Certification: Certificate or reference provided.
Charity number: 278979
UK placements: *England* (London).

SALVATION ARMY
101 Newington Causeway
London
SE1 6BN UK

Tel: +44 (0) 20 7367 4944
Fax: +44 (0) 20 7367 4711
Contact: Captain Colin Johnson

There is no voluntary work at the Salvation Army Headquarters and prospective volunteers should contact their local hostel or branch through the telephone directory. We have our own officers and trained resettlement workers so volunteers would only be involved in helping by doing the mundane tasks.

Total projects worldwide: 1

Total UK projects: 1
Starting months: January–December.
Time required: 1–52 weeks.
Age requirement: 18 plus.
Causes: Addicts/ex-addicts, inner city problems, offenders/ex-offenders, poor/homeless, refugees.
Activities: Administration, catering, cooking, religion, social work, technical skills.
Vols under 26 placed each year: 17 of a total of 100.
When to apply: All year.
Work alone/with others: With others.
Volunteers with disabilities: Possible.
Qualifications: Nil.
Health requirements: Nil.
Costs: Nil. We provide insurance.
Training: Many courses run in-house.
Supervision: By trained Salvation Army officers.
UK placements: *England* (throughout); *Scotland* (throughout); *Northern Ireland* (throughout); *Wales* (throughout).

SAMARITANS, THE
10 The Grove
Slough
Berkshire
SL1 1QP UK

Tel: +44 (0) 1753 216500
Fax: +44 (0) 1753 819004
e-mail: admin@samaritans.org.uk
Web: www.samaritans.org.uk
Contact: Julie Alexander

The Samaritans provide confidential emotional support to anyone who is in despair or suicidal 24 hours a day, 365 days a year throughout the UK and the Republic of Ireland. Most contacts are by telephone but people can talk to us face-to-face or correspond by letter or e-mail. The 19,600 people who provide this service are all volunteers and all of the 203 branches are independent charities, responsible for raising their revenue and capital costs. The Samaritans depend on public donations for over 95% of our income. Funds are raised in the branches from public collections, events, companies and charitable trusts. A growing number of branches run charity shops. The Samaritans take volunteers from all walks of life and are non-judgemental. Contact your local Samaritan branch for an application form.

Total projects worldwide: 203 branches
Total UK projects: 203 branches
Starting months: January–December.
Time required: 2–52 weeks.
Age requirement: 18 plus.
Causes: Addicts/ex-addicts, Aids/HIV, disabled (learning and physical), elderly people, health care/medical, human rights, inner city problems, offenders/ex-offenders, poor/homeless, refugees, unemployed, young people.
Activities: Administration, fundraising, marketing/publicity, training.
Vols under 26 placed each year: Unlimited.
When to apply: All year.
Work alone/with others: Others.
Volunteers with disabilities: Possible.
Qualifications: Over 17 years old.
Health requirements: Nil.
Costs: Nil.
Benefits: Expenses will be paid.
Certification: Reference provided.
Charity number: 219432
Worldwide placements: *Europe* (Ireland).
UK placements: *England* (throughout); *Scotland* (throughout); *Northern Ireland* (throughout); *Wales* (throughout).

SAMASEVAYA

National Secretariat
Anuradhapura Road
Talawa
Sri Lanka

Tel: 00 94 25 76266
Fax: 00 94 25 76266
e-mail: samasevaya@dayanet.lk
Contact: Samson Jayasinghe, National Secretary

Samasevaya works for peace through development; believes in the concept of settling disputes and conflicts by mutual understanding. It tolerates views of all parties involved; believes that all humanity is one brotherhood of man. It is against all types of injustice, hatred, violence whether it be national, communal, racial, religious or political; believes in the concept of self-reliance and in the total development of the individual. All individuals must collectively make decisions, plan act and execute on a just basis. It believes in the concept that all humanity by its own strength, labour and hard work should unite to achieve progress towards self-sustainability. Samasevaya helps the poorest in their best interests in the humblest form to attain both social and economic goals. It believes in the rights of women and that all men and women have a very important role in the transformation of the social economic position of women. We provide loans, making them socially mobilized, and also with scientific knowledge in agriculture and other income generating activities. It believes and takes an active interest in the environment. It believes that the environment has to be bequeathed to future generations intact. Present activities are: 1. Educational Programme on Self-reliance; 2. Educational Programme on National Harmony; 3. Samasevaya Children's Foundation; 4. Educational Programme on the Environment; 5. Upliftment of Women. The work camps provide the opportunity for young people of various nationalities and communities to live together for a short period. Volunteers with offending backgrounds are accepted.

Total projects worldwide: 17
Total UK projects: 0
Starting months: January–December.
Time required: 1–48 weeks.
Age requirement: 16 plus.
Causes: Children, conservation, environmental causes, human rights, poor/homeless, refugees, teaching/assisting (primary, secondary, mature, EFL), unemployed, work camps – seasonal, young people.
Activities: Agriculture/farming, community work, conservation skills, development issues, first aid, forestry, fundraising, gardening/horticulture, group work, library/resource centres, manual work, marketing/publicity, music, scientific work, social work, sport, summer camps, teaching, training, work camps – seasonal.
Vols under 26 placed each year: 20 of a total of 25.
When to apply: All year.
Work alone/with others: Both.
Volunteers with disabilities: Possible.
Qualifications: Usually nil.
Health requirements: Nil.
Costs: Everything except accommodation. Food costs approximately US$3 per day. Volunteers are advised to take out all their own insurance.
Benefits: Free accommodation.
Supervision: We have an informal flexible

arrangement. Volunteers are very free and work with one of the officers. The National Executive Committee is responsible for volunteers.

Interview details: No interview necessary.
Certification: Certificate or reference provided if required.
Charity number: S 371
Worldwide placements: *Asia* (Sri Lanka).

SAO CAMBODIA

Bawtry Hall
Bawtry
Doncaster
DN10 6JH UK
Tel: +44 (0) 1302 714004
Fax: +44 (0) 1302 710027
e-mail: saouk@gn.apc.org
Web: www.sao-cambodia.org
Contact: John Heard, International Director

SAO Cambodia is an interdenominational Christian mission and development agency. We are active solely in Cambodia. We were originally established to raise prayer and support for the Cambodian church and nation. Our object is to promote the Christian faith and relieve poverty and distress. This is currently being accomplished through fish farming and craft businesses, with other practical projects being planned. Discreet church-related ministries are undertaken where this is appropriate and acceptable. All our members and volunteers must have active commitment to the Christian faith. They would be commissioned to join us by their home churches. Because of the nature of the work our members and volunteers usually need relevant skills and experience. Cambodia is a very poor developing country, only very slowly recovering from the ravages of the Khmer Rouge 'Killing Fields' of the 1970s when about two million people died, a quarter of the population.

Total projects worldwide: 2 or 3
Total UK projects: 0
Starting months: January–December.
Time required: 2–52 weeks (plus).
Age requirement: 23 plus.
Causes: Children, disabled (physical), health care/medical, poor/homeless, teaching/assisting (EFL), young people.
Activities: Accountancy, administration, agriculture/farming, arts/crafts, building/construction, community work, computers, development issues, DIY, driving, manual work, music, outdoor skills, religion, social work, sport, teaching, technical skills, training, visiting/befriending.
Vols under 26 placed each year: 1 or 2
When to apply: All year.
Work alone/with others: It varies.
Volunteers with disabilities: Not possible.
Qualifications: Nil but the more qualifications the better.
Health requirements: Robust health.
Costs: All costs are met by volunteers.
Benefits: We have a pooled support system. Medical and personal accident insurance is arranged by SAO.
Training: UK orientation, field orientation, language training when appropriate.
Supervision: Full management and pastoral supervision given.
Interview details: Preliminary exploratory interviews take place in Gravesend, Kent or at Bawtry, Yorkshire. Further interviews are normally in London.
Certification: Both field and UK Management debriefing.
Certificate or reference provided on request.
Charity number: 293382
Worldwide placements: *Asia* (Cambodia).

SCHULGEMEINSCHAFT BRACHENREUTHE

Heimsonderschule und Hof Brachenreuthe
D-88662 Uberlingen
Germany

Tel: 00 49 7551 80070
Fax: 00 49 7551 800750
e-mail: Brachenreuthe@t-online.de
Contact: Fiona M. Zahn

Schulgemeinschaft Brachenreuthe is a residential school for mentally handicapped children. It is beautifully situated in the country near Uberlingen, a medium-sized town on Lake Constance (Bodensee) in southern Germany. Brachenreuthe is in itself comparable with a little village, with ten houses, a therapy building, a community hall and also a large garden and farm. The 90 children in our care are aged from 4 to 17 years old and have varied and often severe handicaps. We place special emphasis on catering for the needs of autistic children. Our work is based on the teachings of Rudolf Steiner, known as anthroposophy. Roughly ten children of different ages live in each house together with the permanent staff and their families, teachers, therapists, trainees (on the Camphill Seminar course) and helpers forming a house community. The children live in small groups of two to four with one or two helpers looking after them. Every child goes to school or nursery. Most children also undergo individual therapies according to their specific needs. The house communities are each run autonomously by their members of staff and they try to live as a large family. Meals are cooked and eaten in each of the houses. Most of the cleaning etc. is done by the staff who live there, so that the children are surrounded by a family atmosphere rather than that of an institution. The Christian festivals and cultural activities play an integral part in the life of Brachenreuthe. A clear-cut structured daily, weekly and yearly rhythm plays an important role in our life. As we live together with the children, whose nurture and development is our main concern, this is not a 9–5 job with set working hours, but a rewarding, if demanding, way of life. Staff have one day a week off. There are five weeks staff holidays in the year. Some of the children always remain in residential care even during the school holidays.

Total projects worldwide: 1
Total UK projects: 0
Starting months: January–December.
Time required: 26–52 weeks.
Age requirement: 19 plus.
Causes: Children, disabled (learning), young people.
Activities: Caring (general and residential).
Vols under 26 placed each year: 15
When to apply: All year.
Work alone/with others: With others.
Volunteers with disabilities: Possible.
Qualifications: Basic knowledge of German.
Health requirements: Free from TB and infectious diseases.
Costs: Travel expenses.
Benefits: Board, lodging (shared room) plus insurance plus DM350 per month pocket money. We cover social insurance (health, unemployment and pension) and insurance against accidents while working.
Training: House parents show volunteers the ropes and there is also a weekly course in curative education for volunteers.
Supervision: Volunteers work in a team headed by the house parents and, ultimately,

the directors.
Nationalities accepted: No restrictions but non-EU members may have difficulty in obtaining residency/work permit.
Interview details: No interview necessary.
Certification: We willingly supply volunteers with a reference on request.
Worldwide placements: *Europe* (Germany).

SCOPE – LONDON AND SOUTH EAST REGION
Shackleton Square
Priestley Way
Crawley
West Sussex
RH10 2GZ UK
Contact: The Director

SCOPE – London and South East Region exists to provide support and services for people with cerebral palsy and their families. Cerebral palsy (CP) is damage to parts of the brain which results in physical impairment affecting movement. It is not a disease or an illness. It is most commonly the result of failure of a part of the brain to develop, either before birth or in early childhood. We originally started in life in 1952 as The National Spastics Society. Scope is about opening doors. It is about enabling people with CP to gain access to the opportunities that everyone needs to make the best use of their abilities. Our education services provide training and support for children and adults with CP, and also for parents and helpers. Our living options services provide accommodation, personal support, training, opportunities for further education, personal development and advocacy for adults with CP and other physical and learning disabilities. We run residential and small group homes, supported independent living schemes and day and respite services. Scope is also involved in a Supported Employment Programme which not only provides information for people with CP but also employs people through the scheme. Scope also has two national sources of information for people with CP. There is a freephone Cerebral Palsy Helpline that is open seven days a week and there is a library and information unit, which responds to both telephone and written enquiries. There are 35 local affiliated groups in this area, some of whom provide services and support groups. Volunteers with an offending background may be accepted for some work.

Total projects worldwide: Many.
Total UK projects: Many.
Starting months: January–October.
Time required: 2–52 weeks (plus).
Age requirement: 15 plus.
Causes: Children, Disabled (learning and physical), work camps – seasonal.
Activities: Administration, agriculture/farming, caring (day and residential), catering, community work, computers, driving, fundraising, gardening/horticulture, library/resource centres, newsletter/journalism, outdoor skills, work camps – seasonal.
Vols under 26 placed each year: Hundreds.
When to apply: All year.
Work alone/with others: Usually with others.
Volunteers with disabilities: Possible.
Qualifications: Nil.
Health requirements: Nil, unless it affects the individual's ability to perform the agreed tasks.
Costs: Nil.
Benefits: Out-of-pocket expenses – normally 30p per mile (own car) or bus/rail fares. Lunch allowance.
Interview details: Interviews take place at project location.
Certification: Reference on request.
UK placements: *England* (Kent, London, Surrey, E. Sussex, W. Sussex).

SCOPE – MIDLANDS REGION

Shapland House
Clews Road
Oakenshaw
Redditch
B98 7ST UK

Tel: +44 (0) 1527 550909
Fax: +44 (0) 1527 550808

SCOPE – Midlands Region: for more details of Scope, see Scope – London and South East Region, above.

Total projects worldwide: Many.
Total UK projects: Many.
Starting months: January–October.
Time required: 2–52 weeks (plus).
Age requirement: 15 plus.
Causes: Children, disabled (learning and physical), work camps – seasonal.
Activities: Administration, agriculture/farming, caring (general, day and residential), community work, computers, driving,

fundraising, gardening/horticulture, library/resource centres, newsletter/journalism, outdoor skills, work camps – seasonal.
Vols under 26 placed each year: Hundreds.
When to apply: All year.
Work alone/with others: Usually with others.
Volunteers with disabilities: Possible.
Qualifications: Nil.
Health requirements: Nil, unless it affects the individual's ability to perform the agreed tasks.
Costs: Nil.
Benefits: Out-of-pocket expenses – normally 30p per mile (own car) or bus/rail fares. Lunch allowance.
Interview details: Interviews take place at project location.
Certification: Reference on request.
UK placements: *England* (Buckinghamshire, Derbyshire, Herefordshire, Leicestershire, Nottinghamshire, Oxfordshire, Shropshire, Staffordshire, Warwickshire, West Midlands, Worcestershire).

SCOPE – THE NORTH REGION

8 Brindley Way
41 Business Park North
Wakefield
WF2 OXJ UK

Tel: +44 (0) 1924 828980
Fax: +44 (0) 1924 829037

SCOPE – The North Region. For more details of Scope, see Scope – London and South East Region, above.

Total projects worldwide: Many.
Total UK projects: Many.
Starting months: January–October.
Time required: 2–52 weeks (plus).
Age requirement: 15 plus.
Causes: Children, disabled (learning and physical), work camps – seasonal.
Activities: Administration, agriculture/farming, caring (general, day and residential), community work, computers, driving, fundraising, gardening/horticulture, library/resource centres, newsletter/journalism, outdoor skills, work camps – seasonal.
Vols under 26 placed each year: Hundreds.
When to apply: All year.
Work alone/with others: Usually with others.
Volunteers with disabilities: Possible.
Qualifications: Nil.

Health requirements: Nil, unless it affects the individual's ability to perform the agreed tasks.
Costs: Nil.
Benefits: Out-of-pocket expenses – normally 30p per mile (own car) or bus/rail fares. Lunch allowance.
Interview details: Interviews take place at project location.
Certification: Reference if requested.
UK placements: *England* (Cheshire, Co. Durham, Cumbria, Lancashire, Manchester, Merseyside, Northumberland, Tyne and Wear, N. Yorkshire, S. Yorkshire, W. Yorkshire).

SCOPE – WEST REGION
Olympus House
Brittania Road
Patchway
Bristol
BS34 5TA UK

Tel: +44 (0) 117 906 6333
Contact: Mike Shepherd

SCOPE – West Region: for more details of Scope, see Scope – London and South East Region, above.

Total projects worldwide: Many.
Total UK projects: Many.
Starting months: January–October.
Time required: 2–52 weeks (plus).
Age requirement: 15 plus.
Causes: Children, disabled (learning and physical), work camps – seasonal.
Activities: Administration, agriculture/farming, caring (general, day and residential), community work, computers, driving, fundraising, gardening/horticulture, library/resource centres, newsletter/journalism, outdoor skills, work camps – seasonal.
Vols under 26 placed each year: Hundreds.
When to apply: All year.
Work alone/with others: Usually with others.
Volunteers with disabilities: Possible.
Qualifications: Nil.
Health requirements: Nil, unless it affects the individual's ability to perform the agreed tasks.
Costs: Nil.
Benefits: Out-of-pocket expenses – normally 30p per mile (own car) or bus/rail fares. Lunch allowance.
Interview details: Interviews take place at

project location.
Certification: Reference on request.
Charity number: 208231
UK placements: *England* (Cornwall, Devon, Dorset, Gloucestershire, Somerset, Wiltshire).

SCOTQUEST – YMCA SCOTLAND
11 Rutland Street
Edinburgh
EH1 2AE Scotland

Tel: +44 (0) 131 228 1464
Fax: +44 (0) 131 228 5462
Contact: Nick Lansdell

Scotquest is an innovative project which provides opportunities for outdoor adventure and the creative arts for young people at risk. A mobile expedition unit provides flexibility together with use of YMCA Scotland's outdoor unit at Bonskeid House, Pitlochry, and is available to all agencies working with people in the 'at risk' category. Outdoor adventure and the creative arts are used to enable the learning, growth and personal development of the young people.

Total projects worldwide: 1
Total UK projects: 1
Starting months: January–December.
Time required: 1–52 weeks.
Age requirement: 18–35
Causes: Addicts/Ex-addicts, inner city problems, offenders/ex-offenders, poor/homeless, unemployed, young people.
Activities: Arts/crafts, community work, development issues, music, outdoor skills, sport, theatre/drama, training.
Vols under 26 placed each year: 3
When to apply: All year.
Work alone/with others: With others.
Volunteers with disabilities: Possible.
Qualifications: Nil – outdoor qualifications useful.
Equipment/clothing: Foul weather gear useful for outdoor activities.
Health requirements: Nil.
Costs: Nil.
Benefits: Travel and all expenses.
Interview details: Applicants are interviewed in Edinburgh.
Charity number: 32970
UK placements: *Scotland* (throughout, except for Orkney Islands, Shetland Islands and Western Isles).

SCOTTISH CHURCHES WORLD EXCHANGE
St Colm's International House
23 Inverleith Terrace
Edinburgh
EH3 5NS Scotland

Tel: +44 (0) 131 315 4444
Fax: +44 (0) 131 225 8258
Contact: The Rev. Robert S. Anderson, Director

Scottish Churches World Exchange sends 40 volunteers each year to work in the developing world and assists congregations/ groups planning their own short-term visits/ exchanges. Placements are arranged through partner churches and agencies of the Church of Scotland, the Catholic Church, the Scottish Episcopal Church and the United Reformed Church. We take volunteers of all denominations, experiences and of all ages. Volunteers have worked in Guatemala, El Salvador, Romania, Palestine/Israel, Pakistan, India, South Africa, Kenya, Malawi, Thailand and Lebanon. You would work in health, education, development, church/community and administration according to your skills and experiences. Volunteers are expected to raise money for the World Exchange Travel Fund. This pays for travel/insurance, preparation courses before departure, debriefing weekend upon return and contributes to costs while the volunteer is overseas. (Other overseas costs are borne by the host organization overseas.) In our volunteer placements we hope there is something of value for you, for the host and for the Scottish churches. The time as a volunteer should be a time of growth in terms of both maturity and faith.

Total projects worldwide: 50
Total UK projects: 0
Starting months: January, July, August, September.
Time required: 52 weeks (plus).
Age requirement: 18 plus.
Causes: Children, disabled (learning and physical), elderly people, health care/medical, human rights, poor/homeless, refugees, teaching/assisting (nursery, primary, secondary, mature, EFL), young people.
Activities: Accountancy, administration, agriculture/farming, building/construction, caring (general), community work, computers, cooking, driving, forestry, fundraising, international aid, manual work, marketing/publicity, music, religion, social work, teaching, technical skills, translating, visiting/befriending.
Vols under 26 placed each year: 40
When to apply: By end of February.
Work alone/with others: With others.
Volunteers with disabilities: Possible.
Qualifications: Member of Scottish Church or United Reformed Church, UK.
Health requirements: Have to pass medical – depending on location.
Costs: Raising £2,000 towards cost.
Benefits: Food, accommodation and pocket money are provided by the host and SCWE. Training and resettlement programme with a small resettlement grant. Weekend debriefing programme for returned volunteers.
Training: SCWE provides preparation courses which are held twice a year before departure.
Supervision: We provide support while the volunteers are overseas.
Interview details: Interviews take place in Edinburgh.
Certification: Certificates or references on request.
Charity number: SCO20905
Worldwide placements: *Africa* (Kenya, Malawi, South Africa); *Asia* (India, Israel, Lebanon, Pakistan, Thailand); *Europe* (Romania); *Central America* (El Salvador, Guatemala).

SCOTTISH COMMUNITY FOUNDATION (THE CALEDONIAN CHALLENGE)
27 Palmerston Place
Edinburgh
EH12 5AP Scotland

Tel: +44 (0) 131 225 9810
Fax: +44 (0) 131 225 9818
e-mail: toby@scottishcomfound.org.uk
Web: www.scottishcomfound.org.uk
Contact: Toby Trustram Eve

The Caledonian Challenge is the most gruelling annual fundraising event of its kind. Teams of four, each representing companies from throughout the UK and beyond, all walk 54 miles of the West Highland Way over a 24 hour period in June. The event is the largest of its kind in the Highlands, raising a large amount of money for the support of local charities throughout Scotland and is set to become Scotland's largest charitable fundraising event. Volunteers are needed as support and back-up to help administer this annual event. Every sort of administrative activity is needed, both before the event and during the 24 hours. Volunteers with an offending background will be assessed individually.

Total projects worldwide: 1
Total UK projects: 1
Starting months: June.
Time required: 1–4 weeks.
Age requirement: 16 plus.
Causes: Addicts/ex-addicts, Aids/HIV, animal welfare, children, conservation, disabled (learning and physical), elderly people, environmental causes, health care/medical, heritage, inner city problems, poor/homeless, teaching/assisting, unemployed, wildlife, young people.
Activities: Administration, conservation skills, first aid, fundraising, group work, manual work, marketing/publicity, outdoor skills.
Vols under 26 placed each year: 20 of a total of 200.
When to apply: All year.
Work alone/with others: With others.
Volunteers with disabilities: We are unable to place people with disabilities as the terrain is not suitable.
Qualifications: Nil.
Equipment/clothing: Waterproofs and sun protection.
Health requirements: Nil.
Costs: Travel, accommodation and board.
Benefits: During the event weekend, accommodation and board are provided. Full insurance is provided by the event organizers.
Training: Varied training on location.
Supervision: Full supervision at all times.
Interview details: Interviews take place in Edinburgh.
Certification: Certificate or reference provided.
UK placements: *Scotland* (Argyll and Bute, E. Dunbartonshire, Highland, Stirling).

SCOTTISH WILDLIFE TRUST
Cramond House
Kirk Cramond
Cramond Glebe Road
Edinburgh
EH4 6NS UK

Tel: +44 (0) 131 312 7765
Fax: +44 (0) 131 312 8705

Contact: Jo Hobbett, Education Development Officer

Scottish Wildlife Trust is Scotland's leading voluntary body for nature conservation which works to protect, enhance and promote enjoyment of all aspects of our natural heritage. One important area of our work is environmental training in which we have a long and successful history. We are an approved SCOTVEC centre and involved in the development and implementation of new qualifications for working in environmental conservation. We own and manage over 100 wildlife reserves from the Borders to Orkney. We protect 7,000 wildlife sites. We own large areas of public greenspace in Cumbernauld and Irvine enjoyed by local people and benefiting wildlife. Among our major campaigns, our Peat Project has already led to more gardeners choosing peat-free alternatives which save peat bogs. Volunteers are also needed for environmental education projects and writing management plans for reserves. Volunteers with offending backgrounds may be accepted but checks would be made when working with children.

Total projects worldwide: Lots!
Total UK projects: Lots!
Starting months: January–December.
Time required: 1–52 weeks (plus).
Age requirement: 16 plus.
Causes: Children, conservation, environmental causes, teaching/assisting (nursery, primary, secondary, mature), wildlife.
Activities: Administration, arts/crafts, campaigning, computers, conservation skills, development issues, driving, fundraising, group work, library/resource centres, manual work, newsletter/journalism, outdoor skills, research, teaching, translating.
When to apply: All year.
Work alone/with others: Either.
Volunteers with disabilities: Possible.
Qualifications: Driving licence sometimes required. Other skills depend on type of project.
Equipment/clothing: No special clothing. Equipment provided.
Health requirements: Dependent on the project.
Costs: Nil.
Benefits: Travel. On some projects training courses are paid for. Volunteers are covered

by the Trust's insurance.
Interview details: Interviews are usually conducted – depending on the project.
Certification: Certificate or reference provided.
Charity number: SC 005792
UK placements: *Scotland* (throughout).

SCOUT ASSOCIATION, THE
Gilwell Park
Bury Road
Chingford
London
E4 7QN UK

Tel: +44 (0) 20 8433 7100
Fax: +44 (0) 20 8433 7103
e-mail: development@scout.org.uk
Web: www.scoutbase.org.uk
Contact: Field Development Service

The aim of The Scout Association is to promote the development of young people in achieving their full physical, intellectual, social, and spiritual potentials, as individuals, as responsible citizens and as members of their local, national and international communities. The method of achieving the aim of The Scout Association is by providing an enjoyable and attractive scheme of progressive training, based on the Scout Promise and Law, guided by adult leadership. The Scout Association is the country's largest co-educational youth movement, with over 640,000 voluntary members in the UK. A major priority of The Scout Association's aim and method is youth involvement. Children and young people take part in the progressive training scheme from 6–20 years. From 18 years young people can become leaders, who enable an attractive range of activities for young people which are run by young people. Youth involvement also influences the decision making process of The Scout Association, as more young people join committees which form policies affecting the future of The Scout Association in the UK. A core part of the progressive training scheme in the UK is community involvement, with young people donating their time to help others. This is an integral part of all progressive awards of The Scout Association. On an international level, Scouts are encouraged to learn more about the world environment. More than 13,000 Scouts travel abroad each year, and many complete development projects whilst overseas. These are often run in partnership with Scout Associations from different countries. All projects are planned by young people, under the guidance of leaders. Decisions on travel, accommodation, finance, etc. are taken by young people. Volunteers with an offending background may be accepted – each case is assessed individually.

Total projects worldwide: 10,000
Total UK projects: 10,000
Starting months: January–December.
Time required: 1–52 weeks (plus).
Age requirement: 16 plus.
Causes: Children, conservation, disabled (learning and physical), environmental causes, inner city problems, unemployed, work camps – seasonal, young people.
Activities: Accountancy, arts/crafts, catering, community work, computers, conservation skills, cooking, counselling, development issues, driving, first aid, fundraising, group work, international aid, marketing/publicity, music, newsletter/journalism, outdoor skills, religion, sport, summer camps, theatre/drama, training, work camps – seasonal.
Vols under 26 placed each year: 30,000
When to apply: All year.
Work alone/with others: With others.
Volunteers with disabilities: Possible.
Health requirements: Good health appropriate to activity/role undertaken.
Costs: Dependent on level/degree of involvement and activities involved in.
Benefits: Arrangements can be made to pay costs. Scout Insurance Services (own company) handle all types of insurances.
Interview details: Interviews take place locally.
Certification: Certificate or reference on request.
Charity number: 306101
Worldwide placements: *Africa* (Gambia, Ghana, Kenya, Malawi, Morocco, Namibia, Saint Helena, Seychelles, Sierra Leone, South Africa, Tanzania, Uganda, Zimbabwe); *Asia* (India, Japan, Mongolia, Nepal, Sri Lanka, Turkey); *Australasia* (Australia, Kiribati, Papua New Guinea, Solomon Islands, Tonga, Tuvalu, Vanuatu); *Europe* (Albania, Belarus, Bosnia-Herzegovina, Bulgaria, Croatia, Czech Republic, Estonia, Hungary, Latvia, Lithuania, Macedonia, Poland, Romania, Russia, Slovakia, Slovenia, Turkey, Ukraine, Yugoslavia); *North America* (USA); *Central*

America (Anguilla, Antigua and Barbuda, Belize, Bermuda, Cayman Islands, Costa Rica, Dominica, Mexico, Montserrat, Saint Lucia, Saint Vincent/Grenadines, Trinidad and Tobago, Turks and Caicos Islands, Virgin Islands); *South America* (Argentina, Brazil, Chile, Falkland Islands).
UK placements: *England* (throughout); *Scotland* (throughout); *Northern Ireland* (throughout); *Wales* (throughout).

SCRIPTURE UNION HOLIDAYS
207–209 Queensway
Bletchley
Milton Keynes
Buckinghamshire
MK2 2EB UK

Tel: +44 (0) 1908 856117
Fax: +44 (0) 1908 856+44 (0) 12
e-mail: holidays@scriptureunion.org.uk
Web: www.scripture.org.uk
Contact: Holidays Administrator

Scripture Union needs activity holiday voluntary instructors to work throughout the summer to help organize Christian activity holidays for young people and carry out residential work. Volunteers work on sites for up to ten days in Britain and overseas. You will work with, befriend and take responsibility for a small group of young people or children, present the Gospel in varying ways – stories, drama, games etc. – take part in teaching, outdoor activities, arts and crafts, sports and special interests with the children and young people, join in daily prayer and worship within a team, work hard with others on the team, prepare material to use with the children and young people, have fun and much, much, more. Volunteers with an offending background may be accepted depending on offence.

Total projects worldwide: 109
Total UK projects: 107
Starting months: July, August.
Time required: 1–52 weeks.
Age requirement: 18 plus.
Causes: Children, disabled (learning and physical), holidays for disabled, teaching/assisting (nursery, primary, secondary), young people.
Activities: Accountancy, administration, arts/crafts, catering, computers, cooking, counselling, first aid, group work, music, outdoor skills, religion, sport, summer

camps, teaching.
Vols under 26 placed each year: 1,500 of a total of 5,000.
When to apply: All year. Summer deadline is 1 July.
Work alone/with others: With others.
Volunteers with disabilities: Possible.
Qualifications: Christian plus qualifications in outdoor activities, sports, First aid, life saving, disabled. Fluent English.
Equipment/clothing: Sleeping bag or sheets and towels.
Health requirements: Good general health.
Costs: Contribution of £25–£160 depending on location (some grants available).
Benefits: Youth work training provided, working in a Christian team environment. We hold public liability insurance.
Training: Day/weekend orientation course.
Supervision: By a team leader.
Charity number: 213422
Worldwide placements: *Africa* (South Africa, Uganda, Zimbabwe); *Australasia* (Australia); *Europe* (Hungary, Switzerland, Ukraine).
UK placements: *England* (Berkshire, Cheshire, Cumbria, Devon, Gloucestershire, Hampshire, Herefordshire, Hertfordshire, Kent, Merseyside, Norfolk, Northamptonshire, Shropshire, Somerset, Staffordshire, Suffolk, W. Sussex, Tyne and Wear, Wiltshire, Worcestershire, N. Yorkshire); *Wales* (Powys, Swansea).

SEA CADET CORPS
202 Lambeth Road
London
SE1 7JF UK

Tel: +44 (0) 20 7928 8978
Fax: +44 (0) 20 7928 8914
Contact: Administration Department

Young people with relevant qualifications may be needed to instruct for Sea Cadet Corps. Prospective volunteers should contact their local branch.

Total projects worldwide: 400
Total UK projects: 400
Starting months: January–December.
Time required: 8–52 weeks.
Age requirement: 18 plus.
Causes: Young people.
Activities: Outdoor skills, sport.
When to apply: All year.
Work alone/with others: With others.
Volunteers with disabilities: Not possible.

Qualifications: Instructor level qualifications, RYA, mountaineering, diving, engineering or similar.
Health requirements: Nil.
Costs: Nil.
UK placements: *England* (throughout); *Scotland* (throughout); *Northern Ireland* (throughout); *Wales* (throughout).

SEA RANGER ASSOCIATION
HQTS Lord Amory
Dollar Bay
631 Manchester Road
London
E14 9NU UK

Tel: +44 (0) 20 7987 1757
Contact: Barbara Macdonald

Total projects worldwide: 1
Total UK projects: 1
Starting months: January–December.
Time required: 1–52 weeks.
Age requirement: 14 plus.

SEDEPAC
Apartado Postal 27-054
06760 Mexico DF
Mexico

Fax: 00 52 5 584 3985
e-mail: sedepac@laneta.apc.org
Contact: Ricardo Olvera

Sedepac is a Mexican non-government organization which needs volunteers to work in remote rural villages in Mexico improving and constructing schools or other community facilities and to help with agricultural projects. In turn, the volunteer learns about local culture, women's issues, local politics and indigenous life in Mexico. All Sedepac placements are in indigenous areas. Participants fly to Mexico City, arriving on or before 30 June. Orientation takes place in Zilitla, a ten-hour bus ride from Mexico City. The programme ends in mid-August. Applicants fill out an application form in Spanish, which is evaluated by Sedepac. Other British young volunteers have participated in the past. Contact Sedepac via e-mail for testimonials from past participants.

Total projects worldwide: 1
Total UK projects: 0
Starting months: June–August.
Time required: 7–52 weeks (plus).
Age requirement: 18–26

Causes: Children, conservation, environmental causes, heritage, human rights, poor/homeless, teaching/assisting (nursery, primary, secondary, mature), work camps – seasonal, young people.
Activities: Agriculture/farming, arts/crafts, building/construction, community work, conservation skills, cooking, development issues, forestry, gardening/horticulture, group work, international aid, manual work, music, outdoor skills, social work, sport, teaching, visiting/befriending, work camps – seasonal.
Vols under 26 placed each year: 15 from Europe of a total of 40.
When to apply: Before 1 April.
Work alone/with others: In groups of 10–12.
Volunteers with disabilities: We are unable to place people with disabilities as the atmosphere is rural and rugged.
Qualifications: Fluent spoken Spanish.
Health requirements: Necessary innoculations, otherwise none.
Costs: All travel expenses plus approximately US$450 to cover board, lodging, insurance plus orientation.
Benefits: Limited scholarships available some years.
Nationalities accepted: Each year we accept approximately 10 Europeans/British, 15 North Americans and 15 youths from Mexico and other Latin American countries.
Certification: Certificate or reference provided.
Worldwide placements: *Central America* (Mexico).

SEEABILITY
56–66 Highlands Road
Leatherhead
Surrey
KT22 8NR UK

Tel: +44 (0) 1372 373086
Fax: +44 (0) 1372 370143
Contact: Volunteer Services Co-ordinator

Seeability is the trading name of the Royal School for the Blind. Volunteers are needed to help realize the potential of people who are blind and have other disabilities. Volunteers with an offending background may be accepted depending on the nature of the offence. Each application is judged individually.

Total projects worldwide: 6

Total UK projects: 6
Starting months: January–December.
Time required: 1–52 weeks.
Age requirement: 18 plus.
Causes: Disabled (learning and physical), elderly people, holidays for disabled, young people.
Activities: Administration, arts/crafts, caring (general and day), computers, DIY, driving, fundraising, gardening/horticulture, group work, library/resource centres, marketing/publicity, music, sport, theatre/drama, visiting/befriending.
Vols under 26 placed each year: 10
When to apply: All year.
Work alone/with others: Mixed.
Volunteers with disabilities: Possible.
Qualifications: Oral and written English must be good.
Health requirements: Generally good health. Volunteers must inform us of any ill health.
Costs: Cost of travel between home and Seeability.
Benefits: Out-of-pocket expenses plus lunch where appropriate.
Interview details: Interviews take place at the Leatherhead campus.
Certification: Reference on request.
Charity number: 255913
UK placements: *England* (Devon, Hampshire, Somerset, Surrey, E. Sussex).

SEND A COW
Unit 3 plus 4, Priston Mill
Priston
Bath
Somerset
BA2 9EQ UK

Tel: +44 (0) 1225 447041
Fax: +44 (0) 1225 317627
e-mail: sacuk@sendacow-stockaid.org uk
Web: www.sendacow.stockaid.org.uk
Contact: Kevin Gullick, UK Co-ordinator

Send a Cow works with people in East Africa to overcome poverty and malnutrition in a sustainable manner through the development of animal production and through groups capable of managing their own future. Work began in Uganda in 1988 and is now spreading to Kenya, Ethiopia and Rwanda. Poor households, primarily women, are trained to manage dairy cows and other types of livestock which are procured locally. Training is also given in organic farming and other aspects of sustainable agriculture. The first-born female offspring is passed on as a gift to another needy family identified by the local groups. Send a Cow aims to build the capacity of these local groups to manage projects. The charity was started by dairy farmers motivated by Christian concern and many are still members of the Board of Trustees (11 members). There are five staff in Uganda and three in the UK. The majority of funds are by individual and group donations, with some support from DFID and trusts.

Total projects worldwide: 15
Total UK projects: 7
Starting months: January–December.
Time required: 4–52 weeks.
Age requirement: 18 plus.
Causes: Animal welfare, children, conservation, elderly people, environmental causes, human rights, poor/homeless, young people.
Activities: Accountancy, administration, agriculture/farming, campaigning, computers, conservation skills, development issues, fundraising, gardening/horticulture, group work, international aid, marketing/publicity, newsletter/journalism, research.
Vols under 26 placed each year: 1 of a total of 12.
When to apply: All year.
Volunteers with disabilities: Most of our projects are located in rural areas which may be considered unsuitable.
Qualifications: Post A-level or university level preferred if possible. Must hold a driving licence.
Health requirements: Must be reasonably fit and provide medical details.
Costs: Volunteer to meet all costs including insurance. When overseas we have a £10m liability insurance cover.
Benefits: Good accommodation.
Supervision: Provided by the UK Co-ordinator.
Certification: Certificate or reference provided.
Charity number: 299717
Worldwide placements: *Africa* (Ethiopia, Kenya, Uganda).
UK placements: *England* (Somerset).

SENSE
The National Deafblind and Rubella Association
11–13 Clifton Terrace

London
N4 3SR UK

Tel: +44 (0) 20 7272 7774
Fax: +44 (0) 20 7272 6012
e-mail: sgranger@globalnet.co.uk
Web: www.sense.org.uk
Contact: Sue Granger, Volunteer
Co-ordinator

Sense holidays are for people of varying ages, from the very young to older people all of whom have a sensory impairment and other difficulties. This means people who are: deafblind (hearing and visually impaired); visually impaired with one or more additional disability; hearing impaired with one or more additional disability. Additional disabilities may include, for example, a learning disability or cerebral palsy. A number of Sense holidaymakers use wheelchairs or may need help with mobility. Sense has organized holidays since 1984. The aim is simply for holidaymakers to have fun in a supportive environment, while at the same time gaining new experiences and meeting new people. Importantly, our holidays also give parents and carers a chance to have a well-earned break. Holidays generally last for about a week and take place through the summer months, mostly during the school break. Every holiday is managed by one (or more) experienced, skilled holiday leaders, backed up by a team of volunteers. The ratio of volunteers to holidaymakers is generally at least one to one and usually more. As a group everyone is on holiday together – although Sense holidays may not be as relaxing as holidays you may have experienced in the past!

Total projects worldwide: 1
Total UK projects: 1
Starting months: July, August.
Time required: 1–2 weeks.
Age requirement: 18 plus.
Causes: Children, disabled (learning and physical), holidays for disabled.
Activities: Caring (general, day and residential), Group Work, Summer Camps.
Vols under 26 placed each year: Approximately 50 of a total of 200.
When to apply: Before April (preferably).
Work alone/with others: With others.
Volunteers with disabilities: We have volunteers with a range of disabilities.
Qualifications: Nil.

Health requirements: Nil.
Costs: Cash for personal needs.
Benefits: Accommodation, food and transport.
Training: Information day to attend.
Charity number: 289868
UK placements: *England* (Berkshire, Bristol, Buckinghamshire, Cambridgeshire, Channel Islands, Cheshire, Cornwall, Cumbria, Derbyshire, Devon, Dorset, Essex, Gloucestershire, Herefordshire, Hertfordshire, Isle of Man, Kent, Lancashire, Leicestershire, Lincolnshire, Manchester, Merseyside, Norfolk, Northamptonshire, Nottinghamshire, Oxfordshire, Rutland, Shropshire, Somerset, Staffordshire, Suffolk, Surrey, E. Sussex, W. Sussex, Tyne and Wear, Warwickshire, West Midlands, Wiltshire, Worcestershire, E. Yorkshire, N. Yorkshire, S. Yorkshire, W. Yorkshire); *Northern Ireland* (Fermanagh); *Wales* (Carmarthenshire, Conwy, Pembrokeshire).

SENSE SCOTLAND

5th Floor, 45 Finnieston Street
Clydeway Centre
Glasgow
G3 8JU Scotland

Tel: +44 (0) 141 564 2444
Fax: +44 (0) 141 564 2443
e-mail: personnel@sensescotland.org.uk
Contact: Margaret Watson, Personnel Officer

Sense Scotland is part of Sense, the National Deafblind and Rubella Association. We provide a number of direct services to people who, at birth or from an early age, have impairments to both sight and hearing whether or not they have other disabilities; impairment to sight with other disabilities; and impairment to hearing with other disabilities. The services we provide include respite, day care, holidays, community homes, information and support for families. Our volunteers enable Sense Scotland to provide our clients with services such as playdays and holidays. They can also provide support to our staff or could help out in one of our shops or on a collecting day. Volunteers also help during our summer playscheme, which runs Monday to Friday during the school holidays. Playdays are one-afternoon activity sessions during the school holidays where volunteers help with painting, baking, music playing or visits to the park.

The holidays are 7 or 8 day breaks where volunteers are paired with a client whom they befriend for that week, assisting with care needs of bathing, dressing, feeding as well as other activities such as visits to the zoo, swimming, canoeing etc. Volunteers with an offending background may be accepted, depending on the offence.

Total projects worldwide: 21
Total UK projects: 21
Starting months: January–December.
Time required: 1–52 weeks.
Age requirement: 16 plus.
Causes: Children, disabled (learning and physical), health care/medical, holidays for disabled, young people.
Activities: Arts/crafts, caring (general and residential), cooking, driving, first aid, fundraising, group work, outdoor skills, summer camps, visiting/befriending.
Vols under 26 placed each year: Approximately 27 of a total of 50.
When to apply: All year – for holidays apply by May.
Work alone/with others: With others.
Volunteers with disabilities: Possible.
Qualifications: Nil.
Health requirements: Nil.
Costs: Nil.
Benefits: Travel expenses. Holiday volunteers receive accommodation, food etc. We provide personal accident insurance for volunteers.
Training: There is a specific volunteer training programme for the holiday programme volunteers, plus regular induction programmes throughout the year.
Supervision: Holiday volunteers are supervised by the holiday leader on their holiday.
Interview details: Interviews take place at our premises.
Charity number: SCO22097
UK placements: *Scotland* (Aberdeenshire, Angus, Argyll and Bute, E. Ayrshire, N. Ayrshire, S. Ayrshire, Dumfries and Galloway, E. Dunbartonshire, W. Dunbartonshire, Fife, Glasgow City, Inverclyde, N. Lanarkshire, S. Lanarkshire, Moray, Perth and Kinross, Renfrewshire, E. Renfrewshire, Scottish Borders, Stirling).

SERMATHANG PROJECT
c/o A.J. Lunch
8 Milton Court
Milton Malsor
Northampton
Northants
NN7 3AX UK

Tel: +44 (0) 1604 858617 or 858225
Fax: +44 (0) 1604 859323
e-mail: businesslink1@compuserve.com
Web: www.yangrima.org
Contact: Anthony J. Lunch

Perched 2,700 metres up in the Himalayas, Sermathang is 70 miles from Kathmandu. It is a day's bus ride to the end of the road and then a 15 mile climb through some of the most beautiful trekking scenery in the region. Sermathang is a traditional mountain village with about 80 houses. Farming is the main occupation. The only electricity is via a generator and solar panels. Water is collected from springs. There is a mobile phone in the village for urgent calls. Yangrima School was set up in 1987 by the village community to improve the children's education without having to leave the village. Volunteers started going to Yangrima in 1989 when the school was in a small run-down building. It has now been rebuilt on a hilltop ridge a short walk from the village, with ten classrooms, a library, staff room and basic sports facilities. There are now over 180 pupils from 4 to 17 years old. There is an active support group of ex-volunteers, parents and trekkers. The challenge: volunteers are needed to teach subjects such as English, Geography, Maths and Science, and to run sport and other activities. You will be a full-time member of staff with a normal teaching load. This is unpaid but the rewards are enormous. The older children's English is good and all the children are eager to learn. There are currently nine Nepalese teachers. Most of the children live with their families locally or in the boarding house, so it is easy to become involved with the community. Being part of a different culture, with its own religions and festivals, has been a great experience for past volunteers. In addition to Sermathang, the scheme now places volunteers in two other villages in the same region and in Kathmandu.

Total projects worldwide: 3
Total UK projects: 0
Starting months: February, April, July, October.
Time required: 8–15 weeks.
Age requirement: 18 plus.

Causes: Children, teaching/assisting (primary, secondary, EFL), unemployed, young people.
Activities: Community work, sport, teaching.
Vols under 26 placed each year: 16 of a total of 30.
When to apply: Flexible.
Work alone/with others: With others.
Volunteers with disabilities: Not possible.
Qualifications: A-levels or a degree for graduate volunteers.
Equipment/clothing: Normal clothing plus clothing suitable for trekking.
Health requirements: Innoculations. Volunteers must be in good health as some projects are in fairly remote locations (no electricity or running water).
Costs: Approximately £1,300: travel £450 approximately, subsistence £10 per week = £120 approximately, registration/video £25, help with fundraising for Nepalese teacher salaries = £700. The volunteer is responsible for providing normal travel and health insurance for third world countries.
Benefits: Board and lodging. Trekking, Nepali language classes and cultural orientation in Nepal.
Training: Briefing notes and discussion before departure. Briefing and cultural awareness in Nepal.
Supervision: Project manager is Ranjan Lama in Nepal. Head teacher is Gopal Lama in Nepal.
Interview details: Interviews take place in Kent, London, Northampton, Manchester or Scotland.
Certification: Certificate or reference provided.
Worldwide placements: *Asia* (Nepal).

SERVICE ARCHEOLOGIQUE DE DOUAI
191 Rue St Albin
59500 Douai
France

Tel: 00 33 3 27 71 38 90
Fax: 00 33 3 27 71 38 93
e-mail: arkeos@wanadoo.fr
Web: www.arkeos.org
Contact: The Director

Service Archeologique de Douai conducts archaeological excavations in the medieval town of Douai. Volunteers are needed to assist with the excavations and drawing of maps. Volunteers with an offending background accepted.

Total projects worldwide: 1
Total UK projects: 0
Starting months: July, August.
Time required: 2–8 weeks.
Age requirement: 18 plus.
Causes: Archaeology, work camps – seasonal.
Activities: Technical skills, work camps – seasonal.
Vols under 26 placed each year: 50
When to apply: By 15 June.
Volunteers with disabilities: Not possible.
Qualifications: Spoken English or French.
Equipment/clothing: For outside work.
Health requirements: Innoculation against tetanus.
Costs: Registration fee of FF150, all expenses including pocket money, except accommodation.
Benefits: Accommodation.
Interview details: No interview necessary.
Certification: Certificate or reference on request.
Worldwide placements: *Europe* (France).

SERVICE D'ARCHEOLOGIE DU CONSEIL GENERAL DE VAUCLUSE
Hotel Department, BP 318
F-84021 Avignon Cedex
France

Tel: 00 33 4 90 86 33 33
Contact: Michel-Edouart Bellet

Service d'Archeologie du Conseil General de Vaucluse needs volunteers to participate in excavations on various sites with the aim of protecting, researching and documenting archaeological sites throughout Vaucluse. Recent excavations have included the prehistoric and medieval sites and the Gallo-Roman towns of Vaison-la-Romaine, Cavaillon, Orange, Apt and Avignon. Volunteers should be prepared to do hard physical work: 40 hours per week.

Total projects worldwide: 1
Total UK projects: 0
Starting months: March, April, June, July, August.
Time required: 1–52 weeks.
Age requirement: 18 plus.
Causes: Archaeology, conservation, heritage.
Activities: Conservation skills.
When to apply: As early as possible.

Qualifications: Fluent French essential and some archaeological experience desirable.
Benefits: Accommodation, food and insurance.
Worldwide placements: *Europe* (France).

SERVICE PROTESTANTE DE LA JEUNESSE – ANNÉE DIACONALE
Rue de Champ de Mars 5
1050 Brussels
Belgium

Tel: 00 32 2 513 2401
Contact: Mme M. Ladrière-Abrassart

Total projects worldwide: 1
Total UK projects: 0
Starting months: September.
Time required: 42–52 weeks.
Age requirement: 18–25
Causes: Children, disabled (learning and physical), elderly people, health care/medical, teaching/assisting (nursery).
Activities: Caring (general and residential), teaching.
Vols under 26 placed each year: 20
When to apply: All year.
Qualifications: Basic knowledge of French essential.
Costs: BF500 application fee; insurance and travel costs.
Benefits: Board, lodging, laundry plus BF4,000 per month.
Interview details: No interview necessary.
Worldwide placements: *Europe* (Belgium).

SERVICE REGIONAL DE L'ARCHEOLOGIE
6 rue de la Manufacture
F-45000 Orleans
France

Tel: 00 33 2 38 53 91 38 or 2 38 78 85 43

Service Regional de L'Archeologie requires diggers and draughtsmen to work on an archaeological dig in Orleans or in one of the other digs in Central France. Eight hour day, five day week. No salary.

Total projects worldwide: 1
Total UK projects: 0
Starting months: August.
Time required: 2–52 weeks.
Age requirement: 18 plus.
Causes: Archaeology, conservation, heritage.
Activities: Conservation skills.
Vols under 26 placed each year: 50

When to apply: April.
Qualifications: Relevant archaeological experience and knowledge of French desirable.
Equipment/clothing: Bring sleeping bag.
Health requirements: Anti-tetanus vaccination.
Costs: Registration fee FF100.
Benefits: Free board and lodging.
Worldwide placements: *Europe* (France).

SERVICES FOR OPEN LEARNING
North Devon Professional Centre
Vicarage Street
Barnstaple
Devon
EX32 7HB UK

Tel: +44 (0) 1271 327319
Fax: +44 (0) 1271 376650
e-mail: sol@enterprise.net
Web: www.sol.org.uk
Contact: Mr G. Yeo

Services for Open Learning (SOL) was set up in 1991, as a non-profit organization by its present Director, Grenville Yeo, who for 13 years had been deputy head of a large comprehensive school in Barnstaple, and had had much experience organizing visits and exchanges, including one he set up with Hungary in 1987. The need to support teachers in countries where the demand for English has suddenly mushroomed following the political changes of 1989/90, and where resources were limited, was the driving force behind SOL. We began offering courses in England at much lower prices than commercial schools, and to work in close harmony with schools and their needs. SOL was operating in seven countries during 2000. Each has its own in-country co-ordinator, who is a qualified teacher of English. They are the link between the main office in Barnstaple, and the teachers taking groups to England. Hungary is our most active country. Since 1992 SOL has recruited qualified native-speaking teachers for schools in the indicated countries. This ensures that SOL's help reaches a great many more students than can afford to travel to England. In 2000/01 around 35 such teachers were placed, including some in higher education. A few exchanges between Teachers of English and teachers in Britain, during the summer holidays, can usually be set up.

Unfortunately, the demand far outstrips the supply of British teachers, who are busy and have very short holidays.

Total projects worldwide: 40
Total UK projects: 0
Starting months: September.
Time required: 42–52 weeks (plus).
Age requirement: 21 plus.
Causes: Teaching/assisting (primary, secondary, mature, EFL).
Activities: Teaching.
Vols under 26 placed each year: 10–15 of a total of 40.
When to apply: Any time but main recruiting is in the spring for September.
Work alone/with others: Alone.
Volunteers with disabilities: Possible. Teaching is strenuous. Schools are large, multistorey. Public transport would be used.
Qualifications: Degree or teaching certificate and TEFL qualification or experience. Must be native English speakers.
Health requirements: Good health essential.
Costs: Return travel to destination country only.
Benefits: Accommodation in independent flat and local salary. In Romania free health care cover too. National Health insurance is paid out of salary (10%) giving health insurance as a national of that country. Additional insurance is a matter for the individual.
Training: 3-day in-country induction programme the week before term.
Supervision: In-country co-ordinators maintain contact and provide a permanent link/support.
Interview details: Interviews usually take place in mainland Britain, usually in geographical areas.
Certification: Certificate or reference provided.
Charity number: 1019182
Worldwide placements: *Europe* (Belarus, Bosnia-Herzegovina, Bulgaria, Croatia, Czech Republic, Hungary, Romania, Slovakia).

SHAD – HARINGEY
33 Winkfield Road
London
N22 5RP UK

Tel: + 44 (0) 20 8365 8528
Fax: + 44 (0) 20 8365 8528
e-mail: shad.haringey@mailexcite.com
Contact: Gisela Iveson

SHAD is Support and Housing Assistance for People with Disabilities. SHAD – Haringey was set up by disabled people in the early 1980s; we are a registered charity. Our aim is to enable physically disabled individuals to live independently in their own homes in the community by providing them with a team of 2–4 volunteers, who work on a rota basis assisting with personal care, housework, social activities etc. Volunteers come from Britain and overseas, and do not need to have any previous experience – the most important thing is a positive and flexible attitude and a good sense of humour. We aim to provide volunteers with a friendly, supportive environment and a valuable work experience. Volunteers with an offending background are accepted, subject to relevant references.

Total projects worldwide: 15
Total UK projects: 15
Starting months: January–December.
Time required: 12–52 weeks.
Age requirement: 18 plus.
Causes: Disabled (physical).
Activities: Caring (general and residential), community work, social work, visiting/befriending.
Vols under 26 placed each year: 30 of a total of 40.
When to apply: All year.
Work alone/with others: Alone, but live with other volunteers.
Volunteers with disabilities: Volunteers must be able to lift other people.
Qualifications: Nil.
Health requirements: Volunteers must be able to lift.
Costs: None.
Benefits: £55 per week allowance, plus fares, accommodation.
Nationalities accepted: Only EU volunteers.
Interview details: Interviews take place in London.
Certification: Written reference provided.
Charity number: 1012142
UK placements: *England* (London).

SHAD – WANDSWORTH
5 Bedford Hill
Balham
London
SW12 9ET UK

Tel: + 44 (0) 20 8675 6095
Fax: + 44 (0) 20 8673 2118

Contact: Volunteer Development Officer

SHAD (Support and Housing Assistance for People with Disabilities – Wandsworth): much of the success of SHAD is a result of its ability to recruit full-time volunteers. Volunteers come from all over Britain and Europe. Overseas volunteers are welcome providing they are able to meet their own travel expenses to this country. Volunteers are an essential part of the SHAD set-up and we have enjoyed a very positive working relationship with them over the years: they are people who are responsive, sensitive, vibrant and giving. We hope that we can offer them a new perspective on disability, the possibility of personal/professional development and the opportunity of a busy social life in London. We ask volunteers to stay at least four months each. They usually work with a SHAD member on a 24-hour rota. A volunteer's job is to act as a physical facilitator to a disabled person. They provide physical assistance, enabling a person to get on with their life in a way which suits them. Volunteers act on the direction of the disabled person they are working for and are not expected to initiate actions or decisions themselves. It is SHAD's belief that disabled persons should have control over the decisions which affect every aspect of their lives. Volunteers do not act as care workers. They are recruited so that we can 'borrow their arms and legs' along with their time and energy, to enable our members to lead a full life. We are very fortunate indeed to have such a committed response from so many volunteers every year. Volunteers with an offending background are accepted.

Total projects worldwide: 1
Total UK projects: 1
Starting months: January–December.
Time required: 16–26 weeks.
Age requirement: 18–35
Causes: Disabled (physical).
Activities: Caring (general), community work.
Vols under 26 placed each year: 90.
When to apply: 2 months before starting or immediate start.
Work alone/with others: Both in a team and alone.
Volunteers with disabilities: Possible, if able to lift and handle.
Qualifications: Clean driving licence and good English language. Some non-driving placements.
Health requirements: Physically fit.
Costs: Overseas volunteers pay travel expenses to UK.
Benefits: Accommodation plus £55 per week plus expenses.
Interview details: Applicants are interviewed at SHAD's office.
Certification: Reference provided.
Charity number: 1001264
UK placements: *England* (London).

SHAFTESBURY SOCIETY
16–20 Kingston Road
South Wimbledon
London
SW19 1JZ UK

Tel: + 44 (0) 20 8239 5555
Fax: + 44 (0) 20 8239 5552
e-mail: Personnel@shaftesburysoc.org.uk
Web: www.shaftesburysoc.org.uk
Contact: Personnel Department

The Shaftesbury Society exists to enable people in great need to achieve security, self-worth and significance and through this to show Christian care in action. Shaftesbury provides whole life services for people with a physical and/or learning disability. These include residential care, respite and domiciliary care services. We run three non-maintained schools and two colleges for pupils and students with a disability. We also support people who are disadvantaged and/or on a low income. We do this, in part, by helping churches respond to local community needs. Our services include Shaftesbury's Community Worker Scheme, day care services for older people, affordable furniture, and services for people who are long-term unemployed or homeless. In these ways, Shaftesbury is working every day to help individuals to reach their full potential, make more of their own choices, and live more independent lives. Now one of the country's leading Christian charities, Shaftesbury works in some 100 centres across the country with more than 1,600 staff and volunteers supporting over 2,000 people with disabilities and hundreds of others in need each year. As a charity, we rely on voluntary donations to sustain and grow our work.

Total projects worldwide: 90 plus.
Total UK projects: 90 plus.

Starting months: January–December.
Time required: 1–52 weeks (plus).
Age requirement: 18 plus.
Causes: Children, disabled (learning and physical), elderly people, holidays for disabled, poor/homeless, unemployed, young people.
Activities: Administration, arts/crafts, caring (general, day and residential), catering, computers, cooking, driving, fundraising, gardening/horticulture, group work, marketing/publicity, music, outdoor skills, religion, sport, technical skills, theatre/drama, training.
Vols under 26 placed each year: 60 of a total of 80.
When to apply: All year.
Work alone/with others: Both.
Volunteers with disabilities: Possible, volunteer would have to contact the unit/school directly to find out.
Qualifications: Contact unit to find out.
Equipment/clothing: Contact unit to find out.
Health requirements: Depends on type of work. Some units will involve assisting to move residents.
Costs: Contact unit to find out.
Benefits: Travel expenses, board and lodging etc, depending on type of unit, e.g. residential or not.
Training: This depends on the work the volunteer is undertaking.
Supervision: This depends on the work the volunteer is undertaking.
Certification: Certificate or reference on request.
Charity number: 221948
UK placements: *England* (Dorset, Essex, Gloucestershire, Hampshire, Herefordshire, Hertfordshire, Kent, Lincolnshire, London, Manchester, Northamptonshire, Surrey, E. Sussex, W. Sussex, Wiltshire, Worcestershire, E. Yorkshire, N. Yorkshire, S. Yorkshire, W. Yorkshire).

SHARE HOLIDAY VILLAGE

Smiths Strand
Lisnaskea
Fermanagh
BT92 OEQ N. Ireland

Tel: +44 (0) 28 6772 2122
Fax: +44 (0) 28 6772 1893
e-mail: katie@sharevillage.org
Web: www.sharevillage.org

Contact: Katie Furfey, Volunteer Co-ordinator

Share is a registered charity providing a lakeside residential activity centre, promoting integration between able-bodied and disabled people of all ages, backgrounds and abilities. We welcome over 10,000 people each year, and run a wide range of outdoor sports and creative arts. There is an indoor pool complex on site and a theatre with workshops for pottery, ceramics and dance. Volunteers with offending background may be accepted.

Total projects worldwide: 1
Total UK projects: 1
Starting months: March–October.
Time required: 2–52 weeks.
Age requirement: 18 plus.
Causes: Disabled (learning and physical), elderly people, holidays for disabled, work camps – seasonal, young people.
Activities: Administration, arts/crafts, caring (general, day and residential), catering, cooking, gardening/horticulture, music, outdoor skills, sport, summer camps, theatre/drama, work camps – seasonal.
Vols under 26 placed each year: 140 of a total of 200.
When to apply: Any time but preferably October–March.
Work alone/with others: With others.
Volunteers with disabilities: Possible.
Qualifications: For some positions we require volunteers with skills and experience in outdoor sports or swimming or creative arts.
Health requirements: Good health.
Costs: Travel to Share. We advise volunteers to take out their own travel insurance and/or personal insurance for belongings etc.
Benefits: Short-term volunteers 1–4 weeks get out-of-pocket travel expenses to Share – maximum £10 per week. For long-term volunteers we provide out-of-pocket expenses of £40 per week. Food and accommodation provided. We provide public liability insurance.
Training: Basic training and hands-on training is provided in all areas: outdoor activites, housekeeping, arts etc.
Supervision: The volunteer co-ordinator is available to provide support. During working hours volunteers are directly supervised by trained staff.
Interview details: Interview in person if

possible for long-term placements or by phone if not possible.

Certification: Certificate in some sports available or written reference provided.

Charity number: NI 112023

UK placements: *Northern Ireland* (Fermanagh).

SHATIL

Capacity – Building Center for Social Change Organizations
POB 53395
Jerusalem
Israel 91533

Tel: 00 972 2 6723597
Fax: 00 972 2 6735149
e-mail: volunteer@shatil.nif.org.il
Contact: Miriam Lappin, Volunteer Co-ordinator

Shatil, the New Israel Fund's Capacity-Building Center for Social Change Organizations, co-ordinates a volunteer placement project that matches volunteers and interns with organizations working to strengthen democracy and promote social justice by safeguarding civil and human rights, promoting Jewish-Arab co-existence, advancing the status of women, fostering tolerance and religious pluralism, bridging social and economic gaps, assisting citizen efforts to protect the environment, and increasing government accountability. Volunteers placed by Shatil work side by side with Israeli activists, learn to apply professional skills, and gain first-hand knowledge of the complexities and challenges facing Israeli society. For summer camps volunteers are needed for 2–4 weeks. Short-term placements of 6–7 weeks are now available throughout the year, otherwise volunteers are needed for a minimum of 12 weeks.

Total projects worldwide: 85
Total UK projects: 0
Starting months: January–December.
Time required: 2–52 weeks (plus).
Age requirement: 19 plus.
Causes: Aids/HIV, children, conservation, disabled (learning and physical), environmental causes, health care/medical, heritage, human rights, inner city problems, poor/homeless, teaching/assisting (primary, secondary, EFL).
Activities: Administration, campaigning,

caring (general), community work, computers, conservation skills, counselling, development issues, fundraising, library/resource centres, marketing/publicity, newsletter/journalism, research, scientific work, social work, summer camps, teaching, theatre/drama, translating.

Vols under 26 placed each year: 160 of a total of 216.

When to apply: All year.

Work alone/with others: Usually alone.

Volunteers with disabilities: Possible.

Qualifications: Responsibility, strong writing and teaching skills, good intercultural communication skills, conversant in Hebrew and/or Arabic is a plus, but not a requirement. Opportunities for English speakers as well. Research or Teaching skills also a bonus.

Health requirements: Nil.

Costs: Subsistence and travel to Israel. In rural areas housing (home hospitality) often provided. Volunteers must arrange their own travel insurance. Health insurance is recommended. Organizations are required to insure volunteers for their work time only.

Benefits: Possibly board and lodging. If a volunteer is fluent in Hebrew or Arabic and willing to volunteer long term (6 plus months), subsistence stipends are available.

Training: Training and on-going supervision is provided by the host organizations as well as by Shatil, once volunteers are placed.

Supervision: All organizations are required to provide on-going supervision, training and feedback to volunteers, so as to enable them to complete their tasks.

Interview details: Prospective volunteers are interviewed on arrival in Israel.

Certification: Certificate or reference on request.

Worldwide placements: *Asia* (Israel).

SHEFFIELD WILDLIFE TRUST

Wood Lane House
52 Wood Lane
Sheffield
S. Yorkshire
S6 5HE UK

Tel: + 44 (0) 114 231 0120
Fax: + 44 (0) 114 231 0120
Contact: The Director

Sheffield Wildlife Trust is a member of the Wildlife Trusts, a national partnership of 47 county trusts. For more details of the Wildlife Trusts, see the entry under Cornwall Wildlife Trust.

Total projects worldwide: 1
Total UK projects: 1
Starting months: January–December.
Time required: 1–52 weeks (plus).
Age requirement: 12 plus.
Causes: Conservation, environmental causes, wildlife.
Activities: Conservation skills.
Work alone/with others: Both.
Qualifications: Nil.
Equipment/clothing: Casual work clothes, waterproofs, stout boots for outdoor work. Protective safety gear is provided.
Health requirements: Anti-tetanus innoculation recommended.
Costs: Nil.
Benefits: Out-of-pocket expenses. Volunteers are covered by the Trust's insurance.
UK placements: *England* (S. Yorkshire).

SHEILING COMMUNITY, THE
Horton Road
Ashley
Ringwood
Dorset
BH24 2EB UK

Tel: +44 (0) 1425 477488
Fax: +44 (0) 1425 479536
Contact: Mrs Sian Hornby

The Sheiling Community embraces around 250 adults and children some of whom have special needs. We occupy a 50 acre rural estate and a 100 acre mixed organic farm which supplies much of our food. Young volunteers, 'co-workers', children 'trainees' and 'companions' live together in small family houses and share daily life in the realms of education, training, work, social and cultural activities. The philosophy that forms the basis of both the educational work and the striving for 'social renewal through community living' is inspired by Rudolf Steiner (1861–1925) whose teachings open up an understanding of the spiritual nature of man in the world. Our cultural life includes the celebration of Christian festivals. We ask volunteers simply to come with an open mind and willingness to participate in a therapeutic lifestyle. Further information and literature is available on request.

Total projects worldwide: 35
Total UK projects: 35
Starting months: January–December.
Time required: 26–52 weeks.
Age requirement: 18 plus.
Causes: Children, disabled (learning), teaching/assisting (primary, secondary, mature).
Activities: Agriculture/farming, arts/crafts, caring (general and residential), gardening/horticulture, group work, music, teaching, training.
Vols under 26 placed each year: Approximately 30.
When to apply: All year.
Work alone/with others: In a community with others.
Volunteers with disabilities: Possible, but most work is physically demanding.
Qualifications: Nil.
Health requirements: Yes – questionnaire provided.
Costs: Initial travel to project.
Benefits: Accommodation, food and pocket money of £22 per week paid.
Certification: Certificate or reference provided.
UK placements: *England* (Dorset).

SHELTER
88 Old Street
London
EC1V 9HU UK

Tel: +44 (0) 20 7505 2000
Fax: +44 (0) 20 7505 2164
e-mail: shelter_supporters@compuserve.com
Web: www.shelter.org.uk
Contact: Benita Morris, Human Resources Officer

Over more than three decades Shelter has provided a lifeline to those facing the misery of homelessness and bad housing. We help approximately 118,000 families and individuals and we are the only national provider of free, specialist housing advice for people in desperate housing need.

Total projects worldwide: 47
Total UK projects: 47
Starting months: January–December.
Time required: 1–52 weeks.
Age requirement: 16 plus.
Causes: Poor/homeless.
Activities: Administration, campaigning, fundraising, social work.

When to apply: All year.
Work alone/with others: With others.
Volunteers with disabilities: Possible.
Qualifications: Nil.
Health requirements: Nil.
Costs: Nil.
Benefits: Travel expenses and lunch costs reimbursed.
Charity number: 263710
UK placements: *England* (throughout, except Kent); *Scotland* (throughout).

SHIN SHIZEN JUKU
Tsurui Mura
Akan Gun
085-1207 Hokkaido
Japan

Tel: 00 81 154 64 2821
Contact: Hiroshi Mine

The Shin Shizen Juku (SSJ) (New Nature School) needs volunteers to help teach English to both adults and children. There are usually about five volunteers working at the school at any one time. Some knowledge of Japanese is helpful, though it is not essential. Volunteers need to acquire a tourist visa to work at the school. A work permit is not necessary.

Total projects worldwide: 1
Total UK projects: 0
Starting months: January–December.
Time required: 6–52 weeks.
Age requirement: 18 plus.
Causes: Teaching/assisting (EFL).
Activities: Agriculture/farming, cooking, driving, teaching.
Vols under 26 placed each year: Most of a total of 20.
When to apply: All year, 1 to 2 months before wishing to start. Volunteers are especially needed and most welcome between January and March.
Volunteers with disabilities: We are unable to place people with disabilities as the weather conditions and house construction are not suitable.
Qualifications: English speakers only. International driving licence. Loving heart, honesty and responsibility.
Equipment/clothing: In winter temperature is −20C. Warm clothing is a must.
Health requirements: Nil.
Costs: Air fare and money for free time. Travel/health insurance is the volunteer's

responsibility.
Benefits: Board, lodging and food only.
Interview details: No interview necessary.
Certification: Certificate or reference on request.
Worldwide placements: *Asia* (Japan).

SHROPSHIRE WILDLIFE TRUST
167 Frankwell
Shrewsbury
Shropshire
SY3 8LG UK

Tel: +44 (0) 1743 241691
Fax: +44 (0) 1743 366671
Contact: The Director

Shropshire Wildlife Trust is a member of the Wildlife Trusts, a national partnership of 47 county trusts. For more details of the Wildlife Trusts, see the entry under Cornwall Wildlife Trust.

Total projects worldwide: 1
Total UK projects: 1
Starting months: January–December.
Time required: 1–52 weeks (plus).
Age requirement: 12 plus.
Causes: Conservation, environmental causes, wildlife.
Activities: Conservation skills.
Work alone/with others: Both.
Qualifications: Nil.
Equipment/clothing: Casual work clothes, waterproofs, stout boots for outdoor work. Protective safety gear is provided.
Health requirements: Anti-tetanus innoculation recommended.
Costs: Nil.
Benefits: Out-of-pocket expenses. Volunteers are covered by the Trust's insurance.
UK placements: *England* (Shropshire).

SIERRA CLUB
730 Polk Street
San Francisco
CA 94109
USA

Tel: 00 1 415 923 5527
Contact: The Publicity Manager

Sierra Club subsidizes trips which combine wilderness outings with conservation projects. Volunteers camp out while helping to build and repair trails and restore damaged wilderness areas. All trips incorporate some days free from work.

Total projects worldwide: 20
Total UK projects: 0
Starting months: April–October.
Time required: 1–52 weeks.
Age requirement: 18 plus.
Causes: Conservation, environmental causes.
Activities: Conservation skills, manual work.
Vols under 26 placed each year: 1000
When to apply: As early as possible.
Qualifications: Nil.
Equipment/clothing: All camping equipment.
Costs: £125 plus travel.
Worldwide placements: *Europe* (Austria, Belgium, Denmark, Finland, France, Germany, Greece, Iceland, Ireland, Italy, Luxembourg, Malta, Netherlands, Norway, Portugal, Spain, Sweden, Switzerland); *North America* (USA).

SIGN (ANASTASIA SOCIETY)
13 Station Road
Beaconsfield
Buckinghamshire
HP9 1YP UK

Tel: +44 (0) 1494 816777
Fax: +44 (0) 1494 812555
e-mail:
sign@charityheadoffice.freeserve.co.uk
Contact: Steve Powell, Chief Executive

Sign aims to offer a range of support to deaf people who have experienced mental health difficulties and who are striving to live independently. We offer long-term supportive accommodation and continuing care in the community. Our first day care facility opened in the autumn of 1995 and is based on the Clubhouse principle whereby people join as members (as opposed to 'clients' or 'patients') and are needed as contributors to a programme that cannot function without their input. Sign believes that to achieve a high quality of service it is essential that the language and culture of deaf people should be recognized, respected and understood. We have therefore developed mental health training programmes specifically for deaf people whose preferred language is British Sign Language thereby promoting better opportunities for deaf people to work in services offering care and support to deaf clients. Each housing project has a befriender programme which provides worthwhile voluntary work with training and monitoring for a large number of deaf and hearing people (who have the communication skills necessary).

Total projects worldwide: 7
Total UK projects: 7
Starting months: January–December.
Time required: 1–52 weeks.
Age requirement: 16 plus.
Causes: Children, disabled (learning and physical), elderly people, health care/medical, poor/homeless, unemployed, young people.
Activities: Administration, campaigning, caring (general, day and residential), catering, community work, computers, cooking, counselling, development issues, DIY, driving, fundraising, gardening/horticulture, marketing/publicity, research, social work, training, translating, visiting/befriending.
When to apply: All year.
Work alone/with others: Both – generally with a deaf resident.
Volunteers with disabilities: Deaf people (who share the same sign language as our residents) welcome.
Qualifications: Projects: ability to communicate with deaf people. Head Office: Nil.
Health requirements: Nil.
Costs: Own travel and subsistence costs.
Benefits: Valuable work experience in field of mental health and deafness.
Interview details: Interviews take place at the location where the volunteer wishes to work.
Certification: Certificate or reference provided.
Charity number: 1011056
UK placements: *England* (Buckinghamshire, London, Manchester, W. Yorkshire).

SILATUR
Emek Ishani (Gokdelen)
Kat: 11, No: 1109,
Ankara
Turkey

Tel: 00 90 312 418 13 26

Silatur organizes voluntary work camps in Turkey lasting three weeks. Volunteers are also invited to help in Silatur's office for periods of three weeks around the year.

Total projects worldwide: 1
Total UK projects: 0
Starting months: June–September.
Time required: 3–52 weeks.
Age requirement: 18 plus.

Causes: Environmental causes, heritage.
Activities: Administration, building/
construction, community work, gardening/
horticulture.
Vols under 26 placed each year:
Approximately 75.
When to apply: As early as possible.
Qualifications: Nil.
Benefits: Food and occasionally help towards
travel expenses. No registration fee.
Worldwide placements: *Asia* (Turkey);
Europe (Turkey).

SIMON COMMUNITY (IRELAND)
St Andrew's House
28–30 Exchequer Street
Dublin 2
Ireland

Tel: 00 353 1 671 1606
Fax: 00 353 1 671 1098
e-mail: catri.o'kane@simoncommunity.com
Web: www.simoncommunity.com
Contact: Catri O'Kane

Established in Ireland in 1969, the Simon
Community is a caring and campaigning
organization providing a range of services for
homeless people. We need full-time
volunteers to work in our projects.
Our shelters provide emergency
accommodation for 25–30 people per night,
while our residential houses are smaller,
providing long-term care for 6–9 people in
each house. We also have settlement projects.
They provide a supportive environment in
which residents can develop and move, with
confidence, into their own accommodation.
We invite you to share your life and skills
with our residents. We're looking for people
who are keen to develop their potential and
the potential of others. The full-time
volunteer plays a vital and indispensable role
in the Simon Community. It is an intensive
and demanding experience. Aside from a
range of challenging work you'll benefit from
a lot of personal fulfilment, good team
morale and a lively social scene. Simon
attempts to provide houses where the
atmosphere is friendly and informal and
people can feel 'at home'. Working alongside
paid staff your role includes: companionship
with residents; practical advice and support
to residents; being involved with the day-to-
day running of the house, i.e. cooking and
cleaning; communicating and relating with

residents who may have alcohol, drug or
mental health problems; arranging
recreational activities with residents.

Total projects worldwide: 4
Total UK projects: 0
Starting months: January–December.
Time required: 26–52 weeks (plus).
Age requirement: 18 plus.
Causes: Elderly people, poor/homeless,
unemployed.
Activities: Caring (general and residential),
catering, cooking, group work, visiting/
befriending.
Vols under 26 placed each year: 85 of a total
of 100.
When to apply: All year.
Work alone/with others: With others.
Volunteers with disabilities: Not possible.
Qualifications: Excellent spoken and written
English.
Health requirements: Reasonably healthy as
the work is intense and demanding.
Costs: Travel costs.
Benefits: Board and lodging plus insurance.
plus IR£40 per week plus IR£7 saved for
each week worked.
Training: On-the-job training, supervision,
support and feedback provided.
Supervision: Each project has paid staff
members responsible for the supervision and
support of volunteers. Weekly one-to-one and
team meetings.
Interview details: Interviews take place at our
office in Dublin.
Certification: Reference provided.
Charity number: 8273
Worldwide placements: *Europe* (Ireland).

SIMON COMMUNITY, THE
PO Box 1187
London
NW5 4HW UK

Tel: +44 (0) 20 7485 6639
Contact: Community Leaders

The Simon Community is a small registered
charity living and working with the homeless
and rootless in London. Volunteers are
involved in the running of the shelter and
residential houses, as well as the office. A
genuine desire to help homeless people and
some understanding of the problems of the
homeless is essential. Although volunteers
have to commit themselves to a minimum of
three months, a longer commitment is

preferred. Volunteers with an offending background are accepted. Each application form is judged individually.

Total projects worldwide: 5
Total UK projects: 5
Starting months: January–December.
Time required: 13–52 weeks (plus).
Age requirement: 19 plus.
Causes: Addicts/Ex-addicts, disabled (learning), elderly people, poor/homeless.
Activities: Administration, campaigning, caring (general and residential), cooking, driving, fundraising, group work, social work.
Vols under 26 placed each year: 20-35
When to apply: 1 month in advance.
Work alone/with others: Mostly with others.
Volunteers with disabilities: Possible.
Qualifications: Excellent command of English. Driving licence useful. Volunteers from outside the UK must be a minimum of 20 years old.
Health requirements: Nil.
Costs: Travel to 48 hour interview and to London when accepted. All other expenses paid.
Benefits: Expenses, basic accommodation, food plus £25 per week pocket money plus 2 weeks holiday after every 3 months with allowance.
Interview details: Applicants attend a 48 hour session where people from all the projects answer informal questions about their experience, reasons for wanting to come etc.
Certification: Reference on request.
Charity number: 293938
UK placements: *England* (Kent, London).

SIOUX INDIAN YMCAS
Box 218
Dupree
South Dakota 57623
USA

Contact: The Programme Director

Total projects worldwide: 1
Total UK projects: 0
Starting months: June–August.
Time required: 12–52 weeks.
Age requirement: 18 plus.
Activities: Arts/crafts, community work, counselling, first aid, sport, summer camps.
When to apply: As early as possible.
Qualifications: Previous camp experience.
Costs: Travel and personal expenses.

Benefits: Board and lodging.
Worldwide placements: *North America* (USA).

SKYLIGHT CIRCUS IN EDUCATION
Broadwater Centre
Smith Street
Rochdale
OL16 1HE UK

Tel: +44 (0) 1706 650676
Fax: +44 (0) 1706 713638
Contact: Bob Fell

Skylight Circus in Education is a school for circus arts, a centre for excellence providing circus arts training, a community arts resource, a provider of community animateur training and a circus training performance company. It is a registered charity.

Total projects worldwide: 1
Total UK projects: 1
Starting months: January–December.
Time required: 1–52 weeks.
Age requirement: 16 plus.
Causes: Disabled (learning and physical), teaching/assisting (nursery, primary, secondary), young people.
Activities: Administration, manual work, teaching.
When to apply: All year.
Volunteers with disabilities: Possible.
Qualifications: Nil.
Health requirements: Nil.
Costs: Nil.
UK placements: *England* (N. Yorkshire).

SOCIETY OF VOLUNTARY ASSOCIATES (SOVA)
Croydon Young People's Project
Cornerstone House
14 Willis Road
Croydon
CRO 2XX UK

Tel: +44 (0) 20 7793 0404
Fax: +44 (0) 20 7735 4410
Contact: Keith MacKett

SOVA is a national charity that believes that everybody is touched by crime. We specialize in training volunteers from local communities to work with offenders, their families and young people in trouble. We promote voluntary action in the penal field by recruiting, training and deploying volunteers to work alongside the primary statutory and voluntary agencies serving the criminal justice system. Volunteers with an offending background are accepted providing a time period of two years has elapsed since the offence, and the acceptance also depends on the seriousness of the offence.

Total projects worldwide: 23
Total UK projects: 23
Starting months: January–December.
Time required: 52 weeks.
Age requirement: 18 plus.
Causes: Inner city problems, offenders/ex-offenders, teaching/assisting (mature), young people.
Activities: Counselling, driving, group work, teaching, visiting/befriending.
Vols under 26 placed each year: Varies.
When to apply: All year.
Work alone/with others: Both.
Volunteers with disabilities: Possible.
Qualifications: Nil.
Health requirements: Nil.
Benefits: All expenses paid.
Interview details: Interviews usually take place at the office where the project is based.
Certification: Certificate or reference provided.
Charity number: 269040
UK placements: *England* (Derbyshire, Hampshire, Kent, Lincolnshire, London, Manchester, Surrey, S. Yorkshire); *Wales* (Conwy, Powys).

SOLBORG LANDSBY
N 3520 Jevnaker
Norway

Tel: 00 47 3213 2480
Fax: 00 47 3213 2020
Contact: Karen Nesheim

Solborg is part of the worldwide Camphill Village organization. We are 50 people – co-workers and their families and adults with learning difficulties – living together in five family houses of about ten people each. Each house has also one or two volunteer co-workers who have usually come for one year's experience, from many different lands. We work together in the houses, on the land with bio-dynamic agriculture and horticulture and in craft workshops – woodworkshop, weavery, bakery. Free time is occupied with a wide variety of social activities – folkdancing, drama, lectures, concerts, games, choir and

co-worker meetings. We expect that volunteers are prepared to learn Norwegian and to join in with all aspects of our life, which is based upon the philosophy of Dr Rudolf Steiner. Drugs and alcohol, and the use of these, are not permitted and will lead to dismissal if this is breached.

Total projects worldwide: 1
Total UK projects: 0
Starting months: January–December.
Time required: 52 weeks (plus).
Age requirement: 18–25
Causes: Disabled (learning), environmental causes.
Activities: Agriculture/farming, caring (general and residential), catering, cooking, forestry, gardening/horticulture, group work, outdoor skills, theatre/drama.
Vols under 26 placed each year: 7
When to apply: All year.
Work alone/with others: With others.
Volunteers with disabilities: We are unable to place people with disabilities as we require good physical and mental health.
Qualifications: Willingness to learn Norwegian.
Equipment/clothing: Work clothes. Adequate summer and winter clothing suitable for Norwegian climate. No sheets or towels required.
Health requirements: Good physical and mental health. TB innoculated. No alcohol or drugs allowed.
Costs: Return fare.
Benefits: Food, lodging, medical insurance and tax, 1400 NKR in pocket money per month. 3 weeks paid holiday is included for those who stay 1 year.
Interview details: Interviews are helpful and take place in Norway.
Certification: Written reference provided.
Worldwide placements: *Europe* (Norway).

SOLIDARITÉ JEUNESSE
01 BP 5648
Ouagadougou 01
5648 Burkina Faso

Tel: 00 226 33 71 17
Fax: 00 226 33 71 17
e-mail: moctar.kouanda@messrs.gov.bf
Contact: Moctar Kouanda, President

Volunteers with an offending background are accepted.

Total projects worldwide: 15
Total UK projects: 0
Starting months: June.
Time required: 3–52 weeks.
Age requirement: 18–40
Causes: Addicts/ex-addicts, Aids/HIV, architecture, children, conservation, disabled (learning and physical), environmental causes, health care/medical, human rights, offenders/ex-offenders, refugees, teaching/assisting (nursery, primary, secondary), wildlife, work camps – seasonal, young people.
Activities: Administration, building/construction, campaigning, caring (general), community work, conservation skills, development issues, fundraising, gardening/horticulture, group work, newsletter/journalism, outdoor skills, social work, sport, summer camps, teaching, translating, work camps – seasonal.
Vols under 26 placed each year: 100 of a total of 120.
When to apply: By the end of January.
Work alone/with others: With others.
Volunteers with disabilities: Not possible.
Qualifications: No qualifications needed for the work camps.
Equipment/clothing: Dependent on the work.
Health requirements: Nil.
Costs: Travel, registration, food and medical insurance.
Interview details: No interview necessary.
Charity number: 198/92
Worldwide placements: *Africa* (Burkina Faso).

SOLIDARITÉS JEUNESSES
38 rue du Faubourg Saint Denis
Paris
75010 France

Tel: 00 33 1 48 00 09 05
Fax: 00 33 1 42 46 49 32
e-mail: Sj.Admin@wanadoo.fr
Contact: Thierry Picquart, Secretary General

Solidarités Jeunesses organizes international work camps in France as well as in over 55 countries worldwide. We work in co-operation with partner agencies in these countries, and exchange volunteers through each other. On work camps, volunteers work on a wide variety of projects such as conservation, protection of the environment, construction, renovation of historical sites, social and community work etc. Volunteers are expected to work for about five to six hours each day on the projects.

Total projects worldwide: Approximately 400.
Total UK projects: Approximately 30.
Starting months: January–December.
Time required: 2–52 weeks.
Age requirement: 15–30
Causes: Conservation, disabled (physical), heritage, holidays for disabled, inner city problems, offenders/ex-offenders, poor/homeless, unemployed, work camps – seasonal, young people.
Activities: Administration, building/construction, community work, conservation skills, manual work, work camps – seasonal.
Vols under 26 placed each year: 1,900 of a total of 2,000.
When to apply: All year.
Work alone/with others: With others.
Volunteers with disabilities: Possible.
Qualifications: Nil.
Health requirements: Nil.
Costs: Registration of FF500–FF1,000 and travel costs.
Benefits: Full board and lodging, pocket money sometimes (3–12 months only), occasionally fares.
Certification: Certificate or reference provided.
Worldwide placements: *Africa* (Algeria, Benin, Burkina Faso, Cameroon, Ivory Coast, Ghana, Kenya, Lesotho, Libya, Mauritania, Morocco, Mozambique, Niger, Nigeria, Senegal, Sierra Leone, South Africa, Tanzania, Togo, Tunisia, Uganda, Zambia, Zimbabwe); *Asia* (Bangladesh, Cambodia, China, India, Israel, Japan, Korea (South), Lebanon, Nepal, Thailand, Turkey, Vietnam); *Australasia* (Australia); *Europe* (Albania, Andorra, Armenia, Austria, Azerbaijan, Belarus, Belgium, Bosnia-Herzegovina, Bulgaria, Croatia, Cyprus, Czech Republic, Denmark, Estonia, Finland, France, Georgia, Germany, Gibraltar, Greece, Hungary, Iceland, Ireland, Italy, Latvia, Lithuania, Luxembourg, Macedonia, Malta, Moldova, Netherlands, Norway, Poland, Portugal, Romania, Russia, Slovakia, Slovenia, Spain, Sweden, Switzerland, Turkey, Ukraine, Yugoslavia); *North America* (Canada, Greenland, USA); *Central America* (Guatemala, Martinique, Mexico); *South*

America (Argentina, Bolivia, Ecuador).
UK placements: *England* (Dorset, Essex,
Oxfordshire, E. Sussex, W. Sussex, West
Midlands); *Scotland* (throughout); *Wales*
(throughout).

SOMERSET WILDLIFE TRUST
Fyne Court
Broomfield
Bridgwater
Somerset
TA5 2EQ UK

Tel: +44 (0) 1823 451587
Fax: +44 (0) 1823 451671
Contact: The Director

Somerset Wildlife Trust is a member of the
Wildlife Trusts, a national partnership of 47
County Trusts. For more details of the
Wildlife Trusts, see the entry under Cornwall
Wildlife Trust.

Total projects worldwide: 1
Total UK projects: 1
Starting months: January–December.
Time required: 1–52 weeks (plus).
Age requirement: 12 plus.
Causes: Conservation, environmental causes,
wildlife.
Activities: Conservation skills.
Work alone/with others: Both.
Qualifications: Nil.
Equipment/clothing: Casual work clothes,
waterproofs, stout boots for outdoor work.
Protective safety gear is provided.
Health requirements: Anti-tetanus
innoculation recommended.
Costs: Nil.
Benefits: Out-of-pocket expenses. Volunteers
are covered by the Trust's insurance.
UK placements: *England* (Somerset).

SONS OF DIVINE PROVIDENCE
Westminster House
25 Lower Teddington Road
Hampton Wick
Kingston-upon-Thames
Surrey
KT1 4HB UK

Tel: +44 (0) 20 8977 5130
Fax: +44 (0) 20 8977 0105
e-mail:
london.divineprovidence@btinternet.com
Web: www.sonsofdivineprovidence.org
Contact: Amanda Whyte

The Sons of Divine Providence is a Catholic
charity providing care and accommodation
for elderly people and people with learning
disabilities. We welcome all people to make
use of our services and we are happy to work
with anybody who is in sympathy with our
aims and ethos.

Total projects worldwide: 18
Total UK projects: 10
Starting months: January–December.
Time required: 1–52 weeks.
Age requirement: 18 plus.
Causes: Disabled (learning), elderly people,
young people.
Activities: Caring (general, day and
residential), cooking, driving, gardening/
horticulture, manual work, outdoor skills,
religion, visiting/befriending.
Vols under 26 placed each year: Unlimited.
When to apply: All year.
Work alone/with others: With others.
Volunteers with disabilities: Possible.
Qualifications: Nil.
Health requirements: Nil.
Costs: Nil.
Benefits: Negotiable. We carry public liability
insurance in all our units.
Training: Training in our English units takes
place during placement with induction and
other areas covered.
Supervision: Volunteers receive formal
supervision once a month and will work
alongside staff to whom they can refer in an
informal way.
Certification: Certificate or reference on
request.
Charity number: 220608
Worldwide placements: *Africa* (Ivory Coast,
Kenya); *Asia* (Jordan, Philippines); *Europe*
(France, Ireland, Italy, Poland, Romania,
Spain, Switzerland); *North America* (USA);
Central America (Mexico); *South America*
(Argentina, Brazil, Chile, Paraguay,
Venezuela).
UK placements: *England* (Lancashire,
London, Norfolk, Surrey).

SORT IT – EUROPEAN YOUTH
ENVIRONMENT FESTIVAL
Western Partnership for Sustainable
Development
The Create Centre
Bristol
BS1 6XN UK

Tel: +44 (0) 117 922 4388
Fax: +44 (0) 117 929 7283
e-mail: future@sort-it.org.uk
Web: www.sort-it.org.uk
Contact: Lottie Berthoud, Project Manager

Each year WPSD's Environment Festival becomes even more exciting and effective than before! It comprises a week-long event for young people from all over Europe called SORT IT, which has been partly funded by the Millennium Festival Fund. Up to 1,000 15–18 year olds transform Almondsbury Scout Camp site in South Gloucestershire into a low-impact global workshop. After visiting relevant projects across the region, exchanging ideas and having a great time, they come together at a Great Gathering to put together a Youth Charter for the Environment. Their voices are heard! There are volunteering opportunities: February-May is ideal for people looking for experience of event organization, project management, office administration and international work. Between May and July is the run-up to Sort it and will mostly involve registration and site organization issues.

Total projects worldwide: 1
Total UK projects: 1
Starting months: January–December.
Time required: 2–52 weeks (plus).
Age requirement: 15–30
Causes: Children, conservation, environmental causes, human rights, unemployed, wildlife, young people.
Activities: Administration, building/ construction, community work, computers, conservation skills, fundraising, marketing/ publicity, outdoor skills, research, summer camps.
Vols under 26 placed each year: Approximately 50.
When to apply: As soon as possible.
Work alone/with others: With others.
Volunteers with disabilities: Possible. The Create Centre has disabled access. Office work would be suitable.
Qualifications: Good phone manner; able (i.e. confident enough) to phone lots of people. Computer skills a bonus.
Health requirements: Nil.
Costs: All costs except local travel.
Benefits: Local travel costs up to £20 per week. We are insured for volunteers.
Training: If necessary we shall provide training.
Supervision: 2 supervisors including one experienced manager.
Nationalities accepted: No restrictions but good English is required for phoning.
Interview details: Informal chat interviews are held at the Create Centre in Bristol.
Certification: Certificate or reference definitely provided.
Charity number: 1026651

SOUTHCARE INC.

54 Bickley Crescent
Manning
Perth
6152 Western Australia
Tel: 00 61 8 9450 6233
Fax: 00 61 8 9450 2324
Contact: Diane Porter or Kim Rostant, Program Administrator/Volunteer Co-ordinator

Southcare's mission statement is to 'Offer caring services to residents of the City of South Perth, assisting them to enhance their quality of life'. The objectives of Southcare are to help to develop a community in which fellow members care and assist one another; establish and provide caring services for those who are disadvantaged by age, disability, unemployment, poverty, social or familial stress; link volunteers from within member organizations and elsewhere to participate in the delivery of appropriate services; and promote and make these services available to all members of the local community. Volunteers with an offending background may be accepted, depending on the crime. We have close to 100 volunteers currently working for our agency. We are always on the lookout for more.

Total projects worldwide: 11
Total UK projects: 0
Starting months: January–December.
Time required: 8–52 weeks (plus).
Age requirement: 18 plus.
Causes: Disabled (learning and physical), elderly people, poor/homeless, unemployed.
Activities: Administration, arts/crafts, caring (general, day and residential), community work, computers, driving, visiting/ befriending.
Vols under 26 placed each year: 10 of a total of 100.
When to apply: All year.

Work alone/with others: Both.
Volunteers with disabilities: Possible.
Qualifications: Spoken English, driving
licence preferable, non-judgmental attitude
with different cultures.
Health requirements: Nil.
Costs: All costs except those incurred in the
course of volunteering which are partly
reimbursed.
Benefits: Travel allowance. All volunteers are
insured by us while undertaking work with
the agency.
Training: All volunteers receive orientation to
the agency. Some programmes continue to
receive ongoing training throughout the year.
Supervision: Some one-to-one. Others
through phone calls etc.
Interview details: Interviews take place at the
offices in South Perth.
Certification: Certificate of appreciation after
a certain period of time.
Worldwide placements: *Australasia*
(Australia).

SOUTHERN AFRICA RESOURCE
CENTRE (SARC)
6 West Street
Old Market
Bristol
BS2 0BH UK

Tel: +44 (0) 117 941 1442
Contact: The Secretary

SARC was set up in 1989 to educate the
public in the south-west of England in the
fields of art, culture, history and current
affairs of southern Africa; and to manage
and develop Bristol's link with Beira, a port
on the coast of Mozambique. Opportunities
for self-funded volunteers to participate in
medical, architectural, administrative and
possibly teaching placements in Beira. In
Bristol there are also opportunities for
volunteers to help with educational, cultural,
commercial and social projects; administrative
work; campaigning; press and public
relations, and production of materials.

Total projects worldwide: 1
Total UK projects: 0
Starting months: January–December.
Time required: 12–52 weeks (plus).
Age requirement: 18 plus.
Causes: Architecture, health care/medical,
teaching/assisting.
Activities: Administration, marketing/

publicity, newsletter/journalism, teaching.
When to apply: All year.
Qualifications: For Beira, knowledge of
Portuguese useful.
Costs: All costs including travel, insurance,
board and accommodation.

SPRINGBOARD YOUTH INFORMATION
SHOP
Foothold Youth Enterprise Agency
Lord Arthur Rank Centre
Trostre Park
Llanelli
Dyfed
SA14 9RA Wales

Tel: +44 (0) 1554 749161
Fax: +44 (0) 1554 756700
Contact: Jill Methley

Springboard will provide a starting point
from which young people can gain personal
confidence, social competence and general life
skills, and experience success and a sense of
achievement. These skills will be developed
through a range of challenging opportunities
which will enable young people to bring
about change for themselves, improve the
quality of their lives and the lives of the
communities in which they live. The
overarching principle is to equip young people
with skills which will assist them to compete
efficiently in the employment market. We will
achieve the aims of Springboard through the
following objectives: the organization of a
programme of individual and group activities
and challenges which will be undertaken on a
contract basis; participation in projects
designed to bring about change in the local
community; opportunities to gain measurable
skills which contribute towards recognized
qualifications; engaging in enterprising
employment-related activities in partnership
with new businesses created in Foothold.
Projects under discussion include: clearing,
planning and planting a series of different
types of garden in a large wasteland behind
the main Foothold building; a mobile Rural
Enterprise Project; a disability project
involving Enterprise; a Youth Information
Shop in conjunction with Welsh Youth
Agency; a Detached Youthwork project
housed in Llanelli, possibly in conjunction
with the Youth Information Shop (using the
same premises); Intereg Project with an
Unemployment Project in Wexford, Ireland.

Total projects worldwide: 1
Total UK projects: 1
Starting months: January–December.
Time required: 4–52 weeks.
Age requirement: 16–30
Causes: Conservation, disabled (physical), environmental causes, holidays for disabled, inner city problems, unemployed, wildlife, young people.
Activities: Administration, building/construction, community work, conservation skills, development issues, fundraising, gardening/horticulture, group work, manual work, outdoor skills, training.
Vols under 26 placed each year: 20 plus.
When to apply: Any time.
Work alone/with others: Both.
Volunteers with disabilities: Possible.
Qualifications: Nil.
Health requirements: Nil.
Benefits: Travel costs.
Interview details: Interviews take place at Springboard (Llanelli).
Certification: Certificate or reference provided.
Worldwide placements: *Europe* (Ireland).
UK placements: *Wales* (Carmarthenshire, Pembrokeshire).

ST ANDREW'S EVANGELICAL MISSION

126 Ealing Road
Brentford
Middlesex
TW8 0LD UK

Tel: +44 (0) 20 8840 9066
Fax: +44 (0) 20 8840 9066
Contact: Ray Spencer, Honorary General Secretary

St Andrew's Evangelical Mission runs an orphanage in Peru which has a British support group based in Middlesex. Volunteers are urgently needed as physiotherapists, speech therapists, multi-skilled DIY persons or builders, opticians, nursing staff trained in care of mentally and physically disabled children, and animal farmers (pigs, poultry).

Total projects worldwide: 2
Total UK projects: 0
Starting months: January–December.
Time required: 4–52 weeks.
Age requirement: 21 plus.
Causes: Animal welfare, children, disabled (learning and physical), health care/medical,

teaching/assisting (nursery, primary).
Activities: Agriculture/farming, building/construction, caring (general, day and residential), DIY, gardening/horticulture, manual work, social work, teaching.
Vols under 26 placed each year: 1 or more.
When to apply: All year.
Work alone/with others: With others.
Volunteers with disabilities: Not possible.
Qualifications: Must speak Spanish and love children. No vegetarians/special diets. See notes.
Health requirements: Must be in good general health.
Costs: Air fares to and from Peru. Own spending money. Travel and medical insurance.
Benefits: Only board and lodging provided.
Training: Brian and Betty Attwell provide instruction and training for volunteers at the home in Peru.
Supervision: By Brian and Betty Attwell.
Interview details: No interview necessary for one month's service term.
Charity number: 290252
Worldwide placements: *South America* (Peru).

ST DAVID'S (AFRICA) TRUST

Beaufort Chambers
Beaufort Street
Crickhowell
Powys
NP8 1AA Wales

Tel: +44 (0) 1873 810665
Fax: +44 (0) 1873 810665
e-mail: wales@africatrust.gi
Web: www.africatrust.gi
Contact: Mrs Sue Wintle, Administrator

St David's (Africa) Trust is an educational trust which organizes residential visits to Africa (Morocco, Ghana and Mali) for students either before or after their university studies. There are several scholarships. The visits include language tuition and volunteer work with handicapped, orphaned and blind children as well as animal welfare work in Morocco and Mali. You are encouraged to demonstrate your own team initiative in helping to develop projects with the donation funds which you will have raised.

Total projects worldwide: 8
Total UK projects: 0
Starting months: January, September.

Time required: 14–28 weeks.
Age requirement: 18–25
Causes: Animal welfare, children, disabled (learning and physical), health care/medical, teaching/assisting (nursery, primary, EFL).
Activities: Agriculture/farming, building/construction, caring (residential), community work, development issues, teaching.
Vols under 26 placed each year: 50
When to apply: At least 6 months before.
Work alone/with others: With others.
Volunteers with disabilities: Not possible.
Qualifications: Preferably A-level, at least GCSE French for Morocco. Swim 100 m.
Health requirements: Good health for insurance requirements. Advice provided on health protection.
Costs: £1,500 for 3 months, £2,500 for six months. Registration fee £25.
Benefits: The cost includes French/Arabic language lessons, board and lodging. Compulsory health, emergency repatriation and personal effects insurance is arranged by The Trust.
Training: In UK: 6 months reading material, pre-departure lectures by past volunteers, country experts and Trust officials.
In country: 2 weeks residential training covering language, culture etc.
Nationalities accepted: Passports must be acceptable for visa purposes in host countries.
Interview details: Interviews take place in London and, possibly, South Wales.
Certification: Certificate or reference on request – e.g. Duke of Edinburgh Gold Award.
Charity number: 90 (Gib.)
Worldwide placements: *Africa* (Ghana, Mali, Morocco).

ST JOHN AMBULANCE
1 Grosvenor Crescent
London
SW1X 7EF UK

Tel: +44 (0) 20 7235 5231
Fax: +44 (0) 20 7235 0796
Contact: James Hilder, Youth Services Manager

Total projects worldwide: 1
Total UK projects: 1
Starting months: January–December.
Time required: 1–52 weeks.
Age requirement: 16 plus.

Causes: Disabled (physical), elderly people, health care/medical, teaching/assisting (primary), young people.
Activities: Accountancy, administration, caring (general and day), community work, driving, first aid, outdoor skills, summer camps, teaching, training, visiting/befriending.
When to apply: All year.
UK placements: *England* (throughout); *Scotland* (throughout); *Northern Ireland* (throughout); *Wales* (throughout).

ST JUDE'S RANCH FOR CHILDREN
PO Box 60100
Boulder City
Nevada 89006-0100
USA

Tel: 00 1 702 294 7100
Fax: 00 1 702 294 7171
Contact: Teresa Hein, Educational Co-ordinator

St Jude's Ranch for Children is a non-profit, non-sectarian residential child-care facility founded in 1967. It serves boys and girls, 6–18 (admitted only before they reach 14) who are neglected, abused or homeless or who have had difficulty functioning satisfactorily while living at home. The Ranch does not accept the physically or mentally handicapped or severely emotionally disturbed. Children live in cottages of six where they are supervised by 'cottage parents' and attend the local public schools. The director of 24 years, Fr Herbert A. Ward, is an Episcopal priest and conducts services according to the Episcopal tradition. The Ranch is financially supported in part by Episcopalians, and through special grants and many generous donors. St Jude's needs summer volunteers with life-saving certification to assist with their swimming and recreation programmes (including camping, arts and crafts, music and dramatics). Other full-time positions may be available for volunteers with specific education and/or experience dealing with emotionally disturbed or behaviourally disordered children. Volunteers must be mature, responsible and take strong initiative. You are expected to act at all times as role models in behaviour, manners, speech and values. No alcohol, drugs, heavy metal music, or inappropriate posters are permitted. Attendance at religious services is required.

Service students are considered part of the staff, and are expected to accept the judgement and follow directions of the professional staff as to what is an appropriate response to children, their problems and behaviour.

Total projects worldwide: 1
Total UK projects: 0
Starting months: January–December.
Time required: 6–52 weeks.
Age requirement: 21–30
Causes: Children, conservation, teaching/assisting (primary, secondary), work camps – seasonal, young people.
Activities: Administration, arts/crafts, caring (residential), computers, conservation skills, counselling, gardening/horticulture, outdoor skills, religion, social work, teaching, visiting/befriending, work camps – seasonal.
Vols under 26 placed each year: 3
When to apply: As early as possible – at least 2 months before starting.
Work alone/with others: With others.
Volunteers with disabilities: Not possible.
Qualifications: A level, driving licence, language ability. Some experience in working with at-risk youth.
Health requirements: Good health.
Costs: Travel to the Ranch. Volunteer responsible for own insurance.
Benefits: Food and lodging provided plus US$200 pocket money per month.
Training: An orientation period is given.
Supervision: All volunteers have a direct supervisor over them. Weekly staff meetings and opportunities for daily discussion with supervisors guide the students in their work.
Interview details: Applicants are interviewed by telephone or fax.
Certification: Certificate or reference provided.
Worldwide placements: *North America* (USA).

ST PIERS
St Piers Lane
Lingfield
Surrey
RH7 6PW UK

Tel: + 44 (0) 1342 832243
Fax: + 44 (0) 1342 834639
e-mail: aniven@stpiers.org.uk
Web: www.stpiers.org.uk
Contact: Alec Niven

St Piers is a non-maintained residential special school for children and young adults who have learning difficulties, epilepsy and other neurological disorders. Situated on the Surrey, Sussex and Kent borders we are just 30 miles from Brighton and 20 miles from London. St Piers has built up a worldwide reputation for the excellence of its educational, care and medical facilities. Working at St Piers provides an ideal opportunity for practical experience of living with and caring for children and young adults with various disabilities in an environment offering support and education.

Total projects worldwide: 1
Total UK projects: 1
Starting months: January, April, September.
Time required: 16–52 weeks.
Age requirement: 18 plus.
Causes: Children, disabled (learning and physical), health care/medical, holidays for disabled, teaching/assisting (primary, secondary), young people.
Activities: Agriculture/farming, arts/crafts, caring (general, day and residential), catering, computers, cooking, counselling, first aid, gardening/horticulture, group work, music, outdoor skills, sport, teaching.
Vols under 26 placed each year: 18–25 of a total of 20–30.
When to apply: Term-time only.
Work alone/with others: With trained staff.
Volunteers with disabilities: Possible, but some residential houses have stairs.
Qualifications: Maturity of approach. Our students can be very demanding.
Equipment/clothing: Try to set an example in dress but volunteers must 'muck in' with all sports, personal care etc.
Health requirements: Reasonable fitness required. Manual lifting would be part of the job in some areas.
Costs: Nil, apart from insurance for personal belongings.
Benefits: Travel to and from project each term/half term. Board and lodging. £25 per week pocket money. All other necessary insurance.
Training: Full induction on arrival. Training is given in appropriate areas and all volunteers are encouraged to participate each half term in in-service training days with the other members of staff.
Supervision: Line manager of relevant department plus director responsible for co-

ordination of volunteers and support from personnel.
Interview details: No interview necessary.
Certification: Written reports provided (if required) for volunteers' use in future. Certificate or reference provided.
Charity number: 311877
UK placements: *England* (Surrey).

STAFFORDSHIRE WILDLIFE TRUST
Coutts House
Sandon
Staffordshire
ST18 0DN UK

Tel: +44 (0) 1889 508534
Fax: +44 (0) 1889 508422
Contact: The Director

Staffordshire Wildlife Trust is a member of the Wildlife Trusts, a national partnership of 47 county trusts. For details of the Wildlife Trusts, see the entry under Cornwall Wildlife Trust.

Total projects worldwide: 1
Total UK projects: 1
Starting months: January–December.
Time required: 1–52 weeks (plus).
Age requirement: 12 plus.
Causes: Conservation, environmental causes, wildlife.
Activities: Conservation skills.
Work alone/with others: Both.
Qualifications: Nil.
Equipment/clothing: Casual work clothes, waterproofs, stout boots for outdoor work. Protective safety gear is provided.
Health requirements: Anti-tetanus innoculation recommended.
Costs: Nil.
Benefits: Out-of-pocket expenses. Volunteers are covered by the Trust's insurance.
UK placements: *England* (Staffordshire).

STALLCOMBE HOUSE
Sanctuary Lane
Woodbury Salterton
Nr Exeter
Devon
EX5 1EX UK

Tel: +44 (0) 1395 232373
Fax: +44 (0) 1395 233351
e-mail: stallfarm@eclipse.co.uk
Web: www.stallcombehouse.co.uk
Contact: Christine Jarman, Care Manager

Stallcombe is a working farm community for adults with a learning disability. There is a relaxed atmosphere and an emphasis on people going out to work or taking an active part in their life's decisions. The residents live in four separate houses and we have encouraged them to make it their home. We have a mixed age-range in our staff and we are glad to have volunteers who bring youth and new experiences. We currently have volunteers from all over the world. We like to think of this as a therapeutic community. We care for the land, the environment, for the staff and the residents.

Total projects worldwide: 1
Total UK projects: 1
Starting months: January–December.
Time required: 26–52 weeks.
Age requirement: 18 plus.
Causes: Disabled (learning and physical).
Activities: Agriculture/farming, caring (general, day and residential), gardening/horticulture.
Vols under 26 placed each year: 7 of a total of 8.
When to apply: 6–12 months in advance.
Work alone/with others: as part of a team.
Volunteers with disabilities: Possible, but not much wheelchair access.
Qualifications: Driving is an advantage but not essential.
Health requirements: Nil.
Costs: Travel to and from Stallcombe.
Benefits: Board/lodging plus pocket money of £30 per week plus 2 days holiday for each month worked. We provide public liability, employer's liability and accident insurance.
Supervision: Normally always supervised.
Interview details: No interview necessary.
Certification: Reference provided.
Charity number: 283877
UK placements: *England* (Devon).

STIFTUNG HUMANUS-HAUS
Beitenwil
CH 3076 Worb 2
Switzerland

Tel: 00 41 31 838 11 11
Fax: 00 41 31 839 7579
Contact: The Director

Total projects worldwide: 1
Total UK projects: 0
Starting months: January–December.
Time required: 1–52 weeks.

Age requirement: 14 plus.
Causes: Disabled (learning).
Worldwide placements: *Europe* (Switzerland).

STRATHSPEY RAILWAY COMPANY LTD
Aviemore Station
Dalfaber Road
Aviemore
Inverness-shire
PH22 1PY Scotland

Tel: +44 (0) 1479 810725
e-mail: laurence.grant@strathspey-
railway.freeserve.co.uk
Web: www.btinternet.com/~strathspey.railway
Contact: Laurence Grant, Superintendent of
the Line

The Strathspey Railway seeks to operate a
railway in the Highlands of Scotland. At
present services run between Aviemore and
Boat of Garten but work is being undertaken
to extend the line to Grantown-on-Spey. The
railway employs 3 1/2 full-time staff and the
rest of the workforce is made up of
volunteers. The main areas of work are:
1. Operating the service – drivers, firemen,
guards, booking office and shop staff. A
buffet car also operates on the train. 2.
Workshop staff – repairs to locomotives,
carriages and wagons. 3. Permanent way –
track repair and maintenance. Also
construction work on the extension.
The railway was set up in 1974 and
commenced operating a public service in
1978. A train service has been operated every
summer since then. Much of the work is
carried out by volunteers at weekends and
during their holidays. Volunteers have come
from South Africa, California, Wales,
England as well as many parts of Scotland.

Total projects worldwide: 1
Total UK projects: 1
Starting months: January–December.
Time required: 1–52 weeks.
Age requirement: 16 plus.
Causes: Heritage.
Activities: Catering, DIY, group work,
manual work, outdoor skills.
Vols under 26 placed each year: 10 of a total
of 100.
When to apply: All year – as soon as
possible.
Work alone/with others: With others.
Volunteers with disabilities: Not possible.
Qualifications: Nil.

Equipment/clothing: Safety footwear and
appropriate clothing for work to be
undertaken (i.e. overalls).
Health requirements: Some work is deemed
safety critical. Volunteers should be fit and
healthy for the work.
Costs: Membership £8 under 18s /OAPs,
others £14. Hostel costs £2.50 for members.
Benefits: We have insurance for our own
volunteers and staff as required by law.
Training: Training on the job.
Supervision: Railway staff supervise, directly
to start with. When volunteer demonstrates
that they can carry out task without
supervision they are allowed to get on with
the job.
Interview details: No interview necessary.
Certification: References on request.
UK placements: *Scotland* (Highland).

STUDENT ACTION INDIA (SAI)
c/o HouseNet
Office 20, 30–38 Dock Street
Leeds
LS10 1JF UK

Tel: 07071 225 866
Fax: 07071 225 866
e-mail: stud_act_india@hotmail.com
Web: http://gn.apc.org/sai
Contact: Nicola Stevenson, Volunteer Co-
ordinator

Student Action India (SAI) is a non-
governmental development organization run
by young people for young people. We aim to
promote awareness of development issues
through providing development opportunities
for volunteers in India, thus simultaneously
improving the development of young people
in India. Volunteers work with Indian
development organizations in the areas of
education (formal and non-formal),
researching and administering projects,
nursing and medicine, women's income
generation and with deaf, dumb and blind
children. Our placements also include two
supervisors who research new placements,
support the volunteers and communicate with
the executive committee in the UK. You
would assist our partner organizations and
during your placement are required to
communicate frequently with the UK via the
supervisors. You would be involved in
organizing your own placements and returned
volunteers can continue to work for SAI. We

promote development education in the UK via our Development in Action Project. Return volunteers can use their knowledge and experience gained in India to increase the understanding of development issues in the UK. In the UK SAI is run entirely by returned volunteers, comprising a co-ordinator and executive committee. Fundraising advice will be given to volunteers and comprehensive training including an introduction to Hindi as part of the programme. 'I learnt that development is also a personal process' (quote by a volunteer).

Total projects worldwide: 15
Total UK projects: 0
Starting months: June, September.
Time required: 12–24 weeks.
Age requirement: 18 plus.
Causes: Children, disabled (physical), health care/medical, teaching/assisting (EFL), young people.
Activities: Administration, arts/crafts, community work, development issues, research, teaching, theatre/drama.
Vols under 26 placed each year: Majority of a total of 30.
When to apply: Any time before 30 March.
Work alone/with others: With others, minimum of 2 per placement.
Volunteers with disabilities: We are unable to place people with disabilities as volunteers must be able to travel independently in India.
Qualifications: None but TEFL qualifications, knowledge of Hindi and experience in development work an advantage. Anyone with relevant experience may apply. Willingness to learn is the most important attribute and flexibility to cope with a diversity of challenges.
Equipment/clothing: General equipment for travel and work in India.
Health requirements: Must be reasonably fit and healthy.
Costs: Membership Fee £5 waged, £3 unwaged. Placement fee and accommodation £350 for two months, £725 for 5 months plus flights and insurance.
Benefits: Placement fee covers food and lodging during placement.
Training: Training weekend in the UK.
Supervision: Orientation week in India led by NGO workers. We also have an Indian adviser in India and further support and supervision from our partner organizations.
Nationalities accepted: No restrictions but

should speak English or Hindi and must be able to travel to India.
Interview details: Group and individual interviews take place in the UK.
Certification: Certificate or reference provided on request.
Charity number: 1037554
Worldwide placements: *Asia* (India).

STUDENT CONSERVATION ASSOCIATION INC.
689 River Road
PO Box 550
Charlestown
Sullivan County, NH
03603 USA

Tel: 00 1 603 543 1700
Fax: 00 1 603 543 1828
e-mail: internships@sca-inc.org
Web: www.sca-inc.org
Contact: Recruitment Office

The Student Conservation Association, (SCA) is the oldest and largest provider of national and community service opportunities in conservation in the United States. We involve the efforts of student and adult volunteers in the stewardship of public lands and natural and cultural resources in the US. We recruit and train over 2,200 high school student and adult volunteers annually to help conserve the parks, forest, wildlife refuges and other public and private lands of the United States. SCA volunteers put their energy and talents to work with natural and cultural resource management agencies such as the National Park Service, US Forest Service, Bureau of Land Management, US Fish and Wildlife Service, as well as other federal, state, local and private agencies. The work projects completed at these various sites include visitor services and environmental education, trail maintenance and construction, GIS/GPS, archaeology, engineering, geology and range management. The work done by an SCA volunteer is vital to the agencies and parks in which you serve. Because of budget staffing limitations the various projects might otherwise never be completed, if not for the dedication and hard work of the high school and adult volunteers placed around the country each year.

Total projects worldwide: 2,000
Total UK projects: 0
Starting months: January–December.

Time required: 4–16 weeks.
Age requirement: 16 plus.
Causes: Conservation, environmental causes.
Activities: Building/construction, computers, conservation skills, forestry, gardening/horticulture, manual work, outdoor skills, research, scientific work, teaching, training.
Vols under 26 placed each year: 700 of a total of 2,200.
When to apply: All year but by 15 March for high school students.
Work alone/with others: With others.
Volunteers with disabilities: Possible.
Qualifications: 18 plus years must have high school diploma and speak and write English fairly well. Otherwise willing to work hard.
Equipment/clothing: Hiking gear, e.g. boots, backpack etc.
Health requirements: Medical certificate confirming good health signed by physician.
Costs: All travel costs (except part travel costs within the US), application fees and any personal supplies needed while in residence.
Benefits: High school: food and shelter is provided. College: weekly stipend, some travel, housing, food, uniform allowance. SCA provides 24-hour accident insurance for all participants if not covered under a primary insurance plan.
Training: Each site will specify what/if any training is provided or required in the job description.
Supervision: High school: volunteers are supervised by 1–2 adult crew leaders who have knowledge and experience in all fields including working with teenagers. College: volunteers work alongside other volunteers and agency personnel.
Interview details: High School volunteers are not interviewed. College volunteers are interviewed by telephone unless other arrangements can be made.
Worldwide placements: *North America* (USA).

STUDENTS PARTNERSHIP WORLDWIDE
17 Dean's Yard
London
SW1P 3PB UK

Tel: +44 (0) 20 7222 0138
Fax: +44 (0) 20 7223 0008
e-mail: spwuk@gn.apc.org
Web: www.spw.org
Contact: Juliette Dodds, UK Volunteer Co-ordinator

Students Partnership Worldwide – Aids, gender, hygiene, conservation, nutrition. SPW offers you 4–9 month programmes tackling these challenging issues affecting rural communities in Africa and Asia. Uniquely, you will be working with local partners of your own age. You will use informal methods to influence young people – Aids workshops, community health days, street drama, environmental action.
Total projects worldwide: 7
Total UK projects: 0
Starting months: January–April, September–November.
Time required: 16–48 weeks.
Age requirement: 18–28
Causes: Aids/HIV, children, conservation, disabled (learning and physical), environmental causes, health care/medical, teaching/assisting (nursery, primary, secondary, EFL), young people.
Activities: Caring (general), community work, conservation skills, counselling, development issues, group work, outdoor skills, sport, teaching, theatre/drama, training.
Vols under 26 placed each year: 600
When to apply: Early application advised.
Work alone/with others: All volunteers work in pairs/groups with British and local volunteers – for example Ugandans of similar age and stage in life.
Volunteers with disabilities: Possible.
Qualifications: Enthusiasm, commitment and interest.
Costs: £2,600–£2,900.
Benefits: Self-catering accommodation plus subsistence allowance. Insurance is included in the cost of the programme, comprehensive, tailored for the work underaken.
Training: Briefing in London. 4–6 week training in-country on language, culture, actual technologies, lesson plans etc.
Supervision: In-country office to train and supervise the volunteers. Placement visits before the volunteers arrive and whilst they are there.
Charity number: 292492
Worldwide placements: *Africa* (South Africa, Tanzania, Uganda, Zimbabwe); *Asia* (India, Nepal).

SUDAN VOLUNTEER PROGRAMME
34 Estelle Road
London
NW3 2JY UK

Tel: +44 (0) 20 7485 8619
Fax: +44 (0) 20 7485 8619
e-mail: davidsvp@aol.com
Web: www.arrive.at/svp-uk
Contact: David Wolton

Sudan Volunteer Programme works with undergraduates and graduates who are native English speakers (regional or national accents are not a problem) and are prepared to give the summer vacation (or at least three months at other times of the year) to our urgent cause. Most will have experience of work or travel abroad and some will have experience of teaching English. TEFL certificates and Arabic are helpful but are not mandatory. We do not take gap year students. Volunteers with offending backgrounds may be accepted

Total projects worldwide: 1
Total UK projects: 0
Starting months: January, February, July–December.
Time required: 8–52 weeks (plus).
Age requirement: 19 plus.
Causes: Teaching/assisting (mature, EFL), young people.
Activities: Sport, teaching.
Vols under 26 placed each year: 35 of a total of 40.
When to apply: All year.
Work alone/with others: Mainly in pairs.
Volunteers with disabilities: Not possible.
Qualifications: Undergraduates or graduates. Native English speakers, travel experience.
Health requirements: Medical check and vaccinations required.
Costs: Each volunteer has to raise the cost of their air fare to Sudan, about £430 plus travel expenses in the UK for selection interviews and briefing before the start of the project, making a volunteer's costs about £550 in all.
Benefits: Free lodging, pocket money, medical, accident and standard travel insurance.
Training: Briefing session by TEFL teacher and ex-volunteers plus extensive reading and what-to-take lists.
Supervision: Co-ordinator and office in Khartoum. E-mail access in the British Council.

Interview details: Prospective volunteers are interviewed in London.
Certification: Certificate or reference on request.
Charity number: 1062155
Worldwide placements: *Africa* (Sudan).

SUE RYDER FOUNDATION
Cavendish
Sudbury
Suffolk
CO10 8AY UK

Tel: +44 (0) 1787 280653

The Sue Ryder Foundation is a living memorial to all those millions who gave their lives during two world wars in defence of human values, and to the countless others who are suffering and dying today as a result of persecution. We are a Christian based international foundation which is devoted to the relief of suffering on the widest scale. We seek to render personal service to those in need and to give affection to those who are unloved, regardless of age, race or creed as part of the family of man. There are over 20 Sue Ryder Homes in England and Scotland, caring for the sick and disabled. Certain of the homes provide specific care for those with cancer or Huntington's Disease. The Foundation runs a retreat house at Walsingham in Norfolk and has over 500 shops countrywide.

Total projects worldwide: Varies.
Total UK projects: Varies.
Starting months: January–December.
Time required: 2–52 weeks.
Age requirement: 16 plus.
Causes: Disabled (physical), elderly people.
Activities: Administration, caring (general and residential), catering, DIY, driving, gardening/horticulture.
Vols under 26 placed each year: Approximately 37 of a total of 50.
When to apply: All year – early application for summer.
Work alone/with others: With others.
Volunteers with disabilities: Not possible.
Qualifications: Nil – previous relevant experience an advantage.
Health requirements: Doctor's certificate required.
Costs: Travel to and from service.
Benefits: Free board and lodging and pocket money.

Nationalities accepted: There are some restrictions on nationalities of volunteers, please enquire.
Interview details: If applicants are interviewed, it would be in their home area.
Certification: Certificate or reference on request.
Charity number: 1052076
UK placements: *England* (Norfolk, Suffolk, N. Yorkshire, S. Yorkshire).

SUFFOLK WILDLIFE TRUST
Brooke House
The Green
Ashbocking
Ipswich
Suffolk
IP6 9JY UK

Tel: +44 (0) 1473 890089
Fax: +44 (0) 1473 890165
e-mail: christinel@suffolkwildlife.cix.co.uk
Web: www.wildlifetrust.org/suffolk
Contact: Christine Luxton

Suffolk Wildlife Trust aims to conserve wildlife and wildlife habitats in the County. We do this through: education of young people and adults; managing 57 nature reserves; influencing decision makers; working with communities, other groups and individual volunteers; raising public awareness about issues affecting wildlife. We need the help of volunteers in all aspects of our work, helping with everything from stuffing envelopes to tending the sheep flock. For people wishing to undertake a minimum of a week's work we offer the opportunity to carry out vital practical work on important wildlife sites. Unfortunately we cannot provide transport except for the two midweek teams which visit Trust reserves to undertake vital management work. We may also be able to provide opportunities for groups to carry out coppicing in ancient woodlands, during the winter months by arrangement.
Volunteers with an offending background are accepted on projects supervised by staff and individuals – not groups.

Total projects worldwide: 600
Total UK projects: 600
Starting months: January–April, July–December.
Time required: 1–2 weeks.
Age requirement: 16 plus.
Causes: Conservation, wildlife, work camps

– seasonal.
Activities: Agriculture/farming, conservation skills, manual work, outdoor skills, work camps – seasonal.
When to apply: All year.
Work alone/with others: Both.
Volunteers with disabilities: Possible.
Qualifications: Must understand English.
Equipment/clothing: Outdoor work clothes, work boots and waterproofs.
Health requirements: Must have up-to-date tetanus protection. Be fit for physical work.
Costs: Travel costs.
Benefits: SWT provides public liability and personal accident cover for volunteers and has employer's liability insurance covering staff and volunteers.
Supervision: Volunteers will report to and be supervised by a member of staff.
Interview details: By telephone only.
Certification: Reference on request.
Charity number: 262777
UK placements: *England* (Suffolk).

SUNSEED TRUST, THE
PO Box 2000
Cambridge
CB4 3US UK

Tel: +44 (0) 1273 387731 or +44 (0) 1480 411784
Fax: +44 (0) 1273 387731 / (0) 1480 411784
e-mail: sunseed@clara.net
Web: www.sunseed.clara.net

The Sunseed Trust has three aims: to find ways to help people living in poverty on degraded land (mainly desert fringes); to live an ecological lifestyle; to raise concern and action about these matters. In our simple, residential research centre in Spain, we have the driest, sunniest climate in Europe while living in an oasis. We germinate, grow and plant dry-land trees; grow organic food; grow crops with very little water; recycle our own wastes to nourish trees; develop new solar cookers, solar stills etc; cook; publicize; educate; fundraise; maintain our own buildings and a Moorish irrigation line; and enjoy life. The work is done by volunteers, from raw beginners to experts, under the guidance of skilled voluntary staff. Up to 35 people live on the project at a time. We also run a Solar Family aiming to become self-sufficient in water and energy (implementing

Sunseed's innovations). We welcome volunteers, part time for one week plus, or full time (at slightly less cost) for five weeks plus. You must be suitably qualified and experienced. In the UK volunteers help with publicity, fundraising, development and IT. Families also welcome. Sister charity Sunseed Tanzania. Send £1 for a booklet, £5 for full information on longer-term breaks.

Volunteers with an offending background are acceptable in small numbers if individually suitable.

Total projects worldwide: 5
Total UK projects: 1–5
Starting months: January–December.
Time required: 1–52 weeks.
Age requirement: 16 plus.
Causes: Conservation, environmental causes, teaching (secondary), work camps – seasonal.
Activities: Administration, agriculture/farming, building/construction, catering, computers, conservation skills, cooking, development issues, DIY, forestry, gardening/horticulture, marketing/publicity, research, technical skills, translating.
Vols under 26 placed each year: 800 of a total of approximately 1,600.
When to apply: All year.
Work alone/with others: Either.
Volunteers with disabilities: Possible, but wheelchair users would need to bring a helper.
Qualifications: Enthusiasm.
Equipment/clothing: Reasonably strong shoes.
Health requirements: Any problems must be advised in advance.
Costs: Travel and subsistence: £49–£96 per week (includes travel insurance but not travel).
Benefits: Full board plus lodging and a tiny expense allowance. Training, challenge, convivial community and advice re undergraduate grants. We insure participants.
Training: On-the-job training given.
Supervision: Health and safety are very important and volunteers are supervised by project leader.
Interview details: Longer-term applicants are interviewed in the UK.
Certification: Reference on request.
Charity number: 292511
Worldwide placements: *Africa* (Kenya, Zimbabwe); *Europe* (Spain).
UK placements: *England* (Cambridgeshire,

London).

SURREY WILDLIFE TRUST
School Lane
Pirbright
Woking
Surrey
GU24 0JN UK

Tel: +44 (0) 1483 488055
Fax: +44 (0) 1483 486505
Contact: The Director

Surrey Wildlife Trust is a member of the Wildlife Trusts, a national partnership of 47 county trusts. For details of the Wildlife Trusts, see the entry under Cornwall Wildlife Trust.

Total projects worldwide: 1
Total UK projects: 1
Starting months: January–December.
Time required: 1–52 weeks (plus).
Age requirement: 12 plus.
Causes: Conservation, environmental causes, wildlife.
Activities: Conservation skills.
Work alone/with others: Both.
Qualifications: Nil.
Equipment/clothing: Casual work clothes, waterproofs, stout boots for outdoor work. Protective safety gear is provided.
Health requirements: Anti-tetanus innoculation recommended.
Costs: Nil.
Benefits: Out-of-pocket expenses. Volunteers are covered by the Trust's insurance.
UK placements: *England* (Surrey).

SURVIVAL
11–15 Emerald Street
London
WC1N 3QL UK

Tel: +44 (0) 20 7242 1441
Fax: +44 (0) 20 7242 1771
e-mail: survival@gn.apc.org
Web: www.survival.org.uk/
Contact: Clara Braggio

Survival International is a worldwide organization supporting tribal peoples. It stands for their right to decide their own future and helps them protect their lives, lands, and human rights.
Total projects worldwide: 1
Total UK projects: 1
Starting months: January–December.

Time required: 12–52 weeks.
Age requirement: 16 plus.
Causes: Human rights.
Activities: Administration, campaigning, fundraising, library/resource centres, marketing/publicity, research, translating.
Vols under 26 placed each year: 15 of a total of 20.
When to apply: All year.
Work alone/with others: Both.
Volunteers with disabilities: Possible, but no wheelchair access.
Qualifications: Computer literacy useful but not essential.
Health requirements: Nil.
Costs: Nil, apart from insurance.
Benefits: Travel expenses within Greater London can be paid.
Training: No pre-placement training provided.
Supervision: By relevant department e.g. membership co-ordinator.
Interview details: Interviews take place in London.
Certification: Reference on request.
Charity number: 267444
UK placements: *England* (London).

SWALLOWS IN DENMARK
Østerbrogade 49
DK-2100 Copenhagen Ø
Denmark

Tel: 00 45 35 26 17 47
Fax: 00 45 31 38 17 46
Contact: Per Markmoller

Swallows in Denmark is a non-profit volunteer organization. Our aim is to support grass-root-level movements in Bangladesh and India. The Swallows is also supported by the Danish agency for development – Danida. The Swallows in Denmark is a member of the Emmaus International Community founded by Abbe Pierre. The purpose of the camp is to participate in solidarity work for grass-root level movements in the developing countries Furthermore the camp is a get-together for a lot of people from different countries. The main purpose of the Swallows Camp is to organize a second-hand market. It is our special summer income-generating activity. About 20 international participants will be selected from all over the world. The official language of the camp will be English. The work involves collecting, sorting and

selling various items such as paper, books, clothes, furniture, electronic items and household things. The participants are organized in different day-to-day teams. Monday to Saturday are working days. Saturday will be the day of the market. Sunday is a day off and there is one afternoon off during the week. During the camp there are many opportunities for you to explore Copenhagen where there are a lot of things to do during the summer and many of these activities are either free or very cheap. In the evenings there are social activities at the camp.

Total projects worldwide: 1
Total UK projects: 0
Starting months: June, July.
Time required: 2–4 weeks.
Age requirement: 18 plus.
Causes: Poor/homeless, work camps – seasonal.
Activities: Arts/crafts, DIY, driving, fundraising, group work, international aid, manual work, summer camps, visiting/befriending.
Vols under 26 placed each year: 30
When to apply: Before 1 May.
Qualifications: Knowledge of English preferred.
Equipment/clothing: Working clothes/rainclothes.
Costs: Travel expenses and pocket money (work is unpaid).
Benefits: Board and accommodation.
Interview details: No interview necessary.
Worldwide placements: *Asia* (Bangladesh, India); *Europe* (Denmark).

SWAYTHLING DETACHED YOUTH WORK PROJECT
The Methodist Church
284 Burgess Road
Swaythling
Southampton
Hampshire
SO16 3BE UK

Tel: +44 (0) 23 8055 4936
Fax: +44 (0) 23 8055 4936
Contact: The Project Manager

The Swaythling Youth Project was established in 1979. It arose from the recognition by members of the Methodist Church and local people that a number of local young people were in need of help, advice and support. The aim of the Project is to work with young people aged between 16 and 25 in the Swaythling area. The work takes place in the streets, in cafés, pubs and in young people's homes. The workers offer a confidential service providing support, information, advice, or just a listening ear. The project also has responsibility for the Youth Centre in Swaythling. As well as the Senior Club (14–25 year olds) there is a Junior Club once a week run by volunteers and the Prince's Trust Volunteers are based there running 12-week courses regularly throughout the year for 16–25 year olds.

Total projects worldwide: 1
Total UK projects: 1
Starting months: January–December.
Time required: 12–52 weeks.
Age requirement: 21 plus.
Causes: Children, inner city problems, offenders/ex-offenders, poor/homeless, unemployed, young people.
Activities: Community work, counselling, group work, outdoor skills, summer camps, training.
When to apply: All year.
Work alone/with others: With others.
Volunteers with disabilities: No disabled access to office base.
Qualifications: Youth work experience preferred, driving licence useful, patience and staying power.
Equipment/clothing: Waterproof clothing, strong walking shoes.
Health requirements: Nil.
Costs: Travel, subsistence, accommodation.
Benefits: Out-of-pocket expenses.
Certification: Certificate or reference provided.
UK placements: *England* (Hampshire).

SYLVIA-KOTI
Kyläkatu 140
15700 Lahti
Finland

Tel: 00 358 3 8831 30
Fax: 00 358 3 8831 315
e-mail: sylvia-koti@kolumbus.fi
Contact: Eric Kaufmann

Sylvia-Koti is a Camphill community for developmentally disabled children and youngsters.

Total projects worldwide: 1
Total UK projects: 0
Starting months: August.
Time required: 1–52 weeks (plus).
Age requirement: 19 plus.
Causes: Children, disabled (learning and physical), teaching/assisting (nursery, primary, secondary), young people.
Activities: Arts/crafts, caring (general, day and residential), cooking, gardening/horticulture, group work, social work, teaching, training.
Vols under 26 placed each year: 10 of a total of 40.
When to apply: By 30 April.
Work alone/with others: With others.
Volunteers with disabilities: Not possible.
Qualifications: It would be useful to learn Finnish.
Health requirements: Healthy.
Costs: Travel.
Benefits: Board/lodging and around £100 monthly pocket money. Accident and liability insurance is provided by us during working times.
Training: On-the-job training guided by experienced co-workers.
Supervision: Volunteers work with more experienced co-workers.
Interview details: By letter only.
Certification: Certificate or reference on request.
Worldwide placements: *Europe* (Finland).

SYNDICAT MIXTE MONTAIGU-ROCHESERVIÈRE
35 Avenue Villebois-Mareuil
BP 44
Montaigu Cedex
85607 France

Tel: 00 33 2 51 46 45 45
Fax: 00 33 2 51 46 45 40
e-mail: julie-legree@yahoo.co.uk
Web: www.explomr.com/english
Contact: Mme Julie Legrée

The Syndicat Mixte Montaigu-Rocheservière is a local government organization. The English teaching section of the Syndicat Mixte plays an active role in 23 different villages in the Montaigu/Rocheservière and St Fulgent area. Five teaching posts are available; four in primary schools with pupils between 9 and 11. Each teacher is allocated seven different schools and approximately

200 pupils. The fifth post, working as an assistant in the Montaigu Collège or Lycée, involves teaching pupils aged 15–21 for 20 hours a week. No work in French school holidays or at weekends. This is extremely good training for a future teaching career which would particularly appeal to conscientious hard-working francophiles.

Total projects worldwide: 1
Total UK projects: 0
Starting months: September.
Time required: 32 weeks.
Age requirement: 18–25
Causes: Teaching/assisting (primary, secondary, EFL).
Activities: Teaching.
Vols under 26 placed each year: 5
When to apply: As early as possible.
Work alone/with others: With others.
Volunteers with disabilities: Not possible.
Qualifications: A-level French, interest in teaching and children, experience of staying in France.
Health requirements: Students contribute to French national insurance system.
Costs: Travel costs to and from UK plus insurance (third party). 'Responsabilité Civile' provided by the student and E111. Other accident/life insurance supplied by us.
Benefits: Salary of FF1,700 per month (before national insurance deductions).
Training: 10 days in-house training including training lessons in schools.
Supervision: British-born project co-ordinator is permanently available on a professional and social basis.
Interview details: Applicants are interviewed in July in the UK.
Certification: Certificate or reference provided.
Worldwide placements: *Europe* (France).

T

TADWORTH COURT CHILDREN'S HOSPITAL HOLIDAY PROJECT
Tadworth Court
Tadworth
Surrey
KT20 5RU UK

Tel: +44 (0) 1737 357171
Fax: +44 (0) 1737 373848
Contact: Rachel Turner, Volunteers Organizer

The Tadworth Court Children's Hospital Holiday Project provides a programme of extra social activities for mentally and physically disabled children attending Tadworth Court for respite care. At any one time there are up to 20 children on the unit aged up to 19 years. Help is needed to provide care feeding, bathing and changing the children, organizing play and activities and generally befriending them. Volunteers are needed mainly in the summer but there are occasional voluntary positions open for a minimum of six months which start at any time of the year. Trained staff are available to assist at all times.

Total projects worldwide: 1
Total UK projects: 1
Starting months: January–December.
Time required: 8–52 weeks.
Age requirement: 18 plus.
Causes: Children, disabled (learning and physical).
Activities: Arts/crafts, caring (general), music.
Vols under 26 placed each year: 15
When to apply: As soon as possible – before end April if applying for summer.
Work alone/with others: With others.
Volunteers with disabilities: Possible.
Qualifications: Preferably some experience with children with very severe special needs.
Equipment/clothing: Flat shoes with soft soles and comfortable clothes.
Health requirements: No eczema or open wounds and no one with a bad back should apply.
Costs: Nil.
Benefits: Accommodation, a meal allowance of £6 per day.
Certification: Reference provided.
UK placements: *England* (Surrey).

TAMBOPATA JUNGLE LODGE
PO Box 454
Cusco
Peru

Tel: 00 51 84 225 701
Fax: 00 51 84 238 911

Tambopata Jungle Lodge needs nature guides

to lead nature walks for tourists and accompany them during their stay at a jungle lodge in the rainforest of Southern Peru within the Tambopata-Candamo. Working hours required may be any time between 4 a.m. and 8 p.m. as the tour programme dictates. You can either work 20 days per month and get around £100 per month or work for just ten days per month and get the other 20 days free for research etc.

Total projects worldwide: 1
Total UK projects: 0
Starting months: January–December.
Time required: 13–52 weeks.
Age requirement: 14 plus.
Causes: Environmental causes, wildlife.
Activities: Forestry, gardening/horticulture, research, scientific work.
Qualifications: Nature Studies qualified students and scientists. English and Spanish speakers.
Costs: Travel to Lima.
Benefits: Room, board, £100 and return air travel between Lima or Cusco and Puerto Maldonado.
Worldwide placements: *South America* (Peru).

TANGENTS
8–10 Lauriston Street
West Port
Edinburgh
EH3 9DJ Scotland

Tel: +44 (0) 131 229 1950
Fax: +44 (0) 131 229 1992
e-mail: tangents@tangents7.freeserve.co.uk
Web: www.tangents.org.uk
Contact: Tara McCarthy, Volunteer Co-ordinator

Tangents develops national networks of peer training and empowerment advocacy, information and action. Tangents is run by 16–25 year olds for 16–25 year olds, encouraging and supporting young people to plan and organize activities for themselves. We are always on the lookout for new volunteers from all walks of life aged between 16–25 with any skills to contribute. Volunteers with an offending background are accepted, depending on charges or convictions.

Total projects worldwide: 1
Total UK projects: 1

Starting months: January–December.
Time required: 1–52 weeks (plus).
Age requirement: 16–25
Causes: Addicts/ex-addicts, Aids/HIV, conservation, disabled (learning and physical), environmental causes, health care/medical, offenders/ex-offenders, poor/homeless, unemployed, young people.
Activities: Administration, arts/crafts, campaigning, community work, computers, conservation skills, development issues, fundraising, group work, library/resource centres, music, research, social work, sport, training, visiting/befriending.
Vols under 26 placed each year: 45 of a total of 50.
When to apply: All year.
Work alone/with others: With others.
Volunteers with disabilities: Possible.
Qualifications: Nil.
Health requirements: Nil.
Costs: Nil.
Benefits: Travel, lunch and training.
Interview details: Interviews take place in the office or somewhere suitable for disabled volunteers.
Charity number: SCO23737
UK placements: *Scotland* (throughout).

TAPOLA CAMPHILL YHTEISO
SF 16350 Niinikoski
Finland

Tel: 00 358 18 7795 312
Fax: 00 358 18 7795 368
Contact: The Director

Tapola Camphill Yhteiso is a Camphill village community for adults with special needs.

Total projects worldwide: 1
Total UK projects: 0
Starting months: January–December.
Time required: 1–52 weeks.
Age requirement: 14 plus.
Causes: Disabled (learning).
Worldwide placements: *Europe* (Finland).

TASK BRASIL
PO Box 4901
London
SE16 3PP UK

Tel: +44 (0) 20 7394 1177
Fax: +44 (0) 20 7394 7713
e-mail: taskbr@globalnet.co.uk›

Web: www.taskbrasil.org.uk
Contact: Ligia Da Silva or Elaine Waller or Denia

Task Brasil is a British-based charity. The office in Rio, Brazil runs programmes for street children, most of whom have been either orphaned or abandoned. Deprived of any alternative, these children 'escape' to the streets where they 'settle in' and attempt to carry on with their lives. Nationally our aims are to create media awareness; to encourage interested parties to be project sponsors and donors; to recruit volunteers; to organize all fundraising events; to establish links in other British cities; to establish regular transport for donated items to Brazil; to co-ordinate the projects in Brazil. In Brazil our objectives are to run programmes and home(s) for street children; to provide access to psychological and medical assistance and a secure and loving place for the children; to promote family planning awareness for both the children and their families; to arrange an educational structure and sporting activities for the children; to set up training schemes for older children; to provide alternatives to combat drug and sexual abuse among the children; to maintain a training programme for those directly involved with the children; to heighten public awareness; to organize covenants and fundraising. Task Brasil is concerned with: the needs of children living and working on Brazil's streets; encouraging family ties; training and educating the children in useful and beneficial skills; giving the children an awareness of and a sense of pride in their own cultural roots; helping the children enter the mainstream of society and to learn the value of life; making the children aware of family planning and diseases, e.g. Aids; helping to change attitudes of the Brazilian public towards the street children.

Total projects worldwide: 2
Total UK projects: 2
Starting months: January–December.
Time required: 2–52 weeks (plus).
Age requirement: 21 plus.
Causes: Addicts/ex-addicts, children, health care/medical, human rights, offenders/ex-offenders, teaching (nursery, primary, EFL), young people.
Activities: Accountancy, administration, arts/crafts, campaigning, caring (general, day and residential), computers, driving, fundraising, group work, library/resource centres, marketing/publicity, newsletter/journalism, research, social work, technical skills, translating.
When to apply: All year.
Work alone/with others: Both.
Volunteers with disabilities: Not possible.
Qualifications: Administration, fundraising, PR all useful.
Health requirements: Nil.
Benefits: Fares or petrol.
Interview details: Interviews take place in SE London.
Certification: References supplied.
Charity number: 1030929
Worldwide placements: *South America* (Brazil).
UK placements: *England* (London).

TEACHING AND PROJECTS ABROAD
Gerrard House
Rustington
West Sussex
BN16 1AW UK

Tel: +44 (0) 1903 859911
Fax: +44 (0) 1903 785779
e-mail: info@teaching-abroad.co.uk
Web: www.teaching-abroad.co.uk
Contact: Dr Peter Slowe

The aims of Teaching and Projects Abroad are to help people in developing countries and Eastern Europe learn English, provide volunteers with good work experience and provide all parties with cultural exchange. There are many students and graduates in Britain and Ireland who would like to spend some time abroad doing a useful job in an interesting part of the world. You choose your own country, dates and activities. Teaching and Projects Abroad makes sure that you have good back-up wherever you go. We have staff in all twelve countries where we work. This means you'll have no worries about accommodation or meals, no worries about needing expensive TEFL qualifications, no worries about not being a qualified teacher or other professional, no worries about local travel, exchanging money or confirming air tickets. The money you pay Teaching and Projects Abroad is for setting you up in a job with adequate supervision, making sure you have good food, accommodation and insurance and being there to help. Over eight years, more than

5,000 volunteers have been placed for teaching and the widest range of other placements including medical (200 plus places), journalism, accountancy, law, business, marketing, engineering, conservation and dissertations. Volunteers with an offending background are accepted.

Total projects worldwide: 49
Total UK projects: 0
Starting months: January–December.
Time required: 4–52 weeks.
Age requirement: 17 plus.
Causes: Architecture, conservation, disabled (physical), environmental causes, health care/medical, teaching/assisting (nursery, primary, secondary, mature, EFL), wildlife.
Activities: Accountancy, arts/crafts, conservation skills, marketing/publicity, newsletter/journalism, summer camps, teaching, technical skills, theatre/drama.
Vols under 26 placed each year: 950 of a total of 1,000.
When to apply: All year.
Work alone/with others: Always a local community of our volunteers. Placements can be shared if desired.
Volunteers with disabilities: Possible.
Qualifications: Gap-year, graduates or undergraduates. Near-native English speakers.
Health requirements: Nil.
Costs: Prices are from £795 (without travel). All prices are for up to 3 months. After 3 months we charge £95–£175 per month up to a maximum of 12 months.
Benefits: Board and lodging with local family. Travel and medical cover is provided by us at no extra charge.
Training: Optional open days and TEFL courses.
Supervision: We have an office and our own paid staff at each destination. Each volunteer also has a supervisor at their placement.
Interview details: Applicants are not usually interviewed but visitors to our offices are most welcome by arrangement.
Certification: Certificate or reference on request.
Worldwide placements: *Africa* (Ghana, South Africa, Togo); *Asia* (China, India, Nepal, Thailand); *Europe* (Russia, Ukraine); *Central America* (Mexico); *South America* (Peru).

TEARFUND
100 Church Road
Teddington

Middlesex
TW11 8QE UK

Tel: +44 (0) 20 8943 7750
Fax: +44 (0) 20 8943 3594
e-mail: transform@tearfund.org
Web: www.tearfund.org
Contact: Rachel Spaul, Transform Administrator

The purpose of Tearfund's programme, 'Transform', is to serve Jesus Christ by enabling those who share evangelical Christian beliefs to bring good news to the poor: proclaiming and demonstrating the gospel for the whole person through the support of Christian relief and development; working through a worldwide network of evangelical Christian partners. The work is a mix of practical tasks and developing relationships with local people. All the teams take time to look beyond the surface. You'll come back understanding why people are poor and what the church can do; encouraging partnership in prayer and support from Christians in Britain and Ireland; seeking at all times to be obedient to biblical teaching. Volunteers with an offending background may be accepted. Our main criterion is that they are committed Christians and members of a local church.

Total projects worldwide: 17
Total UK projects: 9
Starting months: July, December.
Time required: 2–7 weeks.
Age requirement: 18–21
Causes: Addicts/ex-addicts, children, conservation, human rights, inner city problems, poor/homeless, teaching/assisting (primary, secondary), work camps – seasonal, young people.
Activities: Arts/crafts, building/construction, caring (general), community work, conservation skills, development issues, DIY, group work, social work, summer camps, teaching, technical skills, work camps – seasonal.
Vols under 26 placed each year: 200
When to apply: February for overseas, May for UK.
Work alone/with others: In teams.
Volunteers with disabilities: Possible.
Qualifications: Christian. Unskilled welcome. UK residents.
Health requirements: Candidates need to pass a medical check.

Costs: Overseas £1,200 approximately plus personal spending money. UK £95.
Benefits: Orientation, travel, accommodation, food, insurance but not personal spending money.
Training: Residential orientation.
Supervision: We provide team leaders and work alongside national organizations.
Nationalities accepted: UK residents only.
Interview details: Interviews take place at regional selection venues.
Charity number: 265464
Worldwide placements: *Africa* (Burkina Faso, Ethiopia, Ghana, Kenya, South Africa, Tanzania, Uganda, Zimbabwe); *Asia* (India, Lebanon, Philippines, Thailand); *Europe* (Portugal); *Central America* (Haiti, Honduras, Jamaica).
UK placements: *England* (London, Manchester, Merseyside, W. Yorkshire); *Scotland* (E. Ayrshire, N. Ayrshire, Glasgow City, N. Lanarkshire, S. Lanarkshire, Renfrewshire); *Northern Ireland* (Belfast City).

TEES VALLEY WILDLIFE TRUST
Bellamy Pavilion
Kirkleatham Old Hall
Kirkleatham
Redcar
Cleveland
TS10 5NW UK

Tel: +44 (0) 1642 759900
Fax: +44 (0) 1642 480401
e-mail: teesvalleywt@cix.co.uk
Contact: Steve Ashton, Education Officer

Tees Valley Wildlife Trust is an independent voluntary nature conservation organization first set up in 1979, currently managing 130 ha of land. It is a member of the Wildlife Trusts, a national partnership of 47 county trusts. For details of the Wildlife Trusts, see the entry under Cornwall Wildlife Trust.

Total projects worldwide: 20
Total UK projects: 20
Starting months: January–December.
Time required: 1–52 weeks (plus).
Age requirement: 16 plus.
Causes: Conservation, environmental causes, wildlife.
Activities: Administration, building/construction, community work, computers, conservation skills, forestry, gardening/horticulture, group work, manual work, outdoor skills.
Vols under 26 placed each year: 1–2
When to apply: All year.
Work alone/with others: With others.
Volunteers with disabilities: Possible.
Qualifications: Nil but practical skills useful.
Equipment/clothing: Casual work clothes, waterproofs, stout boots. Protective safety boots, gloves etc. provided.
Health requirements: Any medical conditions (illness, allergy or physical disability) that may require treatment/medication or which affect the volunteer working with machinery must be notified to us in advance. Tetanus injections must be up to date.
Costs: Bring own packed lunch.
Benefits: Out-of-pocket expenses. Insurance is covered through the Trust.
Training: Introduction session.
Supervision: Constant supervision.
Interview details: Interviews at our office.
Certification: Reference on request.
Charity number: 511068
UK placements: *England* (Co. Durham, N. Yorkshire).

TEJO (TUTMONDA ESPERANTISTA JUNULARA ORG.)
Nieuwe Binnenweg 176
3015 BJ Rotterdam
The Netherlands

Tel: 00 31 10 436 1044
Fax: 00 31 10 436 1751
e-mail: tejo-oficejo@esperanto.org
Web: www.esperanto.org/internacia/tejo
Contact: The Director

TEJO needs volunteers to join work camps in various European countries arranged by TEJO, the World Organization of Young Esperantists. All camps include Esperanto lessons for beginners. TEJO's principal objectives are to serve the interests of young speakers of Esperanto throughout the world, and to spread the use and practical application of the international language in youth circles. We are concerned with present-day youth problems, especially those requiring international understanding and co-operation. We are completely neutral in regard to nationality, race, sex, religion and politics with the exception of cases in which human rights are violated. We have 41 national sections in all parts of the world. TEJO and the national sections organize frequent meetings, conferences, seminars and congresses. A number of young activists from all over the world serve every year for short periods in order to acquire organizational experience.

Total projects worldwide: 1–2
Starting months: June–August.
Time required: 2–5 weeks.
Age requirement: 18 plus.
Causes: Archaeology, architecture, conservation, heritage, work camps – seasonal.
Activities: Building/construction, conservation skills, gardening/horticulture, group work, outdoor skills, summer camps, work camps – seasonal.
Vols under 26 placed each year: 10–50
When to apply: All year.
Work alone/with others: With others.
Volunteers with disabilities: Not usually.
Qualifications: Basic knowledge of Esperanto or interest in learning Esperanto.
Health requirements: Nil.
Costs: Travel costs – sometimes a small registration fee.
Benefits: Board and lodging.
Worldwide placements: *Asia* (Turkey); *Europe* (Albania, Andorra, Armenia, Austria, Azerbaijan, Belarus, Belgium, Bosnia-Herzegovina, Bulgaria, Croatia, Cyprus, Czech Republic, Denmark, Estonia, Finland, France, Georgia, Germany, Gibraltar, Greece, Hungary, Iceland, Ireland, Italy, Latvia, Liechtenstein, Lithuania, Luxembourg, Macedonia, Malta, Moldova, Monaco, Netherlands, Norway, Poland, Portugal, Romania, Russia, San Marino, Slovakia, Slovenia, Spain, Sweden, Switzerland, Turkey, Ukraine, Vatican City, Yugoslavia).
UK placements: *England* (throughout); *Scotland* (throughout); *Northern Ireland* (throughout); *Wales* (throughout).

TEL AVIV UNIVERSITY – YAVNEH-YAM PROJECT
Department of Classics
69978 Ramat Aviv
Tel Aviv
Israel

Tel: 00 972 3 6409938
Fax: 00 972 3 6409457
e-mail: fischer@ccsg.tau.ac.il
Contact: Professor Moshe Fischer

Tel Aviv University needs volunteers to take part in archaeological excavations at the ancient port site of Yavneh Yam. Volunteers are recruited for two week periods in July and August. It is possible to stay for more than one period. Previous archaeological experience is an advantage but not essential. Groups of volunteers are particularly welcome.

Total projects worldwide: 1
Total UK projects: 0
Starting months: June–August.
Time required: 2–8 weeks.
Age requirement: 16 plus.
Causes: Archaeology.
Activities: Research, scientific work.
Vols under 26 placed each year: 40–50
When to apply: March.
Work alone/with others: With others.
Volunteers with disabilities: We are unable to place people with disabilities.
Qualifications: Not important.
Equipment/clothing: Working clothes and shoes and bathing equipment.
Health requirements: Normal good health. Insurance necessary, will be checked on arrival.
Costs: Food and accommodation (approximately US$300 per week).
Benefits: Evening courses and trips with emphasis on archaeology and history of Israel.
Interview details: No interview necessary.
Certification: Certificate of participation at archaeological excavation in the Holy Land and if necessary back-up letter.
Worldwide placements: *Asia* (Israel).

TEL DOR EXCAVATION PROJECT
Institute of Archaeology
Hebrew University
Mt Scopus
Jerusalem
Israel 30815

Tel: 00 972 2 5882403
Fax: 00 972 2 5825548 Attn Tel Dor
Contact: Dr Ilan Sharon

Tel Dor was a major Canaanite, Phoenician, Hellenistic and Roman port and trading emporium on the Carmel coast. The Centre of Nautical and Regional Archaeology at Dor (CONRAD), housed in a historic glass factory, on the grounds of Kibbutz Nasholim, is home of the Tel Dor excavation project and museum. Volunteers are needed during the season (July–August) for excavation. Restoration, conservation, exhibit preparation and maintenance, analysis of the finds, and conservation work on the building go on year-round.

Total projects worldwide: 1
Total UK projects: 0
Starting months: July, August.
Time required: 2–52 weeks.
Age requirement: 17 plus.
Causes: Archaeology, architecture, heritage, work camps – seasonal.
Activities: Administration, computers, outdoor skills, research, training, work camps – seasonal.
Vols under 26 placed each year: 70 of a total of 100.
When to apply: All year until 31 May.
Work alone/with others: With others.
Volunteers with disabilities: Possible.
Qualifications: Hebrew or English.
Equipment/clothing: Hat, sun screen lotion, strong shoes.
Health requirements: Must hold health insurance for Israel.
Costs: All costs including accommodation, food, personal possesions (theft and damage) insurance.
Training: Lectures and tours are given during the day.
Supervision: One area manager working with about 20 volunteers.
Interview details: No interview necessary.
Certification: Participation certificates are issued at end of stay. University credits may be obtained from participating institutions (usually entailing additional demands such as attending field-school lectures, etc. and also extra fees).
Worldwide placements: *Asia* (Israel).

TERRENCE HIGGINS TRUST LIGHTHOUSE, THE
52–54 Grays Inn Road
London
WC1X 8JU UK

Tel: +44 (0) 20 7831 0330
Fax: +44 (0) 20 7816 4561
e-mail: katie.ryan@tht.org.uk
Web: www.tht.org.uk
Contact: Volunteer Co-ordinator

The Terrence Higgins Trust Lighthouse was founded in 1983 to inform, advise and help people affected by HIV and Aids. Today, we are the UK's largest HIV and Aids voluntary organization, providing a range of high quality services which are responsive to the needs of people living with or affected by HIV and Aids. You will be joining 1,000 other volunteers and 80 staff who work in partnership to achieve our Mission. Our volunteers and staff come from all sections of the community and are committed to providing services to anyone affected by HIV and Aids. All aspects of selection and training are covered by our equal opportunities policy, which ensures that selection for volunteering or training is based on personal ability. Our mission is to: reduce the spread of HIV; provide services which improve the health and quality of life of those affected; campaign for greater public understanding of the personal, social and medical impact of HIV and Aids. Volunteers with an offending background may be accepted. Volunteers are asked to self disclose certain un-spent convictions.

Total projects worldwide: 1
Total UK projects: 1
Starting months: January–December.
Time required: 26–52 weeks.
Age requirement: 18 plus.
Causes: Addicts/ex-addicts, Aids/HIV, health care/medical.
Activities: Administration, campaigning, caring (general), computers, DIY, driving, fundraising, gardening/horticulture, training, translating, visiting/befriending.
Vols under 26 placed each year: 15–20 of a total of 150.
When to apply: All year.
Work alone/with others: Both.
Volunteers with disabilities: Possible.
Qualifications: Nil.
Costs: Must be resident in London as accommodation not provided.
Benefits: Travel and lunch expenses and insurance.
Training: We ask all volunteers to attend an initial orientation event to help volunteer and THT to match skills and interests. Basic skills training (2 days). We also provide ongoing training as well as regular information updates.
Supervision: Support through volunteer group and regular meetings.
Interview details: Interviews take place in London.
Certification: Reference on request.

Charity number: 288527
UK placements: *England* (London,
Oxfordshire, E. Sussex, W. Sussex, West
Midlands, W. Yorkshire).

THISTLE CAMPS
The National Trust for Scotland
Wemyss House
28 Charlotte Square
Edinburgh
EH2 4ET Scotland

Tel: +44 (0) 131 243 9470
Fax: +44 (0) 131 243 9593
e-mail: conservationvolunteers@nts.org.uk
Contact: Julia Downes, CV Manager

Thistle Camps are open to all volunteers over
18 years of age. (Some camps are open to
those over 16 as well but these are limited.)
They provide opportunities for you to see
new places, meet new people and contribute
to the conservation of Scotland's wild places.
All volunteers are expected to work a 9–5
day and help out with domestic duties when
not on site. A day off is programmed to visit
nearby places of interest. Volunteers must be
prepared for physically demanding tasks and
bad weather.

Total projects worldwide: 36
Total UK projects: 36
Starting months: March–November.
Time required: 1–3 weeks.
Age requirement: 16 plus.
Causes: Archaeology, conservation,
environmental causes, heritage, wildlife,
work camps – seasonal.
Activities: Building/construction,
conservation skills, gardening/horticulture,
group work, manual work, outdoor skills,
summer camps, training, work camps –
seasonal.
Vols under 26 placed each year: 260 of a
total of 370.
When to apply: January–September.
Work alone/with others: With others.
Volunteers with disabilities: Not possible.
Qualifications: Willingness to work hard and
mix in.
Equipment/clothing: Work clothes/overalls,
waterproofs, steel toe-capped boots/
wellingtons.
Health requirements: Should be reasonably
fit. Anti-tetanus innoculation recommended.
Costs: Travel to pick-up point in Scotland.
Camp costs start at £45 (£30 unwaged,

retired, student).
Benefits: Accommodation plus food provided.
Public liability insurance provided by the
Trust.
Training: Training given on the job.
Supervision: By staff and camp leaders.
Interview details: No interview necessary.
Charity number: SCO07410
UK placements: *Scotland* (throughout, except
for Fife and Orkney Islands).

THOMAS-HAUS BERLIN FÜR HEILPÄDOGOGIK UND SPRACHTHERAPIE e.V.
Peter-Lenné-Str. 42
D-14195 Berlion (Dahlem)
Germany

Tel: 00 49 30 832 64 53
Contact: The Director

Thomas-Haus Berlin für Heilpädogogik und
Sprachtherapie is a Camphill curative
therapeutic centre for young children with
special needs.

Total projects worldwide: 1
Total UK projects: 0
Starting months: January–December.
Time required: 1–52 weeks.
Age requirement: 14 plus.
Causes: Children, disabled (learning).
Worldwide placements: *Europe* (Germany).

TIME FOR GOD SCHEME, THE
7 Colney Hatch Lane
Muswell Hill
London
N10 1PN UK

Tel: +44 (0) 20 8883 1504
Fax: +44 (0) 20 8365 2471
e-mail: OfficeTFG@cs.com
Web: www.timeforgod.org
Contact: Roger Taylor/Tracy Phillips,
Director/Deputy Director

The Time for God Scheme offers 9–12
month volunteer placements for Christian
young people aged 18–25. Opportunities
include working with churches and
community projects, the elderly, mentally ill,
ex-offenders, disabled children, youth and
homeless. Volunteers are supported by field
staff. The TFG programme, established 33
years ago, operates by matching young people
to church and community projects working
with a variety of client groups in numerous

settings throughout the UK and more recently abroad. TFG helps young people develop new skills, take a year out from education, serve God in a new way, explore a vocation or simply try something new.

Total projects worldwide: Various.
Total UK projects: 150
Starting months: January, September.
Time required: 40–52 weeks.
Age requirement: 18–25
Causes: Addicts/ex-addicts, Aids/HIV, children, disabled (learning and physical), elderly people, health care/medical, inner city problems, offenders/ex-offenders, poor/homeless, teaching (nursery), unemployed, young people.
Activities: Administration, campaigning, caring (general, day and residential), community work, computers, cooking, counselling, group work, manual work, marketing/publicity, music, outdoor skills, religion, social work, sport, teaching, theatre/drama, training, visiting/befriending.
Vols under 26 placed each year: 200
When to apply: 2–8 months in advance.
Work alone/with others: Both.
Volunteers with disabilities: Possible.
Qualifications: Committed Christians or honestly exploring Christian faith.
Health requirements: Nil.
Costs: Home church contributes approximately £600 towards training costs. Non-UK volunteers need health care insurance.
Benefits: We pay for day-to-day living costs plus £25 per week. End-of-service conference. Overseas volunteers have 3-day debriefing event.
Training: TFG provides three 4-day residential training conferences for all volunteers with opportunities for worship, Bible study, reflection, training and a monthly spiritual development programme.
Supervision: Supervisor in placement gives weekly supervision. Pastoral support and placement visits by field officers ensure the volunteer is well supported.
Interview details: We interview all applicants who attend one of our briefing days which take place throughout the year.
Certification: Certificate or reference provided.
Charity number: 206163
Worldwide placements: *Europe* (Austria, Belgium, Denmark, Finland, France, Germany, Ireland, Italy, Netherlands, Norway, Portugal, Sweden); *North America* (USA).
UK placements: *England* (throughout); *Scotland* (throughout); *Northern Ireland* (throughout); *Wales* (throughout).

TLHOLEGO DEVELOPMENT PROJECT
PO Box 1668
Rustenburg 0300
North West Province
South Africa

Tel: 00 27 14 592 7090
Fax: 00 27 11 486 0279
e-mail: tlholego@iafrica.com
Contact: Mr Paul Cohen

Tlholego Development Project provides a rural educational environment based on ecological principles, with the purpose of training people in the design and implementation of sustainable land use and village settlements. Tlholego is a living model village for those ecological principles, consisting of a community of 50 plus members, many of whom were formerly disadvantaged under the apartheid regime. These principles are continually refined and improved through the community's activities and experiences. Volunteers play an active part in the community, not only living alongside its members, but assisting in tending the permaculture garden, in the building and maintaining of the buildings constructed using sustainable building technologies, and in the community decision-making processes. It is an opportunity to be an active part, rather than an observer, of a vibrant developing rural community.
Tlholego Development Project also operates a series of workshops covering Permaculture, Eco-village Design, building using sustainable building technology and landcare through the Keyline Design and Earthworks Engineering Design system. The leading authorities in their field facilitate these workshops. Volunteers are automatically able to attend these workshops. Volunteers with an offending background would be considered individually.

Total projects worldwide: 1
Total UK projects: 0
Starting months: January–December.
Time required: 4–24 weeks.
Age requirement: 16–25

Causes: Environmental causes, heritage, young people.
Activities: Agriculture/farming, building/ construction, development issues, fundraising, gardening/horticulture.
Vols under 26 placed each year: 1 of a total of 2.
When to apply: All year – as early as possible before starting.
Work alone/with others: Both.
Volunteers with disabilities: Possible.
Qualifications: Nil.
Health requirements: Nil.
Costs: All travel, personal expenses and insurance.
Benefits: Food and accommodation.
Supervision: Project directors supervise.
Interview details: No interview necessary.
Certification: Certificate or reference on request.
Worldwide placements: *Africa* (South Africa).

TOC H
1 Forest Close
Wendover
Aylesbury
Buckinghamshire
HP22 6BT UK

Tel: +44 (0) 1296 623911
Fax: +44 (0) 1296 696137
e-mail: info@toch.org.uk
Web: www.toch.org.uk
Contact: Projects Office

Toc H was conceived in 1915 just behind the front lines in Flanders where it ran a house for all ranks for rest and recreation where, in the midst of all the horror and futility of the trenches, men discovered friendships which crossed the normal barriers of rank and class. And they discovered peace, hope and God. At the end of the Great War the international Toc H movement sprang up, open to men and women from all walks of life and committed to the same principles experienced in Talbot House: Friendship – to love widely, Service – to build bravely, Fair-mindedness – to think fairly, and the Kingdom of God – to witness humbly. Throughout the Second World War Toc H was active across the world in providing creature comforts and friendships for service men and women. For more than 80 years Toc H has brought together thousands of people. All discover extraordinary friendships; work together

serving their community; welcome, listen and learn from those with very different opinions; and, through the challenge of testing the Christian way by trying it, discover a faith to live by. Volunteers with an offending background are accepted.

Total projects worldwide: 54
Total UK projects: 50
Starting months: January–December.
Time required: 1–2 weeks.
Age requirement: 16 plus.
Causes: Children, conservation, disabled (learning and physical), elderly people, environmental causes, inner city problems, offenders/ex-offenders, poor/homeless, unemployed, work camps – seasonal.
Activities: Arts/crafts, building/construction, caring (general, day and residential), community work, conservation skills, counselling, fundraising, group work, manual work, outdoor skills, religion, summer camps, training, visiting/befriending, work camps – seasonal.
Vols under 26 placed each year: 400 of a total of 500.
When to apply: All year.
Work alone/with others: With others.
Volunteers with disabilities: Possible – enquire before submitting application.
Qualifications: Nil.
Equipment/clothing: Not unless notified by project leader before commencement of project.
Health requirements: Nil.
Costs: Registration fee £10, plus possible supplementary fee. Insurance for personal belongings.
Benefits: Travel bursary for low waged/ unemployed. Board and lodging. Toc H covers project insurance for personal accident and public liability.
Supervision: 2 leaders over 18 sharing responsibility. All new leaders trained in accordance with our guidelines. Project support groups/regional committees as back-up.
Nationalities accepted: No restrictions but EU member countries are favoured.
Interview details: No interviews – we operate a 'first come, first served' policy – sight unseen but references required for work with children.
Certification: Certificate or reference and volunteer log provided.
Charity number: 211042

Worldwide placements: *Africa* (South Africa, Zimbabwe); *Australasia* (Australia); *Europe* (Belgium).
UK placements: *England* (Bedfordshire, Berkshire, Buckinghamshire, Cheshire, Co. Durham, Cumbria, Derbyshire, Devon, Essex, Hampshire, Hertfordshire, London, Norfolk, Northamptonshire, Oxfordshire, Somerset, Staffordshire, Suffolk, Tyne and Wear, West Midlands, Wiltshire, N. Yorkshire, S. Yorkshire, W. Yorkshire); *Scotland* (E. Ayrshire, N. Ayrshire, Falkirk, Glasgow City, N. Lanarkshire, S. Lanarkshire, Renfrewshire); *Wales* (Gwynedd, Swansea).

TOPS DAY NURSERIES
104 and 106 Herbert Avenue
Parkstone
Poole
Dorset
BH12 4HU UK

Tel: +44 (0) 1202 716130
Fax: +44 (0) 1202 382165
e-mail: tops@iname.com
Contact: Maria Thomas

TOPS provides a childcare service to the community, offering 80 places for children aged 6 weeks to 8 years. Volunteers can help with: playing with the children, reading stories 1:1, inside and outside, helping with swimming and/or tumble tots, and trips further afield e.g. farms, monkey world; providing a clean, tidy, safe environment including preparation for/clearing up after meals; photocopying, filing, children's work. We have lots of pets (birds, rabbits, guinea pigs, hamsters, fish) on site that need handling and care too.

Alternative addresses:
1 Carey Road
Wareham
Dorset
Tel: +44 (0) 01929 555051

Royal Bournemouth Hospital
East Castle Lane
Bournemouth
Dorset
Tel: +44 (0) 0589 244182

Total projects worldwide: 1
Total UK projects: 1
Starting months: January–December.
Time required: 1–52 weeks.

Age requirement: 16 plus.
Causes: Animal welfare, children, teaching/assisting (nursery).
Activities: Administration, arts/crafts, caring (day), community work, computers, cooking, first aid, fundraising, group work, music, teaching, technical skills, theatre/drama.
Vols under 26 placed each year: 8 of a total of 10.
When to apply: All year.
Work alone/with others: With others.
Volunteers with disabilities: Possible.
Qualifications: Police check and Social Service forms completed before starting voluntary work. GBH/ABH/Drugs/Child Abuse will disallow.
Health requirements: Nil.
Costs: Nil. Our insurance covers volunteers.
Benefits: Training on site.
Training: Induction training on site.
Supervision: Nursery/NVQ assessors are supervisors.
UK placements: *England* (Dorset).

TRAILBLAZERS, WALES
c/o Scope
Brunel House
5 Ynys Bridge Court
Gwaelod y Garth
Cardiff
CF4 8SS Wales

Tel: +44 (0) 29 2081 3913
Fax: +44 (0) 29 2081 3866
e-mail: neil.taylor@cwmpascymru.org.uk
Contact: Neil Taylor, Development Officer

Trailblazers is a club which offers membership to young disabled children between 9 and 14 years throughout Wales. As members of the Trailblazers club, the children will have the opportunity to participate in a variety of activities, which might otherwise be inaccessible to them. Membership will be offered to those children who find it difficult to be included in out-of-school activities for a variety of reasons, including physical, emotional, sensory and perceptual impairments. Trailblazers is supported by young adult volunteers who wish to contribute their time and skills to enhance their own development. It is hoped that we will be providing out-of-school hours activities starting in 2001. Volunteers with an offending background may be accepted sometimes, depending on the offence.

Total projects worldwide: 1
Total UK projects: 1
Starting months: January–December.
Time required: 1–9 weeks.
Age requirement: 16 plus.
Causes: Children, disabled (physical), holidays for disabled.
Activities: Arts/crafts, caring (general, day and residential), driving, fundraising, group work, music, outdoor skills, sport, summer camps, theatre/drama, visiting/befriending.
Vols under 26 placed each year: 45 of a total of 70 plus.
When to apply: Any time.
Work alone/with others: With others.
Volunteers with disabilities: Possible. They can befriend the children and act as role models.
Qualifications: Nil.
Equipment/clothing: Nil.
Health requirements: Good in general.
Costs: Nil.
Benefits: All out-of-pocket expenses are covered. Each volunteers is covered under Scope's insurance.
Training: Child protection, lifting and handling training and also induction.
Supervision: By an experienced volunteer enabler.
Interview details: Applicants are interviewed and must attend training days for child protection and moving and handling.
Certification: Certificate or reference provided.
UK placements: *Wales* (throughout).

TRAVEL ACTIVE
PO Box 107
5800 AC Venray
The Netherlands

Tel: 00 31 478 551 900
Fax: 00 31 478 551 911
e-mail: info@travelactive.nl
Web: www.travelactive.nl
Contact: Esther Busink

Travel Active needs camp counsellors to work either directly with children on summer camps in America or to work in the kitchens etc., 8–10 hours per day, six days per week. Work and Travel Europe: working on a farm in Norway or Switzerland, or restoration projects in France, Italy etc. Working on an Israeli Kibbutz. Work and Travel Australia and Canada: conservation programmes.

Volunteer work in Africa and Latin-America. Volunteers with an offending background may be accepted depending on the situation and the programme.

Total projects worldwide: 30
Total UK projects: 0
Starting months: January–December.
Time required: 3–52 weeks.
Age requirement: 16–30
Causes: Architecture, children, conservation, disabled (physical), environmental causes, poor/homeless, unemployed, wildlife, work camps – seasonal, young people.
Activities: Administration, agriculture/farming, arts/crafts, building/construction, catering, conservation skills, forestry, gardening/horticulture, manual work, marketing/publicity, outdoor skills, social work, sport, summer camps, work camps – seasonal.
Vols under 26 placed each year: 200 of a total of 1,000.
When to apply: Depends on the programme.
Work alone/with others: Depends on the programme.
Volunteers with disabilities: Possible.
Qualifications: Must be citizens of the EU.
Equipment/clothing: Depends on the programme.
Health requirements: Depends on the programme.
Costs: Depends on the programme. Sometimes insurance is provided but we recommend the Travel Active Insurance. The volunteer is responsible for providing this.
Benefits: Depends on the programme.
Training: Depends on the programme. For most of the programmes, we organize orientation programmes in Holland and also in the desired country.
Supervision: Depends on the programme. Usually there is supervision in the workplace.
Worldwide placements: *Africa* (Benin, Ivory Coast, Nigeria, Senegal); *Asia* (Israel); *Australasia* (Australia); *Europe* (Austria, Finland, France, Italy, Netherlands, Norway, Switzerland); *North America* (Canada, USA); *Central America* (Costa Rica, Guatemala, Mexico); *South America* (Ecuador, Peru).

TRAVELLERS
7 Mulberry Close
Ferring
West Sussex
BN12 5HY UK

Tel: +44 (0) 1903 700478
Fax: +44 (0) 1903 502595
e-mail: teach@travellersworldwide.com
Web: www.travellersworldwide.com
Contact: Philip Perkes, Director

Travellers offers a unique opportunity to live and teach in a different and fascinating ethnic environment with a different lifestyle – and to experience a different culture from the 'inside'. An unforgettable experience! Do gratifying and much-needed work in less advantaged countries – and add an impressive entry on your CV! Placements are open to all – no formal teaching qualifications needed. You don't need to speak the local language. Your travel arrangements can allow time to explore the country. This is not a salaried position. The work is voluntary but all your food and accommodation for the entire length of your programme is included in our charge – all you need is pocket money (a meal in India can cost less than 30p). In India placement locations include: Shimla, Dehra Dun, Mussoorie, Palampur, Kulu, Chandigarh, Meerut City, Dalhousie, Delhi, Panipat, or Lucknow in the north and Madras, Madurai, Kanyakummari, Kotagiri, Blue Mountains Kerala or Hyderabad in the south. Teaching in all countries is generally in state schools with some private tutoring. There will be plenty of time for sightseeing – you work a minimum of 18 hours a week, maximum 24 hours per week. Travellers now offer placements in three new destinations: South Africa, Cuba and Malaysia. Volunteers with offending backgrounds may be accepted subject to interview.

Total projects worldwide: 10
Total UK projects: 0
Starting months: January–December.
Time required: 2–52 weeks.
Age requirement: 17 plus.
Causes: Children, teaching/assisting (primary, secondary, mature, EFL).
Activities: Arts/crafts, computers, music, outdoor skills, summer camps, teaching, theatre/drama.
Vols under 26 placed each year: 80 of a total of 100.
When to apply: All year.
Work alone/with others: With others.
Volunteers with disabilities: Possible.
Qualifications: Good English. Gap year

students before university, undergraduates or graduates.
Health requirements: Nil. Volunteers take any necessary medication with them and inform us. There are always local doctors on call.
Costs: India from £1,425 (£925 excluding flights). Russia £1,245 (£895 excluding flights). Ukraine £1,080 (£775 excl. flights); Sri Lanka £1,495 (£995 excluding flights). Nepal £1,475 (£975 excluding flights).
Benefits: All food and accommodation whilst teaching. All travel inside the countries to schools. Free travel passes provided for Moscow, St Petersburg and Kiev. In Sri Lanka all travel to the schools is provided by car. Comprehensive advice on insurance is given. Excellent cover is offered. Volunteers to choose insurance providers.
Training: Guideline booklet and notes prior to leaving. Teacher assistance in all destinations.
Supervision: You will be supervised and given all the help you need.
Nationalities accepted: No restrictions but good spoken English.
Interview details: Personal interviews where necessary. Telephone interviews are standard.
Certification: Certificate or reference on request.
Worldwide placements: *Africa* (South Africa); *Asia* (India, Kuwait, Malaysia, Nepal, Sri Lanka); *Europe* (Russia, Ukraine); *Central America* (Cuba).

TREE IS LIFE VEGETABLE SOCIETY
c/o Non-Formal Education Division
PO Box 6, Walewale
Janga
Northern Region
Ghana

Tel: 00 233 71 22647
Fax: 00 233 71 23088
Contact: J.B. Ibrahim Tahiru

Tree is Life Vegetable Society has the following aims and activities: 1. to overcome specific problems that affect the rural youth, e.g. unemployment; 2. to help the people in the rural community to improve upon their living standards through self-generating income; 3. to improve the quality and quantity of vegetables and fruits. e.g. tomatoes, cashew nuts, sunflowers, peanuts and many others; 4. we also aim to link the rural community to the urban people through improved and modern methods of vegetable and fruit production. It is in the light of the above aims that we find it necessary to mobilize the rural youth for effective work. The Tree is Life Vegetable Society would be more effective with more help. Alternative address for J.B. Ibrahim Tahiru: Johnson Farms Complex Ltd, PO Box 14448, Accra, Tel: 00 233 21 400271, 00 233 21 401515 or 00 233 21 401212. Fax 00 233 21 400593.

Total projects worldwide: 3
Total UK projects: 0
Starting months: June.
Time required: 2–10 weeks.
Age requirement: 16 plus.
Causes: Animal welfare, environmental causes, health care/medical, unemployed, work camps – seasonal.
Activities: Agriculture/farming, arts/crafts, community work, development issues, forestry, fundraising, gardening/horticulture, group work, marketing/publicity, social work, sport, training, translating, visiting/befriending, work camps – seasonal.
Vols under 26 placed each year: 75 of a total of 100.
When to apply: By 5 May.
Work alone/with others: With others.
Volunteers with disabilities: Possible – weaving and carving.
Qualifications: Nil.
Equipment/clothing: Depends on the project to be undertaken.
Health requirements: Nil except malarial prophylactics.
Costs: Registration £10, fares to Ghana plus £15, subsistence £50 per annum. Insurance.
Benefits: Accommodation.
Supervision: By the organizer.
Interview details: No interviews before arriving at the worksite.
Certification: Written reference provided.
Worldwide placements: *Africa* (Ghana).

TREKFORCE EXPEDITIONS
34 Buckingham Palace Road
London
SW1W 0RE UK

Tel: +44 (0) 20 7828 2275
Fax: +44 (0) 20 7828 2276
e-mail: trekforce@dial.pipex.com
Web: www.trekforce.org.uk

Contact: Lucy Helberg

Trekforce Expeditions – adventure with a purpose: Trekforce offers you a once in a lifetime opportunity to play your part in international conservation, scientific and community projects. Expeditions last from two to five months to Belize (incorporating a month of learning Spanish in Guatemala and teaching in Belizean villages) and two months also in South East Asia and East Africa. Each volunteer has to fundraise for our parent charity. If you are looking for a fun, challenging adventure, come and find out more on one of our introduction days.

Total projects worldwide: 7
Total UK projects: 0
Starting months: January–December.
Time required: 8–20 weeks.
Age requirement: 17 plus.
Causes: Animal welfare, children, conservation, environmental causes, teaching/assisting (primary, EFL), wildlife, young people.
Activities: Building/construction, community work, conservation skills, development issues, forestry, fundraising, group work, international aid, manual work, outdoor skills, scientific work, teaching.
Vols under 26 placed each year: 170 of a total of 200.
When to apply: All year.
Work alone/with others: In expedition of usually about 20 people.
Volunteers with disabilities: Each case considered with safety as a priority.
Qualifications: Good spoken English.
Equipment/clothing: Expedition equipment, boots, rucksack etc. Advice given.
Health requirements: Yes.
Costs: £2,350 plus flights for 8 weeks. £3,500 plus flights for 5 months (Belize only). We recommend that volunteers take out baggage insurance.
Benefits: Contribution includes all expenses, training, board and accommodation, medical insurance. A chance to work on very worthwhile projects in fascinating parts of the world.
Training: Introduction day and briefing day before departing UK. In-country training before every expedition.
Supervision: By fully qualified and experienced expedition staff and medical teams with full back-up. Help and advice are

provided throughout.
Interview details: Introduction days are run in Central London every other Sunday and take place occasionally in North England and Scotland.
Charity number: 1005452
Worldwide placements: *Africa* (Kenya, Uganda); *Asia* (Indonesia, Malaysia); *Central America* (Belize, Guatemala).

TRELOAR TRUST
Upper Froyle
Alton
Hampshire
GU34 4JX UK

Tel: +44 (0) 1420 526407
Fax: +44 (0) 1420 23957
e-mail: personnel@treloar.org.uk
Web: www.treloar-trust.org.uk
Contact: Catherine Short

The Treloar Trust supports The Treloar School, a non-maintained residential special school for 130 young people aged 8–16, and Treloar National Specialist College providing further education for 170 residential students aged 16–25. On both sites the students have a wide range of physical disabilities including cerebral palsy, muscular dystrophy, spina bifida, epilepsy, haemophilia, various forms of ataxia, heart conditions and the results of serious accidents. Many students have associated specific or moderate learning difficulties. Over 80% use wheelchairs. Students at the School follow a curriculum based on the National Curriculum with a wide range of GCSEs available in Years 10 and 11 and individually constructed programmes for those who are not able to do GCSEs. In the College some students take A-levels in conjunction with the local tertiary college; others follow pre-vocational, vocational or ACCESS programmes according to their individual abilities. Treloar volunteers are required in several departments of the School and College to assist the professional staff with their duties associated with caring for the students. A period of work of one academic year is preferred but one or two terms could be acceptable.

Total projects worldwide: 1
Total UK projects: 1
Starting months: September
Time required: 37 weeks.
Age requirement: 18–25

Causes: Children, Disabled (physical), health care/medical, teaching/assisting (primary, secondary), young people.
Activities: Caring (general, day and residential), computers, group work, sport, teaching, theatre/drama.
Vols under 26 placed each year: 30
When to apply: September–March.
Work alone/with others: With others.
Volunteers with disabilities: We are unable to place people with disabilities as volunteers give physical help including handling clients who are all physically disabled.
Qualifications: Enthusiasm and commitment. Excellent knowledge of English is essential.
Health requirements: Need to be fit and strong.
Costs: Travel costs to and from home at start and end of every term.
Benefits: £42 per week pocket money.
Training: Pre-placement training given one week before start of term.
Supervision: By permanent members of staff in each department.
Interview details: Interviews take place at Alton. and travel costs are provided.
Certification: Certificate or reference provided.
Charity number: 307103
UK placements: *England* (Hampshire).

TRIFORM CAMPHILL COMMUNITY
20 Triform Road
Hudson
NY 12534
USA

Tel: 00 1 518 851 9320
Fax: 00 1 518 851 2864
e-mail: triform@epix.net
Contact: Tim Paholak

Triform Camphill Community is an intentional therapeutic community of 45 people, about half of whom are young adults with disabilities. Located on beautiful farmland in upstate New York, Triform offers a unique opportunity to live and work full time with handicapped young people: full participation in all aspects of Community life; experience in curative education and social therapy; work with handicapped young adults in gardening, farming, weaving, artistic and cultural activities, household management, courses and workshops, outings; opportunities to travel to nearby places of interest. Volunteers live in a house, usually with a family, one or two other volunteers and four to six young adults with disabilities. You will have your own bedroom and be able to have some time in the day for yourself, as well as one day off per week. You will be one of a number of international and American volunteers who come for short term stays, e.g. 12 months, as well as the long term volunteers who either live here for some years or who regard Triform as their permanent home. We hope you find this information helpful and positive, and we welcome any questions you may have. Triform recognizes the great contribution made by short-term volunteers, who bring vibrancy, energy and questions. We appreciate your interest and willingness to participate, and encourage your application. Volunteers with an offending background may be accepted – individually specific – no blanket policy.

Total projects worldwide: 1
Total UK projects: 0
Starting months: June, August.
Time required: 6–52 weeks (plus).
Age requirement: 18 plus.
Causes: Disabled (learning and physical), environmental causes, young people.
Activities: Agriculture/farming, arts/crafts, building/construction, caring (general), catering, driving, forestry, gardening/ horticulture, manual work, outdoor skills, social work, teaching, theatre/drama, training, visiting/befriending.
Vols under 26 placed each year: 7–10
When to apply: As early as possible.
Work alone/with others: With others.
Volunteers with disabilities: Possible.
Qualifications: No minimum education or skills necessary.
Equipment/clothing: Work clothes, winter clothes.
Health requirements: Must provide own medical insurance for first 6 months.
Costs: All travel costs.
Benefits: US$100 pocket money per month plus US$20 for phone bills. After one year US$400 vacation money.
Interview details: If we need to interview an applicant the interview would take place in Britain.
Certification: Certificate or reference provided on completion of contracted time.
Worldwide placements: *North America*
(USA).

TRINITY YOUTH AND COMMUNITY CENTRE
265 Burrage Road
Plumstead
London
SE18 7JW UK

Tel: +44 (0) 20 8317 7940
Fax: +44 (0) 20 8855 2732
Contact: Louise Winstanley, Senior Youth Worker

Total projects worldwide: 1
Total UK projects: 1
Starting months: January–December.
Time required: 1–52 weeks.
Age requirement: 14 plus.
Causes: Children, inner city problems, offenders/ex-offenders, poor/homeless, teaching (nursery, primary, secondary), unemployed, young people.
Activities: Administration, arts/crafts, community work, computers, counselling, development issues, fundraising, group work, library/resource centres, music, newsletter/ journalism, research, social work, sport.
When to apply: All year.
UK placements: *England* (London).

TURICOOP
Rua Pascoal-Melo
15-1DTO
P-1000 Lisbon
Portugal

Total projects worldwide: 1
Starting months: July–September.
Time required: 2–12 weeks.
Age requirement: 14 plus.
Activities: Summer camps.
Vols under 26 placed each year: 150
When to apply: From April.
Qualifications: Must speak English.
Benefits: Board and accommodation.
Worldwide placements: *Europe* (Portugal).

U

UK YOUTH

Kirby House
20–24 Kirby Street
London
EC1N 8TS UK

Tel: +44 (0) 20 7242 4045
Fax: +44 (0) 20 7242 4125
e-mail: executive@youthclubs.org.uk
Web: www.youthclubs.org.uk
Contact: John Bateman, Chief Executive

UK Youth, a national registered charity, promotes opportunities for young people to develop skills and interests which will help them to become fulfilled adults and effective citizens. We are the largest non-uniformed youth organization in the United Kingdom supporting a network that reaches more than 700,000 young people in clubs and projects and includes about 45,000 youth workers with other 30,000 volunteers. We initiate a range of projects that young people enjoy, promoting sports and outdoor activities, art, drama and dance, health education, action to improve the environment, community work, international exchanges to name but a few. Our organization also works with particular disadvantaged groups such as homeless young people or those involved with car crime, drugs, alcohol or solvents. The key aim of all our work is to give young people, whatever their starting point, the skills and information they need to make constructive decisions, and plan and manage their own activities and projects. Volunteers with an offending background accepted.

Total projects worldwide: 1
Total UK projects: 1
Starting months: March, April.
Time required: 2–12 weeks.
Age requirement: 18 plus.
Causes: Children, conservation, environmental causes, holidays for disabled, unemployed, wildlife, work camps – seasonal, young people.
Activities: Administration, community work, conservation skills, driving, gardening/horticulture, group work, manual work, outdoor skills, sport, summer camps, theatre/drama, work camps – seasonal.
Costs: Travel costs to Avon Tyrrell.

Certification: Certificate or reference provided.
Charity number: 306066
UK placements: *England* (throughout); *Scotland* (throughout); *Northern Ireland* (throughout); *Wales* (throughout).

ULSTER WILDLIFE TRUST

3 New Line
Crossgar
Co. Down
BT30 9EP UK

Tel: +44 (0) 1396 830282
Fax: +44 (0) 1396 830888
Contact: The Director

Ulster Wildlife Trust is a member of the Wildlife Trusts, a national partnership of 47 county trusts. For details of the Wildlife Trusts, see the entry for Cornwall Wildlife Trust.

Total projects worldwide: 1
Total UK projects: 1
Starting months: January–December.
Time required: 1–52 weeks (plus).
Age requirement: 12 plus.
Causes: Conservation, environmental causes, wildlife.
Activities: Conservation skills.
Work alone/with others: Both.
Qualifications: Nil.
Equipment/clothing: Casual work clothes, waterproofs, stout boots for outdoor work. Protective safety gear is provided.
Health requirements: Anti-tetanus innoculation recommended.
Costs: Nil.
Benefits: Out-of-pocket expenses. Volunteers are covered by the Trust's insurance.
UK placements: *Northern Ireland* (throughout).

UNION REMPART

(Pour la Réhabilitation et L'Entretien des Monuments et du Patrimoine Artistique)
1 rue des Guillemites
75004 Paris
France

Tel: 00 33 1 42 71 96 55
Fax: 00 33 1 42 71 73 00
e-mail: contact@rempart.com
Web: www.rempart.com
Contact: Sabine Guilbert

Union Rempart needs volunteers to help

restore and preserve various castles, fortresses, churches, chapels, abbeys, monasteries, farms, ancient villages, Gallo-Roman amphitheatres and underground passages on the 140 sites organized by Rempart each year during holidays. Work includes masonry, woodwork, carpentry, interior decorating, restoration and clearance work. Opportunities for swimming, tennis, riding, water sports, cycling, climbing, rambling, exploring the region, crafts, music, cinema and taking part in local festivities. You can choose the camp in which you would like to take part.

Total projects worldwide: 130
Total UK projects: 0
Starting months: February–November.
Time required: 2–52 weeks.
Age requirement: 13 plus.
Causes: Archaeology, conservation, heritage, work camps – seasonal.
Activities: Building/construction, conservation skills, gardening/horticulture, manual work, sport, technical skills, theatre/drama, training, work camps – seasonal.
Vols under 26 placed each year: 3,520 of a total of 4,000.
When to apply: By the end of April.
Work alone/with others: Work in groups.
Volunteers with disabilities: Not possible.
Qualifications: Some knowledge of French but no experience in restoration needed.
Equipment/clothing: Sleeping bag, work clothes, strong work boots, swimsuit and pocket money.
Health requirements: Anti-tetanus injection.
Costs: Approximately £4–£5 per day covers board and accommodation. Fees for insurance are FF220 for one year – to be taken out by volunteer.
Supervision: Every work camp has leaders, some of them for technical work and others for pedagogical aspects.
Interview details: Applicants should phone each camp director for interview before applying.
Worldwide placements: *Europe* (France).

UNIPAL (UNIVERSITIES' EDUCATIONAL TRUST FOR PALESTINIANS)
BCM UNIPAL
London
WC1N 3XX UK

Tel: +44 (0) 20 8299 1132

Fax: +44 (0) 20 8299 1132
Contact: Brenda Hayward

UNIPAL sends volunteers to take part in short-term projects during July and August in the Israeli-occupied West Bank and Gaza Strip, as well as with Palestinian communities elsewhere. There are also opportunities for long-term work for a minimum period of six months. Most projects involve teaching English, but there are also possibilities of other work of an educational kind – from occupational therapy to helping build a school. A university degree and TEFL qualification are essential for the long-term work. Short-term volunteers must be at least 20 years old and long-term volunteers at least 22. Short-term volunteers are provided with food and accommodation, but must pay their own air fares and insurance. Long-term volunteers have their air fares paid and receive an allowance. Applicants should send a stamped self-addressed envelope to the above address before the end of February.

Total projects worldwide: 3
Total UK projects: 0
Starting months: July.
Time required: 4–52 weeks.
Age requirement: 20 plus.
Causes: Children, teaching (secondary, mature, EFL), young people.
Activities: Summer camps, teaching.
Vols under 26 placed each year: 20–30
When to apply: Before the end of March.
Work alone/with others: With others.
Volunteers with disabilities: Not possible.
Qualifications: Short-term A-levels. Long-term: TEFL qualification and experience preferred.
Equipment/clothing: Sleeping bag, modest summer clothes.
Health requirements: Immunizations required.
Costs: Short-term: £250 for flight and £50 insurance. Long-term: None.
Benefits: Short-term: board and lodging provided. Long-term: flights, insurance, food, board all paid for.
Training: There are briefings in June for those selected.
Interview details: Interviews take place in Durham and London and are held before the Easter vacation.
Certification: Certificate or reference on request.
Charity number: 325007

Worldwide placements: *Asia* (Israel, Jordan, Lebanon).

UNITED KINGDOM ANTARCTIC HERITAGE TRUST

The Blue House
East Marden
Chichester
West Sussex
PO18 9JE UK

Tel: +44 (0) 1243 535256
Fax: +44 (0) 1243 535256
Contact: Captain Pat McLaren (RN)

United Kingdom Antarctic Heritage Trust objectives: to promote an educational programme aimed at British youth to stimulate interest in science, the global environment and Antarctic research through the inspiration of earlier British Antarctic endeavours; to conserve selected early British scientific bases on the Antarctic Peninsula for the education and enjoyment of visitors; to help with the acquisition and preservation of Antarctic memorabilia; to help New Zealand's AHT conserve Scott's and Shackleton's bases.

Total projects worldwide: 1
Total UK projects: 0
Starting months: January–December.
Time required: 1–52 weeks.
Age requirement: 14 plus.
Charity number: 1024911

UNITED NATIONS ASSOCIATION (WALES)

International Youth Service
The Temple of Peace
Cathays Park
Cardiff
CF10 3AP Wales

Tel: +44 (0) 29 2022 3088
Fax: +44 (0) 29 2066 5557
e-mail: unaiys@btinternet.com
Web: www.btinternet.com/~unaiys.office
Contact: The International Officer

United Nations Association International Youth Service (UNAIYS) is an organization that recruits international volunteers for community projects in Wales and sends UK-based volunteers to similar projects overseas. The aims of UNAIYS are to work for the ideals of global peace and social justice set down in the United Nations Charter, but

specifically: to promote international understanding through the medium of voluntary service; to assist in community development by acting as a means to stimulate new ideas and projects; to encourage the concept of voluntary service as a force in the common search for peace, equality and social justice; to provide opportunities for the people of Wales to understand international issues through direct contact with people from other countries. International Volunteer Projects are organized throughout the world all year round, but the majority are concentrated during the summer. They provide the opportunity for international discovery, not through tourism, but work with local people and volunteers from other countries. They offer an educational experience – volunteers learn from each other, the local community and (perhaps most of all) themselves. Work involved varies from one area to the next but generally is unskilled work which would not be done without voluntary effort, so does not replace paid labour.

Total projects worldwide: 1,500 plus
Total UK projects: 40
Starting months: April–August.
Time required: 2–26 weeks.
Age requirement: 14 plus.
Causes: Archaeology, architecture, children, conservation, disabled (learning and physical), elderly people, environmental causes, heritage, inner city problems, poor/homeless, teaching/assisting work camps – seasonal, young people.
Activities: Arts/crafts, building/construction, community work, conservation skills, cooking, development issues, forestry, gardening/horticulture, group work, manual work, music, outdoor skills, research, social work, sport, summer camps, teaching, theatre/drama, training, work camps – seasonal.
Vols under 26 placed each year: 270 of a total of 300.
When to apply: April–July.
Work alone/with others: With others.
Volunteers with disabilities: Enquiries welcome and encouraged.
Qualifications: Nil except age – generally 18 plus (14 plus for some).
Equipment/clothing: Sleeping bag. Strong footwear on environmental projects.
Health requirements: E111 usually required.

Costs: £50–£125 registration fee plus travel costs which vary according to country plus pocket money. All volunteers must have their own travel and health insurance.
Benefits: Free board and lodging.
Training: Optional one day training for Eastern Europe/North Africa/Turkey. Mandatory weekend training for rest of Africa, Central and South America, Asia (except Japan).
Supervision: All projects have at least one trained leader.
Certification: A reference/certificate can often be provided.
Charity number: 700760
Worldwide placements: *Africa* (Botswana, Burkina Faso, Ivory Coast, Ghana, Kenya, Lesotho, Morocco, Mozambique, Senegal, South Africa, Swaziland, Tanzania, Togo, Tunisia, Uganda, Zambia, Zimbabwe); *Asia* (Bangladesh, Cambodia, China, India, Indonesia, Japan, Korea (South), Nepal, Philippines, Thailand, Turkey, Vietnam); *Europe* (Albania, Belarus, Belgium, Bulgaria, Croatia, Czech Republic, Denmark, Estonia, Finland, France, Germany, Greece, Hungary, Italy, Latvia, Lithuania, Netherlands, Poland, Portugal, Romania, Russia, Slovakia, Slovenia, Spain, Switzerland, Turkey, Ukraine); *North America* (Canada, Greenland, USA); *Central America* (Barbados, Costa Rica, Dominica, Guatemala, Martinique, Mexico); *South America* (Argentina, Bolivia, Brazil, Chile). UK placements: *Wales* (throughout).

UNITY NORWOOD RAVENSWOOD
25 Bourne Court
Southend Road
Woodford Green
Essex
IG8 8HD UK

Tel: +44 (0) 20 8550 6114
Fax: +44 (0) 20 8551 3951
Contact: Raina Gee

Unity Norwood Ravenswood is a play and youth service for children and young people of mixed abilities aged between 5 and 18. Our aim is to provide integrated activities through our weekly clubs, holiday schemes and residential holidays, whilst maintaining a safe and stimulating environment. We offer a balanced programme to meet individual needs which may include integration into mainstream provisions. Unity has four age groups: 5–8s, 8–11s, 11–14s and 14–18s. Volunteers can be involved in the care of a young person and/or planning and running the activity at one of the clubs. There are programmed day schemes during all school holidays, and a holiday in the UK for the 8–11s and 11–18s, during the summer holiday. There is always a new experience for a Unity member to enjoy. Volunteers with an offending background may be accepted depending on the offence.

Total projects worldwide: 4
Total UK projects: 4
Starting months: January–December.
Time required: 4–52 weeks (plus).
Age requirement: 16 plus.
Causes: Children, disabled (learning and physical), young people.
Activities: Arts/crafts, caring (general and day), cooking, music.
Vols under 26 placed each year: 50
When to apply: All year.
Work alone/with others: With others.
Volunteers with disabilities: Possible.
Qualifications: Willingness to work with children plus young people and ability to communicate. EU residents.
Equipment/clothing: Casual old clothing.
Health requirements: Some.
Costs: Nil.
Benefits: Approved travel, board and lodging (residentials). Out-of-pocket expenses.
Training: Training is provided to all volunteers. These sessions include emergency first aid, lifting and handling people, programming skills, child centred care, etc.
Interview details: Applicants are interviewed at local offices in Redbridge or Hendon.
Certification: Ravenswood certificates provided. Reference if applied for.
Charity number: 1059050
UK placements: *England* (Berkshire, Essex, Hertfordshire, London).

UNIVERSITIES AND COLLEGES CHRISTIAN FELLOWSHIP (UCCF)
38 De Montfort Street
Leicester
LE1 7GP UK

Tel: +44 (0) 116 255 1700
Fax: +44 (0) 116 255 5672
e-mail: relay@uccf.org.uk
Web: www.uccf.org.uk

Contact: Andy Shudall, Relay Co-ordinator

UCCF needs one-year Relay volunteers to support the work of Christian Unions in universities and colleges. Relay is a discipleship and training programme aimed at developing Christian graduates in personal, spiritual and emotional maturity. All activities have an evangelical Christian basis.

Total projects worldwide: 50
Total UK projects: 50
Starting months: September.
Time required: 44 weeks.
Age requirement: 21–25
Causes: Young people.
Activities: Group work, music, religion, theatre/drama, training.
Vols under 26 placed each year: 50
When to apply: Deadline 28 February. Start 1 September.
Work alone/with others: Work as part of a regional team alongside UCCF staff worker.
Volunteers with disabilities: Possible, but a high degree of mobility is needed for the programme.
Qualifications: Committed Christians who are recent graduates of a university or college.
Health requirements: Able to cope with physically and emotionally demanding schedule.
Costs: Living costs plus £475 for training.
Benefits: 4-day debriefing residential conference in June. We cover public liability insurance but not personal accident. We cover travel overseas.
Training: 6 days at beginning of placement, 6 days in January (both residential) plus ongoing training throughout the year.
Supervision: Regular one-on-one supervision by regional staff worker.
Interview details: Interviews are arranged with regional team leader and staff worker.
Certification: References arranged on an individual basis.
Charity number: 273458
UK placements: *England* (throughout); *Scotland* (throughout); *Northern Ireland* (throughout); *Wales* (throughout).

UNIVERSITY RESEARCH EXPEDITIONS PROGRAM (UREP)
University of California
2223 Fulton Street, Desk M31
Berkeley
CA 94720 – 7050
USA

Tel: 00 1 510 642 6586
Fax: 00 1 510 642 6791
e-mail: urep@uclink.berkeley.edu
Web: www.mip.berkeley.eduurep
Contact: The Secretary

UREP provides opportunities for people to participate in scientific discoveries by acting as field assistants on a university research expedition. Research topics offered in a large number of countries include animal behaviour, archaeology and anthropology.

Total projects worldwide: 18–20
Total UK projects: 2–3
Starting months: February–September.
Time required: 1–52 weeks.
Age requirement: 16 plus.
Causes: Animal welfare, archaeology, conservation, environmental causes, heritage.
Activities: Conservation skills, outdoor skills.
Vols under 26 placed each year: 200
When to apply: 15 March.
Work alone/with others: With others.
Volunteers with disabilities: Not possible.
Qualifications: Varies.
Equipment/clothing: Varies.
Health requirements: Varies.
Costs: Equal share of project's costs (£350–£800) plus travel to site.
Benefits: The cost covers all equipment including meals and accommodation.

UPPER CONNING: SOUTHERN WINGONG CATCHMENT TEAM
P O Box 51
Armadale
Western Australia

Tel: 00 61 8 9399 0622
Fax: 00 61 8 9399 0184
e-mail: cthomas@armadale.wa.gov.co
Contact: Colleen Martin, Catchment Co-ordinator

The Upper Conning and Southern Wingong Catchment Team is a community group interested in the conservation of the Upper Conning and Southern River. The team has obtained funding support from local and state government to carry out on-ground works which aim to restore the rivers. Projects include tree planting, weed pulling/spraying, shopping centre and show displays, yellow fish drain stencilling, newsletter publications, school talks, water quality monitoring, habitat surveys, creating rock rittles and ponds in rivers and research. Volunteers with an offending background are accepted.

Total projects worldwide: 15
Total UK projects: 0
Starting months: January–December.
Time required: 1–52 weeks.
Age requirement: 16 plus.
Causes: Conservation, environmental causes, wildlife.
Activities: Community work, conservation skills, forestry, gardening/horticulture, group work, marketing/publicity, newsletter/journalism, outdoor skills, research.
Vols under 26 placed each year: 5 of a total of 30.
When to apply: All year.
Work alone/with others: Both.
Volunteers with disabilities: We are unable to place people with disabilities.
Qualifications: Driving licence and if possible vehicle.
Equipment/clothing: Nil – hat, sunscreen and closed shoes.
Health requirements: Nil.
Costs: Travel, board and lodging.
Benefits: Full personal and public insurance is covered.
Training: On site if required.
Supervision: On-site co-ordinator.
Interview details: Interviews take place at the City of Armadale Council Offices.
Certification: Certificate or reference on request.
Worldwide placements: *Australasia* (Australia).

UPPER NENE ARCHAEOLOGICAL SOCIETY
Toad Hall
86 Main Road
Hackleton
Northampton
NN7 2AD UK

Tel: +44 (0) 1604 870312
e-mail: unarchsoc@aol.com
Contact: Mrs D.E. Friendship-Taylor

The Upper Nene Archaeological Society oversees the excavation of a Romano-British villa and underlying Iron Age settlement. Volunteers are required to help with trowelling and a variety of excavation and post-excavation procedures.

Total projects worldwide: 1
Total UK projects: 1
Starting months: August.
Time required: 2–3 weeks.
Age requirement: 16 plus.
Causes: Archaeology.
Vols under 26 placed each year: Approximately 25.
When to apply: February – July.
Work alone/with others: With others.
Volunteers with disabilities: We are unable to place people with disabilities as it is difficult for people with limited mobility.
Qualifications: English speaking.
Equipment/clothing: 4″ mason's pointing trowel, all other equipment supplied. Clothing for all weathers.
Health requirements: Reasonably fit. Not suitable for severe asthmatics or anyone with severe respiratory problems.
Costs: Specified contribution towards everyday excavation expenses.
Benefits: Basic campsite.
Charity number: 286966
UK placements: *England* (Northamptonshire).

USDA FOREST SERVICE
PO Box 96090
Room 1010 RPE/HRP
Washington DC
20090-6090 USA

Tel: 00 1 703 235 8855
Contact: The Volunteer Co-ordinator

The USDA Forest Service maintains 19 national forests in Oregon and Washington. Volunteers are needed to maintain trails, campgrounds, wildlife and timber. They are also required to help with recreation, range activities, office work, interpretation and the visitor information services.

Total projects worldwide: 1
Starting months: January–December.
Time required: 1–52 weeks.
Age requirement: 14 plus.
Causes: Conservation, environmental causes.
Activities: Administration, conservation skills, forestry, manual work, outdoor skills, translating.
When to apply: All year.
Work alone/with others: With others.
Volunteers with disabilities: Possible.
Qualifications: English speaking. Those under 18 years of age need the written

permission of their parents.
Costs: Travel, accommodation for short-term volunteers.
Benefits: Food and incidental expenses reimbursed. Accommodation for long-term volunteers.
Worldwide placements: *North America* (USA).

USPG AND THE METHODIST CHURCH – EXPERIENCE EXCHANGE PROGRAMME
The United College of the Ascension
Weoley Park Road
Selly Oak
Birmingham
B29 6RD UK

Tel: +44 (0) 121 472 1667
Fax: +44 (0) 121 472 4320
e-mail: uca@sellyoak.ac.uk
Contact: Mandy Quayle, Root Groups International Development Officer

USPG and the Methodist Church – Experience Exchange Programme enables people over 18 to work alongside local people in church-based projects such as schools, community development programmes and hostels for six months to a year. No specific skills are required although applicants should be flexible, adaptable and open to new ideas. Those with specific skills can be placed accordingly. Placements are constantly being reviewed and new ones set up. Through living in another culture you experience new challenges and opportunities and discover much about yourself. You would be strongly encouraged to share what you learn from your experience on your return. The Experience Exchange Programme is one of two volunteer programmes run jointly by the United Society for the Propagation of the Gospel (USPG) and the Methodist Church. Both USPG and the Methodist Church are involved in supporting the mission of the church worldwide through the exchange of people, prayer, resources and ideas. Volunteers with an offending background may be considered.

Total projects worldwide: 1
Total UK projects: 0
Starting months: January, February, August–December.
Time required: 27–52 weeks.
Age requirement: 18 plus.

Causes: Aids/HIV, children, disabled (physical), elderly people, health care/medical, human rights, poor/homeless, refugees, teaching/assisting (nursery, primary, secondary, mature, EFL), unemployed, young people.
Activities: Administration, agriculture/farming, arts/crafts, building/construction, caring (general), community work, computers, counselling, development issues, DIY, driving, international aid, manual work, music, newsletter/journalism, religion, social work, sport, teaching, technical skills, translating, visiting/befriending.
Vols under 26 placed each year: 17 of a total of 25.
When to apply: Before middle of June for September start.
Work alone/with others: With others.
Volunteers with disabilities: Possible.
Qualifications: Christian commitment, flexibility and an ability to learn from a new experience.
Equipment/clothing: Varies according to placement.
Health requirements: Health clearance to ensure individual can endure the climate of the placement.
Costs: Varies – usually £2,000–£2,500.
Interview details: Interviews take place in London and exploration weekends in Birmingham.
Certification: Written reference on request.
Charity number: 234518
Worldwide placements: *Africa* (Angola, Botswana, Egypt, Gambia, Ghana, Kenya, Lesotho, Madagascar, Malawi, Namibia, South Africa, Tanzania, Zambia, Zimbabwe); *Asia* (Bangladesh, India, Israel, Japan, Korea (North), Pakistan, Philippines, Sri Lanka); *Europe* (Estonia, Poland); *Central America* (Barbados, Belize, Saint Vincent/Grenadines, Trinidad and Tobago); *South America* (Brazil, Chile, Guyana, Uruguay).

USPG AND THE METHODIST CHURCH – ROOT GROUPS INTERNATIONAL
The United College of the Ascension
Weoley Park Road
Selly Oak
Birmingham
B29 6RD UK

Tel: +44 (0) 121 472 1667
Fax: +44 (0) 121 472 4320
e-mail: uca@sellyoak.ac.uk

Contact: Mandy Quayle, Root Groups International Development Officer

USPG and the Methodist Church – Root Groups International are for people, aged 18–30, who are looking for a challenge as they try to discover how Christianity should affect their lifestyle and attitudes. Participants from all parts of the world church live together in community. You live and work alongside local communities, often in areas of high unemployment. The groups work in partnership with a local church exploring a way of mission that is practical and challenging. Activities vary widely according to personality and placement: they often include elements of youthwork, befriending the lonely and disadvantaged, worship and Bible study, and volunteering at local community centres. In all their work, Root Groups are building relationships with their local community and developing links between church and community. Root Groups International is one of two short-term experience programmes run jointly by the United Society for the Propagation of the Gospel (USPG) and the Methodist Church. USPG is a mission agency of the Anglican church. Both USPG and the Methodist Church are involved in supporting the mission of the church worldwide through the exchange of people, prayer, resources and ideas. Volunteers with an offending background may be considered.

Total projects worldwide: 5–6
Total UK projects: 3–4
Starting months: September, October.
Time required: 45–52 weeks.
Age requirement: 18–30
Causes: Addicts/Ex-addicts, children, disabled (learning and physical), elderly people, human rights, inner city problems, poor/homeless, teaching/assisting (nursery), unemployed, young people.
Activities: Administration, arts/crafts, campaigning, caring (general and day), community work, counselling, group work, music, religion, social work, sport, teaching, theatre/drama, training, visiting/befriending.
Vols under 26 placed each year: 9 of a total of 10.
When to apply: Before end of June for September start.
Work alone/with others: With others.

Volunteers with disabilities: Possible.
Qualifications: Christian commitment and a willingness to try anything once.
Health requirements: Good health.
Costs: Root Groups are self-supporting and members staying in the UK work part time to fund the group. Those joining an overseas group would be required to raise £2,500 through trust funds etc.
Interview details: Interviews and Exploration Weekends take place in Birmingham.
Certification: Written reference on request.
Charity number: 234518
Worldwide placements: *Africa* (Zambia, Zimbabwe); *Central America* (Belize).
UK placements: *England* (throughout); *Scotland* (throughout); *Northern Ireland* (throughout); *Wales* (throughout).

V

VADHU
Dogra Estate
Ganiadeoli
Ranikhet 263645
India

Tel: 00 91 5966 2506
Contact: Narendra Rautela, Secretary

Vadhu stands for Voluntary Organisation for the Development of the Hills of Uttarakahnd, a non-governmental, non-profit group aimed at creating a model of sustainable mountain development in the Ghatgar watershed area, near Ranikhet in the Himalayan foothills, 4,000–6,700 feet above sea level. This includes an agricultural programme; establishing measures to improve soil and moisture conservation; horticulture, vegetable and fodder production; energy conservation; and appropriate technology for villages. Volunteers must be prepared to work hard and learn from others. You should have a belief in basic human values and be ready to experience a different culture and respect it. Those wishing to take up skilled positions must have relevant experience in various aspects of watershed management.

Total projects worldwide: 1
Total UK projects: 0

Starting months: January–December.
Time required: 4–52 weeks.
Age requirement: 18–40
Causes: Conservation, environmental causes, poor/homeless, teaching/assisting.
Activities: Agriculture/farming, conservation skills, development issues, forestry, gardening/horticulture, manual work, outdoor skills, training.
Vols under 26 placed each year: 24
When to apply: At least 6 months in advance.
Work alone/with others: With others.
Volunteers with disabilities: Possible, but they must be able to manage in hilly terrain.
Qualifications: 4 qualified skilled, 20 unskilled volunteers needed a year.
Volunteers with relevant skills assist with watershed management and administration of the project. Unskilled volunteers work in plant nurseries, planting seedlings and levelling the land.
Costs: £70 per month skilled, £80 per month unskilled. Travel and insurance.
Benefits: Food and accommodation.
Worldwide placements: *Asia* (India).

VALLERSUND GÅRD
N-7167 Vallersund
Norway

Tel: 00 47 725 27740 (9 a.m. – 12 noon)
Fax: 00 47 725 27895
Contact: The Director

Vallersund Gård is a Camphill village community with handicapped adults and ex-drug addicts.

Total projects worldwide: 1
Total UK projects: 0
Starting months: January–December.
Time required: 1–52 weeks.
Age requirement: 14 plus.
Causes: Addicts/ex-addicts, disabled (learning).
Worldwide placements: *Europe* (Norway).

VALLEY AND VALE ARTS PROJECT
Blaengarw Workmen's Hall
Blaengarw
Mid Glamorgan
CF32 8AW Wales

Tel: +44 (0) 1656 871911 or 729246
Contact: Tracy McCoy

Total projects worldwide: 1

Total UK projects: 1
Starting months: January–December.
Time required: 1–52 weeks.
Age requirement: 14 plus.

VALUED INDEPENDENT PEOPLE
49 Templeton Crescent
Girrawheen
Western Australia

Tel: 00 61 8 924 72517
Fax: 00 61 8 924 72516
e-mail: vip@iinet.net.au
Contact: Margaret Walsh

Valued Independent People provides a flexible, home and neighbourhood, daytime occupation community access and participation service to people with a disability according to their needs. We also provide occasional emergency respite for consumers. We provide an intensive Alternative to Employment service, under the Post School Options Program, to school leavers who live either at home with families or in hostels, according to individual needs. Activities include community access, e.g. newspaper deliveries, horseriding, bowling, shopping, dining out, movies, picnics, swimming, library, or centre-based activities e.g. craft, music, cooking, exercise, independent living skills, sensory stimulation. The organization is funded by the state government, managed by an independent Board of Management and staffed by 'facilitators' or carers, some of whom are 'social trainers', i.e. with a Human Services qualification.

Total projects worldwide: 2
Total UK projects: 0
Starting months: January–December.
Time required: 1–52 weeks.
Age requirement: 16 plus.
Causes: Disabled (learning and physical).
Activities: Caring (day), community work.
Vols under 26 placed each year: 5 of a total of 10.
When to apply: All year.
Work alone/with others: With others.
Volunteers with disabilities: Possible.
Qualifications: Interest in working with people with disability.
Health requirements: Nil.
Costs: Fares to Perth, board and lodging.
Benefits: A$5 a day for reimbursement of expenses. We have volunteer insurance.

Training: Normal training provided to all staff and volunteers.

Supervision: Volunteers always work with experienced staff.

Certification: Certificate or reference on request.

Worldwide placements: *Australasia* (Australia).

VENTURE SCOTLAND

Norton Park
57 Albion Road
Edinburgh
EH7 5QY Scotland

Tel: + 44 (0) 131 475 2395
Fax: + 44 (0) 131 475 2396
e-mail: hq@venturescotland.force9.co.uk
Contact: Rob Bushby

Venture Scotland volunteers take groups of 16–25 year olds on residential weekends and weeks, who would not normally get the opportunity to go away on this type of break, e.g. the unemployed or homeless. We focus on personal and social development through working together on various outdoor and conservation activities. Volunteers with an offending background are accepted providing it does not compromise the 'working with young adults' aspect. We do not offer year out placements.

Total projects worldwide: 1
Total UK projects: 1
Starting months: January–March.
Time required: 1–52 weeks.
Age requirement: 21 plus.
Causes: Addicts/ex-addicts, conservation, environmental causes, inner city problems, offenders/ex-offenders, poor/homeless, unemployed, young people.
Activities: Administration, building/ construction, community work, computers, conservation skills, cooking, driving, first aid, fundraising, group work, manual work, marketing/publicity, newsletter/journalism, outdoor skills, training.
Vols under 26 placed each year: 30 of a total of 60.
When to apply: All year – induction January-March.
Work alone/with others: With others.
Volunteers with disabilities: Not possible.
Qualifications: First Aid, youthwork, outdoor and lifesaving qualifications helpful.
Equipment/clothing: Sleeping bag, heavy duty waterproofs, boots, torch.

Health requirements: Reasonable for working outdoors.

Costs: £15 membership fee/£5 concession.

Benefits: Food, accommodation and travel costs. We carry public and employer's liability insurance.

Training: Induction training provided between January and March each year.

Supervision: Each programme has a leader responsible for supervision. All supervised by co-ordinator.

Nationalities accepted: Volunteers from Scotland only.

Interview details: Interviews take place either at volunteer's place of work or our office.

Charity number: ED8089MEB

UK placements: *Scotland* (throughout).

VENTURECO WORLDWIDE LTD

Pleck House
Middletown
Moreton Morrell
Warwickshire
CV35 9AU UK

Tel: + 44 (0) 1926 651 071
Fax: + 44 (0) 1926 650 120
e-mail: Mail@Ventureco-worldwide.com
Web: www.ventureco-worldwide.com
Contact: Mr Mark Davison

VentureCo Worldwide provide exciting four-month programmes in South America and Asia that form a focus for your gap year. Each programme consists of three phases: cultural orientation, aid project work and a long-range expedition. In South America expect to learn/improve Spanish, care for orphans and trek to Machu Picchu. In Asia we learn about Indian culture, survey the tiger population and trek to Everest Base Camp. Volunteers with offending backgrounds are accepted.

Total projects worldwide: 4
Total UK projects: 0
Starting months: January–March.
Time required: 15–16 weeks.
Age requirement: 18–20
Causes: Animal Welfare, children, conservation, environmental causes, poor/ homeless, teaching/assisting (primary, secondary), work camps – seasonal, young people.
Activities: Agriculture/farming, arts/crafts, building/construction, caring (general),

catering, community work, conservation skills, cooking, development issues, DIY, forestry, international aid, manual work, outdoor skills, religion, sport, summer camps, teaching, theatre/drama, visiting/befriending, work camps – seasonal.

Vols under 26 placed each year: 96
When to apply: As early as possible.
Work alone/with others: With others.
Volunteers with disabilities: We are unable to place people with disabilities as we work in developing countries with very basic facilities.
Qualifications: Post A-level students.
Equipment/clothing: Yes – full details available in a booklet.
Health requirements: Full details available after offer of a place.
Costs: Overall budget in the region of £4,000.
Benefits: Develop foreign language skills, understand the plight of developing countries and gain leadership experience. Group insurance available.
Training: UK build-up weekend before departure. VentureCo leaders provide necessary training during the venture.
Supervision: 1 guide accompanies team throughout. 1 expedition leader joins for expedition.
Interview details: Interviews take place in Leamington Spa.
Certification: Written reference on request.
Worldwide placements: *Asia* (India, Nepal); *South America* (Bolivia, Chile, Ecuador, Peru).

VEREINIGUNG JUNGER FREIWILLIGER EV (VJF)
Muggelstrasse 22a
Berlin
10247 Germany

Tel: 00 49 30 588 38 14

VJF organizes international work camps, most of which are social or ecological projects, but there are also special programmes which focus on issues such as the history of Jewish people in Germany. In most cases volunteers have to do easy manual work on the camps. VJF places 500 international volunteers a year and 500 German volunteers. Please apply through Concordia, International Voluntary Service or Quaker International Social Projects. All three have entries on this database.

Total projects worldwide: 1
Total UK projects: 0
Starting months: May–September.
Time required: 2–4 weeks.
Age requirement: 18–30
Causes: Conservation, environmental causes.
Activities: Conservation skills.
Vols under 26 placed each year: 500
When to apply: As early as possible.
Work alone/with others: With others.
Qualifications: Nil.
Equipment/clothing: Outdoor working clothes.
Costs: Application fee of DM200 plus travel expenses.
Benefits: Accommodation.
Worldwide placements: *Europe* (Germany).

VIDARÅSEN LANDSBY
N 3240 Andebu
Norway

Tel: 00 47 3344 41 00 (9 00 am 3 00 pm)
Fax: 00 47 3344 01 91
Contact: The Director

Vidaråsen Landsby is a Camphill Village community.

Total projects worldwide: 1
Total UK projects: 0
Starting months: January–December.
Time required: 1–52 weeks.
Age requirement: 14 plus.
Causes: Disabled (learning).
Activities: Agriculture/farming, arts/crafts, caring (residential), gardening/horticulture.
When to apply: All year.
Work alone/with others: With others.
Volunteers with disabilities: Not possible.
Qualifications: Nil.
Health requirements: Nil.
Worldwide placements: *Europe* (Norway).

VIGYAN SHIKSHA KENDRA
c/o Vigyan Sanchar Sansthan
Civil Lines
Banda
Uttar Pradesh State
210001 India

Tel: 00 91 5192 24587
Contact: Dr Bharatendu Prakash, Convenor

Vigyan Shiksha Kendra was set up in 1974 with an aim to research and improve traditional systems and seed farming techniques. 5–10 hardworking volunteers are

neded for four-plus months. Projects include training of farmers, artisans and village youth, and publishing a rural newspaper. We organize traditional health practitioners and train the next generation. We run an Ayurvedic hospital. We organize women and train them for self-employment. We work towards self-reliant education for children. We are working to establish a medicinal garden and encourage farmers to grow herbs. We plan to set up an Institute of Environmental Engineering and Management to prepare an environment-friendly, sustainable society.
Total projects worldwide: 3–4
Total UK projects: 0
Starting months: January–December.
Time required: 20–30 weeks.
Age requirement: 18 plus.
Causes: Animal welfare, children, conservation, elderly people, environmental causes, health care/medical, heritage, teaching/assisting (primary, secondary, EFL), work camps – seasonal, young people.
Activities: Agriculture/farming, arts/crafts, campaigning, community work, computers, conservation skills, counselling, development issues, first aid, forestry, gardening/ horticulture, group work, library/resource centres, manual work, music, newsletter/ journalism, research, scientific work, social work, teaching, technical skills, theatre/ drama, training, work camps – seasonal.
Vols under 26 placed each year: 5–10
When to apply: All year.
Work alone/with others: With others.
Volunteers with disabilities: Difficult as we work in difficult rural areas.
Qualifications: Scientific, technical or medical background desirable. Above all, commitment is essential. Some knowledge of Hindi desirable.
Health requirements: Very good health.
Costs: Travel and personal necessities. Insurance is desirable – we can provide general insurance which is nominal.
Benefits: Board and lodging. Simple vegetarian food as we eat here.
Supervision: We have a built-in process of supervision.
Certification: Certificate or reference provided.
Worldwide placements: *Asia* (India).

VILLAGE AIGUES-VERTES
29 Route de Chèvres
CH 1233 Chèvres-Bernex
Genève
Switzerland

Tel: 00 41 22 757 17 21
Fax: 00 41 22 757 36 09
Contact: The Director

Village Aigues-Vertes is a Camphill Village community with adults with special needs.

Total projects worldwide: 1
Total UK projects: 0
Starting months: January–December.
Time required: 1–52 weeks.
Age requirement: 14 plus.
Causes: Disabled (learning).
Worldwide placements: *Europe* (Switzerland).

VILLAGE CAMPS INC.
Department 840
Rue de la Morache 14
CH-1260 Nyon
Switzerland

Tel: 00 41 22 990 9405
Fax: 00 41 22 990 9494
e-mail: personnel@villagecamps.ch
Web: www.villagecamps.com
Contact: Rebecca Meaton

Village Camps need volunteers to work 12 hours a day in summer and winter holiday camps. Experience in working with young people, sports and organizational ability are also necessary. Must have a desire to live and work with young people of various nationalities. Also staff are required with certification in ski-ing, canoeing, rock climbing, teaching, sailing, archery, swimming, football, arts/crafts, outdoor pursuits.

Total projects worldwide: 10
Total UK projects: 1
Starting months: February, May–August, December.
Time required: 6–8 weeks.
Age requirement: 21–40
Causes: Children, conservation, environmental causes, teaching/assisting (nursery, primary, secondary, EFL), wildlife, young people.
Activities: Arts/crafts, caring (general, day and residential), catering, community work, computers, conservation skills, cooking,

counselling, development issues, driving, international aid, music, newsletter/journalism, outdoor skills, research, sport, summer camps, teaching, theatre/drama, training, translating.
Vols under 26 placed each year: 200 of a total of 300.
When to apply: February–May (summer camps), October (winter camps).
Work alone/with others: With others in a community of 40. Must get along with others.
Volunteers with disabilities: Possible.
Qualifications: Good sports (parallel skiers, winter), speak English, know French/Spanish/Italian/German.
Health requirements: Must be in good health.
Costs: Nil, apart from health insurance.
Benefits: Pocket money plus food, accommodation, ski pass in winter and accident and liability insurance.
Training: Full 7 day in-house training a week before work starts.
Supervision: Trained management staff oversee and supervise volunteers.
Interview details: We interview by phone.
Certification: Certificate or reference on request.
Worldwide placements: *Europe* (Austria, France, Netherlands, Switzerland).
UK placements: *England* (E. Sussex, W. Sussex).

VILLAGE EDUCATIONAL PROJECT (KILIMANJARO)
Mint Cottage
Prospect Road
Sevenoaks
Kent
TN13 3UA UK

Tel: +44 (0) 1732 459799
Contact: Katy Allen

Village Education Project (Kilimanjaro) was set up as a UK registered charity in 1994. The overall aim is to improve the education of primary school children by renovating government school buildings, providing books and teaching aids, and sponsoring in-service teacher training. The gap year Student Project is one of the charity's more recent projects. The students help to teach English in village schools. Students are encouraged to provide extra curricular activities such as sport, art and music for the pupils who are between 7

and 14 years old. The students accompany parties of children on school outings to a National Park and to the coast. Students live in their own village house, and their life in the village involves lots of walking each day up and down the lush countryside of Kilimanjaro's slopes. School holidays provide an opportunity for further travel – Zanzibar being a favourite destination. Katy Allen, the Project Leader, lived in Kilimanjaro for three years and now visits the region for at least four months each year, and is there to meet the gap year students and help them to settle in to their village and their schools, giving advice and guidance. They have at all times the full support of the local community and church, and specifically of the ex-head of a local school now seconded to work for the charity.

Total projects worldwide: 1
Total UK projects: 0
Starting months: January.
Time required: 32–48 weeks.
Age requirement: 18–25
Causes: Teaching/assisting (primary, EFL).
Activities: Arts/crafts, sport, teaching.
Vols under 26 placed each year: 8 plus
When to apply: September (18 months ahead of departure date).
Work alone/with others: Both.
Volunteers with disabilities: Not possible.
Qualifications: Clear speech.
Health requirements: Nil.
Costs: £1,700 (subject to change) fee plus full medical repatriation and other insurance and subsistence.
Benefits: Return air ticket, village accommodation in Kilimanjaro.
Training: A pre-departure two-week training course is given in Sevenoaks, Kent.
Supervision: On arrival students are met by Katy Allen and introduced to villages. Dilly Mtui, working for the charity, has responsibility when Katy returns to the UK.
Nationalities accepted: No restrictions but British passport-holders preferred.
Interview details: Interviews take place in Sevenoaks, Kent.
Certification: Certificate or reference on request.
Charity number: 1041672
Worldwide placements: *Africa* (Tanzania).

VILLAGES YOUTH PROJECT, THE
37 Bridlington Street
Hunmanby
N. Yorkshire
UK

Tel: +44 (0) 1723 891521
Contact: Mrs Dee Heim, Project Worker

The Villages Youth Project operates in
Hunmanby, Muston, Reighton, Speeton,
Wold Newton and surrounding villages. It is
a youthwork project initiated by local
churches and local people of Hunmanby and
those in surrounding villages. This project
began in 1989. It was developed to meet the
needs and help address the real problems
facing young people in rural areas such as
unemployment and homelessness, isolation
and boredom. During the last five years the
project volunteers have converted a double
decker bus for use as a youth centre to work
with the young people in the villages. We
have come across young people who have
problems relating to drugs, alcohol,
gambling, homelessness, health issues,
teenage pregnancies and juvenile offending.
As well as providing recreational facilities on
the bus, there has been liaison with police,
courts and other organizations to help
support young people with various
difficulties. What are our aims? The overall
objectives are: (a) to provide facilities for
meeting the needs of young people aged 11–
25 in Hunmanby, Muston, Reighton,
Speeton, Wold Newton and the surrounding
area; (b) to offer support and assistance to
young people to enable them to make
informed choices in the areas of education,
health, training, independence and recreation
so that their conditions of life may be
improved and they may develop their
physical, mental and spiritual capacities so as
to grow to full maturity as individuals and
members of society.

Total projects worldwide: 1
Total UK projects: 1
Starting months: January–December.
Time required: 12–52 weeks.
Age requirement: 19 plus.
Causes: Conservation, environmental causes,
unemployed, young people.
Activities: Administration, arts/crafts,
conservation skills, counselling, development
issues, driving, fundraising, group work,
outdoor skills, religion, visiting/befriending.

Vols under 26 placed each year: 8
When to apply: All year.
Work alone/with others: With others.
Volunteers with disabilities: All applications
warmly welcomed. Some access issues need
addressing.
Qualifications: Any relative to working with
young people.
Health requirements: Nil.
Costs: Nil.
Benefits: Travel costs.
Interview details: Interviews take place at
project office.
Certification: Certificate or reference
provided.
UK placements: *England* (N. Yorkshire).

VINCENTIAN SERVICE CORPS
7800 Natural Bridge Road
St Louis
Missouri 63121
USA

Tel: 00 1 314 382 2800 ext 291
Fax: 00 1 314 382 8392
e-mail: vsccentral@juno.com
Web: www.vscorps.org
Contact: The Director

The Vincentian Service Corps/Central is part
of the national Vincentian Service Corps. The
other office is in New York. We invite men
and women, 20 years and older to serve the
poor for one year. The VSC/Central is
sponsored by the Daughters of Charity of the
Midwest and all placements from our office
are in the central area of the United States.
Our volunteers (members) serve in many
aspects of social work, health care, education
and parish ministry. We offer a one-year
programme each year. Application forms are
available upon request from which we can
learn the applicant's background, interests,
education, family history, medical history and
experiences. We ask for five personal
references that we follow up for their
recommendation regarding the applicant's
ability to work in the programme.
Evaluations are conducted twice a year with
input from the member and from the work
supervisor. We strive to place members in
community settings whenever possible or
preferred. Proximity to Daughters of Charity
or Vincentian priests is always a part of the
assignment to ensure their inclusion in the
Vincentian family. Because of the difficulty of

getting a visa for the USA, we ask applicants from outside the USA to apply for their visa as soon as possible.

Total projects worldwide: 1
Total UK projects: 0
Starting months: January, August.
Time required: 1–52 weeks.
Age requirement: 22 plus.
Causes: Aids/HIV, children, disabled (physical), elderly people, health care/medical, human rights, inner city problems, poor/homeless, refugees, teaching/assisting (nursery, primary, mature, EFL), young people.
Activities: Building/construction, caring (general and residential), community work, computers, fundraising, religion, social work, teaching.
Vols under 26 placed each year: 6 of a total of 7.
When to apply: At least 3 months in advance.
Work alone/with others: Both.
Qualifications: All applicants must speak very good English because they will be in positions of leadership or role models for those they serve. Spanish is also useful.
Costs: Fares to St Louis.
Benefits: Accommodation plus US$100 per month plus US$100 per month for food, health insurance and 3 renewal weekends during the year.
Training: There is a week of orientation at the beginning of the programme introducing the member to the charisma of the Vincentian family, to service, community living, cultural diversity and living gospel values.
Interview details: Interviews are by telephone.
Worldwide placements: *Australasia* (New Zealand); *North America* (USA).

VISIONS IN ACTION
2710 Ontario Road NW
Washington
DC 20009
USA

Tel: 00 1 202 625 7402
Fax: 00 1 202 625 2353
e-mail: visions@igc.apc.org
Web: www.visionsinaction.org
Contact: Shaun Skelton

Visions in Action is an international not-for-profit organization founded in 1988 out of the conviction that much can be learned from and contributed to the developing world by working as part of a community of volunteers committed to achieving social and economic justice. Visions in Action co-ordinates volunteers with non-profit development organizations. Volunteers are matched according to skills, interest and experience to one of any number of overseas non-profit organizations operating in both rural and urban settings. They work in such diverse fields as business management, law, health care, environmental concerns, journalism, youth and children's programmes, scientific research, women's issues, housing, agriculture, building and manual trades, democratization, human rights and social justice. Visions in Action volunteers interact on a daily basis with host country nationals and development professionals. You work within the local culture while participating as members of the international development community. Visions in Action's mission statement: participants in the Visions in Action programme support the following precepts: grass-roots approach: development occurs best when we are as close as possible to the standard of living of those we are trying to assist. Therefore, a modest, low overhead, grass-roots approach is taken in all that Visions does. Voluntarism: there is much that can be done in the spirit of true voluntarism – giving of oneself and making personal sacrifices for the betterment of others, expecting nothing in return. Community development occurs best in a community of inspired, informed individuals, living together and supporting one another throughout the volunteer experience. Self-reliance: participants are self-reliant, mirroring the same type of self-reliance that those in developing countries are trying to achieve. Social justice: all of our efforts are directed at achieving social and economic justice for those in the developing world. Volunteers possess a range of skills, experience, education, age and nationality.

Total projects worldwide: Numerous
Total UK projects: 0
Starting months: January–December.
Time required: 26–52 weeks.
Age requirement: 19 plus.
Causes: Addicts/Ex-addicts, Aids/HIV, animal welfare, archaeology, architecture, children, conservation, disabled (learning and

physical), elderly people, environmental causes, health care/medical, heritage, holidays for disabled, human rights, inner city problems, offenders/ex-offenders, poor/homeless, refugees, teaching/assisting (nursery, primary, secondary, mature, EFL), unemployed, wildlife, work camps – seasonal, young people.

Activities: Administration, agriculture/farming, caring (general), community work, conservation skills, development issues, international aid, newsletter/journalism, research, social work, training, work camps – seasonal.

Vols under 26 placed each year: 40 of a total of 65.

When to apply: At least 90 days before departure.

Work alone/with others: Work for local non-profit organizations (not with other volunteers).

Volunteers with disabilities: Possible.

Qualifications: University degree or equivalent work experience for all programmes except 6 month South Africa and Mexico programmes.

Equipment/clothing: No specific equipment. Clothing depends on programme.

Health requirements: Good general health.

Costs: Travel plus programme fees which average US$3,800 for one year.

Benefits: Housing, monthly stipend, medical insurance and training in development and the local language.

Training: A thorough one-month orientation in-country, including local language training, homestays, visits to development projects and guest speakers.

Supervision: By staff at local development organizations.

Interview details: Interviews by phone.

Certification: Written reference provided.

Charity number: 52-1659822

Worldwide placements: *Africa* (Burkina Faso, South Africa, Tanzania, Uganda, Zimbabwe); *Central America* (Mexico).

VISWADARSANAM

Feny Land
Nariyapuram – 689 513
Pathanamthitta District
Kerala
India

Tel: 00 91 473 350543
Fax: 00 91 473 322264

e-mail: viswadarsanam@hotmail.com
Contact: Mrs Janee Babu, Programme Director

Viswadarsanam is a voluntary organization located in Kerala in South India. It started on world environment day, 5 June 1987. Our aim is to make nature truly natural and human lives more cheerful and thus bring health, happiness and peace to society to prevent further deterioration of natural wealth and promote a sustainable utilization of natural resources for human welfare. Essentially we are an environmental organization. The activities included are the following: 1. Establishing a development centre for humanity and nature. 2. Preparing newsletters, books, information sheets and audio visuals. 3. Conducting guided educative wilderness trips, nature walks and trekking for interested groups. Our interests also extend into rural development, cottage industry, art and cultural heritage, flora and fauna, travel and tourism. We need administrative volunteers for planning and implementation of long- and short-term projects such as nature camps, environmental programmes and green health programmes. Volunteers also help with international correspondence, computer work and publication of a souvenir handbook to cover a decade of work at Viswadarsanam. We need volunteers for alternative lifestyle experiments/holistic way of life. We need volunteers for teaching spoken English to the local school and university students. Apart from work involvement, the volunteers will get the opportunity to relax with cultural programmes, interact with local people, travel the countryside, and trek nature trails. There are forests and rivers nearby. There is also the opportunity to experience local fairs and festivals. There are numerous sites in the area. See the Viswadarsanam home district handbook for more information about the area. Sightseeing trips to experience Kerala will be arranged upon request. The asset of Viswadarsanam is the grace of kind-hearted and service-minded people. Their might is our strength. Volunteers are welcome to stay and acclimatize before committing.

Total projects worldwide: 5
Total UK projects: 0
Starting months: January–December.
Time required: 1–12 weeks.

Age requirement: 18 plus.
Causes: Animal welfare, conservation, environmental causes, health care/medical, heritage, human rights, teaching/assisting (EFL), wildlife, work camps – seasonal.
Activities: Administration, agriculture/farming, arts/crafts, building/construction, campaigning, community work, conservation skills, cooking, development issues, forestry, fundraising, gardening/horticulture, group work, manual work, marketing/publicity, newsletter/journalism, outdoor skills, teaching, work camps – seasonal.
Vols under 26 placed each year: 30 of a total of 40–50.
When to apply: All year.
Work alone/with others: With others.
Volunteers with disabilities: Not possible.
Qualifications: Post A-level or university preferred. Above all social commitment and dedication. Any skill is particularly welcome such as computer knowledge, photography and cinematography, arts and crafts, language ability and/or project planning.
Equipment/clothing: Raincoat, sleeping bag, mosquito net, torch etc.
Health requirements: Good health, not been in contact with any infectious diseases.
Costs: Registration fee £10. £40 per week, £140 for one month, £350 for 3 months. Travel to India. Insurance.
Benefits: The cost covers board and lodging.
Training: Training in local customs and manners.
Supervision: Maximum supervision by the camp directors.
Interview details: Selection by application form, then informal induction on arrival.
Certification: Certificate or reference provided.
Charity number: Q 915
Worldwide placements: *Asia* (India).

VOLUNTARY SERVICE BELFAST (VSB)

70–72 Lisburn Road
Belfast
Antrim
BT9 6AF N. Ireland

Tel: +44 (0) 28 9020 0850
Fax: +44 (0) 28 9020 0860
Contact: Jim Woods

The VSB Volunteer Centre is concerned with promoting, supporting and developing voluntary activity within the Greater Belfast community. It provides the link between people interested in voluntary work, and organizations or individuals who can benefit from the services provided by the volunteers. Volunteering is about becoming involved in the community to benefit others, by doing something because you want to. You do not have to possess special skills or experience, but it helps to be patient, tolerant, understanding and reliable. Volunteers with an offending background are accepted but generally placed where they can be closely supervised – at least to begin with. It depends on the nature of the offence. We are unlikely to recruit sex offenders for any type of placement.

Total projects worldwide: 7
Total UK projects: 5
Starting months: January–December.
Time required: 12–52 weeks (plus).
Age requirement: 16 plus.
Causes: Addicts/Ex-addicts, children, conservation, disabled (learning and physical), elderly people, poor/homeless, young people.
Activities: Administration, arts/crafts, caring (general), community work, conservation skills, counselling, DIY, driving, fundraising, gardening/horticulture, manual work, marketing/publicity, research, visiting/befriending.
Vols under 26 placed each year: 300
When to apply: One month prior to starting.
Work alone/with others: Both.
Volunteers with disabilities: Possible, if sufficient time for forward planning.
Qualifications: Nil.
Health requirements: Nil.
Costs: Accommodation.
Benefits: Travel costs up to £3 per day. Lunch allowance of £1.50 per day.
Interview details: Interviews take place in our head office in Lisburn Road.
Certification: Certificate or reference provided.
Charity number: XN48736
Worldwide placements: *Asia* (India, Israel); *Europe* (Germany, Romania).
UK placements: *Northern Ireland* (Antrim, Belfast City, Down).

VOLUNTARY SERVICE OVERSEAS

317 Putney Bridge Road
London
SW15 2PN UK

Tel: +44 (0) 20 8780 2266
Fax: +44 (0) 20 8780 1326
e-mail: enquiry@vso.org.uk
Contact: Atha Murphy

Voluntary Service Overseas (VSO) enables
men and women to work alongside people in
poorer countries in order to share skills, build
capabilities and promote international
understanding and action, in the pursuit of a
more equitable world. Placements are in
education, health, natural resources, technical
trades, engineering, business, communications
and social development. Over 1,750
volunteers work in 57 countries. Posts are
overseas for two years (some new six-month
posts). It is important to think seriously
about the implications of volunteering before
applying. Volunteers are highly motivated,
flexible and adaptable individuals who have
made a commitment to VSO and the
employer overseas. You may be living in
circumstances that are a good deal less
comfortable than the UK and away from
family and friends. It won't be easy – but it
will be the experience of a lifetime.
Volunteers with an offending background are
accepted.

Total projects worldwide: 1,800
Total UK projects: 0
Starting months: January, February, April,
May, September.
Time required: 26–52 weeks (plus).
Age requirement: 20 plus.
Causes: Children, conservation, disabled
(learning and physical), environmental
causes, health care/medical, inner city
problems, teaching/assisting (primary,
secondary, mature, EFL), wildlife.
Activities: Accountancy, administration,
agriculture/farming, arts/crafts, building/
construction, catering, community work,
computers, conservation skills, forestry,
fundraising, gardening/horticulture, library/
resource centres, marketing/publicity, music,
newsletter/journalism, social work, sport,
teaching, technical skills, training.
Vols under 26 placed each year: 50 (short-
term).
When to apply: All year – only on standard
application form.
Work alone/with others: Either.
Volunteers with disabilities: Applications
welcome. Nature of disability and skills
determines overseas placements.

Qualifications: Professional qualification plus
usually 2 years' work experience in a trade or
profession. No dependent children volunteers
must have unrestricted access to the UK and
be willing to work for a modest living
allowance.
Equipment/clothing: TBA.
Health requirements: Yes.
Costs: Negligible.
Benefits: Modest living allowance plus
accommodation.
Nationalities accepted: Certain restrictions on
nationalities of volunteers.
Interview details: Interviews take place in
London, Manchester, Glasgow, Netherlands,
Canada.
Certification: Certificate or reference
provided.
Charity number: 313757
Worldwide placements: *Africa* (Gambia,
Ghana, Guinea-Bissau, Kenya, Malawi,
Namibia, Nigeria, Sierra Leone, South
Africa, Tanzania, Uganda, Zambia,
Zimbabwe); *Asia* (Bangladesh, Bhutan,
Cambodia, China, Indonesia, Laos,
Mongolia, Nepal, Pakistan, Philippines, Sri
Lanka, Thailand, Vietnam); *Australasia* (Fiji,
Kiribati, Papua New Guinea, Solomon
Islands, Tonga, Tuvalu, Vanuatu); *Europe*
(Albania, Bulgaria, Czech Republic, Estonia,
Hungary, Latvia, Lithuania, Poland,
Romania, Russia, Slovakia); *Central America*
(Anguilla, Antigua and Barbuda, Belize,
Dominica, Grenada, Montserrat, Saint Lucia,
Saint Vincent/Grenadines); *South America*
(Guyana).

VOLUNTARY WORKCAMPS
ASSOCIATION OF GHANA
PO Box 1540
Accra
Ghana

Tel: 00 233 21 663486
Fax: 00 233 21 665960
Contact: Francis Atta Donkor, General
Secretary

Voluntary Workcamps Association of Ghana
organizes work camps in the rural areas of
Ghana for international volunteers. Campers
work about seven hours a day, mostly
unskilled manual digging, clearing bush,
mixing cement or building. The projects are
mostly roads, schools, street drains, latrines,
hospitals or clinics, social centres, bridges etc.

in villages and small towns which villagers themselves are carrying out through voluntary communal labour. In some camps there is a programme of educational work for girls among the village women. The function of the camps is not to do the work for the people but to help them to help themselves by working with them. In selecting and arranging the projects the Association co-operates closely with some government departments.

Total projects worldwide: 12–20
Total UK projects: 0
Starting months: January, June, July, August, September, October, December.
Time required: 3–52 weeks.
Age requirement: 16 plus.
Causes: Children, conservation, disabled (physical), environmental causes, work camps – seasonal.
Activities: Agriculture/farming, building/construction, community work, conservation skills, forestry, group work, manual work, outdoor skills, social work, summer camps, work camps – seasonal.
Vols under 26 placed each year: 1,500
When to apply: February.
Work alone/with others: With others – 25–50 per camp.
Volunteers with disabilities: Possible.
Qualifications: Nil.
Equipment/clothing: Working clothes, boots, gloves, torch, raincoat, mosquito net plus repellent, sleeping bag, water purifier.
Costs: Inscription fee of approximately £120 and travel.
Benefits: Accommodation, administration expenses and food at campsite.
Certification: Certificate or reference on request.
Worldwide placements: *Africa* (Ghana).

VOLUNTARY WORKCAMPS ASSOCIATION OF NIGERIA
PO Box 2189
Lagos
Nigeria

Tel: 00 234 1951290 or 821568
Fax: 00 234 1 2663294
e-mail: Voworan@nipost.pinet.net
Contact: The Secretary-General

Voluntary Workcamps Association of Nigeria organizes work camps centred around community projects for youths of different cultural backgrounds and nationalities throughout Nigeria. Between 120 and 150 volunteers per year participate in the work camps; the work is mainly skilled and unskilled manual labour. This includes bricklaying, carpentry, sports, games, excursions, debates and discussions. We also undertake short and medium term programmes in the year. The usual length of placement is between one and two months (i.e. July to September). Application forms are available at US$20 for volunteers to receive brochure and placement for the camps. Only applications received with the fee before the month of May will be considered.

Total projects worldwide: 1
Total UK projects: 0
Starting months: July, August.
Time required: 4–8 weeks.
Age requirement: 14 plus.
Causes: Environmental causes, health care/medical, poor/homeless, work camps – seasonal, young people.
Activities: Building/construction, community work, DIY, sport, work camps – seasonal.
Vols under 26 placed each year: 120–150
When to apply: Before May.
Work alone/with others: With others.
Volunteers with disabilities: Not possible.
Qualifications: Knowledge of English.
Health requirements: Volunteers must be physically fit.
Costs: US$20 for application form. US$200 registration fee plus travel and upkeep.
Benefits: Board and lodging.
Worldwide placements: *Africa* (Nigeria).

VOLUNTARY YEAR
Stora Sköndal
128 85 Sköndal
Sweden

Tel: 00 46 8 605 0927
Contact: The Director

Total projects worldwide: 1
Total UK projects: 0
Starting months: January–December.
Time required: 40–52 weeks.
Age requirement: 18–25
Activities: Community Work, Religion.
Worldwide placements: *Europe* (Sweden).

VOLUNTEER NEPAL
GPO Box 11535
Dilli Bazar
Kathmandu
Nepal

Tel: 00 977 1 426996
Fax: 00 977 1 416417/428925
e-mail: cdnnepal@wlink.com.np
Web: www.volunteernepal.org.np
Contact: Rajesh Shrestha, Director

Volunteer Nepal is the name of a promising programme aiming to introduce participants in individually differentiated grades to Nepal's diverse geographical and cultural environment and to promote general intercultural understanding through experiential learning in Nepal. We are dedicated to the promotion of worldwide understanding of cultural differences. We are engaged in service to humanity right on the spot. This is perfect for volunteers who are interested in more than pure vacation-stay. This programme is designed for those people who wish to visit Nepal and contribute their time and skills to benefit the community as well as learn Nepalese culture and customs by living as a member of a Nepali family and doing volunteer work in various fields. By participating in this programme, we hope that you will experience personal growth as well as open communication channels among different countries and cultures. Other starting dates can be arranged. Nepal is a country of amazing extremes where one can find compacted within its small area a roster of the highest mountains on earth, a repertoire of enchanting cultures and exquisite temples, thick tropical jungles holding a wealth of wildlife, thundering rivers swollen by the snow of Himalayas, and most of all, the friendliest people you have ever met. As diverse as the land on which they live, the people of Nepal represent distinct cultures and races, speaking a variety of tongues and practising different religions. A delightful similarity is that they all speak the language of courtesy, and hospitality is a national culture. Volunteers with an offending background are accepted.

Total projects worldwide: 3
Total UK projects: 0
Starting months: February–April, August–October.
Time required: 8–16 weeks.

Age requirement: 18 plus.
Causes: Addicts/ex-addicts, Aids/HIV, children, disabled (learning and physical), environmental causes, health care/medical, human rights, poor/homeless, teaching/assisting (nursery, primary, secondary), young people.
Activities: Administration, arts/crafts, community work, computers, group work, manual work, music, social work, sport, teaching, technical skills, training.
Vols under 26 placed each year: 50 of a total of 75.
When to apply: Three months before programme commencement.
Work alone/with others: With others.
Volunteers with disabilities: Not possible.
Qualifications: Minimum A-level (high school diploma), language requirement is English.
Health requirements: Nil.
Costs: Application fee US$50, Registration US$650. Return air fare to Nepal. Visa fee. Personal money. Essential health and any other insurance required.
Benefits: Accommodation, breakfast and dinner. Free trekking, rafting, jungle safari, language training, homestay, lectures, cross-cultural orientation, study tour and other cultural activities.
Training: 2-weeks pre-service training is provided. This includes language training, lectures, cross-cultural orientation, orientation tour, practice teaching, class observation, schooling system and so on.
Supervision: By the host organization and constant communication is carried out by us.
Interview details: No interview necessary.
Certification: Certificate or reference provided.
Charity number: 5663/110
Worldwide placements: *Asia* (Nepal).

VOLUNTEER TASK FORCE INC.
194 Loftus Street
North Perth
6006 Western Australia

Tel: 00 61 8 932 85388
Fax: 00 61 8 932 85385
e-mail: Task1@Smartchat.net.au
Contact: Pamela Coates, Manager

Volunteer Task Force has been operating for 30 years. We are a registered charitable organization with Public Benevolent Institution (PBI) status. We recruit, train and manage volunteers to perform gardening, home maintenance and voluntary transport for the frail aged, those on disability pensions and their carers. The aim of our programme is to provide services so these clients can remain in their own homes for as long as possible and not have to go into a nursing home or hostel. We have 85 volunteers, four full-time and two part-time employees. Volunteers with an offending background are accepted with the exception of theft, violent or sexual offences.

Total projects worldwide: 1
Total UK projects: 0
Starting months: January–December.
Time required: 1 week.
Age requirement: 17 plus.
Causes: Disabled (physical), elderly people, unemployed.
Activities: Community work, manual work, outdoor skills.
Vols under 26 placed each year: 10–15 of a total of 80–90.
When to apply: Any time, Monday to Friday 9 a.m.–4 p.m. Call to make an appointment.
Work alone/with others: With others.
Volunteers with disabilities: We are unable to place people with disabilities as most of our work is physically demanding, e.g. gardening, yard clean-up, driving etc.
Qualifications: All skills and qualifications, honesty, reliability. English language proficiency.
Equipment/clothing: Covered shoes, hat plus long-sleeved shirt for protection from sun, insects, plus irritating plants.
Health requirements: Volunteers are required to manage their own health condition, e.g. schizophrenia, depression.
Costs: Flights to Australia, board and lodging.
Benefits: Reimbursement of local fares to and from agency. Volunteer personal accident, vehicle, public liability insurance all paid for by us.
Training: Orientation day at the agency on the first day.
Supervision: By a trained, paid staff member.
Interview details: Prospective volunteers are interviewed at the agency, given a volunteer handbook and asked to read the literature and sign an enrolment form, accepting mutual duty of care obligations between volunteer employer and employee.
Certification: Written reference on request.

Charity number: 18037
Worldwide placements: *Australasia* (Australia).

VOLUNTEERS FOR OUTDOOR COLORADO
600 South Marion Parkway
Denver
Colorado
80209 USA

Tel: 00 1 303 715 1010 ext 12
Fax: 00 1 303 715 1212
e-mail: voc@voc.org
Web: www.voc.org
Contact: Dusty Martin, Youth Program Co-ordinator

Volunteers for Outdoor Colorado (VOC) is a non-profit organization formed in 1984 to engage volunteers in improving Colorado's public lands. Each year VOC performs between 10 and 12 weekend outdoor service projects. These projects vary in size from 75 to 1,000 volunteers. We travel all over the state to find fun, interesting and worthwhile service projects for our volunteers. VOC provides all the tools, crew leading and food for these projects. VOC also serves as a clearinghouse for other volunteer opportunities and internships around the state of Colorado. Included are more than 720 volunteer opportunities with agencies such as the National Park Service, US Forest Service, Bureau of Land Management and Colorado State Parks and other non-profit organizations. Positions vary from one-time events to summer-long internships. Volunteers should visit our website for the most current information on volunteer positions throughout the year. Individuals or groups wishing to pursue any of these volunteer possibilities should contact our office by phone, fax, e-mail or postal mail. Indicate which opportunities interest you by listing the four-digit code following each project description. Once we receive your request, we will then send you more information on each position, including the appropriate person to contact. Volunteers with an offending background are accepted.

Total projects worldwide: 700 plus.
Total UK projects: 0
Starting months: January–December.
Time required: 1–26 weeks.
Age requirement: 12 plus.

Causes: Archaeology, conservation, environmental causes, wildlife, young people.
Activities: Building/construction, community work, conservation skills, forestry, gardening/horticulture, group work, manual work, outdoor skills, scientific work, training.
Vols under 26 placed each year: 600 of a total of 4,000 plus.
When to apply: All year.
Work alone/with others: With others.
Volunteers with disabilities: Possible.
Qualifications: Dependent on the position.
Equipment/clothing: Volunteers must have their own transport and overnight gear if they are planning on camping out.
Health requirements: Dependent on the position.
Costs: Dependent on the project.
Benefits: Some positions offer housing, stipend, travel allowance.
Training: Dependent on the position.
Supervision: Dependent on the position.
Interview details: Prospective volunteers may be interviewed, depending on the project.
Worldwide placements: *North America* (USA).

W

WAR ON WANT
37–39 Great Guildford Street
London
SE1 OES UK

Tel: +44 (0) 20 7620 1111
Fax: +44 (0) 20 7261 9291
e-mail: rcartridge@waronwant.org
Web: www.waronwant.org
Contact: Rob Cartridge, Campaigns Director

War on Want was established over 40 years ago. It is a membership organization working with project partners overseas. We do not administer relief aid but financial support for long-term development programmes. We also believe in the need to raise awareness in Britain about the causes of world poverty. This is essential in order to promote the fundamental changes in international policies that are needed before a permanent improvement in the lives of the world's poor can be made. As with all charities, volunteers are used extensively at War on Want. They are required only at our London office, primarily for administrative support. However, there are occasional campaign-based tasks, e.g. attending conferences, representing WOW at NGO meetings etc.

Total projects worldwide: 19 plus.
Total UK projects: Varies.
Starting months: January–December.
Time required: 4–52 weeks.
Age requirement: 21 plus.
Causes: Human rights, inner city problems, young people.
Activities: Administration, campaigning, computers, development issues, fundraising, international aid.
Vols under 26 placed each year: 2 of a total of 20.
When to apply: All year.
Work alone/with others: Both.
Volunteers with disabilities: Possible if properly qualified.
Qualifications: Excellent English, A-levels or computer skills or willingness to learn quickly.
Benefits: £3.50 for lunch and travel costs. Insurance provided by us on the same basis as for full-time employees.
Training: Through briefings. Most training is on the job.
Supervision: All volunteers allocated one member of staff or supervisor.
Certification: Written reference provided.
Charity number: 208724
Worldwide placements: *South America* (Brazil).
UK placements: *England* (London).

WARWICKSHIRE ASSOCIATION OF YOUTH CLUBS
Arno House
63 Willes Road
Leamington Spa
Warwickshire
CV31 1BN UK

Tel: +44 (0) 1926 450156
Fax: +44 (0) 1926 313328
e-mail: warks.youthclubs.uk@ukonline.co.uk
Contact: William Clemmey, Executive Director

Warwickshire Association of Youth Clubs is an association of 115 youth clubs working with over 9,000 young people and over 900 youth workers in Warwickshire, Coventry and Solihull. We were established as a charity in 1954 to meet the needs of youth organizations working with young people up to the age of 25. We also work directly with young people, regardless of race, creed, sex or disability. We are affiliated to Young Warwickshire and to Youth Clubs UK. The support we offer includes: helping to set up new youth groups; providing a comprehensive insurance package for clubs; arranging events and activities to enhance their programmes; support and training for youth workers, some of whom are paid part time but the majority of whom are volunteers; a newsletter six times a year to keep clubs up to date with what is on offer; help with fundraising ideas including running an annual golf tournament. Our Sport and Arts Programmes enable youngsters to take part in a variety of games and activities in village and church halls. We also offer drama, dance, video and digital photography workshops as part of our Arts Development programme, Youth Achievement Award and First Year Course opportunities. Our events and competitions programme includes: netball, pool, ice skating, dance, five-a-side football and unihoc. Young people are also involved in international youth work. In Easter 2000 we were involved in a quadrilateral youth exchange with Russia, Denmark and Belarus. Our Environmental Springboard Project offers young people the opportunity to explore environmental issues and take part in action that means something to them. We have a new 12-berth narrowboat *Dream Catcher* which can be borrowed by youth groups, schools and disabled groups. We are seeking volunteer helmsmen for this.

Total projects worldwide: 1
Total UK projects: 1
Starting months: January–December.
Time required: 1–52 weeks.
Age requirement: 16 plus.
Causes: Children, environmental causes, young people.
Activities: Administration, arts/crafts, computers, driving, fundraising, group work, marketing/publicity, music, newsletter/journalism, outdoor skills, sport, summer camps, theatre/drama, training.
Vols under 26 placed each year: 40–45 of a total of 50–60.
When to apply: All year.

Work alone/with others: Both.
Volunteers with disabilities: We are unable to place people with disabilities as unfortunately the building is inaccessible at present.
Qualifications: Nil. Driving licence, IT skills, coaching awards, arts background all desirable.
Health requirements: Nil.
Costs: Subsistence only. We have public liability insurance but volunteers may wish to take out additional cover, particularly for personal belongings.
Benefits: Travel costs.
Training: Induction plus ongoing training as well as access to accredited training courses, i.e. Level 1 and 2 Youth Work Training.
Supervision: By volunteer programme worker.
Certification: Certificate or reference provided.
Charity number: 1056035
UK placements: *England* (Warwickshire, West Midlands).

WARWICKSHIRE WILDLIFE TRUST
Brandon Marsh Nature Centre
Brandon Lane
Coventry
Warwickshire
CV3 3GW UK

Tel: +44 (0) 24 7630 8975
Fax: +44 (0) 24 7663 9556
e-mail: PDickin@warkswt.cix.co.uk
Contact: Phil Dickin, Community and Education Manager

Warwickshire Wildlife Trust is the leading local environmental charity, dedicated to protecting wildlife and natural habitats throughout Warwickshire, Coventry and Solihull. It is one of 47 independent trusts forming the Wildlife Trusts – the largest body in the UK concerned with all aspects of nature conservation. The Trust manages over 50 nature reserves totalling over 2,000 acres, including woodlands, meadows and wetlands. Practical work on these reserves is carried out by a network of local volunteers. The Trust also works to protect wildlife by campaigning on nature conservation issues, by liaising with other organizations, individuals and community groups, and by promoting a greater awareness of conservation to the general public. The Trust promotes wildlife education in schools, colleges and local communities through talks, exhibitions and guided walks. The Trust's junior membership is part of the national environment club – WILDLIFE WATCH – which provides projects for members and affiliated schools, so involving them directly with environmental issues. The Trust's flagship Nature Centre at Brandon Marsh just outside Coventry was opened by Sir David Attenborough in 1992. Its 200 acres of pools and wetlands are now visited by over 25,000 people each year, including over 5,000 children on organized educational activities. The Centre is open every day from 9–5 (10–5 at weekends). In addition to income from membership, the Trust raises funds by sponsorship, grants, donations and legacies. The Trust is organized through a Council of Trustees elected from its members, who provide the overall direction for the development of the Trust. On a day-to-day basis conservation work is carried out by a staff of 32, based at the Trust offices at Brandon Marsh Nature Centre. Volunteers with an offending background may be accepted but not for work with children.

Total projects worldwide: 50 plus.
Total UK projects: 50 plus.
Starting months: January–December.
Time required: 1–52 weeks (plus).
Age requirement: 14 plus.
Causes: Animal welfare, children, conservation, environmental causes, heritage, inner city problems, teaching/assisting (primary, secondary, mature), unemployed, wildlife, young people.
Activities: administration, arts/crafts, campaigning, community work, conservation skills, development issues, forestry, fundraising, gardening/horticulture, group work, library/resource centres, manual work, marketing/publicity, newsletter/journalism, outdoor skills, research, scientific work, teaching, training.
Vols under 26 placed each year: 20
When to apply: All year.
Work alone/with others: With others.
Volunteers with disabilities: Possible.
Qualifications: Nil.
Equipment/clothing: Loaned.
Health requirements: Nil.
Costs: Nil.
Benefits: Travel costs and expenses reimbursed. We provide insurance whilst working for the Trust.
Training: Depends on the person and the

opportunity we offer.
Supervision: All volunteers are closely supervised. Responsibility will be given to individuals who have shown a clear ability to take on responsibility.
Interview details: Interviews take place at Brandon Marsh Nature Centre.
Certification: Certificate or reference provided if required.
Charity number: 209200
UK placements: *England* (Warwickshire, West Midlands).

WATERWAY RECOVERY GROUP – CANAL CAMPS
PO Box 114
Rickmansworth
WD3 1ZY UK
Tel: +44 (0) 1923 711114
Fax: +44 (0) 1923 897000
e-mail: wrg@waterways.org.uk
Web: www.wrg.org.uk
Contact: Enquiries Officer

Waterway Recovery Group – Canal Camps. In helping to restore one of Britain's derelict canals, you will have the opportunity to do a hundred and one things that you have never done before and earn yourself a place in canal restoration history! You will be meeting all sorts of new people, having a lively social life in the evenings and you could find yourself doing any, if not all of the following: restoring industrial archaeology; demolishing old brickwork structures; bricklaying and pouring concrete; driving a dumper truck; clearing a lock chamber of 'orrible black slimy silt; helping to run a major national waterways festival; cooking for 20 hungry volunteers; clearing vegetation and felling trees. For a worthwhile and fun-filled week with about 20 or so like-minded people, all you need is to be reasonably fit, over 17, and able to cope with the basic facilities of village hall accommodation. All applicants are treated equally with no special qualifications or restrictions.

Total projects worldwide: 50
Total UK projects: 50
Starting months: January–December.
Time required: 1–52 weeks.
Age requirement: 17 plus.
Causes: Archaeology, conservation, environmental causes, work camps – seasonal.

Activities: Building/construction, conservation skills, forestry, manual work, summer camps, work camps – seasonal.

Vols under 26 placed each year: 1,000 of a total of 2,000.

When to apply: All year.

Work alone/with others: With others.

Volunteers with disabilities: Not usually.

Qualifications: Nil.

Equipment/clothing: Outdoor working clothes, strong work or wellington boots (steel toe capped), sleeping bag.

Health requirements: Reasonable fitness.

Costs: £35 per week towards food and accommodation or £5 per day.

Benefits: Accommodation in village halls or similar. Waterway Recovery Group is insured for workers over 17 years of age.

Training: All training is provided at the camp although there is an optional annual training weekend.

Supervision: Each residential camp has leaders responsible for supervising the work tasks.

Interview details: No interview necessary.

Certification: Written reference if requested.

Charity number: 212342

UK placements: *England* (Cornwall, Derbyshire, Devon, Essex, Gloucestershire, Herefordshire, Hertfordshire, Lincolnshire, Shropshire, Surrey, E. Sussex, W. Sussex, Wiltshire, Worcestershire, N. Yorkshire, W. Yorkshire).

WEC INTERNATIONAL

Bulstrode
Oxford Road
Gerrards Cross
Buckinghamshire
SL9 8SZ UK

Tel: +44 (0) 1753 884631
Fax: +44 (0) 1753 278166
e-mail: trek.bulstrode@talk21.com
Web: www.wec-int.org
Contact: Sheila Kilkenny, Short-term Co-ordinator

WEC International is an interdenominational mission agency with workers in many countries around the world. Our aim is to share the Gospel with people who have never heard it. As well as church-related activities, workers are involved in community development projects, rehabilitation programmes, medical work, teaching (primary, secondary and TEFL), administration and working with children. Small numbers of volunteers are needed for various tasks in a number of countries to help long-term personnel.

Total projects worldwide: 50 plus

Total UK projects: 2

Starting months: January–December.

Time required: 4–36 weeks.

Age requirement: 18 plus.

Causes: Addicts/ex-addicts, Aids/HIV, children, health care/medical, refugees, teaching/assisting (nursery, primary, secondary, EFL), unemployed, young people.

Activities: Accountancy, administration, agriculture/farming, arts/crafts, building/construction, caring (general), catering, community work, computers, cooking, counselling, development issues, DIY, driving, first aid, library/resource centres, manual work, music, outdoor skills, religion, research, social work, sport, summer camps, teaching, technical skills, theatre/drama, training, translating, visiting/befriending, work camps – seasonal.

Vols under 26 placed each year: About 10 of a total of 20 plus.

When to apply: At least 4 months in advance.

Work alone/with others: Frequently with others in a team.

Volunteers with disabilities: There are no projects for volunteers with disabilities.

Qualifications: Evangelical Christians. Teachers, maintenance/mechanical and general help/medical doctors, nurses, obstetricians, midwives/secretaries.

Equipment/clothing: Information from country of service.

Health requirements: Good health is necessary.

Costs: All costs are paid by the volunteers. including the necessary travel and medical insurance.

Training: WEC Trek has 5 days training for short placements. For one year or more there is a 4-week training programme. All volunteers are required to attend an orientation course before final acceptance for any position.

Supervision: The leader of each placement has full responsibility for supervision.

Interview details: Interviews take place at WEC HQ, Gerrards Cross or at the nearest WEC base in the UK.

Certification: Reference on request.
Charity number: 237005
Worldwide placements: *Africa* (Burkina Faso, Chad, Ivory Coast, Equatorial Guinea, Gambia, Ghana, Guinea, Guinea-Bissau, Senegal, South Africa); *Asia* (Cambodia, Japan, Korea (South), Nepal, Taiwan, Thailand); *Australasia* (Australia, Fiji, New Zealand); *Europe* (Albania, Bulgaria, France, Greece, Italy, Portugal, Spain); *Central America* (Mexico); *South America* (Brazil, Colombia, Venezuela).
UK placements: *England* (Buckinghamshire, London, West Midlands).

WELSH WILDLIFE CENTRE, THE
Cilgerran
Cardigan
SA43 2TB Wales

Tel: +44 (0) 1239 621212
Fax: +44 (0) 1239 613211
e-mail: wildlife@wtww.co.uk
Web: www.wildlife-wales.org.uk
Contact: Mrs J. Glennerster

The Welsh Wildlife Centre manages Skomer Island which is a National Nature Reserve. The island is internationally famous for its seabird colonies. Our volunteers help us with a wide variety of tasks, including the repair and maintenance of buildings, hides and footpaths, and at appropriate times may help with scientific work, bird surveys and generally contribute to the island's records. Help will also be needed to meet the boats which bring day visitors to the island, collecting landing fees and patrolling the reserve. We are very keen to have help from good birdwatchers during the last week of May and the first two weeks of June as during this time a great deal of seabird census work is carried out.

Total projects worldwide: 1
Total UK projects: 1
Starting months: March–October.
Time required: 1–2 weeks.
Age requirement: 16 plus.
Causes: Conservation, environmental causes.
Activities: Conservation skills, DIY, group work, manual work, outdoor skills, scientific work.
Vols under 26 placed each year: 88 of a total of 110.
When to apply: 1 September for the following year.

Work alone/with others: With others.
Volunteers with disabilities: Not possible.
Qualifications: Nil – interest in natural history an advantage.
Equipment/clothing: Stout walking boots, waterproof clothing and bedding (pillow case, sheet and duvet).
Health requirements: Good general health.
Costs: Everything free but bring your own food.
Benefits: Accommodation and travel from mainland to Skomer. We have joint employer's public liability insurance cover.
Training: Introductory talk and health and safety talk given on arrival.
Supervision: Under direct supervision of island warden and assistant warden.
Interview details: No interview necessary.
Certification: Certificate or reference on request.
Charity number: 227996
UK placements: *Wales* (Pembrokeshire).

WELSHPOOL AND LLANFAIR LIGHT RAILWAY
The Station
Llanfair
Caereinion
Welshpool
Powys
SY21 0SF Wales

Tel: +44 (0) 1938 810441
Contact: Frank Cooper

Welshpool and Llanfair Light Railway is a restored Edwardian railway in beautiful Mid-Wales countryside.

Total projects worldwide: 1
Total UK projects: 1
Starting months: January–December.
Time required: 1–52 weeks.
Age requirement: 16 plus.
Causes: Conservation, heritage.
Activities: Building/construction, conservation skills, forestry, manual work, outdoor skills, summer camps, technical skills.
Vols under 26 placed each year: 70 of a total of 350.
When to apply: All year.
Work alone/with others: With others.
Volunteers with disabilities: Very restricted.
Qualifications: Nil.
Equipment/clothing: Overalls, steel capped work boots.

Health requirements: Fit, healthy, no medication which may affect work ability.
Costs: Travel, board, lodging and pocket money.
Benefits: Subsidized accommodation. Public/employers liability and personal accident insurance is provided by us.
Training: As required, depending on actual job.
Supervision: We have paid management and 'regular' volunteer supervisors.
Charity number: 1000378
UK placements: *Wales* (Powys).

WEST MOORS OUT OF SCHOOL CLUB
113 Heathfield Road
West Moors
Ferndown
Dorset
BH22 0DE UK

Tel: +44 (0) 1202 876269
Contact: Mrs Anne Whittle-Lord

West Moors Out of School Club is held at the Community Centre, Bond Avenue, West Moors. It provides activities for children aged 5–13 years, in a safe, happy environment, supervised by professional, experienced and caring staff at a minimum ratio of 1 adult to 8 children. Social Services regulations are adhered to and registration has been obtained, together with membership of Kids Clubs Network. The varied programme includes arts, crafts, sports, recreational and educational activities. A quiet area will be set aside where children can complete homework, read or rest and a television and video are available, if necessary, to watch suitably monitored programmes for relaxation or educational purposes. Sports and active games will be arranged outside supervised by the appropriate number of staff. We also have two play parks nearby and a yard attached to the building. In bad weather conditions, suitable games will be arranged indoors under close supervision. Regular outings will be arranged during school holiday-time. The Club sessions start at 3.00pm in term-time and 8.30 a.m. in the school holidays, ending at 6.00 p.m. for both types of session; however, shorter sessions will be available upon request.

Total projects worldwide: 1
Total UK projects: 1
Starting months: January–December.

Time required: 1–52 weeks.
Age requirement: 16 plus.
Causes: Children.
Activities: Arts/crafts, caring (general), sport.
Vols under 26 placed each year: 6
When to apply: All year.
Work alone/with others: With others.
Volunteers with disabilities: Possible if capable of supervising children.
Qualifications: Communication skills and an ability to relate to children aged 5–13.
Equipment/clothing: Nil – some activities can be messy e.g. painting, papier mache etc.
Health requirements: Nil other than Social Services recommendations.
Costs: Nil but any travel costs to and from work.
Interview details: Applicants are interviewed in Ferndown, Dorset.
Certification: Written reference or assessment on request.
UK placements: *England* (Dorset).

WEST YORKSHIRE YOUTH ASSOCIATION
Investing in Success Project
Kettlethorpe Youth Centre
Standbridge Lane
Kettlethorpe
WF2 7NW UK

Tel: +44 (0) 1924 256686
Fax: +44 (0) 1924 256686
Contact: Helen Thompson

The West Yorkshire Youth Association has always made the needs and welfare of young people central to the activities and organization, since its inception in 1907. Now it is a dynamic organization running nine projects. We are looking to continue that development beyond the year 2000 as we build on our work to meet the needs of many young people, within cities, rural communities and on a county-wide basis. The Association works to provide opportunities and support for young people in training and employment, housing, the arts, involvement in the community, sports and outdoor pursuits and the running of a residential centre open to all young people. In order that we can convert ideas and needs into reality we work with communities, local authorities and trusts to continue to meet more of the needs and develop the aspirations of young people across West Yorkshire.

Volunteers with an offending background may be accepted depending on the role and the offence.

Total projects worldwide: 9
Total UK projects: 9
Starting months: January–December.
Time required: 1–52 weeks.
Age requirement: 16 plus.
Causes: Young people.
Activities: Arts/crafts, outdoor skills, sport.
When to apply: All year.
Work alone/with others: With others.
Volunteers with disabilities: Possible.
Qualifications: Nil.
Health requirements: Nil.
Costs: Nil.
Benefits: Depending on budgets of individual projects.
Interview details: Applicants are interviewed at the base/office of the particular project.
Certification: Reference on request.
Charity number: 519883
UK placements: *England* (W. Yorkshire).

WESTERN AUSTRALIAN AIDS COUNCIL
664 Murray Street
West Perth
6005 Australia

Tel: 00 61 8 9429 9900
Fax: 00 61 8 9429 9901
e-mail: waHIV@waHIV.asn.au
Web: www.waHIV.asn.au
Contact: Volunteer Co-ordinator

The West Australian AIDS Council needs the support of volunteers. Without this support vital services would not be able to function. HIV/Aids affects the lives of hundreds of people in Western Australia. We need your support to continue to help people living with HIV/Aids and to prevent the further transmission of HIV. Support Services: volunteers help to improve the quality of life for people living with HIV/Aids. Volunteers provide transport and other practical assistance in the home, as well as emotional support. Qualified practitioners of complementary therapies such as massage, volunteer their skills in our Living Well Program. Volunteers of Support Services give approximately four hours per week with the majority of volunteer work occurring during weekdays. Community Education: volunteers play a vital role in improving the general communities' understanding and knowledge of HIV/Aids and accompanying issues. Education on safer practices aims to prevent the further transmission of HIV. There are a number of ways volunteers can make a difference in the community. Some of these include providing resources, information and referrals on the AIDSline, and through the Needle and Syringe Exchange Program. Volunteers can also provide informative presentations to schools and other community groups. Weekday work is available with some weekend and after hours work also available. Peer Education: Volunteers reduce the impact and further transmission of HIV/Aids through work with men who have sex with men. There are plenty of opportunities to become involved in the community. Volunteers provide outreach services, groups and workshops and a telephone information and referral service. Peer Education programmes mostly operate in the evening, with limited weekday work available. Freedom Centre: Volunteers provide support and information to young people with same sex attractions through a youth drop-in centre. Shifts are available in the evenings and volunteers must be 27 years old or under.

Total projects worldwide: 15
Total UK projects: 0
Starting months: January–December.
Time required: 26–52 weeks (plus).
Age requirement: 16 plus.
Causes: Addicts/Ex-addicts, Aids/HIV, young people.
Activities: Administration, caring (day), community work, fundraising, visiting/befriending.
Vols under 26 placed each year: 100 of a total of 300.
When to apply: When the volunteer arrives in Perth.
Work alone/with others: With others.
Volunteers with disabilities: Possible.
Qualifications: Own transport occasionally. Volunteer training day required by some projects.
Health requirements: Nil.
Costs: Training Course A$20.
Benefits: Out-of-pocket expenses reimbursed.
Training: 4–5 days training provided.
Supervision: Volunteers are supervised.
Interview details: Interview required.
Certification: Certificate for training. Reference on request.
Worldwide placements: *Australasia*

(Australia).

WESTON SPIRIT, THE
5th Floor
Cotton House
Old Hall Street
Liverpool
Merseyside
L3 9WS UK

Tel: +44 (0) 151 258 1066
Fax: +44 (0) 151 258 1388
e-mail: ben@weston-spirit.org.uk
Contact: Ben Harrison, Chief Executive

The Weston Spirit works in the inner city areas of Britain offering young people, who may experience feelings of isolation and hopelessness, a real alternative to problems such as unemployment, drugs, alcohol misuse, homelessness and abuse, amongst other things. Our aim is to encourage young people aged 16–18 from major British cities to reassess their attitude and their role within the communities in which they live.
Programme Path: Recruitment: talks are carried out in youth training centres, schools, youth clubs, through outreach workers and word of mouth, as well as referrals from the social, careers and probation services. Any young person aged between 16–18 and living within commuting distance of a city centre base is eligible for the programme. Intro Day: interested individuals attend a day of activities which include team building, discussions and ice-breaking exercises before participating in a residential course. Residential Experience: a week-long intensive course towards the development of team-building values, community involvement and inter-personal skills. This is the foundation of The Weston Spirit membership. Membership: continued development in your home area through a positive programme of activities run from a city base. These include educational, training and employment opportunities, group work and social awareness, enterprise skills and project work, counselling and community involvement. Volunteers with an offending background are accepted – depending on offence.

Total projects worldwide: 4
Total UK projects: 4
Starting months: January–December.
Time required: 1–52 weeks.
Age requirement: 16 plus.

Causes: Inner city problems, poor/homeless, unemployed, young people.
Activities: Administration, community work, cooking, counselling, driving, fundraising, group work, library/resource centres, marketing/publicity.
Vols under 26 placed each year: 240
When to apply: All year.
Work alone/with others: Both.
Volunteers with disabilities: Possible.
Qualifications: Nil.
Health requirements: Nil.
Costs: Cost of weekly visits to drop-in centres.
Benefits: Most expenses are paid by TWS.
Interview details: Interviews are conducted in relevant city centre base or national office.
Certification: City and Guilds Profile of Achievement available to both members and volunteers.
Charity number: 327937
UK placements: *England* (Merseyside, Tyne and Wear); *Wales* (Cardiff, Vale of Glamorgan).

WILDERNESS TRUST, THE
The Oast House
Hankham
Nr Pevensey
East Sussex
BN24 5AP UK

Tel: +44 (0) 1323 461730
Fax: +44 (0) 1323 461730
e-mail: wilderness.trust@dial.pipex.com
Contact: Chris Blessington, Director

The Wilderness Trust does not employ volunteers as such. We do provide opportunities for young people and adults to take part in wilderness journeys in the UK, South Africa, Canada and very shortly in Italy. These are journeys of self-discovery as well as insights into the ecology and wildlife of the wilderness areas in which you travel. The journeys are self-financing. In South Africa the leadership is provided by the Wilderness Leadership School which employs fully qualified field officers and guides to conduct the journeys into the wilderness areas. In Wales, Canada and soon in Italy, the journeys are conducted by guides selected for their experience and qualifications. A programme of journey dates is available on request. Special journeys can be arranged to suit schools, colleges, universities and other organizations as well as those with special physical needs.

Total projects worldwide: 1
Total UK projects: 1
Starting months: January–November.
Time required: 1–3 weeks.
Age requirement: 16 plus.
Causes: Conservation, environmental causes, wildlife, young people.
Activities: Conservation skills, development issues, outdoor skills.
Vols under 26 placed each year: 40–50
When to apply: All year.
Work alone/with others: With others.
Volunteers with disabilities: Special trails may be organized for special needs parties.
Qualifications: Nil.
Equipment/clothing: Walking boots and personal clothing. All else provided. Kit list sent with joining instruction.
Health requirements: Reasonably fit, able to carry a rucksack and walk up to 10 miles a day.
Costs: Trail costs including accommodation available on request.
Certification: Certificate or reference provided.
Charity number: 1005826
Worldwide placements: *Africa* (South Africa); *Europe* (Italy); *North America* (Canada).
UK placements: *Wales* (Conwy).

WILDFOWL AND WETLANDS TRUST (WWT)
Slimbridge
Gloucestershire
GL2 7BT UK

Tel: +44 (0) 1453 891900 ext 115
Fax: +44 (0) 1453 891941
e-mail: daphne.chin@wwt.org.uk
Web: www.wwt.org.uk
Contact: Mrs Daphne Chin, Office Manager

Wildfowl and Wetlands Trust is a registered charity whose aim is to preserve and protect wetlands through programmes of scientific study, education and the operation of eight visitor centres around the UK. Volunteers are needed at the visitor centres to help with a variety of practical conservation tasks including grounds maintenance (planting, weeding, trimming etc.), reserve management, looking after the birds at the centres (feeding, making nest boxes etc.) and also as visitor centre staff working on the information desk, helping with school parties, envelope stuffing. There is also the opportunity to learn a lot about the unique environments of the wetlands themselves.

Total projects worldwide: 8
Total UK projects: 8
Starting months: January–December.
Time required: 12–52 weeks (plus).
Age requirement: 16 plus.
Causes: Animal welfare, conservation, environmental causes, wildlife.
Activities: Administration, conservation skills, gardening/horticulture, manual work, outdoor skills.
Vols under 26 placed each year: 20
When to apply: All year.
Work alone/with others: Both.
Volunteers with disabilities: Possible in the Visitor Services Deptartment. Work on grounds/reserve is demanding.
Qualifications: Driving Licence is useful.
Equipment/clothing: Outside gear – waterproof coat and wellies are useful.
Health requirements: Need to be fit and healthy.
Costs: Own food. If not full time, accommodation.
Benefits: For full-time volunteers there is limited space in the hostel at Slimbridge which is free. We have employer's liability insurance.
Training: General induction given at commencement of placement plus more specific training as required.
Supervision: Work alongside other staff with a line manager who supervises and delegates.
Interview details: Interviews take place at the respective WWT Centre.
Certification: Reference on request.
Charity number: 1030884
UK placements: *England* (Cambridgeshire, Gloucestershire, Lancashire, W. Sussex, Tyne and Wear); *Scotland* (Dumfries and Galloway); *Northern Ireland* (Down); *Wales* (Pembrokeshire).

WILDLIFE TRUST FOR BEDS, CAMBS, NORTHANTS AND PETERBOROUGH
3B Langford Arch
London Road
Sawston
Cambridge
Cambridgeshire
CB2 4EE UK

Tel: +44 (0) 1223 712400
Fax: +44 (0) 1223 712412
e-mail: cambswt@cix.co.uk
Web: www.wildlifetrust.org.uk/bcnp
Contact: Sue Bashford

The Wildlife Trust for Bedfordshire, Cambridgeshire and Northamptonshire is a voluntary organization totally committed to protecting the local countryside and its inhabitants. Our concern is for wildlife of all types, rare and common, ranging from orchids to otters, barn owls to badgers, securing their survival for future generations. Our vitally important work will ensure the existence of our precious countryside and the many endangered species currently under threat. Our Wildlife Trust is part of a nation-wide network of local Trusts dedicated to all aspects of wildlife protection. It is because of this dedication that the Wildlife Trusts collectively manage 2,000 nature reserves which include some of the most important sites for wildlife in the UK. Our effectiveness comes from working in partnership with local communities with the common purpose of conserving the countryside. In Bedfordshire, Cambridgeshire and Northamptonshire we manage over 130 nature reserves, screen planning applications and fight to save sites where there is a threat to the survival of wildlife. The Trust has 11,000 members throughout its three counties. Volunteers with an offending background may be accepted for certain jobs but not those working with children.

Total projects worldwide: 1
Total UK projects: 1
Starting months: January–December.
Time required: 1–52 weeks (plus).
Age requirement: 12 plus.
Causes: Conservation, environmental causes, wildlife.
Activities: Administration, conservation skills, forestry, manual work, marketing/publicity, newsletter/journalism, outdoor skills.
Vols under 26 placed each year: Many of a total of 1,000.
When to apply: All year.
Work alone/with others: With others.
Volunteers with disabilities: Not possible.
Qualifications: Nil. Training/advice given where necessary.
Equipment/clothing: Outdoor clothing / waterproofs/boots if appropriate. Safety gear

provided if necessary.
Health requirements: Depends on task – general good health preferred.
Costs: Travel costs and a lunch box.
Benefits: Our insurance cover 'protects' our volunteers as well as our staff.
Training: All training is given on the job.
Supervision: It is the responsibility of the person taking on the volunteers to supervise them. By the nature of the job, it cannot be close supervision.
Interview details: No interview necessary.
Certification: Certificate or reference provided if appropriate.
Charity number: 11000412
UK placements: *England* (Bedfordshire, Cambridgeshire, Northamptonshire).

WILTSHIRE WILDLIFE TRUST
Elm Tree Court
Long Street
Devizes
Wiltshire
SN10 1NJ UK

Tel: +44 (0) 1380 725670
Fax: +44 (0) 1380 729017
e-mail: wio@wiltshirewildlife.org
Web: www.wiltshirewildlife.org
Contact: Wildlife Information Officer

The Wiltshire Wildlife Trust is the largest voluntary organization in the county concerned with nature conservation. The Trust manages over 40 nature reserves including woodland, chalk downland, watermeadows and streams. With experts and skilled staff, the Trust is the charity best able to protect Wiltshire and Swindon's wildlife. Although much of our work depends on the financial support of over 10,000 members, just as important is the enormous contribution of time given by volunteers.

Total projects worldwide: 1
Total UK projects: 1
Starting months: January–December.
Time required: 1–52 weeks (plus).
Age requirement: 14 plus.
Causes: Children, conservation, environmental causes, wildlife.
Activities: Administration, campaigning, conservation skills, fundraising, marketing/publicity, outdoor skills.
Vols under 26 placed each year: 55 of a total of approximately 500.
When to apply: All year.

Work alone/with others: With others.
Volunteers with disabilities: Possible.
Qualifications: Nil.
Health requirements: Nil.
Costs: Travel to work.
Benefits: All expenses reimbursed. We have insurance for volunteers.
Training: Any necessary training is carried out.
Supervision: By a Trust member of staff or key volunteers.
Interview details: Interviews are conducted at the Devizes head office or at our offices in Swindon or Salisbury.
Charity number: 266202
UK placements: *England* (Wiltshire).

WINANT CLAYTON VOLUNTEER ASSOCIATION

Davenant Centre
179 Whitechapel Road
London
E1 1DU UK

Tel: +44 (0) 20 7375 0547
e-mail: wcva@dircon.co.uk
Web: www.wcvr.dircon.co.uk
Contact: Tessa Crichton-Miller, Co-ordinator

Winant Clayton Volunteers travel as a group to New York City in late June to undertake two months community/social work, followed by 2 1/2 weeks travel. Placements are with different groups; the homeless, elderly, children, HIV/Aids, mental health etc. The work is full-time, up to 40 hours per week over five days. It can be challenging and exhausting but the rewards are great, and there is a real opportunity to make a valuable contribution to people in need. Volunteers are supervised and given support by our US Board, which, like the UK Committee, is made up of returned volunteers. It is a reciprocal scheme, with a similar group of US volunteers coming to work each summer in the East End of London. Ability to be flexible and open-minded is more important than qualifications. Some volunteers fundraise towards their costs and are supported in this by Winant Clayton. Volunteers with an offending background may be accepted – minor offences to be cleared with the US Embassy.

Total projects worldwide: 25
Total UK projects: 13
Starting months: June–September.

Time required: 12 weeks.
Age requirement: 19 plus.
Causes: Aids/HIV, children, disabled (learning and physical), elderly people, health care/medical, inner city problems, poor/homeless, young people.
Activities: Caring (day), community work, counselling, social work.
Vols under 26 placed each year: 10 of a total of 20.
When to apply: Before end of January.
Work alone/with others: Both alone and with others.
Volunteers with disabilities: Possible.
Qualifications: UK or Irish passports essential, volunteer work and/or social community work experience desirable.
Equipment/clothing: General.
Health requirements: Reasonable level of mobility and fitness required.
Costs: Air fare, insurance, visa and travel expenses.
Benefits: Food, accommodation and pocket money while on placement. Travel insurance is arranged by us. Full details provided.
Training: 2-day orientation in London, 1 day in New York and induction at work placement.
Supervision: Volunteers have supervisor at their project. In addition they have an American 'link' for support, as well as the New York based Winant Clayton co-ordinator.
Nationalities accepted: Must be from the UK or Ireland.
Interview details: Interviews take place in London during February.
Charity number: 296101
Worldwide placements: *North America* (USA).
UK placements: *England* (London).

WIND SAND AND STARS

2 Arkwright Road
London
NW3 6AD UK

Tel: +44 (0) 20 7433 3684
Fax: +44 (0) 20 7431 3247
e-mail: office@windsandstars.co.uk
Web: www.windsandstars.co.uk
Contact: Janina Stajic

Wind Sand and Stars is a small company that specializes in projects and journeys in the desert and mountain regions of Sinai. Each summer we organize an expedition for young people combining desert travel and adventure with the opportunity to work on projects with the local Bedouin people and to develop expedition and leadership skills.

Total projects worldwide: 3–5
Total UK projects: 0
Starting months: June–August.
Time required: 4 weeks.
Age requirement: 16–25
Causes: Environmental causes.
Activities: Community work, group work, outdoor skills, research.
Vols under 26 placed each year: 20–25
When to apply: October–April.
Work alone/with others: With others.
Volunteers with disabilities: Minor disabilities may be accommodated – this would need to be confirmed.
Qualifications: Good level of fitness and stamina.
Equipment/clothing: Tough, light desert clothing and some camping equipment.
Health requirements: A medical form will be provided for completion.
Costs: Approximately £2,000.
Benefits: Support given for fundraising activities. Full insurance covered in the cost.
Training: One day pre-departure training.
Supervision: Qualified leaders.
Nationalities accepted: No restrictions but an Egyptian visa is required.
Interview details: Prospective applicants are occasionally interviewed at our office.
Certification: Personal reference provided.
Worldwide placements: *Africa* (Egypt).

WINGED FELLOWSHIP TRUST
Angel House
20–32 Pentonville Road
London
N1 9XD UK

Tel: +44 (0) 20 7833 2594
Fax: +44 (0) 20 7278 0370
e-mail: admin@wft.org.uk
Web: www.wft.org.uk
Contact: Karen Atwell

The Winged Fellowship provides respite for carers and quality holidays for people with severe physical disabilities. We would not be able to cope without the much appreciated help of our volunteers. Our volunteers are asked to be the hands and feet of our disabled guests and to be their companions and friends. The tasks, undertaken include: 1. Helping one of the guests wash and dress in the mornings. 2. Helping feed those who need assistance. 3. Transferring people from wheelchair to the toilet and vice-versa, or from their wheelchair to an ordinary chair. 4. Accompanying them in a group on outings to places of interest, the theatre or shopping. 5. Serving meals. 6. Generally assisting in the everyday running of the centres. Volunteers work long hours and the work is physically and emotionally very demanding but we hope also interesting and rewarding. Many of our volunteers return again and again. There are opportunities for volunteers to work in Europe on the Overseas and Discovery Holidays programme but these volunteers are only selected after completing voluntary work with Winged Fellowship in the UK. We require references before accepting any volunteer. Volunteers with an offending background may be accepted but not offences against the person or sexual offences.

Total projects worldwide: Approximately 10.
Total UK projects: 5
Starting months: February–December.
Time required: 1–2 weeks.
Age requirement: 16 plus.
Causes: Children, disabled (learning and physical), elderly people, holidays for disabled.
Activities: Arts/crafts, caring (general and residential), fundraising, sport.
Vols under 26 placed each year: 3,000 of a total of 4,500.
When to apply: All year.
Work alone/with others: With others.
Volunteers with disabilities: Possible, but they must be able to push wheelchairs on day trips.
Qualifications: Must be able to speak and understand spoken English.
Health requirements: Reasonably fit.
Costs: Pocket money only.
Benefits: Free board and lodging. Travel expenses refunded. We have public liability and employer's liability insurance to cover volunteers helping at the centres.
Training: Written information and induction training, ongoing support, supervision and feedback sessions.
Supervision: Constant access to professional staff. Buddy system of supervision.
Nationalities accepted: No restrictions but we do not assist volunteers to obtain visas to

enter Britain.

Interview details: No interview necessary – if a volunteer is found to be unsuitable they will be asked to leave.

Certification: Written reference as required plus certificate of achievement.

Charity number: 295072

UK placements: *England* (Essex, Hampshire, Merseyside, Nottinghamshire).

WOMANKIND WORLDWIDE

Viking House
3rd Floor
5–11 Worship Street
London
EC2A 2BH UK

Tel: +44 (0) 20 7588 6099
Fax: +44 (0) 20 7588 6101
e-mail: info@womankind.org.uk
Web: www.womankind.org.uk
Contact: Brita Schmidt

Womankind Worldwide is a development agency set up in 1989 to assist women in developing countries in their efforts to overcome poverty and ill health, to gain access to education and training, to eliminate violence and to take greater control of their lives. Our vision is of a society, just, equitable and peaceful, in which women are equal partners in determining the values, direction and governance of society at all levels both national and international, for the benefit of all. Our guiding principles are: listen to women's own needs; respect their knowledge and experience; take a broad view of development and be imaginative and responsive in our support; encourage women to use all their skills and develop those skills; work in partnership with women; co-operate with organizations with similar aims; support a wide range of women's projects; collaborate with men working towards women's advancement. All volunteering places are in our London office and there are no opportunities to volunteer abroad.

Total projects worldwide: 19
Total UK projects: 1
Starting months: January–December.
Time required: 12–52 weeks (plus).
Age requirement: 24–34
Causes: Human rights, inner city problems, young people.
Activities: Administration, development issues, first aid, library/resource centres, marketing/publicity, newsletter/journalism, research, translating.

Vols under 26 placed each year: 10 of a total of 20.

When to apply: All year.
Work alone/with others: Both.
Volunteers with disabilities: Possible.

Qualifications: English essential. Spanish desirable. Computer skills, writing skills, database if possible.

Health requirements: Nil.
Costs: Nil.

Benefits: Travel expenses (up to London area Zone IV) and £3 lunch.

Supervision: The line manager responsible for the area of work supervises the volunteer.

Interview details: Interviews are conducted in our office.

Certification: Reference if required.
Charity number: 328206
UK placements: *England* (London).

WOMEN'S ENVIRONMENTAL NETWORK (WEN)

P O Box 30626
London
E1 1TZ UK

Tel: +44 (0) 20 7481 9004
Fax: +44 (0) 20 7481 9144
e-mail: info@wen.org.uk
Web: www.gn.apc.org/wen
Contact: Ann Link

WEN is a unique, vital and innovative campaigning organization, which represents women and campaigns on issues which link women, environment and health. We are a non-profit membership organization. Putting Breast Cancer on the Map is a National Lottery-funded project involving individuals and communities drawing a map of their own locality, highlighting any breast cancer incidence and local sources of environmental pollution which they think have adversely influenced the incidence rate in the area. Waste Prevention Campaign initiated the Waste Minimization Bill, which now has government support. We inform councils and individuals on alternatives to wasteful products and packaging, and are involved with a waste prevention project at Spitalfields Market. The Taste of a Better Future Campaign encourages people to grow their own organic foods and supports growing groups. The Real Nappy Project/Campaign promotes the use of 'real' nappies to replace the use of disposable nappies.

Total projects worldwide: 5
Total UK projects: 5
Starting months: January–December.
Time required: 6–52 weeks (plus).
Age requirement: 20 plus.
Causes: Environmental causes.
Activities: Administration, campaigning, group work, newsletter/journalism, research.
Vols under 26 placed each year: Varies.
When to apply: All year.
Work alone/with others: Both.
Volunteers with disabilities: Possible, the office has a lift but is not very disabled-friendly.
Qualifications: Good written English, adaptability. Other specific skills are required at times.
Health requirements: Nil.
Costs: Nil.
Benefits: £3 for cost of lunch and £3–£4 travel per day if total of 6 hours are worked.
Training: An induction for half a day.
Supervision: By campaign co-ordinator.
Interview details: After sending a CV, prospective volunteers will need to attend an interview in London.
Certification: Certificate or reference provided.
UK placements: *England* (London).

WOMEN'S ROYAL VOLUNTARY SERVICE
Milton Hill House
Milton Hill
Abingdon
Oxon
OX13 6AF UK

Tel: +44 (0) 1235 442961
Fax: +44 (0) 1235 861166
e-mail: enquiries@wrvs.org.uk
Web: www.wrvs.org.uk
Contact: Pauline Pope, Volunteer Development Manager

WRVS is one of Britain's largest active volunteering organization with over 100,000 members, 12,000 of whom are men, working in four core areas of emergency, community, food and hospital services on such projects as meals on wheels, hospital shops, contact centres where divorced parents can meet their children and support to the 'blue light'

emergency services. Our vision is to be the premier provider of voluntary assistance to those in need within their local community.

Total projects worldwide: 5,000
Total UK projects: 5,000
Starting months: January–December.
Time required: 1–52 weeks.
Age requirement: 14 plus.
Causes: Children, elderly people, offenders/ex-offenders, poor/homeless.
Activities: Administration, caring (general, day and residential), community work, driving, social work, visiting/befriending.
Vols under 26 placed each year: 1,150 of a total of 100,000.
When to apply: All year.
Work alone/with others: With others.
Volunteers with disabilities: Possible.
Qualifications: Varied.
Costs: Nil.
Benefits: Travel costs. Out-of-pocket expenses of volunteering are met. Personal accident cover for all volunteers and public liability insurance cover on all projects provided by us.
Training: Relevant training provided, usually at project.
Supervision: Supervision of young volunteers will meet good practice guidelines appropriate for the project.
Interview details: No interview necessary. Two references required.
UK placements: *England* (throughout); *Scotland* (throughout); *Wales* (throughout).

WOODLAND TRUST, THE
Autumn Park
Dysart Road
Grantham
Lincolnshire
NG31 6LL UK

Tel: +44 (0) 1476 581111
e-mail: personnel@woodland-trust.org.uk
Web: www.woodland-trust.org.uk
Contact: Julie Beals, Personnel Officer

The Woodland Trust is Britain's largest conservation organization concerned solely with the acquisition and management of woodland. The Trust protects Britain's heritage of native and broad leaved trees by acquiring existing woodland and open land on which to plant trees for the future, and by managing those woods in perpetuity. This ownership ensures that the woods are open to all for quiet, informal recreation and that they remain integral parts of familiar landscapes providing habitats for wildlife benefit. Opportunities for woodland conservation include tree planting, path and weed clearance. Volunteers are also required to help with local fundraising campaigns, act as speakers to inform the public about Woodland Trust and develop new ways to raise funds in order to purchase threatened woodland.

Total projects worldwide: Varies.
Total UK projects: Varies.
Starting months: January–December.
Time required: 1–48 weeks.
Age requirement: 16 plus.
Causes: Conservation, environmental causes, wildlife.
Activities: Conservation skills, forestry, fundraising, manual work, outdoor skills.
When to apply: All year.
Work alone/with others: Either.
Volunteers with disabilities: Possible.
Qualifications: Nil.
Equipment/clothing: Warm waterproof clothing with stout shoes or boots for practical work.
Health requirements: Nil.
Costs: Nil.
Benefits: Travel expenses depending on project. We provide accident and public liability cover for those up to 60 years old.
Interview details: Interviewed at project.
Certification: None.
Charity number: 294344
UK placements: *England* (throughout); *Scotland* (throughout); *Northern Ireland* (Antrim, Armagh, Derry/Londonderry, Down, Fermanagh, Tyrone); *Wales* (throughout).

WOODLARKS CAMP SITE TRUST
Tilford Road
Farnham
Surrey
GU10 3RN UK

Tel: +44 (0) 1252 716279
e-mail: woodlarks1@aol.com
Web: www.woodlarks.org.uk
Contact: Mrs Sue Lewis, Honorary Secretary

Woodlarks Camp Site Trust offers the opportunity for physically disabled children and adults to have a traditional camping holiday as part of an organized group on our peaceful wooded campsite. Facilities include a heated outdoor swimming pool, trampoline, archery, barbecue and campfire sites, and an aerial runway. Various groups make use of the site between May and September, many requiring volunteers to assist in supporting their disabled participants. The Trust organizes six week-long camps that are open to public application. Each camp is aimed at a specific group and is organized by a different camp leader. Adventurers for boys aged 10–18 (male volunteers only). Explorers for girls aged 10–18 (female volunteers only). Odyssians for men and women aged 18 to 35 Pathfinders for women aged over 18 (female volunteers only). Pioneer 1 for men aged over 18 (female volunteers are accepted). Volunteers are normally taken on for a period of one week (the duration of a single camp), but some do stay for longer. When the campsite is closed (between October and April) there are often opportunities for skilled volunteers to assist in the maintenance and repair of the facilities. Those interested should contact the Honorary Secretary.

Total projects worldwide: 1
Total UK projects: 1
Starting months: May–September.
Time required: 1 week.
Age requirement: 12 plus.
Causes: Children, disabled (physical), holidays for disabled.
Activities: Caring (residential), summer camps.
When to apply: January–April.
Work alone/with others: With others.
Volunteers with disabilities: Possible, provided they can make a personal contribution either to administration, leadership or care.
Qualifications: Nil.
Equipment/clothing: Sleeping bag, torch, waterproof gear.
Health requirements: Physical health necessary for physically demanding work.
Costs: Camps charge different amounts, normally in the region of £30–£100. Insurance necessary if coming from abroad.
Interview details: Camp leaders may wish to interview prospective volunteers at the site.
Certification: Certificate or reference on request and by arrangement with the campleader.
Charity number: 305148
UK placements: *England* (Surrey).

WORCESTER LIFESTYLES
Woodside Lodge
Lark Hill Road
Worcester
Worcestershire
WR5 2EF UK

Tel: +44 (0) 1905 350686
Fax: +44 (0) 1905 350684
e-mail: worcslifestyles@care4.free.net
Contact: Sue Abbott

Worcester Lifestyles is an independent
registered charity established in 1991 to assist
people with disabilities to exercise freedom of
choice, extend their horizons and make
decisions about the lifestyle they wish to
enjoy. Lifestyles recruit volunteer workers, on
behalf of Social Services, to provide full-time
support and assistance to people with
disabilities to enable them to lead the
independent lifestyle of their choice, in the
counties of Worcestershire and Herefordshire.
Volunteers work on a one-to-one basis to
assist individuals or families to undertake
everyday tasks and pursuits, for example:
personal assistance, sharing leisure pursuits,
shopping, cooking. Volunteers are: people
who have just left school/college looking for
a worthwhile experience; people taking time
out to develop themselves or decide on their
career path; people who need relevant
experience for their chosen career, for
example, nursing, social work, probation
work, occupational therapist, speech therapist
or physiotherapy. Volunteers must be able to
make a commitment of between four and
twelve months. Volunteers with an offending
background may be accepted. This depends
on the offence as volunteers usually work on
a one-to-one basis with someone with a
disability.

Total projects worldwide: 1
Total UK projects: 1
Starting months: January–December.
Time required: 18–52 weeks.
Age requirement: 17 plus.
Causes: Disabled (learning).
Activities: Caring (general and day).
Vols under 26 placed each year:
Approximately 50 of 80.
When to apply: All year.
Work alone/with others: Both.
Volunteers with disabilities: Possible, but
volunteers act as the arms and legs of people
with disabilities.

Qualifications: Good spoken English. Caring,
honest, reliable and adaptable.
Health requirements: Mentally and physically
fit.
Costs: No costs (volunteers from abroad must
pay their own travel costs to England).
Benefits: Weekly pocket money of £57.16.
Return fares from home to the project at the
start and finish of placement, within the UK.
Bonus paid on satisfactory completion of
agreed commitment. Invaluable experience
and references. Our insurance covers
volunteers from within the EU.
Training: Moving and handling training
provided by Social Services. New volunteers
shadow existing volunteers.
Supervision: By Social Services Volunteer
Supervisors.
Nationalities accepted: Providing the
volunteer can obtain a visa allowing them to
be a full-time volunteer with us, they will be
considered for a placement.
Interview details: UK volunteers interviewed
in Worcester. Overseas volunteers are asked
to complete a more detailed application form.
Certification: A certificate is provided.
Volunteers can use Lifestyles as a referee.
Charity number: 1068883
UK placements: *England* (Herefordshire,
Worcestershire).

WORKERS' MOSHAV MOVEMENT IN ISRAEL, THE
19 Leonardo da Vinci Street
Tel Aviv 64733
Israel

Tel: 00 972 3 258473

Total projects worldwide: 1
Total UK projects: 0
Starting months: January–December.
Time required: 1–52 weeks (plus).
Age requirement: 12 plus.
Activities: Agriculture/farming.
Worldwide placements: *Asia* (Israel).

WORLD ASSEMBLY OF YOUTH (WAY)
Ved Ballahoj 4 e
Bronshoj
Copenhagen
DK – 2700 Denmark

Tel: 00 45 3160 7770
Fax: 00 45 3160 5797
e-mail: wayouth centrum.dk
Contact: Mr Heikki Pakarinen, Secretary

General

WAY recognizes the Universal Declaration of Human Rights as the basis of its action and services and works for the promotion of youth and youth organizations in programme areas such as: democracy, environment, human rights, population, health, drugs, community development, and leadership training.

Total projects worldwide: 10
Total UK projects: 0
Starting months: January–December.
Time required: 26–52 weeks.
Age requirement: 20–30
Causes: Young People.
Activities: Administration, computers, development issues, group work, library/resource centres, newsletter/journalism, training, translating.
Vols under 26 placed each year: 2–3
When to apply: All year.
Work alone/with others: Both.
Volunteers with disabilities: Not possible.
Qualifications: Fluent English, Spanish or French.
Health requirements: Good health essential. Travelling in the tropics is required.
Costs: Nil.
Benefits: Accommodation and 3,000DK per month. Travel costs to Denmark reimbursed.
Certification: Certificate or reference provided.
Worldwide placements: *Europe* (Denmark).

WORLD CHALLENGE EXPEDITIONS
Black Arrow House
2 Chandos Road
London
NW10 6NF UK

Tel: +44 (0) 20 8728 7200
Fax: +44 (0) 20 8961 1551
e-mail: welcome@world-challenge.co.uk
Web: www.world-challenge.co.uk
Contact: Rosie Bozman

World Challenge Expeditions (WCE) was established to provide educational adventure opportunities for young people. WCE have been organizing expeditions throughout the developing world for over 13 years. We offer an extensive range of skills development courses which range from short residential courses to 18 month programmes which culminate in an overseas expedition. The ethos behind every programme is challenge, participation and environment and every participant is encouraged to take on as much responsibility as they can. The entire expedition process encourages the development of skills for life, such as leadership, teamwork and decision making. Team Challenge is the core programme of WCE. A typical team consists of approximately fifteen 16–18 year olds together with their teacher and a WCE leader, who during the four week expedition take part in a physically challenging itinerary and a cultural project phase. Under the guidance of their leader, the students take control of all aspects of their expedition, including budget, travel and catering, taking it in turns to act as group leader. To date, over 10,000 students have participated in expeditions which are currently based in over 40 developing countries including Nepal, Bolivia, Mongolia and Indonesia. Each expedition is the culmination of 18 months of preparation. Teams spend this time researching and planning their itinerary, whilst raising their funds towards the overall cost. Throughout this period, they work closely with an expedition manager from World Challenge Expeditions. The expert knowledge that these managers can provide combines with the introduction of the Money Management programme.

Total projects worldwide: 1
Total UK projects: 0
Starting months: June, July.
Time required: 4 weeks.
Age requirement: 16–18
Causes: Children, conservation, environmental causes, inner city problems, poor/homeless, teaching/assisting (secondary), wildlife, young people.
Activities: Agriculture/farming, building/construction, community work, conservation skills, forestry, fundraising, manual work, social work, teaching.
Vols under 26 placed each year: Over 3,000.
Work alone/with others: School teams.
Equipment/clothing: Information provided on suitable clothing for expeditions.
Health requirements: All applicants are asked to disclose pre-existing conditions.
Costs: Cost includes 15–20 month training, travel, insurance, in-country costs, 24-hour emergency London back-up.
Training: During the 15–18 month

programme, teams learn how to plan their expedition, money management and also attend a training course.

Supervision: Each school team is accompanied by a qualified leader and teacher from their school. There is also a 24-hour emergency back-up support from World Challenge HQ in London.

Certification: Reference on request.

Worldwide placements: *Africa* (Botswana, Kenya, Madagascar, Malawi, Morocco, Namibia, South Africa, Swaziland, Tanzania, Uganda, Zambia, Zimbabwe); *Asia* (India, Indonesia, Jordan, Kyrgyzstan, Malaysia, Mongolia, Nepal, Pakistan, Thailand, Tibet, Vietnam); *Australasia* (Australia); *North America* (Canada); *Central America* (Belize, Costa Rica, Honduras, Mexico); *South America* (Argentina, Bolivia, Brazil, Ecuador, Guyana, Peru, Venezuela).

WORLD EXCHANGE
St Colm's International House
23 Inverleith Terrace
Edinburgh
EH3 5NS UK

Tel: +44 (0) 131 315 4444
Fax: +44 (0) 131 315 2222
e-mail: we@stcolms.org
Web: www.worldexchange.org.uk
Contact: Robert S. Anderson

World Exchange draws on an extensive network of international church-related contacts to provide opportunities for people of all ages and skills to live and work overseas for a year. Volunteers are sent to work and to live as part of the local community. World Exchange funds a suitable placement for each successful applicant and provides an excellent training and support package. Short-term visits, work camps and exchanges for individuals and groups can also be organized and appropriate briefings for travellers provided.

Total projects worldwide: Many
Total UK projects: 1
Starting months: June–September.
Time required: 4–52 weeks (plus).
Age requirement: 17 plus.
Causes: Aids/HIV, children, health care/medical, human rights, poor/homeless, teaching/assisting (primary, secondary, mature, EFL), work camps – seasonal, young people.

Activities: Accountancy, administration, agriculture/farming, arts/crafts, building/construction, community work, computers, conservation skills, development issues, music, religion, social work, teaching, technical skills, theatre/drama, work camps – seasonal.

Vols under 26 placed each year: 30 of a total of 50.

When to apply: All year.

Work alone/with others: Both.

Volunteers with disabilities: Yes.

Qualifications: Commitment and flexibility.

Health requirements: Yes.

Costs: £2,000 for one year overseas.

Benefits: The cost includes travel, accommodation, allowance and insurance. We hold a return volunteers weekend.

Training: Two preparation weekends in April and July.

Supervision: Locally arranged to high standards.

Nationalities accepted: British only.

Interview details: Interviews are held in Edinburgh and London.

Certification: Certificate or reference provided.

Worldwide placements: *Africa* (Egypt, Kenya, Malawi, Mauritius, Nigeria, Rwanda, South Africa, Zimbabwe); *Asia* (Bangladesh, India, Israel, Pakistan, Thailand); *Europe* (Hungary, Romania); *Central America* (Guatemala, Trinidad and Tobago).

WORLD HORIZONS
Centre for the Nations
North Dock
Llanelli
Dyfed
SA15 2LF UK

Tel: +44 (0) 1554 750005
Contact: The Director

Total projects worldwide: 1
Total UK projects: 0
Starting months: January–December.
Time required: 1–52 weeks (plus).
Age requirement: 14 plus.

WORLD LAND TRUST
Blyth House
Bridge Street
Halesworth
Suffolk
IP19 8AB UK

Tel: +44 (0) 1986 874422
Fax: +44 (0) 1985 874425
e-mail: worldlandtrust@btinternet.com
Web: www.worldlandtrust.org
Contact: Cindy Engel, Volunteer Co-ordinator

The World Land Trust is an international conservation charity based in Halesworth, Suffolk. A small team of five employees manage and administer a range of overseas projects in which land is purchased and protected from destruction. In the first ten years of our existence, we have saved over 250,000 acres of endangered rainforest habitat. So, although our projects are global, the day-to-day work is all done from Halesworth and this is where most volunteers are based. In return for voluntary assistance with our work, we offer in-house training in conservation management and support in the form of references, CV development and job search. The precise work you would do is carefully matched to your skills and experience. All volunteers need to be literate and numerate as we are working with large sums of money and communicating with professional conservation bodies around the world. Our Belize volunteers will need to work, for a short period, in the office at Halesworth (Suffolk) before going abroad.

Total projects worldwide: 1
Total UK projects: 1
Starting months: January–December.
Time required: 4–26 weeks.
Age requirement: 21 plus.
Causes: Conservation, environmental causes, heritage, wildlife.
Activities: Accountancy, administration, agriculture/farming, arts/crafts, computers, conservation skills, development issues, forestry, fundraising, library/resource centres, marketing/publicity, newsletter/journalism, research.
Vols under 26 placed each year: 2 of a total of 10.
When to apply: All year.
Work alone/with others: Both.
Volunteers with disabilities: At Halesworth we can offer facilities for disabled volunteers.
Qualifications: A good level of literacy and numeracy.
Health requirements: Non-smoking policy.
Costs: Accommodation and travel to and from the office.

Benefits: Travel and lunch expenses up to a maximum of £10 per day. Support in the form of references, CV development and job search. Insurance is provided.
Training: One week induction course in Halesworth.
Supervision: Volunteers are never left unsupervised and have a manager to go to at all times.
Interview details: Usually in London.
Certification: Written references.
Charity number: 1001291
Worldwide placements: *Central America* (Belize, Turks and Caicos Islands) *South America* (Argentina, Ecuador).
UK placements: *England* (Suffolk).

WORLDTEACH

Center for International Development
Harvard University
79 John F. Kennedy Street
Cambridge
Massachusetts
02138 USA

Tel: 00 1 617 495 5527
Fax: 00 1 617 495 1599
e-mail: info@worldteach.org
Web: www.worldteach.org
Contact: Admissions and Alumni Co-ordinator

Based in Cambridge, Massachusetts, WorldTeach is a non-profit organization which sends volunteers overseas to teach English in developing countries. Working in educational settings ranging from primary schools to adult education centres, WorldTeach volunteers teach English as a foreign language and, in some cases, maths and science. Outside traditional school settings, volunteers develop curriculum and provide contextualized English training for guides working in national parks and reserves in Honduras, Mexico and South Africa. There are year-long opportunities in Costa Rica, Ecuador and Namibia, six-month programs in China, and Honduras. We also have a summer programme for undergraduate students in those countries.

Total projects worldwide: 7
Total UK projects: 0
Starting months: January, April, June, August, September, December.
Time required: 7–52 weeks.
Age requirement: 18 plus.

Causes: Environmental causes, teaching/assisting (primary, secondary, mature, EFL).
Activities: Teaching.
Vols under 26 placed each year: 150 of a total of approx. 200.
When to apply: Any time but approximately 4 months in advance – rolling admissions.
Work alone/with others: Summer – with others; nature guide training – with others; others – individual placements.
Volunteers with disabilities: Possible.
Qualifications: Native English fluency required. Bachelor's degree (except summer programme), 25 hours teaching English experience or TEFL course after acceptance recommended.
Health requirements: Health examination.
Costs: From US$3,950–$5,990 including air fare from US, insurance, training and support.
Benefits: Accommodation with family or in apartment plus small living allowance. End of service conference and alumni networking opportunities. WorldTeach volunteers are covered by CISI (Cultural Insurance Services International).
Training: There is a 3–4 week orientation on arrival (includes language lessons, training on how to teach English, and cross-cultural adjustment sessions) for year-long and semester volunters; summer volunteers receive 3–4 days of orientation.
Supervision: A field co-ordinator resides in each country to offer support to our volunteers.
Interview details: Interviews are in Cambridge, Massachusetts or if not possible with individuals who have experience in the region.
Certification: Certificate of Completion issued to each volunteer.
Worldwide placements: *Africa* (Namibia, South Africa); *Asia* (China); *Central America* (Costa Rica, Honduras, Mexico); *South America* (Ecuador).

WORLD VISION UK

World Vision House
599 Avebury Boulevard
Central Milton Keynes
Buckinghamshire
MK9 3PG UK

Tel: +44 (0) 1908 841000
Fax: +44 (0) 1908 841 + 44 (0) 14
e-mail: peter.scott@worldvision.org.uk

Web: www.worldvision.org.uk
Contact: Peter Scott, Church Relations Manager

World Vision UK: the Student Challenge is aimed at students between 19 and 28 years of age and takes place for five weeks over the summer vacation. It seeks to help you understand issues of development from a Christian perspective. Due to World Vision's network of offices throughout the world and many years of development expertise, we are able to offer a unique student experience in the Middle East, Africa and Asia. Placement examples: World Vision is working among Palestinian people for justice and peace. As the peace process flounders World Vision is seeking to draw people together in order to bring about reconciliation. After a one-week orientation in Jerusalem your work placement will take place in a Palestinian community. It will involve working with children in a nearby refugee camp and helping to develop Bethlehem Bible College. You may be asked to do a number of other tasks. You do not have to be an expert, just flexible and keen. World Vision is working to help alleviate crippling poverty in both a rural and urban setting in Ghana and to bring freedom to those bound by poverty. You will receive one week's orientation in Accra, Ghana's capital. There you will meet development specialists, politicians, church leaders and human rights experts. You will then begin a two week placement in local villages where you will help build classrooms with the rest of the community and work with children from that area. In the Philippines you will meet men and women who are working with the poor as an expression of their service to God. They have given their lives to working with the poor and their faith is expressed in words and actions. You will experience a holistic conception of development that does not ignore an individual's spiritual needs but sees them as a central component towards developing the person. You will have a life-changing experience working with the urban poor of the Philippines.

Total projects worldwide: 5
Total UK projects: 0
Starting months: June.
Time required: 3–5 weeks.
Age requirement: 19–29
Causes: Children, human rights, poor/

homeless, refugees.

Activities: Building/construction, community work, development issues, fundraising, group work, international aid, religion, research, sport, summer camps, teaching.

Vols under 26 placed each year: 18–27 of a total of 20–30.

When to apply: Before February.

Work alone/with others: With others.

Volunteers with disabilities: Not possible.

Qualifications: Experience in areas of interest (academic and experience).

Equipment/clothing: Each location differs.

Health requirements: Full medical prior to posting.

Costs: Self funded £1,000–£1,500.

Benefits: Organization caters for insurance and day to day living costs. One-day debrief on return, with group work and counselling if necessary.

Training: We hold a 2 1/2 day orientation each spring. For Palestine we hold a one week orientation in Jerusalem. For Ghana, you will receive one week's orientation in Accra.

Supervision: By World Vision in the project country.

Interview details: 2 hour interview in Milton Keynes.

Certification: Reference on completion.

Charity number: 285908

Worldwide placements: *Africa* (Ghana, Zambia); *Asia* (Bangladesh, Israel, Philippines); *Europe* (Armenia).

WORLDWIDE FUND FOR NATURE
Panda House
Weyside Park
Godalming
Surrey
GU7 1XR UK

Tel: +44 (0) 1483 426444
Contact: Susie Hall

Total projects worldwide: 1
Total UK projects: 1
Starting months: January–December.
Time required: 1–52 weeks.
Age requirement: 14 plus.

WORTHING CVS
Methold House
North Street
Worthing
BN11 1DU UK

Contact: Mark Roberts

Total projects worldwide: 1
Total UK projects: 1
Starting months: January–December.
Time required: 1–52 weeks (plus).
Age requirement: 12 plus.

WWOOF – AUSTRALIA
RSD Buchan
Victoria
3885 Australia

Tel: 00 61 3 515 50218
Fax: 00 61 3 515 50342
e-mail: wwoof@net-tech.com.au
Web: www.wwoof.com.au
Contact: Garry Ainsworth, Managing Director

WWOOF is a form of cultural exchange in which volunteers live and work as a family to learn about farming and gardening, as well as about life in Australia. Working for 3–6 hours a day in exchange for board and lodging is the basis of all WWOOFing. The hosts are mostly people who are involved in alternative lifestyles, and most of them are organic growers, many practise permaculture and biodynamics. Work includes gardening, planting trees, woodcutting, weeding, cooking – anything!

Total projects worldwide: 1
Total UK projects: 0
Starting months: January–December.
Time required: 1–52 weeks.
Age requirement: 16 plus.

Causes: Conservation, environmental causes, wildlife.

Activities: Agriculture/farming, building/construction, conservation skills, forestry, gardening/horticulture, manual work, outdoor skills.

Vols under 26 placed each year: 8,000 of a total of 10,000.

When to apply: About 2 weeks prior to starting.

Work alone/with others: With others.

Volunteers with disabilities: Generally not.

Qualifications: Nil.

Equipment/clothing: Work clothes and good boots.

Health requirements: Nil.

Costs: To book costs £18 for one and £20 for 2 people travelling together.

Benefits: Board and lodging. We offer a small insurance policy to help with medical

expenses for accidents incurred while working.
Supervision: By the host farmer.
Interview details: No interview necessary.
Worldwide placements: *Australasia* (Australia).

WWOOF – CANADA
RR2
S.18, C.9
Nelson
British Columbia
VIL 5P5 Canada

Tel: 00 1 250 354 4417
Fax: 00 1 250 354 4417
e-mail: wwoofcan@uniserve.com
Web: www.members.tripod.com/wwoof
Contact: John Vanden Heuvel

WWOOF is a very popular and successful programme in which hundreds of UK young people have participated. It has been a wonderful way to meet Canadians, live with a family (total integration!), see Canada and pick up valuable life skills and experiences. You can choose from 400 farms and homesteads. (Separate booklet for USA and Hawaii.) Please send three international postal coupons (available from the post office) and C$30 cash with application.

Total projects worldwide: 400
Total UK projects: 0
Starting months: January–December.
Time required: 1–26 weeks.
Age requirement: 17 plus.
Causes: Animal welfare, children, conservation, environmental causes, teaching (primary, secondary, EFL).
Activities: Agriculture/farming, building/construction, conservation skills, forestry, gardening/horticulture, manual work, teaching.
Vols under 26 placed each year: 900 of a total of 1,000.
When to apply: All year.
Work alone/with others: With others.
Volunteers with disabilities: Not possible.
Qualifications: Only a willingness to try to the best of one's ability.
Equipment/clothing: Nil except good footwear.
Health requirements: Provide own medical insurance.
Costs: Travel costs plus registration C$30 (cash), city-host/lodging and meals while

travelling. Approximately £200 per 1, 2, 3 months. Any insurance required must be provided by the volunteer.
Benefits: Board, lodging and a wonderful experience.
Supervision: By your host.
Nationalities accepted: No restrictions but a tourist visa necessary.
Interview details: No interview necessary.
Certification: Certificate or reference provided.
Worldwide placements: *North America* (Canada).

WWOOF/FIOH
PO Box TF 154
Trade Fair Site,
Accra
Ghana

Tel: 00 233 21 766825
Fax: 00 233 21 766825
Contact: Ebenezer Nortey-Mensah, Co-ordinator

WWOOF/FIOH is affiliated to WWOOF. Voluntary farm workers work on both organic and traditional farms. Work includes weeding with a hoe or cutlass and harvesting of food and cash crops including maize, cassava, oranges, cocoa etc. Volunteers also needed to teach English, French, science, music and mathematics – mostly in primary and secondary schools. Placements throughout the year. Volunteers with skills in bicycle repairs and maintenance are invited to work in a bicycle repair workshop. The workshop trains apprentices to repair bicycles. Street children are trained here and are assisted with tools and some funds to set up wayside bicycle repair works. All volunteers are offered the security of arriving to pre-arranged work and family. This allows you to integrate more easily, without the stress of having to find a position. Two summer work-camps (July and August) available. Send two International Reply Coupons (IRCs) available at post offices, for enquiries and programme details and each time they write.

Total projects worldwide: 7
Total UK projects: 0
Starting months: January–December.
Time required: 1–12 weeks.
Age requirement: 18 plus.
Causes: Conservation, teaching/assisting

(nursery), work camps – seasonal.

Activities: Agriculture/farming, arts/crafts, catering, community work, conservation skills, development issues, music, social work, summer camps, teaching, theatre/drama, training, work camps – seasonal.

Vols under 26 placed each year: 38 of a total of 50.

When to apply: One month in advance.

Work alone/with others: With others.

Volunteers with disabilities: We are unable to place people with disabilities.

Qualifications: Nil but volunteers with teaching, organic farm or bicycle repair experience especially welcome.

Equipment/clothing: Working/wellington boots, hand gloves (garden), mosquito net (c. $10 in Ghana).

Health requirements: Yellow Fever vaccination.

Costs: Programme fee: $30 for farm placements, $200 for teaching, $250 for each work camp. Board: £10 per week. Health insurance is imperative and to be provided by the volunteer.

Benefits: Accommodation free usually.

Training: Volunteers are taken through all basics for each project.

Supervision: By the co-ordinator and the farm manager at all times.

Interview details: No interview necessary.

Certification: Written reference provided – certificates also available.

Charity number: G.717

Worldwide placements: *Africa* (Ivory Coast, Ghana, Togo).

WWOOF – NEW ZEALAND

PO Box 1172
Nelson
New Zealand

Tel: 00 64 3 544 9890
Fax: 00 64 3 544 9890
e-mail: atj@wwoof.co.uk
Web: www.wwoof.co.nz
Contact: Jane and Andrew Strange

WWOOF (Willing Workers on Organic Farms) has as its aims: to enable people to learn first hand organic growing techniques; to enable town-dwellers to experience living and working on a farm; to show alternative ways of life; to improve communication within the organic movement; to help develop confidence in becoming self-sufficient; to meet interesting people and make useful contacts. WWOOF – NZ provides the opportunity for you to live and experience life on New Zealand organic properties. You learn organic farming methods by helping on the farm and having 'hands-on' experience. Uusually you live with the family and are expected to join in and co-operate with the day-to-day activities. The success of WWOOF depends on mutual co-operation. There is a variety of properties spread throughout NZ, including farms, market gardens, communities and ventures in self-sufficiency in which organic growing plays some part. Currently there are over 500 host farms.

Total projects worldwide: 1

Total UK projects: 0

Starting months: January–December.

Time required: 1–14 weeks.

Age requirement: 16 plus.

Causes: Conservation, environmental causes, heritage.

Activities: Agriculture/farming, arts/crafts, building/construction, conservation skills, cooking.

Vols under 26 placed each year: 2,200 of a total of 3,000.

When to apply: All year.

Work alone/with others: 50% of the time with other young volunteers.

Volunteers with disabilities: Possible.

Qualifications: Enthusiasm is the prime requisite.

Equipment/clothing: Sturdy shoes and work clothes.

Health requirements: Nil.

Costs: £12 membership fee. Travellers should have normal travel/medical insurance.

Benefits: Full board and lodging.

Training: Written guidelines are given.

Supervision: Volunteers may be left to work alone – but not usually for extended periods.

Interview details: No interview necessary.

Worldwide placements: *Australasia* (New Zealand).

WWOOF – TOGO

BP 25
Agou Nyogbo
Togo

Tel: 00 228 47 10 30
Fax: 00 228 47 10 12
e-mail: wwooftogo@hotmail.com
Contact: Prosper Komla Agbeko, Co-

ordinator

WWOOF (Willing Workers on Organic Farms) – Togo: Every summer we organize an adventure camp on Bethel, the highest mountain in Togo, which includes walking trips, reforestation, discovering wild vegetation and tropical species. You are invited to return to the rural life with Jeunesse en Action. You can experience a completely calm and dark night except for the light of the moon and stars, cook over wood fires, and learn about African family life. Volunteers are also needed all year to help work on organic farms in all areas on Togo. Aims of WWOOF: to get first-hand experience of organic farming and growing; to get into the countryside; to help the organic movement; to make contact with other people in the organic movement. Please send two International Reply Coupons with each letter. Letters received without IRCs will not be answered.

Total projects worldwide: 3
Total UK projects: 0
Starting months: January–December.
Time required: 3–52 weeks.
Age requirement: 17 plus.
Causes: Animal welfare, children, conservation, environmental causes, health care/medical, heritage, poor/homeless, teaching/assisting (nursery, EFL), unemployed, wildlife, work camps – seasonal, young people.
Activities: Agriculture/farming, arts/crafts, building/construction, caring (general), community work, conservation skills, counselling, development issues, DIY, first aid, forestry, fundraising, gardening/horticulture, group work, international aid, library/resource centres, manual work, marketing/publicity, research, sport, summer camps, teaching, training, work camps – seasonal.
Vols under 26 placed each year: 20–30
When to apply: 30 days in advance.
Work alone/with others: With others.
Qualifications: French or English speaking.
Equipment/clothing: Workclothes, mosquito net and cream, suncream, torch, sleeping bag.
Health requirements: Water filters, anti-malarial pills and anti-diarrhoea pills.
Costs: All travel, FF150 inscription plus FF150 per week board.Summer camp FF250

per week, FF900 per month.
Benefits: Nil financial because Togo is so poor with a very low standard of living.
Certification: Certificate or reference on request.
Charity number: 3939
Worldwide placements: *Africa* (Togo).

WYCLIFFE BIBLE TRANSLATORS
Horsleys Green
High Wycombe
Buckinghamshire
HP14 3XL UK

Tel: + 44 (0) 1494 682259
Fax: + 44 (0) 1494 682300
e-mail: short_termers_uk@wycliffe.org
Web: www.wycliffe.org.uk
Contact: Hilary Greenwood

'By the year 2025, together with partners worldwide, we aim to see a Bible translation programme begun in every language that needs one.' Do you want to help fulfil this vision? Wycliffe can use your skills, even as a short-term volunteer. What could I do? Imagine what it means for a harassed mother to have a break from tutoring her own children or for an overworked administrator to have an assistant. Do you have skills in finance, computing or word processing? Could you organize a library? Help with maintenance? Look after a guesthouse? Or are you willing simply to offer an extra pair of hands, doing whatever will help the existing Bible translation team? Most opportunities are in the developing world, though we sometimes need help in the UK. What happens next? We will send you as much information as possible about the country and project where you will be going. We'll also send you a copy of our *One-to-One Handbook*, which will help you with practical preparations such as arranging vaccinations, booking a flight and obtaining a visa. As part of your preparations we will invite you to a Simulator weekend at the Wycliffe Centre. This programme is specially designed to help you cope with some of the situations you may face overseas. Then, almost before you know it, Lift Off!

Total projects worldwide: 1,000 plus
Total UK projects: 2
Starting months: January–December.
Time required: 6–52 weeks.
Age requirement: 17 plus.

Causes: Children, teaching/assisting (nursery, primary, secondary, mature).

Activities: Accountancy, administration, building/construction, community work, computers, manual work, marketing/publicity, outdoor skills, religion, research, summer camps, teaching, technical skills, training, translating, visiting/befriending.

Vols under 26 placed each year: 30 of a total of approximately 65.

When to apply: Any time – by April for summer placements.

Work alone/with others: Not usually with other young volunteers.

Volunteers with disabilities: Possible for UK placement only.

Qualifications: Foreign languages (especially French) and/or 1 other skill (computer, secretarial, teacher etc.) are useful but not essential.

Equipment/clothing: Full advice will be given, depending on destination country.

Health requirements: Must be able to cope with the demands of placement – often in tropical conditions.

Costs: Participants pay own costs including travel, vaccinations, insurance, plus minimal living costs.

Benefits: We can give details of trusts to which volunteers can apply.

Training: Simulator weekend at the Wycliffe Centre.

Supervision: By senior members – usually on an individual basis.

Interview details: Interviews take place at High Wycombe or by area representative.

Certification: References and official thank-you letter.

Worldwide placements: *Africa* (Benin, Burkina Faso, Cameroon, Central African Republic, Chad, Ivory Coast, Gambia, Ghana, Guinea, Kenya, Liberia, Mali, Nigeria, Senegal, Sierra Leone, Tanzania, Togo, Uganda); *Asia* (Indonesia, Philippines); *Australasia* (Papua New Guinea).

UK placements: *England* (Buckinghamshire, Devon).

Y

YMCA
YMCA England
640 Forest Road
London
E17 3DZ UK

Tel: +44 (0) 20 8520 5599
Fax: +44 (0) 20 8509 3190
Contact: David Pendle, Human Resources Department

YMCA volunteering opportunities are based in autonomous local units. The range of work in the UK includes accommodation for the homeless; sport, recreation and fitness; outdoor education, working with children and young people; specialist services for the disadvantaged and vulnerable in society. The YMCA is a Christian organization, open to all irrespective of gender, race or faith but requires all volunteers at least to be in sympathy with the Christian basis of the movement. Volunteers with an offending background are sometimes accepted.

Total projects worldwide: 250
Total UK projects: 250
Starting months: January–December.
Time required: 1–52 weeks.
Age requirement: 16 plus.
Causes: Addicts/ex-addicts, children, disabled (learning and physical), offenders/ex-offenders, poor/homeless, young people.
Activities: Community work, counselling, development issues, fundraising, group work, sport, summer camps.
Vols under 26 placed each year: 60 plus.
When to apply: All year.
Work alone/with others: With others.
Volunteers with disabilities: Possible.
Qualifications: Nil (some countries request another language as well as English).
Equipment/clothing: Supplied if required for specialist volunteering job.
Health requirements: Good health.
Costs: Nil (some overseas opportunities may require volunteer to pay for travel).
Benefits: Personal development and training, accommodation, pocket money (varies).
Interview details: Interviews normally take place on site..
Certification: Reference, achievement certificates, sometimes opportunity for NVQ

etc.
Charity number: 212810
UK placements: *England* (Bedfordshire,
Berkshire, Bristol, Buckinghamshire,
Cambridgeshire, Channel Islands, Cheshire,
Cornwall, Co. Durham, Cumbria,
Derbyshire, Devon, Dorset, Essex,
Gloucestershire, Hampshire, Herefordshire,
Hertfordshire, Isle of Man, Kent, Lancashire,
Leicestershire, Lincolnshire, London,
Manchester, Merseyside, Norfolk,
Northamptonshire, Northumberland,
Nottinghamshire, Oxfordshire, Rutland,
Shropshire, Somerset, Staffordshire, Suffolk,
Surrey, E. Sussex, W. Sussex, Tyne and
Wear, Warwickshire, West Midlands,
Worcestershire, E. Yorkshire, N. Yorkshire,
S. Yorkshire, W. Yorkshire); *Scotland*
(throughout); *Northern Ireland* (throughout);
Wales (throughout).

YMCA (UNION CHRETIENNE DE JEUNES GENS) (UCJG)
Secretariat General
18 Bd Mobutu Sese Seko, BP 02
Lomé
Togo

UCJG–Togo is an international Christian
voluntary organization dedicated to
improving the standard of living in Togo.
The organization is involved in a wide range
of activities offering many opportunities for
volunteers. As well as organizing summer
work camps, the organization runs education
and training programmes, community
development programmes, environmental
projects, cultural programmes and biblical
study retreats.

Total projects worldwide: 1
Total UK projects: 0
Starting months: January–December.
Time required: 4 weeks.
Age requirement: 12 plus.
Costs: $350 plus travel costs.
Benefits: The cost covers board and
accommodation. Volunteers are included in
our employer's liability and personal accident
insurance, made by each YMCA.
Supervision: By experienced and even
specialized managers.
Worldwide placements: *Africa* (Togo).

YORK STUDENT COMMUNITY ACTION
Daw Suu Student Centre
University of York
Heslington
York
N. Yorkshire
YO10 5DD UK

Tel: +44 (0) 1904 433133
Fax: +44 (0) 1904 434664
e-mail: su-ysca@york.ac.uk
Contact: Robert Holt, Camp Organizer

York Student Community Action runs three
types of holiday for a total of 200 children
who would not normally get a holiday. Most
have special needs because they come from
low income, broken or unsettled family
backgrounds.

Total projects worldwide: 7
Total UK projects: 7
Starting months: March–April, June–July.
Time required: 1–3 weeks.
Age requirement: 18–30
Causes: Children, disabled (learning), poor/
homeless, young people.
Activities: Arts/crafts, catering, driving, first
aid, group work, music, outdoor skills,
sport, summer camps.
Vols under 26 placed each year: 95 of a total
of 100.
When to apply: 2 months before.
Work alone/with others: With others.
Volunteers with disabilities: Possible.
Qualifications: Nil – experience with young
people and first aid helpful.
Equipment/clothing: Rucksack, boots and
waterproofs if possible plus sleeping bag if
wanted.
Health requirements: Nil.
Costs: Nil except travel costs to York.
Benefits: Accommodation and food.
Certification: Reference on request.
UK placements: *England* (Derbyshire, N.
Yorkshire).

YORKSHIRE DALES FIELD CENTRE
The Square House
Church Street
Giggleswick
Settle
N. Yorkshire
BD24 OBE UK

Tel: +44 (0) 1729 824180
Fax: +44 (0) 1729 824180

Contact: Peter Fish

The Yorkshire Dales Field Centre: individual requests considered in advance only.

Total projects worldwide: 1
Total UK projects: 1
Starting months: January–December.
Time required: 1–52 weeks.
Age requirement: 18 plus.
Causes: Conservation, environmental causes, teaching/assisting (primary, secondary).
Activities: Catering, conservation skills, DIY, outdoor skills, research, scientific work, teaching.
When to apply: Negotiated.
Work alone/with others: Alone.
Volunteers with disabilities: Not possible.
Qualifications: Environmental qualifications.
Health requirements: Must be medically fit.
Benefits: Negotiated.
UK placements: *England* (N. Yorkshire, S. Yorkshire, W. Yorkshire).

YORKSHIRE WILDLIFE TRUST
10 Toft Green
York
YO1 1JT UK

Tel: +44 (0) 1904 659570
Fax: +44 (0) 1904 613467
Contact: The Director

Yorkshire Wildlife Trust is a member of the Wildlife Trusts, a national partnership of 47 county trusts. For details of the Wildlife Trusts, see the entry Cornwall Wildlife Trust.

Total projects worldwide: 1
Total UK projects: 1
Starting months: January–December.
Time required: 1–52 weeks (plus).
Age requirement: 12 plus.
Causes: Conservation, environmental causes, wildlife.
Activities: Conservation skills.
Work alone/with others: Both.
Qualifications: Nil.
Equipment/clothing: Casual work clothes, waterproofs, stout boots for outdoor work. Protective safety gear is provided.
Health requirements: Anti-tetanus innoculation recommended.
Costs: Nil.
Benefits: Out-of-pocket expenses. Volunteers are covered by the Trust's insurance.
UK placements: *England* (N. Yorkshire, S. Yorkshire, W. Yorkshire).

YOUNG DISABLED ON HOLIDAY
Flat 4, 62 Stuart Park
Corstorphine
Edinburgh
EH12 8YE Scotland

Tel: +44 (0) 131 339 8866
e-mail: aliwalker1@aol.com
Contact: Alison Walker

The Young Disabled on Holiday organization runs a wide range of interesting holidays in the UK and abroad purely for the young with an age limit for both disabled and helpers of 18–35. In addition to holidays at fixed locations there are boating and camping trips. Activities on the holidays include discotheques, swimming, horseriding, wheelchair sports, barbecues and banquets. Please send SAE for information.

Total projects worldwide: 2
Total UK projects: 2
Starting months: January, May–September.
Time required: 1–52 weeks.
Age requirement: 18–35
Causes: Disabled (physical), holidays for disabled, young people.
Activities: Caring (general).
Vols under 26 placed each year: 36 of a total of 45.
When to apply: From January onwards.
Work alone/with others: Both.
Volunteers with disabilities: Not possible.
Qualifications: Patience, be fit and willing to work as a team.
Health requirements: Must be generally fit.
Costs: 50% of cost of holiday abroad; 50% of cost of UK holiday.
Benefits: Half board. We arrange appropriate insurance.
Supervision: 2 holiday organizers supervise.
Interview details: No interview necessary – send CV and complete application.
Certification: Certificate or reference on request.
Charity number: 200644
Worldwide placements: *Asia* (Turkey); *Europe* (France, Ireland, Netherlands, Spain, Turkey); *North America* (USA).
UK placements: *England* (throughout); *Scotland* (throughout); *Wales* (throughout).

YOUNG POWER IN SOCIAL ACTION (YPSA)
House # 2, Road # 1, Block # B
Chandgaon R/A

Chittagong – 4212
Bangladesh

Tel: 00 880 31 653088 ext. 123
Fax: 00 880 31 650145
e-mail: ypsa@abnetbd.com
Contact: Md. Arifur Rahman, Chief
Executive

Young Power in Social Action (YPSA) is a voluntary organization working with social development issues, which has been running in the southern part of Bangladesh since 1985. The majority of the work focuses on women and children, adolescents and youth and some of our projects include non-formal primary education for poor children, community-based rehabilitation of people with disabilities, advocacy, reforestation, health and sanitation, STD treatment, mother and child care and micro-credit finance for women and youths etc. YPSA has a strong network with like-minded organizations at home and abroad. We have a Centre for Youth and Development (YPSA-CYD) which aims to work for and with young people for their development. We also lead a networking group of youth organizations called Pro Youth Network. We organize individual volunteer placements, internships and work camps for national and international volunteers who are interested in participating in our development projects. Volunteers can participate in both short- and long-term periods. YPSA won the International Youth Peace Prize from Bolivia for outstanding social activities in 1999.

Total projects worldwide: 1
Total UK projects: 0
Starting months: January–December.
Time required: 12–24 weeks.
Age requirement: 18–35
Causes: Disabled (learning and physical), environmental causes, health care/medical, teaching/assisting (primary, EFL), work camps – seasonal, young people.
Activities: Administration, agriculture/farming, community work, computers, development issues, forestry, fundraising, gardening/horticulture, manual work, newsletter/journalism, research, social work, teaching, training, work camps – seasonal.
Vols under 26 placed each year: 7 of a total of 10.
When to apply: All year.
Work alone/with others: With others.

Volunteers with disabilities: Not possible.
Qualifications: At least A-level.
Equipment/clothing: Modest dress and/or sub-continental dress is preferred.
Health requirements: Innoculation as recommended by your doctor.
Costs: Return travel to Bangladesh plus registration and administrative fee of US$100. Small contribution for host family. All insurance.
Benefits: Free board and lodging, local transport and local sightseeing with a guide.
Training: An orientation course on YPSA and its ongoing projects and local culture.
Supervision: Volunteers are directed and supervised by the chief executive of YPSA.
Nationalities accepted: No restrictions providing a visa can be obtained.
Interview details: No interview necessary.
Certification: Certificate and a crest is provided.
Worldwide placements: *Asia* (Bangladesh).

YOUTH ACCOMMODATION CENTRES INTERNATIONAL
188 St Lucia Street
Valetta
VLT 06 Malta

e-mail: myha@keyworld.net
Contact: Manwel Cutajar, Secretary.

Youth Accommodation Centres International. Interested persons are asked to send three international reply coupons for programme and an application form.

Total projects worldwide: 1
Total UK projects: 0
Starting months: January–November.
Time required: 2–8 weeks.
Age requirement: 16 plus.
Causes: Young people.
Activities: Fundraising, newsletter/journalism.
Vols under 26 placed each year: 10
When to apply: All year.
Work alone/with others: Alone.
Volunteers with disabilities: Not possible.
Qualifications: Enthusiasm, initiative.
Health requirements: Nil.
Costs: Deposit and postage expenses plus travel costs to Malta.
Benefits: Lodging.
Interview details: No interview necessary.
Worldwide placements: *Europe* (Malta).

YOUTH ACTION

Youth House
Unit 1, 38 Hangingroyd Lane
Hebden Bridge
W. Yorkshire
HX7 7DD UK

Tel: +44 (0) 1422 842308
Contact: Larraine Longbottom

Youth Action aims to create dynamic groups
of young people who can be a driving force
for inspired action and leadership in the
community. This involves young people in
voluntary community action and activity
responding to local community needs. We
aim to offer an accredited training package of
personal development. The project works
with the 14–21 age group from a cross-
section of social backgrounds.

Total projects worldwide: 1
Total UK projects: 1
Starting months: January–December.
Time required: 1–52 weeks.
Age requirement: 21–25
Causes: Young people.
Activities: Arts/crafts, campaigning,
community work, computers, fundraising,
group work, newsletter/journalism, outdoor
skills, theatre/drama.
Vols under 26 placed each year: 1
When to apply: All year.
Work alone/with others: With an adult
worker.
Volunteers with disabilities: We are unable to
place people with disabilities at present as the
building has steps to the entrance and limited
access within it.
Qualifications: Motivation, leadership
qualities and commitment.
Health requirements: Nil.
Costs: Nil.
Benefits: All costs paid by project.
Certification: Certificate or reference
provided.
UK placements: *England* (W. Yorkshire).

YOUTH ACTION FOR PEACE

8 Golden Ridge
Freshwater
Isle of Wight
PO40 9LE UK

Tel: +44 (0) 1983 752557
Fax: +44 (0) 1983 756900
e-mail: yapuk@ukonline.co.uk
Web: www.yap-uk.org

Contact: Cedric Medland, Secretary

The international branches of Youth Action
for Peace co-ordinate hundreds of projects
each year, mainly within Europe. The variety
of work undertaken on these projects is
enormous, ranging from conservation in rural
France, restoration of historic buildings in
Italy, development construction and
conservation in Africa or Asia and
disarmament action in Germany. The projects
allow you to serve in an area of need, whilst
working in a community atmosphere with
other volunteers and local people. There is
also a great opportunity to get to know a
particular region and its culture.
The majority of projects last two to four
weeks with 10 to 20 participants. They are
normally held in the months from June to
September, but a few projects happen in the
winter and spring too. Knowing a foreign
language is not essential. Volunteers with an
offending background are accepted.

Total projects worldwide: 700
Total UK projects: 2
Starting months: April–December.
Time required: 2–6 weeks.
Age requirement: 18 plus.
Causes: Archaeology, architecture, children,
conservation, disabled (learning and
physical), elderly people, environmental
causes, health care/medical, heritage, human
rights, inner city problems, poor/homeless,
refugees, teaching/assisting (primary),
wildlife, work camps – seasonal, young
people.
Activities: Agriculture/farming, arts/crafts,
building/construction, campaigning,
community work, conservation skills,
forestry, gardening/horticulture, group work,
international aid, library/resource centres,
manual work, music, social work, sport,
summer camps, teaching, theatre/drama,
work camps – seasonal.
Vols under 26 placed each year: 70 of a total
of 80.
When to apply: From March onwards. Send
£1 worth stamps for project list. For wildlife
projects please apply from December
onwards.
Work alone/with others: With others.
Volunteers with disabilities: Possible.
Qualifications: No skills but English is
desirable. Official language on camps abroad
is often English.

Equipment/clothing: Sleeping bag, sleeping mat, working clothes.
Health requirements: Nil.
Costs: Travel costs to and from the project vary. Registration fee in UK £80.
Membership fee £15. Extra fee for projects in Africa, Asia or Latin America. This is stated on programme descriptions. Some insurance is provided. Volunteers provide their own insurance for certain items and full insurance for developing countries.
Benefits: Food and accommodation are provided. In some funded programmes all costs are covered.
Training: Training weekends for specified destinations.
Supervision: By responsible volunteer co-ordinators of the hosting organization.
Interview details: For certain specified destinations interviews take place in various offices.
Certification: Reference is available after a successful project.
Worldwide placements: *Africa* (Ivory Coast, Ghana, Morocco, South Africa, Tanzania, Zimbabwe); *Asia* (Bangladesh, Cambodia, Indonesia, Israel, Japan, Mongolia, Nepal, Turkey); *Europe* (Armenia, Belarus, Belgium, Czech Republic, Denmark, Estonia, France, Germany, Greece, Hungary, Italy, Netherlands, Poland, Portugal, Romania, Russia, Slovakia, Turkey, Yugoslavia); *North America* (USA); *Central America* (Mexico); *South America* (Chile, Ecuador).
UK placements: *England* (Co. Durham, Essex); *Scotland* (Edinburgh, E. Lothian, W. Lothian).

YOUTH AND STUDENT CND (CAMPAIGN FOR NUCLEAR DISARMAMENT)

162 Holloway Road
London
N7 8DQ UK

Tel: +44 (0) 20 7607 3616 or +44 (0) 20 7700 2393
Fax: +44 (0) 20 7700 2357
e-mail: youth_cnd@hotmail.com
Contact: Heather

Youth CND: We will accept volunteers for anything from one week to a year. There is a variety of mostly office-based work. In summer, there is also campaigning, stall holding and bar work to be done at festivals.

Total projects worldwide: 1
Total UK projects: 0
Starting months: January–December.
Time required: 1–52 weeks.
Age requirement: 16–23
Causes: Environmental causes, young people.
Activities: Administration, campaigning, computers, fundraising, group work, marketing/publicity, newsletter/journalism.
Vols under 26 placed each year: 90% of total.
When to apply: All year.
Work alone/with others: With others.
Volunteers with disabilities: We are unable to place people with disabilities as there are difficulties with access.
Qualifications: Nil.
Health requirements: Nil.
Costs: Nil.
Benefits: Travel expenses and lunch.
Training: Basic (as required).
Supervision: Part-time, help available from other office workers if needed.
Interview details: Informal.
UK placements: *England* (London, W. Yorkshire).

YOUTH EXCHANGE CENTRE

The British Council
10 Spring Gardens
London
SW1A 2BN UK

Tel: +44 (0) 20 7389 4030
Fax: +44 (0) 20 7389 4033
Contact: Julie Stimpson

The Youth Exchange Centre is the British national agency for the European Voluntary Service Scheme which is open to all young people with no qualification requirement. For more details of the European Voluntary Service Scheme, see the entry under European Voluntary Service.

Total projects worldwide: 1,500 plus
Total UK projects: 0
Starting months: January–December.
Time required: 26–52 weeks.
Age requirement: 18–25
Causes: Addicts/ex-addicts, Aids/HIV, animal welfare, archaeology, architecture, children, conservation, disabled (learning and physical), elderly people, environmental causes, health care/medical, heritage, holidays for disabled, human rights, inner city problems, offenders/ex-offenders, poor/

homeless, refugees, unemployed, wildlife, work camps – seasonal, young people.

Activities: Accountancy, administration, agriculture/farming, arts/crafts, building/construction, campaigning, caring (general, day and residential), catering, community work, computers, conservation skills, cooking, counselling, development issues, DIY, driving, first aid, forestry, fundraising, gardening/horticulture, group work, international aid, library/resource centres, manual work, marketing/publicity, music, newsletter/journalism, outdoor skills, religion, research, scientific work, social work, sport, summer camps, teaching, technical skills, theatre/drama, training, translating, visiting/befriending, work camps – seasonal.

When to apply: All year.

Work alone/with others: Both.

Qualifications: Nil.

Equipment/clothing: Any special equipment or clothing supplied.

Health requirements: Any special health requirements for a specific project would be notified to prospective volunteers.

Benefits: Board and lodging plus pocket money approximately £20 per week. Travel money and special equipment.

Training: You will be given preparatory training before you leave including language training and preparation for the new culture you will be living in. You will also attend an in-service training event during the course of your assignment.

Supervision: As well as a job supervisor, you will have a personal supervisor unconnected with your project to whom you can turn for personal support if needed.

Certification: Certificate or reference provided – European approved certificate.

Worldwide placements: *Europe* (Austria, Belgium, Denmark, Finland, France, Germany, Greece, Iceland, Ireland, Italy, Liechtenstein, Luxembourg, Netherlands, Norway, Portugal, Spain, Sweden).

YOUTH HOSTELS ASSOCIATION (ENGLAND AND WALES)

PO Box 11
Matlock
Derbyshire
DE4 2XA UK

Tel: +44 (0) 1629 822074
e-mail: recruitment@yha.org.uk

Web: www.yha.org.uk
Contact: Edwina Edwards, National Volunteer Co-ordinator

Youth Hostels Association (England and Wales). 16–25 year olds can volunteer for activities such as hostel and grounds maintenance. Alternatively countryside work, fundraising, publicity and promotion professional services. All skills and interests welcomed. For more information contact the National Volunteer Co-ordinator at the above address for a Volunteering in YHA information pack.

Total projects worldwide: 1
Total UK projects: 1
Starting months: January–December.
Time required: 1–52 weeks.
Age requirement: 14 plus.
Causes: Conservation, environmental causes, heritage.
Activities: Administration, building/construction, catering, computers, conservation skills, DIY, forestry, fundraising, gardening/horticulture, group work, manual work, marketing/publicity, newsletter/journalism, outdoor skills, translating.
When to apply: All year.
Work alone/with others: Both.
Qualifications: All skills and interests welcomed.
Equipment/clothing: Depends on the activity.
Benefits: Some expenses reimbursed. Opportunity to self-develop through new challenges.
Nationalities accepted: No restrictions but must be resident in the UK.
Interview details: Tele-interviews conducted by volunteer co-ordinators. Volunteers must complete a volunteer registration form.
Charity number: 301657
UK placements: *England* (throughout); *Wales* (Cardiff, Conwy, Powys).

YOUTH ROUTE 70

Douglas Primary School
Ayr Road
Douglas
South Lanarkshire
ML11 0QA Scotland

Tel: +44 (0) 1555 851166
Contact: Paul Smith

Total projects worldwide: 1
Total UK projects: 1

Starting months: January–December.
Time required: 1–52 weeks.
Age requirement: 18 plus.
Causes: Children, teaching/assisting
(secondary), unemployed, young people.
Activities: Administration, arts/crafts,
community work, computers, counselling,
development issues, DIY, driving, first aid,
fundraising, group work, music, newsletter/
journalism, outdoor skills, research, social
work, sport, summer camps, teaching,
technical skills, theatre/drama, training,
visiting/befriending.
Vols under 26 placed each year: 5
When to apply: All year.
Work alone/with others: Varies.
Volunteers with disabilities: Possible.
Qualifications: Nil.
Equipment/clothing: If special equipment/
clothing is required it can be supplied.
Health requirements: Nil.
Costs: Nil.
Benefits: Food and accommodation when
working away from project and travel costs.
Interview details: Interviews take place –
arrangements can be made to suit the
volunteer.
Certification: Certificate or reference
provided.
Charity number: SC 020206
UK placements: *Scotland* (E. Ayrshire, N.
Ayrshire, S. Ayrshire, Glasgow City, N.
Lanarkshire, S. Lanarkshire, Renfrewshire).

YOUTH WITH A MISSION
Highfield Oval
Ambrose Lane
Harpenden
Hertfordshire
AL5 4BX UK

Tel: +44 (0) 1582 463216
Fax: +44 (0) 1582 463213
e-mail: enquiries@oval.com
Web: www.ywam-england.com
Contact: Public Relations Manager

Youth With a Mission is an international,
interdenominational Christian missionary
organization working in over 132 nations
worldwide. YWAM was founded in 1960 and
is committed to training people to care for
those in need, through short-term relief and
long-term community development projects.
Our desire for those who work with us is
that they 'know God and make Him known'.

As a volunteer on one of YWAM's short term
projects, you will get the opportunity to share
your Christian faith with those you meet,
take part in building and development
projects, work alongside permanent staff in
urban community work in cities such as
Amsterdam and London. You will be able to
work with children in orphanages and on the
street in some of the poorest of the world's
cities. We need people who have a wide
variety of skills from cooks to secretaries,
people who are willing to have a hands-on
experience, to work in a team with other
volunteers in order to get the job done.

Total projects worldwide: 15
Total UK projects: 15
Starting months: January, April, June, July,
September.
Time required: 2–52 weeks.
Age requirement: 16 plus.
Causes: Addicts/ex-addicts, Aids/HIV,
children, health care/medical, human rights,
inner city problems, offenders/ex-offenders,
poor/homeless, teaching (primary), young
people.
Activities: Accountancy, administration,
building/construction, catering, community
work, computers, cooking, group work,
manual work, music, religion, summer
camps, teaching, theatre/drama, training.
Vols under 26 placed each year: 600 of a
total of 1,000.
When to apply: 2–6 months before start
date.
Work alone/with others: With teams.
Volunteers with disabilities: Possible.
Qualifications: Christian faith and to be a
member of a church.
Equipment/clothing: Nothing specific –
Bible.
Health requirements: Depends on location
but generally, no.
Costs: Given as a lump sum which YWAM
will take care of. Approximately £3,000 for 6
months, £150 for 2 weeks. Volunteers must
take out their own insurance if they wish.
Benefits: The cost covers food, board, travel
etc.
Training: We have training weekends for
short-term outreaches or placements are part
of a training school.
Supervision: All volunteers come under the
leadership structure of our organization.
Interview details: Prospective volunteers may
be interviewed, depending on the length of

placement.
Certification: Certificate or reference provided within YWAM.
Charity number: 264078
Worldwide placements: *Africa* (Ghana, Kenya, Malawi, Mali, Mauritania, Morocco, Mozambique, Nigeria, South Africa, Tanzania, Uganda, Zimbabwe); *Asia* (Cambodia, China, Hong Kong, India, Indonesia, Japan, Nepal, Philippines, Singapore, Taiwan, Thailand); *Australasia* (Australia, New Zealand); *Europe* (Albania, Bosnia-Herzegovina, Croatia, Cyprus, Denmark, France, Ireland, Italy, Moldova, Netherlands, Norway, Portugal, Romania, Russia, Slovakia, Spain, Sweden, Switzerland, Turkey, Ukraine); *North America* (Canada, USA); *Central America* (Barbados, Mexico); *South America* (Bolivia, Brazil, Colombia, Paraguay).
UK placements: *England* (Derbyshire, Devon, Herefordshire, Hertfordshire, London, Merseyside, Nottinghamshire, E. Sussex, W. Sussex, Warwickshire); *Scotland* (E. Ayrshire, N. Ayrshire, S. Ayrshire, Edinburgh, Glasgow City, Renfrewshire); *Northern Ireland* (Down); *Wales* (Cardiff, Rhondda, Cynon, Taff, Vale of Glamorgan).

YWCA OF GREAT BRITAIN
Clarendon House
52 Cornmarket Street
Oxford
OX1 3EJ UK

Tel: +44 (0) 1865 304200
Fax: +44 (0) 1865 204805
Contact: Wendy Dawson, Director, Youth and Community

YWCA of GB works for social justice and equality for young women. Volunteering opportunities within the YWCA vary each year depending on priorities and programmes; best to contact Youth and Community Department at Headquarters, Oxford. Volunteers with an offending background may be accepted, depends on the offence, e.g. child offenders not accepted. For opportunities in Scotland, contact YWCA of GB, Scottish National Council, 7 Randolph Crescent, Edinburgh EH3 7TH.

Total projects worldwide: 30
Total UK projects: 30
Starting months: January–December.
Time required: 1–52 weeks.

Age requirement: 16 plus.
Causes: Addicts/ex-addicts, conservation, environmental causes, health care/medical, human rights, inner city problems, poor/homeless, refugees, unemployed, young people.
Activities: Administration, arts/crafts, campaigning, caring (general), community work, computers, conservation skills, counselling, development issues, driving, first aid, fundraising, group work, international aid, library/resource centres, marketing/publicity, newsletter/journalism, religion, sport, summer camps, theatre/drama, training.
Vols under 26 placed each year: 250 of a total of 500.
When to apply: All year.
Work alone/with others: With others.
Volunteers with disabilities: Possible.
Qualifications: Nil – understanding issues affecting women desirable.
Health requirements: Nil.
Costs: Nil – volunteer takes out own insurance if they wish.
Benefits: Experience in working with young women in participative environment.
Training: Specific training may be available.
Supervision: Variable.
Interview details: Applicants are interviewed at their nearest centre in the UK.
Certification: Certificate or reference provided.
Charity number: 249895
UK placements: *England* (throughout); *Scotland* (throughout); *Northern Ireland* (throughout); *Wales* (throughout).

Index by Worldwide Placement

SOUTH AMERICA

Argentina

Bolivia

Brazil

Chile

Colombia

Youth With a Mission, 443

Sweden
Apare/Gec, 25
Associazione Italiana Soci
 Costruttori – I.B.O., 35
BSES Expeditions, 61
Camphill Rudolf Steiner Schools,
 80
Camphill Village Trust (HQ), 85
Camphill Village Trust Ltd, 86
Co-ordinating Committee for
 International Voluntary
 Service, 123
Diakonala Aret, 140
E.I.L., 148
European Voluntary Service, 157
Foreningen Staffansgaarden, 164
Global Outreach Mission UK,
 182
Groupe Archeologique du
 Mesmontois, 192
GSM – Gençlik Servisleri Merkezi
 / Youth Services Centre, 193
Intercultural Youth Exchange,
 219
International Voluntary Service
 (IVS – N. Ireland), 223
International Voluntary Service
 (IVS – North), 224
International Voluntary Service
 (IVS – Scotland), 224
International Voluntary Service
 (IVS – South), 225
National Federation of City
 Farms, 289
Operation New World, 302
Prince's Trust, 315
Sierra Club, 354
Solidarités Jeunesses, 359
TEJO (Tutmonda Esperantista
 Junulara Org.), 379
Time for God Scheme, 382
Voluntary Year, 409
Youth Exchange Centre, 441
Youth With a Mission, 443

Switzerland
Apena, 25
Associazione Italiana Soci
 Costruttori – I.B.O., 35
Camphill Rudolf Steiner Schools,
 80
Camphill Village Trust (HQ), 85
Camphill Village Trust Ltd, 86
Concordia, 120
Co-ordinating Committee for
 International Voluntary
 Service, 123
Crusaders, 132
E.I.L., 148
Ecumenical Network for Youth

Action, 150
Enseignants Sans Frontières, 154
Groupe Archeologique du
 Mesmontois, 192
Gruppo Voluntari Della Svizzera
 Italiana, 193
GSM – Gençlik Servisleri Merkezi
 / Youth Services Centre, 193
Guide Association, 195
Intercultural Youth Exchange,
 219
International Voluntary Service
 (IVS – N. Ireland), 223
International Voluntary Service
 (IVS – North), 224
International Voluntary Service
 (IVS – Scotland), 224
International Voluntary Service
 (IVS – South), 225
Jesuit Volunteer Community:
 Britain, 236
L'Arche – UK, 252
Prince's Trust, 315
Scripture Union Holidays, 342
Sierra Club, 354
Solidarités Jeunesses, 359
Sons of Divine Providence, 360
Stiftung Humanus-Haus, 366
TEJO (Tutmonda Esperantista
 Junulara Org.), 379
Travel Active, 386
United Nations Association
 (Wales), 393
Village Aigues-Vertes, 402
Village Camps Inc., 402
Youth With a Mission, 443

Turkey
Apare/Gec, 25
Associazione Italiana Soci
 Costruttori – I.B.O., 35
BTCV – HQ, 62
Christians Abroad, 108
Concordia, 120
Co-ordinating Committee for
 International Voluntary
 Service, 123
Earthwatch, 149
Genctur (Tourism and Travel
 Agency Ltd), 176
GSM – Gençlik Servisleri Merkezi
 / Youth Services Centre, 193
Guide Association, 195
IJGD – Internationale
 Jugendgemeinschaft Dienste
 E.v., 209
International Voluntary Service
 (IVS – N. Ireland), 223
International Voluntary Service
 (IVS – North), 224
International Voluntary Service
 (IVS – Scotland), 224

International Voluntary Service
 (IVS – South), 225
Interserve, 229
Lisle Inc. 259
Prince's Trust, 315
Proyecto Ambiental Tenerife, 319
Quaker Voluntary Action (QVA),
 320
Scout Association, 341
Silatur, 355
Solidarités Jeunesses, 359
TEJO (Tutmonda Esperantista
 Junulara Org.), 379
United Nations Association
 (Wales), 393
Young Disabled on Holiday, 438
Youth Action for Peace, 440
Youth With a Mission, 443

Ukraine
Apare/Gec, 25
Associazione Italiana Soci
 Costruttori – I.B.O., 35
Christians Abroad, 108
Church Mission Society –
 Encounter, 111
Church Mission Society – Make a
 Difference (Overseas), 112
Concordia, 120
Co-ordinating Committee for
 International Voluntary
 Service, 123
Ecumenical Network for Youth
 Action, 150
Global Outreach Mission UK,
 182
Groupe Archeologique du
 Mesmontois, 192
IJGD – Internationale
 Jugendgemeinschaft Dienste
 E.v., 209
International Exchange Center,
 221
International Voluntary Service
 (IVS – N. Ireland), 223
International Voluntary Service
 (IVS – North), 224
International Voluntary Service
 (IVS – Scotland), 224
International Voluntary Service
 (IVS – South), 225
Internationaler Bauorden –
 Deutscher Zweig, 228
Prince's Trust, 315
Scout Association, 341
Scripture Union Holidays, 342
Solidarités Jeunesses, 359
Teaching and Projects Abroad,
 377
TEJO (Tutmonda Esperantista
 Junulara Org.), 379
Travellers, 386

Index by Cause

Arranged alphabetically by cause and organisation.
See How To Use This Book page xv. for a full list of causes.

Addicts/Ex-Addicts

Addaction – Community Drug and Alcohol Initiatives, 8
AFS International Youth Development, 15
Année Diaconale, 23
Associazione Italiana Soci Costruttori – I.B.O., 35
ATD Fourth World, 36
Baptist Missionary Society, 39
Barnardo's – Lease Children's Services, 41
Barnardo's – North East, 42
Befrienders International, 46
Brethren Volunteer Service, 57
Britain – Tanzania Society, 59
Caisse Populaire d'Assurance-Maladies des Travailleurs Salaries, 67
Cambridge Cyrenians, 68
Careforce, 91
Centre 63, 95
Cheshire and Wirral Federation of Youth Clubs, 102
Church Mission Society – Make a Difference (Overseas), 112
Church of England Youth Service, 113
Community for Creative Non-Violence, 117
Community Service Volunteers, 118
Dale View, 135
Devon Youth Association, 139
Diakonala Aret, 140
Ecumenical Network for Youth Action, 150
Edinburgh Cyrenians, 151
Emmaus House/Harlem, 153
Espaco T, 156
European Voluntary Service, 157
Fairbridge, 159
Glasgow Simon Community, 179
Global Education: International Co-op Thailand, 181
Great Georges Project – the Blackie, 188
Hope UK, 207
Intercultural Youth Exchange, 219
International Volunteer Program, 226

Interserve, 229
Iona Community, 232
Jesuit Volunteer Community: Britain, 236
Kristoffertunet, 247
Land Use Volunteers, 249
Llanelli Centre Project, 263
Mansfield Outdoor Centre, 272
Ministry of Youth and Sports, Enugu State, Nigeria, 278
National Association of Citizens Advice Bureaux, 286
Network Drugs Advice Projects (Youth Awareness Prog.), 294
PACT Centre for Youth Ltd, 306
Partnership for Service Learning, 308
Prince's Trust, 315
Quit, 322
Red Cross Voluntary Social Year, 325
Richmond Fellowship, 327
Salvation Army, 333
Samaritans, 333
Scotquest – YMCA, 338
Scottish Community Foundation (The Caledonian Challenge), 339
Simon Community, 356
Solidarité Jeunesse, 358
Tangents, 376
Task Brasil, 377
Tearfund, 378
Terrence Higgins Trust Lighthouse, 381
Time for God Scheme, 382
USPG and the Methodist Church – Root Groups International, 397
Vallersund Gård, 399
Venture Scotland, 400
Visions in Action, 405
Voluntary Service Belfast (VSB), 407
Volunteer Nepal, 410
WEC International, 415
Western Australian Aids Council, 418
YMCA, 436
Youth Exchange Centre, 441
Youth With a Mission, 443
YWCA of Great Britain, 444

AIDS/HIV

1990 Trust, 1
Abantu for Development, 1
ACET (Aids Care Education and

Training), 3
Across Trust, 4
Action Health / Skillshare International, 6
AFS International Youth Development, 15
Année Diaconale, 23
ATD Fourth World, 36
Baptist Missionary Society, 39
Barnardo's – Lease Children's Services, 41
Barnardo's – North East, 42
Barnardo's – North West, 42
Befrienders International, 46
Brethren Volunteer Service, 57
Britain – Tanzania Society, 59
Caisse Populaire d'Assurance-Maladies des Travailleurs Salaries, 67
Cambridge Aids Action, 67
Careforce, 91
Centre for Environment and Development, 96
Christians Abroad, 108
Community Service Volunteers, 118
Corps Volontaires Congolais au Developpement (COVOCODE), 127
Dale View, 135
Devon Youth Association, 139
Diakonisches Jahr, 141
Ecumenical Network for Youth Action, 150
Emmaus House/Harlem, 153
Espaco T, 156
European Voluntary Service, 157
Gap Activity Projects, 175
GOAL, 185
Human Service Alliance (HSA), 208
IILOS-Tanzania, 210
India Development Group (UK) Ltd, 212
Institute of Cultural Affairs, 216
Intercultural Youth Exchange, 219
International Volunteer Program, 226
Interserve, 229
Iona Community, 232
Jesuit Volunteer Community: Britain, 236
Land Use Volunteers, 249
Latin Link, 253
Mansfield Outdoor Centre, 272
Mouvement Twiza, 284
National Association of Citizens

478

Disabled – Physically

Elderly People

Environmental Causes

Health Care/Medical

Heritage

Holidays for Disabled

Human Rights

Inner City Problems

Teaching – Nursery

Teaching – Primary

Teaching – Secondary

Work Camps – Seasonal

Young People